ATHENAEUS

I

LCL 204

ATHENAEUS

THE LEARNED BANQUETERS

BOOKS I–III.106e

EDITED AND TRANSLATED BY

S. DOUGLAS OLSON

HARVARD UNIVERSITY PRESS
CAMBRIDGE, MASSACHUSETTS
LONDON, ENGLAND
2006

Library of Congress Catalog Card Number 2006041321
CIP data available from the Library of Congress

ISBN-13: 978-0-674-99620-5
ISBN-10: 0-674-99620-8

*Composed in ZephGreek and ZephText by
Technologies 'N Typography, Merrimac, Massachusetts.
Printed and bound by Edwards Brothers,
Ann Arbor, Michigan, on acid-free paper.*

CONTENTS

INTRODUCTION

We know little about the historical Athenaeus except that he was born in the Egyptian city of Naucratis.[1] The *Suda* reports that he lived (less likely "was born") in the time of the emperor Marcus Aurelius (reigned 161–180 CE; cf. 1.2c), although *The Learned Banqueters* itself refers more often—and in a consistently favorable fashion—to Hadrian (reigned 117–138 CE).[2] The latest reference to external events in the text (12.537f) is to Commodus (reigned 180–192 CE), who appears no longer to be alive, and the general consensus today is that the work was composed (or at least completed) early in the reign of Septimius Severus (reigned 193–211 CE). At 7.211a, one of the dinner guests refers to a history of the kings of Syria written by "our companion Athenaeus" (*FGrH* 166 F 1), and the author in question may well be the historical Athenaeus, not just the fictional character who shares his name. The work is otherwise lost.[3]

---

[1] Thus *Suda* α 731 (cited again below) and the inscriptions on the manuscripts of *The Learned Banqueters*. Cf. 7.312a (perhaps to be understood as a momentary intrusion of the author's own voice); Thompson, in Braund and Wilkins pp. 77–84, esp. 82.

[2] 3.115b; 8.361f; 13.574f; 15.677e.

[3] It is nonetheless worth noting that that the sole fragment of the history is an anecdote about the dubious behavior of a philoso-

Larensius, who hosts the party (or series of parties; see below) described in *The Learned Banqueters*, is said at 1.2c to have been given substantial responsibility for religious matters by Marcus Aurelius, and claims at 9.398e to have been appointed procurator (governor) of Moesia by "the lord emperor" (i.e. Commodus?). Larensius speaks on only a few occasions in *The Learned Banqueters*, but Athenaeus lavishes praise on him at the beginning of the text not just for his learning but for his hospitality and the size of his library (1.2b–3f). That Larensius represents a real person is made likely by the presence of the cognomen Larensis in *CIL* 6.212, an epitaph for L. Livius Larensis, who is said only to have been a *pontifex minor*, with no mention of the more important and prestigious procuratorship, strongly suggesting that he is a different member of the family. The most likely conclusion would seem to be that the historical Larensis was the historical Athenaeus' friend and patron; that the elaborate praise at 1.3c–d of the character Larensius' hospitality, and in particular his ability to make men from other cities feel that Rome was their home, represents a heartfelt expression of thanks for the historical Athenaeus' own experiences in Larensis' house; and that much of the research for *The Learned Banqueters* was carried out in Larensis' personal library.[4] If Athenaeus' history of the kings of Syria was not pro-

---

pher at a symposium—making it easy to believe that it was produced by the same man who wrote *The Learned Banqueters*.

[4] See in general Braund, in Braund and Wilkins pp. 3–22, esp. 3–12. For personal libraries in this period, see Jacob, in Braund and Wilkins pp. 87–9.

duced there as well, it may have been the work that attracted Larensis' attention to him and introduced him into a sophisticated Roman cultural and literary circle dominated by Greek expatriates.

The Learned Banqueters is a sprawling and oddly structured work, whose sheer mass regularly threatens to overwhelm its modest literary pretensions. But as C. B. Gulick, the original Loeb editor, noted long ago, it is also "in some respects . . . the most important work of later antiquity."[5] Athenaeus quotes over 1000 authors and over 10000 lines of verse, many of them known from no other source. We are particularly indebted to him for 100s of fragments of the tragic and comic poets; for numerous, frequently substantial excerpts from lost historians; for what appear to be extended citations from several Hellenistic scholarly treatises on Homer; and for everything we know of authors as diverse as Archestratus of Gela, Lynceus of Samos, and Agallis of Corcyra. Had *The Learned Banqueters* not survived, our knowledge of classical Greek literature and its reception in the Hellenistic and Roman periods would have been immensely poorer; and whatever the work's other virtues or failings, it represents an extraordinary trove of texts and authors that would otherwise have perished entirely.

Like the Platonic dialogues it imitates (1.2a with n.), *The Learned Banqueters* features action on two basic narrative levels. The first (which frames the second) is a conversation between Timocrates, who has heard rumors of a brilliant dinner party and would like to learn more, and a character named Athenaeus, who was present at the

5 Vol. I p. xv.

events in question. The second level is an account of the banquet itself, and although the character Athenaeus mostly quotes the other guests directly, he also describes in his own words what was served, how the company reacted to their companions' speeches, and the like. The most outspoken guest is the grammarian Ulpian of Tyre, who is the symposiarch and plays the provocateur, posing questions for the other guests,[6] evaluating their answers, responding to their claims and queries, and generally dominating the conversation. His constant interlocutor and intellectual rival is the sharp-tongued Cynic philosopher Theodorus, referred to throughout as Cynulcus and only identified by his proper name at 15.669e (cf. 15.692b). After they are introduced at 1.1d–e, both men are characterized primarily via the brief remarks that begin and end their speeches; otherwise, they serve as little more than vehicles for long strings of quotations, anecdotes, and catalogues.

19 other guests are referred to by name at one point or another in *The Learned Banqueters*. These men generally make fewer and shorter speeches, many appropriate to their individual interests; musicians commonly discuss music, for example, while physicians quote medical texts. Among the physicians is Galen of Pergamum, who is identified as a prolific author and must stand in somehow for the historical individual of the same name and city, who was born in 129 CE and survived into the reign of Septimius Severus. If Athenaeus and Larensius also repre-

---

[6] He thus takes over the role seemingly reserved for Larensius at 1.2b.

sent real people (above), it becomes tempting to try to discover other historical individuals mentioned or at least alluded to within the company. At 15.686c, the narrator reports that Ulpian died peacefully shortly after the party described in *The Learned Banqueters* was over. Kaibel[7] argued that this ought to be understood as a reference to the death of the famous jurist Ulpian of Tyre in 228 CE, and went on to suggest that a number of other dinner guests stand in for famous men from a variety of periods: the grammarian Plutarch of Alexandria is really the philosopher Plutarch of Chaeroneia (c. 50–120 CE); the philosopher Philadelphus of Ptolemais is really the Egyptian king Ptolemy Philadelphus (reigned 282–246 BCE); the physicians Daphnus of Ephesus and Rufinus of Nicaea combine to suggest the physician Rufus of Ephesus (late 1st century CE); the jurist, poet, and musician Masurius is really the jurist Masurius Sabinus (early 1st century CE); the philosopher Democritus of Nicomedia represents the atomist philosopher Democritus of Abdera (5th century BCE); and so forth. These identifications are far more tenuous than the ones discussed above, and require that the dinner party be made up of guests from different historical periods, depriving it of much of its nominally realistic character. Nor is Kaibel's identification of Athenaeus' Ulpian with the historical Ulpian of Tyre—the idea that serves as the linchpin of his argument—compelling, for the Ulpian of *The Learned Banqueters* is a grammarian rather than a jurist; the historical Ulpian did not die happily, but was

---

7 On pp. v–vii of vol. I of his Teubner edition (see below).

executed, and not at the end of the 2nd century but a generation later; and if Athenaeus' Ulpian represents a real person, it is most likely another, older member of the family. Nor does Kaibel's theory add much to our appreciation of the text; and while it is possible that the members of Larensis' intellectual and social circle would have recognized allusions to their friends, contemporaries, and predecessors in Athenaeus' patently over-the-top recollection of the many (doubtless often brilliant and fascinating) dinner parties they attended together, we can no longer do the same with any degree of assurance.

The Learned Banqueters is, among other things, the tale of an extraordinarily extravagant dinner and drinking party, and a rough framework for the second level of the narrative is provided by the normal order of events on such occasions: dishes and accessories come and go in something approximating the normal order; washing-water is poured over the guests' hands, and wine distributed at the proper times; and the cook interrupts occasionally with announcements and banter. But Athenaeus' narrative pays less attention to the dinner itself than to the discussion that springs from and accompanies it. Plato's Socrates (*Prt.* 347c–8a) insists that educated men have no need of pipe-girls or the like at their symposia, since they can entertain themselves with conversation; and the guests at Larensius' dinner party are indeed relentless talkers. Better than that, they are capable of stringing together long series of poetic fragments that touch on obscure topics, quoting extensive passages of prose, and knowing where rare words can be found—all seemingly off the top of their heads. By Athenaeus' time, the type of literary symposia in which

the author's attention focussed more on the conversation than the food was a well-established genre.[8] Plato and Xenophon each produced one; Athenaeus, quoting Herodicus, makes numerous reference to a *Symposium* by Epicurus, in which philosophical topics were discussed; and his rough contemporary Lucian wrote a *Symposium or Lapiths* that tells the story of a learned—if quarrelsome—wedding feast, at which the guests quote a considerable quantity of literature.[9] But perhaps the most striking parallel to Athenaeus' description of Larensius' dinner party is the fragment of the letter of Parmeniscus (1st century BCE or later) preserved at 4.156d–7d, 157f–8a. Parmeniscus addresses a certain Molpis and describes a dinner he attended but Molpis did not. The other guests are a half-dozen Cynic philosophers, including a Cynic Master *(Kunoulkos)*, who are joined by a pair of courtesans. The meal is simple, but Parmeniscus is in any case more concerned to report the conversation, which was sparked by the arrival (or failure to arrive) of various menu items. Most of the discussion consists of quotations or

[8] Plu. *Mor.* 612d–e also mentions *Symposia* by Aristotle, Speusippus, Prytanis, Hieronymus, and Dio. All these works are lost except for a few stray bits of Aristotle's *Symposium* (frr. 47–53), which appears to have had to do with symposium procedures, and what may be a trace of Dio's *Symposium* at 1.34b (where see n.). Contrast texts such as Matro fr. 1 Olson–Sens = *SH* 534, quoted at 4.134d–7c; Hippolochus' *Letter to Lynceus*, quoted at 4.128c–30d; and Anaxandrides fr. 42, quoted at 4.131a–f, all of which focus on the food and utensils, and ignore the conversation.

[9] Cf. also Plutarch's *Convivial Questions*.

parodies thereof from tragic and lyric poetry or from various philosophers and historians. The Cynics are learned and witty, if unintentionally comic, while the courtesans are raucously abusive, but no less well-versed in literature than their hosts.[10] Although Athenaeus was certainly working within the broad literary tradition defined by Plato and Xenophon, therefore, he also had more specific models, now mostly lost; and his great innovation was perhaps simply to extend the form to enormous length.

The Learned Banqueters consists of 15 Books, which cover an immense range of topics, often in a seemingly unorganized way. The narrator initially appears to be describing a single great meal (1.2a) and, as noted above, this provides a fundamental structuring device for the text as a whole; but it gradually becomes clear that conversations at a whole series of banquets are being reported.[11] In addition, notices at a number of points in the manuscripts tell us that "this is the end of (e.g.) number five and the beginning of (e.g.) number six of the division into 30." Kaibel[12] took all these peculiarities to mean that *The Learned Banqueters* was originally much longer than it is now, and that what has been passed down to us is a crudely trun-

[10] Guests at Greek symposia seem to have mocked and abused one another routinely (cf. Ar. V. 1224–48, 1308–21 with MacDowell on 1308–13; Rosen, *Pallas* 61 [2003] 131–5), and the fact that this goes on at Larensius' party is thus not an aberration but expected.

[11] Contrast 3.99e (the meal is going on during the dog-days in mid-summer) with 8.361f (the Parilia festival, in April, is being celebrated) and 9.372b, c (it is January); and cf. 11.459c; 14.613d; 15.665a, 699d.

[12] Pp. xxi–xl of vol. I of his Teubner.

cated version of the text. As Rodríguez-Noriega Guillén[13] has shown, however, this is unlikely to be true. The text preserved for us is carefully divided into 15 units, which routinely begin and end with a framing dialogue between the narrator Athenaeus and Timocrates; the oddities and obscurities to which Kaibel pointed are better explained as a consequence of the author's haphazard narrative style; and the "division into 30" must represent an early stage in the history of the text, when it occupied 30 scrolls, each containing about half a Book.

The Learned Banqueters we have is thus most likely the text Athenaeus produced, and the fact that it consists of an extraordinary jumble of material raises the vexed problem of the author's sources. Athenaeus quotes thousands of different works, but it is unclear whether he knew them all at first hand or has simply taken over his citations from other, earlier scholarly treatises. Larensis' library was apparently substantial—although certainly not as substantial as Athenaeus claims (1.3a)—but it is difficult to believe that complete copies of e.g. the plays of the early Athenian comic poets or the mimes of Sophron were available in Rome at the end of the 2nd century CE. In addition, Athenaeus certainly quotes at length and without attribution from Hellenistic scholarship at several points (e.g. 1.8e–11b; 5.215c–18e), while at others he appears to be moving back and forth between two or more unacknowledged sources (e.g. 5.185f–6d). Most likely, therefore, *The Learned Banqueters* is heavily dependent on the work of earlier scholars, even if it has been enriched by Athenaeus'

13 In Braund and Wilkins pp. 244–55.

own reading. Close attention to individual passages should allow more progress to be made on this question.

The Manuscript Tradition

The Learned Banqueters is preserved in three manuscripts and two different forms. Venetus Marcianus 447 (traditionally referred to as "A") represents an unabridged version of the text, but has been badly damaged and now lacks everything before 3.74a, as well as a few other scattered folios. Parisinus suppl. gr. 841 (traditionally referred to as "C") and Laurentianus LX.2 (traditionally referred to as "E") are independent witnesses to the complete text of an epitomized (shortened) version of the text apparently made from the manuscript from which A is also descended. The Epitomator (who wrote 1.1 as a preface to his version of *The Learned Banqueters*, which properly begins at 1.2a) has aggressively condensed the work, *inter alia* by omitting the names of most of the speakers at Larensius' dinner party, as well as the titles of many of the poems and plays they cite. The Epitome is nonetheless of enormous value, since it preserves a version of the portions of the text missing from A and can occasionally be used to correct A's readings elsewhere. In addition, the *Suda* offers a large number of quotations from the opening sections of *The Learned Banqueters*, and these can be used to supplement the Epitome. Eustathius (12th century CE) appears to have had his own copy of the Epitome, which may have been superior in some respects to the version of the text represented by CE; but for the current edition, the point is of limited significance.

INTRODUCTION

This Edition

The Learned Banqueters was first printed by the Aldine editor, Marcus Musurus (relying on a copy of A, now lost), in Venice in 1514. The standard enumeration of the text is drawn from the edition of Isaac Casaubon (Heidelberg, 1597). Casaubon's pages are generally divided into six sections (a–f), which consist for the most part of ten, or sometimes 11 lines of text; the f-sections may be longer or shorter than the others, and are occasionally omitted, e.g. in the first page of a Book. Because Casaubon's indications of section-divisions are not neatly aligned with his Greek text, I have at times been forced to guess as to where they should be placed. In addition, his sections fail to take account not just of punctuation but even of word-division, and I have chosen to mark them after the words in which they fall, so as to keep my text as readable as possible.

The standard modern critical edition of *The Learned Banqueters* is the Teubner of Georg Kaibel (3 vols.; Leipzig, 1887, 1890). My text is based on Kaibel, supplemented by my own collations of the manuscripts; for the reader's convenience, I retain Kaibel's paragraph divisions, which were altered by Gulick. Where Athenaeus is our only authority for a fragmentary text, I have given it as it appears in the best modern editions and thus not infrequently in a substantially emended form. When Athenaeus quotes a variant form of a text we know from other sources, on the other hand, I have generally given it in the form he knows. As the Loeb format does not allow for a substantial *apparatus criticus*, readers concerned about exactly what the

manuscripts of *The Learned Banqueters* read at any particular point should refer to Kaibel, to S. P. Peppink's edition of the Epitome (Leiden, 1937–9), or to the standard major critical edition of the author in question.

I cite comic fragments from *PCG*; tragic fragments from *TrGF*; the fragments of Alcaeus and Sappho from Voigt; the fragments of Pindar and Bacchylides from Maehler; the fragments of the presocratic philosophers from Diels-Kranz; the fragments of the historians from *FGrH* or (where *FGrH* is not available) *FHG*; the fragments of Aristotle from Gigon; the fragments of Theophrastus from Fortenbaugh et al.; and the fragments of Callimachus from Pfeiffer. I cite Pollux from Bethe; Hesychius from Latte (a-o), Hansen (π-σ), and Schmidt (τ-ω); the paroemiographers from Leutsch–Schneidewin; and the *Suda* from Adler. For other fragmentarily preserved authors and works, I have made a systematic effort to indicate the edition or editor whose numbering I have taken over. Historical individuals are identified by Berve, Billows, *PA*, *PAA*, Poralla, or Stephanis numbers (with Appendix i or ii specified for Berve), or by Bradford page, wherever possible. Names of ancient authors and works are abbreviated as in LSJ[9], although I have generally omitted "Hom." (for "Homer").

I would like to express my gratitude to Dean Steven Rosenstone of the College of Liberal Arts at the University of Minnesota for his continuing support of my research. Thanks are also due my research assistant Timothy Beck, and Christy Marquis, whose work on the text of Books 1–5 was generously supported by a grant from the Graduate

Research Partnership Program. This volume is dedicated to Rachel Bruzzone, who grew up on a Christmas-tree farm on the shores of Lake Wobegon, and whose steady kindness and support over the last few years have made me happier than she can possibly imagine.

ABBREVIATIONS

Berve	H. Berve, *Das Alexanderreich auf prosopographischer Grundlage* ii *Prosopographie* (Munich, 1926)
Billows	R. A. Billows, *Antigonos the One-Eyed and The Creation of the Hellenistic State* (Berkeley, Los Angeles, and London, 1990)
Bradford	A. S. Bradford, *A Prosopography of Lacedaimonians from the Death of Alexander the Great, 323 B.C., to the Sack of Sparta by Alaric, A.D. 396* (Vestigia 27: Munich, 1977)
Braund and Wilkins	D. Braund and J. Wilkins (eds.), *Athenaeus and His World: Reading Greek Culture in the Roman Empire* (Exeter, 2000)
FGE	D. L. Page (ed.), *Further Greek Epigrams* (Cambridge, 1981)
FGrH	F. Jacoby (ed.), *Die Fragmente der Griechischen Historiker* (Leiden, 1923–69)
FHG	C. and T. Müller, *Fragmenta Historicorum Graecorum* (5 vols.: Paris, 1841–70)
GGM	C. Müller, *Geographi Graeci Minores* (3 vols.: Paris, 1855–61)
GPh	A. S. F. Gow and D. L. Page (eds.), *The Greek Anthology: The Garland of Philip* (Cambridge, 1968)

ABBREVIATIONS

HE	A. S. F. Gow and D. L. Page (eds.), *The Greek Anthology: Hellenistic Epigrams* (Cambridge, 1965)
IG	*Inscriptiones Graecae*
K–A	see *PCG*
PA	J. Kirchner, *Prosopographia Attica* (Berlin, 1901–3)
PAA	J. Traill (ed.), *Persons of Ancient Athens* (Toronto, 1994–)
PCG	R. Kassel and C. Austin (eds.), *Poetae Comici Graeci* (Berlin and New York, 1983–)
PMG	D. L. Page (ed.), *Poetae Melici Graeci* (Oxford, 1962)
Poralla	P. Poralla, *A Prosopography of Lacedaimonians from the Earliest Times to the Death of Alexander the Great (X–323 B.C.)*² (revised by A. S. Bradford: Chicago, 1985)
SH	H. Lloyd-Jones and P. Parsons (eds.), *Supplementum Hellenisticum* (Texte und Kommentar, Band 11: Berlin and New York, 1983)
SSR	G. Giannantoni, *Socratis et Socraticorum Reliquiae* (4 vols.; n.p., 1990)
Stephanis	I. E. Stephanis, Διονυσιακοὶ Τεχνίται (Herakleion, 1988)
SVF	J. van Arnim (ed.), *Stoicorum Veterum Fragmenta* (3 vols.; Leipzig, 1921, 1903)
TrGF	B. Snell *et al.* (eds.), *Tragicorum Graecorum Fragmenta* (Göttingen, 1971–)
West, *AGM*	M. L. West, *Ancient Greek Music* (Oxford, 1992)

THE CHARACTERS

ATHENAEUS, the narrator; also a guest at the dinner party
TIMOCRATES, Athenaeus' interlocutor

AEMILIANUS MAURUS, grammarian (e.g. 3.126b)
ALCEIDES OF ALEXANDRIA, musician (1.1f; 4.174b)
AMOEBEUS, citharode (14.622d–e)
ARRIAN, grammarian (3.113a)
CYNULCUS, Cynic philosopher whose given name is
    Theodorus (e.g. 1.1d; 3.97c)
DAPHNUS OF EPHESUS, physician (e.g. 1.1e; 2.51a)
DEMOCRITUS OF NICOMEDIA, philosopher (1.1e; 3.83c)
DIONYSOCLES, physician (3.96d, 116d)
GALEN OF PERGAMUM, physician (e.g. 1.1e–f, 26c)
LARENSIUS, Roman official and also host of the party
    (e.g. 1.2b–3c; 2.50f)
LEONIDAS OF ELIS, grammarian (1.1d; 3.96d)
MAGNUS (e.g. 3.74c)
MASURIUS, jurist, poet, musician (e.g. 1.1c; 14.623e)
MYRTILUS OF THESSALY, grammarian (e.g. 3.83a)
PALAMEDES THE ELEATIC, lexicographer (9.379a)
PHILADELPHUS OF PTOLEMAIS, philosopher (1.1d)*
PLUTARCH OF ALEXANDRIA, grammarian (e.g. 1.1c–d;
    3.83b)
PONTIANUS OF NICOMEDIA, philosopher (1.1d; 3.109b)

CHARACTERS

RUFINUS OF NICAEA, physician (1.1f)*

ULPIAN OF TYRE, grammarian and also symposiarch
 (e.g. 1.1d–e; 2.49a)

VARUS, grammarian (3.118d)

ZOILUS, grammarian (e.g. 1.1d; 7.277c)

---

* Neither Philadelphus nor Rufinus is said to speak anywhere
in the preserved text of *The Learned Banqueters*, and most likely
some of the anonymous speeches in 1.2a–3.73e (represented in
the Epitome manuscripts only) belong to them.

THE LEARNED BANQUETERS

ΑΘΗΝΑΙΟΥ ΝΑΥΚΡΑΤΙΤΟΥ

ΔΕΙΠΝΟΣΟΦΙΣΤΩΝ

ΕΚ ΤΟΥ ΠΡΩΤΟΥ ΒΙΒΛΙΟΥ

1   Ἀθήναιος μὲν ὁ τῆς βίβλου πατήρ· ποιεῖται δὲ τὸν λόγον πρὸς Τιμοκράτην[1]. Δειπνοσοφιστὴς δὲ ταύτῃ τὸ ὄνομα. ὑπόκειται δὲ τῷ λόγῳ Λαρήνσιος Ῥωμαῖος, ἀνὴρ τῇ τύχῃ περιφανής, τοὺς κατὰ πᾶσαν παιδείαν ἐμπειροτάτους ἐν τοῖς αὑτοῦ δαιτυμόνας ποιούμενος· ἐν οἷς οὐκ ἔσθ᾽ οὗτινος τῶν καλλίστων οὐκ ἐμνημόνευσεν. ἰχθῦς τε γὰρ τῇ βίβλῳ ἐνέθετο καὶ τὰς τούτων χρείας καὶ τὰς τῶν ὀνομάτων ἀναπτύξεις καὶ λαχάνων

---

[1] ἐχεκράτην E: ἐχικράτην C. See 1.2a n.

THE LEARNED BANQUETERS

OF ATHENAEUS OF NAUCRATIS

FROM BOOK I

Athenaeus is the father of the book and is offering his account to Timocrates; the book's title is *The Learned Banqueter*.[1] The central character is Larensius of Rome, a conspicuously wealthy man who is entertaining the greatest experts in every field of knowledge at a banquet in his own house. [Athenaeus] omits no one's finest sayings; for he included fish in his book, and the ways they are prepared and the derivations of their names,[2] as well as every sort of veg-

---

[1] Literally *"The Dinner-Sophist,"* as again in 1.2a (where the plural is used). 1.1a–f is not by Athenaeus, but is a brief introduction to the work composed by the Epitomator. The (condensed version of the) text itself begins at 1.2a.

[2] Especially Book 7.

γένη παντοῖα καὶ ζῴων παντοδαπῶν καὶ ἄνδρας ἱστορίας συγγεγραφότας καὶ ποιητὰς καὶ φιλοσόφους².
b καὶ ὄργανα μουσικὰ | καὶ σκωμμάτων εἴδη μυρία καὶ
ἐκπωμάτων διαφορὰς καὶ πλούτους βασιλέων διηγή-
σατο καὶ νηῶν μεγέθη καὶ ὅσα ἄλλα οὐδ' ἂν εὐχερῶς
ἀπομνημονεύσαιμι, ἢ ἐπιλίποι μ' ⟨ἂν⟩ ἡ ἡμέρα κατ'
εἶδος διεξερχόμενον. καί ἐστιν ἡ τοῦ λόγου οἰκονομία
μίμημα τῆς τοῦ δείπνου πολυτελείας καὶ ἡ τῆς βίβλου
διασκευὴ τῆς ἐν τῷ δείπνῳ³ παρασκευῆς. τοιοῦτον ὁ
θαυμαστὸς οὗτος τοῦ λόγου οἰκονόμος Ἀθήναιος ἥδιστον λογόδειπνον εἰσηγεῖται κρείττων τε αὐτὸς ἑαυτοῦ γινόμενος, ὥσπερ οἱ Ἀθήνησι ῥήτορες, ὑπὸ τῆς ἐν
c τῷ λέγειν θερμότητος πρὸς τὰ | ἑπόμενα τῆς βίβλου
βαθμηδὸν ὑπεράλλεται.

Οἱ δ' ἐν τῷ δείπνῳ δῆθεν ἐπιδημήσαντες δειπνοσο-
φισταὶ ἦσαν Μασούριος, νόμων ἐξηγητὴς καὶ πάσης
παιδείας οὐ παρέργως ἐπιμέλειαν ποιούμενος, δαιμό-
νιος⁴ ποιητής, ἀνὴρ καὶ κατὰ τὴν ἄλλην παιδείαν
οὐδενὸς δεύτερος καὶ τὴν ἐγκύκλιον οὐ παρέργως
ἐζηλωκώς· ἕκαστον γὰρ ὧν ἐπεδείκνυτο ὡς μόνον
τοῦτο ἠσκηκὼς ἐφαίνετο, τοιαύτῃ πολυμαθείᾳ ἐκ παίδων συνετράφη· ἰάμβων δὲ ἦν ποιητὴς οὐδενὸς δεύτερος, φησί, τῶν μετ' Ἀρχίλοχον ποιητῶν. παρῆν δὲ καὶ
Πλούταρχος καὶ Λεωνίδης ὁ Ἠλεῖος καὶ Αἰμιλιανὸς ὁ

---

² φιλοσόφους Wilamowitz: ὅλους σοφοὺς C: ὅλως σοφοὺς
E   ³ δείπνῳ Kaibel: λόγῳ CE
⁴ δαιμόνιος Harrison: μόνιος E: μόνος C

4

etable,[3] animals of every kind, and authors of historical works, poets, and philosophers. He also described musical instruments,[4] a million types of jokes, different styles of drinking cups,[5] the wealth of kings,[6] huge ships[7]—and so many other items that I could not easily mention them all, or else the day would end as I was still going through them category by category. The account is arranged to imitate the extravagance of the dinner party, and the book's structure reflects how the dinner was organized. This is the sort of delightful feast of words this marvellous chief literary steward Athenaeus introduces. And driven by his ardor for language, like the orators in Athens he outdoes even himself and sets off by leaps and bounds to the later portions of his book.

The learned banqueters attending the meal were supposedly:[8] Masurius, a legal scholar who paid serious attention to learning of every sort, an extraordinary poet, and a man second to none in other sorts of culture, who had shown great eagerness for getting a comprehensive education. He made every topic he discussed seem like the one subject he had studied, so encyclopedic was his training from childhood. [Athenaeus] reports that he was an iambic poet inferior to none of Archilochus' successors. Also present were Plutarch, Leonides of Elis, and Aemilianus

3 E.g. 2.58f–60b, 62d–3a.

4 Especially 4.174a–85a; 14.633f–7f.

5 Especially Book 11.

6 E.g. 5.194c–203e.

7 See 5.203e–9e.

8 For possible connections between real historical individuals and the guest-list, see the Introduction.

Μαυρούσιος καὶ Ζωίλος, γραμματικῶν οἱ χαριέστα-
d τοι. | φιλοσόφων δὲ παρῆσαν Ποντιανὸς καὶ Δημόκρι-
τος οἱ Νικομηδεῖς, πολυμαθείᾳ πάντας ὑπερηκοντικό-
τες, Φιλάδελφός τε ὁ Πτολεμαεύς, ἀνὴρ οὐ μόνον ἐν
φιλοσόφῳ θεωρίᾳ τεθραμμένος, ἀλλὰ καὶ κατὰ τὸν
ἄλλον βίον ἐξητασμένος. τῶν δὲ κυνικῶν εἷς ἦν ὃν
Κύνουλκον καλεῖ· ᾧ οὐ μόνον

< . . . > δύο κύνες ἀργοὶ ἕποντο,

ὡς τῷ Τηλεμάχῳ ἐκκλησιάζοντι, ἀλλὰ τῶν Ἀκταίωνος
πολὺ πλείονες. ῥητόρων τε ἦν ἄγυρις τῶν κυνικῶν κατ'
οὐδὲν ἀπολειπομένη· ὧν κατέτρεχε μετὰ καὶ τῶν ἄλλων ὅσοι τι ἐφθέγγοντο Οὐλπιανὸς ὁ Τύριος, ὃς διὰ
τὰς συνεχεῖς ζητήσεις, ἃς ἀνὰ πᾶσαν ὥραν ποιεῖται
e ἐν ταῖς ἀγυιαῖς, περιπάτοις, | βιβλιοπωλείοις, βαλα-
νείοις, ἔσχεν ὄνομα τοῦ κυρίου διασημότερον Κειτού-
κειτος. οὗτος ὁ ἀνὴρ νόμον εἶχεν ‹ἴδιον›[5] μηδενὸς
ἀποτρώγειν πρὶν εἰπεῖν "κεῖται ἢ οὐ κεῖται;", οἷον εἰ
κεῖται ὥρα ἐπὶ τοῦ τῆς ἡμέρας μορίου, ‹εἰ ὁ μέθυσος
ἐπὶ ἀνδρός,›[6] εἰ ἡ μήτρα κεῖται ἐπὶ τοῦ ἐδωδίμου
βρώματος[7], εἰ σύαγρος κεῖται τὸ σύνθετον ἐπὶ τοῦ

---

[5] from S δ 359   [6] from S δ 359   [7] τοῦ ἐδωδίμου
βρώματος S δ 359: τῶν ἐδωδίμων βρωμάτων CE

[9] Literally "Hound-Master," i.e. "Cynic Master"; cf. 4.156e.
Cynulcus' real name is eventually revealed to be Theodorus
(15.669e).

[10] "Cynic" is literally "dog-like" (i.e. shameless; cf. Il. 1.225,

Maurus and Zoilus, who were the wittiest of the grammarians. As for philosophers, Pontianus and Democritus, both of whom were from Nicomedia and excelled all men in the range of their learning, were present, as was Philadelphus of Ptolemais, who had not only been educated in philosophic inquiry but had experience in the rest of life as well. Representing the Cynics was a man [Athenaeus] calls Cynulcus[9]; because it was not just (*Od.* 2.11)

> two white dogs that followed him,

as they followed Telemachus when he entered the assembly, but many more than were in Actaeon's pack.[10] The crowd of orators was even larger than the crowd of Cynics; they were attacked by Ulpian of Tyre, as well as by everyone else who spoke. Because of the constant inquiries he made at every hour in the streets, covered walkways, bookshops, and bathhouses, Ulpian had a nickname that identified him more precisely than the one he had been given at birth: *Keitoukeitos*.[11] This man observed a custom, unique to himself, of never eating anything until he asked "Is it attested or isn't it?" *(keitai ē ou keitai?)*, as, for example, if the word *hōra* ("hour, season") is attested for a portion of the day, or *methusos* ("drunken") for a man,[12] or if *mētra* ("womb") is attested for edible food,[13] or if the compound *suagros* ("wild-pig") is attested for a pig.[14] The physicians

quoted at 1.11b), hence the pun. Actaeon was torn to pieces by his own hunting-dogs after he accidentally spied Artemis bathing and she transformed him into a stag ([Apollod.] *Bib.* 3.4.4).
  [11] "Mr. Attested-or-not-attested."   [12] Phryn. *Ecl.* 122 claims that for a man the proper form of the adjective is instead *methustikos*.   [13] See 3.96f.   [14] See 9.401c–d.

συός. ἰατρῶν δὲ παρῆσαν Δάφνος Ἐφέσιος, ἱερὸς τὴν τέχνην καὶ κατὰ τὰ ἤθη, τῶν Ἀκαδημαϊκῶν λόγων οὐ παρέργως ἁπτόμενος, Γαληνός τε ὁ Περγαμηνός, ὃς τοσαῦτ᾽ ἐκδέδωκε συγγράμματα φιλόσοφά τε καὶ ἰατρικὰ ὡς πάντας ὑπερβαλεῖν τοὺς πρὸ αὐτοῦ, καὶ κατὰ τὴν ἑρμηνείαν οὐδενὸς ὢν τῶν ἀρχαίων ἀδυνατώτερος,
f Ῥουφῖνός τε ὁ Νικαεύς. μουσικὸς δὲ παρῆν Ἀλκείδης ὁ Ἀλεξανδρεύς. καὶ ἦν ὁ κατάλογος οὗτος στρατιωτικός, φησί, μᾶλλον ἢ συμποτικός.

Δραματουργεῖ δὲ τὸν διάλογον ὁ Ἀθήναιος ζήλῳ Πλατωνικῷ· οὕτως γοῦν ἄρχεται·‖

2 Αὐτός, ὦ Ἀθήναιε, μετειληφὼς τῆς καλῆς ἐκείνης συνουσίας τῶν νῦν ἐπικληθέντων δειπνοσοφιστῶν, ἥτις ἀνὰ τὴν πόλιν πολυθρύλητος ἐγένετο, ἢ παρ᾽ ἄλλου μαθὼν τοῖς ἑταίροις[8] διεξῄεις;—αὐτός, ὦ Τιμόκρατες, μετασχών.—ἆρ᾽ οὖν ἐθελήσεις καὶ ἡμῖν τῶν καλῶν ἐπικυλικίων λόγων μεταδοῦναι—

b τρὶς δ᾽ ἀπομαξαμένοισι θεοὶ διδόασιν ἄμεινον, |

ὥς πού φησιν ὁ Κυρηναῖος ποιητής—ἢ παρ᾽ ἄλλου τινὸς ἡμᾶς ἀναπυνθάνεσθαι δεῖ·

---

[8] ἑταίροις Casaubon: ἑτέροις CE

---

[15] As a servant of the god Asclepius.

[16] Probably an allusion to Archestratus fr. 4 Olson–Sens, quoted at 1.4e and eluded to again at 15.671a.

[17] Cf. Pl. *Phd.* 57d (whence the name Echecrates has made its way into the first line of Athenaeus in place of "Timocrates"); *Smp.*

8

present were Daphnus of Ephesus, who was holy in his trade[15] and his manners, and had a firm grasp of the doctrines of the Academy; Galen of Pergamum, who had published more medical and philosophical treatises than all his predecessors and was not inferior to any of the ancient doctors in his diagnoses; and Rufinus of Nicaea. The musician Alceides of Alexandria was also there. In fact, says [Athenaeus], the list was more like a military muster-roll than a catalogue of guests at a symposium.[16]

Athenaeus imitates Plato in his dramatization of the dialogue.[17] It begins, at any rate, as follows:

"Did you yourself, Athenaeus, participate in that wonderful party of men now referred to as 'learned banqueters', which was widely discussed in the city? Or did you learn about it from someone else and pass along the description to your companions?" "I myself participated, Timocrates." "Will you then agree to share some of the fine talk you had over your cups with us as well?

> The gods give a better portion to those who wipe
>   their mouths three times,

as the Cyrenaean poet (Eratosth. fr. 30, p. 65 Powell) says somewhere.[18] Or do we need to ask someone else?"

172a–3b (where Apollodorus, however, readily concedes that he was *not* at the famous party and only knows about what was said there at second hand).

[18] Timocrates is worried that Athenaeus may be weary of repeating the story, and the quotation is intended to suggest that repetition, even if it seems tiresome, produces better results than when something is done only once.

Εἶτα εἰσβάλλει μετ' ὀλίγον εἰς τὸν τοῦ Λαρηνσίου
ἔπαινον καὶ λέγει· ὃς ὑπὸ φιλοτιμίας πολλοὺς τῶν ἀπὸ
παιδείας συναθροίζων οὐ μόνον τοῖς ἄλλοις ἀλλὰ καὶ
λόγοις εἰστία, τὰ μὲν προβάλλων τῶν ἀξίων ζητή-
σεως, τὰ δὲ ἀνευρίσκων, οὐκ ἀβασανίστως οὐδ' ἐκ τοῦ
παρατυχόντος τὰς ζητήσεις ποιούμενος, ἀλλ' ὡς ἔνι
μάλιστα μετὰ κριτικῆς τινος καὶ Σωκρατικῆς ἐπιστή-
c μης, ὡς πάντας θαυμάζειν τῶν ζητήσεων | τὴν τήρη-
σιν. λέγει δ' αὐτὸν καὶ καθεσταμένον ἐπὶ τῶν ἱερῶν
εἶναι καὶ θυσιῶν ὑπὸ τοῦ πάντα ἀρίστου βασιλέως
Μάρκου καὶ μὴ ἔλαττον τῶν πατρίων τὰ τῶν Ἑλλήνων μεταχειρίζεσθαι. καλεῖ δὲ αὐτὸν καὶ Ἀστεροπαῖόν
τινα, ἐπ' ἴσης ἀμφοτέρων τῶν φωνῶν προϊστάμενον.
λέγει δ' αὐτὸν καὶ ἔμπειρον εἶναι ἱερουργιῶν τῶν
νομισθεισῶν ὑπό τε τοῦ τῆς πόλεως ἐπωνύμου Ῥωμύ-
λου καὶ Πομπιλίου Νουμᾶ καὶ ἐπιστήμονα νόμων
πολιτικῶν. πάντα δὲ ταῦτα μόνον ἐξευρεῖν ἐκ παλαιῶν
d ψηφισμάτων καὶ δογμάτων | τηρήσεως, ἔτι δὲ νόμων
συναγωγῆς οὓς οὐκέτι[9] διδάσκουσιν, ὡς τὰ Πινδάρου
3 ⟨ὁ⟩ κωμῳδιοποιὸς ‖ Εὔπολίς φησιν ἤδη κατασεσι-
γασμένα ὑπὸ τῆς τῶν πολλῶν ἀφιλοκαλίας. ἦν δέ,
φησί, καὶ βιβλίων κτῆσις αὐτῷ ἀρχαίων Ἑλληνικῶν
τοσαύτη ὡς ὑπερβάλλειν πάντας τοὺς ἐπὶ συναγωγῇ
τεθαυμασμένους, Πολυκράτην τε τὸν Σάμιον καὶ Πει-

---

[9] οὐκέτι Kaibel: ἔτι CE

---

[19] Marcus Aurelius, reigned 161–180 CE.

Shortly after this, he launches into his eulogy of
Larensius and says: [He was a man] whose love of distinction caused him to assemble many educated people and
feast them not just on the expected items but on words as
well, proposing some topics generally thought worthy of
debate, coming up with others of his own, and not raising
questions for discussion without due consideration or at
random, but in such a way that they contained considerable critical, even Socratic insight, so that everyone was
astonished at the care he took with the topics posed. He
also says that Larensius had been put in charge of offerings
and sacrifices by the most excellent emperor Marcus,[19]
and was as involved in Greek ceremonies as in those of his
fatherland. And he refers to him as a sort of Asteropaeus,
because he was equally outstanding in both languages,[20]
and notes that he was both experienced in the sacred rites
established by Romulus, who gave his name to the city,
and Numa Pompilius,[21] and knowledgeable about political
customs. Larensius recovered all this information personally, by examining ancient decrees and ordinances and
collecting laws that are no longer taught but are, as the
comic poet Eupolis (fr. 398) says of Pindar's poems, now
condemned to silence by the decay of popular taste.
[Athenaeus] says that Larensius owned more old Greek
books than any of the people regarded as having marvellous collections: Polycrates of Samos;[22] Pisistratus the ty-

[20] Asteropaeus was an ambidextrous ally of the Trojans (*Il.*
21.163), and the point is that Larensius' Greek was as good as his
Latin.

[21] Rome's second king.

[22] Tyrant of Samos *c*.535–522 BCE.

σίστρατον τὸν Ἀθηναίων τυραννήσαντα Εὐκλείδην τε
τὸν καὶ αὐτὸν Ἀθηναῖον καὶ Νικοκράτην τὸν Κύπριον
ἔτι τε τοὺς Περγάμου βασιλέας Εὐριπίδην τε τὸν
ποιητὴν Ἀριστοτέλην τε τὸν φιλόσοφον καὶ τὸν τὰ
b   τούτων διατηρήσαντα βιβλία Νηλέα· | παρ' οὗ πάντα,
φησί, πριάμενος ὁ ἡμεδαπὸς βασιλεὺς Πτολεμαῖος,
Φιλάδελφος δὲ ἐπίκλην, μετὰ τῶν Ἀθήνηθεν καὶ τῶν
ἀπὸ Ῥόδου εἰς τὴν καλὴν Ἀλεξάνδρειαν μετήγαγε.
διόπερ ἐκεῖνα τῶν Ἀντιφάνους ἐρεῖ τις εἰς αὐτόν·

αἰεὶ δὲ πρὸς Μούσαισι καὶ λόγοις πάρει,
ὅπου ⟨τι⟩ σοφίας ἔργον ἐξετάζεται.

ἀγλαΐζεται δὲ καὶ
μουσικᾶς ἐν ἀώτῳ,
οἷα παίζομεν φίλαν
ἄνδρες ἀμφὶ θαμὰ τράπεζαν,

c   κατὰ τὸν Θηβαῖον μελοποιόν. | καὶ ἐπὶ τὰς ἑστιάσεις
δὲ παρακαλῶν πατρίδα, φησί, τὴν Ῥώμην πᾶσιν
ἀποφαίνει. τίς γὰρ τὰ οἴκοι ποθεῖ τούτῳ ξυνὼν ἀναπε-
πταμένην ἔχοντι τοῖς φίλοις τὴν οἰκίαν; κατὰ γὰρ τὸν
κωμῳδιοποιὸν Ἀπολλόδωρον·

εἰς οἰκίαν ὅταν τις εἰσίῃ φίλου,
ἔστιν θεωρεῖν, Νικοφῶν, τὴν τοῦ φίλου

---

23 Pisistratus (*PAA* 771760) controlled Athens briefly beginning *c.*560, and then continuously from *c.*546–527 BCE. For his
library, cf. Gell. *NA* 7.17.1.   24 *PAA* 436020. Not otherwise
identified; the name is a common one.

rant of Athens;[23] Eucleides, who was also an Athenian;[24] Nicocrates of Cyprus;[25] and also the Pergamene kings;[26] the poet Euripides and the philosopher Aristotle; and Neleus, who got control of their books. It was from Neleus, Athenaeus says, that our king Ptolemy (nicknamed Philadelphus)[27] bought them all and transferred them to his beautiful Alexandria, along with the books he got from Athens and Rhodes. One is therefore inclined to apply to him[28] the well-known verses of Antiphanes (fr. 272):

> You are always in the company of the Muses and
>   literature
> when any work of art is examined.

As the lyric poet from Thebes (Pi. *O*. 1.14–17) puts it:

> He finds glory
> in the finest songs,
> such as we men often perform in play
> around the friendly table.

And by inviting these men to his feasts, [Athenaeus] says, he made Rome seem like a native land for all of them. Because who longs for what he has at home, when he is with a friend whose house is open wide to his friends? As the comic poet Apollodorus (fr. 15) puts it:

> Whenever someone enters a friend's house,
> he can see, Nicophon, his friend's

---

[25] Otherwise unknown.   [26] Eumenes II (reigned 197–159 BCE), founder of the library in Pergamum, and his successors.

[27] Ptolemy II (reigned 285/3–246 BCE). A different tradition about the fate of Aristotle's library is preserved at 5.214d.

[28] Larensius.

εὔνοιαν εὐθὺς εἰσιόντα τὰς θύρας.
ὁ θυρωρὸς ἱλαρὸς πρῶτόν ἐστιν, ἡ κύων
d ἔσηνε καὶ προσῆλθ᾽, ὑπαντήσας δέ τις |
δίφρον εὐθέως ἔθηκε, κἂν μηδεὶς λέγῃ
μηδέν.

Τοιούτους ἔδει καὶ τοὺς λοιποὺς εἶναι πλουσίους[10],
ὡς τοῖς γε μὴ τοῦτο ποιοῦσιν ἐρεῖ τις· "τί μικρολόγος
εἶ; πλεῖαί τοι οἴνου κλισίαι· δαίνυ δαῖτα γέρουσι
θάλειαν· ἔοικέ τοι." τοιοῦτος ἦν τῇ μεγαλοψυχίᾳ ὁ
μέγας Ἀλέξανδρος. Κόνων δὲ τῇ περὶ Κνίδον ναυμα-
χίᾳ νικήσας Λακεδαιμονίους καὶ τειχίσας τὸν Πειραιᾶ
ἑκατόμβην τῷ ὄντι θύσας καὶ οὐ ψευδωνύμως πάντας
e Ἀθηναίους εἱστίασεν. Ἀλκιβιάδης δὲ Ὀλύμπια | νική-
σας ἅρματι πρῶτος καὶ δεύτερος καὶ τέταρτος, εἰς ἃς
νίκας καὶ Εὐριπίδης ἔγραψεν ἐπινίκιον, θύσας Ὀλυμ-
πίῳ Διὶ τὴν πανήγυριν πᾶσαν εἱστίασε. τὸ αὐτὸ
ἐποίησε καὶ Λεώφρων Ὀλυμπίασιν, ἐπινίκιον γρά-
ψαντος τοῦ Κείου Σιμωνίδου. Ἐμπεδοκλῆς δ᾽ ὁ Ἀκραγαντῖνος ἵπποις Ὀλύμπια νικήσας, Πυθαγορικὸς ὢν
καὶ ἐμψύχων ἀπεχόμενος, ἐκ σμύρνης καὶ λιβανωτοῦ
καὶ τῶν πολυτελεστάτων ἀρωμάτων βοῦν ἀναπλάσας

[10] πλουσίους Adam: πλείους CE

---

29 Cf. 6.270f, where Amips. fr. 18 (which expresses a senti-
ment very much like this) is quoted and said to apply to Larensius.
30 Adapted from Il. 9.70–1.
31 In 394 BCE.

14

affection the moment he enters the door.
The doorkeeper, first of all, is cheerful; the dog
wags its tail and comes up to him; and a slave
    immediately
greets him and offers him a chair—all without
    anyone saying
a word.

Other rich people ought to be like this;[29] and to those who do not behave thus one is inclined to say: "Why are you so stingy? Your huts are full of wine; spread a handsome feast for the elders! This befits you!"[30] Alexander the Great showed this sort of magnanimity. Conon, after he defeated the Spartans in the naval battle off Cnidus[31] and erected a wall around the Piraeus, sacrificed a real hecatomb,[32] not something merely called by that name, and invited all the Athenians to a feast. When Alcibiades took first-, second- and fourth-place at Olympia in the chariotrace[33]—Euripides (*PMG* 755) wrote the victory ode for the victories—he sacrificed to Olympian Zeus and invited everyone at the festival to the feast. Leophron did the same at Olympia when Simonides of Cos wrote the victory ode (*PMG* 515).[34] Empedocles of Acragas was victorious in the horse-race at Olympia; since he was a Pythagorean and did not eat meat, he made an ox out of myrrh, frankincense, and the most expensive spices and divided it up

---

[32] I.e. a sacrifice consisting of 100 oxen, as properly, although the word was often used hyperbolically of smaller sacrifices.

[33] In 420 BCE; see Th. 6.16.2.

[34] Simonides died in 467 BCE, but the victory is otherwise undated.

f διένειμε τοῖς εἰς τὴν πανήγυριν ἀπαντήσασιν. | ὁ δὲ
Χῖος Ἴων τραγῳδίαν νικήσας Ἀθήνησιν ἑκάστῳ τῶν
Ἀθηναίων ἔδωκε Χίου κεράμιον.

  τοῦδε † γάρ τις ἄλλου πρὸς θεῶν οὕνεκα
  εὔξαιτο πλουτεῖν εὐπορεῖν τε χρημάτων
  ἢ τοῦ δύνασθαι παραβοηθεῖν τοῖς φίλοις
  σπείρειν τε καρπὸν Χάριτος, ἡδίστης θεῶν;
  τοῦ μὲν πιεῖν γὰρ καὶ φαγεῖν τὰς ἡδονὰς
  ἔχομεν ὁμοίας· † οὐχὶ δὲ τοῖς λαμπροῖσι γὰρ
  δείπνοις τὸ πεινῆν παύεται,

Ἀντιφάνης φησίν.

Ὅτι Ξενοκράτης ὁ Χαλκηδόνιος καὶ Σπεύσιππος ὁ
Ἀκαδημαϊκὸς καὶ Ἀριστοτέλης βασιλικοὺς νόμους
4 ἔγραψε. ‖

Ἀλλὰ μὴν καὶ ὁ Ἀκραγαντῖνος Τελλίας, φιλόξενος
ὢν καὶ πάντας πολυωρῶν, πεντακοσίοις ἱππεῦσιν ἐκ
Γέλας ποτὲ καταλύσασιν ὡς αὐτὸν χειμῶνος ὥρᾳ
ἔδωκεν ἑκάστῳ χιτῶνα καὶ ἱμάτιον.

Ὁ τρεχέδειπνος, φησί, σοφιστής.

Κλέαρχός φησι Χάρμον τὸν Συρακούσιον εὐτρεπί-
σθαι στιχίδια καὶ παροιμίας εἰς ἕκαστον τῶν ἐν τοῖς
δείπνοις παρατιθεμένων· εἰς μὲν τὸν ἰχθύν·

---

35 This is in fact a different Empedocles (Moretti #170), mistakenly identified here with the philosopher. His victory (in horse-
back-riding) dates to 496 BCE.

among the people attending the festival.[35] When Ion of Chios (*TrGF* 19 T 3) was victorious in a tragic competition in Athens, he gave every Athenian a jar of Chian wine.[36]

> This † for why else would one pray to the gods for
> wealth and an abundance of goods,
> except to be able to help one's friends
> and sow a crop of Gratitude, the most delightful god?
> For we all take the same pleasure in drinking
> and eating; † and hunger is not eliminated
> by brilliant dinner parties,

says Antiphanes (fr. 226).

Xenocrates of Chalcedon (fr. 49 Isnardi Parente), Speusippus of the Academy (test. 47 Tarán), and Aristotle (fr. 466) wrote treatises on how the symposiarch ought to behave.[37]

On one occasion when 500 Gelan horsemen stopped at his house during the winter season, Tellias of Acragas, a hospitable man who lavished attention on all comers, gave each of them a tunic and a robe.

[Athenaeus] uses the phrase "the sophist who chases dinner."[38]

Clearchus (fr. 90 Wehrli) says that Charmus of Syracuse[39] had appropriate verses and proverbs ready for each dish served at his dinner parties. For the fish:

---

[36] A particularly fine local variety; cf. the material quoted at 1.28d–f.

[37] Cf. 5.186b.

[38] Cf. 6.242c.

[39] Presumably to be identified with the gluttonous pipe-player (Stephanis #2621) referred to at 8.344c.

SPRING CREEK CAMPUS

ἥκω λιπὼν Αἰγαῖον ἁλμυρὸν βάθος,

εἰς δὲ τοὺς κήρυκας·

χαίρετε, κήρυκες, Διὸς ἄγγελοι,

b εἰς δὲ τὴν | χορδήν·

ἑλικτὰ κοὐδὲν ὑγιές,

εἰς δὲ τὴν ᾠνθυλευμένην τευθίδα·

σοφὴ σοφὴ σύ,

εἰς δὲ τὸ ἐν τοῖς ἑψητοῖς ὡραῖον·

οὐκ ἀπ᾽ ἐμοῦ σκεδάσεις ὄχλον;,

εἰς δὲ τὴν ἀποδεδαρμένην ἔγχελυν·

οὐ προκαλυπτομένα βοστρυχώδεα.[11]

τοιούτους πολλούς φησι τῷ Λαρηνσίου παρεῖναι δείπνῳ, ὥσπερ συμβολὰς κομίζοντας τὰ ἀπὸ τῶν στρω-
ματοδέσμων γράμματα. φησὶ δὲ καὶ ὅτι ὁ Χάρμος εἰς
ἕκαστον τῶν παρατιθεμένων ἔχων τι πρόχειρον, ὡς
c προείρηται, ἐδόκει τοῖς Μεσσηνίοις πεπαιδευμένος |
εἶναι, ὡς καὶ Καλλιφάνης ὁ τοῦ Παραβρύκοντος κληθεὶς ἀρχὰς ποιημάτων πολλῶν ⟨καὶ λόγων⟩[12] ἐκγρα-

---

[11] The traditional text of Euripides has genitive βοστρυ-
χώδεος.   [12] from S κ 243

[40] The name means literally "heralds."

I have come, leaving the salty depth of the Aegean.
  (E. *Tr.* 1)

For the trumpet-shells[40]:

Greetings, heralds, messengers of Zeus! (*Il.* 1.334)

For the sausage:

twisted and utterly unsound. (E. *Andr.* 448)[41]

For the stuffed squid:

You are wise, wise! (E. *Andr.* 245)

For the stewed *fruits-de-mer*:

Scatter the mob from my presence! (*Cypr.* fr. 16
  Bernabé = Bion of Borysthenes fr. 25.4
  Kindstrand)[42]

For the skinned eel:

hidden by no clustering curls. (E. *Ph.* 1485)

[Athenaeus] reports that many men of this sort attended Larensius' dinner party, and that as their contribution to it they brought knapsacks full of literature.[43] He also says that by having something ready for each dish that was served, as was noted above, Charmus got a reputation among the Messenians for being educated. Likewise Calliphanes, nicknamed "Son of Gorger," copied out the be-

---

[41] Sausage-casings were made of animal intestines, hence the reference to sausages as "twisted."

[42] A more complete version of the line is quoted at D.L. 2.117.

[43] Cf. 2.67f; 7.277b–c; 8.331b–c; Gell. *NA* 7.13.1–2.

ψάμενος ἀνειλήφει μέχρι τριῶν καὶ τεσσάρων στίχων,
πολυμαθείας δόξαν προσποιούμενος.

Πολλοὶ δὲ καὶ ἄλλοι διὰ στόματος εἶχον τὰς ἐν τῷ
Σικελικῷ μυραίνας, τὰς πλωτὰς ἐγχέλεις, τῶν Παχυ-
νικῶν θύννων τὰς ἠτριαίας, τοὺς ἐν Μήλῳ ἐρίφους,
τοὺς ἐν Σκιάθῳ[13] κεστρέας· καὶ τῶν ἀδόξων δὲ τὰς
Πελωρίδας κόγχας, τὰς ἐκ Λιπάρας μαινίδας, τὴν
d Μαντινικὴν γογγυλίδα, τὰς ἐκ Θηβῶν βουνιάδας | καὶ
τὰ παρ᾽ Ἀσκραίοις τεῦτλα.

Κλεάνθης δὲ ὁ Ταραντῖνος, ὥς φησι Κλέαρχος,
πάντα παρὰ τοὺς πότους ἔμμετρα ἔλεγε, καὶ Πάμφιλος δὲ ὁ Σικελός, ὡς ταῦτα·

ἔγχει πιεῖν μοι καὶ τὸ πέρδικος σκέλος.
ἀμίδα δότω τις ἢ πλακοῦντά τις δότω.

Τὸν βίον, φησίν, εὐσταθεῖς, οὐκ ἐγχειρογάστορες.

γυργαθοὺς ψηφισμάτων ⟨ . . . ⟩
φέροντες,

Ἀριστοφάνης φησίν.

Ὅτι Ἀρχέστρατος ὁ Συρακούσιος ἢ Γελῷος ἐν τῇ
e ὡς Χρύσιππος ἐπιγράφει | Γαστρονομίᾳ, ὡς δὲ Λυγ-
κεὺς καὶ Καλλίμαχος Ἡδυπαθείᾳ, ὡς δὲ Κλέαρχος

---

13 Σκιάθῳ Gesner, from Clem. Al. *Paid*. 2.1.3: συμαίθῳ CE

44 Probably a prose adaptation of a comic banquet catalogue
resembling Antiph. fr. 191 (quoted at 7.295c–d).

ginnings of many poems and speeches, memorized three or four lines at most, and got a false reputation for wide learning.

Many others had their mouths full of Sicilian morays, "floating" eels, belly-sections of Pachynian tuna, Melian kids, and Sciathic mullets; and of foods of lesser reputation, Pelosian shellfish, sprats from the Lipari Islands, Mantinean turnip, French turnips from Thebes, and beets from Ascra.[44]

According to Clearchus (fr. 89 Wehrli), Cleanthes of Tarentum spoke exclusively in meter when he was drinking, as did Pamphilus the Sicel. For example:

Pour me a drink and [give me] a partridge leg!
Someone give me a pisspot! Or give me a cake!

Those who enjoy a settled prosperity, he says, do not live from hand to mouth.[45]

Aristophanes (fr. 226.1–2) says:

men carrying baskets
full of decrees.[46]

Archestratus of Syracuse or Gela (test. 2 Olson–Sens), in the work entitled according to Chrysippus (xxviii fr. 6, *SVF* iii.199) the *Gastronomy*, but according to Lynceus (fr. 21a Dalby) and Callimachus (fr. 436) the *Life of Pleasure*, and according to Clearchus (fr. 79a Wehrli) the *Science*

[45] *Men Who Live from Hand to Mouth* (*Encheirogastores*; an extremely rare word) is the title of a comedy by Nicophon quoted by Athenaeus at 3.126e; 9.389a; 14.645b, and presumably referred to here as well.　　[46] Probably cited in connection with the "knapsacks full of literature" referred to above.

Δειπνολογίᾳ, ὡς δ' ἄλλοι Ὀψοποιίᾳ—ἐπικὸν δὲ τὸ ποίημα, οὗ ἡ ἀρχή·

ἱστορίης ἐπίδειγμα ποιούμενος Ἑλλάδι πάσῃ—

φησί·

πρὸς δὲ μιῇ πάντας δειπνεῖν ἁβρόδαιτι τραπέζῃ·
ἔστωσαν δ' ἢ τρεῖς ἢ τέσσαρες οἱ ξυνάπαντες
ἢ τῶν πέντε γε μὴ πλείους· ἤδη γὰρ ἂν εἴη
μισθοφόρων ἁρπαξιβίων σκηνὴ στρατιωτῶν.

f ἀγνοεῖ δ' ὅτι οἱ ἐν τῷ Πλάτωνος συσσιτίῳ[14] ὀκτὼ | καὶ εἴκοσι ἦσαν.

οὗτοι δὲ ⟨πρὸς⟩ τὰ δεῖπνα τῶν ἐν τῇ πόλει
ἀφορῶσι ⟨ . . . ⟩ καὶ πέτονται δεξιῶς
ἐπὶ ταῦτ' ἄκλητοι,

Ἀντιφάνης φησί. καὶ ἐπάγει·

οὓς ⟨ . . . ⟩ ἐκ κοινοῦ ⟨ . . . ⟩
5   ἔδει τρέφειν τὸν δῆμον, ‖ ἀεί θ' † ὥσπερ
Ὀλυμπίασί φασι ταῖς μυίαις ποιεῖν
βοῦν τοῖς ἀκλήτοις προκατακόπτειν πανταχοῦ.

[14] συμποσίῳ S a 731

---

[47] Cf. 1.1f with n.

of Dining, but according to other authorities the *Art of Cooking*—the poem is in epic verse and begins (Archestr. fr. 1 Olson–Sens = *SH* 132):

> Making a display of the results of my research to all
> Greece

—says (Archestr. fr. 4 Olson–Sens = *SH* 191):

> Everyone should dine at a single table set for an
> elegant meal.
> Let the company total three or four,
> or at any rate no more than five; after that you would
> have
> a mess-group of rapacious mercenary soldiers.[47]

He is unaware that there were 28 people in Plato's mess-hall.[48]

> These fellows are always on the lookout for dinner
> parties
> held by the city's inhabitants, and they shrewdly fly
> off to them uninvited,

says Antiphanes (fr. 227). He continues:

>   men whom the people
> ought to support from the public treasury and †
> routinely
> do what, they say, is done for the flies at Olympia,
> by butchering an ox everywhere for the uninvited
> guests.

---

[48] Presumably a reference to the *Symposium*, although Plato never specifies the number of guests at the party described there.

23

ATHENAEUS

< . . . > τὰ μὲν θέρεος, τὰ δὲ γίνεται ἐν χειμῶνι,

φησὶν ὁ Συρακούσιος ποιητής. οὐχ ἅμα μὲν οὖν πάντα παρασκευάζεσθαι δυνατόν, λέγεσθαι δὲ ῥάδιον.

῞Οτι δείπνων ἀναγραφὰς πεποίηνται ἄλλοι τε καὶ
Τιμαχίδας ὁ ῾Ρόδιος δι᾽ ἐπῶν ἐν ἕνδεκα βιβλίοις ἢ καὶ
πλείοσι καὶ Νουμήνιος <ὁ> ῾Ηρακλεώτης, ὁ Διεύχους
τοῦ ἰατροῦ μαθητής, καὶ Ματρέας[15] ὁ Πιταναῖος ὁ
b παρῳδὸς καὶ ῾Ηγήμων ὁ Θάσιος ὁ ἐπικληθεὶς | Φακῆ,
ὃν τῇ ἀρχαίᾳ κωμῳδίᾳ τινὲς ἐντάττουσιν.

῞Οτι ᾿Αρτεμίδωρος ὁ Ψευδαριστοφάνειος ὀψαρτυτι-
κὰς λέξεις συνήγαγε. τοῦ Φιλοξένου δὲ τοῦ Λευκαδίου
Δείπνου Πλάτων ὁ κωμῳδιοποιὸς μέμνηται·

(Α.) ἐγὼ δ᾽ ἐνθάδ᾽ ἐν τῇ ἐρημίᾳ
τουτὶ διελθεῖν βούλομαι τὸ βιβλίον

15 Μάτρων Schweighäuser

49 The next line in Theocritus ("so that I could not bring all
these things at the same time") makes the point of the quotation
clear. What follows in Athenaeus is apparently intended as a further gloss or elaboration of it, and is most likely the beginning of a
speech.

50 Athenaeus cites the poem at least four times (3.82d; 7.283c;
15.682c, 684f).

51 A mistake for Matro of Pitane, whose *Dinner Party* Athenaeus quotes at length at 4.134d–7c. For Matreas of Alexandria
and his parodies, see 1.19d with n.

52 No fragments of his plays (if he wrote any) survive.

53 As at 4.182d; 9.387d; 14.485d, 662d. Artemidorus dates to
the 1st century BCE and presumably identified himself (or was

Some flowers appear in summer, others in winter,

says the Syracusan poet (Theoc. 11.58).[49] Not everything can be prepared at the same time, but it can all be discussed quite easily.

Descriptions of dinner parties have been produced by a number of poets, including Timachidas of Rhodes (*SH* 769) in 11 books of epic verse or perhaps more;[50] Numenius of Heracleia (*SH* 596), the student of the physician Dieuches (fr. 1 Bertier); the parodist Matreas of Pitane;[51] and Hegemon of Thasos (test. 1), nicknamed Lentil Soup, whom some authorities include among the authors of Old Comedy.[52]

Artemidorus, who is falsely identified as a student of Aristophanes,[53] collected culinary terms. The comic poet Plato (fr. 189) mentions the *Dinner Party* of Philoxenus of Leucas:[54]

(A.) Here in this deserted spot I
want to go through this book

identified by others) as a member of Aristophanes of Byzantium's school rather than as his actual student. The work referred to here is cited at 9.387d; 14.662d, 663c–d; and almost certainly also at 3.111c; 4.171b; cf. 11.485e.

[54] From *Phaon* (the name of a mortal man with whom Aphrodite fell in love; cf. 2.69d). The recipes Speaker A consults mostly involve aphrodisiac foods (for the hyacinth bulb and the octopus, cf. Xenarch. fr. *1, quoted at 2.63f–4a), and this is presumably Phaon himself, who is looking for ways to cope with the immense sexual demands being made on him; cf. Pl. Com. fr. 188, quoted at 10.441e. Philoxenus of Leucas and Philoxenus of Cythera are hopelessly confused in ancient sources; cf. 1.5f. For Philoxenus' *Dinner Party*, see 4.146f with n.

πρὸς ἐμαυτόν. (Β.) ἔστι δ', ἀντιβολῶ σε, τοῦτο
    τί;
(Α.) Φιλοξένου καινή τις ὀψαρτυσία.
(Β.) ἐπίδειξον αὐτὴν ἥτις ἔστ'. (Α.) ἄκουε δή.
"ἄρξομαι ἐκ βολβοῖο, τελευτήσω δ' ἐπὶ θύννον."
c   (Β.) ἐπὶ θύννον; οὐκοῦν † τῆς τελευτ † πολὺ |
    κράτιστον ἐνταυθὶ τετάχθαι τάξεως.
    (Α.) "βολβοὺς μὲν σποδιᾷ δαμάσας καταχύσματι
        δεύσας
    ὡς πλείστους διάτρωγε· τὸ γὰρ δέμας ἀνέρος
        ὀρθοῖ.
    καὶ τάδε μὲν δὴ ταῦτα· θαλάσσης δ' ἐς τέκν'
        ἄνειμι."

εἶτα μετὰ μικρόν·

    "οὐδὲ λοπὰς κακόν ἐστιν· ἀτὰρ τὸ τάγηνον
        ἄμεινον,
    οἶμαι."

καὶ μετ' ὀλίγα·

    "ὀρφὼν αἰολίαν συνόδοντά τε καρχαρίαν τε
d   μὴ τέμνειν, μή σοι νέμεσις θεόθεν καταπνεύσῃ, |
    ἀλλ' ὅλον ὀπτήσας παράθες· πολλὸν γὰρ
        ἄμεινον.
    πουλύποδος † πλεκτὴ δ' ἂν ἐπιλήψῃ † κατὰ
        καιρόν,
    ἐφθὴ τῆς ὀπτῆς, ἢν ᾖ μείζων, πολὺ κρείττων·
    ἢν ὀπταὶ δὲ δύ' ὦσ', ἐφθῇ κλαίειν ἀγορεύω.

privately. (B.) Tell me, please, what's this?
(A.) A new cookbook by Philoxenus.
(B.) Give me a sample of it! (A.) Alright, listen.
"I shall begin with hyacinth bulb and conclude with
    tuna."
(B.) With tuna? Well, it's [corrupt] much
better to be posted here in the rear then!
(A.) "Subdue the hyacinth bulbs with hot ash; drench
    them with sauce;
and eat as many as you can. For this makes a man's
    body stand up straight.
So much for that; I move on to the children of the
    sea."

Then after a bit:

"Nor is a casserole-dish bad; but a frying pan is
    better,
I think."

And after a few verses:

"As for the perch, the speckle-fish, the four-toothed
    sea-bream, and the shark,
do not cut them up, lest vengeance from the gods
    breathe down upon you,
but roast and serve them whole; for this is much
    better.
† If you get hold of the tentacle † of an octopus at the
    right season,
a stewed one is much better than a roasted one—
    provided it's bigger.
But if there are two roasted ones, I say to hell with
    the stewed one.

τρίγλη δ' οὐκ ἐθέλει νεύρων ἐπιήρανος εἶναι·
παρθένου Ἀρτέμιδος γὰρ ἔφυ καὶ στύματα μισεῖ.
σκορπίος αὖ—" (Β.) παίσειέ γέ σου τὸν πρωκτὸν
ὑπελθών.

ἀπὸ τούτου τοῦ Φιλοξένου καὶ Φιλοξένειοί τινες πλα-
e κοῦντες | ὠνομάσθησαν. περὶ τούτου Χρύσιππός φη-
σιν· ἐγὼ κατέχω τινὰ ὀψοφάγον ἐπὶ τοσοῦτον ἐκπε-
πτωκότα τοῦ μὴ ἐντρέπεσθαι τοὺς πλησίον ἐπὶ τοῖς
γινομένοις ὥστε φανερῶς ἐν τοῖς βαλανείοις τήν τε
χεῖρα συνεθίζειν πρὸς τὰ θερμὰ καθιέντα εἰς ὕδωρ
θερμὸν καὶ τὸ στόμα ἀναγαργαριζόμενον θερμῷ,
ὅπως δηλονότι ἐν τοῖς θερμοῖς δυσκίνητος ᾖ. ἔφασαν
γὰρ αὐτὸν καὶ τοὺς ὀψοποιοῦντας ὑποποιεῖσθαι, ἵνα
θερμότατα παρατιθῶσι καὶ μόνος καταναλίσκῃ αὐτὸς
f τῶν λοιπῶν | συνακολουθεῖν μὴ δυναμένων. τὰ δ' αὐτὰ
καὶ περὶ τοῦ Κυθηρίου Φιλοξένου ἱστοροῦσι καὶ Ἀρ-
χύτου καὶ ἄλλων πλειόνων, ὧν τις παρὰ Κρωβύλῳ τῷ
κωμικῷ φησιν·

(Α.) ἐγὼ δὲ πρὸς τὰ θερμὰ ταῦθ' ὑπερβολῇ
τοὺς δακτύλους δήπουθεν Ἰδαίους ἔχω
καὶ τὸν λάρυγγ' ἥδιστα πυριῶ τεμαχίοις.
(Β.) κάμινος, οὐκ ἄνθρωπος.

---

[55] For *neuron* (properly "sinew, tendon") in the sense "penis,"
cf. the proverb quoted at 2.64b.

[56] An early 4th-century Pythagorean philosopher (D–K 6).

The mullet refuses to be of assistance to the male
   muscle;[55]
for it is devoted to virgin Artemis and hates hard-ons.
The bullhead, on the other hand—" (B.) Will, I hope,
   sneak up and sting you in the ass!

Certain types of cakes came to be called "Philoxenian"
from this Philoxenus. Chrysippus (xxviii fr. 10, SVF iii.200)
says about him: I recall a certain gourmand who had so
completely abandoned any concern for what others
thought of his behavior that at the baths he openly tried to
accustom his hand to heat by plunging it into hot water,
and his mouth by gargling with it. He did this, of course, to
make himself difficult to dislodge when hot dishes were
served; they claimed that he tried to convince the cooks
to serve the food as hot as possible, so that he could gobble
it down alone while the others were unable to follow his
example. The same stories are told about Philoxenus of
Cythera, Archytas[56], and many others, one of whom says in
a play by the comic poet Crobylus (fr. 8):

   (A.) As for these extremely hot items,
   of course, I've got Idaean fingers;[57]
   and I love giving my throat a steam-bath with fish-
      steaks.
   (B.) He's a kiln, not a human being!

[57] A reference to Mt. Ida in Crete, so that "Idaean" means
"covered in snow" (cf. Thphr. HP 4.1.3), i.e. "able to endure tremendous heat"; but also a punning allusion to the Idaean Dactyls
(literally "Fingers"), small magical creatures who are said to have
invented iron-working at e.g. Hes. fr. 282.

Κλέαρχος δέ φησι Φιλόξενον προλουόμενον ⟨ἐν τῇ πατρίδι κἀν ἄλλαις πόλεσι⟩[16] περιέρχεσθαι τὰς οἰκί-
6 ας, ἀκολουθούντων αὐτῷ παίδων φερόντων ‖ ἔλαιον, οἶνον, γάρον, ὄξος, καὶ ἄλλα ἡδύσματα· ἔπειτα εἰσι- όντα εἰς τὰς ἀλλοτρίας οἰκίας τὰ ἑψόμενα τοῖς ἄλλοις ἀρτύειν ἐμβάλλοντα ὧν ἐστι χρεία, καθ᾽ οὕτως ⟨εἰς ἑαυτὸν⟩ κύψαντα[17] εὐωχεῖσθαι. οὗτος εἰς Ἔφεσον καταπλεύσας εὑρὼν τὴν ὀψοπώλιδα κενὴν ἐπύθετο τὴν αἰτίαν· καὶ μαθὼν ὅτι πᾶν εἰς γάμους συνηγόρασται λουσάμενος παρῆν ἄκλητος ὡς τὸν νυμφίον. καὶ μετὰ τὸ δεῖπνον ᾄσας ὑμέναιον, οὗ ἡ ἀρχὴ

Γάμε θεῶν λαμπρότατε,

b πάντας ἐψυχαγώγησεν· ἦν δὲ διθυραμβοποιός. καὶ ‖ ὁ νυμφίος, "Φιλόξενε," εἶπε, "καὶ αὔριον ὧδε δειπνήσεις;" καὶ ὁ Φιλόξενος, "ἂν ὄψον," ἔφη, "μὴ πωλῇ τις."

Θεόφιλος δέ φησιν· οὐχ ὥσπερ Φιλόξενον τὸν Ἐρύξιδος· ἐκεῖνος γάρ, ὡς ἔοικεν, ἐπιμεμφόμενος τὴν φύσιν εἰς τὴν ἀπόλαυσιν ηὔξατό ποτε γεράνου τὴν φάρυγγα σχεῖν· ἀλλὰ πολὺ μᾶλλον ἵππον ὅλως ἢ βοῦν ἢ κάμηλον ἢ ἐλέφαντα δεῖ σπουδάζειν γενέσθαι. οὕτω γὰρ καὶ αἱ ἐπιθυμίαι καὶ αἱ ἡδοναὶ πολλῷ μείζους καὶ σφοδρότεραι· πρὸς γὰρ τὰς δυνάμεις
c ποιοῦνται τὰς ἀπολαύσεις. Κλέαρχος δὲ Μελάνθιόν ‖

16 from S φ 395
17 εἰς ἑαυτὸν κύψαντα S φ 395: ἀνακάμψαντα CE

30

Clearchus (fr. 57 Wehrli) reports that Philoxenus, in his native city and elsewhere, would bathe and then go around from one house to the next, with his slaves following him carrying oil, wine, fermented fish-sauce, vinegar, and other seasonings. Then he would go into other people's houses; season whatever was being cooked for everyone, adding what was needed; and lower his head, ignoring everyone else, and enjoy the feast. This fellow sailed into Ephesus once and found the fish-stall empty. He asked the reason, and when he found out that everything had been purchased for a wedding feast, he bathed and showed up at the bridegroom's house uninvited. After dinner he sang a marriage-song, the first line of which (Philox. Cyth. *PMG* 828) is:

Marriage, most radiant of gods,

and charmed them all; he was a dithyrambic poet. The bridegroom said "Philoxenus, will you dine with us here tomorrow as well?" And Philoxenus said "[I will] if there's no fish for sale."

Theophilus (fr. 6, *FHG* iv.516) says: Unlike Philoxenus son of Eryxis. For he, it seems, found fault with what nature provided for enjoying food, and prayed on one occasion to have a crane's neck.[58] But one ought to be eager to become a horse, an ox, a camel, or an elephant instead. Because that way one's desires and pleasures would be much greater and more intense; for they produce enjoyment in proportion to their strength. Clearchus (fr. 55

[58] Cf. 8.341d.

φησι τοῦτ᾽ εὔξασθαι λέγων· Τιθωνοῦ Μελάνθιος ἔοικε
βουλεύσασθαι βέλτιον. ὁ μὲν γὰρ ἀθανασίας ἐπιθυ-
μήσας ἐν θαλάμῳ[18] κρέμαται πάντων ὑπὸ γήρως
ἐστερημένος τῶν ἡδέων· Μελάνθιος δὲ τῶν ἀπολαύ-
σεων ἐρῶν ηὔξατο τῆς μακραύχενος ὄρνιθος τὸν τράχηλον ἔχειν, ἵν᾽ ὅτι πλεῖστον τοῖς ἡδέσιν ἐνδιατρίβῃ.
ὁ αὐτός φησι Πίθυλλον τὸν Τένθην καλούμενον οὐ
περιγλωττίδα μόνον ὑμενίνην φορεῖν, ἀλλὰ καὶ προσ-
d ελυτροῦν τὴν γλῶσσαν πρὸς τὰς ἀπολαύσεις· | καὶ
τέλος ἰχθύαν τρίβων ἀπεκάθαιρεν αὐτήν. μόνος δ᾽
οὗτος τῶν ἀπολαυστικῶν καὶ δακτυλήθρας ἔχων ἐσθίειν λέγεται τὸ ὄψον, ἵν᾽ ὡς θερμότατον ὁ τρισάθλιος
ἀναδιδῷ τῇ γλώττῃ. ἄλλοι δὲ φίλιχθυν τὸν Φιλόξενόν
φασιν· Ἀριστοτέλης δὲ φιλόδειπνον ἁπλῶς, ὃς καὶ
γράφει που ταῦτα· δημηγοροῦντες ἐν τοῖς ὄχλοις
κατατρίβουσιν ὅλην τὴν ἡμέραν ἐν τοῖς θαύμασι καὶ
πρὸς τοὺς ἐκ τοῦ Φάσιδος ἢ Βορυσθένους καταπλέ-
οντας, ἀνεγνωκότες οὐδὲν πλὴν εἰ τὸ Φιλοξένου Δεῖ-
e πνον οὐχ ὅλον. |

Φαινίας δέ φησιν ὅτι Φιλόξενος ὁ Κυθήριος ποιητής, περιπαθὴς ὢν τοῖς ὄψοις, δειπνῶν ποτε παρὰ

18 ταλάρῳ Adam

59 A late 5th-century Athenian tragic playwright (*PAA* 638275;
TrGF 23), also mocked as a glutton at e.g. Ar. *Pax* 1009–15.
60 Cf. 12.548f–9a. Tithonus was a mortal lover of the goddess Dawn, who asked Zeus to make him immortal but forgot to
ask that he also be made ageless; cf. *h.Ven.* 218–38. According

Wehrli) reports that this was Melanthius'[59] prayer, saying: Melanthius appears to have planned more effectively than Tithonus. For Tithonus desired immortality but now hangs in his bedroom, deprived of all pleasures by old age.[60] But Melanthius in his lust to enjoy himself prayed to have the gullet of a long-necked bird, in order to spend as much time as possible enjoying himself. The same authority reports that Pithyllus[61], who was called "the Glutton," not only used to wear a covering of skin over his tongue,[62] but applied additional sheathing to it to increase his enjoyment; and afterward he would grind up some fish-skin to clean his tongue. He is the only hedonist said to have eaten fish using finger-guards, the lousy bastard, so that he could deliver it to his tongue as hot as possible. Other authorities call Philoxenus *philichthus* ("a fish-lover"); but Aristotle (fr. 793) simply refers to him as *philodeipnos* ("a dinner-lover"), writing somewhere as follows: They deliver speeches to the crowds and waste the whole day at freakshows and among people who have sailed in from the Phasis or the Borysthenes[63]; and they've never read anything except Philoxenus' *Dinner Party*, and not all of that.

Phaenias (fr. 13 Wehrli) reports that Philoxenus the poet from Cythera (*PMG* 816) had strong feelings about

to Hellanicus (*FGrH* 4 F 140) and Clearchus (fr. 56 Wehrli), Tithonus was eventually transformed into a cicada, which may be the point of the claim that he "hangs" in his bedroom (sc. in a wicker cage).   [61] Otherwise unknown.

[62] To keep it from being burnt by the food (cf. his use of fingerguards below). But why further protection was required is unclear, and the clause that follows may be an intrusive gloss.

[63] Two northern rivers (referred to today as the Rioni and the Dnieper) that flow into the Black Sea.

Διονυσίῳ ⟨τῷ τυράννῳ⟩[19] ὡς εἶδεν ἐκείνῳ μὲν μεγάλην τρίγλαν παρατεθεῖσαν, ἑαυτῷ δὲ μικράν, ἀναλαβὼν αὐτὴν εἰς τὰς χεῖρας πρὸς τὸ οὖς προσήνεγκε. πυθομένου δὲ τοῦ Διονυσίου τίνος ἕνεκεν τοῦτο ποιεῖ, εἶπεν ὁ Φιλόξενος ὅτι γράφων τὴν Γαλάτειαν βούλοιτό τινα παρ᾽ ἐκείνης τῶν κατὰ Νηρέα πυθέσθαι· τὴν δὲ ἠρω-
f τημένην ἀποκεκρίσθαι[20] διότι νεωτέρα ἁλοίη· | διὸ μὴ παρακολουθεῖν· τὴν δὲ τῷ Διονυσίῳ παρατεθεῖσαν πρεσβυτέραν οὖσαν εἰδέναι πάντα σαφῶς ἃ βούλεται μαθεῖν. τὸν οὖν Διονύσιον γελάσαντα ἀποστεῖλαι αὐτῷ τὴν τρίγλαν τὴν παρακειμένην αὐτῷ. συνεμέθυε δὲ τῷ Φιλοξένῳ ἡδέως ὁ Διονύσιος. ἐπεὶ δὲ τὴν ἐρω-
7 μένην Γαλάτειαν[21] ἐφωράθη διαφθείρων, ‖ εἰς τὰς λατομίας ἐνεβλήθη· ἐν αἷς ποιῶν τὸν Κύκλωπα συνέθηκε τὸν μῦθον εἰς τὸ περὶ αὐτὸν γενόμενον πάθος, τὸν μὲν Διονύσιον Κύκλωπα ὑποστησάμενος, τὴν δ᾽ αὐλητρίδα Γαλάτειαν, ἑαυτὸν δ᾽ Ὀδυσσέα.

Ἐγένετο δὲ κατὰ τοὺς Τιβερίου χρόνους ἀνήρ τις Ἀπίκιος, πλουσιώτατος τρυφητής, ἀφ᾽ οὗ πλακούντων γένη πολλὰ Ἀπίκια ὀνομάζεται. οὗτος ἱκανὰς μυρι-

---

[19] from S φ 395   [20] ἀποκεκρίσθαι S φ 395: οὐκ ἀποκεκρίσθαι CE   [21] Γαλάτειαν ought perhaps to be expelled from the text as an intrusive superlinear gloss on τὴν ἐρωμένην, in which case τὴν Γαλάτειαν above is probably an alternative title for the poem referred to below as τὸν Κύκλωπα.

---

[64] Dionysius I, who controlled Syracuse from the end of the 5th century until his death in 367 BCE.   [65] One of the sea-

seafood and was dining once with the tyrant Dionysius.[64] When he saw that Dionysius had been served a large red mullet, whereas he had been served a small one, Philoxenus took his fish in his hands and held it up to his ear. Dionysius asked him why he was doing this, and Philoxenus said that he was writing about Galateia[65] and wanted to ask the fish about some matters involving Nereus; but that when it was questioned, the fish responded that it had been too young when it was caught and therefore was not part of Nereus' circle, although the mullet Dionysius had been served was older and therefore well-informed about everything Philoxenus wanted to know. So Dionysius laughed and sent him the mullet he had been served himself. Dionysius enjoyed getting drunk with Philoxenus. But when Philoxenus was caught trying to seduce Dionysius' mistress Galateia, he was thrown into the stone-quarries. He wrote his *Cyclops* there, connecting the story with the trouble he had gotten into by portraying Dionysius as the Cyclops, the pipe-girl as Galateia, and himself as Odysseus.[66]

In Tiberius'[67] time, there was an extremely wealthy pleasure-seeker named Apicius,[68] from whom many types of cakes get the name "Apician." This fellow spent an in-

nymphs and thus a daughter of Nereus (*Il.* 18.45 ~ Hes. *Th.* 250), the Old Man of the Sea (cf. 3.107b with n.); but supposedly also the name of Dionysius' mistress (see below), although that may be an ancient scholarly error.   [66] Cf. 13.564e, citing a fragment of the *Cyclops* (*PMG* 821) in which the monster praises Galateia's beauty.   [67] Roman emperor, 14–37 CE.

[68] M. Gavius Apicius, who wrote on sauces and to whom a 4th-century CE cookbook (*De re coquinaria*) is falsely attributed.

άδας ⟨ἀργυρίου⟩²² καταναλώσας εἰς τὴν γαστέρα ἐν
Μιντούρναις (πόλις δὲ Καμπανίας) διέτριβε τὰ πλεῖ-
b στα καρίδας ἐσθίων πολυτελεῖς, | αἳ γίνονται αὐτόθι
ὑπέρ γε τὰς ἐν Σμύρνῃ μέγισται καὶ τοὺς ἐν Ἀλεξανδρείᾳ ἀστακούς. ἀκούσας ⟨οὖν⟩²³ καὶ κατὰ Λιβύην
γίνεσθαι ὑπερμεγέθεις ἐξέπλευσεν οὐδ' ἀναμείνας μίαν ἡμέραν. καὶ πολλὰ κακοπαθήσας κατὰ τὸν πλοῦν
ὡς πλησίον ἧκε τῶν τόπων πρὶν ἐξορμῆσαι τῆς νεὼς
(πολλὴ δ' ἐγεγόνει παρὰ Λίβυσι φήμη τῆς ἀφίξεως
αὐτοῦ), προσπλευσάντες ἁλιεῖς προσήνεγκαν αὐτῷ
τὰς καλλίστας καρίδας. ὁ δ' ἰδὼν ἐπύθετο εἰ μείζους
ἔχουσιν· εἰπόντων δὲ μὴ γίνεσθαι ὧν ἤνεγκαν, ὑπο-
c μνησθεὶς | τῶν ἐν Μιντούρναις ἐκέλευσε τῷ κυβερ-
νήτῃ τὴν αὐτὴν ὁδὸν ⟨αὖθις⟩²⁴ ἐπὶ Ἰταλίαν ἀναπλεῖν
μηδὲ προσπελάσαντι τῇ γῇ.

Ἀριστόξενος δ' ὁ Κυρηναῖος φιλόσοφος, ὁ ὄντως
μετελθὼν τὴν πάτριον φιλοσοφίαν, ἀφ' οὗ καὶ κωλήν
τις καλεῖται Ἀριστόξενος ἰδίως σκευαζόμενος, ὑπὸ
τῆς ἀνυπερβλήτου τρυφῆς καὶ τὰς ἐν τῷ κήπῳ γινομένας θριδακίνας οἰνομέλιτι ἐπότιζεν ἑσπέρας καὶ ὑπὸ
τὴν ἔω λαμβάνων χλωροὺς ἔχειν ἔλεγε πλακοῦντας
ὑπὸ τῆς γῆς ἀναπεμπομένους αὐτῷ.

d   Τραιανῷ | δὲ τῷ αὐτοκράτορι ἐν Παρθίᾳ ὄντι καὶ

²² from S α 3207
²³ from S α 3207
²⁴ from S α 3207

36

finite amount of money on his belly and generally passed his time in Minturnae (a city in Campania) eating expensive shrimp, which grow very large there, larger even than the shrimp in Smyrna or the lobsters in Alexandria. So when he heard that there were extraordinarily large shrimp in Libya, he sailed off without a day's delay. After much trouble at sea, he approached those regions; but before he disembarked from his ship—there had been much discussion among the Libyans of his arrival—fishermen sailed out to meet him, bringing him their best shrimp. After he saw them, he asked if they had any that were bigger; when they said that they did not grow any larger than the ones they had brought, his thoughts returned to the shrimp in Minturnae, and he ordered the helmsman to sail back to Italy again by the same route without even putting in to shore.

Aristoxenus the Cyrenaic philosopher, who unambiguously pursued the philosophy of his fatherland,[69] and from whom a specially prepared type of ham is called "Aristoxenus ham," was so profoundly devoted to luxury that he used to water the lettuce he grew in his garden with honeyed wine in the evening. When he picked it at dawn, he would say that he had green cakes which the earth sent up to him.

When the emperor Trajan[70] was in Parthia and was

[69] The Cyrenaics were a philosophical sect who believed that pleasure was the supreme good. Aristoxenus (not to be confused with the Peripatetic author on music cited frequently by Athenaeus) is otherwise unknown.

[70] Roman emperor, 98–117 CE. The Parthian campaign took place in 115–116.

τῆς θαλάσσης ἀπέχοντι ἡμερῶν παμπόλλων ὁδὸν
Ἀπίκιος ‹ὁ ὀψοφάγος›[25] ὄστρεα νεαρὰ διεπέμψατο
ὑπὸ σοφίας αὐτοῦ τεθησαυρισμένα· καὶ οὐχ ὡς Νικο-
μήδει τῷ Βιθυνῶν βασιλεῖ[26] ἐπιθυμήσαντι ἀφύης (μακρὰν δὲ καὶ οὗτος ἦν τῆς θαλάσσης) μάγειρός τις
μιμησάμενος τὸ ἰχθύδιον παρέθηκεν[27]. ὁ γοῦν παρ᾽
Εὔφρονι τῷ κωμικῷ μάγειρός φησιν·

(A.) ἐγὼ μαθητὴς ἐγενόμην Σωτηρίδου,
e   ὃς ἀπὸ θαλάττης Νικομήδει δώδεκα |
    ὁδὸν ἀπέχοντι πρῶτος ἡμερῶν ποτε
    ἀφύης ἐπιθυμήσαντι χειμῶνος μέσου
    παρέθηκε νὴ Δί᾽, ὥστε πάντας ἀνακραγεῖν.
    (B.) πῶς δὲ δυνατὸν τοῦτ᾽ ἐστι; (A.) θήλειαν
        λαβὼν
    γογγυλίδα ταύτην ἔτεμε λεπτὰ ‹ . . . ›,
    τὴν ὄψιν αὐτῆς τῆς ἀφύης μιμούμενος,
    ἀποζέσας, ἔλαιον ἐπιχέας, ἅλας
    δοὺς μουσικῶς, μήκωνος ἐπιπάσας ἄνω
    κόκκους μελαίνης τὸν ἀριθμὸν δισχιλίους,
f   περὶ τὴν Σκυθίαν ἔλυσε τὴν ἐπιθυμίαν. |
    καὶ Νικομήδης γογγυλίδα μασώμενος
    ἀφύης τότ᾽ ἔλεγε τοῖς φίλοις ἐγκώμιον.
    οὐδὲν ὁ μάγειρος τοῦ ποιητοῦ διαφέρει·
    ὁ νοῦς γάρ ἐστιν ἑκατέρῳ τούτων τέχνη.

[25] from S o 720, cf. a 4660
[26] τῷ Βιθυνῶν βασιλεῖ S a 4660: τῷ Βιθυνῷ τῷ βασιλεῖ CE
[27] παρέθηκεν ὡς ἀφύας CE

many days away from the sea, the glutton Apicius[71] had
fresh oysters sent to him packed in a clever way he devised
himself. Matters were different when Nicomedes king of
Bithynia[72] had a yearning for small-fry (he too was a long
way from the sea), and a cook made something that resembled the fish and served it to him. The cook in the comic
poet Euphro (fr. 10), at any rate, says:

> (A.) I was a student of Soterides,
> who, when Nicomedes was twelve days'
> journey away from the sea once and had a yearning
> for small-fry in mid-winter, was the first
> to serve him some, by Zeus; he made them all cry out
>   in amazement.
> (B.) How's this possible? (A.) He took a soft
> turnip like this one; cut it in thin slices,
> so that it looked like small-fry;
> stewed it thoroughly; poured oil over it; salted
> it artfully; sprinkled 2000
> black-poppy seeds on top;
> and satisfied the king's desire in Scythia.
> And as Nicomedes chewed on turnip,
> he sang the praises of small-fry to his friends.
> The cook's no different from the poet;
> for the genius of each consists of his technical skill.

[71] Presumably a descendant of the Apicius referred to above.

[72] Nicomedes I, king of Bithynia (a region in northwest Asia
Minor) 280–255/3 BCE.

Ὅτι περὶ Περικλέους φησὶν Ἀρχίλοχος ὁ Πάριος
ποιητὴς ὡς ἀκλήτου ἐπεισπαίοντος εἰς τὰ συμπόσια

< . . . > Μυκονίων δίκην.

δοκοῦσι δ᾽ οἱ Μυκόνιοι διὰ τὸ πένεσθαι καὶ λυπρὰν
νῆσον οἰκεῖν ἐπὶ γλισχρότητι καὶ πλεονεξίᾳ διαβάλ-
8 λεσθαι· ‖ τὸν γοῦν γλίσχρον Ἰσχόμαχον Κρατῖνος
Μυκόνιον καλεῖ· † πῶς ἂν Ἰσχομάχου γεγονὼς Μυκο-
νίου Φιλόδωρος εἴης; †

Ἀγαθὸς πρὸς ἀγαθοὺς ἄνδρας ἑστιασόμενος ἧκον·

< . . . > κοινὰ γὰρ τὰ τῶν φίλων.

                    πολλὸν δὲ πίνων καὶ χαλίκρητον μέθυ,
οὔτε τῖμον εἰσενείκας < . . . >
οὐδὲ μὲν κληθεὶς < . . . > ἦλθες οἷα δὴ φίλος,
b ἀλλά σεο γαστὴρ νόον τε καὶ φρένας |
        παρήγαγεν
εἰς ἀναιδείην,

Ἀρχίλοχος φησίν. Εὔβουλος ὁ κωμικός φησί που·

εἰσὶν ἡμῖν τῶν κεκλημένων δύο
ἐπὶ δεῖπνον ἄμαχοι, Φιλοκράτης καὶ
        Φιλοκράτης[28].

[28] Φιλοκράτης[2] Turnebus: Φιλοκτήτης CE

---

[73] *PAA* 542570.   [74] A reference to the proverb quoted at
5.178b, and probably the beginning of a speech.

The Parian poet Archilochus (fr. 124a West[2]; see below) claims that Pericles used to burst into drinking parties uninvited

in Myconian style.

The inhabitants of Myconos seem to have been criticized for greed and avarice because they were poor and inhabited a miserable island. Cratinus (fr. 365, unmetrical), for example, calls the greedy Ischomachus[73] a Myconian: †How could *you*, the son of Myconian Ischomachus, be named "Generous"? †

I am a good man come to dine in the company of good men;[74]

for friends' possessions are held in common. (E. *Or.* 735 ~ Men. fr. 13)[75]

Archilochus (fr. 124b West[2]) says:[76]

Although you drink much unmixed wine,
you neither contributed any money . . .
And you came uninvited, as a friend would do;
but your belly led your mind and heart astray
into shamelessness.

The comic poet Eubulus (fr. 117) says somewhere:

Two of our guests are
invincible at dinner: Philocrates and Philocrates.[77]

---

[75] Also proverbial.   [76] The individual attacked is the Pericles mentioned in fr. 124a above (not to be confused with the Athenian statesman).   [77] Perhaps the late 4th-century Athenian politician (*PA* 14599) also mentioned at 8.343e.

ἕνα γὰρ ἐκεῖνον ὄντα δύο λογίζομαι
μεγάλους < . . . > μᾶλλον δὲ τρεῖς.
ὅν φασί ποτε κληθέντ᾽ ἐπὶ δεῖπνον † ὡς φίλου
   καὶ τῶ τινος †

c εἰπόντος αὐτῷ τοῦ φίλου, ὁπηνίκ᾽ ἂν |
εἴκοσι ποδῶν μετροῦντι τὸ στοιχεῖον ᾖ,
ἥκειν, ἔωθεν αὐτὸν εὐθὺς ἡλίου
μετρεῖν ἀνέχοντος, μακροτέρας δ᾽ οὔσης ἔτι
πλεῖν ἢ δυοῖν ποδοῖν παρεῖναι τῆς σκιᾶς,
† ἔπειτα φάναι † μικρὸν ὀψιαίτερον
δι᾽ ἀσχολίαν ἥκειν, παρόνθ᾽ ἅμ᾽ ἡμέρᾳ.

ἀσυμβόλου δείπνου γὰρ ὅστις ὑστερεῖ,
τοῦτον ταχέως νόμιζε κἂν τάξιν λιπεῖν,

Ἄμφις φησὶν ὁ κωμικός. Χρύσιππος δέ φησιν·

d ἀσύμβολον κώθωνα μὴ παραλίμπανε. |
κώθων δ᾽ οὐ παραλειπτὸς ἀσύμβολος, ἀλλὰ
   διωκτός.

Ἀντιφάνης δέ φησι·

βίος θεῶν γάρ ἐστιν, ὅταν ἔχῃς ποθὲν
τἀλλότρια δειπνεῖν, μὴ προσέχων λογίσμασι.

For although there's only one of him, I count him as
    two
big ones . . . rather as three.
They say that once, when he was invited to dinner
    [corrupt],
his friend told him to come when
the sundial's shadow measured 20 feet.
So he began to measure it at dawn, as soon as
the sun came up; and when the shadow was still
more than two feet too long, he appeared.
† And then he said † he'd come a bit late,
because he'd been busy—even though he was there
    at daybreak!

The comic poet Amphis (fr. 39) says:

Because if someone's late to a dinner party for which
    no contribution is required,
you can assume he would quickly desert his place in
    the battle-line as well.

Chrysippus (xxviii fr. 15, *SVF* iii.200) says:

Do not neglect the drinking party that requires no
    contribution.
A drinking party that requires no contribution is not
    to be neglected but sought after.

Antiphanes (fr. 252) says:

For this is the life of the gods—when you have the
    chance
to eat someone else's food and not worry about the
    bills.

καὶ πάλιν·

μακάριος ὁ βίος † ᾧ δεῖ μ' ἀεὶ καινὸν πόρον
εὑρίσκειν † ὡς μάσημα ταῖς γνάθοις ἔχω.

Ταῦτα οἴκοθεν ἔχων εἰς τὸ συμπόσιον ἦλθον καὶ
προμελετήσας, ἵνα κἀγὼ τὸ στεγανόμιον κομίζων
παραγένωμαι·

e   ἄκαπνα γὰρ αἰὲν ἀοιδοὶ |
θύομεν.

Ὅτι τὸ μονοφαγεῖν ἐστιν ἐν χρήσει τοῖς παλαιοῖς.
Ἀντιφάνης·

⟨ . . . ⟩ μονοφαγεῖς ἤδη τι καὶ βλάπτεις ἐμέ.

Ἀμειψίας·

ἔρρ' ἐς κόρακας, μονοφάγε καὶ τοιχωρύχε.[29]

Ὅτι Ὅμηρος ὁρῶν τὴν σωφροσύνην οἰκειοτάτην
ἀρετὴν οὖσαν τοῖς νέοις καὶ πρώτην, ἔτι δὲ ἁρμόττου-

[29] CE preface what follows with the subtitle περὶ τοῦ τῶν
ἡρώων καθ' Ὅμηρον βίου ("On the Life of the Heroes according to Homer").

---

[78] The comment is in fact cynical and disaffected.

[79] Presumably jokes or quotations, by means of which the
speaker will earn his dinner; cf. 1.4b. This remark clearly comes at
the beginning or end of a speech, which most likely begins with a
response to a philological question posed by Ulpian. The quota-

And again (fr. 253):[78]

> A happy life I lead—† when I must always try to
>   discover
> some new trick † to have a morsel for my jaws!

I came to the symposium bringing these items[79] from
my own house, and I took care to be here with my rent-
money in hand;

> because we singers always make smokeless
> sacrifices. (Call. fr. 494)

The word *monophagein* ("to eat alone, without sharing") is used by the ancients. Antiphanes (fr. 291):

> You're eating privately *(monophageis)* now and doing
>   me an injury.

Amipsias (fr. 23):

> Go to hell, you solo-eating *(monophage)* burglar!

Homer saw[80] that moderation is the most appropriate
and foremost virtue of young men, and also that it inte-

tion from Callimachus suggests that a musician is speaking.

[80] The *Suda* (o 251) assigns 1.8e–9c to Dioscurides, *On Homeric Law*. Dioscurides is cited explicitly by Athenaeus at 1.11a
(for a variant reading in Homer that supports the general line of
interpretation adopted throughout this section), and Weber argued that all of 1.8e–11b ought to be assigned to him on that basis
(= *FGrH* 594 F *8). In any case, the speaker argues that Homer
was making a moralizing point by presenting the life of his heroes
as extremely simple and constrained; contrast 1.11b n.; 1.24b n.

σαν καὶ πάντων τῶν καλῶν χορηγὸν οὖσαν, βουλόμε-
νος ἐμφῦσαι πάλιν αὐτὴν ἀπ᾽ ἀρχῆς καὶ ἐφεξῆς, ἵνα
f τὴν σχολὴν καὶ τὸν ζῆλον ἐν | τοῖς καλοῖς ἔργοις
ἀναλίσκωσι καὶ ὦσιν εὐεργετικοὶ καὶ κοινωνικοὶ[30]
πρὸς ἀλλήλους, εὐτελῆ κατεσκεύασε πᾶσι τὸν βίον
καὶ αὐτάρκη, λογιζόμενος τὰς ἐπιθυμίας καὶ τὰς ἡδονὰς ἰσχυροτάτας γίνεσθαι ‹καὶ πρώτας ἔτι τε καὶ
ἐμφύτους τὰς›[31] περὶ ἐδωδὴν καὶ πόσιν, τοὺς δὲ δια-
μεμενηκότας ἐν εὐτελείᾳ εὐτάκτους καὶ περὶ τὸν ἄλλον
βίον γίνεσθαι ἐγκρατεῖς. ἁπλῆν οὖν ἀποδέδωκε τὴν
δίαιταν πᾶσι καὶ τὴν αὐτὴν ὁμοίως βασιλεῦσιν ἰδιώ-
9 ταις νέοις πρεσβύταις ‖ ‹λέγων·

παρὰ δὲ ξεστὴν ἐτάνυσσε τράπεζαν.
σῖτον δ᾽ αἰδοίη ταμίη παρέθηκε φέρουσα,
δαιτρὸς δὲ κρειῶν πίνακας παρέθηκεν ἀείρας,

καὶ τούτων ὀπτῶν καὶ ὡς ἐπὶ τὸ πολὺ βοείων· παρὰ δὲ
ταῦτα οὔτε ἐν ἑορταῖς οὔτ᾽ ἐν γάμοις οὔτ᾽ ἐν ἄλλῃ
συνόδῳ παρατίθησιν οὐδέν, καίτοι πολλάκις τὸν Ἀγα-
μέμνονα ποιήσας δειπνίζοντα τοὺς ἀρίστους›[32]. καὶ
οὐ θρῖα καὶ κάνδυλον καὶ ἄμητας μελίπηκτά τε τοῖς

30 κοινωνικοὶ Kuster: κοινοὶ CE S o 251
31 from S o 251   32 from S o 251. CE have only ὀπτὰ
παρατιθεὶς πᾶσι κρέα καὶ ταῦτα ὡς ἐπὶ τὸ πολὺ βόεια ἔν τε
ἑορταῖς καὶ γάμοις καὶ ἄλλῃ συνόδῳ.

---

81 The omitted verse 140 describes how the housekeeper offered "foods of many kinds," and is thus inconvenient for the argu-

46

grates and coordinates all good qualities. And because he wished to implant it again forever, so that they would spend their leisure time and energy on noble deeds and be good to and sociable with one another, he made the lives of all his characters frugal and simple. For he calculated that desires and pleasures are very powerful, and that those that involve food and drink are the most basic and deeply engrained, and that people who have lived in a consistently frugal manner are orderly and self-disciplined in other aspects of their lives as well. He therefore gives them all a simple way of life, drawing no distinction between kings and commoners, young and old, saying (e.g. *Od.* 1.138–9, 141):[81]

> and she stretched out a polished table
>   beside them.
> And the respectful housekeeper brought bread and
>   set it by their side.
> And the carver picked up platters of meat and set
>   them by their side.

This meat was roasted and was generally beef. He serves them nothing except this at festivals, wedding feasts, and other parties, even though he often represents Agamemnon as entertaining the leading warriors at dinner. Nor does Homer serve his kings stuffed fig-leaves, *kandulos*[82], or fine wheat-cakes and honey-cakes as their special por-

---

ment, as is 142, which reports that the meat was "of every sort." Cf. 5.193b, where an argument is made for expelling either 140 or 141 from the text; and contrast 1.25e.

[82] An exotic Lydian dish; see 4.132f n.; 12.516c–d.

βασιλεῦσιν ἐξαίρετα παρατίθησιν Ὅμηρος, ἀλλ᾽ ἀφ᾽
ὧν εὖ ἕξειν ἔμελλον τὸ σῶμα καὶ τὴν ψυχήν. Αἴαντα
γοῦν μετὰ τὴν μονομαχίαν

> νώτοισι < . . . > γέραιρεν

ὁ Ἀγαμέμνων· καὶ Νέστορι δ᾽ ἤδη ὄντι γηραιῷ καὶ
b Φοίνικι κρέας ὀπτὸν δίδωσι[33], ἀφιστῶν | ἡμᾶς τῶν
ἀτάκτων ἐπιθυμιῶν. καὶ Ἀλκίνους δὲ ὁ τὸν τρυφερὸν
ᾑρημένος βίον <τοὺς τρυφερωτάτους ἑστιῶν Φαίακας
καὶ τὸν Ὀδυσσέα ξενίζων, ἐπιδεικνύμενος αὐτῷ τὴν
τοῦ κήπου κατασκευὴν καὶ τῆς οἰκίας καὶ τὸν αὐτοῦ
βίον, τοιαύτας παρατίθεται τραπέζας>[34]. καὶ Μενέλα-
ος δὲ τοὺς τῶν παίδων γάμους ποιούμενος <καὶ τοῦ
Τηλεμάχου πρὸς αὐτὸν παραγενομένου>[35]

> νῶτα βοὸς < . . . > παρέθηκεν[36]
> <ὄπτ᾽ ἐν χερσὶν ἑλών,>[37] τά ῥά οἱ γέρα
> πάρθεσαν αὐτῷ.

καὶ Νέστωρ δὲ βόας θύει Ποσειδῶνι παρὰ τῇ θαλάσσῃ διὰ τῶν φιλτάτων καὶ οἰκειοτάτων τέκνων, βασιλεὺς ὢν καὶ πολλοὺς ἔχων ὑπηκόους, <τάδε παρακε-
λευόμενος·

> ἀλλ᾽ ἄγ᾽ ὁ μὲν πεδίονδ᾽ ἐπὶ βοῦν ἴτω

[33] The order of the words that follow in the text has been altered by Kaibel to take account of the material preserved in the
Suda (below); CE have δίδωσι καὶ Ἀλκίνῳ δὲ τῷ τὸν τρυφερὸν
ᾑρημένῳ βίον, ἀφιστῶν κτλ.   [34] from S ο 251

tion, but foods likely to keep their bodies and souls healthy. In the case of Ajax after his one-on-one duel, for example, Agamemnon (*Il.* 7.321)

honored him with chine.

Homer also gives roast meat to Nestor (*Od.* 3.32–3), who was an old man by now, and to Phoenix (cf. *Il.* 9.206–17), as a way of restraining us from unruly desires. So too, although Alcinous has adopted a pampered way of life, when he feasts the luxury-loving Phaeacians and entertains Odysseus, he shows him the layout of his garden and his house and how he himself lives, but serves him the same type of food.[83] Likewise Menelaus, when he was holding a marriage feast for his children and Telemachus was with him (*Od.* 4.65–6),

took in his hand and served him the roasted beef chine they served him as his portion of honor.

Nestor as well sacrifices cattle to Poseidon on the seashore, relying on his children, who are nearest and dearest to him, to do this, although he is a king and has many servants. He gives them the following orders (*Od.* 3.421):

Come now! One of you go to the field for a heifer,

83 In fact, Odysseus sees the palace and its grounds as he enters alone (*Od.* 7.81–132), and is never given a tour.

---

35 from S o 251. CE have only Τηλεμάχῳ.

36 The standard text of Homer has παρὰ πίονα θῆκεν rather than Athenaeus' παρέθηκεν.

καὶ τὰ ἑξῆς>[38]· ὁσιωτέρα γὰρ αὕτη ἡ θυσία θεοῖς καὶ
προσφιλεστέρα ἡ διὰ τῶν οἰκείων καὶ εὐνουστάτων
ἀνδρῶν. καὶ τοὺς μνηστῆρας δὲ ὑβριστὰς ὄντας καὶ
c πρὸς ἡδονὰς ἀνειμένους | οὔτε ἰχθῦς ἐσθίοντας ποιεῖ
οὔτε ὄρνιθας οὔτε μελίπηκτα, περιελὼν παντὶ σθένει
τὰς μαγειρικὰς μαγγανείας καὶ τά, ὡς ὁ Μένανδρός
φησιν,

> < . . . > ὑποβινητιῶντα βρώματα

καὶ τὸ παρὰ πολλοῖς λασταυροκάκαβον καλούμενον
βρῶμα, ὥς φησι Χρύσιππος <ἐν τῷ Περὶ Καλοῦ καὶ
Ἡδονῆς>[30], οὗ ἡ κατασκευὴ περιεργοτέρα.

Πρίαμος δὲ παρὰ τῷ ποιητῇ καὶ ὀνειδίζει τοῖς υἱοῖς
ἀναλίσκουσι τὰ μὴ νενομισμένα·

> ἀρνῶν ἠδ᾽ ἐρίφων ἐπιδήμιοι ἁρπακτῆρες.

Φιλόχορος δὲ ἱστορεῖ καὶ κεκωλῦσθαι Ἀθήνησιν
d ἀπέκτου | ἀρνὸς μηδένα γεύεσθαι, ἐπιλιπούσης ποτὲ
τῆς τῶν ζῴων τούτων γενέσεως.

Ἑλλήσποντον δὲ Ὅμηρος ἰχθυόεντα προσαγορεύ-
ων καὶ τοὺς Φαίακας πλωτικωτάτους ποιῶν καὶ ἐν τῇ
Ἰθάκῃ εἰδὼς λιμένας πλείους καὶ νήσους προσεχεῖς
πολλάς, ἐν αἷς ἰχθύων ἐγίνετο πλῆθος καὶ ἀγρίων
ὀρνίθων, καὶ εἰς εὐδαιμονίαν δὲ καταριθμῶν τὸ τὴν
θάλασσαν ἰχθῦς παρέχειν, ὅμως τούτων οὐδὲν οὐδένα
ποιεῖ προσφερόμενον· καὶ μὴν οὐδ᾽ ὀπώραν παρατίθη-

[37] from S o 251   [38] from S o 251   [39] from S λ 140

and so forth. For a sacrifice made by the members of one's household and one's loyal friends is holier in the gods' eyes and more pleasing. Homer even represents the suitors, violent and devoted to pleasure though they are, as eating neither fish nor birds nor honey-cakes. And he vigorously excludes culinary trickery and what Menander calls (fr. 351.11)[84]

lecherous foods,

along with what many authors refer to as "food stewed in depravity," as Chrysippus puts it in *On the Good and Pleasure* (xxviii fr. 9, *SVF* iii.199–200), that is, food that is quite elaborately prepared.

Homer's Priam faults his sons for consuming foods that fall outside the norm (*Il.* 24.262):

plunderers of the common people's lambs and kids.

Philochorus (*FGrH* 328 F 169a)[85] records that in Athens it was forbidden to taste the meat of a lamb that had never been shorn, since at one point an insufficient number of these creatures was born.

Homer refers to the Hellespont as "full of fish" (*Il.* 9.360); represents the Phaeacians as very fond of sailing (e.g. *Od.* 6.270–2); knows that there are numerous harbors on Ithaca (cf. *Od.* 1.185–6; 2.391; 13.96–101) and many islands full of fish and wild birds nearby (e.g. *Od.* 9.22–4); and counts the sea's supply of fish as an element of prosperity (*Od.* 19.113). But he nonetheless does not represent anyone consuming these foods. Indeed, he serves no one

[84] Quoted in more complete form at 4.132e–f.
[85] Cf. 9.375c.

e σί τινι καίπερ οὖσαν πολλὴν καὶ ἥδιστα | ταύτης
μνημονεύων καὶ πάντα χρόνον παρασκευάζων ἀθά-
νατον·

ὄγχνη (γάρ, φησίν,) ἐπ᾽ ὄγχνη

καὶ τὰ ἑξῆς. ἀλλὰ μὴν οὐδὲ στεφανουμένους οὐδὲ
μυρουμένους ποιεῖ ὥσπερ οὐδὲ θυμιῶντας, ἀλλὰ πάντων τούτων ἀπολυομένους τοὺς ἀνθρώπους εἰς ἐλευ-
θερίαν καὶ αὐτάρκειαν ἐξαιρεῖται τοὺς πρώτους.[40] καὶ
θεοῖς δὲ ἁπλῆν ἀποδίδωσι δίαιταν νέκταρ καὶ ἀμβροσίαν. καὶ τοὺς ἀνθρώπους δὲ ποιεῖ τιμῶντας αὐτοὺς
f ἀπὸ τῆς | διαίτης, ἀφελὼν λιβανωτὸν καὶ σμύρναν καὶ
στεφάνους καὶ τὴν περὶ ταῦτα τρυφήν. καὶ τῆς ἁπλῆς
δὲ ταύτης διαίτης οὐκ ἀπλήστως ἀπολαύοντας παρί-
στησιν, ἀλλ᾽ ὡς οἱ κράτιστοι τῶν ἰατρῶν ἀφαιρεῖ τὰς
πλησμονάς,

αὐτὰρ ἐπεὶ πόσιος καὶ ἐδητύος ἐξ ἔρον ἕντο.

καὶ τὴν ἐπιθυμίαν πληρώσαντες οἱ μὲν ἐξώρμων ἐπὶ
10 μελέτην ἀθλητικὴν δίσκοισι ‖ τερπόμενοι καὶ αἰγανέ-
αις, τῇ παιδιᾷ τὰ πρὸς σπουδὴν ἐκμελετῶντες· οἱ δὲ
κιθαρῳδῶν ἠκροῶντο τὰς ἡρωικὰς πράξεις ἐν μέλει
καὶ ῥυθμῷ ποιούντων. διὸ οὐδὲν θαυμαστὸν τοὺς οὕτω
τεθραμμένους ἀφλεγμάντους εἶναι τὰ σώματα καὶ τὰς
ψυχάς. ἐνδεικνύμενος οὖν καὶ τὴν εὐταξίαν ὡς ὑγιεινόν

---

[40] This sentence (ἀλλὰ μὴν . . . πρώτους) is omitted by E
and preserved in C only in the margin.

any fruit, although there is plenty of it and he mentions it in a delightful passage, where he presents it as never failing in any season. For, he says (*Od.* 7.120),

> pear follows pear,

and so forth. He also does not represent them as wearing garlands or using perfume, or similarly as burning incense, but instead distinguishes the foremost individuals as free and self-sufficient, by keeping them away from such luxuries. He even ascribes a simple regimen of nectar and ambrosia to the gods; and he represents human beings as honoring the gods by the way they live, letting them have nothing to do with frankincense, myrrh, garlands, and the luxury that goes with them. Nor does he depict men enjoying this simple diet greedily, but like the best doctors he forbids satiety (e.g. *Od.* 1.150):

> But when they put away their desire for food and
> drink.

And after they satisfied their appetite, some of them would set off for athletic exercise, enjoying themselves with discuses and hunting-spears (cf. *Od.* 4.625–7), using games to train for serious pursuits. Others listened to citharodes[86] describe heroic deeds in rhythmic melody (cf. *Od.* 1.325–7). It is accordingly no wonder that people brought up this way do not suffer from overheated bodies or souls. As a means, therefore, of showing that discipline is healthy

---

[86] Men who played the lyre and sang.

ἐστι καὶ εὔχρηστον καὶ κοινὸν τὸν σοφώτατον Νέστο-
ρα πεποίηκε Μαχάονι τῷ ἰατρῷ τετρωμένῳ τὸν δεξιὸν
ὦμον προσφέροντα οἶνον, ταῖς φλεγμοναῖς ἐναντιώ-
b τατον ὄντα, καὶ τοῦτον Πράμνειον, ὃν ἴδμεν | παχὺν
καὶ πολύτροφον (οὐ διψήσεως ἄκος, ἀλλ᾽ ἐμφορήσεως
ἕνεκα· πεπωκότι γοῦν παρακελεύεται συνεχῶς τοῦτο
ποιεῖν·

　　< . . . > σὺ μέν, (φησί,) < . . . πῖνε> καθήμενος),

καὶ ἐπιξύοντα τυρὸν αἴγειον, ἐπὶ δὲ κρόμυον ποτοῦ
ὄψον, ἵνα πλεῖον πίνῃ, καίτοι ἀλλαχοῦ λέγων τὸν
οἶνον ἐκλύειν τὴν ἰσχὺν καὶ ἀπογυιοῦν. περὶ δὲ τοῦ
Ἕκτορος Ἑκάβη οἰομένη μενεῖν αὐτὸν τὸ καταλει-
πόμενον τῆς ἡμέρας παρακαλεῖ πιεῖν σπείσαντα, προ-
τρεπομένη εἰς θυμηδίαν· ὁ δ᾽ ὑπερτίθεται πρὸς πρᾶξιν
c ἐξιών. καὶ ἡ μὲν ἀπερισπάστως | ἐπαινεῖ τὸν οἶνον, ὁ
δὲ μετὰ ἄσθματος ἥκων ἀπωθεῖται· καὶ ἡ μὲν ἀξιοῖ
σπείσαντα πιεῖν, ὁ δὲ καθημαγμένος ἀσεβὲς ἡγεῖται.
οἶδε δὲ ὁ Ὅμηρος καὶ τὸ ὠφέλιμον καὶ τὸ σύμμετρον
τοῦ οἴνου <ἐν> οἷς τὸν χανδὸν ἕλκοντα αὐτὸν βλά-
πτεσθαί φησι. καὶ κράσεων δὲ γένη διάφορα ἐπίστα-
ται· οὐκ ἂν γὰρ Ἀχιλλεὺς τὸ ζωρότερον κεραίρειν

---

[87] The material that follows (to 1.10d) appears to come from a
different source from what surrounds it.

[88] It is not actually Nestor who does any of this, but his slave-
woman Hecamede.

[89] In fact, Hecabe claims in verses 261–2 that drinking wine

54

and useful for everyone,[87] he represents Nestor, the wisest of men, as offering wine to the physician Machaon after Machaon had been wounded in the right shoulder (*Il.* 11.638–41), even though Nestor was utterly opposed to heated behavior; and Pramneian wine at that, which we know is substantial and filling. (This was not to cure his thirst but to fill his belly; because even after Machaon has drunk, Nestor continues to urge him on (*Il.* 14.5);

Sit down and drink!,

he says.) Nestor also grates goat-cheese on top and adds an onion as a garnish (*Il.* 11.639–40, 630)[88] to make him drink more, even though Homer says elsewhere that wine dissipates a man's strength and disables him. In the case of Hector, Hecabe expects that he will remain there for the rest of the day, and urges him to pour a libation and have a drink, and encourages him to enjoy himself (*Il.* 6.258–60).[89] But he puts this off and goes out to complete his business (esp. *Il.* 6.264–5, 313). She insistently praises the wine; but although he arrived panting for breath (cf. *Il.* 6.261–2), he refuses it. She thinks it right that he pour a libation and have a drink; whereas he considers this impious, because he is stained with blood (*Il.* 6.266–8). But Homer recognizes both the usefulness of wine and the need to drink it in moderation in the passage where he says that the man who drains his cup greedily does himself an injury (*Od.* 21.293–4). He also understands that there are different ways of mixing wine; for Achilleus would not have ordered that the wine be mixed "purer" (*Il.* 9.203) un-

---

will restore Hector's strength (sc. for battle), and she does not insist when he rejects her suggestion.

διέστειλε, μὴ οὔσης τινὸς καθημερινῆς κράσεως. ἴσως
οὖν οὐκ ἐγίνωσκεν αὐτὸν εὐδιαφόρητον ἄνευ στερεμ-
νίου σιτίου μίγματος, ὃ τοῖς ἰατροῖς διὰ τὴν τέχνην
d ἐστὶ δῆλον· | τοῖς γοῦν καρδιακοῖς μετὰ οἴνου σιτῶδες
ἀναμίσγουσί τι πρὸς κατοχὴν τῆς δυνάμεως. ἀλλ᾽
ἐκεῖνος τῷ μὲν Μαχάονι μετ᾽ ἀλφίτου καὶ τυροῦ δέδω-
κε τὸν οἶνον, τὸν δ᾽ Ὀδυσσέα ποιεῖ συνάπτοντα τὴν
ἀπὸ τῶν σιτίων καὶ οἴνου ὠφέλειαν·

    ὃς δέ κ᾽ ἀνὴρ οἴνοιο κορεσσάμενος καὶ ἐδωδῆς.

τῷ δὲ κωθωνιζομένῳ δίδωσι τὸν ἡδύποτον, οὕτω καλέ-
υας αὐτόν·

    ἐν δὲ πίθοι οἴνοιο παλαιοῦ ἡδυπότοιο.

e   Ποιεῖ δὲ Ὅμηρος καὶ τὰς κόρας καὶ τὰς γυναῖκας |
λουούσας τοὺς ξένους, ὡς οὔτε φλεγμονὴν οὔτε ἀκρα-
σίαν τῶν εὖ βεβιωκότων καὶ σωφρόνως ἁπτομένας.
ἀρχαῖον δὲ τοῦτο ἔθος· λούουσι γοῦν καὶ αἱ κωκάλου
θυγατέρες, ὡς νενομισμένον, τὸν Μίνω παραγενόμε-
νον εἰς Σικελίαν.

    Τῆς μέθης δὲ κατατρέχων ὁ ποιητὴς τὸν τηλικοῦ-
τον Κύκλωπα ὑπὸ μικροῦ σώματος διὰ ταύτην ἀπολ-
λύμενον παρίστησι καὶ Εὐρυτίωνα τὸν Κένταυρον·
τούς τε παρὰ Κίρκῃ λέοντας ποιεῖ καὶ λύκους ταῖς

---

90 Minos was tracking down Daedalus, who fled Crete after he
helped Theseus negotiate the Labyrinth. Athenaeus fails to note
that Cocalus' daughters murdered their guest with scalding water
([Apollod.] *Epit*. 1.15 with Frazer ad loc.).

less there were some conventional proportion. Perhaps, therefore, he was unaware that wine passes easily through the body if solid food is not mixed into it, a fact that is obvious to physicians from their work. For cardiac patients, for example, they mix something solid into the wine to contain its effect. But Homer gives wine mixed with barley-meal and cheese to Machaon (*Il*. 11.639–40), and represents Odysseus as conflating the benefits derived from solid food and from wine (*Il*. 19.167):

whenever a man gets his fill of wine and food.

And Homer provides "sweet wine" for the man who intends to do serious drinking, referring to it as follows (*Od*. 2.340):

And in there were storage-jars full of old sweet wine.

Homer also represents his girls and his women as bathing their guests, in the conviction that passion and lust have no effect on men who have led good, modest lives. This is an ancient custom; the daughters of Cocalus, for example, give Minos a bath when he visits them in Sicily, as if this were normal.[90]

The poet disparages drunkenness by representing it as the means by which the Cyclops, big as he is, is defeated by a tiny person (cf. *Od*. 9.515–16), as also in the case of the centaur Eurytion (*Od*. 21.295–302). And he represents the lions and wolves at Circe's house as pursuing pleasure,[91]

[91] I.e. as men lured on by their appetites and transformed by the sorceress, in the same way Odysseus' men were transformed into pigs. But Homer's account (*Od*. 10.212–13) makes it clear that these are real wild animals Circe has captured.

f ἡδοναῖς ἐπακολουθήσαντας. τὸν | δὲ Ὀδυσσέα σῴζει
τῷ Ἑρμοῦ λόγῳ πεισθέντα· διὸ καὶ ἀπαθὴς γίνεται.
Ἐλπήνορα δὲ πάροινον ὄντα καὶ τρυφερὸν κατακρημ-
νίζει. καὶ Ἀντίνοος δ᾽ ὁ λέγων πρὸς Ὀδυσσέα·

οἶνός σε τρώει μελιηδής,

αὐτὸς οὐκ ἀπείχετο τοῦ πώματος· διὸ καὶ τρωθεὶς
ἀπώλετο, ἔτι κρατῶν τὸ ποτήριον. ποιεῖ δὲ καὶ τοὺς
Ἕλληνας ἐν τῷ ἀπόπλῳ μεθύοντας, διὸ καὶ στασιά-
11 ζοντας· ὅθεν καὶ ἀπόλλυνται. ‖ ἱστορεῖ δὲ καὶ τὸν
δεινότατον[41] τῶν Τρώων ἐν τῷ βουλεύεσθαι διὰ τὴν ἐν
τῇ μέθῃ παρρησίαν καὶ τὰς ἀπειλὰς ἃς Τρωσὶν ὑπ-
έσχετο οἰνοποτάζων ὑπομείναντα τὴν Ἀχιλλέως ὁρ-
μὴν καὶ μικροῦ παραπολλύμενον. καὶ Ἀγαμέμνων δὲ
λέγει που περὶ αὐτοῦ·

ἀλλ᾽ ἐπεὶ ἀασάμην φρεσὶ λευγαλέῃσι πιθήσας
ἢ᾽ οἴνῳ μεθύων ἤ μ᾽ ἔβλαψαν θεοὶ αὐτοί,

εἰς τὴν αὐτὴν τιθεὶς πλάστιγγα τὴν μέθην τῇ μανίᾳ.
οὕτω δὲ καὶ τὰ ἔπη ταῦτα προηνέγκατο Διοσκουρίδης
b | ὁ Ἰσοκράτους μαθητής. καὶ ὁ Ἀχιλλεὺς δ᾽ ὀνειδίζων
τῷ Ἀγαμέμνονί φησιν·

---

[41] τὸν δεινότατον Αἰνείαν CE

---

[92] Aeneas, whose name (originally added above the line as an
explanatory gloss, and deleted here) has made its way into the text
of the Epitome.

but keeps Odysseus safe because he listens to what Hermes tells him (*Od.* 10.277ff); this is why nothing happens to him. He throws the drunken, dissolute Elpenor, on the other hand, off a roof (*Od.* 10.552–60). So too Antinoos, who tells Odysseus that (*Od.* 21.293)

> the sweet wine is doing you harm,

did not himself avoid drinking; as a consequence, he was "done harm" and died still clutching his goblet (*Od.* 22.8–20). Homer also represents the Greeks as drunk when they sailed away from Troy and as quarreling because of that (*Od.* 3.136–50, esp. 139), as a result of which they perished. And he recounts that the cleverest Trojan when it came to making plans[92] resisted Achilleus' onslaught because of his outspokenness when he was drunk and the threats he made against the other Trojans when he was consuming wine, and nearly died (*Il.* 20.79ff, esp. 83–5). Likewise Agamemnon says about himself somewhere (*Il.* 9.119–19a):[93]

> But since I acted recklessly by yielding to my baleful
> inclinations
> or by being drunk on wine; or else the gods
> themselves smote me,

balancing drunkenness against madness. Isocrates' student Dioscurides (fr. 25 Weber) also cited these verses in this form.[94] When Achilleus abuses Agamemnon, he says (*Il.* 1.225):

[93] The second verse does not appear in the manuscripts of Homer and is not printed by modern editors.
[94] See 1.8e n.

οἰνοβαρές, κυνὸς ὄμματ᾽ ἔχων.

Ταῦτ᾽ εἶπε τὸ Θετταλὸν σόφισμα ἤτοι ὁ ἐκ Θετταλίας σοφιστής· παίζει δ᾽ ἴσως πρὸς τὴν παροιμίαν ὁ Ἀθήναιος.

Ὅτι τροφαῖς ἐχρῶντο ⟨οἱ⟩ ἥρωες παρ᾽ Ὁμήρῳ πρῶτον μὲν τῷ καλουμένῳ ἀκρατίσματι, ὃ λέγει ἄριστον· οὗ ἅπαξ μέμνηται ἐν Ὀδυσσείᾳ·

Ὀδυσεὺς καὶ δῖος ὑφορβὸς
c   ἐντύνοντ᾽ ἄριστον ⟨ . . . ⟩ κηαμένω πῦρ, |

καὶ ἅπαξ ἐν Ἰλιάδι·

ἐσσυμένως ἐπένοντο καὶ ἐντύνοντ᾽ ἄριστον.

λέγει δὲ τὸ πρωινὸν ἔμβρωμα, ὃ ἡμεῖς ἀκρατισμὸν καλοῦμεν διὰ τὸ ἐν ἀκράτῳ βρέχειν καὶ προσίεσθαι ψωμούς, ὡς Ἀντιφάνης·

ἄριστον ἐν ὅσῳ ⟨ . . . ⟩ ὁ μάγειρος ποεῖ.

εἶτ᾽ ἐπάγει·

συνακρατίσασθαι πῶς ἔχεις μετ᾽ ἐμοῦ;

---

95 I.e. shameless; but perhaps also a hostile reference to the Cynics attending the party.

96 Myrtilus; cf. 7.308b. For *Thettalon sophisma* as a proverb applied to sharp dealing, see Macar. 4.66; Suda θ 291.

97 Unlike Myrtilus, the character who now takes over the conversation (and whose name has been removed by the Epitomator)

Heavy with wine! Dog-eyed![95]

Thus spoke the Thessalian wit, or rather the sophist from Thessaly;[96] Athenaeus is perhaps playing on the proverb.

The meals Homer's heroes eat were, first, what is referred to as *akratisma*, which he calls *ariston*.[97] He mentions this once in the *Odyssey* (16.1–2):

> Odysseus and the divine swineherd
> kindled a fire . . .   and prepared *ariston*;

and once in the *Iliad* (24.124):

> They quickly got to work and prepared *ariston*.

He is referring to the early morning meal, which we call *akratismon*, because we dip bits of food in undiluted wine *(akratos)* and consume them, as for example Antiphanes (fr. 271, encompassing both quotations):

> while the cook is making *ariston*.

He then continues:

> How do you feel about having *akratismon* with me?

argues that Homer's characters ate birds and fish in addition to roast beef. But his main interest is in exactly how Homeric banquets were organized and the contrast with how "we" do things "today," and comparison with very similar material by Herodicus the Cratetean in Book 5 suggests that much of what follows ought to be attributed to him as well. Homeric terminology for meals appears to have been a traditional topic of learned discussion (cf. Plu. *Mor.* 726c–d; *AB* p. 23.16–26), and the treatment of the problem here does nothing to clarify it.

καὶ Κάνθαρος·

(A.) οὐκοῦν ἀκρατισώμεθ᾽ αὐτοῦ. (B.) μηδαμῶς·
Ἰσθμοῖ γὰρ ἀριστήσομεν.

d Ἀριστομένης· |

ἀκρατιοῦμαι μικρόν, εἶθ᾽ ἥξω πάλιν,
ἄρτου δὶς ἢ τρὶς ἀποδακών.

Φιλήμων δέ φησιν ὅτι τροφαῖς τέσσαρσιν ἐχρῶντο οἱ
παλαιοί, ἀκρατίσματι, ἀρίστῳ, ἑσπερίσματι, δείπνῳ.
τὸν μὲν οὖν ἀκρατισμὸν διανηστισμὸν ἔλεγον, τὸ δ᾽
ἄριστον < . . . > δορπηστόν, τὸ δὲ δεῖπνον ἐπιδορπίδα.
ἐστὶ δ᾽ ἡ τάξις καὶ παρ᾽ Αἰσχύλῳ τῶν ὀνομάτων ἐν οἷς
ὁ Παλαμήδης πεποίηται λέγων·

καὶ ταξιάρχας † καὶ στρατάρχας καὶ
    ἑκατοντάρχας †
e ἔταξα, σῖτον δ᾽ εἰδέναι διώρισα, |
ἄριστα, δεῖπνα δόρπα θ᾽ αἱρεῖσθαι τρίτα.

τῆς δὲ τετάρτης τροφῆς οὕτως Ὅμηρος μέμνηται·

< . . . > σὺ δ᾽ ἔρχεο δειελιήσας,

ὃ καλοῦσί τινες δειλινόν, ὅ ἐστι μεταξὺ τοῦ ὑφ᾽ ἡμῶν
λεγομένου ἀρίστου καὶ δείπνου. καὶ ἄριστον μέν ἐστι

---

98 Cf. 5.193a–b.
99 Literally "the evening (meal)."

Also Cantharus (fr. 10):

> (A.) So then, we'll eat our *akratismon* here. (B.)
>   Absolutely not;
> we'll have our *ariston* at the Isthmus!

Aristomenes (fr. 14):

> I'll eat a little *akratismon*; then I'll return
> after I've had a bite or two of bread.

But Philemon says that the ancients had four meals:[98] *akratisma*, *ariston*, *hesperisma*[99], and *deipnon*; they used the word *akratismon* to refer to breakfast, *ariston* to refer to . . . the evening meal, and *deipnon* to refer to the second course. The words appear in this order also in Aeschylus (fr. *182), in the verses where Palamedes[100] is represented as saying:

> And I appointed company commanders † and army
>   commanders and
> division commanders †, and I created distinctions
>   among their meals:
> breakfasts *(arista)*, dinners *(deipna)*, and suppers
>   *(dorpa)* to be taken third.

Homer mentions the fourth meal, as follows (*Od.* 17.599):

> Go after you have had your evening meal!

Some authorities call this *deilinon*, which comes between what we refer to as *ariston* and *deipnon*. *Ariston* is the meal one has at daybreak; *deipnon* (which we call *ariston*)

---

[100] A proverbially clever member of the Achaean expedition against Troy; cf. Eup. fr. 385.6, quoted at 1.17e.

τὸ ὑπὸ τὴν ἔω λαμβανόμενον, δεῖπνον δὲ τὸ μεσημβρινόν, ὃ ἡμεῖς ἄριστον, δόρπον δὲ τὸ ἑσπερινόν. μήποτε δὲ καὶ συνωνυμεῖ τὸ ἄριστον τῷ δείπνῳ. ἐπὶ γὰρ τῆς πρωινῆς που τροφῆς ἔφη·

οἱ δ' ἄρα δεῖπνον ἕλοντο < . . . >,

f   < . . . > ἀπὸ δ' αὐτοῦ θωρήσσοντο. |

μετὰ γὰρ τὴν ἀνατολὴν εὐθὺς δειπνοποιησάμενοι προέρχονται εἰς τὴν μάχην.

Εὐωχοῦνται δὲ παρ' Ὁμήρῳ καθήμενοι. οἴονται δέ τινες καὶ ἑκάστῳ τῶν δαιτυμόνων κατ' ἄνδρα παρακεῖσθαι τράπεζαν. τῷ γοῦν Μέντῃ, φασίν, ἀφικομένῳ πρὸς Τηλέμαχον τῶν τραπεζῶν παρακειμένων ξεστὴ παρετέθη τράπεζα. οὔκ ἐστι δὲ τοῦτο ἐμφανῶς τοῦ προκειμένου κατασκευαστικόν· δύναται γὰρ ἡ Ἀθηνᾶ ἀπὸ τῆς Τηλεμάχου τραπέζης δαίνυσθαι. παρ' ὅλην 12 δὲ τὴν συνουσίαν παρέκειντο || αἱ τράπεζαι πλήρεις, ὡς παρὰ πολλοῖς τῶν βαρβάρων ἔτι καὶ νῦν ἔθος ἐστί,

< . . . > κατηρεφέες παντοίων ἀγαθῶν,

κατὰ Ἀνακρέοντα. μετὰ δὲ τὴν ἀναχώρησιν αἱ δμωαὶ

ἀπὸ μὲν σῖτον πολὺν ἥρεον καὶ τράπεζαν[42] καὶ δέπα'.

---

[42] The traditional text of Homer has ἠδὲ τραπέζας ("and the tables") rather than Athenaeus' καὶ τράπεζαν (unmetrical).

is the midday meal; and *dorpon* is the evening meal. But sometimes Homer uses the same term for breakfast *(ariston)* as he does for dinner *(deipnon)*; for in reference to the morning meal he says somewhere (*Il.* 8.53–4):

> Then they had their *deipnon* . . .
> . . . and afterward they put on their armor.

Because they make their *deipnon* immediately after sunrise and then go forth to battle.

Homer's characters feast sitting down. Some authorities believe that an individual table is set for each diner. In the case of Mentes, for example, they say, when he comes to visit Telemachus, a polished table was set beside him (*Od.* 1.138), even though the tables were already in place (*Od.* 1.111–12). But this is obviously not conclusive proof of the thesis; for Athena[101] might eat from Telemachus' table. The tables remained there beside them covered with food throughout the entire party, as is still the custom today among many uncivilized peoples,

> covered with dainties of every sort,

as Anacreon (*PMG* 435) puts it. After the guests left, the slavewomen (*Od.* 19.61–2)

> removed much food, along with the table
> and the goblets.

[101] In her disguise as the visitor Mentes.

ἰδιάζον δὲ τὸ παρὰ Μενελάῳ εἰσάγει συμπόσιον. δει-
πνήσαντας γὰρ ποιεῖ ὁμιλοῦντας· εἶτ' ἀπονιψαμένους
ποιεῖ πάλιν δειπνοῦντας καὶ δόρπου ἐξαῦτις μεμνη-
μένους μετὰ τὸν κλαυθμόν. τῷ δὲ μὴ αἴρεσθαι τὰς
b τραπέζας ἐναντιοῦσθαι δοκεῖ τὸ ἐν Ἰλιάδι ω· |

ἔσθων καὶ πίνων· ἔτι καὶ παρέκειτο τράπεζα.

ἀναγνωστέον οὖν οὕτω·

ἔσθων καὶ πίνων ἔτι· καὶ παρέκειτο τράπεζα,

ἢ τὸν καιρὸν αἰτιᾶσθαι τὸν παρόντα δεῖ. πῶς γὰρ ἦν
πρέπον τῷ Ἀχιλλεῖ πενθοῦντι παρακεῖσθαι τράπεζαν
καθάπερ τοῖς εὐωχουμένοις παρ' ὅλην τὴν συνουσίαν;
παρετίθεντο δὲ οἱ μὲν ἄρτοι σὺν τοῖς κανοῖς, τὰ δὲ
δεῖπνα κρέα μόνον ἦν ὀπτά. ζωμὸν δὲ οὐκ ἐποίει
Ὅμηρος θύων βοῦς,

c   οὐδ' ἧψεν κρέα |
οὐδ' ἐγκέφαλον· ὤπτα δὲ καὶ τὰς κοιλίας.
οὕτω σφόδρ' ἦν ἀρχαῖος,

Ἀντιφάνης φησί.

Καὶ τῶν κρεῶν δὲ μοῖραι ἐνέμοντο· ὅθεν ἔίσας φησὶ
τὰς δαῖτας ἀπὸ τῆς ἰσότητος. τὰ γὰρ δεῖπνα δαῖτας
ἔλεγον ἀπὸ τοῦ δατεῖσθαι, οὐ μόνον τῶν κρεῶν δια-

---

102 The reference to a passage of Homer by Book-number is
extremely unusual in Athenaeus; contrast e.g. 1.15d, 16b, 18b,
25d, where titles of episodes are used.   103 The word in
fact appears to be derived from *daiomai* (as is asserted below).

But Homer makes the symposium in Menelaus' house unusual. For he presents them as dining (*Od*. 4.54–67) and afterward having a conversation (*Od*. 4.68–215); then after they wash their hands (*Od*. 4.216–17), he presents them as eating again and as thinking of dinner *(dorpon)* a second time after they burst into tears (*Od*. 4.213, 218). The idea that the tables were not removed seems to be contradicted by the passage in *Iliad* 24[102] (476):

> eating and drinking, and a table was still set beside
> > him.

One must therefore read as follows:

> eating and drinking still, and a table was set beside
> > him.

Or else the situation must be responsible for it being there; for how could it have been appropriate that a table was set beside Achilleus when he was in mourning, as it is for guests at a feast throughout the whole party? The loaves of bread were served in baskets, and the dinners consisted of roast meat only. Homer did not make broth when he sacrificed cattle,

> and he didn't stew the meat
> or the brains, but he used to roast even the entrails.
> That's how extraordinarily old-fashioned he was,

says Antiphanes (fr. 248).

The meat was divided into portions, and he therefore refers to meals as "equal" because of the equality observed; for they called their dinner parties *daites* from the verb *dateisthai* ("to divide"),[103] since it was not just the

νεμομένων ἀλλὰ καὶ τοῦ οἴνου·

ἤδη μὲν δαιτὸς κεκορήμεθα ⟨ . . . ⟩ ἐίσης.

καί·

χαῖρ', Ἀχιλεῦ· δαιτὸς μὲν ἐίσης οὐκ ἐπιδευεῖς.

d ἐκ τούτων δ' ἐπείσθη Ζηνόδοτος δαῖτα ἐίσην τὴν |
ἀγαθὴν λέγεσθαι. ἐπεὶ γὰρ ἡ τροφὴ τῷ ἀνθρώπῳ
ἀγαθὸν ἀναγκαῖον ἦν, ἐπεκτείνας, φησίν, εἴρηκεν ἐί-
σην· ἐπεὶ οἱ πρῶτοι ἄνθρωποι, οἷς δὴ οὐ παρῆν ἄφθο-
νος τροφή, ἄρτι φαινομένης ἀθρόον ἐπ' αὐτὴν ἰόντες
βίᾳ ἥρπαζον καὶ ἀφῃροῦντο τοὺς ἔχοντας, καὶ μετὰ
τῆς ἀκοσμίας ἐγίνοντο καὶ φόνοι. ἐξ ὧν εἰκὸς λεχθῆ-
ναι καὶ τὴν ἀτασθαλίαν, ὅτι ἐν ταῖς θαλίαις τὰ πρῶτα
ἐξημάρτανον οἱ ἄνθρωποι εἰς ἀλλήλους. ὡς δὲ παρ-
e εγένετο αὐτοῖς πολλὴ ἐκ τῆς Δήμητρος, διένεμον |
ἑκάστῳ ἴσην, καὶ οὕτως εἰς κόσμον ἦλθε τοῖς ἀνθρώποις τὰ δόρπα. διὸ ἄρτου τε ἐπίνοια πέμματός τε εἰς
ἴσον διαμεμοιραμένου καὶ τοῖς διαπίνουσιν ἄλεισα·
καὶ γὰρ ταῦτα εἰς ⟨τὸ⟩ ἴσον χωρούντων ἐγίνετο. ὥστε
ἡ τροφὴ δαὶς ἐπὶ τῷ δαίεσθαι λέγεται, ὅ ἐστι δια-
μοιρᾶσθαι ἐπ' ἴσης· καὶ ὁ τὰ κρέα ὀπτῶν δαιτρός, ἐπεὶ
ἴσην ἑκάστῳ μοῖραν ἐδίδου. καὶ ἐπὶ μόνων ἀνθρώπων

---

104 The quotations are intended to show not that in Homer the
wine too was divided up equally, but that meals were referred to as
"equal."

105 eisos ("equal") is thus fancifully derived from eus ("good,
noble").

meat that was portioned out but the wine as well (*Od.* 8.98):

Now we have had enough of the equal meal;[104]

and (*Il.* 9.225):

Cheers, Achilleus! We are not lacking an equal meal.

These passages convinced Zenodotus that a good feast is referred to as "equal"; because since food was a good human beings had to have, he says, Homer used an extended form of the word and said "equal."[105] For primitive human beings, who of course lacked plentiful food, used to all go after it the moment it appeared, seize it aggressively, and wrench it away from anyone who had it; this disorder was even accompanied by murder. This is most likely also the source of the term *atasthalia* ("reckless wickedness"), because people first committed crimes against one another during *thaliai* ("festivities").[106] But after Demeter provided them with large amounts of food, they divided it up so that everyone had an equal share, and human meals took on an orderly character. This was the source of the idea that bread and cakes should be divided into equal shares, and of sharing goblets when we drink; because these practices are all characteristic of individuals moving toward equality. Food is therefore called *dais* ("a meal") from *daiomai*, which means "divide into equal portions." And the man who roasts the meat was the *daitros*, since he gave each person an equal portion. The poet uses the word *dais* in connection with human beings only, and no

[106] Another fanciful etymology, the first element in *atasthalia* supposedly being supplied by *atē* ("blind folly").

δαῖτα λέγει ὁ ποιητής, ἐπὶ δὲ θηρίων οὐκ ἔτι. ἀγνοῶν
δὲ ταύτης τῆς φωνῆς τὴν δύναμιν Ζηνόδοτος ἐν τῇ
f κατ᾽ | αὐτὸν ἐκδόσει γράφει·

> αὐτοὺς δὲ ἑλώρια τεῦχε κύνεσσιν
> οἰωνοῖσί τε δαῖτα,

τὴν τῶν γυπῶν καὶ τῶν ἄλλων οἰωνῶν τροφὴν οὕτω
καλῶν, μόνου ἀνθρώπου χωροῦντος ⟨εἰς⟩ τὸ ἴσον ἐκ
13 τῆς πρόσθεν βίας. διὸ καὶ μόνου τούτου | ἡ τροφὴ
δαίς· καὶ μοῖρα τὸ ἑκάστῳ διδόμενον. οὐκ ἔφερον δὲ
οἴκαδε παρ᾽ Ὁμήρῳ οἱ δαιτυμόνες τὰ λειπόμενα, ἀλλὰ
κορεσθέντες κατέλιπον παρ᾽ οἷς ἦν ἡ δαίς· καὶ ἡ
ταμία λαβοῦσα εἶχεν, ἵνα ἄν τις ἀφίκηται ξένος, ἔχοι
δοῦναι αὐτῷ.

Καὶ ἰχθύσι δὲ Ὅμηρος ποιεῖ χρωμένους τοὺς τότε
καὶ ὄρνισι. κατὰ γοῦν τὴν Θρινακίαν οἱ Ὀδυσσέως
ἑταῖροι θηρεύουσιν

> ἰχθῦς ὄρνιθάς τε, φίλας θ᾽ ὅ τι χεῖρας ἵκοιτο,
> γναμπτοῖς ἀγκίστροισιν.

b οὐ γὰρ ἐν τῇ Θρινακίᾳ ἐκεχάλκευτο τὰ ἄγκιστρα, |
ἀλλ᾽ ἐπεφέροντο ἐν τῷ πλῷ δηλονότι· ὥστε ἦν αὐτοῖς
θήρας ἰχθύων ἐπιμέλεια καὶ τέχνη. εἰκάζει δὲ καὶ τοὺς
ὑπὸ Σκύλλης ἁρπαζομένους Ὀδυσσέως ἑταίρους
ἰχθύσι προμήκει ῥάβδῳ ἁλισκομένοις καὶ θύραζε

longer uses it when referring to wild animals. But because Zenodotus is ignorant of the meaning of the word, he writes in his edition of Homer (*Il.* 1.4–5):[107]

> and he made them spoil for dogs
> and a meal *(dais)* for birds,

referring thus to the food consumed by vultures and other birds, although only human beings are making progress from primitive violence toward equality. Human food alone is therefore called a *dais*; and a *moira* ("portion") is what each individual is given.[108] Banqueters in Homer did not take the leftovers home, but ate as much as they wanted and left the rest behind with their hosts. The housekeeper took this food and kept it, so that she would have something to offer any stranger who arrived.

Homer represents the people of those times as eating both fish and birds. On Thrinacia, for example, Odysseus' companions hunt (*Od.* 12.331–2)

> fish and birds, and whatever they could get their
>   hands on,
> with curved hooks.

The hooks had not been forged on Thrinacia, but were obviously brought along on the voyage, showing that the characters were both interested in and skilled at catching fish. Homer also compares the companions of Odysseus who were grabbed by Scylla to fish caught with a long pole and thrown out of the water (*Od.* 12.251–5). He is thus

---

[107] Zenodotus substituted *daita* ("meal") for the metrically equivalent *pasi* ("all"; to be taken with "birds").

[108] The same word is used of an individual's "fate."

ῥιπτομένοις. οὕτω καὶ ταύτην τὴν τέχνην ἀκριβοῖ
μᾶλλον τῶν τοιαῦτα προηγουμένως ἐκδεδωκότων ποι-
ήματα ἢ συγγράμματα, Καίκαλον[43] λέγω τὸν Ἀργεῖον καὶ Νουμήνιον τὸν Ἡρακλεώτην, Παγκράτην τὸν
Ἀρκάδα, Ποσειδώνιον τὸν Κορίνθιον καὶ τὸν ὀλίγῳ |
πρὸ ἡμῶν γενόμενον Ὀππιανὸν τὸν Κίλικα· τοσούτοις
γὰρ ἐνετύχομεν ἐποποιοῖς Ἁλιευτικὰ γεγραφόσι·
καταλογάδην δὲ τοῖς Σελεύκου τοῦ Ταρσέως καὶ Λεω-
νίδου τοῦ Βυζαντίου ⟨καὶ Ἀγαθοκλέους τοῦ Ἀτρα-
κίου⟩[44]. οὐ μνημονεύει δὲ τοιαύτης ἐδωδῆς ἐπὶ τῶν
δείπνων, ὡς οὐκ οἰκείας νομιζομένης τῆς τροφῆς τοῖς
ἐν ἀξιώμασιν ἥρωσι κειμένοις, ὡς οὐδὲ τῆς τῶν νεο-
γνῶν ἱερείων. οὐ μόνον δὲ ἰχθύσιν ἀλλὰ καὶ ὀστρείοις
ἐχρῶντο, καίτοι τῆς τούτων ἐδωδῆς οὐ πολὺ ἐχούσης
τὸ ὠφέλιμον καὶ ἡδύ, ἀλλὰ κἂν τῷ βυθῷ | κατὰ βάθος
κειμένων. καὶ οὐκ ἔστιν εἰς ταῦτα ἄλλῃ τινὶ τέχνῃ
χρήσασθαι ἢ δύντα κατὰ βυθοῦ.

⟨ . . . ⟩ ἢ μάλ' ἐλαφρὸς ἀνήρ, ὃς[45] ῥεῖα κυβιστᾷ,

ὃν καὶ λέγει πολλοὺς ἂν κορέσαι τήθεα διφῶντα.

Ἑκάστῳ δὲ τῶν δαιτυμόνων παρ' Ὁμήρῳ παρά-
κειται ποτήριον. ⟨Δημοδόκῳ⟩[46] γοῦν παρατίθεται κά-
νεον καὶ τράπεζα καὶ δέπας

---

43 Καίκαλον Meineke: καικλον CE: Κικίλιον S κ 1596
44 from S κ 1596
45 Most witnesses have ὡς.
46 add. Schweighäuser

more accurate about this art too than are the authors who
have published poems or treatises directly concerned with
such matters; I am referring to Caecalus of Argos (*SH*
237); Numenius of Heracleia (*SH* 568); Pancrates of Arcadia (*SH* 601); Posidonius of Corinth (*SH* 709); and Oppian
of Cilicia,[109] who lived shortly before our time. These are
all the epic poets we have encountered who have written on fishing, although I have also encountered prose
works by Seleucus of Tarsus, Leonidas of Byzantium, and
Agathocles of Atrax.[110] But Homer does not mention such
food at dinner parties, since it was considered inappropriate for heroes with great reputations. He likewise makes
no mention of eating immature animals. But they did eat
not only birds but shellfish as well, although doing so produces little benefit or pleasure, and although they are
found deep down in the depths of the sea and it is impossible to consume them except by diving into the depths.

Quite a nimble fellow, who dives easily! (*Il.* 16.745)

Homer also says about this man that he could satisfy many
people by searching for sea-squirts (*Il.* 16.747).

A drinking cup is set beside each banqueter in Homer.
Demodocus, for example, has a bread-basket, a table, and
a goblet set beside him (*Od.* 8.69–70)

[109] Oppian's *Halieutica* (unlike any of the other works referred
to here) is preserved entire. Athenaeus cites Pancrates' poem
(otherwise lost) at 7.283a, 305c, 321e.

[110] Athenaeus cites Seleucus very briefly at 7.320a; his work is
otherwise lost. Leonidas was used by Aelian (*NA* 2.6, 50; 3.18;
12.42) and probably by Athenaeus as well; he most likely dates to
*c.*100 BCE. Agathocles is otherwise unknown.

< . . . > πιεῖν ὅτε θυμὸς ἀνώγοι.

ἐπιστέφονται δὲ ποτοῖο οἱ κρητῆρες, ἤτοι ὑπερχειλεῖς
οἱ κρατῆρες ποιοῦνται, ὥστε διὰ τοῦ ποτοῦ ἐπιστε-
e φανοῦσθαι, καὶ | ταῦτα ἔπρασσον πρὸς οἰωνοῦ τι-
θέμενοι. κοῦροι δὲ διανέμουσι

< . . . > πᾶσιν ἐπαρξάμενοι δεπάεσσι.

τὸ δὲ πᾶσιν οὐ τοῖς ποτηρίοις, ἀλλὰ τοῖς ἀνδράσιν.
Ἀλκίνους γοῦν τῷ Ποντονόῳ φησί·

μέθυ νεῖμον
πᾶσιν ἀνὰ μέγαρον.

καὶ ἑξῆς ἐπάγει·

νώμησεν δ᾽ ἄρα πᾶσιν ἐπαρξάμενος δεπάεσσιν.

Εἰσὶ δὲ καὶ τοῖς ἀρίστοις κατὰ δεῖπνα τιμαί. Τυδεί-
δης γοῦν καὶ κρέασι καὶ πλείοις δεπάεσσι τιμᾶται καὶ
f | Αἴας

νώτοισι < . . . > διηνεκέεσσι

γεραίρεται, καὶ οἱ βασιλεῖς δὲ τοῖς αὐτοῖς·

νῶτα βοὸς < . . . >
< . . . >, τά ῥά οἱ < . . . > πάρθεσαν αὐτῷ.[47]

καὶ Ἰδομενέα δὲ Ἀγαμέμνων πλείῳ δέπᾳ τιμᾷ. καὶ

[47] After this quotation CE preserve the intrusive gloss Με-
νέλαος δηλονότι.

74

to drink from, when his heart urged him.

The mixing-bowls are "crowned with drink" (e.g. *Il.* 1.470), which means that they are filled to the brim, so that the liquid is like a crown around the top; they acted this way because they regarded these as good omens. The young men distribute the wine (*Il.* 1.471),

> pouring a libation into all the guests' goblets;

the word "all" refers not to the drinking cups but to the men. Alcinous, for example, tells Pontonous (*Od.* 7.179–80):

> Give a share of wine
> to everyone in the hall!

And immediately after this the poet continues (*Od.* 7.183):

> and he distributed it, pouring a libation into
> everyone's goblet.

The most distinguished men were shown honors at their dinner parties. Tydeides, for example, is honored "with meat and full goblets" (cf. *Il.* 8.161–2); Ajax is given a special portion of (*Il.* 7.321)

> chine cut straight across the back;

and the nobles get the same (*Od.* 4.65–6):

> beef chine   . . . ,
> . . . which they served . . . him.

Likewise Agamemnon honors Idomeneus with a full gob-

Σαρπηδὼν δὲ παρὰ Λυκίοις τοῖς αὐτοῖς τιμᾶται καὶ ἕδρῃ καὶ κρέασιν.

Ἦν δέ τις αὐτοῖς καὶ διὰ τῆς προπόσεως ἀσπασμός· οἱ γοῦν θεοὶ

χρυσέοις δεπάεσσι

δειδέχατ᾽ ἀλλήλους,

ἤτοι ἐδεξιοῦντο προπίνοντες ἑαυτοῖς ταῖς δεξιαῖς. καί 14 ‖ τις δὲ

< . . . > δείδεκτ᾽ Ἀχιλῆα

ἀντὶ τοῦ ἐδεξιοῦτο, ὅ ἐστι προέπινεν αὐτῷ τῇ δεξιᾷ διδοὺς τὸ ποτήριον. ἐδωροῦντο δὲ καὶ ἀπὸ τῆς αὐτῶν μοίρας οἷς ἐβούλοντο, ὡς Ὀδυσσεὺς

νώτου ἀποπροταμὼν

οὗ αὐτῷ παρέθεντο τῷ Δημοδόκῳ.

Ἐχρῶντο δ᾽ ἐν τοῖς συμποσίοις καὶ κιθαρῳδοῖς καὶ ὀρχησταῖς, ὡς οἱ μνηστῆρες. καὶ παρὰ Μενελάῳ[48]

ἐμέλπετο θεῖος ἀοιδὸς
< . . . > δύο δὲ κυβιστητῆρες < . . . >
μολπῆς ἐξάρχοντες ἐδίνευον.

μολπῆς δὲ ἀντὶ τοῦ παιδιᾶς. σῶφρον δέ τι ἦν τὸ τῶν

---

[48] The Homeric duals in 17 and 18 have been replaced in Athenaeus' quotation by more modern forms; cf. 1.15c n.; 1.24d n. For further discussion of this passage (allegedly interpolated by Aristarchus), see 5.180c–e.

let (*Il.* 4.262–3), and Sarpedon has the same honors among the Lycians, as well as a special seat and share of the meat (*Il.* 12.310–12).

When they toasted one another, there was friendly physical contact. The gods, for example (*Il.* 4.3–4),

> hailed one another
> with gold goblets,

which is to say that they clasped right hands as they drank one another's health.[111] And someone (*Il.* 9.224)[112]

> hailed Achilleus,

which means that he took his right hand, that is, drank his health and handed him the drinking cup with his right hand. They would also present anyone they wished with some of their own portion, as Odysseus does by (*Od.* 8.475)

> cutting off some of the chine

they served him for Demodocus.

At their drinking parties they employed citharodes and dancers, as the suitors do, for example. And in Menelaus' house (*Od.* 4.17–19)

> a divine bard was singing,
> . . . and a pair of tumblers . . .
> led the song, whirling about among them.

The word "song" is used here to mean "fun." Bards were

111 The discussion here is repeatedly self-contradictory.
112 The individual in question is Odysseus.

b ἀοιδῶν γένος | καὶ φιλοσόφων διάθεσιν ἐπέχον. Ἀγα-
μέμνων γοῦν τὸν ἀοιδὸν καταλείπει τῇ Κλυταιμνή-
στρᾳ φύλακα καὶ παραινετῆρά τινα· ὃς πρῶτον μὲν
ἀρετὴν γυναικῶν διερχόμενος ἐνέβαλλέ τινα φιλοτιμίαν εἰς καλοκἀγαθίαν, εἶτα διατριβὴν παρέχων ἡδεῖαν ἀπεπλάνα τὴν διάνοιαν φαύλων ἐπινοιῶν. διὸ Αἴ-
γισθος οὐ πρότερον διέφθειρε τὴν γυναῖκα πρὶν τὸν
ἀοιδὸν ἀποκτεῖναι ἐν νήσῳ ἐρήμῃ. τοιοῦτός ἐστι καὶ ὁ
παρὰ τοῖς μνηστῆρσιν ἀείδων ἀνάγκῃ, ὃς τοὺς ἐφε-
c δρεύοντας τῇ | Πηνελόπῃ ἐβδελύττετο. κοινῶς δέ που
πάντας τοὺς ἀοιδοὺς αἰδοίους τοῖς ἀνθρώποις εἶναί
φησι·[49]

τοὔνεκ' ἄρα σφέας
οἴμας Μοῦσ' ἐδίδαξε φίλησέ τε φῦλον ἀοιδῶν.

ὁ δὲ παρὰ Φαίαξι Δημόδοκος ᾄδει Ἄρεος καὶ Ἀφροδίτης συνουσίαν, οὐ διὰ τὸ ἀποδέχεσθαι τὸ τοιοῦτον
πάθος, ἀλλ' ἀποτρέπων αὐτοὺς παρανόμων ἔργων[50],
⟨ἢ⟩ εἰδὼς ἐν τρυφερῷ τινι βίῳ τεθραμμένους κἀν-
τεῦθεν ὁμοιότατα τοῖς τρόποις αὐτῶν τὰ πρὸς ἀνάπαυ-
d σιν προφέρων. καὶ τοῖς μνηστῆρσιν ᾄδει πρὸς τὴν |
αὐτὴν βουλὴν ὁ Φήμιος νόστον Ἀχαιῶν. καὶ αἱ Σει-
ρῆνες δὲ ᾄδουσι τῷ Ὀδυσσεῖ τὰ μάλιστα αὐτὸν τέρ-
ψοντα καὶ τὰ οἰκεῖα τῇ φιλοτιμίᾳ αὐτοῦ καὶ πολυ-

---

[49] The traditional version of the text has οὔνεκα rather than
Athenaeus' τοὔνεκα in 480, and δέ rather than Athenaeus' τε in
481.   [50] ἔργων Kaibel: ὀρέων CE

thoughtful people, who occupied the position of philosophers. Agamemnon, for example, leaves his bard behind to guard Clytemnestra and serve as a sort of advisor (*Od.* 3.267–8). The fellow used to offer her, first of all, a detailed account of feminine virtue, to inspire her with eagerness to become a noble person, while also providing a pleasant way of passing the time so as to divert her attention from base thoughts. Aegisthus was therefore unable to seduce the woman until he put the bard to death on a desert island (*Od.* 3.269–72). The man who was forced to sing for the suitors and was appalled at their plotting against Penelope resembled him.[113] In general, Homer says, people ought to show all bards respect (*Od.* 8.480–1)

> because the Muse taught them
> the paths of song and showed her affection for the
> tribe of bards.

The Phaeacian bard Demodocus sings about the lovemaking of Ares and Aphrodite (*Od.* 8.266–367) not because he approves of this sort of passion, but as a way of dissuading his audience from illicit longings. Or perhaps he recognizes that they have been brought up in a voluptuous environment, and therefore offers them entertainment that fits their manners. Phemius has the same motivation when he sings to the suitors about the homecoming of the Achaeans.[114] Likewise the Sirens sing Odysseus the songs they know will please him most, by discussing matters that

---

113 Phemius; cf. *Od.* 1.154; 22.351–3.

114 Because he knew that they would be pleased by tales of the disastrous homecoming of the other heroes from Troy, as what follows makes clear.

μαθείᾳ λέγουσαι. "ἴσμεν γάρ," φασί, "τά τ' ἄλλα καὶ
ὅσσα γένηται ἐν χθονὶ πολυβοτείρῃ."

Ὀρχήσεις δ' εἰσὶ παρ' Ὁμήρῳ αἱ μέν τινες τῶν
κυβιστητήρων, αἱ δὲ διὰ τῆς σφαίρας· ἧς τὴν εὕρεσιν
Ἀγαλλὶς[51] ἡ Κερκυραία γραμματικὴ Ναυσικάᾳ ἀνα-
τίθησιν ὡς πολίτιδι χαριζομένη, Δικαίαρχος δὲ Σι-
e κυωνίοις, Ἵππασος δὲ Λακεδαιμονίοις ταύτην | τε καὶ
τὰ γυμνάσια πρώτοις. ταύτην δὲ μόνην τῶν ἡρωίδων
Ὅμηρος παράγει σφαιρίζουσαν. διαβόητοι δὲ ἐπὶ
σφαιρικῇ Δημοτέλης ὁ Θεοκρίτου[52] τοῦ Χίου σοφι-
στοῦ ἀδελφὸς καί τις Χαιρεφάνης· ὃς ἀσελγεῖ τινι νέῳ
παρακολουθῶν οὐ διελέγετο μέν, ἐκώλυε δὲ πράττειν
τὸν νεανίσκον. εἰπόντος δὲ ὅτι "Χαιρέφανες, ἐὰν παύσῃ ἀκολουθῶν, πάντα σοι ἔσται παρ' ἡμῶν," "ἐγὼ δ'
ἄν," ἔφη, "σοὶ διαλεχθείην;" "τί οὖν," εἶπε, "παρακο-
f λουθεῖς;" "χαίρω σε θεωρῶν," ἔφη, "τὸ δὲ ἦθος | οὐ
δοκιμάζω."

Ὅτι τὸ φούλλικλον καλούμενον (ἦν δὲ ὡς ἔοικε
σφαιρίσκιόν τι) εὗρεν Ἀττικὸς Νεαπολίτης παιδοτρίβης γυμνασίας ἕνεκα Πομπηίου Μάγνου.[53] τὸ δὲ κα-

---

[51] Ἀναγαλλὶς S a 1817   [52] Θεοκρίτου Jacobs: θεόγνι-
δος CE   [53] E omits this sentence and C has it immediately
after Σικυωνίοις in the preceding paragraph. Schweighäuser restored it here; presumably it stood in the margin of the exemplar,
and was ignored by E-copyist and added in the wrong place by the
C-copyist.

---

[115] Corcyra was identified with the Homeric Phaeacia (home
of the princess Nausicaa) already in the 5th century BCE (Th.

appeal to his ambition and love of learning. "For we know," they say, "whatever goes on on the fruitful earth, and other things as well" (cf. *Od.* 12.189–91).

Some Homeric dances are performed by tumblers (*Il.* 18.604/5; *Od.* 4.18), while others involve a ball (*Od.* 6.100–1; 7.370–9). The grammarian Agallis of Corcyra shows favoritism to a fellow-citizen when she attributes the invention of the ball-game to Nausicaa.[115] Dicaearchus (fr. 62 Wehrli) attributes it to the Sicyonians, Hippasus (*FGrH* 589 F 1) to the Spartans, whom he identifies as innovators in other sports as well. Nausicaa is the only heroine Homer introduces playing ball.[116] Demoteles, the brother of the Chian sophist Theocritus,[117] was a famous ballplayer, as was a certain Chairephanes. Chairephanes was dogging the steps of a sluttish boy, and was not talking to him but nonetheless preventing him from doing any business. When the young man said "Chairephanes, if you'll stop following me, I'll let you have whatever you want," Chairephanes said "Do you think I'd have sex with you?" He said "Why are you following me then?"; and Chairephanes said "I like looking at you; but I don't approve of your behavior."

The so-called *phoulliklos*[118] (this was apparently a small ball of some sort) was invented by the athletic trainer Atticus of Naples for Pompey the Great's[119] workouts. The

---

1.25.4; 3.70.4). For Nausicaa playing ball, see *Od.* 6.100–1; and cf. S. test. 28 at 1.20f. Agallis is otherwise unknown.

[116] The material that follows is evidently drawn from a different source (or set of sources).   [117] Cf. 1.21c with n.

[118] Latin *folliculus*, "inflated ball."

[119] A Roman general and statesman (106–48 BCE).

λούμενον διὰ τῆς σφαίρας ἁρπαστὸν φαινίνδα ἐκαλεῖτο, ὃ ἐγὼ πάντων μάλιστα ἀσπάζομαι.

Πολὺ δὲ τὸ σύντονον καὶ καματηρὸν τῆς περὶ τὴν
σφαιριστικὴν ἁμίλλης τό τε κατὰ τοὺς τραχηλισμοὺς
ῥωμαλέον. Ἀντιφάνης·

οἴμοι κακοδαίμων, τὸν τράχηλον ὡς ἔχω.

διηγεῖται δὲ τὴν φαινίνδα παιδιὰν οὕτως Ἀντιφάνης· ‖

15   σφαῖραν λαβὼν
τῷ μὲν διδοὺς ἔχαιρε, τὸν δ᾽ ἔφευγ᾽ ἅμα,
τοῦ δ᾽ ἐξέκρουσε, τὸν δ᾽ ἀνέστησεν πάλιν,
κλαγκταῖσι φωναῖς < . . . >
"ἔξω, μακράν, παρ᾽ αὐτόν, ὑπὲρ αὐτόν, κάτω,
ἄνω, βραχεῖαν † ἀπόδοσιν ἐγκαταστρέφει". †

ἐκαλεῖτο δὲ φαινίνδα ἀπὸ τῆς ἀφαιρέσεως[54] τῶν σφαι-
ριζόντων, ἢ ὅτι εὑρετὴς αὐτοῦ, ὥς φησιν Ἰόβας ὁ
Μαυρούσιος, Φαινέστιος ὁ παιδοτρίβης. καὶ Ἀντι-
φάνης·

φαινίνδα παίζων † ἤεις ἐν Φαινεστίου.

b   ἐφρόντιζον δὲ εὐρυθμίας οἱ σφαιρίζοντες. Δαμόξενος |
γοῦν φησι·

νεανίας τις ἐσφαίριζεν εἷς

---

[54] ἀφαιρέσεως Olson: ἀφέσεως CE

---

[120] From *harpazō*, "snatch"; cf. Latin *harpastum*.

ballgame we refer to as *harpaston*[120] used to be called *phaininda*; this is my favorite game.

Playing ball involves a great deal of exertion and fatigue, and requires considerable strength for when one is grabbed about the neck. Antiphanes (fr. 277):

Miserable me! how my neck hurts!

Antiphanes (fr. 231) describes the game of *phaininda* as follows:

He grabbed the ball
and gleefully offered it to one player, while
    simultaneously escaping another;
knocked it out of someone's hands; helped a different
    player up;
with shrill cries . . .
"Out of bounds! Long! Past him! Over him! Down!
Up! Not far enough!" [corrupt]

It was called *phaininda* either because the players took the ball away from one another[121] or because the person who invented the game was, as Juba of Mauretania (*FGrH* 275 F 80) asserts, the athletic trainer Phaenestius. Also Antiphanes (fr. 278):

You were † playing *phaininda* at Phaenestius' place.

Ballplayers were concerned to move gracefully. Damoxenus (fr. 3), for example, says:

One particular young man was playing ball,

---

[121] As if the word were derived from *aphaireō*, "take away" (which it almost certainly is not).

ἐτῶν ἴσως < . . . > ἑπτακαίδεκα,
Κῷος· θεοὺς γὰρ φαίνεθ' ἡ νῆσος φέρειν.
ὃς ἐπεί ποτ' ἐμβλέψειε τοῖς καθημένοις,
ἢ λαμβάνων τὴν σφαῖραν ἢ διδούς, ἅμα
πάντες ἐβοῶμεν· < . . . >
ἡ δ' εὐρυθμία τό τ' ἦθος ἡ τάξις θ' ὅση
ἐν τῷ τι πράττειν ἢ λέγειν ἐφαίνετο.
c   πέρας ἐστὶ κάλλους, ἄνδρες. οὔτ' ἀκήκοα |
ἔμπροσθεν οὔθ' ἑόρακα τοιαύτην χάριν.
κακὸν ἄν τι μεῖζον ἔλαβον, εἰ πλείω χρόνον
ἔμεινα· καὶ νῦν δ' οὐχ ὑγιαίνειν μοι δοκῶ.

ἐσφαίριζε δ' οὐκ ἀηδῶς καὶ Κτησίβιος <ὁ> Χαλκιδεὺς
φιλόσοφος· καὶ πολλοὶ διὰ τὴν σφαιρικὴν αὐτῷ συν-
απεδύοντο τῶν Ἀντιγόνου τοῦ βασιλέως φίλων. συνέ-
γραψε δὲ περὶ σφαιριστικῆς Τιμοκράτης ὁ Λάκων.

Οἱ Φαίακες δὲ παρ' Ὁμήρῳ καὶ ἄνευ σφαίρας
ὀρχοῦνται. καὶ ὀρχοῦνταί που ἀνὰ μέρος πυκνῶς
d   (τοῦτο γάρ ἐστι τὸ |

ταρφέ' ἀμειβόμενοι),

ἄλλων ἐφεστώτων καὶ ἐπικροτούντων τοῖς λιχανοῖς
δακτύλοις, ὅ φησι ληκεῖν. οἶδε δὲ ὁ ποιητὴς καὶ τὴν
πρὸς ᾠδὴν ὄρχησιν· Δημοδόκου γοῦν ᾄδοντος κοῦροι

---

[122] Antigonus Gonatus, king of Macedon c.277/6–239 BCE.
For Ctesibius, cf. 4.162e–f.

84

perhaps seventeen years old
and from Cos—the island evidently produces gods!
Whenever he cast a glance at us sitting there,
as he was receiving the ball or passing it to someone
     else, we all
immediately began to shout. . . .
How graceful he appeared, and how he handled and
held himself, whatever he said or did!
He's as beautiful as they come, gentlemen; I've never
     heard
or seen anything so lovely before.
I would have suffered an even greater injury, if I'd
     stayed
longer; as it is, I'm not entirely in my right mind.

The philosopher Ctesibius of Chalcideus (*SSR* III.H.2)
enjoyed playing ball, and many of King Antigonus'[122] clos-
est associates used to strip down and play with him.[123]
Timocrates the Spartan wrote a treatise on ballplaying.

   Homer's Phaeacians also dance without a ball. They apparently take rapid turns as they do so (because this is what

   switching off at brief intervals[124] (*Od*. 8.379)

means), while the others stand by and clap time with
their hands, for which he uses the word *lēkein*. The poet
is also familiar with dance accompanied by song. When
Demodocus sang, for example, adolescent boys were

---

[123] This observation is probably taken from Antigonus of
Carystus' *Life of Menedemus* (p. 102 Wilamowitz).
[124] Homer's dual has been replaced by a plural; and what is being described is in fact a ballgame, and the words mean "swiftly
passing it back and forth."

πρωθῆβαι ὠρχοῦντο· καὶ ἐν τῇ Ὁπλοποιίᾳ δὲ παιδὸς
κιθαρίζοντος ἄλλοι ἐναντίοι μολπῇ τε ὀρχηθμῷ τε
ἔσκαιρον. ὑποσημαίνεται δὲ ἐν τούτοις ὁ ὑπορχηματι-
κὸς τρόπος, ὃς ἤνθησεν ἐπὶ Ξενοδήμου καὶ Πινδάρου.
καὶ ἔστιν ἡ τοιαύτη ὄρχησις μίμησις τῶν ὑπὸ τῆς
e   λέξεως ἑρμηνευομένων πραγμάτων· ἣν | παρίστησι
γινομένην Ξενοφῶν ὁ καλὸς ἐν τῇ Ἀναβάσει ἐν τῷ
παρὰ Σεύθῃ τῷ Θρᾳκὶ συμποσίῳ. φησὶ γοῦν· ἐπειδὴ
σπονδαί τε ἐγένοντο καὶ ἐπαιώνισαν, ἀνέστησαν πρῶτοι Θρᾷκες καὶ πρὸς αὐλὸν ὠρχοῦντο σὺν ὅπλοις καὶ
ἥλλοντο ὑψηλά τε καὶ κούφως καὶ ταῖς μαχαίραις
ἐχρῶντο· τέλος δ᾽ ὁ ἕτερος τὸν ἕτερον παίει, ὡς πᾶσι
δοκεῖν πεπληγέναι τὸν ἄνδρα. ὁ δ᾽ ἔπεσε τεχνικῶς
πως, καὶ πάντες ἀνέκραγον οἱ συνδειπνοῦντες Παφλαγόνες[55]. καὶ ὁ μὲν σκυλεύσας τὰ ὅπλα τοῦ ἑτέρου ἐξῄει
f   ᾄδων Σιτάλκαν, ἄλλοι δὲ τῶν Θρᾳκῶν τὸν ἕτερον |
ἐξέφερον ὡς τεθνηκότα· ἦν δὲ οὐδὲν πεπονθώς. μετὰ
τοῦτον Αἰνιᾶνες καὶ Μάγνητες ἀνέστησαν, οἳ ὠρχοῦντο τὴν καρπαίαν καλουμένην ἐν τοῖς ὅπλοις. ὁ δὲ
τρόπος τῆς ὀρχήσεως ἦν· ὁ μὲν παραθέμενος τὰ ὅπλα
σπείρει καὶ ζευγηλατεῖ πυκνὰ μεταστρεφόμενος ὡς
φοβούμενος, λῃστὴς δὲ προσέρχεται· ὁ δὲ ἐπὰν προΐ-
δηται ἁρπάσας τὰ ὅπλα μάχεται πρὸ τοῦ ζεύγους ἐν
ῥυθμῷ πρὸς τὸν αὐλόν· καὶ τέλος ὁ λῃστὴς δήσας τὸν

---

[55] οἱ συνδειπνοῦντες Παφλαγόνες is preserved in the margin in E and has been added above the line in C.

dancing (*Od*. 8.262–4); and in the *Forging of the Arms* a boy was playing the lyre while others frisked about opposite him, singing and dancing (*Il*. 18.569–72). There is an allusion here to the hyporchemic style, which was popular in the time of Xenodamus and Pindar;[125] this type of dance imitates what is expressed in the lyrics. The noble Xenophon in his *Anabasis* (6.1.5–8) describes a dance of this sort that took place at the symposium in the house of Seuthes the Thracian.[126] He says, at any rate: After they made libations and sang the paean, some Thracians rose up first and began to dance in armor to the music of a pipe, leaping high and lightly and brandishing their knives. Finally one struck the other, and everyone thought the fellow had been mortally wounded. He fell artfully, and all the Paphlagonians dining with us shouted loudly. The first man stripped the other of his equipment and went out singing the Sitalcas song, while other Thracians carried off the other man, as if he were dead; but he had not been hurt at all. After this, some Aenianians and Magnesians got up and began to dance the so-called *karpaia* in armor. The dance was of the following sort: one man sets his armor aside, and sows and drives a yoke of oxen, turning around frequently, as if he were afraid. A bandit approaches; as soon as the sower sees him coming, he snatches up his arms and fights to save his oxen, moving in time with the pipe-music. Finally the bandit ties the man up and drives

---

[125] Xenodamus of Cythera dates to the 7th century BCE; none of his poetry survives. Pindar's *floruit* was the first half of the 5th century BCE.   [126] The party referred to in this passage was actually hosted by Corylas the Phrygian; Seuthes the Thracian hosts a different party at 7.3.21–33 (cf. 2.49b).

16 ἄνδρα τὸ ζεῦγος ἀπάγει, ‖ ἐνίοτε δὲ καὶ ὁ ζευγηλάτης
τὸν λῃστήν· εἶτα παρὰ τοὺς βοῦς δήσας ὀπίσω τὼ
χεῖρε δεδεμένον ἐλαύνει. καί τις, φησί, τὸ Περσικὸν
ὠρχεῖτο καὶ κροτῶν τὰς πέλτας ὤκλαζε καὶ ἐξανί-
στατο· καὶ ταῦτα πάντα ῥυθμῷ πρὸς τὸν αὐλὸν ἐποίει.
καὶ Ἀρκάδες δέ, φησίν, ἀναστάντες ἐξοπλισάμενοι
ᾖσαν ἐν ῥυθμῷ πρὸς τὸν ἐνόπλιον ῥυθμὸν αὐλούμε-
νοι καὶ ἐνωπλίσαντο καὶ ὠρχήσαντο.

Ἐχρῶντο δὲ καὶ αὐλοῖς καὶ σύριγξιν ‹οἱ› ἥρωες. ὁ
γοῦν Ἀγαμέμνων

b   αὐλῶν συρίγγων τ᾽ ἐνοπήν |

ἀκούει. εἰς δὲ τὰ συμπόσια οὐ παρήγαγε· πλὴν ἐν τῇ
Ὁπλοποιίᾳ γάμων γινομένων αὐλῶν μνημονεύει. τοῖς
δὲ βαρβάροις ἀποδίδωσι τοὺς αὐλούς· παρὰ Τρωσὶ
γοῦν ἦν αὐλῶν συρίγγων τ᾽ ἐνοπή.

Ἔσπενδον δὲ ἀπὸ τῶν δείπνων ἀναλύοντες καὶ τὰς
σπονδὰς ἐποιοῦντο Ἑρμῇ καὶ οὐχ ὡς ὕστερον Διὶ
Τελείῳ· δοκεῖ γὰρ Ἑρμῆς ὕπνου προστάτης εἶναι.
σπένδουσι δ᾽ αὐτῷ καὶ ἐπὶ ταῖς γλώσσαις ἐκ τῶν
δείπνων ἀπιόντες. προσνέμονται δ᾽ αὐτῷ αἱ γλῶσσαι
διὰ τὴν ἑρμηνείαν.

Οἶδε δ᾽ Ὅμηρος καὶ ποικίλας ἐδωδάς· λέγει γοῦν

                    ἐδωδὴν
παντοίην,

off the oxen; or sometimes the master of the team ties the bandit up, fastens him alongside the oxen with his hands bound behind his back, and drives him off. Someone else, Xenophon reports (*An*. 6.1.10–11), began doing the "Persian dance," banging light shields together as he alternately squatted down and leapt up; and he did all this in time with the pipe-music. The Arcadians too, he reports, got up in full armor and marched in step with an enoplian meter as the pipe played, displaying their fighting ability as they danced.

The heroes used both pipes and pan-pipes. Agamemnon, for example, hears (*Il*. 10.13)

the voice of pipes and pan-pipes.

But Homer does not introduce them into his symposia, except that in the *Forging of the Arms*, when a wedding celebration is going on, he mentions pipes (*Il*. 18.495). He gives the pipes to non-Greek peoples; it was the Trojans, at any rate, who were responsible for the "voice of pipes and pan-pipes."

They poured libations when they were leaving their dinner parties, and they made their libations to Hermes (*Od*. 7.137) rather than to Zeus the Fulfiller, as in later times; because Hermes is considered the patron of sleep. They also pour libations to him over the tongues as they leave their dinner parties (*Od*. 3.341); the tongues were his share because he is the god of interpretation.

Homer is also familiar with food of different sorts; he refers (e.g. *Od*. 6.76–7), for example, to

food

of every sort,

καί·

c   ὄψα < . . . > οἷα ἔδουσι διοτρεφέες βασιλῆες. |

οἶδε δὲ καὶ πᾶσαν τὴν νῦν πολυτέλειαν. οἴκων μὲν οὖν
λαμπρότατος ὁ Μενελάου. τοιοῦτον δέ τινα ὑφίσταται
τῇ κατασκευῇ καὶ λαμπρότητι ⟨οἷανπερ⟩ Πολύβιος
Ἴβηρός τινος βασιλέως οἰκίαν· ὃν καὶ ἐζηλωκέναι
λέγει τὴν τῶν Φαιάκων τρυφὴν πλὴν τοῦ τοὺς κρατῆρας ἐν μέσῳ τῆς οἰκίας ἑστάναι πλήρεις οἴνου κριθί-
d   νου, ἀργυροῦς ὄντας καὶ χρυσοῦς. Ὅμηρος δὲ | τοπο-
γραφῶν καὶ τὴν Καλυψοῦς οἰκίαν ἐκπλήττει τὸν
Ἑρμῆν.

Ἀπολαυστικὸς δέ ἐστι παρ' αὐτῷ καὶ ὁ τῶν Φαιάκων βίος·

αἰεὶ γὰρ[56] ἡμῖν δαίς τε φίλη κίθαρίς τε

καὶ τὰ ἑξῆς. < . . . >[57] ἃ ἔπη Ἐρατοσθένης οὕτω
γεγράφθαι φησίν·

     οὐ γὰρ ἔγωγέ τί φημι τέλος χαριέστερον εἶναι
     ἢ ὅταν εὐφροσύνη μὲν ἔχῃ κακότητος ἀπούσης,
e   δαιτυμόνες δ' ἀνὰ δώματ' ἀκουάζωνται ἀοιδοῦ, |

---

[56] The traditional text has δ' rather than Athenaeus' γάρ
(unmetrical).

[57] A portion of the text, in which Od. 9.5–7 was cited in its normal form, with κατὰ δῆμον ἅπαντα ("among all the people")
rather than Eratosthenes' κακότητος ἀπούσης ("and wickedness
was absent") at the end of 6, has been lost. Athenaeus' version

and to (*Od.* 3.480)

> dainties of the type Zeus-nourished princes eat.

He is also familiar with every sort of modern luxury. Menelaus' house is the most luxurious (cf. *Od.* 4.45–6); Homer conceives of it as being as gloriously well-furnished as the home of a certain Iberian chieftain described by Polybius (34.9.14–15), who says that he had imitated the luxury of the Phaeacians except that the mixing-bowls standing in the middle of his house, although made of gold and silver, were full of barley wine.[127] When Homer describes Calypso's home, he has Hermes be astonished at it (*Od.* 5.73–5).

The life of the Phaeacians as Homer presents it is devoted to pleasure (*Od.* 8.248):

> For what we care about is always feasting and the
> lyre,

and so forth . . . which verses, Eratothenes (pp. 34–5 Bernhardy) says, were actually written thus (cf. *Od.* 9.5–7):

> For I declare that there is no greater height of
> happiness
> than when joy prevails and wickedness is absent,
> and feasters are in the house listening to a bard.

---

[127] Beer, which the Greeks seldom drank but other ancient peoples did; cf. 1.34b; 10.447a–d.

---

of the text also has ὅταν for Homer's ὅτ᾽, as a result of treating ἐΰφρ-as a single syllable, as also at 2.40d; 5.192d.

ATHENAEUS

κακότητος ἀπούσης φάσκων τῆς ἀφροσύνης· ἀδύνατον γὰρ μὴ φρονίμους εἶναι Φαίακας, οἳ μάλα φίλοι
εἰσὶ θεοῖσιν, ὡς ἡ Ναυσικάα φησί.

Καὶ οἱ μνηστῆρες δὲ παρ' αὐτῷ

πεσσοῖσι προπάροιθε θυράων

ἐτέρποντο, οὐ παρὰ τοῦ μεγάλου Διοδώρου[58] μαθόντες
τὴν πεττείαν οὐδὲ τοῦ Μιτυληναίου Λέοντος τοῦ ἀνέ-
καθεν Ἀθηναίου, ὃς ἀήττητος ἦν κατὰ τὴν πεττευτι-
f κήν, ὥς φησι Φαινίας. Ἀπίων δὲ ὁ Ἀλεξανδρεὺς | καὶ
ἀκηκοέναι φησὶ παρὰ τοῦ Ἰθακησίου Κτήσωνος τὴν
τῶν μνηστήρων πεττείαν οἵα ἦν. ὀκτὼ γάρ, φησί, καὶ
ἑκατὸν ὄντες οἱ μνηστῆρες διετίθεσαν ψήφους ἐναν-
τίας ἀλλήλαις, ἴσας πρὸς ἴσας τὸν ἀριθμόν, ὅσοιπερ
ἦσαν καὶ αὐτοί. γίνεσθαι οὖν ἑκατέρωθεν τέσσαρα
καὶ πεντήκοντα. τὸ δ' ἀνὰ μέσον τούτων διαλιπεῖν
ὀλίγον· ἐν δὲ τῷ μεταιχμίῳ τούτῳ μίαν τιθέναι ψῆφον,
17 ἣν καλεῖν μὲν αὐτοὺς Πηνελόπην, ‖ σκοπὸν δὲ ποιεῖ-
σθαι εἴ τις βάλλοι ψήφῳ ἑτέρᾳ· καὶ κληρουμένων τὸν
λαχόντα στοχάζεσθαι ταύτης. εἰ δέ τις τύχοι καὶ
ἐκκρούσειε πρόσω τὴν Πηνελόπην, ἀποτίθεσθαι τὴν
ἑαυτοῦ εἰς τὴν τῆς βληθείσης καὶ ἐξωσμένης χώραν,
ἐν ᾗ πρότερον ἦν· καὶ πάλιν στάντα τὴν Πηνελόπην ἐν
ᾧ τὸ δεύτερον ἐγένετο χωρίῳ ἐντεῦθεν βάλλειν τὴν
ἑαυτοῦ. εἰ δὲ τύχοι ἄνευ τοῦ μηδεμιᾶς τῶν ἄλλων
ψαῦσαι, νικᾶν καὶ ἐλπίδας ἔχειν πολλὰς γαμήσειν

92

BOOK I

When he says "and wickedness is absent," he is referring to thoughtless behavior; because the Phaeacians must have been thoughtful people, given that they were very close to the gods, as Nausicaa says (*Od.* 6.203).

The suitors in Homer used to enjoy themselves (*Od.* 1.107)

with game-pieces before the doors,

although they did not learn the game from the famous Diodorus or from Leon of Mitylene[128], who was of Athenian descent and never lost a game of this sort, according to Phaenias (fr. 18 Wehrli). Apion of Alexandria (*FGrH* 616 F 36) reports that he had heard from Cteson of Ithaca what sort of game the suitors played. Since there were 108 suitors, he says, they lined up pebbles opposite one another, with an equal number on each side, one pebble per suitor; there were thus 54 pebbles on each side. They left a little distance between the lines; and in this no-man's-land they placed a single pebble they called "Penelope," and made hitting this pebble with another one the object of the game. After they drew lots, whoever was chosen took a shot at "Penelope." If he hit her and knocked her forward, he moved his own piece to where she was before she was hit and displaced; then, after moving his own piece, he took another shot from there at "Penelope" in her second position. If he hit his target without touching any other piece, he won and had great hopes of marrying her.

[128] Nothing else is known about either man.

---

[58] Διοδώρου ἢ Θεοδώρου CE; the second name is a variant reading that made its way into the text.

b αὐτήν. τὸν δὲ Εὐρύμαχον πλείστας εἰληφέναι | ταύτῃ
τῇ παιδιᾷ καὶ εὔελπιν εἶναι τῷ γάμῳ. οὕτω δὲ διὰ τὴν
τρυφὴν τὰς χεῖρας οἱ μνηστῆρες ἔχουσιν ἁπαλὰς ὡς
μηδὲ τὸ τόξον ἐντεῖναι δύνασθαι. πολυτελεῖς δ᾽ αὐτοῖς
καὶ οἱ διακονούμενοι.

Δυνατωτάτη δὲ παρ᾽ Ὁμήρῳ καὶ ἡ τῶν μύρων
εὐωδία·

οὗ < . . . > κινυμένου Διὸς ποτὶ χαλκοβατὲς
δῶμα[59]
ἔμπης εἰς γαῖάν τε καὶ οὐρανὸν ἵκετ᾽ ἀυτμή.

Καὶ στρωμνὰς δὲ οἶδε διαπρεπούσας· τοιαύτας
c γοῦν Ἀρήτη Ὀδυσσεῖ ὑποστρωννύειν κελεύει, | καὶ
Νέστωρ αὐχεῖ πρὸς Τηλέμαχον πολλῶν τοιούτων εὐπορεῖν.

Τῶν δ᾽ ἄλλων ποιητῶν ἔνιοι τὰς καθ᾽ αὑτοὺς πολυτελείας καὶ ῥᾳθυμίας ἀνέπεμπον ὡς οὔσας καὶ κατὰ
τὰ Τρωικά. Αἰσχύλος γοῦν ἀπρεπῶς που παράγει
μεθύοντας τοὺς Ἕλληνας, ὡς καὶ τὰς ἀμίδας ἀλλήλοις περικαταγνύναι. λέγει γοῦν·

ὅδ᾽ ἐστίν, ὅς ποτ᾽ ἀμφ᾽ ἐμοὶ βέλος
γελωτοποιόν, τὴν κάκοσμον οὐράνην,
ἔρριψεν οὐδ᾽ ἥμαρτε· περὶ δ᾽ ἐμῷ κάρᾳ
d πληγεῖσ᾽ ἐναυάγησεν ὀστρακουμένη |

[59] The text of this verse is problematic, and κατά ought probably to be printed rather than Athenaeus' ποτί (also found in some
other witnesses).

94

Eurymachus had won this game more times than anyone else and was confident about the marriage. And so, because of the easy life they lead, the suitors' hands are too soft to allow them to bend the bow (cf. *Od.* 21.150–1). Even their servants live in lavish style (cf. *Od.* 15.330–3).

The smell of perfume is extraordinarily potent in Homer (*Il.* 14.173–4):

> the smell of which, when it was shaken in the bronze-floored
> house of Zeus, went out over earth and heaven alike.

Homer is also familiar with magnificent bedding. Arete, for example, orders that this sort of bedding be spread for Odysseus (*Od.* 7.335–8), and Nestor boasts to Telemachus that he is rich in such goods (*Od.* 3.351).

Some other poets retroject the luxury and ease of their own times into the period of the Trojan Wars. Aeschylus (fr. *180), for example, rather inappropriately represents the Greeks as drunk enough to break pisspots over one another's heads. At any rate, he says:[129]

> This is the man who once upon a time threw
> a laugh-producing missile, his stinking pisspot,
> at me and didn't miss. When it hit,
> it broke into shards over my head

---

[129] From a satyr play (perhaps *Bone-collectors*). The speaker may be Odysseus complaining about the suitor Eurymachus; cf. A. fr. 179, quoted at 15.667c.

χωρὶς μυρηρῶν τευχέων πνέουσ᾽ ἐμοί.

καὶ Σοφοκλῆς δὲ ἐν Ἀχαιῶν Συνδείπνῳ·

ἀλλ᾽ ἀμφὶ θυμῷ τὴν κάκοσμον οὐράνην
ἔρριψεν οὐδ᾽ ἥμαρτε· περὶ δ᾽ ἐμῷ κάρᾳ
κατάγνυται τὸ τεῦχος οὐ μύρου πνέον·
ἐδειματούμην δ᾽ οὐ φίλης ὀσμῆς ὕπο.

Εὔπολις δὲ τὸν πρῶτον εἰσηγησάμενον τὸ τῆς ἁμίδος
ὄνομα ἐπιπλήττει λέγων·

(Α.) μισῶ λακωνίζειν, ταγηνίζειν δὲ κἂν
πριαίμην.
(Β.) πολλὰς δ᾽ † οἶμαι νῦν βεβινῆσθαι |
(Α.) < . . . > ὃς δὲ πρῶτος ἐξηῦρον τὸ πρὼ
᾽πιπίνειν
(Β.) πολλήν γε λακκοπρωκτίαν ἡμῖν ἐπίστασ᾽
εὑρών.
(Α.) εἶέν· τίς εἶπεν "ἁμίδα παῖ" πρῶτος μεταξὺ
πίνων;
(Β.) Παλαμηδικόν γε τοῦτο τοὐξεύρημα καὶ
σοφόν σου.

παρ᾽ Ὁμήρῳ δὲ οἱ ἀριστεῖς κοσμίως δειπνοῦσιν ἐν
Ἀγαμέμνονος. εἰ δ᾽ ἐν Ὀδυσσείᾳ φιλονεικοῦσιν Ἀχιλλεὺς καὶ Ὀδυσσεύς, καὶ Ἀγαμέμνων

χαῖρε νόῳ,

and breathed a scent unlike that of perfume-jars over
me.

Also Sophocles in *The Achaeans' Dinner Party* (fr. 565):[130]

But in wrath he hurled his stinking pisspot
at me and didn't miss. The vessel broke
over my head—and it didn't smell like perfume.
I was terrified by the hostile odor.

Eupolis (fr. 385) rebukes the person who first introduced
the word "pisspot," saying:[131]

(A.) I hate living like a Spartan; I'd like to buy a pan
    to fry in.
(B.) Many women, I imagine † now have been fucked
(A.) I, who first invented drinking early in the
    morning
(B.) You need to recognize that what you really
    invented for us was a lot of faggotry!
(A.) Okay—who was the first person to say "Bring me
    a pisspot, slave!" while he was drinking?
(B.) *This* is a brilliant discovery of yours—worthy of
    Palamedes![132]

But in Homer the nobles dine in an orderly way in Agamemnon's residence. And although in the *Odyssey* Achilleus and Odysseus quarrel, and Agamemnon (8.78)

    was secretly pleased,

---

130 Also from a satyr play.
131 Speaker A may be the renegade late 5th-century Athenian
politician and libertine Alcibiades son of Cleinias (*PAA* 121625).
132 See 1.11d n.

ἀλλ' ὠφέλιμοι αἱ φιλοτιμίαι ζητούντων ⟨εἰ⟩ λόγῳ ἢ
f μάχῃ αἱρεθῆναι δεῖ τὸ Ἴλιον. ἀλλ' οὐδ' ὅτε | μνηστῆ-
ρας εἰσάγει μεθύοντας, οὐδὲ τότε τοιαύτην ἀκοσμίαν
εἰσήγαγεν ὡς Σοφοκλῆς καὶ Αἰσχύλος πεποιήκασιν,
ἀλλὰ πόδα βόειον ἐπὶ τὸν Ὀδυσσέα ῥιπτούμενον.

Καθέζονται δ' ἐν τοῖς συνδείπνοις οἱ ἥρωες, οὐ
κατακέκλινται. τοῦτο δὲ καὶ παρ' Ἀλεξάνδρῳ τῷ βασιλεῖ ἐνίοτε ἦν, ὥς φησι Δοῦρις· ἐστιῶν γοῦν ποτε
ἡγεμόνας εἰς ἑξακισχιλίους ἐκάθισεν ἐπὶ δίφρων ἀρ-
γυρῶν καὶ κλιντήρων, ἁλουργοῖς περιστρώσας ἱματί-
18 οις. ‖ Ἡγήσανδρος δέ φησιν οὐδὲ ἔθος εἶναι ἐν
Μακεδονίᾳ κατακλίνεσθαί τινα ἐν δείπνῳ, εἰ μή τις
ἔξω λίνων ὗν κεντήσειεν· ἕως δὲ τότε καθήμενοι ἐδεί-
πνουν. Κάσανδρος οὖν πέντε καὶ τριάκοντα ὢν ἐτῶν
ἐδείπνει παρὰ τῷ πατρὶ καθήμενος, οὐ δυνάμενος τὸν
ἆθλον ἐκτελέσαι καίπερ ἀνδρεῖος γεγονὼς καὶ κυνη-
γὸς ἀγαθός.

Ἐς τὸ πρέπον δὲ Ὅμηρος ἀφορῶν τοὺς ἥρωας οὐ
παρήγαγεν ἄλλο τι δαινυμένους ἢ κρέα καὶ ταῦτα
ἑαυτοῖς σκευάζοντας· οὐ γὰρ ἔχει γέλωτα οὐδ' αἰσχύ-
b νην ὀψαρτύοντας αὐτοὺς | καὶ ἕψοντας ὁρᾶν. ἐπετή-
δευον γὰρ τὴν αὐτοδιακονίαν καὶ ἐκαλλωπίζοντο, φησὶ Χρύσιππος, τῇ ἐν τούτοις εὐστροφίᾳ. Ὀδυσσεὺς
γοῦν δαιτρεῦσαί τε καὶ πῦρ νηῆσαι οἷος οὐκ ἄλλος

---

133 Antipater (Berve i #94; d. 319 BCE), one of the generals of
Philip II of Macedon and Alexander the Great. For Cassander, see
1.19c n.

their rivalry was helpful, since they were debating whether Troy would have to be taken by strategem or in battle. Not even when he presents the suitors as drunk does Homer make the situation as disorderly as it is in Sophocles' and Aeschylus' plays, but a cow's foot is merely thrown at Odysseus (*Od.* 20.299–300).

The heroes sit at their banquets rather than reclining. According to Duris (*FGrH* 76 F 49), this also happened occasionally with King Alexander. On one occasion, for example, when he was giving a feast for 6000 officers, he seated them on silver chairs and couches, which he covered with purple robes. And Hegesander (fr. 33, *FHG* iv.419) says that it was not the custom in Macedon for anyone to recline at dinner unless he had speared a wild boar without using hunting-nets; until they did that, they ate sitting up. Therefore Cassander, although he was 35 years old, used to sit next to his father[133] at dinner, since he was unable to accomplish this feat, despite being brave and a good hunter.

Homer's concern for propriety explains why he presents his heroes as eating nothing but meat and preparing it for themselves; because seeing them fixing their meals and stewing food inspires no laughter or shame. In fact, they deliberately did their own chores and prided themselves, according to Chrysippus (fr. 708, *SVF* iii.177–8), on their versatility in this area. Odysseus, for example, claims that no one is cleverer at cutting up meat and lighting a fire (*Od.* 15.321–4, esp. 322–3);[134] and in the *En-*

---

[134] The hero is, however, pretending to be an impoverished old wanderer.

δεξιὸς εἶναί φησι. καὶ ἐν Λιταῖς δὲ Πάτροκλος[60] πάντα εὐτρεπίζει. καὶ Μενελάου δὲ τελοῦντος γάμους ὁ
νυμφίος Μεγαπένθης οἰνοχοεῖ. νῦν δὲ ἐπὶ τοσοῦτον
ἐκπεπτώκαμεν ὡς κατακεῖσθαι δαινύμενοι.

c   Προσφάτως δὲ καὶ τὰ βαλανεῖα παρῆκται, | τὴν
ἀρχὴν οὐδὲ ἔνδον τῆς πόλεως ἐώντων εἶναι αὐτά, ὧν
τὸ βλαπτικὸν Ἀντιφάνης δηλοῖ·

> εἰς μακαρίαν τὸ λουτρόν, ὡς διέθηκέ με.
> ἐφθὸν κομιδῇ πεποήκεν· ἀποκναίσειεν ἂν
> κἂν ὁστισοῦν μου λαβόμενος τοῦ δέρματος.
> οὕτω στερεόν ⟨τι⟩ πρᾶγμα θερμόν ἐσθ᾽ ὕδωρ.

Ἕρμιππος·

> μὰ ⟨τὸν⟩ Δί᾽ οὐ μέντοι μεθύειν τὸν ἄνδρα χρὴ
> τὸν ἀγαθὸν οὐδὲ θερμολουτεῖν, ἃ σὺ ποεῖς.

ηὔξηται δὲ καὶ ἡ τῶν ὀψοποιῶν περιεργία καὶ ἡ τῶν
μυρεψῶν· ὥστ᾽

d   οὐδ᾽ ἂν κολυμβᾶν εἰς κολυμβήθραν | μύρου

ἀρκεῖσθαί τις ἂν δύναιτο, φησὶν Ἄλεξις. ἀνθοῦσι δὲ
καὶ αἱ τῶν περὶ τὰ πέμματα δημιουργίαι καὶ αἱ περὶ
τὰς συνουσίας περιεργίαι, ὥστ᾽ ἐπιτεχνᾶσθαι σπόγ-
γους ὑποτίθεσθαι· ἐπακτικὸν γὰρ εἶναι τὸ τοιοῦτον

---

[60] Πάτροκλος καὶ Ἀχιλλεὺς CE

treaties Patroclus gets everything ready (*Il*. 9.201–17). So too when Menelaus is celebrating a wedding feast, the bridegroom Megapenthes pours the wine.[135] But today we are so degenerate that we lie down when we dine.

Bathhouses too have been introduced only recently, and originally were not allowed within the city limits. Antiphanes (fr. 239) reveals the damage they do:

> Damn this bath for what it's done to me!
> It's absolutely boiled me! Anyone who
> grabbed hold of me could pull my skin right off!
> That's how cruel hot water is.

Hermippus (fr. 68):

> By Zeus! A decent man, you know, shouldn't spend
> his time
> getting drunk or taking hot baths—which is what you
> do!

Cooks and perfume-makers have also grown increasingly inventive, and the result is that some people would not be satisfied

> even if they dived into a vat of perfume,

as Alexis (fr. 301) puts it. The craftsmanship of cake-makers is likewise in full bloom, as is inventiveness in sex, to the extent that suppository sponges have been created on the theory that this sort of device encourages frequent inter-

---

135 A reference to *Od*. 15.141, by which point the wedding celebrated in Book 4 is long over. The same error appears at 4.192b, which appears to be drawn straight from Herodicus the Cratetean.

πρὸς ἀφροδισίων πλῆθος. Θεόφραστος δ' οὕτω φησί τινας ὀχευτικὰς δυνάμεις εἶναι ὡς καὶ μέχρι ἑβδομή-κοντα συνουσιῶν ἐπιτελεῖν καὶ τὸ τελευταῖον αὐτοῖς αἷμα ἀποκρίνεσθαι. Φύλαρχος δὲ Σανδρόκοττόν φησι

e τὸν Ἰνδῶν βασιλέα Σελεύκῳ μεθ' ὧν ἔπεμψε | δώρων ἀποστεῖλαί τινας δυνάμεις στυτικὰς τοιαύτας ὡς ὑπὸ τοὺς πόδας τιθεμένας τῶν συνουσιαζόντων οἷς μὲν ὁρμὰς ἐμποιεῖν ὀρνίθων δίκην, οὓς δὲ καταπαύειν. ηὔξηται δὲ νῦν καὶ ἡ τῆς μουσικῆς διαστροφή, καὶ ἡ περὶ τὰς ἐσθήσεις καὶ ὑποδέσεις ἐπήκμασε πολυτέ-λεια. Ὅμηρος δὲ τὴν τοῦ μύρου φύσιν εἰδὼς οὐκ εἰσήγαγε μύροις ἀλειφομένους τοὺς ἥρωας πλὴν τὸν Πάριν ἐν οἷς φησί·

κάλλεϊ < . . . > στίλβων,

f ὡς καὶ Ἀφροδίτη κάλλεϊ τὰ πρόσωπα καθαίρει. | ἀλλ' οὐδὲ στεφανουμένους εἰσάγει, καίτοι τῷ ἐκ τῆς μετα-φορᾶς ὁμοιώματι σημαίνεται ὅτι ᾔδει τὸν στέφανον. φησὶ γοῦν· [61]

νῆσος, ἣν πέρι πόντος ἀπείριτος ἐστεφάνωτο,

καί·

[61] In Athenaeus' version of the text, νῆσος is nominative rather than accusative, as in the traditional version; the Homeric relative pronoun τήν has been replaced by the later form ἥν (unmetrical); and Homer's perfect ἐστεφάνωται has been re-placed by a pluperfect.

course. Theophrastus (*HP* 9.18.9) claims that aphrodisiac agents exist powerful enough to allow a man to have sex up to 70 times, and that in the end they ejaculate blood. And Phylarchus (*FGrH* 81 F 35b) says that the Indian king Sandrocottus[136] included among the gifts he sent Seleucus male aphrodisiacs that, when placed under the feet[137] of men having sex, made some of them as randy as birds, but caused others to lose their erections. The perversity of music has also increased in our time, and extravagance in matters of dress and footwear is at a peak. Although Homer was familiar with perfume, he did not introduce his heroes anointed with it, except for Paris in the passage where the poet says (*Il.* 3.392):

glistening with beauty,

in the same way that Aphrodite washes [Penelope's] face with beauty (*Od.* 18.192–4). Nor does he introduce them wearing garlands, although in his metaphorical comparisons he shows that he was familiar with them. He says, for example (*Od.* 10.195),

the island, which the endless sea surrounded like a
    garland;

and (*Il.* 13.736):

136 "Sandrocottus" (Berve i #696) is the Greek form of the name Chandragupta; and the gifts in question must have been sent when the families of Seleucus I (Berve i #700; one of Alexander's generals and successors) and Chandragupta (who controlled much of the subcontinent) formed a marriage alliance at the end of the 4th century.   137 Perhaps a colloquial term for a different (more relevant) part of the male anatomy.

πάντη γάρ σε ⟨ . . . ⟩ στέφανος πολέμοιο δέδηε.

παρατηρητέον δὲ καὶ ὅτι ἐν μὲν Ὀδυσσείᾳ ἀπονιζο-
μένους τὰς χεῖρας ποιεῖ πρὶν μεταλαβεῖν τροφῆς, ἐν
Ἰλιάδι δὲ τοῦτο ποιοῦντας οὐκ ἔστιν εὑρεῖν. σχολα-
ζόντων γὰρ βίος ὁ ἐν Ὀδυσσείᾳ καὶ διὰ τὴν εἰρήνην
19 τρυφώντων· διὸ οἱ ἐνταῦθα ἐθεράπευον τὸ σῶμα διὰ ‖
λουτρῶν καὶ κατανιμμάτων. διὰ τοῦτο καὶ ἀστραγαλί-
ζουσιν ἐν ταύτῃ τῇ πολιτείᾳ καὶ ὀρχοῦνται καὶ σφαι-
ρίζουσιν. Ἡρόδοτος δὲ οὐ καλῶς εἴρηκεν ἐπὶ Ἄτυος
διὰ λιμὸν εὑρεθῆναι τὰς παιδιάς· πρεσβεύει γὰρ τοῖς
χρόνοις τὰ ἡρωικά. οἱ δ' ἐν τῇ Ἰλιακῇ πολιτείᾳ μονο-
νοὺ βοῶσι·

κλῦθ' Ἀλαλά, Πολέμου θύγατερ,
ἐγχέων προοίμιον.

Ὅτι Ἀριστόνικον τὸν Καρύστιον, τὸν Ἀλεξάνδρου
⟨τοῦ βασιλέως⟩[62] συσφαιριστήν, Ἀθηναῖοι πολίτην
ἐποιήσαντο διὰ τὴν τέχνην καὶ ἀνδριάντα ἀνέστησαν.
b | τὰς γὰρ βαναύσους τέχνας Ἕλληνες ὕστερον περὶ
πλείστου μᾶλλον ἐποιοῦντο ἢ τὰς κατὰ παιδείαν γινομένας ἐπινοίας. Ἑστιαιεῖς γοῦν καὶ Ὠρεῖται Θεοδώρου τοῦ ψηφοκλέπτου ἐν θεάτρῳ χαλκῆν εἰκόνα ἀνέ-
θηκαν ψῆφον κρατοῦσαν· ὡς δ' αὕτως Μιλήσιοι
Ἀρχελάου τοῦ κιθαριστοῦ. ἐν δὲ Θήβαις Πινδάρου

---

[62] from S χ 398

---

[138] Used like dice, although they had four sides rather than six.

for the garland of war has leapt into flame
    everywhere (around) you.

It should also be noted that in the *Odyssey* he represents
his characters as washing their hands before they eat (e.g.
1.136–8), whereas in the *Iliad* no one can be found doing this. For the lifestyle depicted in the *Odyssey* is that
of people at leisure, enjoying the luxury associated with
peace; and its characters therefore took good care of their
bodies by bathing and washing. This is also why the members of this society shoot knucklebones,[138] dance, and play
ball. Herodotus (1.94.3–4) is wrong to assert that these
games were invented in Atys' time as the result of a fam-
ine; for the heroic period is earlier than this. The members
of Iliadic society, on the other hand, all but shout (Pi. fr.
78.1–2):

Hear us, Battle-cry, daughter of War,
    prelude of spears!

The Athenians made Aristonicus of Carystus,[139] who
played ball with King Alexander, a citizen because of his
skill and set up a statue of him. For in later times the
Greeks attached much more value to crafts involving man-
ual skill than to intellectual pursuits that require an education. The people of Hestiaea and Oreus, for example,
erected in their theater a bronze statue of Theodorus the
sleight-of-hand artist holding a pebble. The Milesians did
the same for Archelaus the citharode.[140] And in Thebes

---

[139] *PAA* 173985; Berve i #129 ; Billows #130. The grant of citi-
zenship occurred *c*.307–303/2 BCE.

[140] Stephanis #434.

μὲν οὐκ ἔστιν εἰκών, Κλέωνος δὲ τοῦ ᾠδοῦ, ἐφ᾽ ἧς ἐπιγέγραπται·

Πυθέα υἱὸς ὅδ᾽ ἐστὶ Κλέων Θηβαῖος ἀοιδός,
    ὃς πλείστους θνητῶν ἀμφέθετο στεφάνους |
κρατὸς ἐπὶ σφετέρου· καί οἱ κλέος οὐρανόμηκες.
    χαῖρε, Κλέων, Θήβας πατρίδ᾽ ἐπευκλεΐσας.

c

ὑπὸ τούτου τὸν ἀνδριάντα, ὅτε Ἀλέξανδρος τὰς Θήβας κατασκάπτων < . . . > φησὶ Πολέμων φεύγοντά τινα χρυσίον εἰς τὸ ἱμάτιον κοῖλον ὂν ἐνθέσθαι, καὶ ἀνοικιζομένης τῆς πόλεως ἐπανελθόντα εὑρεῖν τὸ χρυσίον μετὰ ἔτη εἴκοσιν[63]. Ἡρόδοτος δὲ ὁ λογόμιμος, ὥς φησιν Ἡγήσανδρος, καὶ Ἀρχέλαος ὁ ὀρχηστὴς παρὰ Ἀντιόχῳ τῷ βασιλεῖ | μάλιστα ἐτιμῶντο τῶν φίλων. ὁ δὲ πατὴρ αὐτοῦ Ἀντίοχος τοὺς Σωστράτου τοῦ αὐλητοῦ υἱεῖς σωματοφύλακας ἐπεποίητο.

d

Ἐθαυμάζετο δὲ παρ᾽ Ἕλλησι καὶ Ῥωμαίοις Ματρέας ὁ πλάνος ὁ Ἀλεξανδρεύς, ὃς ἔλεγε καὶ θηρίον τρέφειν ὃ αὐτὸ ἑαυτὸ κατεσθίει· ὡς καὶ ζητεῖσθαι μέχρι νῦν τὸ Ματρέου θηρίον τί ἐστιν. ἐποίησε δ᾽ οὗτος καὶ παρὰ τὰς Ἀριστοτέλους ἀπορίας καὶ ἀνεγί-

---

[63] εἴκοσιν (i.e. κ′) Casaubon: τριάκοντα (i.e. λ′) CE

---

141 Stephanis #1465.

142 In 335 BCE, after the city revolted against Macedonian authority; Cassander (who ruled Macedon from 316–297; Berve i #414) rebuilt Thebes in 315 (see below). The rest of the sentence has been lost.

there is no statue of Pindar, but there is one of the bard Cleon[141], which bears this inscription (anon. *FGE* 1532–5):

> This is the Theban singer Cleon son of Pytheas,
>> the mortal man who placed the most garlands
> about his own head; and his fame reaches heaven.
>> Hail, Cleon, who brought glory to your fatherland
>> Thebes!

Beneath Cleon's statue, when Alexander was leveling Thebes[142] . . . Polemon (fr. 25 Preller) reports that a refugee put a gold coin inside its robe, which was hollow; when the city was being rebuilt, he returned and found it there twenty years later. According to Hegesander (fr. 13, *FHG* iv.416), King Antiochus[143] showed more honor to Herodotus the mime-actor[144] and Archelaus the dancer[145] than to any of his other close associates. His father Antiochus had made the sons of Sostratus the pipe-player[146] his personal bodyguards.

The itinerant showman Matreas of Alexandria[147] inspired admiration among the Greeks and the Romans. He used to say that he was raising a beast that devoured itself, and a debate continues until today about what Matreas' beast was. He also wrote parodies of Aristotle's *Problems*

---

143 Probably Antiochus IV ("Epiphanes"; reigned 175–164 BCE), son of Antiochus III ("the Great"; reigned 222–187 BCE), to whom Athenaeus refers below.

144 Stephanis #1112.   145 Stephanis #433.

146 Stephanis #2363. For Antiochus III's relationship with Sostratus, see also 6.244f.

147 Stephanis #1619.

νωσκε δημοσίᾳ, διὰ τί ὁ ἥλιος δύνει μὲν κολυμβᾷ δ᾽
οὔ, καὶ διὰ τί οἱ σπόγγοι συμπίνουσι μὲν συγκωθωνί-
e ζονται | δ᾽ οὔ, καὶ ‹διὰ τί›[64] τὰ τετράδραχμα καταλ-
λάττεται μὲν ὀργίζεται δ᾽ οὔ. Ἀθηναῖοι δὲ Ποθεινῷ τῷ
νευροσπάστῃ τὴν σκηνὴν ἔδωκαν ἐφ᾽[65] ἧς ἐνεθουσίων
οἱ περὶ Εὐριπίδην. Ἀθηναῖοι δὲ καὶ Εὐρυκλείδην ἐν τῷ
θεάτρῳ ἀνέστησαν μετὰ τῶν περὶ Αἰσχύλον. ἐθαυμάζετο δὲ καὶ Ξενοφῶν ὁ θαυματοποιός, ὃς μαθητὴν
κατέλιπε Κρατισθένη τὸν Φλιάσιον· ὃς πῦρ τε αὐτό-
ματον ἐποίει ἀναφύεσθαι καὶ ἄλλα πολλὰ φάσματα
ἐτεχνᾶτο, ἀφ᾽ ὧν ἐξίστα τῶν ἀνθρώπων τὴν διάνοιαν.
f τοιοῦτος ἦν καὶ Νυμφόδωρος | ὁ θαυματοποιός, ὃς
προσκρούσας Ῥηγίνοις, ὥς φησι Δοῦρις, εἰς δειλίαν
αὐτοὺς ἔσκωψε πρῶτος. Εὔδικος δὲ ὁ γελωτοποιὸς
ηὐδοκίμει μιμούμενος παλαιστὰς καὶ πύκτας, ὥς φησιν Ἀριστόξενος. Στράτων δ᾽ ὁ Ταραντῖνος ἐθαυμάζετο τοὺς διθυράμβους μιμούμενος· τὰς δὲ κιθαρῳδίας
20 οἱ περὶ τὸν ἐξ Ἰταλίας Οἰνώναν, ὃς καὶ || Κύκλωπα
εἰσήγαγε τερετίζοντα καὶ ναυαγὸν Ὀδυσσέα σολοικί-
ζοντα, ὁ αὐτός φησι. Διοπείθης δὲ ὁ Λοκρός, ὥς φησι
Φανόδημος, παραγενόμενος εἰς Θήβας καὶ ὑποζωννύ-
μενος οἴνου κύστεις μεστὰς καὶ γάλακτος καὶ ταύτας

---

⁶⁴ ‹διὰ τί› Olson   ⁶⁵ ἐφ᾽ Schweighäuser: ἀφ᾽ CE

[148] Literally "How can four-drachma pieces be changed?" (a
verb that can also mean "be reconciled").
[149] *PAA* 776120; Stephanis #2077.

and read them in public: "Why does the sun sink but not dive?"; "Why do sponges soak up wine but not get drunk?"; and "How can accounts be reconciled,[148] if they don't argue with one another?" The Athenians granted the puppeteer Potheinus[149] use of the stage on which Euripides staged his inspired dramas; and they erected a statue of Eurycleides[150] in the theater along with that of Aeschylus. The magician Xenophon[151] was also much admired. He left behind a student, Cratisthenes of Phlius,[152] who could make fire flare up spontaneously and created many other illusions that allowed him to baffle people's minds. The magician Nymphodorus[153] resembled him; according to Duris (*FGrH* 76 F 57), he got angry with the Rhegians and was the first person to mock them for cowardice. The comedian Eudicus[154] won his reputation by imitating wrestlers and boxers, according to Aristoxenus (fr. 135 Wehrli). Straton of Tarentum[155] was admired for his imitations of dithyrambs; and Oenonas of Italy,[156] who brought the Cyclops onstage warbling a tune and the shipwrecked Odysseus speaking bad Greek, was admired for his imitations of harp-songs, according to the same authority. Phanodemus (*FGrH* 325 F 9) reports that when Diopeithes of Locris[157] was in Thebes, he tied bladders full of milk and wine inside his clothes, and then squeezed them and claimed

[150] *PAA* 444767; Stephanis #984. Otherwise unknown.
[151] Stephanis #1914.   [152] Stephanis #1496.
[153] Stephanis #1894; also mentioned at 10.452f.
[154] Stephanis #942.
[155] Stephanis #2316.
[156] Stephanis #1933; called Oenopas at 14.638b.
[157] Stephanis #766.

ἀποθλίβων ἀνιμᾶν ἔλεγεν ἐκ τοῦ στόματος. τοιαῦτα
ποιῶν ηὐδοκίμει καὶ Νοήμων ὁ ἠθολόγος. ἔνδοξοι δ'
ἦσαν καὶ παρ᾽ Ἀλεξάνδρῳ θαυματοποιοὶ Σκύμνος ὁ
Ταραντῖνος, Φιλιστίδης ὁ Συρακούσιος, Ἡράκλειτος
ὁ Μιτυληναῖος. γεγόνασι δὲ καὶ πλάνοι ἔνδοξοι, ὧν
b   Κηφισόδωρος καὶ Πανταλέων. | Φιλίππου δὲ τοῦ γε-
λωτοποιοῦ Ξενοφῶν μνημονεύει.

Ὅρος. οἰκουμένης δῆμον τὴν Ῥώμην φησί. λέγει
δὲ καὶ ὅτι οὐκ ἄν τις σκοποῦ πόρρω τοξεύων λέγοι τὴν
Ῥώμην πόλιν ἐπιτομὴν τῆς οἰκουμένης· ἐν ᾗ συνιδεῖν
ἔστιν οὕτως πάσας τὰς πόλεις ἱδρυμένας, καὶ κατ᾽
ἰδίαν δὲ τὰς πολλάς, ὡς Ἀλεξανδρέων μὲν τὴν χρυ-
σῆν, Ἀντιοχέων δὲ τὴν καλήν, Νικομηδέων δὲ τὴν
περικαλλῆ, προσέτι τε

τὴν λαμπροτάτην πόλεων πασῶν ὁπόσας ὁ Ζεὺς
ἀναφαίνει,

c   τὰς Ἀθήνας λέγω. ἐπιλείποι δ᾽ ἄν με οὐχ ἡμέρα | μία
ἐξαριθμούμενον τὰς ἐν τῇ Ῥωμαίων οὐρανοπόλει[66]
ἀριθμουμένας πόλεις, ἀλλὰ πᾶσαι αἱ κατὰ τὸν ἐνιαυτὸν[67] διὰ τὸ πλῆθος. καὶ γὰρ ὅλα ἔθνη ἀθρόως αὐτόθι

[66] οὐρανοπόλει Ῥωμῇ CE
[67] ἐνιαυτὸν ἀριθμούμενοι CE

---

158 Stephanis #1888.
159 Cf. 12.538e (drawing on Chares).
160 Berve i #713; Stephanis #2285. According to Chares of
Mitylene (*FGrH* 125 F 4; quoted at 12.538e), the three men men-

that the liquid was coming out of his mouth. The mimic Noemon[158] won a reputation by performing similar tricks. Alexander[159] thought highly of the magicians Scymnus of Tarentum,[160] Philistides of Syracuse,[161] and Heracleitus of Mitylene.[162] There have also been famous itinerant showmen, including Cephisodorus[163] and Pantaleon[164]; and Xenophon (*Smp.* 1.11–16) mentions the comedian Philip.[165]

A division.[166] [Athenaeus] refers to Rome as an international community. He also says that you would not be far from the mark if you call the city of Rome an epitome of the inhabited world, since you can see every single city settled in it, many of them in individual neighborhoods, for example golden Alexandria, lovely Antioch, gorgeous Nicomedia, and in addition

> the most radiant of all the cities Zeus reveals (adesp.
>   com. fr. 100),

by which I mean Athens. One day would not be enough, if I tried to offer a complete list of the cities included in the count of the Romans' heavenly city; indeed, there are so many that all the days in a year would be required. The fact is that whole populations have settled there *en masse*,

---

tioned here performed at the mass marriage between Persian woman and Macedonians staged by Alexander in Susa in 324.

   161 Berve i #791; Stephanis #2508.   162 Berve i #351; Stephanis #1092.   163 Stephanis #1395; also mentioned (along with Pantaleon) at 14.615f.   164 Stephanis #1996.

   165 Stephanis #2498.   166 This enigmatic notice falls about halfway through the epitomized version of Book One and probably referred originally to one of the divisions of the work into 30 half-Books; see the Introduction.

συνῴκισται, ὡς τὸ Καππαδοκῶν καὶ Σκυθῶν καὶ Ποντίων καὶ ἄλλων πλειόνων. οὗτοι οὖν πάντες, ὁ σύμπας δῆμος τῆς οἰκουμένης, τὸν ἐφ᾽ ἡμῖν, φησί, φιλόσοφον ὀρχηστὴν Μέμφιν ἐκάλεσαν ἀπαρχαΐζοντες τὴν διὰ τοῦ σώματος αὐτοῦ κίνησιν τῇ τῶν πόλεων ἀρχαιοτάτῃ καὶ βασιλικωτάτῃ, περὶ ἧς Βακχυλίδης | φησί·

d

   τὰν ἀχείμαντόν τε Μέμφιν
   καὶ δονακώδεα Νεῖλον.

οὗτος τὴν Πυθαγόρειον φιλοσοφίαν ἐπιδείκνυσιν ἥτις ἐστί, μετὰ σιωπῆς πάνθ᾽ ἡμῖν ἐμφανίζων σαφέστερον[68] ἢ οἱ τὰς τῶν λόγων τέχνας ἐπαγγελλόμενοι διδάσκειν. τῆς δὲ κατὰ τοῦτον ὀρχήσεως τῆς τραγικῆς καλουμένης πρῶτος εἰσηγητὴς γέγονε Βάθυλλος ὁ Ἀλεξανδρεύς, ὅν φησι παντομίμους[69] ὀρχήσασθαι Σέλευκος. τοῦτον τὸν Βάθυλλόν φησιν Ἀριστόνικος καὶ Πυλάδην, | οὗ ἐστι καὶ σύγγραμμα περὶ ὀρχήσεως, τὴν Ἰταλικὴν ὄρχησιν συστήσασθαι ἐκ τῆς κωμικῆς, ἣ ἐκαλεῖτο κόρδαξ, καὶ τῆς τραγικῆς, ἣ ἐκαλεῖτο ἐμμέλεια, καὶ τῆς σατυρικῆς, ἣ ἐλέγετο σίκιννις (διὸ καὶ οἱ σάτυροι σικιννισταί), ἧς εὑρετὴς Σίκιννός τις βάρβαρος· οἱ δέ φασιν ὅτι Κρὴς ἦν ὁ Σίκιννος. ἦν δὲ ἡ Πυλάδου ὄρχησις ὀγκώδης παθητική τε καὶ πολυπρόσωπος[70], ἡ δὲ Βαθύλλειος ἱλαρωτέρα· καὶ γὰρ ὑπόρχημά τι τοῦτον διατίθεσθαι. Σοφο-

e

---

[68] σαφέστερον Musurus: σαφῶς CE
[69] παντομίμους Herwerden: νομίμως CE

such as the Cappadocians, Scythians, Pontians, and many others. All of them, then, the whole population of the world, says [Athenaeus], called the philosopher-dancer of our time[167] "Memphis," comparing the way he moved his body to the oldest and most regal of cities, about which Bacchylides (fr. 30) says:

and Memphis, which knows no storms,
and the reed-filled Nile.

This fellow demonstrates what Pythagorean philosophy is, and although he remains silent, he makes it all clearer to us than professional teachers of oratory can. The first exponent of his style of dancing (referred to as "tragic") was Bathyllus of Alexandria, who, according to Seleucus (*FGrH* 341 F *5 = fr. 81 Müller), danced pantomimes. Aristonicus (fr. 43 Razzetti) says that this Bathyllus, along with Pylades, who wrote a treatise on dancing, developed the Italian style of dancing from the comic dance referred to as the *kordax*, the tragic dance referred to as the *emmeleia*, and the satyric dance called the *sikinnis*. (This is why satyrs are called *sikinnistai*.) The *sikinnis* was invented by a non-Greek named Sicinnus; but other authorities claim that Sicinnus was from Crete. Pylades' style of dancing was full of bombast, passion, and characterization, whereas Bathyllus' was more cheerful; in fact, he performed a sort

---

[167] Agrippa, a slave of Lucius Verus (co-emperor with Marcus Aurelius 161–169 CE).

---

[70] πολυπρόσωπος Plu. *Mor.* 711e: πολύκοπος CE

κλῆς δὲ πρὸς τῷ καλὸς γεγενῆσθαι τὴν ὥραν ἦν καὶ
f ὀρχηστικὴν | δεδιδαγμένος καὶ μουσικὴν ἔτι παῖς ὢν
παρὰ Λάμπρῳ. μετὰ γοῦν τὴν ἐν Σαλαμῖνι ναυμαχίαν
περὶ τρόπαιον γυμνὸς ἀληλιμμένος ἐχόρευσε μετὰ
λύρας· οἱ δὲ ἐν ἱματίῳ φασί. καὶ τὸν Θάμυριν διδά-
σκων αὐτὸς ἐκιθάρισεν· ἄκρως δὲ ἐσφαίρισεν, ὅτε τὴν
Ναυσικάαν καθῆκε. τῆς δὲ Μέμφιδος ὀρχήσεως ἦρα
καὶ Σωκράτης ὁ σοφὸς καὶ πολλάκις καταλαμβανό-
μενος ὀρχούμενος, ὥς φησι Ξενοφῶν, ἔλεγε τοῖς γνω-
21 ρίμοις παντὸς εἶναι ‖ μέλους τὴν ὄρχησιν γυμνάσιον.
ἔταττον γὰρ τὸ ὀρχεῖσθαι ἐπὶ τοῦ κινεῖσθαι καὶ ἐρε-
θίζεσθαι. Ἀνακρέων·

κλικομοι κοῦραι Διὸς ὠρχήσαντ᾽ ἐλαφρῶς.

Ἴων·

ἐκ τῶν ἀέλπτων μᾶλλον ὤρχησαι φρένας.

Ἕρμιππος δέ φησι Θεόφραστον παραγίνεσθαι εἰς
τὸν περίπατον καθ᾽ ὥραν λαμπρὸν καὶ ἐξησκημένον,
εἶτα καθίσαντα διατίθεσθαι τὸν λόγον οὐδεμιᾶς ἀπε-
b χόμενον κινήσεως οὐδὲ σχήματος | ἑνός. καί ποτε
ὀψοφάγον μιμούμενον ἐξείραντα τὴν γλῶσσαν περι-
λείχειν τὰ χείλη.

Ἔμελε δὲ αὐτοῖς καὶ τοῦ κοσμίως ἀναλαμβάνειν

---

168 Cf. 1.15d–e.
169 A famous musician (*PAA* 601647).
170 In 480 BCE.

of *hyporcheme*.[168] Sophocles (test. 28), in addition to being good-looking in his youth, was also taught dancing and music as a young man by Lamprus.[169] After the sea-battle at Salamis,[170] for example, he danced around the victory monument to lyre-music naked and anointed with oil; although other authorities report that he wore a robe. When he produced *Thamyris*, he played the lyre himself;[171] and he did a neat job of ball-playing when he staged *Nausicaa*. The wise Socrates also loved the Memphian style of dancing; often when he was caught dancing, according to Xenophon (*Smp.* 2.17), he would tell his acquaintances that this was a means for every limb to get some exercise. They used the verb "dance," in fact, to describe physical movement and excitement generally. Anacreon (*PMG* 390):

The fair-tressed daughters of Zeus danced lightly.

Ion (*TrGF* 19 F 50):

to have set my heart dancing at these unexpected events.

Hermippus (Hermipp. Hist. fr. 51 Wehrli = Thphr. fr. 12) says that Theophrastus used to appear at the school at his regular time, shining with oil and neatly dressed, and would then take a seat and deal with the day's topic, using every sort of gesture and expression. Once when he was imitating a glutton, he struck out his tongue and licked his lips.

They were also concerned to drape their clothing in a

---

[171] Thamyris was a Thracian lyre-singer who claimed to be more skilled even than the Muses, who therefore blinded him and stripped him of his abilities (*Il.* 2.594–600).

τὴν ἐσθῆτα καὶ τοὺς μὴ τοῦτο ποιοῦντας ἔσκωπτον.
Πλάτων ἐν Θεαιτήτῳ· πάντα δυναμένους ὀξέως τε καὶ
τορῶς διακονεῖν, ἀναβάλλεσθαι δ' οὐκ ἐπισταμένους
ἐπιδέξι' ἐλευθερίως οὐδ' ἁρμονίαν λόγων λαβόντας
ὀρθῶς ὑμνῆσαι θεῶν τε καὶ ἀνθρώπων εὐδαιμόνων
βίον. Σαπφὼ περὶ Ἀνδρομέδας σκώπτει·

c   τίς δ' ἀγροίωτις | θέλγει νόον < . . . >
       οὐκ ἐπισταμένα τὰ βράκε' ἕλκην ἐπὶ τῶν
           σφύρων;

Φιλέταιρος·

       ἀμφιβάλλου † στέρνοις φᾶρος † οὐ καθήσεις,
           τάλαν,
       μηδ' ἀγροίκως ἄνω γόνατος ἀμφέξει;

Ἕρμιππος δέ φησι Θεόκριτον τὸν Χῖον ὡς ἀπαίδευτον
μέμφεσθαι τὴν Ἀναξιμένους περιβολήν· Καλλίστρα-
τός τε ὁ Ἀριστοφάνειος Ἀρίσταρχον ἐν συγγράμματι
κακῶς εἴρηκεν ἐπὶ τῷ μὴ εὐρύθμως ἀμπέχεσθαι, φέ-
ροντός τι καὶ τοῦ τοιούτου πρὸς παιδείας ἐξέτασιν. διὸ
d   καὶ Ἄλεξίς φησιν· |

       ἐν γὰρ νομίζω τοῦτο τῶν ἀνελευθέρων
       εἶναι, τὸ βαδίζειν ἀρρύθμως ἐν ταῖς ὁδοῖς,

---

172 Athenaeus or his source has replaced many of Sappho's
rare Aeolic forms (restored here) with more common ones, as
again at e.g. 2.39a. Alcaeus is treated similarly at e.g. 1.22e–f.

dignified way, and they made fun of anyone who failed to do so. Plato in the *Theatetus* (175e–6a): men who can render all these services quickly and smartly, but don't know how to wear their robes like free men, over the left shoulder, or how to put words together to properly hymn the life of gods and blessed men. Sappho (fr. 57.1, 3) says scornfully of Andromeda:[172]

> What unsophisticated girl charms your mind . . . ,
> one who does not know how to pull her robes over
>   her ankles?

Philetaerus (fr. 18):

> Wrap around † your breast a robe † Pull it down, fool,
> and don't wrap it above your knee like a bumpkin!

Hermippus (Hermipp. Hist. fr. 78 Wehrli) says that Theocritus of Chios criticized Anaximenes' style of dress as uncultivated;[173] and Aristophanes' pupil Callistratus (p. 313 in A. Nauck (ed.), *Aristophanes of Byzantium*) attacked Aristarchus[174] in a treatise for not putting his robes on gracefully, on the ground that this sort of behavior offers evidence about a man's upbringing. This is why Alexis (fr. 265) says:

> For I consider this to be one mark
> of servility—walking erratically in the street,

[173] Theocritus of Chios (Billows #114; cf. *FHG* ii.86–7) was active in the second half of the 4th century BCE, and the Anaximenes in question is presumably the historian and rhetorician Anaximenes of Lampsacus (*FGrH* 72 T 12).

[174] Aristarchus of Samothrace (c.216–144 BCE), head of the Library at Alexandria c.153–145.

ἐξὸν καλῶς· οὗ μήτε πράττεται τέλος
μηδεὶς ⟨γὰρ⟩ ἡμᾶς, μήτε τιμὴν δόντα δεῖ
ἑτέρῳ λαβεῖν, φέρει δὲ τοῖς μὲν χρωμένοις
δόξης τιν᾽ ὄγκον, τοῖς δ᾽ ὁρῶσιν ἡδονήν,
κόσμον δὲ τῷ βίῳ, τὸ τοιοῦτον γέρας
τίς οὐκ ἂν αὑτῷ κτῷτο φάσκων νοῦν ἔχειν;

Καὶ Αἰσχύλος δὲ οὐ μόνον ἐξεῦρε τὴν τῆς στολῆς
e εὐπρέπειαν | καὶ σεμνότητα, ἣν ζηλώσαντες οἱ ἱερο-
φάνται καὶ δᾳδοῦχοι ἀμφιέννυνται, ἀλλὰ καὶ πολλὰ
σχήματα ὀρχηστικὰ αὐτὸς ἐξευρίσκων ἀνεδίδου τοῖς
χορευταῖς. Χαμαιλέων γοῦν πρῶτον αὐτόν φησι σχη-
ματίσαι τοὺς χοροὺς ὀρχηστοδιδασκάλοις οὐ χρη-
σάμενον, ἀλλὰ καὶ αὐτὸν τοῖς χοροῖς τὰ σχήματα
ποιοῦντα τῶν ὀρχήσεων, καὶ ὅλως πᾶσαν τὴν τῆς
τραγῳδίας οἰκονομίαν εἰς ἑαυτὸν περιιστᾶν. ὑπεκρίνε-
το οὖν μετὰ τοῦ εἰκότος τὰ δράματα. Ἀριστοφάνης
f γοῦν (παρὰ δὲ τοῖς κωμικοῖς | ἡ περὶ τῶν τραγικῶν
ἀπόκειται πίστις) ποιεῖ αὐτὸν Αἰσχύλον λέγοντα·

⟨ . . . ⟩ τοῖσι χοροῖς αὐτὸς τὰ σχήματ᾽ ἐποίουν.

καὶ πάλιν·

(Β.) τοὺς Φρύγας οἶδα θεωρῶν,

when one could walk like a gentleman. Because when
   no one taxes
us for doing something, and you don't have to pay
another person to get it, and it produces a certain
   amount
of distinction for those who act this way, pleasure for
   the onlookers,
and a bit of polish in your life, who that claims to
   have any sense
wouldn't try to get an honor like this for himself?

Aeschylus as well not only invented the elegance and
dignity of costume that the hierophants and torch-
bearers[175] imitate when they dress themselves, but also
created many dance-steps himself and passed them on to
the members of his choruses. Chamaeleon (fr. 41 Wehrli =
A. test. 103), at any rate, says that he was the first to
arrange the dances, and that he did not use special train-
ers, but worked out the dance-steps for his choruses himself and generally took on the entire management of the
tragedy. Most likely, therefore, he acted in his own plays.
Aristophanes (fr. 696, encompassing both quotations), at
any rate—there is credible information about the tragic
poets in the comedians—represents Aeschylus himself as
saying:

I myself used to create the dances for my choruses.

And again:

      (B.) I know from seeing his *Phrygians*,

---

[175] Two of the chief classes of officials at the Eleusinian Mys-
teries.

ὅτε τῷ Πριάμῳ συλλυσόμενοι τὸν παῖδ' ἦλθον
  τεθνεῶτα,
πολλὰ τοιαυτὶ καὶ τοιαυτὶ καὶ δεῦρο
  σχηματίσαντας.

καὶ Τέλεσις δὲ ἢ Τελέστης ὁ ὀρχηστοδιδάσκαλος
πολλὰ ἐξεύρηκε σχήματα, ἄκρως ταῖς χερσὶ τὰ λεγόμενα δεικνύς. Φίλλις ὁ Δήλιος μουσικὸς τοὺς ἀρχαί-
ους φησὶ κιθαρῳδοὺς κινήσεις ἀπὸ μὲν τοῦ προσώπου
μικρὰς φέρειν, ἀπὸ ποδῶν δὲ πλείους, ἐμβατηρίους
22 καὶ χορευτικάς. ‖ Ἀριστοκλῆς γοῦν φησιν ὅτι Τελέστης ὁ Αἰσχύλου ὀρχηστὴς οὕτως ἦν τεχνίτης ὥστε
ἐν τῷ ὀρχεῖσθαι τοὺς Ἑπτὰ Ἐπὶ Θήβας φανερὰ
ποιῆσαι τὰ πράγματα δι' ὀρχήσεως. φασὶ δὲ καὶ ὅτι
οἱ ἀρχαῖοι ποιηταί, Θέσπις, Πρατίνας, Κρατῖνος,
Φρύνιχος, ὀρχησταὶ ἐκαλοῦντο διὰ τὸ μὴ μόνον τὰ
ἑαυτῶν δράματα ἀναφέρειν εἰς ὄρχησιν τοῦ χοροῦ,
ἀλλὰ καὶ ἔξω τῶν ἰδίων ποιημάτων διδάσκειν τοὺς
βουλομένους ὀρχεῖσθαι.

Μεθύων δὲ ἐποίει τὰς τραγῳδίας Αἰσχύλος, ὡς
b φησι Χαμαιλέων. Σοφοκλῆς γοῦν | ὠνείδιζεν αὐτῷ ὅτι
εἰ καὶ τὰ δέοντα ποιεῖ, ἀλλ' οὐκ εἰδώς γε.

Ὀρχήσεις δὲ ἐθνικαὶ αἵδε· Λακωνικαί, Τροιζήνιαι,
Ἐπιζεφύριοι, Κρητικαί, Ἰωνικαί, Μαντινικαί, ἃς προκρίνει Ἀριστόξενος διὰ τὴν τῶν χειρῶν κίνησιν. οὕτως

---

176 Hector, killed by Achilles, who refused to release the body
for burial until Priam came to ransom it personally.
177 Stephanis #2390.

when they came to help Priam get his dead son[176]
    released,
and they did dance-steps like this and that and in this
    direction.

The dance-teacher Telesis (or Telestes)[177] also invented
many steps, neatly illustrating what was said with hand-
gestures. The musician Phillis of Delos (fr. 3, *FHG* iv.476)
says that in the old days citharodes did not make many
facial expressions, but they moved their feet more, producing marching-steps and dance-steps. Aristocles (fr. 11,
FHG iv.332 = A. test. 81), for example, says that Aeschylus'
dancer Telestes was so skilful that when he danced the
Seven Against Thebes he could make the action apparent
simply by his dancing. They also say that the ancient
poets—Thespis, Pratinus, Cratinus[178], and Phrynichus—
were called "dancers" because not only did they integrate
their own dramas with choral dancing, but, quite apart
from their own compositions, they taught anyone who
wanted to learn to dance.

Aeschylus used to write his tragedies drunk, according
to Chamaeleon (fr. 40b Wehrli = A. test. 117b). Sophocles
(test. 52b), at any rate, found fault with him, saying that
even if used the right words, he did so unconsciously.[179]

The following dances are associated with particular
peoples: the Spartan, Troezenian, Epizephyrian, Cretan,
Ionian, and Mantinean, which Aristoxenus (fr. 112 Wehrli)
prefers because of the hand-gestures. Dancing was so re-

---

[178] The mid-5th-century comic poet Cratinus seems out of
place in this list, which otherwise contains the names of early 5th-
century tragic poets.   [179] A more complete version of this
material appears at 10.428f–9a.

δ᾽ ἦν ἔνδοξον καὶ σοφὸν ἡ ὄρχησις ὥστε Πίνδαρος
τὸν Ἀπόλλωνα ὀρχηστὴν καλεῖ·

ὀρχήστ᾽ ἀγλαΐας ἀνάσσων, εὐρυφάρετρ᾽
Ἄπολλον.

καὶ Ὅμηρος ἢ τῶν Ὁμηριδῶν τις ἐν τῷ εἰς Ἀπόλλωνα
ὕμνῳ φησίν·

Ἀπόλλων
c   φόρμιγγ᾽ ἐν χείρεσσιν ἔχων χάριεν κιθάριζε,[71] |
καλὰ καὶ ὕψι βιβάς.[72]

Εὔμηλος δὲ ὁ Κορίνθιος ἢ Ἀρκτῖνος[73] τὸν Δία ὀρ-
χούμενόν που παράγει λέγων·

μέσσοισιν δ᾽ ὠρχεῖτο πατὴρ ἀνδρῶν τε θεῶν τε.

Θεόφραστος δὲ πρῶτόν φησιν Ἄνδρωνα τὸν Κατα-
ναῖον αὐλητὴν κινήσεις καὶ ῥυθμοὺς ποιῆσαι τῷ σώ-
ματι αὐλοῦντα· ὅθεν σικελίζειν τὸ ὀρχεῖσθαι παρὰ
τοῖς παλαιοῖς· μεθ᾽ ὃν Κλεόλαν τὸν Θηβαῖον. ὀρχησταὶ δὲ ἔνδοξοι Βολβὸς μὲν παρὰ Κρατίνῳ καὶ Καλ-
d   λίᾳ, Ζήνων δὲ ὁ Κρὴς ὁ πάνυ Ἀρταξέρξῃ | προσ-
φιλέστατος παρὰ Κτησίᾳ. Ἀλέξανδρος δὲ ἐν τῇ πρὸς

[71] 515 is a troubled verse; but all other witnesses have κιθα-
ρίζων rather than Athenaeus' κιθάριζε.
[72] καὶ Ὅμηρος . . . βιβάς is omitted by E and is preserved in
C only in the margin.
[73] ἢ Ἀρκτῖνος is omitted by E and is preserved in C only in
the margin.

spected and involved so much skill that Pindar (fr. 148) refers to Apollo as a dancer:

Dancer, lord of brilliance, Apollo of the broad quiver!

And Homer or one of the Homeridae says in the *Hymn to Apollo* (514–16):

Apollo,
lyre in hand, was playing a pleasant tune,
stepping high and gracefully.

And Eumelus of Corinth or Arctinus somewhere introduces Zeus dancing, saying (*Titan.* fr. 6 Bernabé):

And the father of men and gods was dancing in their
midst.

Theophrastus (fr. 718) says that Andron of Catana[180] was the first pipe-player to move his body to the rhythm as he played; this is why ancient sources use the verb *sikelizō* ("act like a Sicel") to mean "dance." Cleolas of Thebes[181] came after him. Famous dancers include Bolbus[182], who is mentioned by Cratinus (fr. 425) and Callias (fr. 30); and Zeno of Crete[183], who was a great favorite of Artaxerxes[184] and is mentioned by Ctesias (*FGrH* 688 F 31). Alexander

---

[180] Stephanis #187. Andron and Cleolas are otherwise unknown, but presumably date to the 5th century.

[181] Stephanis #1443.   [182] Stephanis #531.

[183] Stephanis #1027.   [184] Artaxerxes II (king of Persia 405/4–359/8 BCE), in whose court Ctesias served as a physician.

[185] Berve i #363; Stephanis #1163. Philoxenus (Berve i #793) became Alexander's chief financial officer after the flight of Harpalus. For Alexander's letter (which concerned two handsome boys Theodorus wanted to sell), see Plu. *Alex.* 22.1.

Φιλόξενον ἐπιστολῇ μέμνηται Θεοδώρου καὶ Χρυσίππου.

Ὅτι τὸ Μουσεῖον[74] ὁ Φλιάσιος Τίμων ὁ σιλλογράφος τάλαρόν πού φησιν ἐπισκώπτων τοὺς ἐν αὐτῷ τρεφομένους φιλοσόφους, ὅτι ὥσπερ ἐν πανάγρῳ τινὶ σιτοῦνται καθάπερ οἱ πολυτιμότατοι ὄρνιθες·

πολλοὶ μὲν βόσκονται ἐν Αἰγύπτῳ πολυφύλῳ
βυβλιακοὶ χαρακῖται ἀπείριτα δηριόωντες
Μουσέων ἐν ταλάρῳ.

e   Ἕως ἂν τῆς λογοδιαρροίας | ἀπαλλαγῶσιν οὗτοι οἱ τραπεζορήτορες, οἳ ὑπὸ γλωσσαλγίας ἐπιλελῆσθαί μοι δοκοῦσι καὶ τοῦ Πυθικοῦ χρησμοῦ, ὃν ἀναγράφει Χαμαιλέων·

εἴκοσι τὰς πρὸ κυνὸς καὶ εἴκοσι τὰς μετέπειτα
οἴκῳ ἐνὶ σκιερῷ Διονύσῳ χρῆσθαι ἰητρῷ.

καὶ Μνησίθεος δ᾽ ὁ Ἀθηναῖος Διόνυσον ἰατρόν φησι τὴν Πυθίαν χρῆσαι τιμᾶν Ἀθηναίοις. φησὶ δὲ καὶ Ἀλκαῖος ὁ Μιτυληναῖος ποιητής·

τέγγε πνεύμονας οἴνῳ, τὸ γὰρ ἄστρον
περιτέλλεται,

[74] τὸ Μουσεῖον E: τὸ Ἀθήνησι τὸ ἐν πρυτανείῳ Μουσεῖον C

---

[186] Berve i #830; Stephanis #2633.

in his letter to Philoxenus mentions Theodorus[185] and Chrysippus[186].

The satirist Timo of Phlius (*SH* 786) refers somewhere to the Museum as a "bird-cage," as a way of making fun of the philosophers maintained there, because they were fed like expensive birds in a netted enclosure:[187]

> Numerous cloistered papyrus-warblers are fattened
> in Egypt with its many peoples, quarrelling endlessly
> in the Muses' bird-cage.

Until these dinner-table-orators get over their verbal diarrhea; their tongue-disease, it seems to me, has made them forget the Pythian oracle recorded by Chamaeleon (fr. 11 Wehrli = Delphic oracle L103 Fontenrose):

> For 20 days before the dog-star[188] rises and 20 days
>   after,
> use Dionysus as a physician in your shadowy house.

Mnesitheus of Athens (fr. 42 Bertier) also reports that the Pythia in an oracle ordered the Athenians to honor Dionysus as a physician. And Alcaeus the poet from Mitylene (fr. 347.1–2) says:[189]

> Moisten your lungs with wine. For the star is rising,

[187] This quotation and the one that follows are probably part of a transition between speakers; and the abusive tone, the charge of "verbal diarrhea" (cf. 4.159e), the series of positive references to the dog-star, and the retrospective description below of the discussion as "cynical" combine to suggest that Cynulcus is speaking.

[188] Sirius (referred to below simply as "the star"), which rises in mid-summer; see Hes. *Op.* 584–7 with West on 417.

[189] See 1.21c n. The verses are quoted again at 10.430b.

f   ἀ δ' ὥρα | χαλέπα, πάντα δὲ δίψαισ' ὑπὰ
       καύματος.

καὶ ἀλλαχοῦ·

     πώνωμεν, τὸ γὰρ ἄστρον περιτέλλεται.

Εὔπολίς τε τὸν Καλλίαν φησὶν ἀναγκάζεσθαι ὑπὸ
Πρωταγόρου πίνειν,

                        ἵνα
     πρὸ τοῦ κυνὸς τὸν πνεύμον'[75] ἔκπλυτον φορῇ.

ἡμῖν δ' οὐ μόνον ὁ πνεύμων ἀπεξήρανται, κινδυνεύει
δὲ καὶ ἡ καρδία. καίτοι Ἀντιφάνης λέγει·

          τὸ δὲ ζῆν, εἰπέ μοι,
23   τί ἐστι; < . . . > τὸ πίνειν φήμ' ἐγώ. ||
ὁρᾷς παρὰ ῥείθροισι χειμάρροις ὅσα
δένδρων ἀεὶ τὴν νύκτα καὶ τὴν ἡμέραν
βρέχεται, μέγεθος καὶ κάλλος οἷα γίνεται,
τὰ δ' ἀντιτείνοντ' αὐτόπρεμν' ἀπόλλυται.

οὕτω τούτοις, φησί, κυνολογήσασιν ἐδόθη πιεῖν. εἴρηται δὲ τὸ βρέχειν καὶ ἐπὶ τοῦ πίνειν. Ἀντιφάνης·

---

[75] πλεύμον' Plutarch

---

190 From *Flatterers*, in which various hangers-on took relentless advantage of Callias son of Hipponicus (*PAA* 554500), who
was extremely wealthy and was mocked constantly by the comic
poets (cf. 4.169a; 5.218b–c).
191 Quoting and adapting S. *Ant.* 712–14.

the season is a harsh one, and the heat makes
everything thirsty.

And elsewhere (Alc. fr. 352):

Let's drink; for the star is rising.

Eupolis (fr. 158.1–2)[190] says that Callias is forced to drink
by Pythagoras

so that
he may have his lung washed clean before the dog-
star rises.

And it is not just our lungs that have dried out; it is possible
that our heart has as well. Indeed, Antiphanes (fr. 228)[191]
says:

Tell me—what's
the point of life? I say it's to drink.
Look at the trees along torrent streams
that stay moist *(brechetai)* all day and all night;
how large and beautiful they grow!
But those that resist are destroyed root and branch.

After they engaged in this cynical discussion, [Athenaeus]
says, they were offered a drink. The verb *brechō* ("wet,
moisten") is also used to refer to drinking.[192] Antiphanes
(fr. 279):

---

[192] As the verb is used in this sense in the quotation just above,
and as the Epitomator tells us that there was a break in the discussion as drinks were served, what follows is probably a response to a
question (most likely by Ulpian) as to whether *brechō* is used elsewhere in this sense. Presumably he also posed the question which
the remarks about the verb *anapiptō* etc. below address.

δεῖ γὰρ φαγόντας δαψιλῶς βρέχειν.

Εὔβουλος·

          (Α.) Σίκων ἐγὼ
b βεβρεγμένος ἥκω καὶ κεκωθωνισμένος. |
  (Β.) πέπωκας οὗτος; (Α.) < . . . > πέπωκ᾽ ἐγώ,
μὰ ⟨τὸν⟩ Δία τὸν Μενδαῖον.

Ὅτι τὸ ἀναπίπτειν κυρίως ἐπὶ ψυχῆς ἐστιν, οἷον
ἀθυμεῖν, ὀλιγοδρανεῖν[76]. Θουκυδίδης πρώτῃ· νικώμε-
νοι ἐπ᾽ ἐλάχιστον ἀναπίπτουσι. Κρατῖνος δ᾽ ἐπὶ ἐρε-
τῶν χρᾶται τῇ λέξει·

ῥοθίαζε κἀνάπιπτε.

καὶ Ξενοφῶν ἐν Οἰκονομικῷ· διὰ τί ἄλυποι ἀλλήλοις
εἰσὶν οἱ ἐρέται; ἢ ὅτι ἐν τάξει μὲν κάθηνται, ἐν τάξει δὲ
προνεύουσιν, ἐν τάξει δὲ ἀναπίπτουσιν; ἀνακεῖσθαι δέ
c φαμεν | ἐπὶ ἀνδριάντος· ὅθεν τοὺς ἐπὶ κατακειμένων
χρωμένους τῇ λέξει διέσυρον. Δίφιλος· ἐγὼ δ᾽ † ἕως
μέν τινος ἀνεκείμην †. πρὸς ὃν δυσχεραίνων ὁ ἑταῖρός
φησιν· ἀνάκεισο. Φιλιππίδης·

          (Α.) καὶ δειπνῶν ἀεὶ
ἀνακείμενος παρ᾽ αὐτόν.

---

[76] ὀλιγοδρανεῖν Kaibel: ὀλιγωρεῖν CE

---

[193] Sicon is a slave-name, and the oath by Mendaean Zeus is an
allusion to Mendaean wine (for which, see 1.29d–f).

Because those who eat well must drink *(brechein)*.

Eubulus (fr. 123):[193]

> (A.) My name is Sicon
> and I've come drenched *(bebregmenos)* and drunk.
> (B.) Hey you! Have you been drinking? (A.) I have
>   been drinking,
> by Mendaean Zeus!

The verb *anapiptō* ("fall back") is properly used of a person's spirit, in the sense "be discouraged, faint-hearted." Thucydides Book I (70.5): they are minimally discouraged *(anapiptousi)* when defeated. But Cratinus (fr. 332) uses the word to refer to rowers:

> Raise a splash and fall back *(anapipte)!*

Also Xenophon in the *Oeconomicus* (8.8): Why do the rowers not hamper one another? Isn't it because they are seated in order, swing forward in order, and fall back *(anapiptousin)* in order? But we use the verb *anakeimai* (literally "lay up") of statuary; as a result those who used the word to describe people lying down were ridiculed. Diphilus (fr. 124, unmetrical): I † lay back *(anekeimēn)* for a while. † And the man he is with is annoyed and says to him: Go ahead and lay back *(anakeiso)!*[194] Philippides (fr. 31):

> (A.) And all the time I was eating dinner,
> I was laying back *(anakeimenos)* beside him.

194 As if he were a statue—and thus dead.

καὶ ἐπάγει·

(B.) < . . . > πότερον ἀνδριάντας εἱστία;

κατακεῖσθαι δὲ λέγεται καὶ κατακεκλίσθαι, ὡς ἐν Συμποσίοις Ξενοφῶν καὶ Πλάτων. Ἄλεξις·

> ὡς ἔστι κατακεῖσθαι πρὸ δείπνου συμφορά·
d > οὔτε γὰρ ὕπνος δήπουθεν οὐδέν' ἂν λάβοι, |
> οὔθ' ἂν λέγῃ τις οὐδαμῶς μάθοιμεν ἄν·
> ὁ νοῦς γάρ ἐστι τῆς τραπέζης πλησίον.

ἔστι δὲ εὑρεῖν καὶ ἐπὶ τῆς ἐννοίας ταύτης σπανίως τὸ ἀνακεῖσθαι. σάτυρος παρὰ Σοφοκλεῖ τοῦτό φησιν ἐπικαιόμενος τῷ Ἡρακλεῖ·

> ἀνακειμένῳ
> μέσον εἰς τὸν αὐχέν' εἰσαλοίμην.

Ἀριστοτέλης ἐν Τυρρηνῶν Νομίμοις· οἱ δὲ Τυρρηνοὶ δειπνοῦσι μετὰ τῶν γυναικῶν ἀνακείμενοι ὑπὸ τῷ
e αὐτῷ ἱματίῳ. Θεόπομπος· |

> ἐπίνομεν μετὰ ταῦτα < . . . >
> κατακείμενοι μαλακώτατ' ἐπὶ τρικλινίῳ,
> Τελαμῶνος οἰμώζοντες ἀλλήλοις μέλη.

Φιλωνίδης·

> < . . . > κατάκειμαι, ὡς ὁρᾶτε, δεκαπάλαι.

---

195 The hero Telamon was the father of Salaminian Ajax. For *scholia* sung in his honor, carm. conv. *PMG* 898–9; Ar. *Lys*. 1237.

And he continues:

(B.) Was he entertaining statues?

The verbs *katakeimai* ("lie down") and *katakeklina* ("have reclined") are also used, as in the *Symposia* of Xenophon (e.g. 1.13, 15; 2.23) and Plato (e.g. 175a; 177d). Alexis (fr. 279):

What a disaster it is to lie down *(katakeisthai)* before
      dinner is served!
Because naturally you can't fall asleep then,
and neither can we understand anything someone
      else might say;
because our attention's fixed on the table.

One can occasionally find the verb *anakeimai* used in this sense. One of Sophocles' (fr. 756) satyrs is angry with Heracles and says the following:

I'd like to jump
right on his neck as he lies *(anakeimenōi)* there!

Aristotle in the *Customs of the Tyrrhenians* (fr. 472): The Tyrrhenians dine with their wives, lying down *(anakeimenoi)* under the same robe. Theopompus (fr. 65):

After that we began drinking,
lying down *(katakeimenoi)* comfortably on three
      couches,
singing laments for Telamon to one another.[195]

Philonides (fr. 8):

I've been lying down *(katakeimai)*, as you can see, for
      a very long time.

131

Εὐριπίδης Κύκλωπι·

ἀνέπεσε φάρυγος αἰθέρ' ἐξανιεὶς[77] βαρύν.

Ἄλεξις·

μετὰ ταῦτ' ἀναπεσεῖν
ἐκέλευον αὐτὴν παρ' ἐμέ.

Ὅτι τὸ πάσασθαι ἐπὶ τοῦ ἀπογεύσασθαι τίθεται.
f φησὶ γοῦν Φοῖνιξ πρὸς Ἀχιλλέα· | οὐκ ἤθελον ἅμ'
ἄλλῳ ἐν μεγάροισι πάσασθαι. καὶ ἀλλαχοῦ·

εὖθ' οἱ σπλάγχν' ἐπάσαντο.[78]

τῶν γὰρ σπλάγχνων ἀπογεύονται μόνον ὡς ἂν ὀλίγων
24 πολὺς ὅμιλος. καὶ ὁ Πρίαμος δὲ πρὸς Ἀχιλλέα φησί· ‖

νῦν δὴ καὶ σίτου πασάμην.

οἰκεῖον γὰρ τοῦ τηνικάδε ἀτυχήσαντος ἀπογεύσασθαι
μόνον· εἰς κόρον γὰρ ἐλθεῖν οὐκ εἴα τὸ πένθος. διὸ καὶ
ὁ τὸ σύνολον οὐ γευσάμενος τροφῆς

κεῖτ' < . . . > ἄσιτος, ἄπαστος.

ἐπὶ δὲ τῶν ἀποπληρουμένων οὐδέποτε λέγει τὸ πάσα-

---

[77] ἐξανεὶς Porson
[78] The standard text of Homer has σπλάγχνα πάσαντο.

---

[196] This quote and the one that follows use the verb *anapiptō*,
which makes it clear that they belong with the material assembled
at 1.23b.

132

Euripides in *Cyclops* (410):[196]

> He fell on his back *(anepese)*, belching a foul stench
>   from his maw.

Alexis (fr. 295):

>   After this, I told
> her to lie down *(anapesein)* beside me.

The verb *pateomai* ("eat, consume") is used to mean "taste." Phoenix, for example, says to Achilleus: I was unwilling to taste *(pasasthai)* food with anyone else in the house.[197] And elsewhere (*Od.* 3.9):

> when they tasted *(epasanto)* the entrails;

for they only taste the entrails, since there are not many entrails and there is a large group of people. And Priam says to Achilleus (*Il.* 24.641):

> Now I tasted *(pasamēn)* food;

because it is appropriate that when someone is in trouble, he only tastes his food, since his grief does not let him eat to the point that he is full. This is why a man who has tasted no food at all (*Od.* 4.788)[198]

> lay there fasting, eating nothing *(apastos)*.

He never uses *pateomai* to refer to people who eat as much

---

[197] A garbled recollection of *Il.* 9.486–7.
[198] Referring to Penelope grieving for Telemachus, rather than to a man, as Athenaeus suggests.

σθαι, ἀλλ᾽ ὁπόσα δηλοῖ κόρον·

αὐτὰρ ἐπεὶ σίτου τάρφθεν,

καί·

< . . . > ἐδητύος ἐξ ἔρον ἔντο.

οἱ δὲ νεώτεροι καὶ ἐπὶ τοῦ πληρωθῆναι τιθέασι τὸ
b πάσασθαι. Καλλίμαχος· |

μύθου δὲ πασαίμην
ἥδιον.

Ἐρατοσθένης·

ὀπταλέα κρέα
ἐκ τέφρης ἐπάσαντο τά τ᾽ ἀγρώσσοντες ἕλοντο.

ποτίκολλον ἄτε ξύλον παρὰ ξύλῳ,

φησὶν ὁ Θηβαῖος μελοποιός.[79]
῞Οτι Σέλευκός φησι τὴν παρ᾽ Ὁμήρῳ δαῖτα θάλει-
αν στοιχείων μεταθέσει δίαιταν εἶναι· τὸ δὲ ἀπὸ τοῦ
δαίσασθαι λέγειν βιαιότερόν ἐστι.
῞Οτι Καρύστιος ὁ Περγαμηνὸς ἱστορεῖ τὰς Κερκυ-
ραίας γυναῖκας ἔτι καὶ νῦν σφαιριζούσας ᾄδειν. σφαι-

---

[79] C prefaces what follows with the subtitle ἔτι περὶ τοῦ τῶν
ἡρώων βίου ("Further on the Life of the Heroes").

---

199 In both quotations offered in support of this assertion,
however, the normal sense "taste" would do just as well.

as they want, but prefers language that indicates satiety
(*Od.* 6.99):

and when they enjoyed their food,

and (e.g. *Il.* 1.469; *Od.* 1.150):

they put away desire for food.

But more recent authors also use *pateomai* to mean "be
full."[199] Callimachus (fr. 476):

> I'd happily have my fill *(pasaimēn)*
> of story-telling.

Eratosthenes (fr. 29, p. 65 Powell):

> They ate their fill *(epasanto)* of the meat
> they got in the hunt roasted on the coals.

> Glued together like two pieces of wood,

as the Theban lyric poet puts it (Pi. fr. 241).[200]

    Seleucus (fr. 26 Müller) claims that the Homeric
phrase *daita thaleian* ("a substantial meal") is the word
diaita ("way of life, diet") with some letters transposed,
and argues that saying that it comes from the verb *dainumi*
("give a feast") is too forced.

    Carystius of Pergamum (fr. 14, *FHG* iv.359) records
that even in his day the women of Corcyra sang as they

---

[200] The same quotation is used at 6.248c in a transition between speakers, as presumably here. The point of the argument
that follows is that the Homeric lifestyle was quite luxurious; contrast 1.9a n.; 1.11b n.

ρίζουσι δὲ παρ' Ὁμήρῳ οὐ μόνον ἄνδρες ἀλλὰ καὶ
γυναῖκες. καὶ δίσκοις δὲ καὶ ἀκοντίοις μετά τινος
c συμμετρίας ἐχρῶντο· |

δίσκοισιν τέρποντο καὶ αἰγανέῃσιν ἱέντες.

τὸ γὰρ τερπνὸν τὴν κακοπάθειαν κουφίζει. καὶ ἐπὶ
κυνηγέσια δὲ ἐξίασιν οἱ νέοι πρὸς μελέτην τῶν πολε-
μικῶν κινδύνων καὶ ἐπὶ θήρας παντοίας, ἀφ' ὧν ῥωμα-
λεώτεροι καὶ ὑγιεινότεροι διετέλουν, ὡς ὅτε

πυργηδὸν σφέας αὐτοὺς ἀρτύνουσι
καὶ ἀντίον ἱστάμενοι ἀκοντίζουσιν.

ἴσασι δὲ καὶ λουτρὰ ἄκη πόνων παντοῖα, κόπον μὲν
θαλάττῃ λύοντες, ἣ μάλιστα τοῖς νεύροις ἐστὶ πρόσ-
φορος, ἀναχαλῶντες δὲ ταῖς ἐμβάσεσι τὰς τῶν μυῶν
d συντάσεις, | εἶτ' ἐπαλείφοντες λίπα πρὸς τὸ μὴ ξηραν-
θέντος τοῦ ὕδατος ἀπεσκληρυμμένα γίνεσθαι τὰ σώματα. οἱ γοῦν ἀπὸ τῆς σκοπιῆς ἐπανελθόντες

< . . . > ἱδρῶ πολλὸν ἀπενίζοντο θαλάσσῃ
< . . . > κνήμας < . . . > ἰδὲ λόφον ἀμφί τε
μηρούς[80].

καὶ οὕτως ἀναψύξαντες

ἐς < . . . > ἀσαμίνθους βάντες ἐυξέστας
λούσαντο·

[80] μακρούς CE

136

played ball. It is not just men who play ball in Homer, but women as well (*Od.* 6.100–1). His characters also made limited use of discuses and javelins (*Od.* 4.626):

> They enjoyed themselves by throwing discuses and
>   hunting-spears.

Because pleasure makes misery more bearable. In addition, the young men go out hunting both to train themselves for the dangers of war and in pursuit of wild animals of all kinds, as a result of which they remained quite strong and healthy, as when

> they line up in close array
> and stand opposite their quarry and hurl javelins.[201]

They are also familiar with baths of all sorts as a way of curing aches and pains, since they eliminate fatigue with salt-water baths, which are particularly good for the nerves, and loosen the knots in their muscles in bathtubs, and then put on a rich coat of oil to keep their bodies from stiffening up when the water dries. The men who come back from the reconnaissance mission, for example (*Il.* 10.572–3),[202]

> washed much sweat off in the sea
> from their calves, necks, and thighs;

and after they cooled down in this way (*Il.* 10.576–8),

> they got into polished tubs and bathed;

[201] A garbled quotation of *Il.* 12.43–4. The words "as when" (*hōs hote*) in the introduction to the quotation are perhaps drawn from *Il.* 12.41 (introducing the simile).
[202] Of Diomedes and Odysseus at the end of the *Doloneia*.

< . . . > καὶ ἀλειψάμενοι[81] λίπ' ἐλαίῳ
δείπνῳ ἐφιζανέτην.

ἔστι καὶ τρόπος ἕτερος καμάτων λύσεως ἐκ τῶν κατὰ
κεφαλῆς καταιονήσεων·

e   θυμῆρες κεράσασα κατὰ κρατός τε καὶ ὤμων. |

αἱ γὰρ ἐμβάσεις περικεχυμένου πανταχόθεν τοῖς πόροις τοῦ ὕδατος φράττουσι τὴν τῶν ἱδρώτων ἔκκρισιν
καθάπερ ἂν εἴ τις ἠθμὸς εἰς ὕδωρ βληθείς· διέξεισι
γὰρ οὐθέν, εἰ μή τις αὐτὸν μετεωρίσας τοῖς πόροις
ἀναψυχὴν καὶ διέξοδον εἰς τὸ ἔξω παράσχῃ, ὡς Ἀριστοτέλης εἴρηκεν ἐν τοῖς Φυσικοῖς Προβλήμασι, ζητῶν διὰ τί οἱ ἱδροῦντες ἐπὰν ἔλθωσιν εἰς θερμὸν ἢ
ψυχρὸν ὕδωρ οὐκ ἔτι ἱδροῦσιν, ἕως <ἂν> πάλιν ἐπα-
νέλθωσιν ἀπὸ τῶν ἐμβάσεων.

f   Παρετίθετο δὲ τοῖς ἥρωσι δειπνοῦσι καὶ λάχανα. |
ὅτι δὲ οἴδασι τὰς λαχανείας δῆλον ἐκ τῶν

< . . . > παρὰ νείατον ὄρχον

κοσμητῶν πρασιῶν. ἀλλὰ μὴν καὶ <τοῖς> κακοχυμο-
τάτοις κρομύοις ἐχρῶντο·

< . . . > ἐπὶ δὲ κρόμυον ποτοῦ[82] ὄψον.

ἐπιμελουμένους δὲ αὐτοὺς εἰσάγει καὶ τῶν ἀκροδρύων·

---

[81] Athenaeus has replaced Homer's dual ἀλειψαμένω with a
plural.   [82] Most witnesses have ποτῷ, but Plutarch also preserves Athenaeus' ποτοῦ (also in the paraphrase at 1.10b).

and after anointing themselves richly with oil,
they sat down to dinner.

There is another way to eliminate fatigue, by pouring water over the head (*Od.* 10.362):

mixing it so that it was a pleasant temperature over
my head and shoulders.

For because one's pores are completely surrounded by water, tub-baths prevent sweat from being excreted, as when a strainer is immersed in water; nothing passes through it, unless someone lifts it up and gives the pores relief and a way for the liquid to get out. This is what Aristotle says in his *Physical Problems* (fr. 762), when he asks why people who are sweating and enter hot or cold water stop sweating until they get out of the tub again.

The heroes were also served vegetables at dinner. That they are familiar with gardening is apparent from the reference to neatly planted beds (*Od.* 7.127)

beside the furthest row of vines.

Indeed, they also ate onions, even though their juice is quite unhealthy (*Il.* 11.630):

and an onion as a garnish of the drink.

Homer also presents them as taking care of fruit trees:

ὄγχνη γὰρ ἐπ' ὄγχνῃ που γηράσκει[83], ‹ . . . ›

25   ‹   . . .   › σῦκον δ' ‖ ἐπὶ σύκῳ.

διὸ καὶ τῶν δένδρων τὰ μὲν καρποφόρα καλὰ προσ-
αγορεύει·[84]

ἔνθα ‹ . . . › δένδρεα καλὰ πεφύκει ‹ . . . ›,
ὄγχναι καὶ ῥοιαὶ καὶ μηλέαι.

τὰ δ' εἰς ξυλείαν εὔθετα μακρά, τοῖς ἐπιθέτοις τὰς
χρήσεις διαστέλλων·

ἔνθα[85] δένδρεα μακρὰ πεφύκει,
κλήθρη τ' αἴγειρός τ', ἐλάτη τ' ἦν οὐρανομήκης.

ἀρχαιοτέρα δ' ἦν καὶ τῶν Τρωικῶν ἡ τούτων χρῆσις.

b Τάνταλος γοῦν οὐδὲ θανὼν ἀπαλλάττεται τῆς | τούτων
ἐπιθυμίας· εἴπερ ὁ κολάζων αὐτὸν θεὸς προσείων,
καθάπερ οἱ τὰ ἄλογα τῶν ζῴων τοῖς θαλλοῖς ἄγοντες,
τοὺς τοιούτους καρποὺς ἀποκρούεται αὐτὸν τῆς ἀπο-
λαύσεως, ὅτε τῆς ἐλπίδος ἐγγὺς ἔλθοι. καὶ Λαέρτην δ'
Ὀδυσσεὺς ἀναμιμνήσκει ὧν ἔδωκεν αὐτῷ παιδὶ ὄντι·

ὄγχνας μοι δῶκας τρισκαίδεκα,

καὶ τὰ ἑξῆς.

Ὅτι δὲ καὶ ἰχθῦς ἤσθιον Σαρπηδὼν δῆλον ποιεῖ,

---

[83] γηράσκων C: γηράσκουσι E   [84] A reference to *Od.*
7.114–15; but the traditional text of 114 reads ἔνθα δὲ δένδρεα
μακρὰ πεφύκασι.   [85] The traditional text of Homer has
ὅθι for Athenaeus' unmetrical ἔνθα.

for pear somehow follows pear into maturity,
. . .   and fig follows fig.[203]

This is why he calls fruit-trees "lovely":

Lovely trees grew there,
pear, pomegranate, and apple.

He refers to trees suitable for lumber, on the other hand,
as "tall," distinguishing their uses by the adjectives he ap-
plies to them (*Od.* 5.238–9):

Tall trees grew there,
alder and poplar, and pine(s) reached up to heaven.

The use of these predated the Trojan War. Tantalus (cf.
Od. 11.582–92), for example, is not free of his desire for
them even after death, since the god punishing him dan-
gles fruit of this sort in front of him, in the same way people make irrational creatures[204] move forward by using
green branches (cf. Pl. *Phdr.* 230d); and then he keeps him
from enjoying the food when he is on the verge of realizing
his hopes. Likewise Odysseus reminds Laertes of what he
gave him when he was a boy (*Od.* 24.340):

You gave me 13 pear trees,

and so on.

Sarpedon makes it clear that they ate fish when he com-

---

[203] A condensed and slightly garbled quotation of *Od.* 7.120–1.
[204] Perhaps specifically "horses."

ὁμοιῶν τὴν ἅλωσιν πανάγρου δικτύου θήρᾳ. καίτοι

c Εὔβουλος κατὰ τὴν κωμικὴν χάριν φησὶ παίζων· |

ἰχθὺν δ' Ὅμηρος ἐσθίοντ' εἴρηκε πού
τίνα τῶν Ἀχαιῶν; κρέα δὲ μόνον ὤπτων, ἐπεὶ
ἕψοντά γ' οὐ πεπόηκεν αὐτῶν οὐδένα,
ἀλλ' οὐδὲ μικρόν. οὐδ' ἑταίραν εἶδέ τις
αὐτῶν, ἑαυτοὺς δ' ἔδεφον ἐνιαυτοὺς δέκα·
πικρὰν στρατείαν δ' εἶδον, οἵτινες πόλιν
μίαν λαβόντες εὐρυπρωκτότεροι πολὺ
τῆς πόλεος ἀπεχώρησαν ἧς εἷλον τότε.

οὐδὲ τὸν ἀέρα δ' ⟨οἱ⟩ ἥρωες τοῖς ὄρνισιν εἴων ἐλεύ-

d θερον, παγίδας καὶ νεφέλας ἐπὶ ταῖς κίχλαις καὶ |
πελειάσιν ἱστάντες. ἐγυμνάζοντο δὲ πρὸς ὀρνεοθηρευ-
τικὴν τὴν πελειάδα τῇ μηρίνθῳ κρεμάντες ἀπὸ νηὸς
ἱστοῦ καὶ τοξεύοντες ἑκηβόλως εἰς αὐτήν, ὡς ἐν τῷ
Ἐπιταφίῳ δηλοῦται. παρέλιπε δὲ τὴν χρῆσιν τῶν
λαχάνων καὶ ἰχθύων καὶ ὀρνίθων[86] διά τε τὴν λιχνείαν
καὶ προσέτι τὴν ἐν ταῖς σκευασίαις ἀπρέπειαν, ἐλάττω κεκρικὼς ἡρωικῶν καὶ θείων ἔργων. ὅτι δὲ καὶ
ἑφθοῖς ἐχρῶντο κρέασιν ἐμφανίζει ἐν οἷς λέγει·[87]

ὡς δὲ λέβης ζεῖ ⟨ . . . ⟩

e κνίσσῃ μελδόμενος ἀπαλοτρεφέος σιάλοιο. |

---

[86] καὶ τῶν ὀρνίθων CE   [87] Accusative κνίσην should
probably be printed in 363; but Athenaeus' dative is attested in
other witnesses. Athenaeus has also replaced Homer's uncon-
tracted ζέει with the contracted form ζεῖ.

pares being captured to being caught in a fishing net (*Il.* 5.487–8). Eubulus (fr. 118), with typical comic wit, nonetheless jokingly says:

> Where does Homer refer to any Achaean as
> eating fish? And all they did with their meat was roast
>   it;
> he never has any of them stew something,
> not even a little. And none of them laid eyes on a
> courtesan; they had to jerk off for ten years.
> That was a miserable expedition for them; they only
>   captured
> one city, and they left with their assholes enlarged
>   more
> than the gates of the town they captured![205]

Nor did the heroes leave the air free for the birds, since they set out traps and nets for thrushes and doves. And they trained to hunt birds by tying a dove to a ship's mast with a string and shooting at it from a distance, as is clear from the *Funeral Games* (*Il.* 23.852–6). But Homer ignored the fact that they ate vegetables, fish, and birds, because he was concerned about gluttony, and because preparing such foods is an ugly business, which he considered beneath the level of heroic, godlike deeds. But he makes it clear that they also ate stewed meat in the passage where he says (*Il.* 21.362–3):

> as a cauldron boils . . .
> melting down the lard of a fatted hog.

[205] Because (despite line 5) they had buggered one another so long and hard.

καὶ ὁ κατ' Ὀδυσσέως ἀφεθεὶς ποῦς βοὸς τούτου ση-
μεῖον· πόδα γὰρ βόειον οὐδεὶς ὀπτᾷ. καὶ τὸ

     κρειῶν δὲ[88] πίνακας παρέθηκεν ἀείρας
παντοίων

οὐ μόνον τὴν τῶν κρεῶν ἐξαλλαγὴν δηλοῖ, ὡς ὀρνίθεια, χοίρεια, ἐρίφεια, βόεια λέγων, ἀλλὰ τὴν σκευα-
σίαν ὡς ποικίλην ἔχοντα καὶ οὐ μονοειδῆ ἀλλὰ περιτ-
τήν.

Ὡς ἀνακύπτειν τὰς Σικελικὰς καὶ Συβαριτικὰς καὶ
Ἰταλικὰς[89] τραπέζας, ἤδη δὲ καὶ Χίας. μαρτυροῦνται
f γὰρ καὶ Χῖοι οὐκ ἔλαττον τῶν προειρημένων | ἐπὶ
ὀψαρτυτικῇ. Τιμοκλῆς·

     Χῖοι πολὺ
ἄριστ' ἀνευρήκασιν ὀψαρτυσίαν.

Κοιμῶνται δὲ μετὰ γυναικῶν παρ' Ὁμήρῳ οὐ μόνον οἱ νέοι, ἀλλὰ καὶ οἱ γέροντες Φοῖνιξ τε καὶ
Νέστωρ. μόνῳ Μενελάῳ οὐ συνέζευκται γυνὴ διὰ
γυναῖκα γαμετὴν ἡρπασμένην τὴν στρατείαν πεποιη-
μένῳ.

     παλαιὸν μὲν οἶνον, ἄνθεα δ' ὕμνων
νεωτέρων

---

[88] Homer has δὲ κρειῶν.   [89] καὶ Ἰταλικὰς del. Kaibel

---

[206] Contrast 1.9a with n.   [207] The subject of the discussion changes abruptly here, and this quotation is probably part of

144

The cow's-foot thrown at Odysseus (*Od.* 20.299–300) is also evidence of this; because no one roasts a cow's-foot. So too the passage (e.g. *Od.* 1.141–2)

> he picked up platters of meat and set them by
> their side,
> and the meat was of every sort

not only reveals that they ate different types of meat, as if he said "poultry, pork, goat, and beef," but also that it was prepared in various ways, which were not all alike but diverse.[206]

The Sicilian, Sybarite, and Italian culinary styles emerged in this way, as did the Chian style around the same time; for there is evidence that the Chians were as interested in fine dining as the peoples just mentioned. Timocles (fr. 39):

> Chians
> have made the finest innovations in cooking.

It is not just the young men who sleep with women in Homer, but also the old men like Phoenix and Nestor. Only Menelaus is not paired with a woman, since he organized the expedition when the woman to whom he was married was carried off.

Pindar (*O.* 9.48–9) praises[207]

> old wine, but the flowers of hymns
> that are newer.

the introductory remarks of a new speaker (perhaps Galen, although 1.26c more likely represents his entry into the conversation, as he takes up the topic of specifically Italian wines).

Πίνδαρος ἐπαινεῖ. Εὔβουλος δέ φησιν·

ἄτοπόν γε τὸν μὲν οἶνον εὐδοκιμεῖν ἀεὶ
παρὰ ταῖς ἑταίραις τὸν παλαιόν, ἄνδρα δὲ
μὴ τὸν παλαιόν, ἀλλὰ τὸν νεώτερον.

26 τὸ αὐτὸ ‖ δὲ καὶ Ἄλεξις σχεδὸν ἀπαραλλάκτως, τοῦ
σφόδρα μόνου κειμένου ἀντὶ τοῦ ἀεί. ὄντως δὲ ὁ
παλαιὸς οἶνος οὐ πρὸς ἡδονὴν μόνον, ἀλλὰ καὶ πρὸς
ὑγίειαν προσφορώτερος. πέσσει τε γὰρ μᾶλλον τὰ
σῖτα καὶ λεπτομερὴς ὢν εὐανάδοτός ἐστι δύναμίν τε
τοῖς σώμασιν ἐμποιεῖ τὸ αἷμά τε ἐνερευθὲς καὶ εὐανάδοτον κατασκευάζει καὶ τοὺς ὕπνους ἀταράχους
παρέχει. ἐπαινεῖ δὲ Ὅμηρος τὸν ἐπιδεχόμενον ἱκανὴν
κρᾶσιν, ὡς τὸν τοῦ Μάρωνος. ἐπιδέχεται δὲ πλείω
b κρᾶσιν ὁ παλαιὸς οἶνος διὰ τὸ | μᾶλλον θερμὸς
γίνεσθαι παλαιούμενος. ἔνιοι δὲ καὶ τὴν Διονύσου
φυγὴν εἰς τὴν θάλασσαν οἰνοποιίαν σημαίνειν φασὶ
πάλαι γνωριζομένην· ἡδὺν γὰρ εἶναι τὸν οἶνον παρ-
εγχεομένης θαλάσσης. ἐπαινῶν δὲ Ὅμηρος τὸν μέλανα οἶνον πολλάκις αὐτὸν καὶ αἴθοπα καλεῖ· δυναμικώ-
τατος γάρ ἐστι καὶ μένων ἐν ταῖς ἕξεσι τῶν πινόντων
πλεῖστον χρόνον. Θεόπομπος δέ φησι παρὰ Χίοις
πρώτοις γενέσθαι τὸν μέλανα οἶνον, καὶ τὸ φυτεύειν
δὲ καὶ θεραπεύειν ἀμπέλους Χίους πρώτους μαθόντας
c παρ᾽ | Οἰνοπίωνος τοῦ Διονύσου, ὃς καὶ συνῴκισε τὴν

---

208 For Maron, who gave Odysseus the extraordinarily strong

146

And Eubulus (fr. 122) says:

> It's strange that courtesans always have
> a high opinion of old wine; but when it comes to a
>   man,
> it's not an old one they want but someone younger.

Alexis (fr. 284) has almost precisely the same words, except that he says "have a very high opinion" rather than "always have a high opinion." In fact, old wine not only tastes better but is better for one's health. Because it is more effective at promoting the digestion of one's food; since it has broken down more completely, it is more easily absorbed; it supplies the body with energy; it renders the blood redder and makes it more absorptive; and it produces undisturbed sleep. Homer (*Od.* 9.209–11) praises wine like Maron's that can stand up to a substantial admixture of water.[208] Old wine can stand up to more water, because it grows increasingly "hot" as it ages. Some authorities assert that Dionysus' flight into the sea (*Il.* 6.135–6)[209] is an indication that men have known how to make wine for a long time; for wine tastes good when salt-water is poured into it. When Homer praises dark wine, he often refers to it as "fiery red" (e.g. *Il.* 1.462), because it is very potent and and remains in one's system for a long time when one drinks it. Theopompus (*FGrH* 115 F 276) says that dark wine was first produced by the Chians, and that they were the first to learn to grow and care for grapes, from Dionysus' son Oenopion, who also transformed the island into a

wine he offered to the Cyclops, cf. Clearch. Com. fr. *5, quoted at 1.28e, 33d.   [209] Dionysus was fleeing the mad King Lycurgus and found refuge with Thetis.

νῆσον, τοῖς ἄλλοις ἀνθρώποις μεταδοῦναι. ὁ δὲ λευκὸς
οἶνος ἀσθενὴς καὶ λεπτός. ὁ δὲ κιρρὸς πέττει ῥᾷον
ξηραντικὸς ὤν.

Περὶ Ἰταλικῶν οἴνων φησὶν ὁ παρὰ τούτῳ τῷ
σοφιστῇ Γαληνός· ὁ Φαλερῖνος οἶνος ἀπὸ ἐτῶν δέκα
ἐστὶ πότιμος καὶ ἀπὸ πεντεκαίδεκα μέχρι εἴκοσιν· ὁ δ'
ὑπὲρ τοῦτον ἐκπίπτων τὸν χρόνον κεφαλαλγὴς καὶ τοῦ
νευρώδους καθάπτεται. εἴδη δ' αὐτοῦ δύο, ὁ αὐστηρὸς
d καὶ ὁ γλυκάζων· οὗτος δὲ τοιοῦτος γίνεται ὅταν | ὑπὸ
τὸν τρυγητὸν νότοι πνεύσωσι, παρ' ὃ καὶ μελάντερος
γίνεται. ὁ δὲ μὴ οὕτω τρυγηθεὶς αὐστηρός τε καὶ τῷ
χρώματι κιρρός. καὶ τοῦ Ἀλβανοῦ δὲ οἴνου εἴδη δύο,
ὁ μὲν γλυκάζων, ὁ δ' ὀμφακίας· ἀμφότεροι δὲ ἀπὸ
πεντεκαίδεκα ἐτῶν ἀκμάζουσι. Συρεντῖνος δὲ ἀπὸ
πέντε καὶ εἴκοσιν ἐτῶν ἄρχεται γίνεσθαι πότιμος· ὢν
γὰρ ἀλιπὴς καὶ λίαν ψαφαρὸς μόλις πεπαίνεται· καὶ
παλαιούμενος σχεδὸν μόνοις ἐστὶν ἐπιτήδειος τοῖς
χρωμένοις διηνεκῶς. ὁ δὲ Ῥηγῖνος τοῦ Συρεντίνου
e λιπαρώτερος | ὢν χρήσιμος ἀπὸ ἐτῶν πεντεκαίδεκα.
χρήσιμος καὶ ὁ Πριουέρνος λεπτομερέστερος ὢν τοῦ
Ῥηγίνου ἥκιστά τε καθαπτόμενος κεφαλῆς. τούτῳ
ἐμφερὴς ὁ Φορμιανός, ταχὺ δὲ ἀκμάζει καὶ λιπαρώ-
τερός ἐστιν αὐτοῦ. βράδιον δ' ἀκμάζει ὁ Τριφολῖνος,
ἐστὶ δὲ τοῦ Συρεντίνου γεωδέστερος. ὁ δὲ Στατανὸς
τῶν πρώτων ἐστὶν οἴνων, ἐμφερὴς τῷ Φαλερίνῳ, κουφότερος ⟨δὲ⟩, οὐ πληκτικός. ὁ Τιβουρτῖνος λεπτός,
εὐδιάπνευστος, ἀκμάζων ἀπὸ ἐτῶν δέκα· κρείττων δὲ
f γίνεται παλαιούμενος. | ὁ Λαβικανὸς ἡδὺς καὶ λιπα-

single state; and that they passed the knowledge on to others. White wine, on the other hand, is weak and thin-bodied, whereas yellow wine is better for the digestion, since it is drying.

Regarding Italian wines, the Galen who was in this sophist's house says: Falernian wine can be drunk after ten years and especially after 15 to 20; once it is older than that, it causes headaches and attacks the nervous system. There are two varieties of it, one dry, the other sweet. It takes on the latter character whenever southerly winds blow during the grape-harvest; this also makes the wine darker. When not subjected to such harvest conditions, it is dry and yellow-colored. There are also two varieties of Alban wine, one sweet and the other acidic; both are mature after 15 years. Sorrentine begins to be drinkable after 25 years; because it is thin and quite watery, it matures slowly, and even after it ages it appeals almost exclusively to those who drink it regularly. Wine from Rhegium has more body than Sorrentine and can be drunk after 15 years. Privernian is also drinkable, and breaks down more thoroughly than Rhegian does and is quite unlikely to go to one's head. Formian resembles Privernian, but matures quickly and is richer than Privernian. Trifolian matures more slowly and has an earthier character than Sorrentine. Statan is one of the best wines; it resembles Falernian but is lighter and not particularly powerful. Tiburtine is light and quick to evaporate, and is mature after ten years; it improves as it ages. Labian is sweet and rich-tasting,

ρὸς τῇ γεύσει, μεταξὺ Φαλερίνου καὶ Ἀλβανοῦ· ὁ δὲ
ἄρχεται τῆς πόσεως ἀπὸ ἐτῶν δέκα. ὁ Γαυρανὸς δὲ καὶ
ὀλίγος καὶ κάλλιστος, προσέτι τε εὔτονος καὶ παχύς,
Πραινεστίνου δὲ ⟨καὶ⟩ Τιβουρτίνου λιπαρώτερος. ὁ
Μαρσικὸς δὲ πάνυ αὐστηρός, εὐστόμαχος δέ. γίνεται
δὲ περὶ τὴν Καμπανίας Κύμην ὁ καλούμενος Οὐλ-
βανός, κοῦφος, πότιμος ἀπὸ ἐτῶν πέντε. ὁ Ἀγκωνιτα-
27 νὸς[90] χρηστός, λιπαρός, πό[τιμος ‖ ἀπὸ ἐτῶν . . .][91]. ὁ
Βυξεντῖνος ἐμφερῶς[92] ἔχει τῷ Ἀλβανῷ τῷ ὀμφακίᾳ·
ἔστι δὲ δυνάμει ⟨ . . . ⟩ καὶ εὐστόμαχος. ὁ Οὐελίτερνος
δὲ ἡδὺς πινόμενος, εὐστόμαχος· ἴδιον δ' αὐτοῦ τὸ μὴ
δοκεῖν ἀπαρέγχυτος εἶναι· ἐμφαίνει γὰρ ὡς ἐμμεμι-
γμένου αὐτῷ ἑτέρου. ὁ Καληνὸς κοῦφος, τοῦ Φαλερίνου εὐστομαχώτερος. εὐγενὴς δὲ καὶ ὁ Καίκουβος,
πληκτικός, εὔτονος· παλαιοῦται δὲ μετὰ ἱκανὰ ἔτη. ὁ
Φουνδανὸς εὔτονος, πολύτροφος, κεφαλῆς καὶ στομάχου ἅπτεται· διὸ οὐ πολὺς ἐν συμποσίοις πίνεται.
b πάντων | δὲ τούτων ὁ Σαβῖνος κουφότερος, ἀπὸ ἐτῶν
ἑπτὰ ἐπιτήδειος πίνεσθαι μέχρι πεντεκαίδεκα. ὁ δὲ
Σιγνῖνος ⟨ἀπὸ ἐτῶν . . . ⟩ μέχρις ἐτῶν ἑξ χρήσιμος,
παλαιωθεὶς δὲ πολὺ χρησιμώτερος. ὁ Νουμεντανὸς
ἀκμάζει ταχὺ καὶ ἀπὸ ἐτῶν πέντε πότιμός ἐστιν· ἐστὶ
δ' οὔτε λίαν ἡδὺς οὔτε λεπτός. ὁ Σπωλητῖνος οἶνος
⟨ . . . ⟩ καὶ πινόμενος ἡδὺς καὶ τῷ χρώματι χρυσίζει.
Αἰκουανὸς κατὰ πολλὰ τῷ Συρεντίνῳ παρεμφερής. ὁ
Βαρῖνος λίαν αὐστηρὸς καὶ ἀεὶ ἑαυτοῦ κρείττων γίνε-
c ται. εὐγενὴς καὶ ὁ Καυκῖνος | καὶ τῷ Φαλερίνῳ ἐμ-
φερής. ὁ Βενεφρανὸς εὐστόμαχος καὶ κοῦφος. ὁ ἐν

somewhere between Falernian and Alban; it becomes drinkable after ten years. Gauran is rare and excellent, and is in addition full-bodied and substantial, and richer than Praenestian and Tiburtine. Marsic is very dry but easy on the stomach. The so-called Ulban is produced around Cumae in Campania; it is light and can be drunk after five years. Anconitan is fine, rich, and dr[inkable after . . . years]. Buxentine resembles acidic Alban, but in its strength it is . . . and easy on the stomach. Velitern has a sweet taste and is easy on the stomach, but has the peculiar quality of seeming to be diluted; for it gives the impression that some other wine has been mixed in with it. Calenian is light and easier on the stomach than Falernian. Caecuban is also an excellent wine, powerful and with a good body; but it requires quite a number of years to age. Fundan is full-bodied and nourishing, and affects the head and stomach; it is therefore not much drunk in symposia. Sabine is lighter than all of these and is good for drinking after seven to 15 years. Signine can be drunk after . . . to six years, but is much better after it ages. Nomentan matures quickly and can be drunk after five years; it is neither too sweet nor too light. Spoletine wine . . . and has a sweet taste and a golden color. Aequan is like Sorrentine in many respects. Barine is quite dry and continually improves. Caucine is also excellent; it resembles Falernian. Venefran is easy on

---

90 ὁ Ἀγκωνιτανὸς Casaubon: ὁ   νιτάνος C. E omits much of this section, and the text in C contains numerous minor gaps; there can thus be little doubt that a page in their common exemplar was damaged.   91 πό[τιμος ἀπὸ ἐτῶν . . .] Dindorf

92 ἐμφερῶς Schweighäuser: φερες C

Νεαπόλει Τρεβιλλικὸς εὔκρατος τῇ δυνάμει εὐστόμαχος, εὔστομος. ὁ Ἔρβουλος ἐν ἀρχῇ μέν ἐστι
μέλας, μετ᾽ οὐ πολλὰ δὲ ἔτη λευκὸς γίνεται· ἐστὶ δὲ
λίαν κοῦφος καὶ τρυφερός. ὁ Μασσαλιήτης καλός·
ὀλίγος δὲ γίνεται, παχύς, σαρκώδης. Ταραντῖνος δὲ
καὶ οἱ ἀπὸ τοῦ κλίματος τούτου πάντες ἁπαλοί, οὐ
πλῆξιν, οὐ τόνον ἔχοντες, ἡδεῖς, εὐστόμαχοι. ὁ δὲ
d Μαμερτῖνος ἔξω μὲν τῆς Ἰταλίας | γίνεται καὶ γινό-
μενος ἐν Σικελίᾳ καλεῖται Ἰωτάλινος. ἡδὺς δ᾽ ἐστί,
κοῦφος, εὔτονος.

Ὅτι παρ᾽ Ἰνδοῖς τιμᾶται δαίμων, ὥς φησι Χάρης ὁ
Μιτυληναῖος, ὃς καλεῖται Σοροάδειος· ἑρμηνεύεται δὲ
Ἑλλάδι φωνῇ οἰνοποιός.

Ὅτι Ἀντιφάνης που ὁ χαρίεις τὰ ἐξ ἑκάστης πόλεως ἰδιώματα οὕτω καταλέγει·

ἐξ Ἥλιδος μάγειρος, ἐξ Ἄργους λέβης,
Φλιάσιος οἶνος, ἐκ Κορίνθου στρώματα,
e ἰχθῦς Σικυῶνος, Αἰγίου δ᾽ αὐλητρίδες, |
τυρὸς Σικελικός ⟨ . . . ⟩,
μύρον ἐξ Ἀθηνῶν, ἐγχέλεις Βοιώτιαι.

Ἕρμιππος δ᾽ οὕτως·

ἔσπετε νῦν μοι, Μοῦσαι Ὀλύμπια δώματ᾽
ἔχουσαι,
ἐξ οὗ ναυκληρεῖ Διόνυσος ἐπ᾽ οἴνοπα πόντον,

210 Sura appears to be a Sanskrit term for an alcoholic drink of
some sort, but the Sanskrit lexicon has no deity whose name con-

the stomach and light. Neapolitan Trebellic is moderately powerful, easy on the stomach, and pleasant in the mouth. Erbulan is initially dark, but becomes white after a few years; it is very light and delicate. Massilian is good; not much of it is produced, and it is syrupy and full-bodied. Tarentine and all the wines from that region are soft, have little power or body, and are sweet and easy on the stomach. Mamertine is produced outside of Italy, and when produced in Sicily is referred to as Iotaline. It is sweet, light, and full-bodied.

According to Chares of Mytilene (*FGrH* 125 F 17), the Indians worship a divinity called Soroadeios, which when translated into Greek is "Winemaker."[210]

The witty Antiphanes (fr. 233) somewhere offers the following list of every city's specialty:

> A cook from Elis, a cauldron from Argos,
> Phliasian wine, bed-clothes from Corinth,
> Sicyonian fish, pipe-girls from Aegion,
> Sicilian cheese,
> Athenian perfume, Boeotian eels.

Hermippus (fr. 63) puts it thus:[211]

> Tell me now, Muses whose home is on Olympus,
> during the time that Dionysus is a captain on the
>   wine-dark sea

tains this element. Since Chares wrote in the late 4th century BCE, he may be reporting a Middle Indo-Aryan (Prakrit) name of a local deity in either the Punjab (ancient Gandhara) or Sindh (as far as Alexander ventured).

[211] The passage is in epic meter and much of the language is modelled on (or borrowed directly from) Homer.

ὅσσ' ἀγάθ' ἀνθρώποις δεῦρ' ἤγαγε νηὶ μελαίνῃ.
ἐκ μὲν Κυρήνης καυλὸν καὶ δέρμα βόειον,
ἐκ δ' Ἑλλησπόντου σκόμβρους καὶ πάντα
    ταρίχη,
ἐκ δ' αὖ Θετταλίας χόνδρον καὶ πλευρὰ βόεια·
καὶ παρὰ Σιτάλκου ψώραν Λακεδαιμονίοισι,
καὶ παρὰ Περδίκκου ψεύδη ναυσὶν πάνυ
    πολλαῖς. |

αἱ δὲ Συράκουσαι σῦς καὶ τυρὸν παρέχουσαι

        *   *   *

καὶ Κερκυραίους ὁ Ποσειδῶν ἐξολέσειε
ναυσὶν ἐπὶ γλαφυραῖς, ὅτιὴ δίχα θυμὸν ἔχουσι.
ταῦτα μὲν ἐντεῦθεν· ἐκ δ' Αἰγύπτου τὰ κρεμαστὰ
ἱστία καὶ βίβλους, ἀπὸ δ' αὖ Συρίας λιβανωτόν.
ἡ δὲ καλὴ Κρήτη κυπάριττον τοῖσι θεοῖσιν,
ἡ Λιβύη δ' ἐλέφαντα πολὺν παρέχει κατὰ
    πρᾶσιν,
ἡ Ῥόδος ἀσταφίδας ⟨τε⟩ καὶ ἰσχάδας
    ἡδυονείρους.
αὐτὰρ ἀπ' Εὐβοίας ἀπίους καὶ ἴφια μῆλα,
ἀνδράποδ' ἐκ Φρυγίας, ἀπὸ δ' Ἀρκαδίας
    ἐπικούρους.

---

212 A Thracian king (died winter 424/3 BCE) and sometime ally of the Athenians. Mange is a skin disease caused by fleas, and produces intense itching.

213 Perdiccas II, King of Macedon c.454–413 BCE, who made and abruptly renounced numerous alliances with Athens during the Peloponnesian War years.

about all the good things he brings here for men with
    his black ship.
From Cyrene there is silphium stalk and cowhides;
from the Hellespont mackerel and every kind of salt-
    fish;
from Thessaly barley-meal and sides of beef.
And from Sitalces[212] there is mange for the Spartans,
and from Perdiccas[213] a huge number of ships full of
    lies.
Syracuse supplying us with hogs and cheese . . .

        *   *   *

And as for the Corcyreans—may Poseidon destroy
    them
in their hollow ships, for their heart is divided![214]
That's where all these items are from. From Egypt
    comes hanging gear,
that is sails and papyrus ropes;[215] and from Syria
    comes frankincense.
Beautiful Crete furnishes cypress wood for the
    gods,[216]
while Libya has vast amounts of ivory for sale,
and Rhodes offers raisins and dried figs that bring
    sweet dreams.
He brings pears and goodly apples[217] from Euboea,
slaves from Phrygia, and mercenaries from Arcadia.

---

214 Corcyra was torn by a civil war between pro- and anti-
Athenian factions that came to a climax in 427 BCE.

215 Distinguished from "wooden gear" (oars, masts, and the
like).   216 For use in roof-beams and doors in temples; cf. *IG*
I³ 461.35 (the Parthenon); Thphr. *HP* 5.4.2.   217 A play on
a Homeric phrase in which *iphia mēla* means "goodly sheep."

28   αἱ Παγασαὶ δούλους καὶ στιγματίας παρέχουσι. ‖
τὰς δὲ Διὸς βαλάνους καὶ ἀμύγδαλα σιγαλόεντα
Παφλαγόνες παρέχουσι· τὰ γάρ ‹τ᾽› ἀναθήματα
   δαιτός.
† Φοινίκη δ᾽ αὖ † καρπὸν φοίνικος καὶ
   σεμίδαλιν,
Καρχηδὼν δάπιδας καὶ ποικίλα προσκεφάλαια.

Πίνδαρος δ᾽ ἐν τῇ εἰς Ἱέρωνα Πυθικῇ ᾠδῇ·

   ἀπὸ Ταϋγέτοιο μὲν Λάκαιναν
   ἐπὶ θηρσὶ κύνα τρέχειν
   πυκινώτατον ἑρπετόν·
   Σκύριαι δ᾽ ἐς ἄμελξιν γλάγεος αἶγες ἐξοχώταται·
   ὅπλα δ᾽ ἀπ᾽ Ἄργεος, ἅρμα Θη-
b   βαῖον ‹ . . . › ἀπὸ τῆς ἀγλαοκάρπου ǀ
   Σικελίας ὄχημα δαιδάλεον ματεύειν.

Κριτίας δὲ οὕτως·

   κότταβος ἐκ Σικελῆς ‹ἐστι› χθονός, ἐκπρεπὲς
     ἔργον,
   ὃν σκοπὸν ἐς λατάγων τόξα καθιστάμεθα.
   εἶτα δ᾽ ὄχος Σικελὸς κάλλει δαπάνῃ τε κράτιστος

         *   *   *

   Θεσσαλικὸς δὲ θρόνος γυίων τρυφερωτάτη ἕδρα.
   εὐναίου δὲ λέχους † κάλλος ἔχει
   Μίλητός τε Χίος τ᾽ ἔναλος πόλις Οἰνοπίωνος.

---

[218] Cf. 2.53b–d.

Pagasae supplies us with servants and men with
　　tattoos,
and hazelnuts[218] and shining almonds
are provided by the Paphlagonians; for these are the
　　accessories of a feast.
† Phoenicia again † offers dates and wheat,
Carthage blankets and embroidered pillows.

Pindar in his Pythian ode for Hieron (fr. 106):

From Taygetos a Spartan
hound for hunting, the cleverest
four-legged creature at running.
But for giving milk, Scyrian goats are pre-eminent,
as are Argive weapons and Theban
　　chariots. From Sicily
of glorious crops look for the elaborately built mule-
　　cart.

Critias (fr. B 2 West[2]) puts it thus:

The cottabus-stand is from the land of Sicily, a pre-
　　eminent manufacture;
we set it up as a target to shoot our wine-lees at.[219]
And after that a Sicilian chariot, most expensive and
　　beautiful.

　　　　　*　　*　　*

A Thessalian chair is the most luxurious seat for one's
　　limbs.
The † beauty of a bed to sleep in belongs to
Miletus and Chios, Oenopion's city in the sea.[220]

---

[219] For *cottabus* (a symposium game), see 15.665d–8f.
[220] See 1.26b–c.

Τυρσηνὴ δὲ κρατεῖ χρυσότυπος φιάλη,
c   καὶ πᾶς χαλκὸς ὅτις κοσμεῖ δόμον ἔν τινι χρείᾳ. |
Φοίνικες δ' ηὗρον γράμματ' ἀλεξίλογα.
Θήβη δ' ἁρματόεντα δίφρον συνεπήξατο πρώτη·
φορτηγοὺς δ' ἀκάτους Κᾶρες ἁλὸς ταμίαι.
τὸν δὲ τροχὸν γαίας τε καμίνου τ' ἔκγονον ηὗρεν
κλεινότατον κέραμον, χρήσιμον οἰκονόμον,
ἡ τὸ καλὸν Μαραθῶνι καταστήσασα τρόπαιον.

καὶ ἐπαινεῖται ὄντως ὁ Ἀττικὸς κέραμος. Εὔβουλος δέ
φησι· † Κνίδια κεράμια, Σικελικὰ βατάνια, Μεγαρικὰ
d | πιθάκνια †. Ἀντιφάνης δέ·

    ⟨καὶ⟩ νᾶπυ Κύπριον καὶ σκαμωνίας ὀπὸν
    ⟨καὶ⟩ κάρδαμον Μιλήσιον ⟨καὶ⟩ κρόμμυον
    Σαμοθράκιον ⟨καὶ⟩ καυλὸν ἐκ Καρχηδόνος
    καὶ σίλφιον, θύμον ⟨τε τῶν⟩ Ὑμηττίων
    ὀρίγανον ⟨τε⟩ Τενέδιον.

Ὅτι ὁ Περσῶν βασιλεὺς τὸν Χαλυβώνιον μόνον
οἶνον ἔπινεν· ὃν φησι Ποσειδώνιος κἂν Δαμασκῷ τῆς
Συρίας γίνεσθαι, Περσῶν αὐτόθι καταφυτευσάντων
τὰς ἀμπέλους. ἐν δὲ Ἴσσῃ τῇ κατὰ τὸν Ἀδρίαν νήσῳ
Ἀγαθαρχίδης φησὶν οἶνον γίνεσθαι ὃν πᾶσι συγκρι-
e νόμενον | καλλίω εὑρίσκεσθαι. Χίου δὲ οἴνου καὶ
Θασίου μέμνηται Ἐπίλυκος·

---

221 Athens (hence the comment that follows).
222 Pollux 6.67 assigns these verses not to Antiphanes but to
Eubulus' *Glaucus* (= Eub. fr. 18).

Etruscan libation-bowls of hammered gold are
    pre-eminent,
as is all their bronzework that ornaments a house for
    any purpose.
    The Phoenicians discovered the letters that
    preserve our words.
Thebes was the first to bolt together a chariot seat;
    and the Carians, stewards of the sea, built the first
    cargo-ships.
But the potter's wheel and the child of earth and kiln,
    glorious pottery, a useful resident of one's house,
were invented by the city that erected the beautiful
    victory monument at Marathon.[221]

Attic pottery is in fact praised. Eubulus (fr. 130; unmetrical) says: † Cnidian jars, Sicilian cookpans, Megarian casks †. Antiphanes:[222]

and Cyprian mustard and scamony juice
and Milesian cress and Samothracian
onion and silphium stalk and silphium root
from Carthage and Hymettan thyme
and oregano from Tenedus.

The Persian King drank only Chalybonian wine; Posidonius (*FGrH* 87 F 68 = fr. 242 Edelstein–Kidd) claims that it was also produced in Damascus in Syria, because the Persians planted the vines there. Agatharchides (*FGrH* 86 F 18) says that on Issa, which is an island in the Adriatic, wine is produced that everyone judges the best when it is compared with any other kind. Epilycus (fr. 7) mentions Chian and Thasian wines:

< . . . > Χῖος καὶ Θάσιος ἠθημένος.

καὶ[93] Ἀντίδοτος δέ·

       Θάσιον ἔγχει < . . . >
† ὃ γὰρ λαβών μου καταφάγει τὴν καρδίαν,
ὅταν πίω τοῦδ', εὐθὺς ὑγιὴς γίνεται.
Ἀσκληπιὸς κατέβρεξε.

       οἶνος Λέσβιος
ὃν αὐτὸς † ἐποίησεν ὁ Μάρων μοι δοκῶ,

φησὶ Κλέαρχος.

       Λεσβίου <δὲ> πώματος
οὐκ ἔστιν ἄλλος οἶνος ἡδίων πιεῖν,

φησὶν Ἄλεξις.[94]

       Θασίοις οἰναρίοις καὶ Λεσβίοις
τῆς ἡμέρας τὸ λοιπὸν ὑποβρέχει μέρος
καὶ νωγαλίζει.

ὁ αὐτός·

       ἡδύς <γ'> ὁ Βρόμιος. χρῆν ἀτέλειαν Λεσβίοις
f   ποιεῖν τὸν οἶνον εἰσάγουσιν ἐνθάδε· |
       ὃς ἂν εἰς ἑτέραν ληφθῇ δ' ἀποστέλλων πόλιν

---

[93] The quotation that follows is omitted by E and preserved only in the margin in C.   [94] C adds; in the margin: ὅτι ὁ Λέσβιος ἡδίων τῶν ἄλλων πάντων φησὶν Ἄλεξις ("Alexis says that Lesbian (wine) is more pleasant than all the others").

Chian and strained Thasian.

Also Antidotus (fr. 4):

> Pour me some Thasian!
> † After getting which he gnaws at my heart;
> but whenever I drink some of this, immediately it's
>   healed.
> Asclepius watered it.

> Lesbian wine
> that Maron[223] himself † made, I suspect,

says Clearchus (fr. *5).

> There's no other wine that's
> more pleasant to drink than the Lesbian draught,

says Alexis (fr. 276).[224]

> He keeps the rest of the day
> moist with Thasian and Lesbian wines,
> and eats snacks. (Alex. fr. 277)

The same author (Alex. fr. 278):

> Bromius is kind! We ought to exempt the Lesbians
> from taxes when they import their wine here.
> But if anyone is caught exporting even a ladleful

---

[223] See 1.26b n.

[224] The fragment that follows is quoted again at 2.47d, where it is assigned to Alexis; most likely a few linking words such as *kai palin* ("and again") have dropped out of the text.

κἂν κύαθον, ἱερὰν ἐγγράφω τὴν οὐσίαν.

Ἔφιππος·

    φιλῶ γε πράμνιον οἶνον Λέσβιον

            *   *   *

πολλὴ δὲ Λεσβία σταγὼν ἐκπίνεται
ἄγαν.

Ἀντιφάνης·

    ἔστιν ὄψον χρηστόν, ἐπαγωγὸν πάνυ,
    οἶνός τε Θάσιος καὶ μύρον καὶ στέμματα.
    ἐν πλησμονῇ γὰρ Κύπρις, ἐν δὲ τοῖς κακῶς
    πράσσουσιν οὐκ ἔνεστιν Ἀφροδίτη βροτοῖς.

Εὔβουλος·

          Θάσιον ἢ Χῖον λαβὼν
    ἢ Λέσβιον γέροντα νεκταροσταγῆ.

μέμνηται δὲ οὗτος καὶ ψιθίου οἴνου·

    οἶνον γάρ με ψίθιον γεύσας
    ἡδὺν ἄκρατον, διψῶντα λαβὼν
    ὄξει παίει πρὸς τὰ στήθη.

καὶ Ἀναξανδρίδης·

---

225 For Pramnian wine (also mentioned in a fragment of
Aristophanes quoted at 1.29a; the significance of the adjective is
obscure), see 1.30b–e.

to another city, I put his property on the confiscation
   list.

Ephippus (fr. 28):

I love Pramnian wine[225] from Lesbos.

  *   *   *

Many drops of Lesbian are quickly
swallowed down.

Antiphanes (fr. 238):

   Some fine food is there, very enticing,
and Thasian wine, perfume, and garlands.
Because Cypris[226] is found where there's abundance,
   but Aphrodite
keeps no company with mortals who are poor.

Eubulus (fr. 121):

             After getting some Thasian or Chian
or old Lesbian dripping with nectar.

This author also mentions *psithios*[227] wine (Eub. fr. 136):

After giving me a taste of sweet unmixed
psithios wine and catching me thirsty,
he punches me in the chest with vinegar.

Also Anaxandrides (fr. 73):

[226] Another name for Aphrodite, from the island where she
emerged from the sea; cf. Panyas. fr. 17.3 Bernabé (quoted at
2.36d).

[227] The meaning of the adjective is obscure.

χοῦς κεκραμένος

29 ψιθίου. ‖

"Οτι Ἀριστοφάνους τὰς δευτέρας Θεσμοφοριαζού-
σας Δημήτριος ὁ Τροιζήνιος Θεσμοφοριασάσας ἐπι-
γράφει. ἐν ταύτῃ ὁ κωμικὸς μέμνηται Πεπαρηθίου
οἴνου·

οἶνον δὲ πίνειν οὐκ ἐάσω Πράμνιον,
οὐ Χῖον, οὐχὶ Θάσιον, οὐ Πεπαρήθιον,
οὐδ' ἄλλον ὅστις ἐπεγερεῖ τὸν ἔμβολον.

Εὔβουλος·

ὁ Λευκάδιος πάρεστι καὶ † Μιλίττιος
οἰνίσκος οὕτω πότιμος.

b Ἀρχεστράτου τοῦ δειπνολόγου· |

εἶθ' ὁπόταν πλήρωμα Διὸς σωτῆρος ἔλησθε,
ἤδη χρὴ γεραόν, πολιὸν σφόδρα κρᾶτα
    φοροῦντα
οἶνον, ὑγρὴν χαίτην λευκῷ πεπυκασμένον ἄνθει
πίνειν, ἐκ Λέσβου περικύμονος ἐκγεγαῶτα.
τόν τ' ἀπὸ Φοινίκης ἱερῆς τὸν Βίβλινον αἰνῶ,
οὐ μέντοι κείνῳ γε παρεξισῶ αὐτόν. ἐὰν γὰρ
ἐξαίφνης αὐτοῦ γεύσῃ μὴ πρόσθεν ἐθισθείς,
c εὐώδης μέν σοι δόξει τοῦ Λεσβίου εἶναι |

---

228 *Th. II* was apparently set on the final day of the festival, unlike the preserved *Th.*, which takes place on the "middle day."

a mixed pitcher

of *psithios*.

Demetrius of Troezen (*SH* 377) gives Aristophanes'
second *Thesmophoriazusae* ("Women Celebrating the
Thesmophoria Festival") (test. ii) the title *Thesmophori-
asasai* ("Women Who Are Done Celebrating the Thesmophoria Festival").[228] The comic poet (Ar. fr. 334) mentions
Peparethian wine in this play:

I will not allow you to drink Pramnian wine,
or Chian, or Thasian, or Peparethian,
or any other that's going to arouse your ship's-ram.[229]

Eubulus (fr. 129):

The Leucadian is there, as is a little
† Militian wine, quite drinkable.

From Archestratus (fr. 59 Olson–Sens = *SH* 190) the ex-
pert on dinners:

Then, whenever you take up a full measure of Zeus
the Savior,
it ought to be an old, quite gray-haired
wine, its moist head covered with a white flower,
that you drink, a wine from wave-girt Lesbos by
birth.
I also praise the Bibline wine from holy Phoenicia,
although I do not rank it equal to *Lesbian*. Because if
you are previously unacquainted with it and taste it
for the first time,
you will think it more fragrant than Lesbian,

[229] I.e. that will give the man who drinks it an erection.

165

μᾶλλον, ἔχει γὰρ τοῦτο χρόνου διὰ μῆκος
  ἄπλατον·
πινόμενος δ' ἥσσων πολλῷ. κεῖνος δὲ δοκήσει
οὐκ οἴνῳ σοι ἔχειν ὅμοιον γέρας, ἀμβροσίῃ δέ.
εἰ δέ τινες σκώπτουσιν ἀλαζονοχαυνοφλύαροι
ὡς ἅδιστος ἔφυ πάντων Φοινίκιος οἶνος,
οὐ προσέχω τὸν νοῦν αὐτοῖς < . . . >.
ἔστι δὲ καὶ Θάσιος πίνειν γενναῖος, ἐὰν ᾖ
πολλαῖς πρεσβεύων ἐτέων περικαλλέσιν ὥραις.
οἶδα δὲ κἀξ ἄλλων πόλεων βοτρυοσταγῆ ἔρνη
  εἰπεῖν αἰνῆσαί τε καὶ οὔ με λέληθ' ὀνομῆναι. |
ἀλλ' οὐθὲν τἄλλ' ἐστὶν ἁπλῶς πρὸς Λέσβιον
  οἶνον.
ἀλλά τινες χαίρουσιν ἐπαινοῦντες τὰ παρ'
  αὐτοῖς.

Φοινικίκου δὲ οἴνου μέμνηται καὶ Ἔφιππος·

κάρυα, ῥόας, φοίνικας, ἕτερα νώγαλα,
σταμνάριά τ' οἴνου < . . . > τοῦ Φοινικικοῦ.

καὶ πάλιν·

Φοινικικοῦ βῖκός τις ὑπανεῴγνυτο.

---

230 Here, as elsewhere, the manuscripts are hopelessly confused between the adjectives *Phoinikikos* ("Phoenician") and
phoinikinos ("palm"). The second verse is quoted in a more complete form (and accompanied by a third) at 2.57e.

for it retains this quality on account of its tremendous
    age.
But when it is drunk, it is much inferior, whereas
    Lesbian wine
will seem to you to share the rank of ambrosia rather
    than of wine.
And if some emptyheadedbrainlessbullshitartists
    mockingly assert
that Phoenician wine is best of all,
I pay them no attention . . .
Thasian wine as well is good to drink, if it is
the eldest by many lovely seasons of years.
I am able to mention the vine-shoots dripping with
    grape-clusters from other cities as well,
and am not unaware of how to praise and name them.
But the others are just nothing compared with
    Lesbian wine,
although some people like to praise what they have in
    their own land.

Ephippus (fr. 24.1–2) also mentions Phoenician
wine:[230]

nuts, pomegranates, dates, other dainties,
and jars of Phoenician wine.

And again (Ephipp. fr. 8.2):[231]

Someone opened a transport-jar of Phoenician wine.

[231] Quoted in more complete form at 14.642e.

μνημονεύει αὐτοῦ καὶ Ξενοφῶν Ἀναβάσει.[95] Μενδαίου
δὲ Κρατῖνος·

   νῦν δ᾽ ἢν ἴδῃ Μενδαῖον ἡβῶντ᾽ ἀρτίως
   οἰνίσκον, ἕπεται κἀκολουθεῖ καὶ λέγει
e   "οἴμ᾽ ὡς ἁπαλὸς καὶ λευκός· ἆρ᾽ οἴσει τρία;" |

Ἕρμιππος δέ που ποιεῖ τὸν Διόνυσον πλειόνων μεμ-
νημένον·

   † Μενδαίῳ μὲν ἐνουροῦσι καὶ † θεοὶ αὐτοὶ
   στρώμασιν ἐν μαλακοῖς. Μάγνητα δὲ
     μειλιχόδωρον
   καὶ Θάσιον, τῷ δὴ μήλων ἐπιδέδρομεν ὀδμή,
   τοῦτον ἐγὼ κρίνω πολὺ πάντων εἶναι ἄριστον
   τῶν ἄλλων οἴνων μετ᾽ ἀμύμονα Χῖον ἄλυπον.
   ἔστι δέ τις οἶνος, τὸν δὴ σαπρίαν καλέουσιν,
   οὗ καὶ ἀπὸ στόματος στάμνων ὑπανοιγομενάων
f   ὄζει ἴων, ὄζει δὲ ῥόδων, ὄζει δ᾽ ὑακίνθου |
   ὀσμὴ θεσπεσία, κατὰ πᾶν δ᾽ ἔχει ὑψερεφὲς δῶ,
   ἀμβροσία καὶ νέκταρ ὁμοῦ. τοῦτ᾽ ἔστι τὸ νέκταρ,
   τούτου χρὴ παρέχειν πίνειν ἐν δαιτὶ θαλείῃ
   τοῖσιν ἐμοῖσι φίλοις, τοῖς δ᾽ ἐχθροῖς ἐκ
     Πεπαρήθου.

95 This sentence is omitted by E and preserved in C only in the
margin.

---

232 "palm-wine" (not "Phoenician wine").

Xenophon as well mentions it in the *Anabasis* (2.3.14).[232]
Cratinus (fr. *195) mentions Mendaean:[233]

> But now, if he spies a barely adolescent little
> Mendaean wine, he follows it and dogs its tracks and
>   says:
> "Damn! how soft and white it is! Is it strong enough
>   for three?[234]"

Hermippus (fr. 77) somewhere represents Dionysus as mentioning a number of wines:

> † Mendaean even piss † the gods themselves
> in their soft bed-clothes. And as for Magnesia's
>   pleasant gift
> and Thasian, over which drifts a scent of apples,
> I rank this far and away the best of all
> wines except for faultless, painless Chian.
> But there is one particular wine, which they refer to
>   as "mellow";
> when casks of it are tapped, out of its mouth
> comes the divine scent of violets, of roses,
> of hyacinth. And it fills the whole high-roofed house,
> a mix of ambrosia and nectar. *This* is what nectar is;
> *this* is what I need to give my friends to drink
> at a large meal—whereas my enemies can have
>   Peparethan!

---

[233] Probably from *Wineflask*; the personified Comedy complains about the semi-pederastic fascination of the poet to whom she is married with handsome young . . . wines.

[234] I.e. to withstand being mixed with three measures of water for each measure of wine.

φησὶ δὲ Φαινίας ὁ Ἐρέσιος Μενδαίους τοὺς βότρυς
ἐπὶ τῇ ἀμπέλῳ ῥαίνειν τῷ ἐλατηρίῳ· διὸ γίνεσθαι τὸν
οἶνον μαλακόν.

Ὅτι Θεμιστοκλῆς ὑπὸ βασιλέως ἔλαβε δωρεὰν
τὴν Λάμψακον εἰς οἶνον, Μαγνησίαν δ' εἰς ἄρτον,
Μυοῦντα δ' εἰς ὄψον, Περκώτην δὲ καὶ τὴν Παλαί-
σκηψιν εἰς στρωμνὴν καὶ ἱματισμόν. ἐκέλευσε δὲ
τούτῳ στολὴν φορεῖν βαρβαρικήν, ὡς καὶ Δημαράτῳ,
30 ‖ δοὺς τὰ πρότερον ὑπάρχοντα καὶ ⟨εἰς⟩ στολὴν
Γάμβρειον προσθεὶς ἐφ' ᾧ τε μηκέτι Ἑλληνικὸν ἱμάτιον περιβάληται. καὶ Κῦρος δὲ ὁ μέγας Πυθάρχῳ τῷ
Κυζικηνῷ φίλῳ ὄντι ἐχαρίσατο ἑπτὰ πόλεις, ὥς φησιν
ὁ Βαβυλώνιος Ἀγαθοκλῆς, Πήδασον, Ὀλύμπιον,
Ἀκαμάντιον, ⟨Τίον⟩[96], Σκῆπτρα, Ἀρτύψον, Τορτύρην.
ὁ δ' εἰς ὕβριν, φησί, καὶ ἄνοιαν προελθὼν τυραννεῖν
ἐπεχείρησε τῆς πατρίδος στρατιὰν συναγαγών. καὶ οἱ
Κυζικηνοὶ ἐξορμήσαντες ἐπ' αὐτὸν ἐβοηδρόμουν, πρό-
b κροσσοι φερόμενοι ‖ ἐπὶ τὸν κίνδυνον. τιμᾶται δὲ
παρὰ Λαμψακηνοῖς ὁ Πρίηπος ὁ αὐτὸς ὢν τῷ Διονύσῳ, ἐξ ἐπιθέτου καλούμενος οὕτως, ὡς Θρίαμβος καὶ
Διθύραμβος.

[96] add. Casaubon

---

235 Cf. Th. 1.138.5 (mentioning only the first three cities); Plu.
Them. 29.7 (adding Percote and Palaescepsis to the list, and citing
Phaenias fr. 28 Wehrli and Neanthes *FGrH* 84 F 17a as sources
for this information). The Athenian politician Themistocles (*PAA*
502610) fled to Persia around 470 BCE, and the king who gave him

Phaenias of Eresus (fr. 40 Wehrli) reports that the inhabitants of Mende sprinkle their grapes with squirting-cucumber juice while they are still on the vine, and says that the wine is therefore mild.

The Persian King gave Themistocles Lampsacus to supply his wine; Magnesia to supply his bread; Myus to supply the rest of his food; and Percote and Palaescepsis to supply his bedding and his clothing.[235] He ordered him to wear Persian clothes (he did the same with Demaratus[236]) and added Gambreius to what he had already given him, to supply his clothes, on the condition that he no longer wear a Greek robe. According to Agathocles of Babylon (*FGrH* 472 F 6), Cyrus the Great[237] bestowed seven cities on his friend Pytharchus of Cyzicus: Pedasus, Olympium, Acamantium, Tium, Sceptra, Artypsus, and Tortyre. But, Agathocles says, Pytharchus grew overbearing and reckless, and assembled an army and tried to seize control of his native country; and the Cyzicenes rushed out to defend against his attack, drawn up in ranks against the threat. The people of Lampsacus worship Priapus, who is identical with Dionysus and gets his name from an epithet, like Thriambus and Dithyrambus.[238]

control over a number of cities was Artaxerxes I (reigned 465–423); cf. 2.48d; 3.122a with n.   [236] A Spartan king (Poralla #210; reigned *c*.515–491 BCE) who went into exile in Persia after being deposed on charges of Medism. For Darius I's gift of land and cities to him, see Hdt. 6.70.2 (but without any mention of a request that he wear Persian clothing).

[237] Cyrus gradually built his empire beginning in 550 BCE, and died in 530; Pytharchus is otherwise unknown.

[238] Both epithets of Dionysus.

171

ATHENAEUS

Ὅτι Μιτυληναῖοι τὸν παρ' αὐτοῖς γλυκὺν οἶνον
πρόδρομον καλοῦσι, ἄλλοι δὲ πρότροπον[97].

Θαυμάζεται δὲ καὶ ὁ Ἰκάριος οἶνος, ὡς Ἄμφις·

ἐν Θουρίοις τοὔλαιον, ἐν Γέλᾳ φακοί,
Ἰκάριος οἶνος, ἰσχάδες Κιμώλιαι.

c γίνεται δὲ ἐν Ἰκάρῳ, φησὶν Ἐπαρχίδης, ὁ Πράμνιος. |
ἐστὶ δὲ οὗτος γένος τι οἴνου. καί ἐστιν οὗτος οὔτε
γλυκὺς οὔτε παχύς, ἀλλ' αὐστηρὸς καὶ σκληρὸς καὶ
δύναμιν ἔχων διαφέρουσαν· οἵῳ Ἀριστοφάνης οὐχ
ἥδεσθαι Ἀθηναίους φησί, λέγων τὸν Ἀθηναίων δῆμον
οὔτε ποιηταῖς ἥδεσθαι σκληροῖς καὶ ἀστεμφέσιν οὔτε
Πραμνίοις[98] οἴνοις συνάγουσι τὰς ὀφρῦς τε καὶ τὴν
κοιλίαν, ἀλλ' ἀνθοσμίᾳ καὶ πέπονι νεκταροσταγεῖ.
εἶναι γὰρ ἐν Ἰκάρῳ φησὶ Σῆμος Πράμνιον πέτραν καὶ
παρ' αὐτῇ ὄρος μέγα, ἀφ' οὗ τὸν Πράμνιον οἶνον, ὃν
d καὶ | φαρμακίτην τινὰς καλεῖν. ἐκαλεῖτο δὲ ἡ Ἴκαρος
πρότερον Ἰχθυόεσσα διὰ τὸ ἐν αὐτῇ τῶν ἰχθύων
πλῆθος, ὡς καὶ Ἐχινάδες ἀπὸ τῶν ἐχίνων καὶ Σηπιὰς
ἄκρα ἀπὸ τῶν περὶ αὐτὴν σηπιῶν καὶ Λαγοῦσσαι
νῆσοι ἀπὸ τῶν ἐν αὐταῖς λαγωῶν καὶ ἕτεραι Φυκοῦσ-
σαι καὶ Λοπαδοῦσσαι ἀπὸ τῶν παραπλησίων. προσ-

97 πρότροπον ἢ πρόδρομον CE
98 Πραμνίοις σκληροῖσιν CE

239 Cf. 2.45e. Pollux 6.17 and Hesychius π 4020 claim that the
word refers to wine (made from juice) that flowed out before the

172

The Mityleneans refer to the sweet wine produced in their country as *prodromos* ("front-runner"), whereas others call it *protropos*.[239]

Icarian wine is also highly regarded, according to Amphis (fr. 40):

the oil in Thurii, lentils in Gela,
Icarian wine, dried Cimolian figs.

Eparchides (*FGrH* 437 F 1) claims that Pramnian wine is produced in Icarus. This is a type of wine that is neither sweet nor syrupy, but dry, harsh, and very powerful. Aristophanes (fr. 688) claims that the Athenians dislike wine like this, saying that the Athenian people like neither harsh, unflinching poets nor Pramnian wines that furrow their brows and knot their stomachs, but prefer a mature wine that smells of flowers and drips nectar. Semus (*FGrH* 396 F 6a) claims that there is a Pramnian Rock on Icarus and a high mountain beside it, and that this is where Pramnian wine, which some people also refer to as *pharmakitēs* ("adulterated"), gets its name. Icarus was previously known as Ichthyoessa ("Fishy") because of the large number of fish around it, just as the Echinades Islands got their name from their sea-urchins *(echinoi)*, Cape Sepias got its name from the cuttlefish *(sepiai)* in the area, and the Lagoussae Islands got theirs from the hares *(lagōa)* that live on them, and so too with other islands such as Phycussae and Lopadoussae.[240] Eparchides (*FGrH* 437

grapes were pressed, and thus apparently derive it from *pateō* ("trample").

[240] Allegedly from *phukos* ("seaweed") and *lopas* ("shellfish"), respectively.

αγορεύεται δέ, φησὶν Ἐπαρχίδης, ἡ ἄμπελος ἡ τὸν
Ἰκάριον Πράμνιον φέρουσα ὑπὸ τῶν ξένων μὲν ἱερά,
ὑπὸ δὲ τῶν Οἰνοαίων Διονυσιάς. Οἰνόη δὲ πόλις ἐν τῇ
e νήσῳ ἐστί. Δίδυμος | δὲ Πράμνιόν φησιν οἶνον ἀπὸ
πραμνίας ἀμπέλου οὕτω καλουμένης, οἱ δὲ ἰδίως τὸν
μέλανα, ἔνιοι δὲ ἐν τῷ καθόλου τὸν πρὸς παραμονὴν
ἐπιτήδειον οἱονεὶ παραμόνιον ὄντα· οἱ δὲ τὸν πραΰνον-
τα τὸ μένος, ἐπεὶ οἱ πιόντες προσηνεῖς.

Ἐπαινεῖ Ἄμφις καὶ τὸν ἐξ Ἀκάνθου πόλεως οἶνον
λέγων·

(Α.) ποδαπὸς σύ; φράσον. (Β.) Ἀκάνθιος. (Α.)
  εἶτα πρὸς θεῶν
οἴνου πολίτης ὢν κρατίστου στρυφνὸς εἶ
f καὶ τοὔνομ᾿ αὐτὸ τῆς πατρίδος ἐν τοῖς τρόποις |
ἔχεις, τὰ δ᾿ ἤθη τῶν πολιτῶν οὐκ ἔχεις;

Κορινθίου οἴνου Ἄλεξις μνημονεύει ὡς σκληροῦ·

οἶνος ξενικὸς παρῆν· ὁ γὰρ Κορίνθιος
βασανισμός ἐστι.

καὶ Εὐβοϊκοῦ δέ·

< . . . > πολὺν πιὼν Εὐβοϊκὸν οἶνον.

Ἀρχίλοχος τὸν Νάξιον τῷ νέκταρι παραβάλλει· ὃς
καί πού φησιν·

---

[241] *praunonta to menos*, supposedly producing the adjective
Pramneios.

F 1, continued) claims that the vine that produces Icarian Pramnian is called "sacred" by people from elsewhere, but "Dionysias" by the inhabitants of Oenoe; Oenoe is a city on the island. But Didymus (p. 77 Schmidt) says that Pramnian is wine produced from a vine called *pramnia*, while other authorities claim that this is properly a term for dark wine, and some say that it refers generally to wine that can be stored, as if the word was *paramonios* ("enduring"). Others argue that this is wine that makes one's temper milder,[241] since anyone who drinks becomes gentle.

Amphis (fr. 36) also praises the wine from the city of Acanthus, saying:

> (A.) Where are you from? Tell me! (B.) I'm
>   Acanthian. (A.) So then, by the gods—
> although you're a fellow-citizen of the finest wine
>   there is, you're harsh?
> And you act in a way that matches your country's
>   name,[242] but lack the manners of your fellow-
>   citizens?

Alexis (fr. 292) mentions Corinthian wine as being harsh:

> A foreign wine was there; for what you get in Corinth
> is torture.

He also mentions Euboean (Alex. fr. 303):

> after drinking a lot of Euboean.

Archilochus (fr. 290 West²) compares Naxian wine to nectar. He also says somewhere (fr. 2 West²):

[242] I.e. in a prickly manner (punning on *akantha*, "thorn, prickle").

175

ἐν δορὶ μὲν < . . . > μᾶζα μεμαγμένη, ἐν δορὶ δ᾽
οἶνος
Ἰσμαρικός· πίνω δ᾽ ἐν δορὶ κεκλιμένος.

Στράττις δὲ τὸν Σκιάθιον ἐπαινεῖ·

οἶνος κοχύζει τοῖς ὁδοιπόροις πιεῖν
μέλας Σκιάθιος, ἴσον ἴσῳ κεκραμένος.

31 Ἀχαιὸς δὲ τὸν Βίβλινον· ‖

ἐδεξιοῦτο Βιβλίνου μέθης
ἐκπώματι.

ἐκαλεῖτο δ᾽ οὕτως ἀπό τινος χωρίου οὕτω προσαγο-
ρευομένου. φησὶ δὲ Φιλύλλιος ὅτι

παρέξω Λέσβιον,
Χῖον σαπρόν, Θάσιον, < . . . > Βίβλινον,
Μενδαῖον, ὥστε μηδένα κραιπαλᾶν.

Ἐπίχαρμος δὲ ἀπό τινων ὀρῶν Βιβλίνων φησὶν αὐτὸν
ὠνομάσθαι. Ἀρμενίδας δὲ τῆς Θρᾴκης φησὶν εἶναι
χώραν τὴν Βιβλίαν, ἣν Ἀντισάρην[99] καὶ Οἰσύμην
b προσαγορευθῆναι. ἐπιεικῶς δὲ ἡ Θρᾴκη ἐθαυμάζετο |
ὡς ἡδύοινος, καὶ συνόλως τὰ ἀπὸ πλησίον αὐτῆς
χωρία·

νῆες δ᾽ ἐκ Λήμνοιο παρέστασαν οἶνον ἄγουσαι.

Ἵππυς δ᾽ ὁ Ῥηγῖνος τὴν εἰλεὸν καλουμένην ἄμπελον

---

[99] Ἀντισάρην Casaubon: αὖθις τισάρην CE

Because of my spear, I have kneaded barley-cake;
    because of my spear, I have Ismarian
wine; and because of my spear, I'm lying here
    drinking.

But Strattis (fr. 64) praises Sciathian:

Dark Sciathian wine pours forth
for travelers to drink, mixed one-to-one.

Achaeus (*TrGF* 20 F 41) praises Bibline:

He made a toast with a goblet of Bibline
drunkenness.

It got its name from a place called Biblus. Philyllius (fr. 23) says:

I'll furnish Lesbian,
mellow Chian, Thasian, Bibline,
and Mendaean, so that no one gets a hangover.

Epicharmus (fr. 170) says that it is named after certain Bibline mountains, whereas Armenidas (*FGrH* 378 F 3) claims that Biblia is a region in Thrace referred to as Antisara and Oesyme. Thrace was fairly highly regarded for the quality of its wine, as were the regions around it generally:

Ships were there from Lemnos, carrying wine. (*Il.* 7.467)

But Hippys of Rhegium (*FGrH* 554 F *4) says that the so-

βιβλίαν φησὶ καλεῖσθαι, ἣν Πόλλιν τὸν Ἀργεῖον, ὃς
ἐβασίλευσε Συρακουσίων, πρῶτον εἰς Συρακούσας
κομίσαι ἐξ Ἰταλίας. εἴη ἂν οὖν ὁ παρὰ Σικελιώταις
γλυκὺς καλούμενος Πόλλιος ὁ Βίβλινος οἶνος.

Χρησμός. ἐν τῷ χρησμῷ, φησίν, ὁ θεὸς ηὐτομάτι-
σεν·[100]

c   πῖν᾽ οἶνον τρυγίαν, ἐπεὶ οὐκ Ἀνθηδόνα ναίεις |
    οὐδ᾽ ἱερὰν Ὑπέραν, ὅθι γ᾽ ἄτρυγον οἶνον ἔπινες.

ὠνομάζετο δὲ[101] ἄμπελος Ἀνθηδονιὰς καὶ Ὑπερειὰς
ἀπὸ Ἄνθου τινὸς καὶ Ὑπέρου, ὡς καὶ Ἀλθηφιὰς ἀπὸ
Ἀλθηφίου τινός, ἑνὸς τῶν Ἀλφειοῦ ἀπογόνων.

Ἀλκμὰν δέ που "ἄπυρον οἶνον" καὶ "ἄνθεος ὄσδον-
τά" φησι τὸν ἐκ "Πέντε λόφων", ὅς ἐστι τόπος Σπάρτης
ἀπέχων στάδια ἑπτά· καὶ τὸν ἐκ Καρύστου, ὅς ἐστι
πλησίον Ἀρκαδίας·[102] καὶ τὸν ἐκ Δενθιάδων, ἐρύματός
τινος· καὶ τὸν ἐξ Οἰνοῦντος καὶ τὸν ἐξ Ὀνόγλων καὶ
d   Σταθμῶν. χωρία δὲ ταῦτα τὰ καὶ | πλησίον Πιτάνης.
φησὶν οὖν·

[100] ἐν . . . ηὐτομάτισεν is omitted by E and preserved in C
only in the margin.

[101] Kaibel prints ὠνομάζετο δὲ παρὰ Τροιζηνίοις, ὥς φησιν Ἀριστοτέλης ἐν τῇ αὐτῶν Πολιτείᾳ, ἄμπελος, and says
that the additional words are preserved in the margin in C. I see
no sign of them.

[102] The words καὶ τὸν ἐκ Καρύστου . . . Ἀρκαδίας appear in
C after καὶ τὸν ἐκ Δενθιάδων . . . ἢ Σταθμίταν. The latter section is missing in E and was presumably inserted in the wrong
place by the C-copyist.

called *eileos* vine is called "Biblian," and that Pollis of Argos, the tyrant of Syracuse, first imported it into Sicily from Italy.[243] The sweet Sicilian wine called *Pollios* must therefore be Bibline.

An oracle (Delphic oracle L81 Fontenrose). In the oracle, [Athenaeus] says, the god spoke of his own accord:[244]

> Drink wine full of lees, since you do not inhabit Anthedon
> or holy Hypera, where you used to drink wine with no lees.

A variety of vine was called "Anthedonias and Hypereias" after a certain Anthus and Hyperus, in the same way that there is an Althephian vine called after a certain Althephius, who was one of Alpheius' descendants.

Alcman (*PMG* 92(a–c)) somewhere uses the words "fireless wine" that "smells of flowers" to refer to the wine produced at "Five Crests"; this is a place seven stades from Sparta.[245] He also mentions wine from Carystus, which is near Arcadia; from Denthiades, a fortified place of some sort; from Oenous; and from Onogli and Stathmi. These are the regions around Pitane. Thus he says (*PMG* 92(d)):

---

[243] Pollis appears to be a legendary rather than a historical character. Hesychius ι 539 refers to "a type of grape-cluster" called *ileos*.

[244] I.e. without being asked a question, as was normal. See Plu. *Mor.* 295d–f, who offers several stories that tie together the oracle, Alpheius (mentioned below), and Anthus and Hypera (sic).

[245] One stade = approximately 200 yards or slightly more than 1/9 of a mile.

† οἶνον δ᾽ Οἰνουντιάδα ἢ Δένθιν ἢ Καρύστιον
ἢ Ὄνογλιν ἢ Σταθμίταν †.

ἄπυρον δὲ εἶπε τὸν οὐχ ἡψημένον· ἐχρῶντο γὰρ
ἐφθοῖς οἴνοις. Πολύβιος δὲ διάφορον οἶνον ἐν Καπύῃ
φησὶ γίνεσθαι τὸν ἀναδενδρίτην καλούμενον, ᾧ μηδένα συγκρίνεσθαι. Ἀλκίφρων δ᾽ ὁ Μαιάνδριος περὶ
τὴν Ἐφεσίαν φησὶν εἶναι ὀρείαν κώμην τὴν πρότερον
μὲν καλουμένην Λητοῦς, νῦν δὲ Λατώρειαν ἀπὸ Λατω-
ρείας Ἀμαζόνος· ἐν ᾗ γίνεσθαι | τὸν Πράμνιον οἶνον.
Τιμαχίδας δὲ ὁ Ῥόδιος ὑπόχυτόν τινα οἶνον ἐν Ῥόδῳ
καλεῖ παραπλήσιον τῷ γλεύκει. καὶ γλύξις δ᾽ οἶνος
καλεῖται ὁ τὸ ἕψημα ἔχων. Πολύζηλος δὲ αὐτίτην
καλεῖ οἶνον. Πλάτων δ᾽ ὁ κωμικὸς καπνίαν· κάλλιστος
δ᾽ οὗτος γίνεται ἐν Βενεβέντῳ πόλει Ἰταλίας. ἀμφίας
δ᾽ οἶνος ὁ φαῦλος καλεῖται παρὰ Σωσικράτει. ἐχρῶντο
δ᾽ οἱ ἀρχαῖοι καὶ πόματί τινι ἐξ ἀρωμάτων κατασκευ-
αζομένῳ, ὃ ἐκάλουν τρίμμα. Θεόφραστος δὲ ἐν τῇ
Περὶ Φυτῶν | Ἱστορίᾳ φησὶν ἐν Ἡραίᾳ τῆς Ἀρκαδίας
γίνεσθαι οἶνον ὃς τοὺς μὲν ἄνδρας πινόμενος ἐξίστη-
σι, τὰς δὲ γυναῖκας τεκνούσσας ποιεῖ. περὶ δὲ Κερυ-
νίαν τῆς Ἀχαίας ἀμπέλου τι γένος εἶναι, ἀφ᾽ ἧς τὸν
οἶνον ἐξαμβλοῦν ποιεῖν τὰς γυναῖκας τὰς ἐγκύμονας·
κἂν τῶν βοτρύων δέ, φησί, φάγωσιν, ἐξαμβλοῦσιν. ὁ
δὲ Τροιζήνιος οἶνος ἀγόνους, φησί, ποιεῖ τοὺς πίνοντας. ἐν Θάσῳ δὲ λέγει ὡς αὐτοὶ ποιοῦσιν οἶνόν τινα

---

246 "Sauce," from the verb *tribō* ("grind," referring to how the

† wine from Oenous or Denthis or Carystus
or Onogli or Stathmi †.

By "fireless" wine he means wine that has not been boiled;
for they used to drink wine prepared this way. Polybius
(34.11.1) reports that outstanding wine referred to as
anadendritēs ("tree-climber") is produced in Capua and
that nothing compares to it. Alciphron of Maeander says
that there is a mountain village near Ephesus that used
to be called Leto-ville but is now called Latoreia after an
Amazon by that name; Pramnian wine is produced there.
Timachidas of Rhodes (fr. 32 Blinkenberg) refers to a
must-like wine produced in Rhodes as *hypochutos* ("doc-
tored"). Boiled wine is called *gluxis*. Polyzelus (fr. 1.1) refers to *autitēs* ("home-made," or perhaps "from this year's
vintage") wine. The comic poet Plato (fr. 274) mentions
kapnias ("smoky") wine; this is best when produced in
the Italian city of Beneventum. Sosicrates (fr. 4) refers to
bad wine as *amphias*. The ancients also consumed a drink
made from spices, which they referred to as *trimma*.[246]
Theophrastus in his *Research on Plants* (*HP* 9.18.10–11)
says that a wine is produced in Heraea in Arcadia that
makes men who drink it go crazy and women who drink
it fertile.[247] Around Cerynia in Achaea there is a variety
of vine whose wine causes pregnant women to miscarry;
even if they only eat the grapes, he claims, they miscarry.
Troezenian wine, he claims, makes anyone who drinks it
sterile. And he says that on Thasos they make one type of

spices were prepared). But Athenaeus may be in error; see Arnott
on Alex. fr. 193.3.　　　[247] Material very similar to this is preserved at Plin. *Nat.* 14.116–17; Ael. *VH* 13.6.

ὑπνωτικὸν καὶ ἕτερον ἀγρυπνεῖν ποιοῦντα τοὺς πίνοντας.

Περὶ δὲ τῆς τοῦ ἀνθοσμίου οἴνου σκευασίας Φαινίας ὁ Ἐρέσιός φησι τάδε· γλεύκει παραχεῖται παρὰ
32 χοῦς πεντήκοντα εἰς θαλάσσης ‖ καὶ γίνεται ἀνθοσμίας. καὶ πάλιν· ἀνθοσμίας γίνεται ἐκ νέων ἀμπέλων
ἰσχυρότερος ἢ ἐκ παλαιῶν. ἑξῆς τέ φησι· τὰς ὀμφακώδεις συμπατήσαντες ἀπέθεντο καὶ ἀνθοσμίας ἐγένετο.
Θεόφραστος δ᾽ ἐν Θάσῳ φησὶ τὸν ἐν τῷ πρυτανείῳ
διδόμενον θαυμαστὸν εἶναι τὴν ἡδονήν· ἠρτυμένος
γάρ ἐστιν. ἐμβάλλουσι γὰρ εἰς τὸ κεράμιον σταῖς
μέλιτι φυράσαντες, ὥστε τὴν ὀσμὴν ἀπ᾽ αὐτοῦ, τὴν δὲ
γλυκύτητα ἀπὸ τοῦ σταιτὸς λαμβάνειν τὸν οἶνον. καὶ
b ἑξῆς δέ φησιν· ἐάν | τις κεράσῃ σκληρὸν καὶ εὔοσμον
μαλακῷ καὶ ἀόσμῳ, καθάπερ τὸν Ἡρακλεώτην καὶ
τὸν Ἐρυθραῖον, τοῦ μὲν τὴν μαλακότητα, τοῦ δὲ τὴν
εὐοσμίαν[103] παρεχομένου.

Μυρίνης δὲ[104] οἶνος κεῖται παρὰ Ποσειδίππῳ·

διψηρὸς ἄτοπος ὁ μυρίνης ὁ τίμιος.

καὶ Ἑρμῆς δ᾽ εἶδος πόσεως παρὰ Στράττιδι.

[103] εὐοσμίαν Thphr.: εὐστομαχίαν CE
[104] Μυρίνης δὲ Dindorf: μυρτίτης δὲ ἢ μυρρίνης CE

wine that causes sleep and another that keeps anyone who drinks it awake.

Phaenias of Eresus (fr. 41 Wehrli) says the following about how *anthosmias*[248] wine is produced: One *chous*[249] of sea-water is added to every 50 of grape-must, producing *anthosmias*. And again: Stronger *anthosmias* is produced from young vines than from older ones. And immediately after this he says: They trampled out sour grapes and put (the juice) into storage, and it turned into *anthosmias*. Theophrastus (*Od*. 51) says that the wine distributed in the prytaneion[250] on Thasos is remarkably delicious, because it has seasonings added. Because they knead wheat and honey together to produce dough, and put it into the jar, to make the wine retain its own fragrance but take on the sweetness of the dough. And immediately after this he says (*Od*. 52): If you mix a harsh but fragrant wine with a soft but odorless wine, for example Heracleote and Erythraean, the one furnishes its softness, the other its fragrance.

Perfumed wine is attested in Posidippus (fr. 36):

The expensive perfumed wine is strange and thirsty.

"Hermes" is also a type of beverage mentioned by Strattis (fr. 23.1).[251]

[248] Literally "flower-scented."

[249] A *chous* (literally "pitcher") contained about 3.2 litres and was equal to 12 *kotulai* or one-twelfth of an amphora.

[250] The building that housed the city's central hearth, where meals were provided *inter alia* for individuals who had been awarded permanent maintenance as a civic honor. Cf. 4.137e.

[251] Quoted at 11.473c.

Χαιρέας δὲ ἐν Βαβυλῶνι οἶνόν φησι γίνεσθαι τὸν καλούμενον νέκταρ.

c   ἦν ἄρ' ἔπος τόδ' ἀληθές, ὅ τ' οὐ μόνον ὕδατος |
      αἶσαν,
  ἀλλά τι καὶ χλεύης οἶνος ἔχειν ἐθέλει.

οὐ γὰρ ἀπόβλητον Διονύσιον, οὐδὲ γίγαρτον,

ὁ Κεῖός φησι ποιητής.

Τῶν οἴνων ὁ μὲν λευκός, ὁ δὲ κιρρός, ὁ δὲ μέλας. καὶ ὁ μὲν λευκὸς λεπτότατος τῇ φύσει, οὐρητικός, θερμὸς πεπτικός τε ὢν τὴν κεφαλὴν ποιεῖ διάπυρον· ἀνωφερὴς γὰρ ὁ οἶνος. ὁ δὲ μέλας ὁ μὴ γλυκάζων τροφιμώτατος, στυπτικός· ὁ δὲ γλυκάζων καὶ τῶν λευκῶν καὶ τῶν κιρρῶν τροφιμώτατος· λεαίνει γὰρ d κατὰ τὴν πάροδον | καὶ παχύνων τὰ ὑγρὰ μᾶλλον κεφαλὴν ἧττον παρενοχλεῖ. ὄντως γὰρ ἡ τοῦ γλυκέος οἴνου φύσις ἐγχρονίζει περὶ τὰ ὑποχόνδρια καὶ πτυέλου ἐστὶν ἀναγωγός, ὡς Διοκλῆς καὶ Πραξαγόρας ἱστοροῦσι. Μνησίθεος δ' ὁ Ἀθηναῖος φησιν· ὁ μέλας οἶνός ἐστι θρεπτικώτατος, ὁ δὲ λευκὸς οὐρητικώτατος καὶ λεπτότατος, ὁ δὲ κιρρὸς ξηρὸς καὶ τῶν σιτίων πεπτικώτερος. οἱ δ' ἐπιμελέστερον τεθαλαττωμένοι οἶ- νοι ἀκραιπαλοί τέ εἰσι καὶ κοιλίας λύουσιν ἐπιδάκνου- e σί τε τὸν στόμαχον | ἐμφυσήσεις τε ἐνεργάζονται καὶ συγκατεργάζονται τὴν τροφήν. τοιοῦτος δ' ἐστὶν ὅ τε

---

[252] Chaereas of Athens (2nd century BCE or earlier) wrote on

Chaereas[252] says that a wine produced in Babylon is referred to as "nectar."

> This saying is true, then, that wine wants to have not just
> its share of water, but a bit of joking as well.[253]

> Because nothing associated with Dionysus ought to
> be discarded, not even a grapeseed,

says the Cean poet (Simon. fr. 24 West²).

One type of wine is white, one is yellow, and one is dark. The white is naturally the lightest, is diuretic and warm, and because it promotes digestion, inflames the head; for wine travels upward through the body. Dark wine that is not sweet is highly nutritious and astringent. Sweet white and yellow wines are also extremely nutritious, for sweet wine lubricates the tracts it moves through and, because it makes the moist elements in the body thicker, does less damage to the head. For in fact the essence of sweet wine lingers in the soft portions of the abdomen and produces saliva, according to Diocles (fr. 237 van der Eijk) and Praxagoras (fr. 39 Steckerl). But Mnesitheus of Athens (fr. 46 Bertier) says: Dark wine is best at promoting growth; white wine is best at promoting urination, and the lightest; and yellow wine is dry and best at promoting digestion. Wines that have been aggressively treated with sea-water do not cause hangovers; loosen the bowels; eat away at the stomach; produce gas; and aid in the digestion of food.

agricultural topics; this is the only fragment of his work that survives.

[253] An elegiac couplet by an unknown author; probably a transitional remark, introducing a new speech (by a physician?).

Μύνδιος καὶ ὁ ἀπὸ Ἁλικαρνασσοῦ. ὁ γοῦν κυνικὸς
Μένιππος ἁλμοπότιν τὴν Μύνδον φησίν. ἱκανῶς δὲ
καὶ ὁ Κῷος τεθαλάττωται. καὶ ὁ Ῥόδιος δὲ ἐλάττονος
μὲν κεκοινώνηκε[105] θαλάσσης, ὁ δὲ πολὺς αὐτοῦ
ἀχρεῖός ἐστιν. ὁ δὲ νησιώτης εἴς τε τοὺς πότους ἐστὶν
εὖ πεφυκὼς καὶ πρὸς τὴν καθημερινὴν χρῆσιν οὐκ
ἀνοίκειος. ὁ δὲ Κνίδιος αἵματος γεννητικός, τρόφιμος,
f κοιλίαν εὔλυτον κατασκευάζων· | πλείων δὲ πινόμενος
ἐκλύει τὸν στόμαχον. ὁ δὲ Λέσβιος στῦψιν μικροτέ-
ραν ἔχει καὶ μᾶλλον οὐρεῖται. χαριέστατος δ᾽ ἐστὶν ὁ
Χῖος καὶ τοῦ Χίου ὁ καλούμενος Ἀριούσιος. διαφοραὶ
δὲ αὐτοῦ εἰσι τρεῖς· ὁ μὲν γὰρ αὐστηρός ἐστιν, ὁ δὲ
γλυκάζων, ὁ δὲ μέσος τούτων τῇ γεύσει αὐτόκρατος
καλεῖται. ὁ μὲν οὖν αὐστηρὸς εὐστόμαχός[106] ἐστι καὶ
τρόφιμος καὶ μᾶλλον οὐρεῖται, ὁ δὲ γλυκάζων τρόφι-
33 μος, πλήσμιος, κοιλίας μαλακτικός, ‖ ὁ δ᾽ αὐτόκρατος
τῇ χρείᾳ μέσος ἐστί. κοινῶς δ᾽ ὁ Χῖος πεπτικός,
τρόφιμος, αἵματος χρηστοῦ γεννητικός, προσηνέστα-
τος, πλήσμιος διὰ τὸ παχὺς[107] εἶναι τῇ δυνάμει.

Τῶν δ᾽ οἴνων χαριέστατος ὁ κατὰ τὴν Ἰταλίαν
Ἀλβανὸς καὶ ὁ Φαλερνίτης. ὁ δὲ τούτων πεπαλαιωμέ-
νος καὶ κεχρονικὼς φαρμακώδης ὢν καροῖ λίαν ταχέως. ὁ δὲ Ἀδριανὸς καλούμενος εὔπνους, εὐανάδοτος,
ἄλυπος τὸ σύνολον. οἰνοποιητέον δὲ αὐτοὺς πρό τινος
b χρόνου καὶ εἰς ἀναπεπταμένον τόπον | θετέον εἰς τὸ

---

105 κεκοινώνηκε C[s]: τετύχηκε CE
106 εὐστόμαχός Kaibel: εὔστομός CE

Myndian wine and the wine produced in Halicarnassus fall into this category; the Cynic Menippus (fr. V Riese), at any rate, calls Myndus "brine-drinking." Coan wine also has a substantial amount of sea-water added. Rhodian contains a smaller amount of sea-water, but much of it is no good. Island wine is naturally good for drinking and is well-adapted for everyday use. Cnidian encourages the production of blood, is nutritious, and relaxes the bowels; when too much is drunk, it upsets the stomach. Lesbian is less astringent and more diuretic. Chian is the best wine there is, especially the variety of Chian known as Arousian. There are three varieties of it: one is dry, one sweet, and the one whose taste falls in between these is referred to as *autokratos*.[254] The dry variety is easy on the stomach, nutritious, and more diuretic; the sweet variety is nutritious and filling, and has a laxative effect; and the *autokratos* falls mid-way between the others in its effect. In general, Chian wine is good for the digestion and nutritious; promotes the production of good blood; is quite mild; and is filling because of its syrupy quality.

The best wines are Italian Alban and Falernian. Either of these, when aged and kept in storage for a long time, takes on a drug-like character and rapidly knocks one unconscious. The so-called Adriatic has a nice bouquet, is easily absorbed by the body, and generally does no harm. These wines must be produced early in the season and

[254] Apparently "mixed with itself" (< *kerannumi*), i.e. "that does not need to be mixed with anything else."

---

[107] παχὺς Schweighäuser: πολὺς C: πολὺ E

διαπνεῦσαι τὸ παχὺ τῆς δυνάμεως αὐτῶν. χαριέστατος δ' οἶνος εἰς παλαίωσιν ὁ Κερκυραῖος. ὁ δὲ Ζακύν-
θιος καὶ ὁ Λευκάδιος διὰ τὸ γύψον λαβεῖν καὶ κεφαλὴν ἀδικοῦσιν. ὁ δ' ἀπὸ Κιλικίας Ἀβάτης καλούμενος
κοιλίας μόνον ἐστὶ μαλακτικός. Κῴῳ δὲ καὶ Μυνδίῳ
καὶ Ἁλικαρνασσίῳ καὶ παντὶ τῷ ἱκανῶς τεθαλατ-
τωμένῳ συνᾴδει τὰ σκληρὰ τῶν ὑδάτων οἷον κρηναῖα
καὶ ὄμβρια, ἐὰν ᾖ διυλισμένα καὶ πλείονα χρόνον
c καθεσταμένα. | χρήσιμοι δ' εἰσὶν οὗτοι Ἀθήνησι καὶ
Σικυῶνι· ἐν ταύταις γὰρ σκληρὰ τὰ ὕδατα. τοῖς δ'
ἀθαλάσσοις τῶν οἴνων καὶ τοῖς παρέχουσιν ἱκανωτέ-
ραν στύψιν, ἔτι δὲ τῷ Χίῳ καὶ Λεσβίῳ τὰ ἀποιότατα
τῶν ὑδάτων εὐθετεῖ.

ὦ γλῶσσα, σιγήσασα τὸν πολὺν χρόνον,
πῶς δῆτα τλήσῃ πρᾶγμ' ὑπεξελθεῖν τόδε;
ἢ τῆς ἀνάγκης οὐδὲν ἐμβριθέστερον,
ὑφ' ἧς τὸ κρυφθὲν ἐκφανεῖς ἀνακτόρων,

φησὶ Σοφοκλῆς.

Αὐτὸς ἐμαυτοῦ Ἰόλεώς τε καὶ Ἀλκείδης γενήσομαι.[108]

d   Ὅτι ὁ Μαρεώτης οἶνος ὁ Ἀλεξανδρεωτικὸς | τὴν
μὲν προσηγορίαν ἔχει ἀπὸ τῆς ἐν Ἀλεξανδρείᾳ λίμ-

[108] This sentence is omitted by E and preserved in C only in
the margin.

---

[255] This quotation and the remark that follows must have

stored in an open place to allow their syrupy quality to evaporate. The best wine for aging is Corcyran. Zacynthian and Leucadian cause headaches, because chalk is added to them. The Cilician wine referred to as *Abatēs* is merely laxative. Hard waters such as spring-water and rainwater go well with Coan, Myndian, Halicarnassian, and any wine to which a substantial quantity of sea-water has been added, provided that the water has been carefully strained and allowed to stand for a long time. These wines are good to drink in Athens and Sicyon, because the water is hard in these places. But for wines that have not had sea-water added or that are quite astringent, as well as for Chian and Lesbian, waters with no distinguishing characteristics are appropriate.

> O tongue, after you have been silent for so long,
> how will you dare evade this matter?
> Certainly there is nothing more burdensome than
>   necessity,
> which will force you to reveal the secret of the royal
>   house,

says Sophocles (fr. 757).[255]

I will become my own Iolaus, and Alceides as well.[256]

Mareotic wine from Alexandria gets its name from Lake Mareia in Alexandria and from the city called Mareia

stood at the beginning of a new speech, presumably by a guest from Egypt.

[256] Alceides is the name Heracles was given at birth, and Iolaus was his nephew and assistant in his labors. But one of the dinner guests is also named Alceides (1.1f; 4.174b; a musician), and most likely there is a reference to him as well.

νης[109] Μαρείας καὶ τῆς παρ' αὐτὴν πόλεως ὁμωνύμου,
ἣ πρότερον μὲν ἦν μεγίστη, νῦν δὲ κώμης περιείληφε
μέγεθος, τὴν προσηγορίαν λαβοῦσα ἀπὸ Μάρωνος
ἑνὸς τῶν μετὰ Διονύσου τὰς στρατείας πεποιημένων.
πολλὴ δὲ ἡ περὶ τὴν γῆν ταύτην ἄμπελος, ἧς καὶ ἡ
σταφυλὴ πάνυ βρωθῆναι εὔστομος καὶ ὁ γινόμενος
οἶνος κάλλιστος· λευκός τε γὰρ καὶ ἡδύς, εὔπνους,
e   εὐανάδοτος, λεπτός, κεφαλῆς | οὐ καθικνούμενος, διου-
ρητικός. τούτου δὲ καλλίων ὁ Ταινιωτικὸς καλούμενος.
ταινία δ' ἐστὶν ἐπιμήκης περὶ τοὺς αὐτοὺς τόπους, ἀφ'
ἧς οἱ γινόμενοι οἶνοί εἰσι μὲν ἠρέμα ὑπόχλωροι,
ἐμφαίνοντές τι ἐν αὐτοῖς λιπαρόν, ὃ κατὰ τὴν τοῦ
ὕδατος κρᾶσιν ἀναλύεται κατὰ βραχύ, ὡς καὶ τὸ μέλι
τὸ Ἀττικὸν ἀνακιρνάμενον. οὗτος ὁ Ταινιωτικὸς πρὸς
τῷ ἡδὺς εἶναι ἔχει τι καὶ ἀρωματῶδες ἠρέμα ἐπι-
στῦφον. ἡ δὲ περὶ τὸν Νεῖλον ἄμπελος πλείστη μὲν
f   αὐτή, ὅσος καὶ ὁ ποταμός. | καὶ πολλαὶ τῶν οἴνων αἱ
ἰδιότητες κατά τε τὰ χρώματα καὶ τὴν προσφοράν.
τούτους δ' ὑπερβάλλει ὁ κατὰ Ἄντυλλαν πόλιν οὐ
μακρὰν οὖσαν Ἀλεξανδρείας, ἧς τοὺς φόρους οἱ τότε
βασιλεῖς Αἰγύπτιοί τε καὶ Πέρσαι ταῖς γαμεταῖς
ἐδίδοσαν εἰς ζώνας. ὁ δὲ κατὰ τὴν Θηβαΐδα καὶ
μάλιστα ὁ κατὰ τὴν Κόπτον πόλιν οὕτως ἐστὶ λεπτὸς
καὶ εὐανάδοτος καὶ ταχέως πεπτικὸς ὡς καὶ τοῖς
πυρεταίνουσι διδόμενος μὴ βλάπτειν.

[109] λίμνης Meineke: κρήνης CE

beside it. The city was formerly quite large, but is now only as big as a village; it took its name from Maron, who was one of Dionysus' companions during his campaigns.[257] Many vines grow in this country, and their grapes taste delicious and the wine produced from them is excellent; for it is white and sweet, has a fine bouquet, is easily absorbed by the body and light, does not go to the head, and is diuretic. Even better than this is the so-called Taeniotic ("Strip") wine. There is a long strip *(tainia)* of land in this region, and the wines produced there have a slight yellowish-green cast, which shows that they contain an oily element; this is removed by mixing water into them gradually, as when water is mixed into Attic honey. In addition to its pleasant taste, this Taeniotic wine has a slightly aromatic, astringent quality. The quantity of vines planted along the sides of the Nile matches the river's size, and many of the wines have unique colors and flavors. The best of them is the one produced in the city of Antylla not far from Alexandria; the ancient Egyptian and Persian kings used to give the revenues from this place to their wives to buy belts. The wine produced around Thebes, and especially around the city of Coptos, is so thin and easily absorbed by the body, and promotes digestion so rapidly, that even individuals with fevers can be given it without suffering any harm.

[257] When the god travelled the world, spreading knowledge of wine-making and his own cult; cf. 3.111b. This is the same Maron as the man who gave Odysseus the wine with which he overcame the Cyclops; cf. 1.26b n.

34   σαυτὴν ἐπαινεῖς, ὥσπερ Ἀστυδάμας, γύναι. ‖

ἦν δὲ τραγικὸς ποιητὴς ὁ Ἀστυδάμας.

Ὅτι Θεόπομπος ὁ Χῖος τὴν ἄμπελον ἱστορεῖ εὑρεθῆναι ἐν Ὀλυμπίᾳ παρὰ τὸν Ἀλφειόν· καὶ ὅτι τῆς
Ἡλείας τόπος ἐστὶν ἀπέχων ὀκτὼ στάδια, ἐν ᾧ οἱ
ἐγχώριοι κατακλείοντες τοῖς Διονυσίοις χαλκοῦς λέβητας τρεῖς κενοὺς παρόντων τῶν ἐπιδημούντων ἀπο-
σφραγίζονται καὶ ὕστερον ἀνοίγοντες εὑρίσκουσιν
οἴνου πεπληρωμένους. Ἑλλάνικος δέ φησιν ἐν τῇ
Πλινθίνῃ πόλει Αἰγύπτου πρώτῃ εὑρεθῆναι τὴν ἄμπε-
b   λον. διὸ καὶ Δίων ὁ ἐξ Ἀκαδημίας | φιλοίνους καὶ
φιλοπότας τοὺς Αἰγυπτίους γενέσθαι· εὑρεθῆναί τε
βοήθημα παρ᾿ αὐτοῖς ὥστε τοὺς διὰ πενίαν ἀποροῦν-
τας οἴνου τὸν ἐκ τῶν κριθῶν γενόμενον πίνειν· καὶ
οὕτως ἥδεσθαι τοὺς τοῦτον προσφερομένους ὡς καὶ
ᾄδειν καὶ ὀρχεῖσθαι καὶ πάντα ποιεῖν ὅσα τοὺς ἐξοί-
νους γινομένους. Ἀριστοτέλης δέ φησιν ὅτι οἱ μὲν ὑπ᾿
οἴνου μεθυσθέντες ἐπὶ πρόσωπον φέρονται, οἱ δὲ τὸν
κρίθινον πεπωκότες ἐξυπτιάζονται τὴν κεφαλήν· ὁ μὲν
γὰρ οἶνος καρηβαρικός, ὁ δὲ κρίθινος καρωτικός.

---

258 A disparaging response to the preceding speaker, who
must then be from Egypt? The Astydamas in question is
Astydamas II (*TrGF* 60; second half of the 4th century BCE). According to Pausanias Grammaticus σ 6 = Suda σ 161, when
Astydamas' *Parthenopaeus* took the prize at one of their dramatic
festivals, the Athenians ordered a statue of the poet erected in the
Theater of Dionysus and allowed him to write the epigram for it

You praise yourself, woman, as Astydamas did.
(Philem. fr. 160)[258]

Astydamas was a tragic poet.

Theopompus of Chios (*FGrH* 115 F 277) records that the vine was discovered in Olympia along the Alpheius river. He also reports that there is a spot in Elis eight stades from there, where the inhabitants at their Dionysia place lids on three empty bronze cauldrons in the presence of the visitors to the festival; seal them shut; and when they open them later, find them full of wine. But Hellanicus (*FGrH* 4 F 175) claims that the vine was discovered first in Plinthia, an Egyptian city. This is why, according to Dio from the Academy[259], the Egyptians became fond of wine and drinking. They also discovered a way to help those who were too poor to have any wine, by letting them drink barley-wine;[260] those who consume it enjoy it so much that they sing and dance and do everything people drunk on wine do. Aristotle (fr. 666)[261] says that individuals who get drunk on wine fall forward onto their face, whereas the heads of those who have drunk barley-wine fall backward, because wine makes the head heavy, whereas barley-wine is merely stupefying.

(*FGE* 115–18) himself; the tone is in fact immensely self-important.

[259] Plato's school. Dio belongs to the middle of the 1st century BCE, and the passage cited here probably comes ultimately from the records of dinner-table conversations referred to in passing at Plu. *Mor.* 612d–e.

[260] See 1.16c n.

[261] Cf. 10.447a–b, where the philosopher's remarks are reported more fully.

c   Ὅτι δὲ | φίλοινοι Αἰγύπτιοι, σημεῖον καὶ τὸ παρὰ μόνοις αὐτοῖς ὡς νόμιμον ἐν τοῖς δείπνοις πρὸ πάντων ἐδεσμάτων κράμβας ἔσθειν ἐφθὰς † μέχρι τοῦ δεῦρο παρασκευάζεσθαι †. καὶ πολλοὶ εἰς τὰς κατασκευαζομένας ἀμεθύστους προσλαμβάνουσι τὸ τῆς κράμβης σπέρμα. καὶ ἐν ᾧ δ᾽ ἂν ἀμπελῶνι κράμβαι φύωνται, ἀμαυρότερος ὁ οἶνος γίνεται. διὸ καὶ Συβαρῖται, φησὶ Τίμαιος, πρὸ τοῦ πίνειν κράμβας ἤσθιον. Ἄλεξις·

d   ἐχθὲς ὑπέπινες, εἶτα νυνὶ κραιπαλᾷς. |
   κατανύστασον· παύσῃ γάρ. εἶτά σοι δότω
   ῥάφανόν τις ἐφθήν.

Εὔβουλος δέ πού φησι·

                       γύναι,
   ῥάφανόν με νομίσασ᾽ εἰς ἐμέ σου τὴν κραιπάλην
   μέλλεις ἀφεῖναι πᾶσαν, ὡς ἐμοὶ δοκεῖς.

ὅτι δὲ τὴν κράμβην ῥάφανον ἐκάλουν οἱ παλαιοὶ Ἀπολλόδωρος δηλοῖ ὁ Καρύστιος·

   † εἰ δ᾽ ὅτι † καλοῦμεν ῥάφανον, ὑμεῖς δ᾽ οἱ ξένοι
   κράμβην, γυναιξὶ διαφέρειν † οἴονται †.

Ἀναξανδρίδης·

---

262 Referred to here as *krambē*, as also by Timaeus (below); the Attic word for the vegetable was *rhaphanos*. See the passages collected at 1.34d–e.

Further evidence that the Egyptians like wine is that they alone customarily eat boiled cabbage[262] before any other food at their dinner parties † to be prepared until today †.[263] Many people add cabbage seed to their concoctions designed to prevent getting drunk. And in any vineyard where cabbages grow, the wine is darker. According to Timaeus (*FGrH* 566 F 47), this is why the Sybarites used to eat cabbage before drinking. Alexis (fr. 287):

Yesterday you drank a bit, so now you've got a
    hangover.
Take a nap; that will put a stop to it. And then have
    someone
give you boiled cabbage (*rhaphanos*).

And Eubulus (fr. 124) says somewhere:

Woman,
you've apparently decided I'm a cabbage
    (*rhaphanos*), since
you're trying to shift your entire headache onto me.

That the ancients referred to cabbage (*krambē*) as *rhaphanos* is made clear by Apollodorus of Carystus (fr. 32):

† If because † we call it *rhaphanos*, but
you foreigners call it *krambē*, † they think it † makes
    a difference to women.

Anaxandrides (fr. 59):

[263] The final clause sits oddly with the rest of the sentence, and there has apparently been some disturbance in the text.

195

e   ἐὰν λούσησθε νῦν |
ῥάφανόν τε πολλὴν ἐντράγητε, παύσεται
τὸ βάρος, διασκεδᾷ τε τὸ προσὸν νῦν νέφος
ἐπὶ τοῦ μετώπου.

Νικοχάρης·

εἰς αὔριον <δ'> ἀντὶ ῥαφάνων ἑψήσομεν
βαλάνιον, ἵνα νῶν ἐξάγῃ τὴν κραιπάλην.

Ἄμφις·

οὐκ ἔστιν, ὡς ἔοικε, φάρμακον μέθης
οὐδὲν τοιοῦτον ὡς τὸ προσπεσεῖν ἄφνω
λύπην τιν'. οὕτως ἐξελαύνει γὰρ σφόδρα
† λῆρον ὥστε τὰς ῥαφάνους οὕτω δοκεῖν.

περὶ δὲ τῆς δυνάμεως ταύτης ἣν ἡ κράμβη ποιεῖ
ἱστορεῖ καὶ Θεόφραστος φεύγειν φάσκων καὶ ζῶσαν
τὴν ἄμπελον τῆς ῥαφάνου τὴν ὀδμήν.

> If you take a bath now
> and eat a lot of cabbage *(rhaphanos)*, the sluggishness
> will leave you, and the cloud that's currently
> on your brow will scatter.

Nicochares (fr. 18):

> Tomorrow, instead of cabbage *(rhaphanos)*, we'll
> make
> a little acorn stew[264] to take away our hangover.

Amphis (fr. 37):

> It appears that there's no cure for drunkenness
> as effective as having some unhappiness abruptly
> fall upon you. Because this banishes it so forcibly
> that it makes cabbage *(rhaphanos)* seem like †
> nonsense.

Regarding this power that cabbage *(krambē)* has, Theophrastus *(HP* 4.16.6) reports that as the vine grows, it tries to avoid the smell of cabbage *(rhaphanos)*.

---

[264] *balanion*, diminutive of *balanos* ("acorn, acorn-shaped object"). But the word is not attested elsewhere in this sense, and in medical contexts it refers to suppositories of various sorts.

ΕΚ ΤΟΥ ΔΕΥΤΕΡΟΥ ΒΙΒΛΙΟΥ

35   Τὸ πολὺ τῆς ἡμέρας προσεπιμετρεῖ τῷ ὕπνῳ.

Οὐκ εἴων με οἱ λόγοι, οὓς ἀπεμνημόνευσας, ὄντες
ποικίλοι ὕπνῳ διδόναι σχολήν.

Οὐκ ἀπὸ σκοποῦ τοξεύειν.[1]

Ὅτι τὸν οἶνον ὁ Κολοφώνιος Νίκανδρος ὠνομάσθαι φησὶν ἀπὸ Οἰνέως·

Οἰνεὺς δ᾽ ἐν κοίλοισιν ἀποθλίψας δεπάεσσιν
οἶνον ἔκλησε.

φησὶ δὲ καὶ Μελανιππίδης ὁ Μήλιος[2]·

ἐπώνυμον, δέσποτ᾽, οἶνον Οἰνέως.

b   Ἑκαταῖος δ᾽ ὁ Μιλήσιος τὴν ἄμπελον ἐν Αἰτωλίᾳ |
λέγων εὑρεθῆναί φησι καὶ τάδε· Ὀρεσθεὺς ὁ Δευκα-
λίωνος ἦλθεν εἰς Αἰτωλίαν ἐπὶ βασιλείᾳ, καὶ κύων

---

[1] This phrase is omitted by E and is preserved in C only in the
margin.   [2] Μήλιος 14.651f: μιλήσιος CE

---

[1] Perhaps a description of one of the dinner-guests, whose situation is distinguished from Timocrates' (below). But the verb
might also be taken as a 2nd-person singular middle ("You allow

FROM BOOK II

He devotes much of the day to sleep.[1]

These conversations you reported are so complex that they allowed me no leisure for sleep.[2]

Not to be shooting wide of the mark.[3]

Nicander of Colophon (fr. 86 Schneider) asserts that wine *(oinos)* gets its name from Oeneus:[4]

And Oeneus squeezed it into hollow goblets
and called it wine *(oinos)*.

Melanippides of Melos *(PMG* 761) as well says:

Wine *(oinos)*, master, named after Oeneus.

Hecataeus of Miletus *(FGrH* 1 F 15) claims that the grapevine was discovered in Aetolia, and adds the following: Orestheus the son of Deucalion came to Aetolia to claim

yourself to spend most of the day asleep"), in which case the character Athenaeus may be addressing Timocrates, who was up all night pondering what he had heard (see below) and has risen late.

2 Spoken by Timocrates, apparently on the day after the conversation reported in Book I.

3 For the expression, cf. 1.20b.

4 Oeneus (whose name is derived from *oinos* rather than the other way around) was the first mortal entrusted by Dionysus with the grapevine; see [Apollod.] *Bib.* 1.8.1; Hyg. *Fab.* 129.

αὑτοῦ στέλεχος ἔτεκε· καὶ ὃς ἐκέλευσεν αὐτὸ κατο-
ρυχθῆναι, καὶ ἐξ αὐτοῦ ἔφυ ἄμπελος πολυστάφυλος,
διὸ καὶ τὸν αὑτοῦ παῖδα Φύτιον ἐκάλεσε. τούτου δ᾽
Οἰνεὺς ἐγένετο κληθεὶς ἀπὸ τῶν ἀμπέλων· οἱ γὰρ
παλαιοί, φησίν, Ἕλληνες οἴνας ἐκάλουν τὰς ἀμπέλους. Οἰνέως δ᾽ ἐγένετο Αἰτωλός. Πλάτων δ᾽ ἐν Κρατύ-
c λῳ ἐτυμολογῶν τὸν οἶνον οἰόνουν αὐτόν φησιν εἶναι |
διὰ τὸ οἰήσεως ἡμῶν τὸν νοῦν ἐμπιπλᾶν. ἢ τάχα ἀπὸ
τῆς ὀνήσεως κέκληται· παρετυμολογῶν γὰρ Ὅμηρος
τὴν φωνὴν ὧδέ πώς φησιν·

< . . . > ἔπειτα δὲ καὐτὸς ὀνήσεαι, αἴ κε πίῃσθα.

καὶ γὰρ τὰ βρώματα ὀνείατα καλεῖν εἴωθεν ἀπὸ τοῦ
ὀνίσκειν ἡμᾶς.

οἶνόν τοι, Μενέλαε, θεοὶ ποίησαν ἄριστον
θνητοῖς ἀνθρώποισιν ἀποσκεδάσαι μελεδῶνας.

ὁ τῶν Κυπρίων τοῦτό φησι ποιητής, ὅστις ἂν εἴη.[3]
Δίφιλος δ᾽ ὁ κωμικός φησιν·

d ὦ πᾶσι τοῖς φρονοῦσι προσφιλέστατε |
Διόνυσε καὶ σοφώταθ᾽, ὡς ἡδύς τις εἶ·
ὃς τὸν ταπεινὸν μέγα φρονεῖν ποιεῖς μόνος,

---

[3] This sentence is omitted by E and is preserved in C only in
the margin.

---

[5] Hence the name of the region, Aetolia.

the kingship, and his dog gave birth to a root-clump. He ordered that it be buried, and a vine covered with grape-clusters grew *(ephu)* from it; this is why he called his son Phytius. Oeneus was Phytius' son and got his name from his grapevines; for the ancient Greeks, he says, referred to grapevines as *oinai* (e.g. Hes. *Op*. 572). Oeneus' son was Aetolus.[5] Plato in the *Cratylus* (406c) explains the origin of the word *oinos* by saying that it was originally *oionous*, because it fills our minds with false notions.[6] Or perhaps the word comes from *onēsis* ("benefit"); for Homer (*Il*. 6.260) alludes to its etymology when he says something like the following:

> Then you yourself too will get some benefit *(onēseai),*
>   if you drink.

He also tended to refer to food as *oneiata* (literally "benefits"; e.g. *Od*. 10.9), because it does us good *(oniskein).*

> The gods made wine, Menelaus, as the best means
> for mortal men to scatter their cares;

the author of the *Cypria* (fr. 17 Bernabé), whoever he might be, says this. And the comic poet Diphilus (fr. 86) says:

> O Dionysus, dearest and wisest in the eyes
> of all those who have any sense, how kind you are!
> You alone make the humble man proud

---

[6] As if *oionous* (whence allegedly *oinos*) were derived from *oiēsis* + *nous*. What Plato's Socrates actually asserts is that people who are drunk think *(oiomai)* that they have sense *(nous),* although they do not.

τὸν τὰς ὀφρῦς αἴροντα συμπείθεις γελᾶν,
τόν τ' ἀσθενῆ τολμᾶν τι, τὸν δειλὸν θρασύν.

ὁ δὲ Κυθήριος Φιλόξενος λέγει·

< . . . > εὐρείτας οἶνος πάμφωνος.

Χαιρήμων δὲ ὁ τραγῳδὸς παρασκευάζειν φησὶ τὸν
οἶνον τοῖς χρωμένοις

γέλωτα, σοφίαν, εὐμαθίαν[4], εὐβουλίαν.

e   Ἴων δ' ὁ Χῖός φησιν· |

ἄδαμνον
παῖδα ταυρωπόν, νέον οὐ νέον,
ἥδιστον πρόπολον βαρυ-
    γδούπων ἐρώτων,
    οἶνον ἀερσίνοον
ἀνθρώπων πρύτανιν.

36   <ὁ> Μνησίθεος δ' ἔφη ‖ τὸν οἶνον τοὺς θεοὺς
θνητοῖς καταδεῖξαι τοῖς μὲν ὀρθῶς χρωμένοις
ἀγαθὸν μέγιστον, τοῖς δ' ἀτάκτως τοὔμπαλιν.
τροφήν τε γὰρ δίδωσι τοῖς <εὖ> χρωμένοις
ἰσχύν τε ταῖς ψυχαῖσι καὶ τοῖς σώμασιν.

---

[4] εὐμαθίαν Wagner: ἀμαθίαν CE

---

[7] Literally "with raised eyebrows," a sign of arrogance; cf. Bato
fr. 5.13, quoted at 3.103d; anon. *FGE* 1752, quoted at 4.162a;
Olson on Ar. *Ach.* 1069–70.

and persuade the fellow with a haughty expression[7] to
    laugh,
the weak man to take a risk, and the coward to be
    bold.

Philoxenus of Cythera (*PMG* 831) says:

fair-flowing wine full of voices.

The tragic poet Chaeremon (*TrGF* 71 F 15) claims that
wine provides those who consume it with

laughter, wisdom, a quick wit, sound judgment.

And Ion of Chios (*PMG* 744) says:

                    Untamed
bull-faced child,[8] young but not young,
most pleasant servant of the
        loud-thundering love-gods,
    wine that cheers the mind and is
mankind's lord.

(Adesp. com. fr. 101):

Mnesitheus[9] said that the gods introduced
wine to mortals as the greatest good for those
who use it properly, but as the opposite for anyone
        who lacks discipline;
for it nourishes those who use it well
and strengthens their souls and their bodies.

---

[8] Cf. 2.38e with n., below.   [9] Mnesitheus of Athens
(*PAA* 656085; this passage = fr. 41 Bertier) was a mid-4th-century
"Dogmatic" physician who wrote on diaetetic subjects; Athenaeus
cites him at e.g. 1.22e, 32d; 2.54b, 57b.

εἰς τὴν ἰατρικήν τε χρησιμώτατον·
καὶ τοῖς ποτοῖς γὰρ φαρμάκοις κεράννυται,
καὶ τοῖσιν ἑλκωθεῖσιν ὠφελίαν ἔχει.
ἐν ταῖς συνουσίαις τε ταῖς καθ᾽ ἡμέραν

b   τοῖς μὲν μέτριον πίνουσι καὶ κεκραμένον |
εὐθυμίαν, ἐὰν δ᾽ ὑπερβάλῃς, ὕβριν,
ἐὰν δ᾽ ἴσον ἴσῳ προσφέρῃ, μανίαν ποεῖ·
ἐὰν δ᾽ ἄκρατον, παράλυσιν τῶν σωμάτων.

διὸ καὶ καλεῖσθαι τὸν Διόνυσον πανταχοῦ ἰατρόν. ἡ
δὲ Πυθία εἴρηκέ τισι Διόνυσον ὑγιάτην καλεῖν. Εὔβουλος δὲ ποιεῖ τὸν Διόνυσον λέγοντα·

τρεῖς γὰρ μόνους κρατῆρας ἐγκεραννύω
τοῖς εὖ φρονοῦσι· τὸν μὲν ὑγιείας ἕνα,

c   ὃν πρῶτον ἐκπίνουσι, τὸν δὲ δεύτερον |
ἔρωτος ἡδονῆς τε, τὸν τρίτον δ᾽ ὕπνου,
ὃν ἐκπιόντες οἱ σοφοὶ κεκλημένοι
οἴκαδε βαδίζουσ᾽. ὁ δὲ τέταρτος οὐκέτι
ἡμέτερός ἐστ᾽, ἀλλ᾽ ὕβρεως· ὁ δὲ πέμπτος βοῆς·
ἕκτος δὲ κώμων· ἕβδομος δ᾽ ὑπωπίων·
⟨ὁ δ᾽⟩ ὄγδοος κλητῆρος· ὁ δ᾽ ἔνατος χολῆς·
δέκατος δὲ μανίας, ὥστε καὶ βάλλειν ποεῖ

*   *   *

---

[10] Cf. the reference to Mnesitheus at 1.22e, to which, given the reference to Mnesitheus in the comic fragment cited above, this passage most likely also referred originally.

They also made it very useful for medicine,
because it can be mixed together with liquid drugs
and helps the wounded.
And in everyday get-togethers
it makes those who drink it mixed and in moderate
    amounts
happy; but if you drink too much, it produces ugly
    behavior.
If you consume it mixed one-to-one, it drives you
    crazy;
and if you drink it with no water at all, it paralyzes
    your body.

This is why Dionysus is universally referred to as a physician. The Pythia told certain people to address Dionysus as *Hygiatēs* ("Giver of Health").[10] Eubulus (fr. *93) represents Dionysus as saying:

Because I mix up only three bowls of wine for
sensible people. One is dedicated to good health,
and they drink it first. The second is dedicated
to love and pleasure, and the third to sleep;
wise guests finish it up
and go home. The fourth bowl no longer
belongs to me but to outrage. The fifth belongs to
    arguments;
the sixth to wandering drunk through the streets; the
    seventh to black eyes;
the eighth to the bailiff; the ninth to an ugly black
    humor;
and the tenth to madness extreme enough to make
    people throw stones.

*   *   *

πολὺς γὰρ εἰς ἓν μικρὸν ἀγγεῖον χυθεὶς
ὑποσκελίζει ῥᾷστα τοὺς πεπωκότας.

Ἐπίχαρμος δέ φησιν·

        (Α.) † ἐκ μὲν θυσίας θοίνα < . . . >,

d   ἐκ δὲ | θοίνας πόσις ἐγένετο. (Β.) χαρίεν, ὥς γ᾽
    ἐμοὶ <δοκεῖ>.
    (Α.) ἐκ δὲ πόσιος κῶμος, ἐκ κώμου δ᾽ ἐγένεθ᾽
      ὑανία,
    ἐκ δ᾽ ὑανίας δίκα, <᾽κ δίκας δ᾽ ἐγένετο
      καταδίκα>[5],
    ἐκ δὲ καταδίκας πέδαι τε καὶ σφαλὸς καὶ ζαμία.

Πανύασις δ᾽ ὁ ἐποποιὸς τὴν μὲν πρώτην πόσιν ἀπονέ-
μει Χάρισιν, Ὥραις καὶ Διονύσῳ, τὴν δὲ δευτέραν
Ἀφροδίτῃ καὶ πάλιν Διονύσῳ, Ὕβρει δὲ καὶ Ἄτῃ τὴν
τρίτην.[6] Πανύασίς φησι·

    πρῶται μὲν Χάριτές τ᾽ ἔλαχον καὶ εὔφρονες
      Ὧραι
    μοῖραν καὶ Διόνυσος ἐρίβρομος, οὗπερ ἔτευξαν.
    τοῖς δ᾽ ἔπι Κυπρογένεια θεὰ λάχε καὶ Διόνυσος.
    ἔνθα τε κάλλιστος πότος ἀνδράσι γίνεται οἴνου·
    εἴ τις <δίς> γε πίοι καὶ ὑπότροπος οἴκαδ᾽
      ἀπέλθοι

---

[5] suppl. Meineke   [6] The two quotations that follow and
the introductory material that accompanies them (Πανύασις . . .
ὀπηδεῖ) is preserved after the end of Book 13 in C and after the

For a great deal of wine poured into one little jar
easily knocks drunks' legs out from under them.

Epicharmus (fr. 146) says:

> (A.) † A sacrifice leads to a feast,
> and a feast leads to drinking. (B.) Sounds good to me,
>   at least!
> (A.) But drinking leads to wandering the streets
>   drunk, and wandering the streets drunk leads to
>   acting like a pig,
> and acting like a pig leads to a lawsuit, ‹and a lawsuit
>   leads to being found guilty,›
> and being found guilty leads to shackles, stocks, and a
>   fine.

The epic poet Panyasis assigns the first round of drinks to
the Graces, the Seasons, and Dionysus; the second to Aphrodite and Dionysus again; but the third to Outrage and
Folly. Panyasis (fr. 17 Bernabé) says:

> The first lot fell to the Graces, the cheerful Seasons,
>   and
> loud-roaring Dionysus, out of whom they made it.[11]
> After them the lot fell to the Cyprus-born goddess
>   and Dionysus.
> Up to this point, drinking wine is excellent for men;
> if someone drank twice and turned around and went
>   home

---

[11] I.e. the contents of the mixing-bowl that was their share.

---

end of Book 15 in E, and has been added here on the theory that it
must originally have stood somewhere in this section of Book 2.

δαιτὸς ἀπὸ γλυκερῆς, οὐκ ἄν ποτε πήματι
   κύρσαι·
ἀλλ' ὅτε τις μοίρης τριτάτης πρὸς μέτρον
   ἐλαύνοι
πίνων ἀβλεμέως, τότε δ' Ὕβριος αἶσα καὶ Ἄτης
γίνεται ἀργαλέη, κακὰ δ' ἀνθρώποισιν ὀπάζει.
ἀλλὰ πέπον—μέτρον γὰρ ἔχεις γλυκεροῖο
   ποτοῖο—
στεῖχε παρὰ μνηστὴν ἄλοχον, κοίμιζε δ'
   ἑταίρους·
δείδια γὰρ τριτάτης μοίρης μελιηδέος οἴνου
πινομένης, μή σ' Ὕβρις ἐνὶ φρεσὶ θυμὸν ἀέρσῃ,
ἐσθλοῖς δὲ ξενίοισι κακὴν ἐπιθῇσι τελευτήν.
ἀλλὰ πιθοῦ καὶ παῦε πολὺν πότον.

καὶ ἑξῆς περὶ ἀμέτρου οἴνου·

ἐκ γάρ οἱ Ἄτης τε καὶ Ὕβριος αἶσ' ⟨ἄμ'⟩
   ὀπηδεῖ.

κατὰ γὰρ τὸν Εὐριπίδην·

πληγὰς ὁ κῶμος λοίδορόν θ' ὕβριν[7] φέρει.

ὅθεν τινὲς τὴν Διονύσου γένεσιν καὶ τὴν τῆς Ὕβρεως
κατὰ ταὐτὰ γενέσθαι φασίν.

e   Ἄλεξις δέ πού φησιν ὡς |

---

[7] The traditional text of Euripides has πυγμὰς . . . λοιδορόν
τ' ἔριν.

from the pleasant feast, he would never meet with
    any harm.
But when a man proceeds to measure out a third
    portion,
drinking aggressively, then comes the painful turn of
    Outrage and
Folly, and it brings human beings trouble.
So then, my friend, since you've had a share of sweet
    drink,
go home to the woman you married, and let your
    companions go to sleep!
I'm afraid that, while the third share of wine sweet as
    honey
is being drunk, Outrage may excite your heart in your
    chest
and put an ugly end to our fine festivities.
But take my advice and stop drinking so much!

And immediately after this, on the topic of immense
amounts of wine (Panyas. fr. 18 Bernabé):

For the turn of Folly and Outrage follows next for
    him.

As Euripides (*Cyc.* 534) says:

Wandering the streets drunk produces blows, verbal
    abuse, and outrage.

This is why some authorities claim that Dionysus and Outrage were born at the same time.

    Alexis (fr. 46)[12] says somewhere that

---

[12] Identified by Stobaeus (who cites precisely the same verses)
as a fragment of *Demetrius or Philetaerus*.

ATHENAEUS

ὁμοιότατος ἄνθρωπος οἴνῳ τὴν φύσιν
τρόπον τιν᾽ ἐστί. τὸν γὰρ οἶνον τὸν νέον
πολλή 'στ᾽ ἀνάγκη καὶ τὸν ἄνδρ᾽ ἀποζέσαι
πρώτιστον ἀφυβρίσαι τ᾽, ἀπανθήσαντα δὲ
σκληρὸν γενέσθαι, παρακμάσαντα δ᾽ ὧν λέγω
τούτων ἁπάντων, ἀπαρυθέντα τὴν ἄνω
ταύτην ἄνοιαν ἐπιπολάζουσαν, τότε
πότιμον γενέσθαι καὶ καταστῆναι πάλιν
ἡδύν θ᾽ ἅπασι τοὐπίλοιπον διατελεῖν.

f κατὰ δὲ τὸν Κυρηναῖον ποιητήν· |

οἶνός τοι πυρὶ ἶσον ἔχει μένος, εὖτ᾽ ἂν ἐς ἄνδρας
    ἔλθῃ· κυμαίνει δ᾽, οἶα Λίβυσσαν ἅλα
βορρῆς ἠὲ νότος, τὰ δὲ ⟨καὶ⟩ κεκρυμμένα φαίνει
    βυσσόθεν, ἐκ δ᾽ ἀνδρῶν πάντ᾽ ἐτίναξε νόον.

ἀλλαχοῦ δὲ τοὐναντίον φησὶν Ἄλεξις·

οὐδὲν ⟨ . . . ⟩ ἔοικ᾽ ἄνθρωπος οἴνῳ τὴν φύσιν·
ὁ μὲν ἀπογηράσκων ἀηδὴς γίγνεται,
οἶνον δὲ τὸν παλαιότατον σπουδάζομεν·
ὁ μὲν δάκνει γάρ, ὁ δ᾽ ἱλαροὺς ἡμᾶς ποεῖ.

37 Πανύασις δὲ λέγει· ‖

οἶνος ⟨γὰρ⟩ πυρὶ ἶσον ἐπιχθονίοισιν ὄνειαρ

210

Human nature is, in a way,
a lot like wine. Because new wine
and a young man—there's no escaping it—boil
    intensely
at first and run wild. Then, when their bloom is off,
they turn sour. But when the peak years for all the
    tendencies
I'm talking about are over, and this foolishness has
    been
skimmed off the top of him, then
he becomes drinkable, settles down again,
and remains pleasant to everyone thereafter.

As the Cyrenean poet (Eratosth. fr. 36, p. 67 Powell)
puts it:

Wine is in fact as strong as fire, when men go head-
    to-head
    with it. It whirls them around, as the north or
      south wind
does the Libyan sea; and it reveals what is hidden
    in their depths and shakes all the sense out of
      men.

But elsewhere Alexis (fr. 280) says the opposite:

Human nature's not at all like wine.
When a man gets old, he becomes unpleasant,
whereas we're eager to have the oldest wine;
because an old man causes grief, but old wine makes
    us cheerful.

Panyasis (fr. 16.12–15, 17–19 Bernabé) says:

For wine benefits men on earth as much as fire does:

ἐσθλόν, ἀλεξίκακον, πάσῃ συνοπηδὸν ἀνίῃ.
ἐν μὲν γὰρ θαλίης ἐρατὸν μέρος ἀγλαΐης τε,
ἐν δὲ χοροιτυπίης, ἐν δ' ἱμερτῆς φιλότητος.

        *   *   *

τῷ σε χρὴ παρὰ δαιτὶ δεδεγμένον εὔφρονι θυμῷ
πίνειν, μηδὲ βορῆς κεκορημένον ἠΰτε παῖδα[8]
ἧσθαι πλημύροντα, λελησμένον εὐφροσυνάων.

καὶ πάλιν·

b   <ὡς> οἶνος θνητοῖσι θεῶν πάρα δῶρον ἄριστον |
ἀγλαός· ᾧ πᾶσαι μὲν ἐφαρμόζουσιν ἀοιδαί,
πάντες δ' ὀρχηθμοί, πᾶσαι δ' ἐραταὶ φιλότητες.
πάσας δ' ἐκ κραδίης ἀνίας ἀνδρῶν ἀλαπάζει
πινόμενος κατὰ μέτρον· ὑπὲρ μέτρον δὲ χερείων.

Τίμαιος δὲ ὁ Ταυρομενίτης ἐν Ἀκράγαντι οἰκίαν
τινά φησι καλεῖσθαι Τριήρη ἐξ αἰτίας τοιαύτης. νεανίσκους τινὰς ἐν αὐτῇ μεθυσκομένους ἐς τοσοῦτον
c ἐλθεῖν μανίας ἐκθερμανθέντας ὑπὸ τῆς | μέθης ὡς
νομίζειν μὲν ἐπὶ τριήρους πλεῖν, χειμάζεσθαι δὲ χαλεπῶς κατὰ τὴν θάλασσαν· καὶ τοσοῦτον ἔκφρονας
γενέσθαι ὡς τὰ ἀπὸ τῆς οἰκίας πάντα σκεύη καὶ
στρώματα ῥίπτειν ὡς εἰς τὴν θάλασσαν, τὴν ναῦν διὰ
τὸν χειμῶνα ἀποφορτίζεσθαι δόξαν αὑτοῖς λέγειν τὸν
κυβερνήτην. συναθροιζομένων οὖν πολλῶν καὶ τὰ

---

[8] Stobaeus (who preserves the entire fragment) has γῦπα
("vulture") for Athenaeus' παῖδα.

it's good, keeps trouble away, and is by one's side in
    any sort of grief.
Lovely feasting and splendor belong partially to its
    sphere,
as does choral dancing and the love-making we long
    for.

*   *   *

Therefore you should make a toast at the feast with a
    happy heart
and drink, and not sit there like a child, sated and
stuffed full of food, oblivious to the good time
    going on.

And again (Panyas. fr. 19 Bernabé):

that wine is the gods' best gift to mortals,
shining wine. All songs go well with it,
and all dances, and all sensuous love-making.
It drains all the troubles from men's hearts
when drunk in moderation; but in excess it is not so
    good.

Timaeus of Tauromenium (*FGrH* 566 F 149) reports
that there is a house in Acragas referred to as the Trireme
for the following reason. Some young men were getting
drunk inside; and their drunkenness made them so fever-
ishly crazy that they thought they were sailing on a trireme
and had run into a terrible storm at sea. They were so out
of their minds that they started throwing all the furniture
and bedding out of the house, thinking that they were
throwing it into the sea because the pilot was telling them
that the ship's cargo needed to be jettisoned on account of
the storm. And even though a crowd began to gather and

ῥιπτόμενα διαρπαζόντων οὐδ᾽ ὡς παύεσθαι τῆς μανίας τοὺς νεανίσκους. καὶ τῇ ἐπιούσῃ τῶν ἡμερῶν παρα-
γενομένων τῶν στρατηγῶν ἐπὶ τὴν οἰκίαν ἐγκληθέντες

d   οἱ | νεανίσκοι ἔτι ναυτιῶντες ἀπεκρίναντο πυνθανομέ-
νων τῶν ἀρχόντων ὑπὸ χειμῶνος ἐνοχλούμενοι ἠναγ-
κάσθαι ἀποφορτίσασθαι τῇ θαλάσσῃ τὰ περιττὰ τῶν
φορτίων. θαυμαζόντων δὲ τῶν στρατηγῶν τὴν ἔκ-
πληξιν τῶν ἀνδρῶν εἷς τῶν νεανίσκων, καίτοι δοκῶν
τῶν ἄλλων πρεσβεύειν κατὰ τὴν ἡλικίαν, "ἐγὼ δ᾽,"
ἔφη, "ἄνδρες Τρίτωνες, ὑπὸ τοῦ δέους καταβαλὼν
ἐμαυτὸν ὑπὸ τοὺς θαλάμους ὡς ἔνι μάλιστα κατωτάτω
ἐκείμην." συγγνόντες οὖν τῇ αὐτῶν ἐκστάσει ἐπιτιμή-

e   σαντες μὴ πλείονος οἴνου | ἐμφορεῖσθαι ἀφῆκαν. καὶ
οἱ χάριν ἔχειν ὁμολογήσαντες ⟨ . . . ⟩ "ἂν λιμένος,"
ἔφη, "τύχωμεν ἀπαλλαγέντες τοσούτου κλύδωνος, Σω-
τῆρας ὑμᾶς ἐπιφανεῖς μετὰ τῶν θαλασσίων δαιμόνων
ἐν τῇ πατρίδι ἱδρυσόμεθα ὡς αἰσίως ἡμῖν ἐπιφα-
νέντας." ἐντεῦθεν ἡ οἰκία Τριήρης ἐκλήθη.

Φιλόχορος δέ φησιν ὅτι οἱ πίνοντες οὐ μόνον
ἑαυτοὺς ἐμφανίζουσιν οἵτινές εἰσιν, ἀλλὰ καὶ τῶν
ἄλλων ἕκαστον ἀνακαλύπτουσι παρρησίαν ἄγοντες.
ὅθεν

οἶνος ⟨ . . . ⟩ καὶ ἀλαθέα

f   λέγεται καὶ |

   ⟨ . . . ⟩ ἀνδρὸς δ᾽ ⟨οἶνος⟩ ἔδειξε νόον,

καὶ τὸ νικητήριον ἐν Διονύσου τρίπους· καὶ γὰρ ἐκ

214

steal the items being thrown out, the young men continued to act crazily. The next day the city's chief officials[13] came to the house, and a charge was issued against the young men, who were still seasick; when the magistrates questioned them, they responded that a storm had caused them trouble and forced them to jettison their excess cargo into the sea. When the officials expressed astonishment at their lunacy, one of the young men, who seemed in fact to be older than the others, said: "Triton sirs,[14] I was so afraid, that I had thrown myself under the third course of rowing benchs, since that seemed like the lowest part of the ship, and was lying there." They therefore forgave them for their craziness, ordered them not to consume any more wine, and let them go; and the young men expressing their gratitude . . . "If," he said, "we escape this rough sea and reach a harbor, we will set up altars in our fatherland to you, along with the other sea-divinities, as manifest Savior gods, since you revealed yourselves to us at a crucial moment." The house therefore came to be referred to as the Trireme.

Philochorus (*FGrH* 328 F 170) says that drinkers not only show who they really are themselves, but also reveal other people's secrets by speaking freely. Hence the sayings (Alc. fr. 366.1)

wine and truth

and (Thgn. 500)

Wine reveals a man's mind,

and the fact that the victory monument set up in Dionysus'

---

[13] Literally "generals."   [14] As if he were addressing sea-gods who had suddenly appeared.

τρίποδος λέγειν φαμὲν τοὺς ἀληθεύοντας. δεῖ δὲ νοεῖν
τρίποδα τοῦ Διονύσου τὸν κρατῆρα· ἦν γὰρ τὸ ἀρχαῖον δύο γένη τριπόδων, οὓς καλεῖσθαι λέβητας
συνέβαινεν ἀμφοτέρους· ἐμπυριβήτης ὁ καὶ λοετρο-
χόος. Αἰσχύλος·

> τὸν μὲν τρίπους ἐδέξατ᾽ οἰκεῖος λέβης
> αἰεὶ φυλάσσων τὴν ὑπὲρ πυρὸς στάσιν. ‖

38

ὁ δ᾽ ἕτερος κρατὴρ καλούμενος. Ὅμηρος·

> ἕπτ᾽ ἀπύρους τρίποδας.

ἐν τούτοις δὲ τὸν οἶνον ἐκίρνων· καὶ οὗτός ἐστιν ὁ τῆς
ἀληθείας οἰκεῖος τρίπους. διὸ Ἀπόλλωνος μὲν οἰκεῖος
διὰ τὴν ἐκ μαντικῆς ἀλήθειαν, Διονύσου δὲ διὰ τὴν ἐν
μέθῃ. Σῆμος δ᾽ ὁ Δήλιός φησι· τρίπους χαλκοῦς, οὐχ
ὁ Πυθικός, ἀλλ᾽ ὃν νῦν λέβητα καλοῦσιν. οὗτοι δ᾽
ἦσαν οἱ μὲν ἄπυροι, εἰς οὓς τὸν οἶνον εἰσεκεράννυον,
οἱ δὲ λοετροχόοι, ἐν οἷς τὸ ὕδωρ ἐθέρμαινον, καὶ
ἐμπυριβῆται. καὶ τούτων | ἔνιοι ὠτώεντες, τρίποδα δὲ
τὴν ὑπόβασιν ἔχοντες τρίποδες ὠνομάζοντο. φησί
που Ἔφιππος·

> (Α.) οἴνου σε πλῆθος πόλλ᾽ ἀναγκάζει λαλεῖν.

b

---

15 But the point is clearly that tripods of this sort were normally placed on the fire and were thus of the same sort as those
mentioned by Aeschylus (above).

16 The Pythia, Apollo's priestess at his oracular shrine in Delphi, is sometimes represented sitting in a tripod.

temple is a tripod. For we say that those who speak the truth are "speaking from a tripod"; and it must be recognized that the mixing-bowl is Dionysus' tripod. Because in the old days there were two types of tripods, both of which happened to be referred to as cauldrons *(lebētes)*. The type used for heating bathwater went on the fire. Aeschylus (fr. *1):

> The three-legged household cauldron *(lebēs)*, which always
> stays in its spot over the fire, received him.

The other type was the so-called *kratēr* ("mixing-bowl"). Homer (*Il.* 9.122):

> seven tripods never placed over a fire.[15]

They mixed wine in this type, which is also the tripod associated with truth. This is why it is associated both with Apollo, because of the truth that comes from prophecy,[16] and with Dionysus, because of the truth discovered in drunkenness. Semus of Delos (*FGrH* 396 F 16) says: a bronze tripod, not the Delphic tripod, but what they refer to nowadays as a cauldron *(lebēs)*. Some of these did not go over a fire, but were used for mixing wine; others were for bathwater, which was warmed up in them, and went over the fire. Some also had handles;[17] and because they had a three-legged base, they were called tripods. Ephippus (fr. 25) says somewhere:

> (A.) All the wine you've drunk is making you

[17] Literally "ears."

(B.) οὐκοῦν μεθύοντάς φασι τἀληθῆ λέγειν.

Ἀντιφάνης·

κρύψαι, Φειδία,
ἄπαντα τἆλλά τις δύναιτ' ἂν πλὴν δυοῖν,
οἶνόν τε πίνων εἰς ἔρωτά τ' ἐμπεσών.

c   ἀμφότερα μηνύει γὰρ ἀπὸ τῶν βλεμμάτων |
καὶ τῶν λόγων ταῦθ'· ὥστε τοὺς ἀρνουμένους
μάλιστα τούτους καταφανεῖς ποεῖ.

Φιλόχορος δέ φησιν Ἀμφικτύονα τὸν Ἀθηναίων
βασιλέα μαθόντα παρὰ Διονύσου τὴν τοῦ οἴνου
κρᾶσιν πρῶτον κεράσαι· διὸ καὶ ὀρθοὺς γενέσθαι τοὺς
ἀνθρώπους οὕτω πίνοντας, πρότερον ὑπὸ τοῦ ἀκράτου
καμπτομένους. καὶ διὰ τοῦτο ἱδρύσασθαι βωμὸν Ὀρ-
θοῦ Διονύσου ἐν τῷ τῶν Ὡρῶν ἱερῷ· αὗται γὰρ καὶ
τὸν τῆς ἀμπέλου καρπὸν ἐκτρέφουσι. πλησίον δ' αὐ-
d τοῦ καὶ ταῖς νύμφαις | βωμὸν ἔδειμεν, ὑπόμνημα τοῖς
χρωμένοις τῆς κράσεως ποιούμενος· καὶ γὰρ Διονύσου τροφοὶ αἱ νύμφαι λέγονται. καὶ θέσμιον ἔθετο
προσφέρεσθαι μετὰ τὰ σιτία ἄκρατον μόνον ὅσον
γεύσασθαι, δεῖγμα τῆς δυνάμεως τοῦ Ἀγαθοῦ Θεοῦ,
τὸ δὲ λοιπὸν ἤδη κεκραμένον, ὁπόσον ἕκαστος βούλε-

---

[18] Quoted again, in slightly different form, at 15.693d–e.
[19] Cf. the more complete account at 5.179e.
[20] Because nymphs are frequently associated with springs and rivers.

talkative.

(B.) Well, they say that drunks speak the truth.

Antiphanes (fr. 232):

A man can conceal
anything else, Pheidias, but there are two things he
    can't:
that he's drinking wine and that he's fallen in love.
Because both conditions betray themselves from the
    expression on his face
and the words he speaks; in the end those who
    deny it
are the ones they most obviously convict.

Philochorus (*FGrH* 328 F 5b[18]) says that Amphictyon
the king of Athens learned how to mix wine from Dionysus
and was the first person to do this. As a result, when people
drank wine this way, they stood up straight, whereas before
they were doubled over from drinking it undiluted. This is
also why he established an altar of Upright Dionysus in the
sacred precinct of the Seasons,[19] because they cause the
grapes to mature. Close to this he built an altar to the
nymphs, to remind those who consume wine to mix it;[20]
and in fact the nymphs are said to be Dionysus' nurses (e.g.
h.Hom. 26.3–5). He also made it a custom that, after the
food, we drink just enough unmixed wine to get a taste, as a
demonstration of the Good Divinity's[21] power; and that, after that, the wine is drunk mixed and everyone has as much

---

[21] For the Good Divinity (here presumably to be identified
with Dionysus), e.g. Ar. *Eq.* 85; Nicostr. Com. fr. 19 (quoted at
15.693b); Antiph. fr. 135.

ται· προσεπιλέγειν δὲ τούτῳ τὸ τοῦ Διὸς Σωτῆρος
ὄνομα διδαχῆς καὶ μνήμης ἕνεκα τῶν πινόντων, ὅτι
οὕτω πίνοντες ἀσφαλῶς σωθήσονται. Πλάτων δ᾽ ἐν
e δευτέρῳ Νόμων τὴν τοῦ οἴνου χρῆσίν φησιν ὑγιείας |
ἕνεκα ὑπάρχειν.

Ἀπὸ τοῦ κατὰ μέθην δὲ καταστήματος καὶ ταύρῳ
παρεικάζουσι τὸν Διόνυσον καὶ παρδάλει διὰ τὸ πρὸς
βίαν τρέπεσθαι τοὺς ἐξοινωθέντας. Ἀλκαῖος·

    ἄλλοτα μὲν μελιάδεος, ἄλλοτα
        δ᾽ ὀξυτέρω τριβόλων ἀρυτήμενοι.

εἰσὶ δ᾽ οἳ καὶ θυμικοὶ γίνονται· τοιοῦτος δ᾽ ὁ ταῦρος.
Εὐριπίδης·

f   ταῦροι δ᾽ ὑβρισταὶ κἀς κέρας θυμούμενοι. |

διὰ δὲ τὸ μάχιμον καὶ θηριώδεις ἔνιοι γίνονται· ὅθεν
καὶ τὸ παρδαλῶδες.

Καλῶς οὖν Ἀρίστων ὁ Κεῖός φησιν ἥδιστον ποτὸν
εἶναι τὸν ἅμα μὲν γλυκύτητος, ἅμα δ᾽ εὐωδίας κοινω-
νοῦντα. διὸ καὶ τὸ καλούμενον νέκταρ κατασκευάζειν
τινὰς περὶ τὸν Λυδίας Ὄλυμπον οἶνον καὶ κηρία
39 συγκιρνάντας εἰς ταὐτὰ καὶ τὰ τῶν ἀνθῶν εὐώδη. ||
οἶδα δ᾽ ὅτι Ἀναξανδρίδης τὸ νέκταρ οὐ ποτόν, ἀλλὰ
τροφὴν εἶναι λέγει θεῶν·

                    τὸ νέκταρ ἐσθίω πάνυ

as he wants. And also that we pronounce the name of Zeus the Savior over the mixed wine, so that those who are drinking can learn the name and remember that, if they drink this way, their safety is assured. Plato in Book II of the *Laws* (674b) says that we drink wine for our health.

They compare Dionysus to a bull[22] because of the condition drunks are in, and to a leopard because those who consume too much wine are prone to violence. Alcaeus (fr. 369):

> sometimes drawing themselves wine sweet as honey,
>   at other times some with a bite harsher than
>   brambles.

Some people become quarrelsome; this is what a bull is like. Euripides (*Ba.* 743):

> bulls that were violent, with anger in their horns.

And because they like to fight, some become like wild animals; hence the comparison to a leopard.

Ariston of Chios (fr. 23 Wehrli) was therefore right to say that the most pleasant drink combines sweetness and a fine bouquet, and that this is why the people who live around Mount Olympus in Lydia prepare what they refer to as nectar by mixing wine and honeycomb together with sweet-smelling flowers. I am aware that Anaxandrides (fr. 58) refers to nectar not as what the gods drink, but as what they eat:[23]

I wolf down the nectar

---

[22] E.g. S. fr. 959.2; E. *Ba.* 100; and cf. Ion *PMG* 744.2 (quoted at 2.35e).   [23] Ganymede is speaking.

μάττων διαπίνω τ' ἀμβροσίαν καὶ τῷ Διὶ
διακονῶ καὶ σεμνός εἰμ' ἑκάστοτε
Ἥρᾳ λαλῶν καὶ Κύπριδι παρακαθήμενος.

καὶ Ἀλκμὰν δέ φησι τὸ

< . . . > νέκταρ ἔδμεναι

αὐτούς. καὶ Σαπφὼ δέ φησιν·

      ἀμβροσίας μὲν
κράτηρ ἐκέκρατ',
     Ἔρμαις δ' ἔλων ὄλπιν θέοισ' ἐοινοχόησε. |

b

ὁ δ' Ὅμηρος θεῶν πόμα τὸ νέκταρ οἶδεν. Ἴβυκος δέ
φησι τὴν ἀμβροσίαν τοῦ μέλιτος κατ' ἐπίτασιν ἐννεα-
πλασίαν ἔχειν γλυκύτητα, τὸ μέλι λέγων ἔνατον εἶναι
μέρος τῆς ἀμβροσίας κατὰ τὴν ἡδονήν.

οὐδεὶς φιλοπότης ἐστὶν ἄνθρωπος κακός.
ὁ γὰρ διμάτωρ Βρόμιος οὐ χαίρει συνὼν
ἀνδράσι πονηροῖς οὐδ' ἀπαιδεύτῳ βίῳ,

φησὶν Ἄλεξις, καὶ ὅτι οἶνος φιλολόγους πάντας ποιεῖ
τοὺς πλείονα πίνοντας αὐτόν. ὁ δὲ ποιήσας τὸ | εἰς
Κρατῖνον ἐπίγραμμά φησιν·

οἶνός τοι χαρίεντι πέλει μέγας ἵππος ἀοιδῷ,

c

---

[24] See 1.21b n.

as I knead it, and drink up the ambrosia, and provide
personal services to Zeus; and I routinely act haughty
as I chat with Hera and sit beside Cypris.

Alcman (*PMG* 42) too says that they

eat nectar.

And Sappho (fr. 141.1–3)[24] says:

a bowl of ambrosia
had been mixed up,
and Hermes picked up a vessel and poured wine
for the gods.

But Homer knows nectar as what the gods drink (e.g. *Il.*
1.598). Ibycus (*PMG* 325) asserts that ambrosia is in its in-
tensity nine times as sweet as honey, when he says that in
the pleasure it provides, honey is a ninth-share of ambrosia.

No one who likes to drink is a bad person;
because the two-mothered Bromius[25] does not enjoy
spending time
with nasty people or unrefined ways,

says Alexis (fr. 285), adding that wine makes anyone who
drinks a lot of it talkative. The author of the epigram on
Cratinus (Nicaen. *AP* 13.29 = *HE* 2711–16 = Cratin. test.
45) says:

Wine is a mighty steed for a witty bard;

[25] Referring to the fact that, when Dionysus' mother Semele
was killed while he was still in her womb, he was sewn up temporarily for safekeeping in Zeus' thigh (e.g. E. *Ba.* 88–98).

ὕδωρ δὲ πίνων χρηστὸν οὐδὲν ἂν τέκοις.
ταῦτ' ἔλεγεν, Διόνυσε, καὶ ἔπνεεν οὐχ ἑνὸς ἀσκοῦ
    Κρατῖνος, ἀλλὰ παντὸς ὠδώδει πίθου.
τοιγαροῦν στεφάνων δόμος ἔβρυεν, εἶχε δὲ
    κισσῷ
μέτωπον οἷα καὶ σὺ κεκροκωμένον.

Πολέμων φησὶν ἐν Μουνυχίᾳ ἥρωα Ἀκρατοπότην τι-
μᾶσθαι, παρὰ δὲ Σπαρτιάταις Μάττωνα καὶ Κεράωνα
d ἥρωας ὑπό τινων μαγείρων ἱδρῦσθαι ἐν τοῖς | φειδιτί-
οις. τιμᾶται δὲ καὶ ἐν Ἀχαίᾳ Δειπνεὺς ἀπὸ τῶν δείπνων σχὼν τὴν προσηγορίαν.

    Ἐκ τροφῆς ξηρᾶς
            οὔτ' ἂν σκώμματα
    γένοιτ' ⟨ἂν⟩ οὔτ' αὐτοσχέδια ποιήματα,

ἀλλὰ μὴν οὐδὲ κόμπος οὐδὲ ψυχῆς ἀλαζονεία. καλῶς
οὖν ἐν τῷ πῆ ἔβαν εὐχωλαὶ ἃς ἐν Λήμνῳ ἠγοράασθε,
ἔσθοντες κρέα πολλὰ καὶ πίνοντες οἴνου κρατῆρας
ἐπιστεφέας ἐπεσημήνατο ὁ γραμματικὸς Ἀρίσταρχος
e περιγράφων | τὸν στίχον, ὃς περὶ κρεοφαγίας αὐχεῖν
ποιεῖ τοὺς Ἕλληνας· οὐ γὰρ ἀπὸ πάσης εὐθυμίας καὶ
πληρώσεως τὸ καυχᾶσθαι καὶ σκώπτειν καὶ γελοι-
άζειν, ἀπὸ δὲ τῆς ἀλλοιούσης τὴν γνώμην καὶ πρὸς τὸ
ψευδὲς τρεπούσης, ἣ γίνεται κατὰ τὴν μέθην. διὸ

---

[26] This verse = Cratin. fr. *203 (dubiously assigned to *Wine-flask*).
[27] Cf. Demetrius of Scepsis fr. 10 Gaede, quoted at 4.173f.

but if you drink water, you could never produce
anything good.[26]
This is what Cratinus used to say, Dionysus; and his
breath didn't smell
of just one sack of wine, but reeked of the whole
cask.
That's why his house was full of victory garlands, and
his head
was wrapped with yellowish ivy, like yours.

Polemon (fr. 40 Preller) claims that a hero named Akra-
topotēs ("Drinker of Unmixed Wine") is worshipped in
Munychia, and that in Sparta some cooks erected altars
in the public messes to the heroes Mattōn ("Kneader")
and Keraōn ("Mixer").[27] And in Achaea they worship Dei-
pneus, whose name is derived from *deipna* ("dinner parties").

From dry food (adesp. com. fr. *102)
could arise neither
jokes nor improvised verses,

and certainly no bragging or bombastic spirits. In the passage (*Il.* 8.229–32, condensed) "Where did those boasts go
that you made on Lemnos, as you ate much meat and drank
mixing-bowls filled to the brim with wine?", the grammarian Aristarchus is right to add a marginal note marking the
line (*Il.* 8.231) that represents the Greeks as boasting because they eat meat as spurious. For boastfulness, mock-
ery, and laughter are not the product of every sort of good
cheer and satiety, but of the kind that alters the way one
looks at the world and inclines one to lie, which is what
happens when one gets drunk. This is why Bacchylides (fr.

225

Βακχυλίδης φησί·

           γλυκεῖ' ἀνάγκα
σευομενᾶν κυλίκων θάλπησι θυμόν,
Κύπριδος τ' ἐλπὶς διαιθύσσηι φρένας

f   ἀμμειγνυμένα Διονυσίοισι δώροις· |
ἀνδράσι δ' ὑψοτάτω πέμπει μερίμνας·
αὐτίκα μὲν πολίων κράδεμνα λύει,
πᾶσι δ' ἀνθρώποις μοναρχήσειν δοκεῖ·
χρυσῷ δ' ἐλέφαντί τε μαρμαίρουσιν οἶκοι,
πυροφόροι δὲ κατ' αἰγλάεντα ⟨πόντον⟩
νᾶες ἄγουσιν ἀπ' Αἰγύπτου μέγιστον
πλοῦτον· ὣς πίνοντος ὁρμαίνει κέαρ.

40 Σοφοκλῆς δέ φησι· ‖

   ⟨ . . . ⟩ τὸ μεθύειν πημονῆς λυτήριον.

οἱ δ' ἄλλοι ποιηταί φασι τὸν

   ⟨ . . . ⟩ οἶνον εὔφρονα, καρπὸν ἀρούρης.

καὶ ὁ τῶν ποιητῶν δὲ βασιλεὺς τὸν Ὀδυσσέα παράγει
λέγοντα·

   ὃς δέ κ' ἀνὴρ οἴνοιο κορεσσάμενος καὶ ἐδωδῆς
   ⟨   . . .   ⟩ πανημέριος πολεμίζῃ,
   θαρσαλέον νύ οἱ ἦτορ,

καὶ τὰ ἑξῆς.

   Ὅτι Σιμωνίδης τὴν αὐτὴν ἀρχὴν τίθησιν οἴνου καὶ
μουσικῆς.[9] ἀπὸ μέθης καὶ ἡ τῆς κωμῳδίας καὶ ἡ τῆς

*20b.6–16) says:

> A sweet compulsion
> warms the heart when the cups move quickly,
> and hope of Cypris, mixed up with
> Dionysus' gifts, rushes through the mind
> and sends men's thoughts sky-high.
> It immediately strips cities of their battlements,
> and everyone thinks that he is going to be king.
> Houses glitter with gold and ivory,
> and ships laden with wheat bring
> immense wealth over the shining sea
> from Egypt. This is how a man thinks when he's
>> drinking.

Sophocles (fr. 758) says:

> Being drunk is a release from pain.

Other poets refer to the

> cheerful wine, crop of the field. (*Il.* 3.246)

And the king of poets introduces Odysseus saying (*Il.* 19.167–9):

> Whenever a man is full of wine and food
> . . .   and wages war all day long,
> his heart is still confident,

and so forth.

Simonides (*PMG* 647) claims that wine and music originated together. Drunkenness also resulted in the inven-

---

9 This sentence is omitted by E and is preserved in C only in the margin.

b τραγῳδίας εὕρεσις ἐν Ἰκαρίῳ τῆς Ἀττικῆς | εὑρέθη,
καὶ κατ᾽ αὐτὸν τὸν τῆς τρύγης καιρόν· ἀφ᾽ οὗ δὴ καὶ
τρυγῳδία τὸ πρῶτον ἐκλήθη ἡ κωμῳδία.

> τὴν παυσίλυπον ἄμπελον δοῦναι βροτοῖς.
> οἴνου δὲ μηκέτ᾽ ὄντος οὐκ ἔστιν Κύπρις
> οὐδ᾽ ἄλλο τερπνὸν οὐδὲν ἀνθρώποις ἔτι,

Εὐριπίδης ἐν Βάκχαις φησί. καὶ Ἀστυδάμας δέ φησι·

> θνητοῖσι τὴν ἀκεσφόρον
> λύπης ἔφηνεν οἰνομήτορ᾽ ἄμπελον.

c συνεχῶς μὲν ἐμπιμπλάμενος | ἀμελὴς γίνεται
ἄνθρωπος, ὑποπίνων δὲ πάνυ φροντιστικός,

Ἀντιφάνης φησίν.

> οὐχὶ μεθύω τὴν φρόνησιν, ἀλλὰ τὸ τοιοῦτον
>   μόνον,
> τὸ διορίζεσθ᾽ ⟨οὐ⟩ βεβαίως τῷ στόματι τὰ
>   γράμματα,

φησὶν Ἄλεξις.

Σέλευκος δέ φησι τὸ παλαιὸν οὐκ εἶναι ἔθος οὔτ᾽
οἶνον ἐπὶ πλεῖον οὔτ᾽ ἄλλην ἡδυπάθειαν προσφέρεσθαι, μὴ θεῶν ἕνεκα τοῦτο δρῶντας. διὸ καὶ θοίνας

---

[28] Both Susarion (who is supposed to have produced the first
comedies) and Thespis (who is supposed to have produced the
first tragedies) are associated with the deme Icarion, which was lo-

tion of comedy and tragedy in Icarion in Attica[28] around the time of the grape-harvest *(trugē)*. As a consequence, comedy was originally referred to as "trugedy."[29]

> He gave mortals the vine that puts an end to pain.
> If there is no wine, there is no longer Cypris[30]
> nor any other pleasure for human beings,

says Euripides in *Bacchae* (772–4). Astydamas (*TrGF* 60 F 6) too says:

> > He revealed to mortals the grapevine,
> > mother of wine and a cure for their grief.

> If someone constantly fills himself with wine, he grows
> careless; but if he drinks only a little, he grows quite thoughtful,

says Antiphanes (fr. 268).

> I'm not so drunk that I can't think; I'm just drunk enough
> that my mouth doesn't pronounce the letters clearly,

says Alexis (fr. 304).

Seleucus (fr. 78 Müller) claims that in the old days it was not the custom to indulge excessively in wine or any other luxury, except in honor of the gods. This is why they

cated on the north slope of Mount Pentelicon not far from Marathon.

[29] The word (which puns on "tragedy") and its cognates are used occasionally by the late 5th-century comic poets (Ar. *Ach.* 499 with Olson ad loc.), but are not attested earlier.

[30] Cf. 2.39e n.

καὶ θαλείας[10] ὠνόμαζον· τὰς μὲν ὅτι διὰ θεοὺς οἰνοῦ-
σθαι δεῖν ὑπελάμβανον, τὰς δ᾽ ὅτι θεῶν χάριν ἠλί-
d ζοντο καὶ συνῄεσαν. | τοῦτο γάρ ἐστι τὸ "δαῖτα θά-
λειαν". τὸ δὲ μεθύειν φησὶν Ἀριστοτέλης τὸ μετὰ τὸ
θύειν αὐτῷ χρῆσθαι.

θεοῖσι μικρὰ θύοντας τέλη
τῶν βουθυτούντων ὄντας εὐσεβεστέρους,

Εὐριπίδης φησί. καὶ σημαίνει ὧδε τὸ τέλος τὴν θυ-
σίαν. καὶ Ὅμηρος·

οὐ γὰρ ἔγωγέ τί φημι τέλος χαριέστερον εἶναι
ἢ ὅταν εὐφροσύνη μὲν ἔχῃ κατὰ δῆμον ἅπαντα.[11]

e τελετάς τε καλοῦμεν τὰς ἔτι μείζους καὶ μετὰ | τινος
μυστικῆς παραδόσεως ἑορτὰς τῶν εἰς αὐτὰς δαπανη-
μάτων ἕνεκα· τελεῖν γὰρ τὸ δαπανᾶν καὶ πολυτελεῖς οἱ
πολλὰ ἀναλίσκοντες καὶ εὐτελεῖς οἱ ὀλίγα. φησὶν
Ἄλεξις·

τοὺς εὐτυχοῦντας ἐπιφανῶς
δεῖ ζῆν φανεράν τε τὴν δόσιν τὴν τοῦ θεοῦ
ποιεῖν· ὁ γὰρ ⟨θεὸς⟩ δεδωκὼς τἀγαθὰ

---

[10] θαλείας καὶ μέθας CE   [11] See 1.16d n.

---

[31] As if thoinai were derived from theous oinoumai.
[32] As if thaliai were derived from theōn . . . hēlizo.
[33] Cf. 1.24b.
[34] Identified by Stobaeus as coming from Danae.

230

called them *thoinai* ("feasts") and *thaleiai* ("festivities")—the former because they thought they should drink on the gods' account,[31] the latter because they gathered together and formed groups for the gods' sake.[32] This is what is meant by "a substantial meal."[33] Aristotle (fr. 667) says that the verb *methuō* ("be drunk") refers to the fact that one consumes wine *meta to thuein* ("after making sacrifice").

> Who make small sacrifices *(telē)* to the gods,
> but are more pious than those who sacrifice bulls,

says Euripides (fr. 327.6–7).[34] He thus shows that a *telos* ("rite") is a sacrifice. Also Homer (*Od.* 9.5–6):[35]

> For I declare that there is no greater height *(telos)* of happiness
> than when joy prevails among all the people.

We use the term *teletai* to describe festivals that are larger than this and involve some mystic tradition, because of the money expended on them; for *telein* means "to spend," and people who consume a lot of money are referred to as *poluteleis* ("spendthrifts"), while those who spend only a little are referred to as *euteleis* ("cheap"). Alexis (fr. 267) says:

> Anyone who's doing well ought to live
> ostentatiously and put what the god has given him
> on display. Because the god who has conferred these benefits

---

[35] The speaker (Odysseus) is referring to the pleasure of a banquet, which implies a sacrifice; but *telos* is not used in the sense Athenaeus suggests.

ὧν μὲν πεπόηκεν οἴεται χάριν τινὰ
ἔχειν ἑαυτῷ, τοὺς ἀποκρυπτομένους δὲ καὶ
πράττειν μετρίως φάσκοντας ἀχαρίστους ὁρῶν |
ἀνελευθέρως τε ζῶντας ἐπὶ καιροῦ τινος
λαβὼν ἀφείλεθ᾽ ὅσα δεδωκὼς ἦν πάλαι.

Τοσαῦτα οἰνολογήσαντος ἤτοι περὶ οἴνων εἰπόν-
τος· λαφύσσοντος οἴνων ὀνόματα.[12]
Οὐ χαίρει τῷ πόματι ἐκ πρώτης ἐθισθεὶς ἀνατρο-
φῆς ὑδροποτεῖν. ἡδύ ἐστιν

ἐν δαιτὶ καὶ εἰλαπίνῃ τεθαλυίῃ
τέρπεσθαι μύθοισιν, ἐπὴν δαιτὸς κορέσωνται,

Ἡσίοδος ἐν τῇ Μελαμποδίᾳ φησίν. οὔ τινι ὑμῶν
ἐπῆλθε περὶ ὕδατος εἰπεῖν τι ἀφ᾽ οὗ καὶ ὁ οἶνος
φύεται[13], καίτοι Πινδάρου τοῦ μεγαλοφωνοτάτου ἄριστον πάντων εἶναι τὸ ὕδωρ φήσαντος. ‖ Ὅμηρος μὲν
οὖν ὁ θειότατος καὶ τροφιμώτατον αὐτὸ οἶδεν ἐν οἷς

< . . . > αἰγείρων ὑδατοτρεφέων

ἄλσος λέγει. ἐπαινεῖ δὲ καὶ τὸ διαγὲς αὐτοῦ·

κρῆναι < . . . > πίσυρες ῥέον ὕδατι λευκῷ.

τὸ δὲ δὴ κοῦφον καὶ πλείονος τιμῆς ἄξιον ἱμερτὸν
καλεῖ· ἱμερτὸν οὖν φησι τὸν Τιταρήσιον, ὃς τῷ

---

[12] This sentence is omitted by E and is preserved in C only in the margin.
[13] ἀφ᾽ ὧν καὶ ὁ οἶνος ἀφύεται CE

expects that he'll get some thanks
for what he's done. He regards those who conceal
their wealth and claim that they're no richer than
    anyone else as ingrates
who live meanly; and when the right time comes,
he grabs everything he gave them previously and
    takes it away.

Oenologizing to this extent, or speaking about wine;
gulping down the names of wines.[36]

Someone accustomed from earliest childhood to drink
water does not enjoy drinking wine. It is nice for people

    at a meal and a substantial banquet
to enjoy conversation, after they have had enough to
    eat,

says Hesiod in the *Melampodia* (fr. 274). It did not occur to
any of you to say something about water, from which wine
comes, even though the grandiloquent Pindar (*O.* 1.1)
claimed that water is the best thing there is. The divine
Homer (*Od.* 17.208) shows an awareness that it is nourishing in the passage where he refers to a grove

    of poplars fed by water.

He also praises its clarity (*Od.* 5.70):

    Four springs flowed with clear water.

And he refers to water that is light and valuable as "desirable"; thus he says (*Il.* 2.751) that the Titaresius, which (*Il.*
2.753)

---

[36] A summary description of the behavior of one of the guests;
what follows represents the beginning of a new speech.

< . . . > Πηνειῷ συμμίσγεται.

καὶ τοῦ ῥυπτικοῦ δὲ ὕδατος μέμνηται· ὃ ἀποδεχόμενος
καὶ Πραξαγόρας ὁ Κῷος < . . . > καλὸν εἶναι λέγει·

b   καλὸν ὑπεκπρορέει μάλα περ ῥυπόωντα καθῆραι. |

διαστέλλει δὲ καὶ γλυκὺ ὕδωρ ἀπὸ πλατέος, τὸν μὲν
Ἑλλήσποντον εἶναι λέγων "πλατύν", ὑπὲρ δὲ θατέρου
φράζων·

    στήσαμεν <   . . .   > νῆας[14]
    ἀγχ᾽ ὕδατος γλυκεροῖο.

οἶδε δὲ καὶ τὴν ⟨τοῦ⟩ χλιαροῦ φύσιν πρὸς τὰ τραύ-
ματα. τὸν γοῦν Εὐρύπυλον τρωθέντα ἐκ τούτου καται-
ονᾷ· καίτοι εἰ ἐπισχεῖν ἔδει τὴν αἱμορραγίαν, τὸ
ψυχρὸν ἐπιτήδειον ἦν συστρέφον καὶ συσφίγγον. εἰς
δὲ τὸ παρηγορῆσαι τὰς ὀδύνας τῷ θερμῷ ἐπαιονᾷ
c   θέλγειν δυναμένῳ. ἐστὶ δὲ | παρ᾽ αὐτῷ τὸ "λιαρὸν"
θερμόν. ἐναργῶς δὲ τοῦτο δείκνυσιν ἐν τῷ περὶ τῶν
Σκαμάνδρου πηγῶν·

    ἡ μὲν γὰρ (φησίν) ὕδατι λιαρῷ ῥέει, ἀμφὶ δὲ
       καπνὸς
    γίνεται ἐξ αὐτῆς ὡς εἰ πυρὸς αἰθομένοιο.

ἆρά γε τοῦτο λιαρόν ἐστιν ἀφ᾽ οὗ πυρὸς ἀτμὶς καὶ
καπνὸς ἔμπυρος ἀναφέρεται; περὶ δὲ τῆς ἑτέρας πη-
γῆς λέγει ὡς θέρους

---

[14] The traditional text of Homer has the singular νῆα ("ship").

234

is mixed together with the Peneius,

is "desirable." He also mentions water used for washing clothes. Praxagoras of Cos (fr. 40 Steckerl) approves of this passage . . . says that it is good (*Od*. 6.87):

It pours out forward, good for washing even very
    dirty clothing.

He also distinguishes fresh water from broad water by describing the Hellespont as "broad" (*Il*. 7.86), but saying about the other type (*Od*. 12.305–6):

We moored   . . .   our ships
near fresh water.

In addition, he is familiar with how warm water affects wounds. When Eurypylus is wounded, for example, Homer has this poured over it (*Il*. 11.829–30); although if it had been necessary to stop the flow of blood, cold water would have been useful, since it tightens and compresses the flesh. But for soothing pains he has hot water poured over the wound, since it can control them. Homer uses the word *liaros* (properly "warm") to mean "hot"; he shows this clearly in the passage that describes Scamander's springs (*Il*. 22.149–50):

For one of them (he says) flows with *liaros* water, and
    smoke
comes off of it all around, as if from a blazing fire.

Is this merely warm (*liaros*) water, from which a fiery vapor and burning hot smoke rise? But regarding the other spring, he says that in summer (*Il*. 22.151–2)

ῥέει εἰκυῖα χαλάζῃ
d   ἢ χιόνι ψυχρῇ ἢ᾽ ἐξ ὕδατος κρυστάλλῳ. |

εἰωθὼς δὲ λέγειν καὶ τοὺς νεοτρώτους θερμῷ περιρ-
ρεῖσθαι αἵματι ἐπὶ μὲν Ἀγαμέμνονός φησιν·

ὄφρα οἷ αἷμ᾽ < ... > θερμὸν ἀνήνοθεν ἐξ
ὠτειλῆς.

ἐπὶ δὲ τοῦ φεύγοντος μετὰ τὸ βληθῆναι ἐλάφου μετα-
φράζων φησίν·

< ... > ὄφρ᾽ αἷμα λιαρὸν καὶ γούνατ᾽ ὀρώρῃ.

Ἀθηναῖοι δὲ μετάκερας καλοῦσι τὸ χλιαρόν, ὡς Ἐρατοσθένης φησίν. ὑδαρῆ φησὶ καὶ μετάκερας.
      Τῶν δ᾽ ἄλλων ὑδάτων τὰ μὲν ἐκ πετρῶν φερόμενα
e   δνοφερὰ καλεῖ ὡς ἀχρεῖα δηλονότι· | τὰ δὲ κρηναῖα
καὶ διὰ πλείονος γῆς καὶ εὐκάρπου φερόμενα τῶν
ἄλλων προκρίνει, ὡς καὶ Ἡσίοδος·

κρήνης < ... > αἰενάου[15] καὶ ἀπορρύτου, ἥ τ᾽
ἀθόλωτος.

καὶ Πίνδαρος·

μελιγαθὲς ἀμβρόσιον ὕδωρ
Τιλφώσσας ἀπὸ καλλικράνου.

κρήνη δ᾽ ἐν Βοιωτίᾳ ἡ Τιλφῶσσα· ἀφ᾽ ἧς Ἀριστο-

────────
[15] ἀενννάου CE

236

> its flow resembles hail,
> cold snow, or ice.

Since he customarily says that fresh wounds flow with hot blood, he says of Agamemnon (*Il.* 11.266):

> while the blood was rising hot *(thermon)* from his
>   wound.

And changing the word he uses, he says about the deer that tries to escape after it has been shot (*Il.* 11.477):

> so long as the blood is hot *(liaron)* and its limbs are
>   moving.

According to Eratosthenes (pp. 236–7 Bernhardy), the Athenians refer to warm water as *metakeras*.[37] Watery, he says[38], and warm *(metakeras)*.

Of other types of water, Homer refers to those that emerge from rock-faces as "dark" (*Il.* 9.15; 16.4), since they are, of course, useless. He prefers spring-water that runs through deep, fertile soil over all other kinds, as Hesiod (*Op.* 595) does as well:

> of an everflowing, running spring which is
>   untroubled.

Likewise Pindar (fr. 198b):

> honey-sweet ambrosial water
> from Tilphossa with its lovely spring.

Tilphossa is a spring in Boeotia. Aristophanes (*FGrH* 379 F

---

[37] Literally "intermixed"; see 3.123d–e for a number of comic fragments offered in support of this assertion.   [38] It is unclear whether this refers to Eratosthenes or Athenaeus.

φάνης φησὶ Τειρεσίαν πιόντα διὰ γῆρας οὐχ ὑπο-
f μείναντα τὴν ψυχρότητα ἀποθανεῖν. Θεόφραστος | δέ
φησιν ἐν τῷ Περὶ Ὑδάτων τὸ Νείλου ὕδωρ πολυ-
γονώτατον καὶ γλυκύτατον· διὸ καὶ λύειν τὰς κοιλίας
τῶν πινόντων μῖξιν ἔχον λιτρώδη. ἐν δὲ τῷ Περὶ
Φυτῶν ἐνιαχοῦ φησιν ὕδωρ γίνεσθαι παιδογόνον ὡς
ἐν Θεσπιαῖς, ἐν Πύρρᾳ δὲ ἄγονον. καὶ τῶν γλυκέων δέ
φησιν ὑδάτων ἔνια ἄγονα ἢ οὐ πολύγονα, ὡς τὸ ἐν
42 Φέτᾳ καὶ τὸ ἐν Πύρρᾳ. ‖ αὐχμῶν δέ ποτε γενομένων
περὶ τὸν Νεῖλον ἐρρύη τὸ ὕδωρ ἰῶδες καὶ πολλοὶ τῶν
Αἰγυπτίων ἀπώλοντο. μεταβάλλειν τέ φησιν οὐ μόνον
τὰ πικρὰ τῶν ὑδάτων, ἀλλὰ καὶ τὸ ἁλυκὸν καὶ ὅλους
ποταμούς, καθὰ τὸν ἐν Καρίᾳ, παρ' ᾧ Ζηνοποσει-
δῶνος ἱερόν ἐστιν· αἴτιον δὲ τὸ πολλοὺς κεραυνοὺς
πίπτειν περὶ τὸν τόπον. ἄλλα δὲ τῶν ὑδάτων καὶ
σωματώδη ἐστὶ καὶ ἔχει ὥσπερ τι βάρος ἐν ἑαυτοῖς,
ὡς τὸ ἐν Τροιζῆνι· τοῦτο γὰρ καὶ τῶν γευομένων εὐθὺς
b ποιεῖ πλῆρες τὸ στόμα. τὰ δὲ πρὸς τοῖς περὶ | Πάγ-
γαιον μετάλλοις τοῦ μὲν χειμῶνος τὴν κοτύλην ἄγου-
σαν ἔχει ἐνενήκοντα ἕξ, θέρους δὲ τεσσαράκοντα ἕξ·
συστέλλει δὲ αὐτὸ καὶ πυκνοῖ μᾶλλον τὸ ψῦχος. διὸ
καὶ ⟨τὸ⟩ ἐν τοῖς γνώμοσι ῥέον οὐκ ἀναδίδωσι τὰς
ὥρας ἐν τῷ χειμῶνι, ἀλλὰ περιττεύει βραδυτέρας
οὔσης τῆς ἐκροῆς διὰ τὸ πάχος. καὶ ταὐτὰ περὶ
Αἰγύπτου φησίν, ὅπου μαλακώτερος ὁ ἀήρ. τὸ δὲ

4) says that when Teiresias drank from it, he was too old to stand its cold and died. Theophrastus says in his *On Waters* (fr. 214a, including the material assigned to *On Plants* below) that the Nile's water promotes fertility and is very sweet; this is why it relaxes the bowels of those who drink it, since soda ash is mixed in with it. In his *On Plants* he claims that in some places the water promotes the conception of children, as for example in Thespiae, whereas in Pyrrha it produces sterility. And he says that some fresh water promotes sterility or hinders fertility, as for example the water in Pheta and Pyrrha. Once when there were droughts in the Nile Valley, the river's flow turned poisonous and many Egyptians died. He also says that it is not just saltwater that varies in character, but also brackish water and entire rivers, for example the river in Caria beside which there is a temple of Zeus-Poseidon; the reason for this is that many lightning-bolts fall in the region. Other types of water are substantial and have, as it were, a certain density to them, as for example the water in Troezen, which immediately fills your mouth when you taste it. The water near the mines around Mt. Pangaeum weighs 96 units per cup in the winter, but 46 in the summer; the cold compresses it and increases its density. This is why the water that flows in water-clocks[39] does not measure the hours correctly in the winter, but runs too long; for the outflow is slower because of the water's thickness. He says the same about Egypt, where the air is softer. Brackish water con-

[39] *gnōmōn* has this sense nowhere else, but it is difficult to see what else the text could be referring to.

ATHENAEUS

ἁλυκὸν ὕδωρ γεωδέστερόν ἐστι καὶ πλείονος δεῖται
κατεργασίας, ὡς τὸ θαλάσσιον, θερμοτέραν ἔχον τὴν
φύσιν καὶ μὴ ὁμοίως πάσχον. μόνον δ' ἀτέραμνον |
τῶν ἁλυκῶν τὸ τῆς Ἀρεθούσης. χείρω δ' ἐστὶ τὰ
βαρυσταθμότερα καὶ τὰ σκληρότερα καὶ τὰ ψυχρό-
τερα διὰ τὰς αὐτὰς αἰτίας· δυσκατεργαστότερα γάρ
ἐστι τὰ μὲν τῷ πολὺ τὸ γεῶδες ἔχειν, τὰ δὲ ψυχρό-
τητος ὑπερβολῇ. τὰ δὲ ταχὺ θερμαινόμενα κοῦφα καὶ
ὑγιεινά. ἐν Κραννῶνι δ' ἐστὶν ὕδωρ ἡσυχῇ θερμόν, ὃ
διατηρεῖ κραθέντα τὸν οἶνον ἐπὶ δύο καὶ τρεῖς ἡμέρας.
τὰ δ' ἐπίρρυτα καὶ ἐξ ὀχετοῦ ὡς ἐπίπαν βελτίω τῶν
στασίμων, κοπτόμενά τε μαλακώτερα γίνεται. διὰ
τοῦτο καὶ <τὰ> ἀπὸ τῆς χιόνος | δοκεῖ χρηστὰ εἶναι·
καὶ γὰρ ἀνάγεται τὸ ποτιμώτερον καὶ τοῦτο κεκομ-
μένον ἐστὶ τῷ ἀέρι. διὸ καὶ τῶν ὀμβρίων βελτίω· καὶ
τὰ ἐκ κρυστάλλου δὲ διὰ τὸ κουφότερα εἶναι. σημεῖον
δ' ὅτι καὶ ὁ κρύσταλλος αὐτὸς κουφότερος τοῦ ἄλλου
ὕδατος. τὰ δὲ ψυχρὰ σκληρά, διότι γεωδέστερα. τὸ δὲ
σωματῶδες καὶ θερμανθὲν θερμότερον καὶ ψυχθὲν
ψυχρότερόν ἐστι. κατὰ τὴν αὐτὴν δ' αἰτίαν καὶ τὰ ἐν
τοῖς ὄρεσι ποτιμώτερα τῶν ἐν τοῖς πεδίοις· ἧττον γὰρ
μέμικται τῷ γεώδει. ποιεῖ δὲ τὸ γεῶδες καὶ τὰς ἐπι-
χρόας τῶν | ὑδάτων. τὸ γοῦν τῆς ἐν Βαβυλῶνι λίμνης
ἐρυθρὸν γίνεται ἐπί τινας ἡμέρας· τὸ δὲ τοῦ Βορυσθένους κατά τινας χρόνους ἰοβαφὲς καίπερ ὄντος καθ'
ὑπερβολὴν λεπτοῦ. σημεῖον δέ· τοῦ Ὑπάνιος ἐπάνω

---

40 I.e. the application of more heat to make it boil, as what fol-

240

tains more sediment and requires more treatment[40] in comparison to sea-water, which is naturally warmer and less inert. The only brackish water that does not respond at all[41] comes from the Arethousa spring. Heavier, harsher, and colder waters are inferior for the same reasons, since they are quite difficult to bring to a boil, some of them because of the larger amount of sediment they contain, others because they are extremely cold. But water that can be warmed up quickly is light and healthy. In Crannon the water is slightly warm and keeps wine that is mixed into it this way for two or three days. Running water, including that from streams, is generally superior to standing water and becomes softer when agitated. This is why water from melting snow is thought to be good; because the more drinkable portion rises to the top and is broken up by contact with the air. For this reason it is superior to rainwater, as is water from ice, since it is quite light; evidence of this is the fact that ice itself is lighter than any other form of water. Cold water is harsh because it contains more sediment. Water that has substance is warmer when heated, and colder when cooled. For the same reason, mountain water is more drinkable than water from the plains, because it contains less sediment. The sediment also affects the color of the water. The water in the lake in Babylon, for example, is red for days on end, while the water of the Borysthenes is sometimes purple, even though it is very insubstantial; evidence of this is the fact that the north winds lift it higher than they do the Hypanus, because it is so light. There

lows makes clear. There were springs called Arethousa in Syracuse and near Chalcis on Euboea (cf. 8.331e–f).

[41] I.e. that will not boil, no matter what is done to it.

γίνεται διὰ κουφότητα τοῖς βορείοις. πολλαχοῦ δ' εἰσὶ
κρῆναι αἱ μὲν ποτιμώτεραι καὶ οἰνωδέστεραι, ὡς ἡ
περὶ Παφλαγονίαν, πρὸς ἥν φασι τοὺς ἐγχωρίους
ὑποπίνειν προσιόντας, ἁλμώδεις δ' ἅμα τῷ ὀξεῖ ἐν
f Σικανοῖς τῆς Σικελίας. ἐν τῇ Καρχηδονίων δὲ | ἐπι-
κρατείᾳ κρήνη ἐστὶν ᾗ τὸ ἐφιστάμενον ἐλαίῳ ἐστὶν
ὅμοιον, μελάντερον ⟨δὲ⟩ τὴν χρόαν· ὃ ἀποσφαιροῦν-
τες χρῶνται πρὸς τὰ πρόβατα καὶ τὰ κτήνη. καὶ παρ'
ἄλλοις δ' εἰσὶ λίπος ἔχουσαι τοιοῦτον, ὡς ἡ ἐν Ἀσίᾳ,
ὑπὲρ ἧς Ἀλέξανδρος ἐπέστειλεν ὡς ἐλαίου κρήνην
εὑρηκώς. καὶ τῶν θερμῶν δ' ἐκ φύσεως ὑδάτων ἔνια
43 γλυκέα ἐστίν, ὡς τὰ ἐν Αἰγαῖς ‖ ⟨τῆς⟩ Κιλικίας καὶ
περὶ Παγασὰς τά τ' ἐν τῇ Τρωικῇ Λαρίσσῃ καὶ περὶ
Μαγνησίαν καὶ ἐν Μήλῳ καὶ Λιπάρᾳ· ἐν δὲ Προύσῃ
τῇ πρὸς τὸν Μύσιον Ὄλυμπον τὰ βασιλικὰ καλούμενα. τὰ δ' ἐν Ἀσίᾳ περὶ Τράλλεις καὶ τὸν Χαρακωμή-
την ποταμόν, ἔτι δὲ Νῦσαν πόλιν οὕτως ἐστὶ λιπαρὰ
ὡς μὴ δεῖσθαι τοὺς ἐναπολουμένους ἐλαίου. τοιαῦτα
καὶ τὰ ἐν Δασκύλου κώμῃ. τὰ δ' ἐν Καρούροις κατά-
ξηρα καὶ σφόδρα θερμά· τὰ δὲ περὶ Μηνὸς κώμην, ἥ
ἐστι Φρυγίας, τραχύτερά ἐστι καὶ λιτρωδέστερα, ὡς
b καὶ ⟨τὰ⟩ ἐν τῇ καλουμένῃ | Λέοντος κώμῃ τῆς Φρυ-
γίας. τὰ δὲ περὶ Δορύλαιον καὶ πινόμενά ἐστιν ἥδι-
στα· τὰ γὰρ περὶ Βαΐας ἢ Βαΐου λιμένα τῆς Ἰταλίας
παντελῶς ἄποτα.

Σταθμήσας τὸ ἀπὸ τῆς ἐν Κορίνθῳ Πειρήνης καλουμένης ὕδωρ κουφότερον πάντων εὗρον τῶν κατὰ
τὴν Ἑλλάδα· οὐ γὰρ Ἀντιφάνει τῷ κωμικῷ πεπίστευ-

are springs in many places, some of which are good to
drink from or taste like wine, as for example the spring
in Paphlagonia that the locals are said to visit to do a bit
of drinking, whereas among the Sicanians in Sicily the
springs are simultaneously salty and acidic. In Carthagin-
ian territory there is a spring in which the water on top resembles oil but is darker-colored; they skim it off in glob-
ules and use it for their flocks and cattle. Among other
peoples as well there are springs that are similarly oily, as
for example the one in Asia about which Alexander wrote a
letter claiming to have discovered a well of oil.[42] Some naturally warm water is fresh, such as that in Aegae in Cilicia
and around Pagasae, as well as in Trojan Larissa and Magnesia, Melos, and Lipara; also the so-called "royal water" in
Prusa near Mysian Olympus. But the water in Asia around
Tralles and the Characometes river, and also around the
city of Nysa, is so slick that anyone who bathes in it needs
no oil;[43] the water in the village of Dascylum is like this too.
The water in Carura is drying and very warm, whereas
around the village of Men in Phrygia it is quite harsh and
full of soda ash, as also in the so-called village of Leon in
Phrygia. The water around Dorylaeum is also very pleasant to drink; but that around Baeae or its harbor in Italy is
completely undrinkable.[44]

When I weighed the water from what is referred to as
the Peirene spring in Corinth, I discovered that it was the
lightest water in Greece; for I put no credence in the comic

[42] Cf. Str. 11.518; Plu. *Alex.* 57.5–7.

[43] Sc. to anoint himself with afterward.

[44] The point of the contrast must be that both places had well-
known hot springs.

κα λέγοντι κατὰ πολλὰ τὴν Ἀττικὴν διαφέρουσαν τῶν
ἄλλων καὶ ὕδωρ κάλλιστον ἔχειν. φησὶ γάρ·

        (A.) οἷα δ' ἡ χώρα φέρει
διαφέροντα † πάσης, Ἱππόνικε, τῆς οἰκουμένης,
τὸ μέλι, τοὺς ἄρτους, τὰ σῦκα. (B.) σῦκα | μέν,
   νὴ τὸν Δία,
πάνυ φέρει. (A.) βοσκήματ', ἔρια, μύρτα, θύμα,
   πυρούς, ὕδωρ,
ὥστε καὶ γνοίην ἂν εὐθὺς Ἀττικὸν πίνων ὕδωρ.

Τὸ ὕδωρ ποταμοῦ σῶμά φησί που Εὔβουλος ὁ
κωμῳδιοποιὸς εἰρηκέναι Χαιρήμονα τὸν τραγικόν·

ἐπεὶ δὲ σηκῶν περιβολὰς ἠμείψαμεν
ὕδωρ τε ποταμοῦ σῶμα διεπεράσαμεν.

καὶ ἡμῶν δὲ πᾶσα δύναμις ἐξ ὑδάτων ἄρδεται.

Ἐν Τήνῳ κρήνη ἐστὶν ἧς τῷ ὕδατι οἶνος οὐ μίγνυ-
ται. Ἡρόδοτος δὲ ἐν τετάρτῃ τὸν Ὑπανίν φησιν ἀπὸ
μὲν | τῶν πηγῶν φερόμενον ἐπὶ πέντε ἡμέρας βραχὺν
εἶναι καὶ γλυκύν, μετὰ δὲ ἄλλων τεσσάρων ἡμερῶν
πλόον πικρὸν γίνεσθαι ἐκδιδούσης εἰς αὐτὸν κρήνης
τινὸς πικρᾶς. Θεόπομπος δέ φησι περὶ τὸν Ἐριγῶνα
ποταμὸν ὀξὺ εἶναι ὕδωρ καὶ τοὺς πίνοντας αὐτὸ μεθύ-
σκεσθαι καθὰ καὶ τοὺς τὸν οἶνον. Ἀριστόβουλος δ' ὁ

poet Antiphanes when he claims that Attica is superior to other places in many ways, including in having the best water. He says (fr. 177):[45]

> (A.) The products of this country,
> Hipponicus, better than those in the † whole
> inhabited world!
> Honey! bread! figs! (B.) By Zeus, it certainly
> produces
> figs. (A.) Flocks! wool! myrtle-berries! thyme! wheat!
> water
> such that I'd immediately recognize it as Attic when I
> drank it!

The comic poet Eubulus (fr. 128) says that the tragedian Chaeremon (*TrGF* 71 F 17) refers to water as the body of a river:

> But when we went by the sheep-pen fences
> and crossed the water, which is the body of the river.

And all our strength is irrigated by water.

There is a spring in Tenos with whose water wine does not mix. Herodotus in Book IV (52.2–3) says that the Hypanis, as it moves away from its sources, is small and fresh for five days, but after another four days' sail becomes salty, because a saltwater spring empties into it. Theopompus (*FGrH* 115 F 278a) asserts that the water near the Erigonus river is acidic, and that anyone who drinks it gets as drunk as people do who drink wine. Aristobulus of Casandreia (*FGrH* 139 F 6) says that there

---

[45] Much of this fragment is quoted again at 3.74d–e, where see n.

Κασανδρεύς φησιν ἐν Μιλήτῳ κρήνην εἶναι Ἀχίλ-
λειον καλουμένην, ἧς τὸ μὲν ῥεῦμα εἶναι γλυκύτατον,
τὸ δ᾽ ἐφεστηκὸς ἁλμυρόν· ἀφ᾽ ἧς οἱ Μιλήσιοι περιρ-
e ράνασθαί φασι τὸν ἥρωα, ὅτε | ἀπέκτεινε Τράμβηλον
τὸν τῶν Λελέγων βασιλέα. φασὶ δὲ καὶ ὅτι τὸ περὶ
Καππαδοκίαν ὕδωρ πολύ τε ὂν καὶ κάλλιστον οὐ
σήπεται ἀπόρρυσιν οὐκ ἔχον, πλὴν εἰ μὴ ὑπὸ γῆν
ῥέοι. Πτολεμαῖος δὲ ὁ βασιλεὺς ἐν ἑβδόμῳ Ὑπομνημάτων, ἐπὶ Κορίνθου προάγουσι, φησίν, ἡμῖν διὰ
τῆς Κοντοπορείας καλουμένης κατὰ τὴν ἀκρώρειαν
προσβαίνουσιν εἶναι κρήνην νᾶμα ἀνιεῖσαν χιόνος
ψυχρότερον· ἐξ ἧς πολλοὺς μὴ πίνειν ἀποπαγήσεσθαι
προσδοκῶντας, αὐτὸς δὲ λέγει πεπωκέναι. Φύλαρχος
f δέ φησιν ἐν | Κλείτορι εἶναι κρήνην ἀφ᾽ ἧς τοὺς
πιόντας οὐκ ἀνέχεσθαι τὴν τοῦ οἴνου ὀδμήν. Κλέαρχός φησι τὸ μὲν ὕδωρ ὥσπερ καὶ τὸ γάλα λευκὸν
λέγεσθαι, οἶνον δὲ καθάπερ καὶ τὸ νέκταρ ἐρυθρόν,
μέλι δὲ καὶ ἔλαιον χλωρόν, τὸ δ᾽ ἐκ τῶν μόρων
θλιβόμενον μέλαν.

Εὔβουλος εὑρετικούς φησι τὸ ὕδωρ ποιεῖν τοὺς
πίνοντας αὐτὸ μόνον, τὸν δ᾽ οἶνον ἡμῶν τῷ φρονεῖν
ἐπισκοτεῖν. τὰ αὐτὰ δ᾽ ἰαμβεῖα καὶ Ὠφελίων φησί.

44   Τοιαῦτα ὥσπερ οἱ ῥήτορες πρὸς ὕδωρ εἰπὼν ‖ καὶ
βραχὺ ἀναπαυσάμενος αὖθις ἔφη· Ἄμφις ὁ κωμικὸς
πού φησιν·

is a spring in Miletus referred to as the Achilleion and that the water that comes out of it is entirely fresh, but a layer of saltwater is on top of it. The Milesians claim that the hero[46] purified himself with its water when he killed Trambelus, the king of the Leleges. People also say that the water in Cappadocia is abundant and very good, and does not grow stale even though it lacks an out-channel, unless perhaps it flows underground. King Ptolemy in Book VII of his *Commentaries* (*FGrH* 234 F 6) says: As we were advancing on Corinth and approaching it via what is called the Short Route along the ridge, there was a spring that produced a stream of water colder than snow. Many people refused to drink from it, because they expected to freeze solid; but he says that he drank from it himself. Phylarchus (*FGrH* 81 F 63) claims that there is a spring in Cleiton whose water makes those who drink it unable to stand the smell of wine. Clearchus (fr. 96 Wehrli) says that water is described as "white," as milk is too; that wine, like nectar, is "red"; that honey and olive oil are "greenish yellow"; and that mulberry juice is "black."

Eubulus (fr. 133) claims that water makes people who drink nothing else inventive, but that wine casts shade over our thinking. Ophelio (fr. 4) has the same lines.

After he made remarks of this sort, as the orators do, "with an eye on the water,"[47] and took a brief rest, he resumed: The comic poet Amphis (fr. 41) says somewhere:

---

[46] Achilleus, for whom the spring was named. For Trambelus' death at Achilleus' hands in Miletus, see Σ Lyc. 467; Wüst, *RE*[2] VI.2130–1. [47] A reference to the practice of alloting speaking-time in Athens' courts (and perhaps other public fora as well) by means of water-clocks; cf. 2.42b.

ἐνῆν ἄρ᾽, ὡς ἔοικε, κἀν οἴνῳ λόγος·
ἔνιοι δ᾽ ὕδωρ πίνοντές εἰσ᾽ ἀβέλτεροι.

Ἀντιφάνης δέ·

οἴνῳ < . . . > τὸν οἶνον ἐξελαύνειν,
σάλπιγγι τὴν σάλπιγγα, τῷ κήρυκι τὸν βοῶντα,
κόπῳ κόπον, ψόφῳ ψόφον, τριωβόλῳ δὲ πόρνην,
αὐθαδίαν αὐθαδίᾳ, Καλλίστρατον μαγείρῳ,
στάσιν στάσει, μάχῃ μάχην, ὑπωπίοις δὲ
b   πύκτην, |
πόνῳ πόνον, δίκην δίκῃ, γυναικὶ τὴν γυναῖκα.

Ὅτι καὶ ἐπὶ τοῦ ὕδατος ἔταττον οἱ παλαιοὶ τὸ
ἄκρατον. Σώφρων· ὕδωρ ἄκρατον εἰς τὰν κύλικα.

Ὅτι Φύλαρχός φησι Θεόδωρον τὸν Λαρισσαῖον
ὑδροπότην γενέσθαι, τὸν ἀλλοτρίως ἀεί ποτε πρὸς
Ἀντίγονον ἐσχηκότα τὸν βασιλέα. φησὶ δὲ καὶ τοὺς
Ἴβηρας πάντας ὑδροποτεῖν καίτοι πλουσιωτάτους ἀνθρώπων ὄντας, μονοσιτεῖν τε αὐτοὺς ἀεὶ λέγει διὰ
μικρολογίαν, ἐσθῆτας δὲ φορεῖν πολυτελεστάτας.
c Ἀριστοτέλης | δ᾽ ἢ Θεόφραστος Φιλῖνόν τινα ἱστορεῖ
μήτε ποτῷ χρήσασθαί ποτε μήτε ἐδέσματι ἄλλῳ ἢ
μόνῳ γάλακτι πάντα τὸν βίον. Πύθερμος δὲ ἐν τοῖς

---

48 A small coin, perhaps the standard prostitute's fee.
49 An early 4th-century Athenian politician (PAA 561575),
here implicitly accused of gluttony.
50 Otherwise unknown, like most of the individuals men-

248

It appears that there's some reason in wine as well;
and some water-drinkers are asses.

Antiphanes (fr. 293):

> to try to drive out the wine with wine,
> the trumpet with a trumpet, the fellow who shouts
>   with the herald,
> blow with blow, noise with noise, a whore with a
>   triobol,[48]
> stubbornness with stubbornness, Callistratus[49] with a
>   cook,
> dissension with dissension, a fight with a fight, a
>   boxer with black eyes,
> trouble with trouble, a lawsuit with a lawsuit, your
>   wife with another woman.

The ancients also used the word *akratos* ("unmixed") to
describe water. Sophron (fr. 94): unmixed *(akraton)* water
into the cup.

Phylarchus (*FGrH* 81 F 64) asserts that Theodorus of
Larissa,[50] who was always at odds with King Antigonus,
drank nothing but water. He also claims (*FGrH* 81 F 13)
that the Iberians all drink only water, despite being the
richest people on earth; and he says that they always eat
alone, because of their stinginess, but wear extremely expensive clothing. Aristotle (fr. 668) or Theophrastus (fr.
340) records that a certain Philinus never drank or ate anything in his entire life except milk. Pythermus (*FGrH* 80 F

tioned below. But the Antigonus in question must be Antigonus
Gonatas (reigned *c*.277/6–239 BCE). Cf. 3.73c–d, where another
of Phylarchus' anecdotes about Antigonus is preserved.

Πειραιῶς τυραννεύουσι καταγράφει καὶ Γλαύκωνα ὑδροπότην. Ἡγήσανδρος δ᾽ ὁ Δελφὸς Ἀγχίμολον καὶ Μόσχον φησὶ τοὺς ἐν Ἤλιδι σοφιστεύσαντας ὑδροποτῆσαι πάντα τὸν βίον καὶ μόνα σῦκα προσφερομένους οὐδενὸς ἧττον διακεῖσθαι σώμασιν ἐρρωμενεστέρους· τὸν δ᾽ ἱδρῶτα αὐτῶν δυσώδη οὕτως ἔχειν ὡς

d πάντας αὐτοὺς ἐκκλίνειν ἐν τοῖς βαλανείοις. Μᾶτρις | δ᾽ ὁ Θηβαῖος[16] ὃν ἐβίω χρόνον οὐδὲν ἐσιτεῖτο ἢ μυρρίνης ὀλίγον, οἴνου δὲ καὶ τῶν ἄλλων πάντων ἀπείχετο πλὴν ὕδατος. ὑδροπότης δ᾽ ἦν καὶ Λάμπρος ὁ μουσικός, περὶ οὗ Φρύνιχός φησι·

> λάρους θρηνεῖν, ἐν οἷσι Λάμπρος
>   ἐναπέθνησκεν
> ἄνθρωπος ⟨ὢν⟩ ὑδατοπότης, μινυρὸς
>   ὑπερσοφιστής,
> Μουσῶν σκελετός, ἀηδόνων ἠπίαλος, ὕμνος
>   Ἅιδου.

Μάχων δ᾽ ὁ κωμικὸς ὑδροπότου Μοσχίωνος μέμνηται. Ἀριστοτέλης δ᾽ ἐν τῷ Περὶ Μέθης φησὶν ὅτι ἁλμυράς τινες προσφερόμενοι τροφὰς ἄδιψοι διέμειναν· ὧν ἦν

e Ἀρχωνίδης | ὁ Ἀργεῖος. Μάγων δὲ ὁ Καρχηδόνιος τρὶς τὴν ἄνυδρον διῆλθεν ἄλφιτα ξηρὰ σιτούμενος καὶ μὴ πίνων. Πολέμων δ᾽ ὁ Ἀκαδημαϊκὸς ἀρξάμενος ἀπὸ

---

[16] Θηβαῖος Toup: Ἀθηναῖος CE

---

51 *PAA* 276740. Nothing is known about the "tyrants of the Piraeus"; but Pythermus probably dates to the late 3rd or early

2) includes Glaucon,[51] who drank only water, among the tyrants of the Piraeus. Hegesander of Delphi (fr. 24, *FHG* iv.418) says that Anchimolus and Moschus, who were sophistic teachers in Elis, drank nothing but water all their lives and ate nothing but figs, but were no less physically vigorous than anyone else. Their sweat, however, smelled so bad that everyone tried to avoid them in the baths. Matris of Thebes ate nothing except a few myrtle-berries as long as he lived, and also kept away from wine and everything else except water. Another water-drinker was the musician Lamprus,[52] about whom Phrynichus (fr. 74) says:

> the gulls to wail; and Lamprus lay among
> them dying,
> a person who drinks only water, a warbling super-
> sophist,
> who starves the Muses, gives nightingales a fever, and
> commits murder with his songs.

The comic poet Macho mentions a water-drinker named Moschion.[53] Aristotle in his *On Drunkenness* (fr. 668, continued) claims that some people can consume salty foods without becoming thirsty; Archonidas of Argos was one of them. Mago of Carthage[54] crossed the desert three times, eating only dry barley-meal and drinking nothing. Polemon of the Academy[55] drank only water from the

---

[51] 2nd century BCE.   [52] See 1.20e n.   [53] A reference to Macho 46–50 Gow, quoted at 6.246b, where see n.

[54] Otherwise unknown.   [55] *PAA* 776720; head of the Academy 314/13–270/69 BCE, after Xenocrates. To be distinguished from Polemon of Ilium (early 2nd century BCE), whom Athenaeus cites repeatedly (e.g. 1.19c; 2.39c, 55e).

τριάκοντα ἐτῶν ὑδροπότησε μέχρι θανάτου, ὡς ἔφη
Ἀντίγονος ὁ Καρύστιος. Διοκλῆ τε τὸν Πεπαρήθιόν
φησι Δημήτριος ὁ Σκήψιος μέχρι τέλους ψυχρὸν ὕδωρ
πεπωκέναι. αὐτὸς δὲ περὶ αὑτοῦ μάρτυς ἀξιόχρεως
Δημοσθένης ὁ ῥήτωρ φάσκων χρόνον τινὰ ὕδωρ μόνον πεπωκέναι. καὶ Πυθέας γοῦν φησιν· ἀλλὰ τοὺς νῦν
f δημαγωγοὺς ὁρᾶτε[17] | ὡς ἐναντίως τοῖς βίοις διάκειν-
ται· ὁ μὲν γὰρ ὑδροποτῶν καὶ μεριμνῶν τὰς νύκτας,
ὥς φασιν, ὁ δὲ πορνοβοσκῶν καὶ μεθυσκόμενος κατὰ
τὴν ἡμέραν ἑκάστην προγάστωρ ἡμῖν ἐν ταῖς ἐκκλη-
σίαις ἀνακαλεῖ. Εὐφορίων δὲ ὁ Χαλκιδεὺς οὕτω που
γράφει· Λασύρτας ⟨ὁ⟩ Λασιώνιος οὐδὲν προσεδεῖτο
ποτοῦ καθάπερ οἱ ἄλλοι, οὖρον δὲ προίετο καθάπερ
πάντες ἄνθρωποι. καὶ πολλοὶ διὰ φιλοτιμίαν ἐπεχεί-
ρησαν παρατηρῆσαι καὶ ἀπέστησαν πρὸ τοῦ εὑρεῖν
45 τὸ πραττόμενον· ‖ θέρους γὰρ ὥρᾳ καὶ τριακονθή-
μερον προσεδρεύοντες καὶ οὐδενὸς μὲν ὁρῶντες ἀπ-
εχόμενον ἁλμυροῦ, τὴν κύστιν δ' αὐτοῦ † ἔχοντα †
συνεπείσθησαν ἀληθεύειν. ἐχρῆτο δὲ καὶ τῷ ποτῷ,
ἀλλ' οὐδὲν ἧττον οὐ προσεδεῖτο τούτου.

   μεταλλάξαι διάφορα βρώματα
ἔσθ' ἡδύ,

17 ὁρᾶτε Δημοσθένη καὶ Δημάδην CE

---

56 Identified by the anonymous commentator whose note has
intruded into the text as Demosthenes (*PAA* 318625), while the

time he was 30 until his death, according to Antigonus of Carystus (p. 66 Wilamowitz). And Demetrius of Scepsis (fr. 72 Gaede) claims that Diocles of Peparethus (*FGrH* 820 T 1) drank cold water until the end of his life. The orator Demosthenes (6.30) is himself a credible witness regarding his own habits, when he says that for a while he drank only water. Pytheas (fr. III.2 Baiter–Sauppe), at any rate, says: Look how different the lifestyles of our leading politicians are. One of them[56] drinks only water and spends his nights studying, so they say; but the other is a pimp and a drunk, who makes appeals to us every day at meetings of the Assembly with his belly hanging out. Euphorion of Chalcis (fr. 7, *FHG* iii.73 = fr. 184 van Groningen) writes somewhere as follows: Lasyrtas of Lasion[57] used to feel no need to drink, as other people do, but urinated just like everyone else. Many people tried to win some glory by keeping a watch on him; but they gave up before figuring out how he did it. They used to sit beside him for 30 days at a time in the summer and watch him eating salty foods of all sorts, but as for his bladder † having † ... they were convinced that he was speaking the truth. He did consume liquid; but he nonetheless felt no need for it.[58]

It's nice to vary the food
you eat,

man referred to next is supposed to be Demades son of Demeas (*PAA* 306085).

[57] Otherwise unknown. Euphorion was active in the second half of the 2nd century BCE.

[58] The quotation that follows probably marks the transition to a new speaker, most likely (given the nature of the material cited) one of the physicians.

φησὶν Ἀντιφάνης,

καὶ τῶν πολλάκις θρυλουμένων
διάμεστον ὄντα τὸ παραγεύσασθαί τινος
καινοῦ παρέσχε διπλασίαν τὴν ἡδονήν.

Ὁ Περσῶν βασιλεύς, ὥς φησιν ἐν τῇ πρώτῃ[18]
b Ἡρόδοτος, | ὕδωρ ἀπὸ τοῦ Χοάσπεω πιεῖν ἄγεται τοῦ
παρὰ Σοῦσα ῥέοντος· τοῦ μόνου πίνει ὁ βασιλεύς. τοῦ
δὲ τοιούτου ὕδατος ἀπεψημένου πολλαὶ κάρτα ἅμαξαι
τετράκυκλοι ἡμιόνειαι κομίζουσαι ἐν ἀγγείοις ἀργυ-
ρέοισιν ἕπονταί οἱ. Κτησίας δὲ ὁ Κνίδιος καὶ ἱστορεῖ
ὅπως ἕψεται τὸ βασιλικὸν τοῦτο ὕδωρ καὶ ὅπως ἐν-
αποτιθέμενον τοῖς ἀγγείοις φέρεται τῷ βασιλεῖ, λέγων αὐτὸ καὶ ἐλαφρότατον καὶ ἥδιστον εἶναι. καὶ ὁ
τῆς Αἰγύπτου δὲ βασιλεὺς δεύτερος ὁ Φιλάδελφος
c ἐπίκλην ἐκδοὺς τὴν αὑτοῦ θυγατέρα | Βερενίκην Ἀντι-
όχῳ τῷ Συρίας βασιλεῖ ἐν ἐπιμελείᾳ εἶχε πέμπειν
αὐτῇ τὸ ἀπὸ τοῦ Νείλου ὕδωρ, ἵνα μόνου τούτου[19] ἡ
παῖς πίνῃ, ἱστορεῖ Πολύβιος. Ἡλιόδωρος δέ φησι τὸν
Ἐπιφανῆ Ἀντίοχον, ὃν διὰ τὰς πράξεις Πολύβιος
Ἐπιμανῆ καλεῖ, τὴν κρήνην τὴν ἐν Ἀντιοχείᾳ κεράσαι
οἴνῳ· καθάπερ καὶ τὸν Φρύγα Μίδαν φησὶ Θεόπομπος, ὅτε ἑλεῖν τὸν Σιληνὸν ὑπὸ μέθης ἠθέλησεν. ἐστὶ
δὲ ἡ κρήνη, ὥς φησι Βίων, μέση Μαιδῶν καὶ Παιόνων
Ἴννα καλουμένη. Στάφυλος δέ φησι τὴν τοῦ οἴνου

18 πρώτῃ (i.e. Αʹ) ed. Basel: τετάρτῃ (i.e. Δʹ) CE
19 τούτου τοῦ ποταμοῦ CE

says Antiphanes (fr. 240, including the material that follows),

> and when you're full of the items
> that are repeated constantly, it's twice as nice
> to have a taste of something new.

According to Herodotus in Book I (188), the Persian King has drinking-water brought for him from the Choaspes river, which flows past Susa; this is the only water the King drinks. Large numbers of four-wheeled mule-carts carrying boiled water of this sort in silver vessels follow him. Ctesias of Cnidus (*FGrH* 688 F 37) tells how this royal water is boiled, put into the vessels, and transported for the King; he says that it is very light and pleasant. Likewise when the second king of Egypt, nicknamed Philadelphus,[59] married his daughter Berenice to Antiochus king of Syria,[60] Polybius records (fr. 73 Buettner-Wobst), he was careful to send her Nile water, so that his child could drink nothing except this. Heliodorus (*FGrH* 373 F 8) says that Antiochus Epiphanes,[61] whom Polybius refers to as *Epimanēs* ("the Madman") because of how he acted,[62] mixed wine into the spring in Antioch. Theopompus (*FGrH* 115 F *75a) claims that the Phrygian Midas did the same when he wanted to capture Silenus by getting him drunk.[63] But according to Bion (*FGrH* 14 F 3), the spring is located between the Maedi and the Paeonians, and is called Inna. Staphylus (fr. 9, *FHG* iv.506) says that

---

[59] Ptolemy II; see 1.3b n. [60] Berenice II ("the Syrian") married Antiochus II in 252 BCE. [61] Antiochus IV (reigned 175–164 BCE). [62] Cf. 5.193c–4c.

[63] For the story, cf. Hdt. 8.138.3; X. *An.* 1.2.13; Paus. 1.4.5.

d πρὸς τὸ ὕδωρ κρᾶσιν | Μελάμποδα πρῶτον εὑρεῖν.
φησὶ δὲ καὶ πεπτικώτερον τοῦ οἴνου τὸ ὕδωρ Πλειστό-
νικος.

Ὅτι τοῖς προπίνουσιν ἐπιτεταμένως οὐκ οἰκείως
διατίθεται ὁ στόμαχος, ἀλλὰ μᾶλλον κακοῦται καὶ
πολλάκις φθορὰν τῶν ληφθέντων παρασκευάζει. δεῖ
οὖν τὸν ὑγιείας ἀντιποιούμενον καὶ συμμέτροις γυμνασίοις χρᾶσθαι διὰ τοὺς πολλοὺς ἱδρῶτας καὶ λου-
τροῖς, ὡς διᾶναί τε τὸ σῶμα καὶ μαλαχθῆναι. μετὰ δὲ
ταῦτα προπίνειν ὕδωρ ὡς χρηστότατον, ἐν μὲν χειμῶνι καὶ ἔαρι θερμὸν ὡς μάλιστα, ἐν δὲ τῷ θέρει
e ψυχρόν, ὡς μὴ | προεκλύειν τὸν στόμαχον. προπίνειν
δὲ σύμμετρον τῷ πλήθει χάριν τοῦ προαναληφθῆναι
τοῦτο εἰς τὴν ἕξιν καὶ μὴ ἀκέραιον ἀναδίδοσθαι τὴν
ἀπὸ τοῦ οἴνου δύναμιν μηδὲ τοῖς πέρασι τῶν ἀγγείων
προσπίπτουσαν ἐπιδάκνειν. ἐὰν δέ τις ἡμῶν τοῦτο
δυσκόλως ποιῇ, γλυκὺν ὑδαρῆ θερμὸν προλαμβανέ-
τω, μάλιστα δὲ τὸν καλούμενον πρότροπον[20] ὄντα
εὐστόμαχον. καὶ ὁ γλυκάζων δ᾽ οἶνος οὐ βαρύνει τὴν
κεφαλήν, ὡς Ἱπποκράτης ἐν τῷ Περὶ Διαίτης φησίν, ὅ
f τινες μὲν ἐπιγράφουσι Περὶ Ὀξέων Νόσων, | οἱ δὲ
Περὶ Πτισάνης, ἄλλοι δὲ Πρὸς τὰς Κνιδίας Γνώμας.
λέγει δέ· ὁ γλυκὺς ἧσσόν ἐστι καρηβαρικὸς τοῦ
οἰνώδεος καὶ ἧσσον φρενῶν ἁπτόμενος καὶ διαχωρη-
τικώτερος τοῦ ἑτέρου κατ᾽ ἔντερον. οὐ δεῖ δὲ προπίνειν
καθὰ τοὺς Καρμανούς φησι Ποσειδώνιος· τούτους

---

[20] πρότροπον τὸν γλυκὺν Λέσβιον CE

256

Melampus[64] was the first person to discover mixing wine with water. Pleistonicus (fr. 2 Steckerl) claims that water is also better for the digestion than wine.

If someone drinks constantly without eating, his stomach becomes unsettled, has more problems, and frequently corrupts the food he consumes. Whoever wants to be healthy must therefore get an appropriate amount of exercise, so that he sweats a lot, and bathe, in order that his body can be cleansed and softened. After that, he should drink the best water he can get; it should be as warm as possible in the winter and spring, but cold in the summer, to keep his stomach from relaxing too soon. He should keep his drinking in proportion, so that the food can be absorbed into his system first and the effect of the wine does not make its way through his body in full force and attack the walls of its cavities and eat them away. If any of us regards this as difficult advice, he should drink warm diluted sweet wine first, preferably what is referred to as *protropon*,[65] which is easy on the stomach. Sweet wine does not produce wooziness, according to Hippocrates in his *On Diet* (2.332.5–8 Littré), to which some people give the title *On Acute Diseases*, others *On Barley-Gruel*, and others *A Response to the Cnidian Maxims*.[66] He says: Sweet wine goes to the head less than wine with a more vinous character; and it makes less of an assault on the rational faculties and passes more rapidly through the digestive tract than the other kind does. Posidonius (*FGrH* 87 F 72 = fr. 283 Edelstein–Kidd) says that one should not drink toasts as the Carmani do. Because when they are feeling friendly at

[64] A legendary seer.   [65] Cf. 1.30b.
[66] Further comments on this work at 2.57c.

257

γὰρ φιλοφρονουμένους ἐν τοῖς συμποσίοις λύειν τὰς
ἐπὶ τῷ προσώπῳ φλέβας καὶ τὸ καταρρέον αἷμα
μιγνύντας τῷ πόματι προσφέρεσθαι, τέλος φιλίας
46 νομίζοντας τὸ γεύεσθαι τοῦ ἀλλήλων αἵματος. ‖ μετὰ
δὲ τὴν προσφορὰν ταύτην συγχρίεσθαι τὴν κεφαλὴν
μύρῳ, μάλιστα μὲν ῥοδίνῳ, εἰ δὲ μή, μηλίνῳ, εἰς τὸ
ἀποκρούεσθαί τι ἀπὸ τοῦ πότου καὶ μὴ βλάπτεσθαι
ἀπὸ τῆς τῶν οἴνων ἀναθυμιάσεως· εἰ δὲ μή, ἰρίνῳ ἢ
ναρδίνῳ. οὐ κακῶς οὖν Ἄλεξίς φησιν·

ἐναλείφεται[21] τὰς ῥῖνας· ὑγιείας μέρος
μέγιστον ὀσμὰς ἐγκεφάλῳ χρηστὰς ποεῖν.

ἐκκλίνειν δὲ δεῖ τὰ πάχη τῶν μύρων ὕδωρ τε πίνειν τὸ
b κατὰ πρόσοψιν λεπτὸν καὶ διαυγές, ὃ δὴ καὶ ‖ κατὰ
τὸν σταθμόν ἐστι κοῦφον καὶ οὐδὲν ἐν αὐτῷ γεῶδες
ἔχει. τὸ δὲ συμμέτρως θερμαινόμενον καὶ ψυχόμενον
ὕδωρ χρηστόν ἐστι καὶ εἰς χάλκεον ἢ ἀργύρεον ἄγγος
ἐγχεόμενον οὐ ποιεῖ τὸ ἰῶδες. φησὶ δὲ καὶ Ἱππο-
κράτης· ὕδωρ τὸ ταχέως θερμαινόμενον καὶ ψυχόμενον ἀεὶ κουφότερον. μοχθηρὰ δ᾽ ἐστὶ τὰ βραδέως τὰ
ὄσπρια τήκοντα. τοιαῦτα δὲ τὰ νιτρώδη καὶ ἁλμυρά.
ἐν δὲ τῷ Περὶ Ὑδάτων Ἱπποκράτης καλεῖ τὸ χρηστὸν
ὕδωρ πότιμον. τὰ δὲ τῶν ὑδάτων στάσιμα χαλεπά, ὡς
c τὰ λιμναῖα καὶ τὰ ‖ ἑλώδη. ἐστὶ δὲ καὶ τῶν κρηναίων
τὰ πλεῖστα σκληρότερα. Ἐρασίστρατος δέ φησιν ὡς
δοκιμάζουσί τινες τὰ ὕδατα σταθμῷ ἀνεξετάστως.

---

[21] ὑπαλείφεται Clem. Al.

their symposia, they cut the veins on their foreheads open, mix the blood that runs down their faces into what they are drinking, and consume it; they feel that the perfect expression of friendship is tasting one another's blood. After drinking this way, they rub their heads with perfume, preferably rose perfume, otherwise quince perfume, to dispel some of the effect of their drinking and keep them from being harmed by the wine's vapors. If these perfumes are unavailable, they use iris or spikenard instead. Alexis (fr. 195.2–3) is therefore not wrong to say:

> He rubs perfume on his nostrils; producing smells
> the brain likes is the most significant contribution to
> good health.

One should avoid thick perfumes and drink water that appears thin and transparent, and that is in fact light in weight and contains no sediment. Water that heats up and cools down at the same rate, and that does not tarnish bronze or silver vessels when poured into them, is good. Hippocrates (*Epid.* II 5.88.15–16 Littré; cf. *Aph.* 4.542.1–2 Littré) as well says: Water that heats up and cools down quickly is always lighter. Water that softens peas and beans slowly is of low quality; water that contains soda ash or salt is of this sort. In his *On Waters*, Hippocrates refers to good water as *potimon* ("potable").[67] Standing water, such as lake-water or marsh-water, is problematic; and most spring-water is quite harsh. Erasistratus (fr. 159 Garofalo) says that some people evaluate water by its weight with-

[67] Probably a garbled reference to *Reg.* 6.570.7 Littré.

ἰδοὺ γὰρ τοῦ ἐξ Ἀμφιαράου ὕδατος καὶ <τοῦ> ἐξ
Ἐρετρίας συμβαλλομένων, τοῦ μὲν φαύλου τοῦ δὲ
χρηστοῦ ὄντος, οὐδ᾽ ἥτις ἐστὶ διαφορὰ κατὰ τὸν
σταθμόν. Ἱπποκράτης δ᾽ ἐν τῷ Περὶ Τόπων ἄριστά
φησιν εἶναι τῶν ὑδάτων ὅσα ἐκ μετεώρων χωρίων ῥεῖ
καὶ ἐκ λόφων ξηρῶν. ταῦτα γὰρ λευκὰ καὶ γλυκέα καὶ
τὸν οἶνον ὀλίγον φέρειν οἷά τέ ἐστι, τόν τε χειμῶνα
d θερμαίνεται καὶ τὸ θέρος ψυχρά | ἐστιν. ἐπαινεῖ δὲ
μάλιστα ὧν τὰ ῥεύματα πρὸς ἀνατολὴν ἡλίου ἔρρωγε
καὶ μάλιστα πρὸς τὰς θερινάς· ἀνάγκη γὰρ λαμπρὰ
εἶναι καὶ εὐώδη καὶ κοῦφα. Διοκλῆς δέ φησι τὸ ὕδωρ
πεπτικὸν εἶναι καὶ ἄφυσον ψυκτικόν τε μετρίως ὀξυ-
δερκές τε καὶ ἥκιστα καρηβαρικὸν κινητικόν τε ψυχῆς
καὶ σώματος. Πραξαγόρας τε ταὐτά φησι· ἐπαινεῖ δὲ
τὸ ὄμβριον, Εὐήνωρ δὲ τὰ λακκαῖα· χρηστότερόν τε
εἶναι φάσκει τὸ ἐξ Ἀμφιαράου συμβαλλόμενον τῷ ἐν
Ἐρετρίᾳ. ὅτι δὲ τὸ ὕδωρ ὁμολογουμένως ἐστὶ τρόφι-
e μον | δῆλον ἐκ τοῦ τρέφεσθαί τινα ἐξ αὐτοῦ μόνου τῶν
ζῴων, ὥσπερ τοὺς τέττιγας. πολλὰ δὲ καὶ τῶν ἄλλων
ὑγρῶν ἐστι τρόφιμα, οἷον γάλα, πτισάνη, οἶνος. τὰ
γοῦν ὑποτίτθια γάλακτι διαρκεῖται· καὶ πολλὰ δὲ ἔθνη
γαλακτοποτοῦντα ζῇ. Δημόκριτον δὲ τὸν Ἀβδηρίτην
λόγος ἔχει διὰ γῆρας ἐξάξαι αὐτὸν διεγνωκότα τοῦ

---

68 Literally "toward the rising of the sun, and especially its
summer risings."   69 A well-known late 4th-century BCE
physician (*PAA* 431340); this is the only fragment of his work that
survives.

out really inspecting it. Witness that, when water from
the Amphiaraus spring and from Eretria is compared, although one of them is bad and the other good, there is no
difference in their weights. Hippocrates in his *On Places*
(2.30.5–11 Littré) says that the best water flows from ele-
vated spots and dry hill-crests. For water of this sort is
clear and fresh, and can stand up to only a little wine; and it
is warm in the winter, but cold in the summer. He recommends in particular springs whose streams emerge to the
east and especially the northeast,[68] because they are neces-
sarily bright, sweet-smelling, and light. Diocles (fr. 235 van
der Eijk) says that water is good for the digestion, does not
produce gas, is moderately cooling and good for one's eyesight, does not produce wooziness at all, and makes one's
soul and body energetic. Praxagoras (fr. 41 Steckerl) says
the same, but recommends rainwater; whereas Evenor[69]
recommends cistern-water. He adds that when water from
the Amphiaraus spring is compared with water from
Eretria, it is better.[70] That water is, as is generally agreed,
nutritious is clear from the fact that some creatures get
their nourishment from this alone, as for example cicadas.[71] Many other liquids are also nutritious, such as milk,
barley-gruel, and wine; nursing infants, for example, survive on milk, and many ethnic groups stay alive by drinking it. There is a story that Democritus of Abdera (68 A 29
D–K) had decided to commit suicide because he was old,

---

[70] Probably the opposite of what Erasistratus (fr. 159 Garofalo, above) claimed, although Athenaeus' (or the Epitomator's)
summary of Erasistratus' views is too laconic to make this certain.

[71] Cicadas were thought to live on dew; cf. [Hes.] *Sc.* 393–5;
Call. fr. 1.32–4; Gow on Theoc. 4.16.

ζῆν καὶ ὑφαιροῦντα τῆς τροφῆς καθ᾽ ἑκάστην ἡμέραν,
ἐπεὶ αἱ τῶν Θεσμοφορίων ἡμέραι ἐνέστησαν, δεηθει-
f σῶν τῶν οἰκείων γυναικῶν μὴ ἀποθανεῖν κατὰ | τὴν
πανήγυριν, ὅπως ἑορτάσωσι, πεισθῆναι κελεύσαντα
μέλιτος ἀγγεῖον αὐτῷ πλησίον παρατεθῆναι, καὶ δια-
ζῆσαι ἡμέρας ἱκανὰς τὸν ἄνδρα, τῇ ἀπὸ τοῦ μέλιτος
ἀναφορᾷ μόνῃ χρώμενον, καὶ μετὰ τὰς ἡμέρας βα-
σταχθέντος τοῦ μέλιτος ἀποθανεῖν. ἔχαιρε δὲ ὁ Δημόκριτος ἀεὶ τῷ μέλιτι· καὶ πρὸς τὸν πυθόμενον πῶς ἂν
ὑγιῶς τις διάγοι ἔφη, "εἰ τὰ μὲν ἐντὸς μέλιτι βρέχοι,
τὰ δ᾽ ἐκτὸς ἐλαίῳ." καὶ τῶν Πυθαγορικῶν δὲ τροφὴ ἦν
47 ἄρτος μετὰ μέλιτος, ὥς φησιν Ἀριστόξενος, ‖ τοὺς
προσφερομένους αὐτὰ ἀεὶ ἐπ᾽ ἀρίστῳ λέγων ἀνόσους
διατελεῖν. Λύκος δὲ πολυχρονίους φησὶν εἶναι τοὺς
Κυρνίους²² (οἰκοῦσι δ᾽ οὗτοι περὶ Σαρδόνα) διὰ τὸ
μέλιτι ἀεὶ χρῆσθαι· πλεῖστον δὲ τοῦτο γίνεται παρ᾽
αὐτοῖς.

Ὅρα τὸ "ἀνατιθεμένων πάντων τὴν ζήτησιν" ἤτοι
ἀναβαλλομένων.

Ὅτι τὸ ἄνηστις ἡ νῆστις πλεονασμῷ τοῦ ᾱ, ὡς
στάχυς ἄσταχυς, παρὰ Κρατίνῳ κεῖται·

²² St. Byz. p. 397 Meineke offers πολυχρονιωτάτους and
Κυρναίους.

---

[72] The Thesmophoria was a secret women's festival celebrated
throughout the Greek world in early winter in honor of Demeter
and Persephone.   [73] Similar stories are told by other
authors (esp. Hermipp. Hist. fr. 31 Wehrli ap. D.L. 9.43 = 68 A 1

and was reducing the amount he ate every day. When Thesmophoria-time arrived, the women in his house asked him not to die during the festival, so that they could celebrate it.[72] He agreed and told them to put a jar of honey beside him; and he lived the necessary number of days, getting all his energy from the honey. After the days were up and the honey was gone, he died.[73] Democritus always liked honey, and when someone asked him how a person could live a healthy life, he said: "If he moistens his interior with honey, and his exterior with oil." According to Aristoxenus (fr. 27 Wehrli), the Pythagorean diet consisted of bread and honey; he claims that anyone who regularly eats this for lunch never gets sick. Lycus (*FGrH* 570 F 5) says that the Corsicans, who dwell around Sardinia, live a very long time because they regularly eat honey, a great deal of which is produced in their country.

Note the expression "when they all put up the question" in the sense "put off."[74]

The word *anēstis* ("fasting"), which is equivalent to *nēstis* (also "fasting") with a superfluous *alpha*, like *stachus* and *astachus* (both "ear of grain"), is attested in Cratinus (fr. 47):[75]

D–K), although they report that Democritus survived on loaves of bread rather than honey.

[74] The question referred to was probably posed by Ulpian, who may well have gone on to answer it himself in the section that follows, as at 2.58b; 3.100b–c (cf. 3.96f).

[75] The other witnesses to the fragment (clearly drawing on the same source as Athenaeus) include the word *aklētos* ("uninvited") in the middle of the line, and identify the verse as coming from *Dionysalexandros*.

οὐ γάρ τοι σύ γε πρῶτος < . . . > φοιτᾷς ἐπὶ
b   δεῖπνον ἄνηστις. |

τὸ δὲ ὀξύπεινος παρὰ Διφίλῳ·

            τέρπομαι γυμνοὺς ὁρῶν
τοὺς ὀξυπείνους καὶ πρὸ τῶν καιρῶν ἀεὶ
πάντ᾽ εἰδέναι σπεύδοντας.

καὶ Ἀντιφάνης·

            (Α.) ἓν νόσημα τοῦτ᾽ ἔχει·
ἀεὶ γὰρ ὀξύπεινός ἐστι. (Β.) Θετταλὸν
λέγει κομιδῇ τὸν ἄνδρα.

καὶ Εὔβουλος·

Ζῆθον μὲν ἐλθόνθ᾽ ἁγνὸν ἐς Θήβης πέδον
c   οἰκεῖν κελεύει, καὶ γὰρ ἀξιωτέρους |
πωλοῦσιν, ὡς ἔοικε, τοὺς ἄρτους ἐκεῖ·
ὁ δ᾽ ὀξύπεινος. τὸν δὲ μουσικώτατον
κλεινὰς Ἀθήνας ἐκπερᾶν Ἀμφίονα
οὗ ῥᾷστ᾽ ἀεὶ πεινῶσι Κεκροπιδῶν κόροι
κάπτοντες αὔρας, ἐλπίδας σιτούμενοι.

ὁ δὲ μονοσιτῶν κεῖται παρ᾽ Ἀλέξιδι·

---

76 Thessalians are routinely referred to in Attic comedy as
gluttons; cf. 10.418c–d.
77 Probably from *Antiope*.
78 For Boeotians as gluttons, see 10.417b–18b.

For you're certainly not the first to go to dinner
   hungry *(anēstis)*.

The word *oxupeinos* ("ravenous") is attested in Diphilus
(fr. 95):

> I enjoy seeing ravenous *(oxupeinous)* men
> stripped for action and always eager to know
> everything ahead of time.

Also Antiphanes (fr. 249):

> (A.) He's got this one disease:
> he's constantly ravenous *(oxupeinos)*. (B.) He's calling
>   the fellow
> an outright Thessalian![76]

And Eubulus (fr. *9):[77]

> He orders Zethus to go to the sacred plain
> of Thebes to make his home; because it seems that
> they sell their bread cheaper there,[78]
> and he's ravenous *(oxupeinos)*. But he orders the
>   musical
> Amphion to make his way to famous Athens;
> Cecrops' sons[79] always starve easily there,
> gulping down the breezes and eating hopes.

The participle *monositōn* ("eating alone")[80] is attested in
Alexis (fr. 271):

---

[79] Cecrops was a mythical king of Athens, and his "sons" are
the Athenians generally.

[80] Cf. 1.8e (on the verb *monophageō*). Alternatively, *mono-
siteō* might mean "eating only one meal (per day)."

ἐπὰν ἰδιώτην ἄνδρα μονοσιτοῦντ᾽ ἴδῃς
ἢ μὴ ποθοῦντ᾽ ᾠδὰς ποιητὴν καὶ μέλη,
τὸν μὲν ἰδιώτην τοῦ βίου τὸν ἥμισυν

d ἀπολωλεκέναι νόμιζε, τὸν δὲ τῆς τέχνης |
τὴν ἡμίσειαν· ζῶσι δ᾽ ἀμφότεροι μόλις.

Πλάτων· † οὐ μονοσιτῶν ἑκάστοτε, ἀλλὰ κἀνίοτε
δειπνῶν δὶς τῆς ἡμέρας †.[23]

Ὅτι νωγαλεύματα ἐκάλουν τὰ ἡδέα βρώματα.
Ἀραρώς·

τὰ κομψὰ μὲν ⟨δὴ⟩[24] ταῦτα νωγαλεύματα.

Ἄλεξις·

Θασίοις οἰναρίοις καὶ Λεσβίοις
τῆς ἡμέρας τὸ λοιπὸν ὑποβρέχει μέρος
καὶ νωγαλίζει.

Ἀντιφάνης·

βότρυς, ῥόας, φοίνικας, ἕτερα νώγαλα.

ἀπόσιτον δ᾽ εἴρηκε Φιλωνίδης, αὐτόσιτον δὲ Κρώβυ-
e λος· |

παράσιτον αὐτόσιτον.

[23] This sentence is omitted by E and is preserved in C only in the margin.
[24] cf. 3.86d

266

When you see an ordinary person eating alone
(monositount'),
or a poet with no desire for songs and music,
you may conclude that the ordinary man has lost
half his life and the poet half
his craft. They're both barely alive.

Plato (fr. 296; unmetrical): † not eating alone (monositōn)
all the time, but sometimes attending dinner parties twice
a day †.

They called delicious foods nōgaleumata ("dainties").
Ararus (fr. 8.1):[81]

these sophisticated dainties (nōgaleumata), on the
one hand.

Alexis (fr. 277):

He keeps the rest of the day
moist with Thasian and Lesbian wines,
and eats dainties (nōgalizei).

Antiphanes (fr. 66):

grapes, pomegranates, figs, other dainties (nōgala).

Philonides (fr. 1.1)[82] uses the word apositos ("abstaining
from food"), and Crobylus (fr. 1.1)[83] uses autositos ("providing his own food"):

a parasite who provides his own food.

[81] Quoted at greater length at 3.86d, 105e.
[82] Quoted in full at 6.247e.
[83] Quoted in full at 4.248b.

ATHENAEUS

ἀναρίστητον δ᾽ εἴρηκεν Εὔπολις, ἀναγκόσιτον δὲ
Κράτης. καὶ Νικόστρατος δέ·

      μειράκιον ⟨ . . . ⟩ κατὰ τύχην
ὑποσκαφιόκαρτόν τι κεχλαμυδωμένον
κατάγεις ἀναγκόσιτον.

ἀριστόδειπνον δ᾽ εἶπεν Ἄλεξις·

      ἀφ᾽ ὧν γένοιτ᾽ ἂν ἡμῖν σύντομον
ἀριστόδειπνον.

Μετὰ ταῦτα ἀναστάντες κατεκλίνθημεν ὡς ἕκαστος
ἤθελε, οὐ περιμείναντες ὀνομακλήτορα τὸν τῶν δείπνων ταξίαρχον.

Ὅτι καὶ τρίκλινοι οἶκοι καὶ τετράκλινοι καὶ ἑπτά-
f κλινοι καὶ | ἐννεάκλινοι καὶ κατὰ τοὺς ἑξῆς ἀριθμοὺς
ἦσαν παρὰ τοῖς παλαιοῖς. Ἀντιφάνης·

      συναγαγὼν
τρεῖς ὄντας εἰς τρίκλινον ὑμᾶς.

Φρύνιχος·

      ἑπτάκλινος οἶκος ἦν καλός,
εἶτ᾽ ἐννεάκλινος ἕτερος οἶκος.

Εὔβουλος·

---

84 Literally "lunch-dinner."
85 Ulpian; cf. 2.58b. What follows apparently marks the begin-

Eupolis (fr. 77.1) uses *anaristos* ("lunch-less"). Crates (fr. 50) uses *anangkositos* ("force-fed"), as Nicostratus (fr. 31) does as well:

> Perhaps you bring home
> a force-fed *(anangkositon)* young boy who has a bowl-
> cut and
> is dressed in an ephebe's cloak.

Alexis (fr. 296) uses the word *aristodeipnon* ("brunch"):[84]

> from which we could get a quick
> brunch.

After this we got up and lay down wherever we wanted, without waiting for our dinner-marshal[85] to summon us by name.

The ancients had rooms with space for three couches, four couches, seven couches, nine couches, and even more than that. Antiphanes (fr. 292):

> since there were three of you,
> putting you all together in a room with space for
> three couches.

Phrynichus (fr. 69):

> There was a lovely room with space for seven
> couches,
> and then another with space for nine.

Eubulus (fr. 119.1–3):[86]

ning of a new speech, which explores the history of the dinner-fur-
niture with which the guests are now surrounded.

[86] The rest of the fragment is quoted at 2.49c.

(Α.) θὲς ἑπτάκλινον. (Β.) ἑπτάκλινος οὑτοσί.

(Α.) καὶ πέντε κλίνας Σικελικάς. (Β.) λέγ᾽ ἄλλο τι.

(Α.) Σικελικὰ προσκεφάλαια πέντε.

48   Ἄμφις· ‖

οὐχ ὑποστρώσεις ποτὲ
τρίκλινον;

Ἀναξανδρίδης·

τρίκλινον δ᾽ εὐθέως συνήγετο
καὶ συναυλίαι γερόντων.

ἀλλὰ ξενῶνας οἶγε καὶ ῥᾶνον δόμους
στρῶσόν τε κοίτας καὶ πυρὸς φλέξον μένος,
κρατῆρά τ᾽ αἶρου καὶ τὸν ἥδιστον κέρα.

Νῦν δὲ τὴν τῶν στρωμάτων σύνθεσιν περιβολῇ
χωρίζουσι καὶ ὑποβολῇ, φησὶ Πλάτων ὁ φιλόσοφος.
ὁ δ᾽ ὁμώνυμος αὐτῷ ποιητής φησι·

b   κᾆτ᾽ ἄν | κλίναις ἐλεφαντόποσιν καὶ στρώμασι
πορφυροβάπτοις
κἂν φοινικίσι Σαρδιακαῖσιν κοσμησάμενοι
κατάκεινται.

ἤκμασε δ᾽ ἡ τῶν ποικίλων ὑφὴ μάλιστα ἐντέχνων περὶ

---

[87] Sc. because the one just given has already been accomplished.   [88] To keep down the dust, the floor being dirt.

(A.) Get a room with space for seven couches ready!
   (B.) Here it is!
(A.) And five Sicilian couches! (B.) Give me another
   order![87]
(A.) Five Sicilian pillows!

Amphis (fr. 45):

> Aren't you ever going to lay out the bed-clothes
> in the three-couch room?

Anaxandrides (fr. 72):

> A room with three couches was quickly assembled,
> and a collection of old men.

> But open up the guest-rooms, sprinkle water around
>   the house,[88]
> cover the beds, light a mighty fire,
> and get a mixing-bowl and mix up the best wine!
>   (adesp. tr. fr. 90)

Nowadays, says the philosopher Plato (*Plt*. 280b, cf.
279d),[89] they distinguish the production of rugs by
whether they are wrapped around or go under us. The poet
who shares his name says (Pl. Com. fr. 230):

> And then they lie down on couches with ivory feet
>   and bed-clothes
> dyed purple, dressed up in robes of Sardian red.[90]

The weaving of elaborately patterned fabrics reached its

[89] A garbled reference to a largely irrelevant passage.

[90] See the end of this Book for material that ought probably to
be inserted here.

αὐτὰ γενομένων Ἀκεσᾶ καὶ Ἑλικῶνος τῶν Κυπρίων.
ὑφάνται δ᾽ ἦσαν ἔνδοξοι· καὶ ἦν Ἑλικὼν υἱὸς Ἀκεσᾶ,
ὥς φησιν Ἱερώνυμος. ἐν Πυθοῖ γοῦν ἐπί τινος ἔργου
ἐπιγέγραπται·

> τεῦξ᾽ Ἑλικὼν Ἀκεσᾶ Σαλαμίνιος, ᾧ ἐνὶ χερσὶ
> πότνια θεσπεσίην Παλλὰς ἔχευε χάριν.

τοιοῦτος ἦν καὶ Παθυμίας ὁ Αἰγύπτιος.

c
>   ὡς ἐγὼ | σκιρτῶ πάλαι
> ὅπου ῥοδόπνοα στρώματ᾽ ἐστί, καὶ μύροις
> λοῦμαι ψακαστοῖς,

φησὶν Ἔφιππος. Ἀριστοφάνης·

> ὅστις ἐν ἡδυόσμοις
> στρώμασι παννυχίζων
> τὴν δέσποιναν ἐρείδεις.

Σώφρων δὲ στρουθωτὰ ἑλίγματά φησιν ἐντετιμημένα.
Ὅμηρος δὲ ὁ θαυμασιώτατος τῶν στρωμάτων τὰ μὲν
κατώτερα λῖτα εἶναι φάσκει ἤτοι λευκὰ καὶ μὴ βεβαμ-
μένα ἢ πεποικιλμένα, τὰ δὲ περιστρώματα

>   ῥήγεα καλὰ
> πορφύρεα.

Πρῶτοι δὲ Πέρσαι, ὥς φησιν Ἡρακλείδης, καὶ
d τοὺς λεγομένους στρώτας | ἐφεῦρον, ἵνα κόσμον ἔχῃ ἡ
στρῶσις καὶ εὐάφειαν. τὸν οὖν Τιμαγόραν ἢ τὸν ἐκ

zenith when Acesas and Helicon of Cypris were the chief craftsmen producing such goods. They were famous weavers; according to Hieronymus (fr. 48 Wehrli), Helicon was Acesas' son. At Delphi, at any rate, there is a piece of work that bears the inscription (anon. *FGE* 1544–5):

> Helicon of Salamis, son of Acesas, made this. Lady Athena
> inspired his hands with divine grace.

Pathymias of Egypt was another man of this type.

> Since I've been skipping about for a long time where the rose-scented bed-clothes are, and bathing in drops of perfume,

says Ephippus (fr. 26). Aristophanes (fr. 715):

> you who spend the night
> in sweet-smelling sheets,
> banging your mistress.

Sophron (fr. 95) says: expensive wraps embroidered with birds. The marvellous Homer (*Od.* 10.352–3) says that the bed-clothes that go under a person are white and neither dyed nor embroidered, whereas the covers are

> fine purple

blankets.

According to Heracleides (*FGrH* 689 F 5), the Persians invented what are referred to as "bed-makers" so that their bedding could be neat and soft. According to Phaenias the Peripatetic (fr. 27 Wehrli), Artaxerxes hon-

Γόρτυνος²⁵, ὥς φησι Φαινίας ὁ περιπατητικός, Ἔν-
τιμον, ὃς ζήλῳ Θεμιστοκλέους ἀνέβη ὡς βασιλέα,
τιμῶν Ἀρταξέρξης σκηνήν τε ἔδωκεν αὐτῷ διαφέρουσαν τὸ κάλλος καὶ τὸ μέγεθος καὶ κλίνην ἀργυρόποδα, ἔπεμψε δὲ καὶ στρώματα πολυτελῆ καὶ τὸν
ὑποστρώσοντα, φάσκων οὐκ ἐπίστασθαι τοὺς Ἕλληνας ὑποστρωννύειν. καὶ ἐπὶ τὸ συγγενικὸν ἄριστον
ἐκαλεῖτο ὁ Κρὴς οὗτος, τὸν βασιλέα ψυχαγωγήσας·
e   ὅπερ οὐδενὶ | πρότερον τῶν Ἑλλήνων ἐγένετο, ἀλλ'
οὐδ' ὕστερον· αὕτη γὰρ ἡ τιμὴ τοῖς συγγενέσι διεφυ-
λάττετο. Τιμαγόρᾳ μὲν γὰρ τῷ Ἀθηναίῳ τῷ προσκυ-
νήσαντι βασιλέα καὶ μάλιστα τιμηθέντι τοῦτο οὐχ
ὑπῆρξε· τῶν δὲ παρατιθεμένων βασιλεῖ τούτῳ τινὰ
ἀπὸ τῆς τραπέζης ἀπέστελλε. Ἀνταλκίδᾳ δὲ τῷ Λά-
κωνι τὸν αὑτοῦ στέφανον εἰς μύρον βάψας ἔπεμψε. τῷ
δ' Ἐντίμῳ τοιαῦτα πολλὰ ἐποίει καὶ ἐπὶ τὸ συγγενικὸν
ἄριστον ἐκάλει· ἐφ' ᾧ οἱ Πέρσαι χαλεπῶς ἔφερον ὡς
f   τῆς τε τιμῆς δημευομένης | καὶ στρατείας ἐπὶ τὴν
Ἑλλάδα πάλιν ἐσομένης. ἔπεμψε δὲ καὶ κλίνην αὐτῷ
ἀργυρόποδα καὶ στρωμνὴν καὶ σκηνὴν οὐρανόροφον
ἀνθινὴν καὶ θρόνον ἀργυροῦν καὶ ἐπίχρυσον σκιά-
δειον καὶ φιάλας λιθοκολλήτους χρυσᾶς εἴκοσι²⁶, ἀρ-
γυρίδας²⁷ δὲ μεγάλας ἑκατὸν καὶ κρατῆρας ἀργυροῦς
⟨εἴκοσι⟩²⁸ καὶ παιδίσκας ἑκατὸν καὶ παῖδας ἑκατὸν

²⁵ τὸν οὖν Κρῆτα CE: τὸν οὖν Τιμαγόραν ἢ τὸν ἐκ Γόρ-
τυνος Κρῆτα Voisin   ²⁶ εἴκοσι (i.e. Κ´) Kaibel: καὶ CE
²⁷ ἀργυρίδας Olson: ἀργυρᾶς CE: ἀργυροῦς Kaibel

ored Timagoras[91] or Entimus of Gortyn,[92] who imitated Themistocles by traveling inland to the Persian King,[93] by giving him an extraordinarily large and beautiful tent and a silver-footed chair; he also sent him expensive bed-clothes and a man to arrange them, since he claimed that the Greeks did not know how to make beds. This Cretan[94] was even invited to the family lunch, since the King enjoyed his company. This never happened to any other Greek, before or after, because the honor was reserved for members of the royal family. Even Timagoras of Athens did not have this done for him, although he bowed down before the King and received great honors from him; but the King sent him some of the food that was served to him on his table. The King sent Antalcidas the Spartan[95] his own garland, which he had dipped in perfume. The King did many such kindnesses for Entimus, including inviting him to the family lunch; but the Persians were unhappy about this, since they thought it cheapened the honor and because another expedition against Greece was about to take place. The King also sent him a silver-footed couch and a bed, a tent with a brightly colored canopy, a silver throne, a gilded parasol, 20 gold libation-bowls set with jewels, 100 large silver bowls, 20 silver mixing-bowls, 100 female slaves and

[91] An Athenian (*PA* 13595; see below) sent as an ambassador to Artaxerxes II (for whom, see 1.22c n.) in 367 BCE.

[92] Otherwise unknown.   [93] Cf. 1.29f with n.

[94] Entimus of Gortyn, mentioned above.

[95] Antalcidas (Poralla #97) was repeatedly involved in negotiations with the Persians in the first half of the 4th century.

28 ⟨εἴκοσι⟩ Olson

49 χρυσοῦς τε ἑξακισχιλίους ‖ χωρὶς τῶν εἰς τὰ ἐπιτή-
δεια καθ᾽ ἡμέραν διδομένων.

Τράπεζαι ἐλεφαντόποδες τῶν ἐπιθημάτων ἐκ τῆς
καλουμένης σφενδάμνου πεποιημένων. Κρατῖνος·

γαυριῶσαι δ᾽ ἀναμένουσιν ὧδ᾽ ἐπηγλαϊσμέναι
μείρακες[29] φαιδραὶ τράπεζαι τρισκελεῖς
σφενδάμνιναι.

Εἰπόντος τινὸς κυνικοῦ τρίποδα τὴν τράπεζαν δυ-
σχεραίνει ὁ παρὰ τῷ σοφιστῇ Οὐλπιανὸς καὶ λέγει· †
τήμερον ἐγὼ πράγματα ἔξω ἐξ ἀπραξίας. † πόθεν γὰρ
τούτῳ ὁ τρίπους; εἰ μὴ τὴν Διογένους βακτηρίαν σὺν
b καὶ τὼ πόδε ἀριθμῶν οὗτος τρίποδα | προσηγόρευσε,
πάντων τραπέζας καλούντων τὰς παραθέσεις ταύτας.

Ὅτι Ἡσίοδος ἐν Κήυκος Γάμῳ—κἂν γὰρ γραμματικῶν παῖδες ἀποξενῶσι τοῦ ποιητοῦ τὰ ἔπη ταῦτα,
ἀλλ᾽ ἐμοὶ δοκεῖ ἀρχαῖα εἶναι—τρίποδας τὰς τραπέζας
φησί. καὶ Ξενοφῶν δ᾽ ὁ μουσικώτατος ἐν ἑβδόμῳ
Ἀναβάσεως γράφει· τρίποδες εἰσηνέχθησαν πᾶσιν·
οὗτοι δὲ ὅσον εἴκοσι κρεῶν μεστοὶ νενεμημένων. καὶ

---

[29] γαυριῶσαι . . . μείρακες is omitted by both C and E here,
but C offers the full quotation, along with the lemma, at the end
of Book 13.

---

[96] The final item makes it clear that the other items mentioned
were not gifts Entimus could take home with him, but only things
he was free to enjoy as long as he remained with the King.

[97] This fragment is given in badly damaged form in the manu-

100 male slaves, and 6,000 gold coins in addition to the money he was given to cover his daily expenses.[96]

Ivory-footed tables with their tops made of what is referred to as "Olympian maple." Cratinus (fr. 334):[97]

Awaiting us here are splendid, ornamented,
radiant young women, three-legged maple tables.

When one of the Cynics[98] refers to his table as a "tripod,"[99] the sophist's guest Ulpian becomes annoyed and says (adesp. com. fr. *103, unmetrical): † Today I'm going to have trouble rather than leisure! † Because where does this fellow get the word "tripod" from? Unless he adds Diogenes'[100] stick to his two feet and calls *him* a tripod; because everyone calls these objects set beside us "tables" (*trapezai*).[101]

Hesiod in *The Marriage of Ceyx* (fr. 266b)—even if the grammarians deny these verses to the poet, they seem to me to be ancient—refers to tables as "tripods." Likewise the scholarly Xenophon in Book VII (3.21–2) of the *Anabasis* writes:[102] Tripods were brought in for everyone; there were about 20 of them, piled high with meat. He

scripts here, but is found complete in the supplement to this Book at 2.71e (where see n.).   [98] Most likely Cynulcus.

[99] *Tripous* is properly an adjective ("three-footed"), but was commonly used substantivally to refer to tables of all sorts, as the quotations that follow make clear.

[100] A reference to Diogenes of Sinope (early 4th century BCE), the original Cynic; cf. 3.113f. Cynics commonly carried a stick and a beggar's bag.

[101] A contracted form of *tetrapezai* ("four-footed"), facilitating the pun in Ar. fr. 545 (quoted at 2.49c–d). What follows must be Cynulcus' response to Ulpian's challenge.

ἐπάγει· μάλιστα δ᾽ αἱ τράπεζαι κατὰ τοὺς ξένους ἀεὶ
c ἐτίθεντο. Ἀντιφάνης· |

ἐπεὶ δ᾽ ὁ τρίπους ἤρθη κατὰ χειρῶν τ᾽ εἴχομεν.

Εὔβουλος·

(B.) τρίποδες οὗτοι πέντε σοι.
(A.) καὶ πέντε— (B.) πεντηκοστολόγος
γενήσομαι.

Ἐπίχαρμος·

(A.) τί δὲ τόδ᾽ ἐστί; (B.) δηλαδὴ τρίπους. (A.) τί
μὰν ἔχει πόδας
τέτορας; οὔκ ἐστιν τρίπους, ἀλλ᾽ <ἔστιν> οἶμαι
τετράπους.
(B.) ἔστι δ᾽ ὄνυμ᾽ αὐτῷ τρίπους, τέτοράς γα μὰν
ἔχει πόδας.
(A.) εἰ δίπους τοίνυν ποκ᾽ ἦς, αἰνίγματ᾽
Οἰ<δίπου> νοεῖς.

Ἀριστοφάνης·

d   (A.) τράπεζαν ἡμῖν ἔκφερε |
τρεῖς πόδας ἔχουσαν, τέσσαρας δὲ μὴ 'χέτω.
(B.) καὶ πόθεν ἐγὼ τρίπουν τράπεζαν λήψομαι;

---

102 From the description of the dinner party given by Seuthes
mistakenly referred to at 1.15e.
103 Cf. 2.47f.

278

continues: The tables were consistently placed opposite the visitors. Antiphanes (fr. 280):

> when the tripod was removed and water was poured over our hands.

Eubulus (fr. 119.4–5):[103]

> (B.) Here are five tripods for you.
> (A.) And five—(B.) These fives are going to turn me into a tax-collector![104]

Epicharmus (fr. 147):

> (A.) What's this? (B.) A tripod, obviously. (A.) Then why does it have
> four feet? It's not a tripod; I'd say it's a tetrapod!
> (B.) It's called a tripod; but it's got four feet.
> (A.) If it ever had two feet, you're thinking of Oedipus' riddle![105]

Aristophanes (fr. 545):

> (A.) Bring us out a table *(trapeza)*
> with three feet; I don't want it to have four!
> (B.) And where am I going to get a three-footed table *(tripous trapeza)*?[106]

---

[104] Literally "I'm going to become a collector of the 5% levy!" (Athens' import-export tax).

[105] Actually the riddle of the Sphinx: "What goes on four legs in the morning, two at noon, and three in the evening?" (e.g. E. *Oed*. fr. 540a.20–3; Anaxil. fr. 22.25–7; Asclep. Trag. *FGrH* 12 F 7a (quoted at 10.456b); [Apollod.] *Bib*. 3.5.8).

[106] See the end of this Book for material that ought probably to be inserted somewhere in this area.

Ὅτι ἔθος ἦν ἐν τοῖς δείπνοις τῷ ἑστιάτορι κατα-
κλιθέντι προδίδοσθαι γραμματείδιόν τι περιέχον ἀνα-
γραφὴν τῶν παρεσκευασμένων, ἐφ' ᾧ εἰδέναι ὅ τι
μέλλει ὄψον φέρειν ὁ μάγειρος.

Δαμασκηνά. Δαμασκοῦ τῆς πόλεως ἐνδόξου οὔσης
καὶ μεγάλης πολλοὶ τῶν ἀρχαίων μέμνηνται. ἐπεὶ δὲ
πλεῖστον ἐν τῇ τῶν Δαμασκηνῶν ἐστι χώρᾳ τὸ κοκκύ-
e   μηλον καλούμενον καὶ κάλλιστα | γεωργεῖται, ἰδίως
καλεῖται τὸ ἀκρόδρυον Δαμασκηνὸν ὡς διάφορον τῶν
κατὰ τὰς ἄλλας χώρας γινομένων. κοκκύμηλα οὖν
ἐστι ταῦτα· ὧν ἄλλος τε μέμνηται καὶ Ἱππῶναξ·

στέφανον εἶχον κοκκυμήλων καὶ μίνθης.

Ἄλεξις·

(Α.) καὶ μὴν ἐνύπνιον οἴομαί ⟨γ'⟩ ἑορακέναι
νικητικόν. (Β.) λέγ' αὐτό. (Α.) τὸν νοῦν πρόσεχε
δή·
ἐν τῷ σταδίῳ τῶν ἀνταγωνιστῶν μέ τις
ἐδόκει στεφανοῦν γυμνὸς προσελθὼν ⟨ . . . ⟩
f   στεφάνῳ κυλιστῷ κοκκυμήλων— (Β.) Ἡράκλεις. |
(Α.) πεπόνων.

πάλιν·

ἑόρακας ⟨ἤδη⟩ πώποτ' ἐσκευασμένον
ἤνυστρον ἢ σπλῆν' ὀπτὸν ὠνθυλευμένον
ἢ κοκκυμήλων σπυρίδα πεπόνων; ⟨ . . . ⟩
τοιοῦτ' ἔχει τὸ μέτωπον.

It was the custom at dinner parties for the host to be offered a writing tablet with a list of the dishes when he lay down, so that he would know what food the cook was going to serve.[107]

Damson plums. Many ancient authors mention the city of Damascus, which was large and famous. Because what is referred to as the *kokkumēlon* ("plum tree") is widely and successfully cultivated in the territory of the people of Damascus, its fruit is referred to specifically as the damson, to distinguish it from what is grown in other areas. These are therefore simply *kokkumēla* ("plums"). Someone else mentions them, as does Hipponax (fr. 62 Degani):

I was wearing a garland of plums and mint.

Alexis (fr. 274):

(A.) In fact, I believe I had a dream that
predicts victory. (B.) Tell it to me. (A.) Pay attention!
One of the competitors in the stade-race,
I thought, came up to me naked, and crowned me
with a twined garland of plums—(B.) Heracles![108]
(A.) Ripe ones!

Again (Alex. fr. 275):

Have you ever seen a cooked
cow's stomach, or a roasted stuffed spleen,
or a basket of ripe plums?
That's what his face looks like.

[107] The items discussed in the material that follows are presumably now served to Larensius' guests as appetizers, and a new speaker takes the floor.

[108] The oath generally expresses shock or dismay.

281

Νίκανδρος·

⟨ . . . ⟩ μῆλον ὃ κόκκυγος καλέουσι.

Κλέαρχος δ᾽ ὁ περιπατητικός φησι Ῥοδίους καὶ Σικελιώτας βράβυλα καλεῖν τὰ κοκκύμηλα, ὡς καὶ Θεόκριτος ὁ Συρακούσιος· ‖

50

ὄρπακες βραβίλοισι καταβρίθοντες ἔραζε.

καὶ πάλιν·

ὅσον μῆλον βραβίλοιο
ἥδιον.

ἐστὶ δὲ τοῦτο τὸ ἀκρόδρυον μικρότερον μὲν τῇ περιφορᾷ τῶν κοκκυμήλων, τῇ δ᾽ ἐδωδῇ τὸ αὐτό, πλὴν ὀλίγον δριμύτερον. Σέλευκος δ᾽ ἐν Γλώσσαις βράβιλά φησιν, ἦλα, κοκκύμηλα, μάδρυα, τὰ αὐτὰ εἶναι· τὰ μὲν μάδρυα οἷον μαλόδρυα, τὰ δὲ βράβυλα ὅτι εὐκοίλια καὶ τὴν βορὰν ἐκβάλλοντα, ἦλα δὲ οἷον μῆλα, ὡς Δημήτριος ὁ Ἰξίων λέγει ἐν Ἐτυμολογίᾳ. Θεόφραστος δὲ λέγει· κοκκυμηλέα | καὶ σποδιάς· τοῦτο δ᾽ ἐστὶν ὥσπερ ἀγρία κοκκυμηλέα. Ἀραρὼς δὲ κοκκύμηλον καλεῖ τὸ δένδρον, κοκκύμηλον δὲ τὸ ἀκρόδρυον. Δίφιλος δὲ ὁ Σίφνιος μέσως φησὶν εἶναι ταῦτα εὔχυλα, εὔφθαρτα, εὐέκκριτα, ὀλιγότροφα.

b

___

109 As if the word were derived from *boran ekballonta*.
110 The original point of the observation (which has presum-

Nicander (fr. 87 Schneider):

> the fruit *(mēlon)* they refer to as "the cuckoo's"
> *(kokkugos).*

Clearchus the Peripatetic (fr. 100 Wehrli) says that the Rhodians and Sicilians refer to plums as *brabula*, as Theocritus of Syracuse (7.146) does:

> young trees weighed down to the ground with plums
> *(brabila).*

And again (12.3–4):

> as much as an apple is sweeter
> than a plum *(brabilon).*

The *brabulon* is smaller in circumference than plums *(kokkumēla)* but tastes the same, except that it is slightly more bitter. Seleucus in the *Glossary* (fr. 42 Müller) says that *brabila*, *ēla*, *kokkumēla*, and *madrua* are identical. *Madrua* are, as it were, *malo-drua* ("tree-fruit"); *brabula* are called this because they make one's bowels move and expel the food;[109] and *ēla* are, as it were, *mēla* ("fruit"), as Demetrius Ixion says in the *Etymology* (fr. 42 Staesche). Theophrastus (*HP* 3.6.4) says: plum trees and *spodiai*, which are something like a wild plum tree. Araros (fr. 20) refers to the tree as a *kokkumēlon*, but to the fruit as a *kokkumēlon*.[110] Diphilus of Siphnos says that they produce moderately good *chulē* ("digestive juice") and are easily broken down in the stomach, easily excreted, and not very nutritious.

ably been garbled by the Epitomator) was most likely that Araros treated the tree as masculine, the fruit as neuter; cf. Pollux 1.232.

Κεράσια. Θεόφραστος ἐν τῷ Περὶ Φυτῶν· ἴδιον δὲ
τῇ φύσει δένδρον ὁ κέρασός ἐστι καὶ μεγέθει μέγα·
καὶ γὰρ εἰς εἴκοσι καὶ τέσσαρας πήχεις αὔξεται.
φύλλον δὲ ὅμοιον ἔχει τῷ τῆς μεσπίλης, σκληρὸν δὲ
καὶ παχύτερον, φλοιὸν δ' ὅμοιον φιλύρᾳ, ἄνθος δὲ
λευκόν, ἀπίῳ καὶ μεσπίλῃ ὅμοιον, ἐκ μικρῶν ἀνθῶν
c   συγκείμενον, κηριῶδες. | ὁ δὲ καρπὸς ἐρυθρός, ὅμοιος
διοσπύρῳ τὸ σχῆμα, τὸ δὲ μέγεθος ἡλίκον κύαμος,
πλὴν τοῦ διοσπύρου μὲν ὁ πυρὴν σκληρός, τοῦ δὲ
κεράσου μαλακός. καὶ πάλιν· κράταιγος· οἱ δὲ κραταί-
γονον καλοῦσιν. ἔχει δὲ τὸ μὲν φύλλον τεταμένον
ὅμοιον μεσπίλῃ· πλὴν μεῖζον ἐκείνου καὶ πλατύτερον
ἢ προμηκέστερον· τὸν δὲ χαραγμὸν οὐκ ἔχει ὥσπερ
ἐκεῖνο. γίνεται δὲ τὸ δένδρον οὔτε μέγα λίαν οὔτε
παχύ. τὸ δὲ ξύλον ποικίλον, ξανθόν, ἰσχυρόν. φλοιὸν
d   δ' ἔχει λεῖον ὅμοιον μεσπίλῃ· μονόριζον εἰς βάθος |
ὡς ἐπὶ πολύ. καρπὸν δ' ἔχει στρογγύλον ἡλίκον ὁ
κότινος· πεπαινόμενος δὲ ξανθός τέ ἐστι καὶ ἐπιμελαί-
νεται. ἔχει δὲ τὴν γεῦσιν καὶ τὸν χυλὸν μεσπίλου,
διόπερ ἀγρία μεσπίλη δόξειε ⟨ἂν⟩ μᾶλλον εἶναι. ἐκ
τούτων μοι δοκεῖ, φησίν, ὁ φιλόσοφος τὸ νῦν κερά-
σιον καλούμενον ἐμφανίζειν.

Ἀσκληπιάδης δὲ ὁ Μυρλεανὸς χαμαικέρασόν τινα
καλῶν δένδρον ἔφη οὕτως· ἐν τῇ Βιθυνῶν γῇ γίνεται ἡ
χαμαικέρασος, ἧς ἡ μὲν ῥίζα ἐστὶν οὐ μεγάλη, ἀλλ'
οὐδὲ τὸ δένδρον, ἀλλὰ τῇ ῥόδῃ ἴσον, ὁ δὲ καρπὸς τὰ
e   μὲν ἄλλα πάντα ⟨κεράσῳ⟩ | ὅμοιος, τοὺς δὲ πλείονι
χρησαμένους καθότι οἶνος βαρύνει τε καὶ ἀλγεῖν τὴν

Cherries. Theophrastus in his *On Plants* (*HP* 3.13.1–3, radically condensed): The wild cherry is a peculiar tree and very large, growing as much as 24 cubits high.[111] Its leaf is like the medlar's, but tough and thicker; its bark is like the lime tree's; and its flower is white, like the pear's and the medlar's, composed of a number of small blossoms, and arranged like a honeycomb. The fruit is red and resembles that of the *diospuros* in shape, but is the size of a fava bean, while the stone of the *diospuros* is hard, whereas the cherry's stone is soft. And again (*HP* 3.15.6): *krataigos*; some call it *krataigonos*. Its leaf is organized like the medlar's, but is longer, and is broader than it is wide; and the edge is not jagged like the medlar's. The tree does not grow very tall or thick; its wood is mottled, brown, and strong; and it has smooth bark, like the medlar's, and a single root that goes quite deep. It bears fruit that is round and as large as the wild olive's; when the fruit is ripe, it is brown and then turns black, and it has the taste and flavor of the medlar, as a consequence of which it would seem to be a wild form of that tree. From this description, [Athenaeus] says, the philosopher would appear to be referring to what is today called the wild cherry.

Asclepiades of Myrlea (*FGrH* 697 F *4) mentioned a bush-cherry tree and said the following: The bush-cherry grows in Bithynia. Its root is not large, and neither is the tree, which is the same size as the rose. The fruit is in all other ways like the wild cherry, but it overpowers those who consume a large quantity of it, in the same way wine

[111] A cubit = approximately 1.5 feet.

κεφαλὴν τίθησι. ταῦτα ὁ Ἀσκληπιάδης, φησί, μοι
δοκεῖ λέγειν περὶ τῶν μιμαικύλων. τό τε γὰρ φέρον
αὐτὰ δένδρον τοιοῦτον καὶ ὁ πλέον τῶν ἑπτὰ τοῦ
καρποῦ φαγὼν κεφαλαλγὴς γίνεται. Ἀριστοφάνης·

> ἐν τοῖς ὄρεσιν <δ᾽> αὐτομάτ᾽ αὐτοῖς τὰ μιμαίκυλ᾽
> ἐφύετο πολλά.

Θεόπομπος·

> τρώγουσι μύρτα καὶ πέπονα μιμαίκυλα.

Κράτης·

f πάνυ γάρ ἐστιν ὡρικὰ |
> τὰ τιτθί᾽ ὥσπερ μῆλα καὶ μιμαίκυλα.

Ἄμφις·

> ὁ συκάμινος συκάμιν᾽, ὁρᾷς, φέρει,
> ὁ πρῖνος ἀκύλους, ὁ κόμαρος μιμαίκυλα.

Θεόφραστος· ἡ κόμαρος ἡ τὸ μιμαίκυλον φέρουσα τὸ
ἐδώδιμον.

Ὅτι Ἀγῆνα σατυρικόν τι δρᾶμα ἀμφιβάλλεται
εἴτε Πύθων ἐποίησεν ὁ Καταναῖος ἢ Βυζάντιος ἢ καὶ
αὐτὸς ὁ βασιλεὺς Ἀλέξανδρος.

Φησὶν ὁ παρὰ τῷ ῥήτορι Λαρήνσιος· πολλὰ ὑμεῖς
οἱ Γραικοὶ ἐξιδιοποιεῖσθε ὡς αὐτοὶ ἢ ὀνομάσαντες
ἢ πρῶτοι εὑρόντες. ἀγνοεῖτε δὲ ὅτι Λεύκολλος ὁ Ῥω-

does, and gives them a headache. Asclepiades seems to me, he says, to be referring to arbutus-fruit; because the tree that produces it matches his description, and anyone who eats more than seven arbutus-fruit gets a headache. Aristophanes (fr. 698):

> In the mountains many volunteer arbutus trees grew
> for them.

Theopompus (fr. 68):

> They eat myrtle-berries and ripe arbutus-fruit.

Crates (fr. 43):

>   because her titties are perfectly
> ripe, like apples or arbutus-fruit.

Amphis (fr. 38):

> The mulberry tree, you see, bears mulberries,
> the holm-oak acorns, the arbutus tree arbutus-fruit.

Theophrastus (*HP* 3.16.4): the arbutus tree, which bears the edible arbutus-fruit.

It is a matter of dispute whether Python of Catana or Byzantium (*TrGF* 91) wrote the satyr play *Agēn*, or whether the author was King Alexander himself.[112]

Larensius, the rhetorician's character, says: You Greeks lay claim to many things, alleging that you either gave them their names or discovered them. But you are unaware that the Roman general Lucullus, who defeated

---

[112] See 13.595e–6b (quoting a substantial fragment of the play, which attacked Harpalus). But the point of the remark here is unclear.

51 μαίων στρατηγός, ‖ ὁ τὸν Μιθριδάτην καὶ Τιγράνην
καταγωνισάμενος, πρῶτος διεκόμισεν εἰς Ἰταλίαν
τὸ φυτὸν τοῦτο ἀπὸ Κερασοῦντος Ποντικῆς πόλεως.
καὶ οὗτός ἐστιν ὁ καὶ τὸν καρπὸν καλέσας κέρασον
ὁμωνύμως τῇ πόλει, ὡς ἱστοροῦσιν οἱ ἡμέτεροι συγγραφεῖς. πρὸς ὃν Δάφνος τίς φησιν· ἀλλὰ μὴν παμπόλλοις ‹χρόνοις›[30] πρεσβύτερος Λευκόλλου ἀνὴρ
ἐλλόγιμος Δίφιλος ὁ Σίφνιος, γεγονὼς κατὰ Λυσίμα-
χον τὸν βασιλέα—εἷς δὲ οὗτος τῶν Ἀλεξάνδρου δια-
b δόχων—μνημονεύει τῶν κερασίων λέγων· τὰ ǀ κεράσια
εὔστομα[31], εὔχυλα, ὀλιγότροφα, ἐκ ψυχροῦ δὲ λαμβα-
νόμενα εὐστόμαχα. καλλίω δὲ τὰ ἐρυθρότερα καὶ τὰ
Μιλήσια· εἰσὶ γὰρ διουρητικά.

Συκάμινα. ὅτι πάντων ἁπλῶς οὕτω καλούντων αὐτὰ
Ἀλεξανδρεῖς μόνοι μόρα ὀνομάζουσι. συκάμινα δὲ οὐ
τὰ ἀπὸ τῆς Αἰγυπτίας συκῆς, ἅ τινες συκόμορα
λέγουσιν. ἅπερ οἱ ἐπιχώριοι ἐπὶ βραχὺ κνίσαντες
σιδηρίῳ ἐῶσιν ἐπὶ τοῦ φυτοῦ· καὶ ὑπὸ τοῦ ἀνέμου
κινούμενα ἐντὸς ἡμερῶν τριῶν οὕτω πέπονα καὶ εὐώδη
c γίνονται, ǀ μάλιστα δὲ ζεφύρων πνευσάντων, καὶ ἐδώ-
διμα ὡς ‹διὰ› τὸ ἐν αὐτοῖς ἠρέμα ψυχρὸν καὶ τοῖς
πυρεταίνουσι μετὰ ῥοδίνου ἐλαίου καταπλαττόμενα
ἐπὶ τοῦ στομάχου ἐπιτίθεσθαι καὶ οὐκ ὀλίγα παρηγο-
ρεῖσθαι τοὺς νοσοῦντας. φέρει δὲ τὸν καρπὸν τοῦτον ἡ
Αἰγυπτία συκάμινος ἀπὸ τοῦ ξύλου καὶ οὐκ ἀπὸ τῶν

---

[30] παμπόλλοις χρόνοις Schweighäuser: παμπολ . . . C:
παμπολλῆς . . . ν E   [31] εὔστομα Kaibel: εὐστόμαχα CE

Mithridates and Tigranes,[113] first brought this plant to Italy from the Pontic city of Cerasus. He is also the one who named the fruit the "cherry," after the city, as our historians record. A certain Daphnis answered him: And yet the esteemed Diphilus of Siphnos, who was far earlier than Lucullus, since he lived in the time of King Lysimachus[114]—he was one of Alexander's successors—mentions cherries and says: Cherries are delicious, produce good *chulē*, and are not very nutritious; they are easy on the stomach when eaten cold. Redder ones and the Milesian variety are the best, since they are diuretic.

Mulberries. Although everyone else without exception refers to them this way, the Alexandrians alone call them *mora*. Mulberries *(sukamina)* are not the fruit of the Egyptian fig, which some authorities call *sukomora* ("fig-*mora*").[115] The locals nick the fruit with a knife and leave it on the plant. The breeze moves it about, and within three days it becomes so ripe, fragrant, and edible, especially if the wind is blowing from the west, that, because of its mild coolness, it is made into plasters with rose oil and placed on the stomachs of people suffering from fever, and it offers considerable comfort to the sick. The Egyptian mulberry tree bears this fruit on the wood rather than on fruit-stalks.

[113] L. Licinius Lucullus won a series of victories over Mithridates VI of Pontus and Tigranes II of Armenia in 69–67 BCE.

[114] Lysimachus of Thrace (Berve i #480), reigned 323–281 BCE.

[115] For the information that follows, cf. Thphr. *HP* 4.2.1, on which Athenaeus is perhaps drawing.

ἐπικαρπίων. μόρα δὲ τὰ συκάμινα καὶ παρ' Αἰσχύλῳ
ἐν Φρυξὶν ἐπὶ τοῦ Ἕκτορος·

ἀνὴρ δ' ἐκεῖνος ἦν πεπαίτερος μόρων.

d   ἐν δὲ Κρήσσαις καὶ κατὰ τῆς βάτου· |

λευκοῖς τε γὰρ μόροισι καὶ μελαγχίμοις
καὶ μιλτοπρέπτοις βρίθεται ταὐτοῦ χρόνου.

Σοφοκλῆς·

πρῶτον μὲν ὄψῃ λευκὸν ἀνθοῦντα στάχυν,
ἔπειτα φοινίξαντα γογγύλον μόρον.

καὶ Νίκανδρος δὲ ἐν Γεωργικοῖς ἐμφανίζει καὶ ὅτι
πρότερον τῶν ἄλλων ἀκροδρύων φαίνεται μορέην τε
καλεῖ τὸ δένδρον ἀεί, ὡς καὶ οἱ Ἀλεξανδρεῖς·

e   καὶ μορέης, ἢ παισὶ πέλει μείλιγμα νέοισι |
πρῶτον ἀπαγγέλλουσα βροτοῖς ἡδεῖαν ὀπώρην.

Φαινίας δ' <ὁ> Ἐρέσιος ὁ Ἀριστοτέλους μαθητὴς τὸν
τῆς ἀγρίας συκαμίνου καρπὸν μόρον καλεῖ, ὄντα καὶ
αὐτὸν γλυκύτατον καὶ ἥδιστον ὅτε πεπανθείη. γράφει
δὲ οὕτως· τὸ μόρον τὸ βατῶδες ξηρανθείσης τῆς
σφαίρας τῆς συκαμινώδους σπερματικὰς ἔχει τὰς
συκαμινώδεις διαγονάς, καθάπερ † ὑφάλους[32] † καὶ

---

[32] ὑφάλους C: ὑφάνους E: ὑποφαινούσας Schneider

Aeschylus (fr. 264) also refers to mulberries as *mora* in *Phrygians*, describing Hector:

> That fellow was softer than *mora*.[116]

And in *Cretan Women* (A. fr. 116), referring to the black-berry:

> For it is loaded down simultaneously
> with white, black, and red berries *(mora)*.

Sophocles (fr. 395.1–2):[117]

> First you will see a white, flowering stalk,
> and then a round *moron* that has turned red.

Nicander too in his *Georgics* (fr. 75 Schneider) implies that it appears before other tree-fruit, and consistently refers to the tree as the *moreē*, as the Alexandrians do as well:

> and of the mulberry tree *(moreē)*, which brings little
>   boys joy
> and makes the first announcement of pleasant
>   harvest-time to mortals.

Phaenias of Eresus (fr. 42 Wehrli), the student of Aristotle, refers to the fruit of the wild mulberry as a *moron*;[118] it is quite sweet and enjoyable when ripe. He writes as follows: The blackberry-*moron*, when its mulberry-like sphere has dried, has mulberry-like divisions full of seeds, just like †

---

[116] Despite Athenaeus, the word may just as well refer here to a blackberry.   [117] Probably from *Seers*.

[118] In fact, Phaenias is clearly describing blackberries, which he compares repeatedly to mulberries. The passage is corrupt and probably contains a lacuna.

διαφυὰς[33] ἔχει ψαθυρὰς καὶ εὐχύμους. Παρθένιος δὲ
f ἁβρυνά φησι | συκάμινα, ἃ καλοῦσιν ἔνιοι μόρα·
Σαλαμίνιοι δὲ τὰ αὐτὰ ταῦτα βάτια. Δημήτριος δὲ ὁ
Ἰξίων τὰ αὐτὰ συκάμινα καὶ μόρα οἷον αἱμόροα καὶ
σύκων ἀμείνω. Δίφιλος δὲ ὁ Σίφνιος ἰατρὸς γράφει
οὕτως· τὰ δὲ συκάμινα, ἃ καὶ μόρα λέγεται, εὔχυλα
μέν ἐστιν, ὀλιγότροφα δὲ καὶ εὐστόμαχα καὶ εὐέκκριτα. ἰδίως δὲ τούτων τὰ ἔνωμα ἕλμινθας ἐκτινάσσει.
52 Πύθερμος δὲ ἱστορεῖ, ὥς φησιν Ἡγήσανδρος, ‖ καθ'
αὑτὸν τὰς συκαμίνους οὐκ ἐνεγκεῖν καρπὸν ἐτῶν εἴκοσι καὶ γενέσθαι ἐπιδημίαν ποδαγρικὴν τοσαύτην
ὥστε μὴ μόνον ἄνδρας τῷ πάθει ἐνσχεθῆναι, ἀλλὰ καὶ
παῖδας καὶ κόρας καὶ εὐνούχους, ἔτι δὲ γυναῖκας.
περιπεσεῖν δὲ οὕτω τὸ δεινὸν καὶ αἰπολίῳ ὡς τὰ δύο
μέρη τῶν προβάτων ἐνσχεθῆναι τῷ αὐτῷ πάθει.

Κάρυα. οἱ Ἀττικοὶ καὶ οἱ ἄλλοι συγγραφεῖς κοινῶς
πάντα τὰ ἀκρόδρυα κάρυα λέγουσιν. Ἐπίχαρμος δὲ
b κατ' ἐξοχὴν ὡς ἡμεῖς· |

< . . . > καπυρὰ τρώγων κάρυ', ἀμυγδάλας.

Φιλύλλιος·

< . . . > ᾠά, κάρυ', ἀμυγδάλαι.

Ἡρακλέων δέ φησιν ὁ Ἐφέσιος· κάρυα ἐκάλουν καὶ

[33] διαφυὰς C, ὁρᾷς[s]: διαφορὰς E

salty †; and it has segments that are crumbly and flavorful. Parthenius uses the term *habruna* for mulberries, which some authorities call *mora*; the Salaminians refer to this same fruit as *batia*.[119] Demetrius Ixion says that mulberries *(sukamina)* and *mora* are identical, as if the words were *haimoroa* ("flowing with blood")[120] and *sukōn ameinō* ("better than figs"). The physician Diphilus of Siphnos writes as follows: Mulberries, also referred to as *mora*, produce good *chulē*, are not very nutritious, and are easy on the stomach and easily excreted. The raw ones have the peculiar quality of driving out worms. According to Hegesander (fr. 41, *FHG* iv.421), Pythermus (*FGrH* 80 F 3) records that in his time the mulberry trees produced no fruit for twenty years, and gout became so widespread among the population that it was not just men who were afflicted by it, but boys, girls, eunuchs, and even women. The plague even struck a herd of goats so badly that two-thirds of the animals got the same disease.

Nuts *(karua)*. Attic authors and others refer generically to all tree-fruit as *karua*. But Epicharmus (fr. 148) uses the word in a specific sense, as we do:

eating dried *karua* and almonds.

Philyllius (fr. 24):

eggs, *karua*, almonds.

Heracleon of Ephesus says: They referred to almonds and

---

[119] Simply a diminutive of *batos*, "blackberry."

[120] In reference to the blackberry's dark red juice. Demetrius' claim is that *mora* is a contracted form of *haimoroa*, just as *sukamina* is supposedly contracted from *sukōn ameinō*.

τὰς ἀμυγδάλας καὶ τὰ νῦν καστάνεια. τὸ δὲ δένδρον
καρύα παρὰ Σοφοκλεῖ·

⟨ . . . ⟩ καρύαι μελίαι τε.

Εὔβουλος·

φηγούς, κάρυα Καρύστια.

καλεῖται δέ τινα καὶ μόστηνα κάρυα.
Ἀμυγδάλαι. ὅτι αἱ Νάξιαι ἀμυγδάλαι διὰ μνήμης
ἦσαν τοῖς παλαιοῖς· καὶ γίνονται ὄντως ἐν Νάξῳ τῇ
c νήσῳ διάφοροι, ὡς ἐμαυτόν, φησί, πείθω. | Φρύνιχος·

        τοὺς δὲ γομφίους
    ἅπαντας ἐξέκοψεν, ὥστ᾽
    οὐκ ἂν δυναίμην Ναξίαν
    ἀμυγδάλην κατᾶξαι.

διάφοροι δ᾽ ἀμυγδάλαι γίνονται κἂν Κύπρῳ τῇ νήσῳ·
παρὰ γὰρ τὰς ἀλλαχόθεν καὶ ἐπιμήκεις εἰσὶ καὶ κατὰ
τὸ ἄκρον ἐπικαμπεῖς. Λάκωνας δὲ Σέλευκος ἐν Γλώσσαις φησὶ καλεῖν τὰ μαλακὰ κάρυα μυκήρους, Τηνί-
ους δὲ τὰ γλυκέα κάρυα. Ἀμερίας δέ φησι μύκηρον
d τὴν | ἀμυγδάλην καλεῖσθαι. ἐπακτικώτατα δὲ πρὸς
πότον τὰ ἀμύγδαλα προεσθιόμενα. Εὔπολις·

    δίδου μασᾶσθαι Ναξίας ἀμυγδάλας,
    οἶνόν τε πίνειν Ναξίων ἀπ᾽ ἀμπέλων.

what are now called chestnuts as *karua*. But the tree is called *karúa* in Sophocles (fr. 759):

> nut trees *(karúai)* and ash trees.

Eubulus (fr. 135):

> acorns and Carystian *karua*.[121]

Some *karua* are also called *mostēna*.

Almonds. Naxian almonds were mentioned by the ancients. And I am convinced, he says, that particularly good ones are produced on the island of Naxos. Phrynichus (fr. 73):

> He knocked out
> all my molars, so that
> I wouldn't be able to crack
> a Naxian almond.

Outstanding almonds are also produced on the island of Cyprus; compared to those from elsewhere, they are long and crooked at the tip. Seleucus in the *Glossary* (fr. 61 Müller) says that the Spartans refer to nuts that are still soft as *mukēroi*, and that the inhabitants of Tenos use the word for sweet nuts. But Amerias (p. 7 Hoffmann) says that the almond is referred to as a *mukēros*. Almonds powerfully encourage drinking when eaten ahead of time. Eupolis (fr. 271):

> Give me some Naxian almonds to chew on,
> and some wine from Naxian vines to drink!

[121] Chestnuts?

ἦν δέ τις ἄμπελος Ναξία καλουμένη. Πλούταρχος δὲ ὁ
Χαιρωνεύς φησι παρὰ Δρούσῳ τῷ Τιβερίου Καίσα-
ρος υἱῷ ἰατρόν τινα ὑπερβάντα πάντας ἐν τῷ πίνειν
φωραθῆναι πρὸ τοῦ πότου προεσθίοντα πικρὰς ἀμυ-
e γδάλας πέντε ἢ ἕξ· ἅσπερ | κωλυθεὶς προσενέγκασθαι
οὐδὲ πρὸς τὸ μικρότατον ἀντέσχε τοῦ πότου. αἴτιος
οὖν ἦν ἡ τῆς πικρότητος δύναμις, ξηραντικὴ καὶ
δάπανος ὑγρῶν οὖσα. κληθῆναι δὲ ἀμυγδάλην φησὶν
Ἡρωδιανὸς ὁ Ἀλεξανδρεὺς παρὰ τὸ ἐν τῷ μετὰ τὸ
χλωρὸν ὡσπερεὶ ἀμυχὰς ἔχειν πολλάς.

ὄνος βαδίζεις εἰς ἄχυρα τραγημάτων,

φησί που Φιλήμων.

< . . . > φηγοὶ Πανὸς ἄγαλμα,

φησὶ Νίκανδρος ἐν δευτέρῳ Γεωργικῶν.

f Ὅτι καὶ οὐδετέρως ἀμύγδαλα λέγεται. Δίφιλος· |

τρωγάλια, μυρτίδες, πλακοῦς, ἀμύγδαλα.

Ὅτι περὶ τῆς προφορᾶς τοῦ τόνου τῆς ἀμυγδάλης
Πάμφιλος μὲν ἀξιοῖ ἐπὶ τοῦ καρποῦ βαρύνειν ὁμοίως

---

[122] Athenaeus does not cite Plutarch or Herodian elsewhere,
and Wilamowitz argued that this material must have been added
by the Epitomator (who does not elsewhere, however, appear to
be so ambitious).   [123] Iulius Caesar Drusus (c.13 BCE–
23 CE).   [124] Literally "in the (stage) after the green."
[125] Probably an introductory remark by a new speaker.
[126] Quoted in full at 14.640c–d, where the manuscripts, how-

There was a variety of grapevine called Naxian. Plutarch of Chaeronea (*Mor.* 624c)[122] reports that the circle of Drusus son of Tiberius Caesar[123] included a physician who could drink more than anyone else. Before the party began, he was caught eating five or six bitter almonds; when he was prevented from consuming them, he had no resistance at all to the wine. The reason for this was their bitter character, which is drying and eliminates liquids. Herodian of Alexandria (*Grammatici Graeci* III.1 p. 321.21–2) claims that the almond *(amugdalē)* got its name from the fact that, after the hull is shed,[124] it has what look like numerous scratchs *(amuchas)*.

> You're like a donkey heading off to a bran-pile of
>   dainties,

says Philemon (fr. 158) somewhere.[125]

> Valonia oaks, the delight of Pan,

says Nicander in Book II of the *Georgics* (fr. 69 Schneider).

The neuter plural *amugdala* is used. Diphilus (fr. 80.1):[126]

> snacks, myrtle-berries, a cake, almonds *(amugdala)*.

As for the placement of the accent on the word *amugdalē*, Pamphilus (fr. I Schmidt) believes that an acute should be used for the fruit, as also for the neuter form.[127]

---

ever, have the normal feminine *amugdalai*. The rest of this paragraph appears in virtually identical form at Herodian, *Grammatici Graeci* III.1 pp. 321.22–322.3.

[127] ἀμυγδάλη and ἀμύγδαλον, respectively.

τῷ ἀμυγδάλῳ· τὸ μέντοι δένδρον θέλει περισπᾶν, ἀμυγδαλῆ καὶ ῥοδῆ. καὶ Ἀρχίλοχος·

53   ῥοδῆς τε καλὸν ἄνθος. ‖

Ἀρίσταρχος δὲ καὶ τὸν καρπὸν καὶ τὸ δένδρον ὁμοίως προφέρεται κατ' ὀξεῖαν τάσιν· Φιλόξενος δ' ἀμφότερον περισπᾷ. Εὔπολις·

    ⟨ . . . ⟩ ἀπολεῖς με, ναὶ μὰ τὴν ἀμυγδαλῆν.

Ἀριστοφάνης·

        ἄγε νυν τὰς ἀμυγδαλᾶς λαβὼν
    τασδὶ κάταξον τῇ κεφαλῇ σαυτοῦ λίθῳ.

Φρύνιχος·

    ἀμυγδαλῆ τῆς βηχὸς ἀγαθὸν φάρμακον.

ἄλλοι δὲ ἀμυγδαλᾶς ὡς καλάς. Τρύφων δὲ ἐν Ἀττικῇ
b Προσῳδίᾳ ἀμυγδάλην μὲν τὸν καρπὸν | βαρέως, ὃν ἡμεῖς οὐδετέρως ἀμύγδαλον λέγομεν, ἀμυγδαλᾶς δὲ τὰ δένδρα, κτητικοῦ παρὰ τὸν καρπὸν ὄντος τοῦ χαρακτῆρος καὶ διὰ τοῦτο περισπωμένου.

Ὅτι Πάμφιλος ἐν Γλώσσαις μουκηροβαγόν φησι καλεῖσθαι τὸν καρυοκατάκτην ὑπὸ τῶν Λακώνων ἀντὶ τοῦ ἀμυγδαλοκατάκτην· μουκήρους γὰρ Λάκωνες κα-

---

128 ἀμυγδαλῆ, ῥοδῆ (contrast ῥόδον ("rose")).
129 ἀμυγδάλη.   130 ἀμυγδαλῆ.
131 As if the contracted accusative plural ending -as were actually the genitive singular -ēs/âs.

For the tree, on the other hand, he prefers the circumflex, *amugdalē*, like *rhodē* ("rosebush").[128] Also Archilochus (fr. 30.2 West²):

> and a lovely flower of a rosebush *(rhodē)*.

But Aristarchus pronounces both the fruit and the tree in the same way, with an oxytone accent;[129] whereas Philoxenus (fr. 437 Theodoridis) has them both with a circumflex.[130] Eupolis (fr. 79):

> You'll be the death of me, by the almond *(amugdalē)*!

Aristophanes (fr. 605):

> Come now! Take these almonds *(amugdalās)*
> and use your head as a stone to crack them!

Phrynichus (fr. 64):

> An almond *(amugdalē)* is good medicine for your
> cough.

Others accent the accusative plural *amugdalás*, like *kalás* ("fine, beautiful"). And Tryphon in his *Attic Pronunciation* (fr. 13 Velsen) says that the fruit, for which we use the neuter *amugdalon*, is *amugdále* with an acute accent, whereas the trees are *amugdalás*, which is a possessive form derived from the name of the fruit and therefore takes the circumflex.[131]

Pamphilus in the *Glossary* (fr. XXIII Schmidt) asserts that the Spartans refer to a nutcracker as a *moukērobagos*[132] rather than an *amugdalokataktēs* (literally "almond-

---

[132] From *moukēros* ("nut"; cf. 2.52c) + a verb cognate with *agnumi* ("break"; cf. *bagos ~ agos*, "fragment").

λοῦσι τὰ ἀμύγδαλα.

Ὅτι Ποντικῶν καλουμένων καρύων, ἃ λόπιμά τινες ὀνομάζουσι, μνημονεύει Νίκανδρος. Ἑρμῶναξ δὲ καὶ
c Τιμαχίδας ἐν Γλώσσαις Διὸς βάλανόν | φησι καλεῖσθαι τὸ Ποντικὸν κάρυον.

Ἡρακλείδης δὲ ὁ Ταραντῖνος ζητεῖ πότερον προπαρατίθεσθαι δεῖ τὰ τραγήματα, καθάπερ ἔν τισι
τόποις τῶν κατὰ τὴν Ἀσίαν καὶ τὴν Ἑλλάδα γίνεται,
ἢ οὔ, ἀλλὰ μετὰ τὸ δεῖπνον. ἐὰν μὲν οὖν μετὰ τὸ
δεῖπνον, συμβαίνει πλείονος τροφῆς κειμένης ἐν τῇ
κοιλίᾳ καὶ τοῖς ἐντέροις τὰ ἐπεισφερόμενα κάρυα,
χάριν τῆς πρὸς τὸ πίνειν ὁρμῆς ἐμπλεκόμενα τοῖς
σιτίοις, ἐμπνευματώσεις καὶ φθορὰς τῆς τροφῆς
d παρασκευάζειν | διὰ τὸ παρακολουθοῦν αὐτοῖς ἐπιπολαστικὸν φύσει καὶ δυσκατέργαστον· ἐξ ὧν ἀπεψίαι
γίνονται καὶ κοιλίας καταφοραί.

Τὰ δὲ ἀμύγδαλα, φησὶ Διοκλῆς, τρόφιμα μέν ἐστι
καὶ εὐκοίλια, θερμαντικὰ δὲ διὰ τὸ ἔχειν κεγχρῶδές τι.
λυπεῖ δ' ἧττον τὰ χλωρὰ τῶν ξηρῶν καὶ τὰ βεβρεγμένα τῶν ἀβρόχων καὶ τὰ πεφρυγμένα τῶν ὠμῶν. τὰ δὲ
Ἡρακλεωτικά, καλούμενα δὲ Διὸς βάλανοι, τρέφει μὲν
e οὐχ ὁμοίως τοῖς ἀμυγδάλοις, ἔχει δέ τι κεγχρῶδες |
καὶ ἐπιπολαστικόν· πλείω δὲ βρωθέντα βαρύνει τὴν
κεφαλήν. ἧττον δ' ἐνοχλεῖ καὶ τούτων τὰ χλωρὰ τῶν

---

133 I.e. nuts with a hard shell.
134 The remarks that follow would seem to belong to a physi-

cracker"), because they refer to almonds as *moukēroi*.

Nicander (fr. 77 Schneider) mentions what are referred to as Pontic nuts, to which some authorities give the name "husk-nuts."[133] But Hermonax and Timachidas in the *Glossary* (fr. 18 Blinkenberg) say that the Pontic nut is referred to as a Zeus-acorn.

Heracleides of Tarentum (fr. 71 Guardasole) raises the question of whether snacks ought to be served first, as is done in some regions of Asia and Greece, or not and served after dinner instead.[134] If they are served after dinner, a large amount of food is already in the gut and the intestines; and the nuts, which are introduced in addition to what is already there and are included in the food because they stimulate drinking, tend to produce gas and corrupt what has been eaten, because what is eaten after them naturally rises to the top of the stomach and is difficult to digest. The result is indigestion and diarrhea.

According to Diocles (fr. 202 van der Eijk), almonds are nutritious and easy on the bowels, but are warming because they have some properties of millet. Green almonds are less dangerous than dried almonds, soaked almonds[135] less dangerous than unsoaked almonds, and roasted almonds less dangerous than raw almonds. Heracleot nuts, also referred to as Zeus-acorns, are not as nutritious as almonds, and have some properties of millet and rise to the top of the stomach; when eaten in large quantities, they produce wooziness. Green ones cause fewer prob-

cian, whereas those that preceded are most naturally taken to be by a grammarian.

[135] Probably a reference to the soaking of whole immature almonds in brine.

ξηρῶν. τὰ δὲ Περσικὰ κεφαλαλγικὰ μέν ἐστιν οὐχ
ἧττον τῶν Διὸς βαλάνων, τρέφει δὲ μᾶλλον. φάρυγγα
τραχύνει καὶ στόμα· ὀπτηθέντα δὲ ἀλυπότερα γίνεται·
διαχωρεῖ δὲ μάλιστα τῶν καρύων ἐσθιόμενα μετὰ
μέλιτος. τὰ δὲ πλατέα φυσωδέστερά ἐστιν, ἀλυπότερα
δὲ τὰ ἑφθὰ τῶν ὠμῶν καὶ πεφρυγμένων, τὰ δὲ πεφρυ-
f γμένα τῶν | ὠμῶν. Φιλότιμος δὲ ἐν τοῖς Περὶ Τροφῆς
φησι· τὸ πλατὺ καὶ τὸ καλούμενον Σαρδιανὸν δυσκατέργαστά ἐστιν ὠμὰ πάντα καὶ δυσδιάλυτα, κατεχόμε-
να ὑπὸ τοῦ φλέγματος ἐν τῇ κοιλίᾳ, καὶ στρυφνότητα
ἔχοντα. τὸ δὲ Ποντικὸν λιπαρὸν καὶ δυσκατέργαστον.
τὸ δὲ ἀμύγδαλον ἧττον δυσκατέργαστον· φαγόντες
οὖν πλείονα οὐκ ἐνοχλούμεθα. λιπαρώτερά τε φαίνε-
54 ται καὶ ἀναδίδωσι χυμὸν γλυκὺν καὶ λιπαρόν. ‖ Δίφιλος δ' ὁ Σίφνιος, τὰ κάρυα, φησί, τὰ βασιλικὰ κεφα-
λαλγῆ ἐστι καὶ ἐπιπολαστικά. τούτων δὲ τὰ ἀπαλὰ ἔτι
καὶ λελευκασμένα εὐχυλότερα καὶ κρείττονα ὑπάρχει,
τὰ δ' ἐν τοῖς ἰπνοῖς φρυγόμενα ὀλιγότροφα. τὰ δὲ
ἀμύγδαλά ἐστιν οὐρητικὰ καὶ λεπτυντικὰ καὶ καθαρ-
τικὰ καὶ ὀλιγότροφα. τῶν μέντοι χλωρῶν κακοχύλων
ὄντων καὶ ἀτροφωτέρων πολὺ μᾶλλον φυσωδέστερα
καὶ ἐπιπολαστικώτερά ἐστι τὰ ξηρά. τὰ δὲ ἀπαλὰ καὶ
πλήρη καὶ λελευκασμένα γαλακτώδη ὄντα εὐχυλότε-
b ρά ἐστι. | τῶν δὲ ξηρῶν τὰ Θάσια καὶ Κύπρια ἀπαλὰ
ὄντα εὐεκκριτώτερά ἐστι. τὰ δὲ Ποντικὰ κάρυα κεφα-
λαλγῆ, ἧττον δ' ἐπιπολαστικὰ τῶν βασιλικῶν. Μνησίθεος δ' ὁ Ἀθηναῖος ἐν τῷ Περὶ Ἐδεστῶν, τῶν
Εὐβοικῶν, φησί, καρύων ἢ καστάνων, ἀμφοτέρως γὰρ

lems than dried ones. Persian nuts cause as many headaches as Zeus-acorns, but are more nourishing. They make
the throat and mouth rough, but cause less damage when
roasted, and pass more easily through the system than any
other nut, if eaten with honey. Broad nuts produce more
gas; but they cause less trouble when boiled than when raw
or roasted, and the roasted ones cause less trouble than the
raw ones. Phylotimus (fr. 8 Steckerl) in his *On Food* says:
The broad nut and the so-called Sardis nut are all difficult
to digest and to break down when raw, since the phlegm in
the gut keeps them intact and they have an astringent character. The Pontic nut is oily and difficult to digest. The almond is easier to digest; when we eat a large quantity of
them, therefore, we feel no discomfort. They appear to be
oilier and produce a sweet, oily juice. Diphilus of Siphnos
says: Royal nuts cause headaches and rise to the top of the
stomach. Those that are still soft and have turned white
produce better *chulē* and are of better quality, whereas
those that have been roasted in ovens are not very nutritious. Almonds are diuretic, promote weight-loss, clean
out one's system, and are not very nutritious. Although
green almonds produce bad *chulē* and are lacking in nutritional value, dried almonds produce much more gas and
rise more to the top of the stomach. Those that are soft and
fully developed and have turned white have a milky character and produce better *chulē*. Soft Thasian and Cyprian
almonds are more easily excreted than dried ones. Pontic
nuts cause headaches, but do not rise to the top of the
stomach as much as royal nuts do. Mnesitheus of Athens in
his *On Edible Substances* (fr. 30 Bertier) says: Euboean
nuts or chestnuts—they are referred to in both ways—are

καλεῖται, δύσπεπτος μὲν ἡ κατεργασία τῇ κοιλίᾳ καὶ φυσώδης ἡ πέψις γίνεται, παχύνει δὲ τὰς ἕξεις, ἐάν τις αὐτῶν κρατήσῃ. τὰ δὲ ἀμύγδαλα καὶ τὰ Ἡρακλεωτικὰ καὶ τὰ Περσικὰ κάρυα καὶ τἆλλα τὰ τοιαῦτα χείρω
c ἐστὶ τούτων. χρὴ δὲ | μηδὲν ὅλως τῆς τοιαύτης ἰδέας ἄπυρον ἐσθίειν ἔξω τῶν χλωρῶν ἀμυγδάλων, ἀλλὰ τὰ μὲν ἕψειν, τὰ δὲ φρύγειν. τὰ μὲν γὰρ αὐτῶν ἐστι λιπαρὰ τῇ φύσει, καθάπερ ἀμυγδάλαι τε αἱ ξηραὶ καὶ Διὸς βάλανοι, τὰ δὲ σκληρὰ[34] καὶ στρυφνά, καθάπερ αἵ τε φηγοὶ καὶ πᾶν τὸ τοιοῦτον γένος. τῶν οὖν λιπαρῶν ἀφαιρεῖται τὸ λίπος ἡ πύρωσις· ἐστὶ γὰρ τοῦτο ⟨τὸ⟩ χείριστον. τὰ δὲ σκληρὰ καὶ στρυφνὰ πεπαίνεται, ἐάν τις ὀλίγῳ καὶ μαλακῷ πυρὶ χρῆται. ὁ δὲ Δίφιλος τὰ κάστανα καὶ Σαρδιανὰς βαλάνους κα-
d λεῖ, | εἶναι λέγων αὐτὰς καὶ πολυτρόφους καὶ εὐχύλους, δυσοικονομήτους δὲ διὰ τὸ ἐπιμένειν τῷ στομάχῳ· τὰς δὲ φρυγείσας ἀτροφωτέρας μὲν γίνεσθαι, εὐοικονομήτους δέ· τὰς δὲ ἑψομένας ἐμπνευματοῦν μὲν ἧττον, τρέφειν δὲ τούτων μᾶλλον.

λόπιμον κάρυόν τε
Εὐβοέες, βάλανον δὲ μετεξέτεροι καλέσαντο,

Νίκανδρός φησιν ὁ Κολοφώνιος ἐν Γεωργικοῖς. Ἀγέλοχος δὲ ἄμωτα καλεῖ τὰ καστάνεια· ὅπου δὲ γίνεται
e τὰ κάρυα τὰ Σινωπικά, ταῦτα δένδρα ἐκάλουν | ἄμωτα.
Ἐρέβινθοι. Κρώβυλος·

χλωρὸν ἐρέβινθόν τινα

difficult for the stomach to break down, and the process of digestion produces gas. But they promote weight-gain, if a person can tolerate them. Almonds, Heracleot nuts, Persian nuts, and other nuts of this sort are inferior to them. No nuts of this type should be eaten raw, except green almonds. As for the rest, some should be boiled, others roasted; because some of them are naturally oily, such as dried almonds and Zeus-acorns, while others are harsh and astringent, such as Valonia acorns and all those of this type. Exposure to heat removes the oiliness from the oily ones; for this is their worst characteristic. Harsh, astringent nuts become soft when exposed to a low, slow fire. Diphilus also refers to chestnuts as "Sardian nuts," and says that they are very nutritious and produce good *chulē*, but are hard to digest, because they linger in the stomach. They are less nutritious when roasted, but more easily digested. When boiled, they produce less gas and are more nutritious than the roasted ones.

> The Euboeans referred to it as
> a husk-nut and a *karuon*, but others called it an
>   acorn,

says Nicander of Colophon in the *Georgics* (fr. 76 Schneider). Agelochus refers to chestnuts as *amōta*: Where Sinopic nuts are produced, they called these trees *amōta*.

Chickpeas. Crobylus (fr. 9):

> They were actually playing cottabus

---

34 σκληρὰ Schweighäuser: ξηρὰ CE

ἐκοττάβιζον κενὸν ὅλως. τράγημα δέ
ἐστιν πιθήκου τοῦτο δήπου δυστυχοῦς.

Ὅμηρος·

θρώσκωσιν κύαμοι μελανόχροες ἠ᾽ ἐρέβινθοι.

Ξενοφάνης ὁ Κολοφώνιος ἐν Παρῳδίαις·

πὰρ πυρὶ χρὴ τοιαῦτα λέγειν χειμῶνος ἐν ὥρῃ
ἐν κλίνῃ μαλακῇ κατακείμενον, ἔμπλεον ὄντα,
πίνοντα γλυκὺν οἶνον, ὑποτρώγοντ᾽ ἐρεβίνθους·
"τίς πόθεν εἶς ἀνδρῶν, πόσα τοι ἔτη ἐστί,
    φέριστε;
f   πηλίκος ἦσθ᾽, ὅθ᾽ ὁ Μῆδος ἀφίκετο;" |

Σαπφώ·

χρύσειοι ⟨δ᾽⟩ ἐρέβινθοι ἐπ᾽ ἀιόνων ἐφύοντο.

Θεόφραστος δ᾽ ἐν Φυτικοῖς τῶν ἐρεβίνθων τινὰς καλεῖ
κριούς. καὶ Σώφιλος·

ὁ πατὴρ ὁ ταύτης πολὺ μέγιστός ἐστι ⟨ . . . ⟩
κριὸς ἐρέβινθος.

Φαινίας δ᾽ ἐν τοῖς Περὶ Φυτῶν φησι· τραγήματος ἔχει
χώραν ἁπαλὰ μὲν ὦχρος, κύαμος, ἐρέβινθος, ξηρὰ δὲ
55 ἑφθὰ καὶ φρυκτὰ σχεδὸν τὰ πλεῖστα. Ἄλεξις· ||

ἔστιν ἀνήρ μοι πτωχὸς κἀγὼ

for a hollow green chickpea. This is
a snack for a monkey down on its luck!

Homer (*Il.* 13.589):

Black-skinned fava beans or chickpeas leap about.

Xenophanes of Colophon in the parodies (21 B 22 D–K):

You should say something like this in the winter
    season, when you're lying
beside a fire on a soft couch, with your belly full of
    food,
drinking sweet wine and nibbling on chickpeas:
"Who are you, friend, and where are you from? How
    old are you?
What age were you when the Mede came?"[136]

Sappho (fr. 143):

Golden chickpeas were growing on the shores.

Theophrastus in *On Plants* (*HP* 8.5.1) refers to certain
chickpeas as "rams." Also Sophilus (fr. 9):

This girl's father's the very biggest
ram chickpea there is!

Phaenias in his *On Plants* (fr. 43 Wehrli) says: Birds' pease,
fava beans, and chickpeas are categorized as snacks, when
green; when dried and boiled or roasted, nearly all of them
are. Alexis (fr. 167):

There's my husband, a pauper; and me,

[136] Referring to the Persian invasion of Greece in 480–479
BCE.

γραῦς καὶ θυγάτηρ καὶ παῖς υἱὸς
χἠδ᾽ ἡ χρηστή, πένθ᾽ οἱ πάντες.
τούτων οἱ ⟨μὲν⟩ τρεῖς δειπνοῦμεν,
δύο δ᾽ αὐτοῖς συγκοινωνοῦμεν
μάζης μικρᾶς. φθόγγους δ᾽ ἀλύρους
θρηνοῦμεν, ἐπὰν μηδὲν ἔχωμεν·
χρῶμα δ᾽ ἀσίτων ἡμῶν ὄντων
γίγνεται ὠχρόν. τὰ μέρη δ᾽ ἡμῶν
χἠ σύνταξις τοῦ βίου ἐστὶν
κύαμος, θέρμος, λάχανον, ⟨ . . . ⟩
γογγυλίς, ὦχρος, λάθυρος, φηγός,
βολβός, τέττιξ, ἐρέβινθος, ἀχράς,
τό τε θειοπαγὲς μητρῷον ἐμοὶ
μελέδημ᾽ ἰσχάς,
     Φρυγίας εὑρήματα συκῆς. |

b

Φερεκράτης·

    τακεροὺς ποιῆσαι τοὺς ἐρεβίνθους αὐτόθι.[35]

πάλιν·

    τρώγων ἐρεβίνθους ἀπεπνίγη πεφρυγμένους.

Δίφιλος δέ φησιν· οἱ ἐρέβινθοι δύσπεπτοι, σμηκτικοί,
οὐρητικοί, πνευματικοί. κατὰ δὲ Διοκλέα ζυμωτικοὶ
τῆς σαρκός· κρείττους δ᾽ οἱ λευκοὶ τῶν μελάνων καὶ

---

[35] ποιῆσαι . . . αὐτόθι 9.366d: ποιήσεις . . . εὐθέως CE

an old woman; and my daughter and my young son;
and this fine girl. Five in all.
Three of us are having dinner,
and the other two of us are sharing a little barley-
    cake
with them. We raise our voices
in lyreless lament whenever we have nothing;
and because of our lack of food,
our complexions are pale. Our portion
and our mode of life is:
fava beans, lupine, vegetables,
turnips, birds' pease, grass-peas, Valonia acorns,
hyacinth bulbs, cicadas, chickpeas, wild pears,
and the divinely-planted, maternal
object of my care, a dried fig,
      invention of a Phrygian[137] fig tree.

Pherecrates (fr. 89):[138]

to make the chickpeas soft at once.

Again (Pherecr. fr. 170):

He choked while eating roasted chickpeas.

Diphilus says: Chickpeas are difficult to digest, purgative,
and diuretic, and produce gas. According to Diocles (fr.
194 van der Eijk), they cause the flesh to swell. The white
variety are better than the black variety and resemble box-

---

[137] Most likely a reference not to the region in Asia Minor but
to the Attic village mentioned at Th. 2.22.2. The final three verses
are quoted again at 3.75b.

[138] Also quoted at 9.366d, where the text is slightly different
and the line is identified as coming from *Small Change*.

πυξοειδεῖς καὶ οἱ Μιλήσιοι τῶν λεγομένων κριῶν οἵ τε
χλωροὶ τῶν ξηρῶν καὶ οἱ βεβρεγμένοι τῶν ἀβρόχων.

῞Οτι Ποσειδῶνος εὕρημα οἱ ἐρέβινθοι.

c   Θέρμοι. |

(Α.) μὴ ὥρασι < . . . >
μετὰ τῶν κακῶν ἵκοιθ᾽ ὁ τοὺς θέρμους φαγών,
ἐν τῷ προθύρῳ τὰ λέμμαθ᾽ ὅτιὴ κατέλιπε,
ἀλλ᾽ οὐκ ἀπεπνίγη καταφαγών. μάλιστα δέ

*   *   *

(Β.) Κλεαίνετος μὲν οὐκ ἐδήδοκ᾽ οἶδ᾽ ὅτι
ὁ τραγικὸς αὐτούς· οὐδενὸς γὰρ πώποτε
ἀπέβαλεν < . . . > ὀσπρίου λέπος·
οὕτως ἐκεῖνός ἐστιν εὐχερὴς ἀνήρ.

d   Λυκόφρων δ᾽ ὁ Χαλκιδεὺς ἐν σατυρικῷ δράματι, | ὃ
ἐπὶ καταμωκήσει ἔγραψεν εἰς Μενέδημον τὸν φιλόσοφον, ἀφ᾽ οὗ ἡ τῶν Ἐρετρικῶν ὠνομάσθη αἵρεσις,
διασκώπτων τῶν φιλοσόφων τὰ δεῖπνά φησι·

καὶ δημόκοινος ἐπεχόρευε δαψιλὴς
θέρμος, πενήτων καὶ τρικλίνου συμπότης.

Δίφιλος·

οὐκ ἔστιν οὐδὲν τεχνίον ἐξωλέστερον
τοῦ πορνοβοσκοῦ·
κατὰ τὴν ὁδὸν πωλεῖν περιπατῶν βούλομαι
e   ῥόδα, ῥαφανῖδας, θερμοκυάμους, στέμφυλα, |

310

wood; the Milesian variety are better than what are called "rams"; and they are better green than dried, and soaked than unsoaked.

Chickpeas were discovered by Poseidon.
Lupines.

(A.) May the fellow who ate
the lupines come to a bad, untimely end,
since he left the husks in front of our door
and didn't choke while eating them. And in particular

*   *   *

(B.) I know that the tragic poet Cleaenetus[139]
didn't eat them. Because he never
threw out a single bean-pod;
that's how omnivorous he is! (Alex. fr. 268)[140]

Lycophron of Chalcis, in the satyr play he wrote to make fun of the philosopher Menedemus (*TrGF* 100 F 2.9–10),[141] from whom the Eretrian sect got its name, says in the course of mocking the philosophers' dinners:

and the plentiful common lupine, which drinks
with poor men at their parties, came dancing in.

Diphilus (fr. 87):

There's no occupation more awful
than being a pimp.
I'm willing to walk the streets selling
roses, radishes, lupine-beans, olive pomace,

---

[139] *PAA* 574340; *TrGF* 84. He took third place at the Lenaea in 363 BCE.   [140] Pollux 6.45 (quoting only verses 2–3) identifies the fragment as coming from Alexis.

ἁπλῶς ἅπαντα μᾶλλον ἢ ταύτας τρέφειν.

καὶ σημειωτέον, φησί, τὸ θερμοκυάμους, ἐπεὶ καὶ νῦν
οὕτω λέγεται. Πολέμων δέ φησι τοὺς Λακεδαιμονίους
τοὺς θέρμους λυσιλαίδας καλεῖν. Θεόφραστος δὲ
ἱστορεῖ ἐν Αἰτίοις Φυτικοῖς ὅτι θέρμος καὶ ὄροβος καὶ
ἐρέβινθος μόνα οὐ ζῳοῦται τῶν χεδροπῶν διὰ τὴν
δριμύτητα καὶ πικρότητα· ὁ δ' ἐρέβινθος, φησί, μέλας
γίνεται διαφθειρόμενος. γίνεσθαι δὲ λέγει κάμπας ἐν
f τοῖς ἐρεβίνθοις | ὁ αὐτὸς ἐν τῷ τρίτῳ[36] τῆς αὐτῆς
πραγματείας. Δίφιλος δ' ὁ Σίφνιος τοὺς θέρμους φησὶν εἶναι σμηκτικοὺς καὶ πολυτρόφους, μάλιστα δὲ
τοὺς ἐπὶ πλεῖον ἀπεγλυκασμένους. διὸ καὶ Ζήνων ὁ
Κιτιεύς, σκληρὸς ὢν καὶ πάνυ θυμικὸς πρὸς τοὺς
γνωρίμους, ἐπὶ πλεῖον τοῦ οἴνου σπάσας ἡδὺς ἐγίνετο
καὶ μείλιχος. πρὸς τοὺς πυνθανομένους οὖν τοῦ τρό-
που τὴν διαφορὰν ἔλεγε τὸ αὐτὸ τοῖς θέρμοις πά-
σχειν· καὶ γὰρ ἐκείνους πρὶν διαβραχῆναι πικροτά-
56 τους εἶναι, ποτισθέντας δὲ γλυκεῖς ‖ καὶ προσηνε-
στάτους.

Φάσηλοι. Λακεδαιμόνιοι ἐν τοῖς δείπνοις τοῖς καλουμένοις κοπίσι διδόασι τραγήματα σῦκά τε ξηρὰ
καὶ κυάμους καὶ φασήλους χλωρούς· ἱστορεῖ Πολέμων. Ἐπίχαρμος·

[36] τρίτῳ Kaibel: τετάρτῳ CE

[141] Menedemus of Eretria (c.339–c.265 BCE). The fragment
is quoted in a more complete form at 10.420b and is probably

absolutely anything rather than keep whores.

The word "lupine-beans" should be noted, [Athenaeus] says, since it is still used this way today. Polemon (fr. 91 Preller) says that the Spartans refer to lupines as *lusilaides*. Theophrastus records in his *Aetiology of Plants* (*CP* 4.2.2) that lupine, bitter vetch, and chickpea are the only leguminous plants that do not produce worms, because they are bitter and sour. The chickpea, he reports, turns black as it goes bad. But the same author says in Book III of the same treatise (*CP* 3.22.3) that caterpillars are found among chickpeas. Diphilus of Siphnos says that lupines are purgative and nutritious, especially those that have been treated for a while to make them sweet. This is why Zeno of Citium (fr. 285, *SVF* i.65),[142] although he was harsh and unpleasant with his acquaintances, became affable and gentle after he drank wine for a while. When people asked him to explain the alteration in his behavior, he said that the same change happened to him as to lupines; because they too were very nasty before they were soaked, but after they had a drink, they were sweet and mild.

Phasēloi.[143] Polemon (cf. fr. 86 Preller) reports that at the dinner parties they refer to as *kopides*, the Spartans serve dried figs, fava beans, and green *phasēloi* as dainties.[144] Epicharmus (fr. 149):

drawn from Antigonus of Carystus' *Life of Menedemus* (cited at 10.419e).   [142] The founder of the Stoic movement (335–263 BCE). This anecdote is probably drawn from Antigonus of Carystus' *Life of Zenon* (p. 122 Wilamowitz).

[143] Unidentified, but apparently some sort of nut, pea, or bean.   [144] For the Spartan *kopides*, see 4.138e–9b, 140a–b (drawing once again on Polemon).

< . . . > φασήλους φῶγε θᾶσσον, αἴ χ' ὁ
Διόνυσος φιλῇ.

Δημήτριος·

ἢ σῦκον ἢ φάσηλον ἢ τοιοῦτό τι.

Ἐλᾶαι. Εὔπολις·

σηπίαι
δρυπεπεῖς τ' ἐλᾶαι.

b ταύτας Ῥωμαῖοι δρύππας λέγουσι. Δίφιλος | δέ φησιν
ὁ Σίφνιος τὰς ἐλάας ὀλιγοτρόφους εἶναι καὶ κεφα-
λαλγεῖς, τὰς δὲ μελαίνας καὶ κακοστομαχωτέρας καὶ
βαρύνειν τὴν κεφαλήν, τὰς δὲ κολυμβάδας καλου-
μένας εὐστομαχωτέρας εἶναι καὶ κοιλίας στατικάς,
τὰς δὲ θλαστὰς μελαίνας εὐστομαχωτέρας εἶναι. μνημονεύει τῶν θλαστῶν ἐλαιῶν Ἀριστοφάνης·

< . . . > θλαστὰς ποεῖν ἐλάας.

πάλιν·

οὐ ταὐτόν ἐστιν ἀλμάδες καὶ στέμφυλα.

c καὶ μετ' ὀλίγα· |

θλαστὰς γὰρ εἶναι κρεῖσσόν ἐστιν ἀλμάδος.

Ἀρχέστρατος ἐν τῇ Γαστρονομίᾳ·

Hurry up and parch some *phasēloi*, if Dionysus loves you!

Demetrius (fr. 5):

or a fig or a *phasēlon* or something like that.

Olives. Eupolis (fr. 338.1–2):[145]

squid
and tree-ripened *(drupepeis)* olives.

The Romans call these *druppae*. Diphilus of Siphnos says that olives are not very nutritious and cause headaches; that black olives are harder on the stomach and cause wooziness; that what are referred to as diving olives[146] are easier on the stomach, and slow down the movement of the bowels; and that bruised black olives are easier on the stomach. Aristophanes (fr. 408, encompassing all three quotations) mentions bruised olives:

to make bruised olives.

Again:

Salted olives and olive pomace aren't the same.

And a little further on:

Because it's better that they be bruised than salted.

Archestratus in his *Gastronomy* (fr. 8 Olson–Sens = *SH* 138):

[145] Cf. 2.56e, apparently citing another part of the same fragment.   [146] Olives immersed in a brine-and-oil bath; also called salted olives (Ar. fr. 408, below).

ῥυσαὶ ‹καὶ› δρυπεπεῖς παρακείσθωσάν σοι
ἐλαῖαι.

ὥστε Μαραθῶνος τὸ λοιπὸν ἐπ᾽ ἀγαθῷ
μεμνημένοι
πάντες ἐμβάλλουσιν ἀεὶ μάραθον ἐς τὰς
ἁλμάδας,

φησὶν Ἕρμιππος. Φιλήμων φησίν· πιτυρίδες καλοῦν-
ται αἱ φαυλίαι ἐλᾶαι, στεμφυλίδες δὲ αἱ μέλαιναι.
d Καλλίμαχος δ᾽ ἐν τῇ Ἑκάλῃ γένη ἐλαῶν καταλέγει· |

γεργέριμον πίτυρίν τε.

ἔλεγον δὲ τὰς δρυπεπεῖς ἐλάας καὶ ἰσχάδας καὶ γερ-
γερίμους, ὥς φησι Δίδυμος. καὶ χωρὶς δὲ τοῦ φάσκειν
ἐλάας αὐτὸ καθ᾽ ἑαυτὸ ἔλεγον μόνον δρυπεπεῖς. Τηλε-
κλείδης·

ξυγγενέσθαι διὰ χρόνου † λιπαρείτω με
δρυπεπέσι μάζαις καὶ διασκανδικίσαι †.

Ἀθηναῖοι δὲ τὰς τετριμμένας ἐλαίας στέμφυλα ἐκάλουν, βρύτεα δὲ τὰ ὑφ᾽ ἡμῶν στέμφυλα, τὰ ἐκπι-
έσματα τῆς σταφυλῆς· παρὰ δὲ τοὺς βότρυς γέγονεν
ἡ φωνή.

e Ῥαφανίδες. αὗται κέκληνται διὰ τὸ | ῥᾳδίως φαίνε-
σθαι. καὶ ἐκτεταμένως δὲ καὶ κατὰ συστολὴν λέγεται

---

147 Cognate words always refer to olive pomace (the flesh left
behind when olives are pressed for oil; see 2.56d).

Let wrinkled, tree-ripened olives be served to you.

And so thereafter remembering Marathon to good
      end
they all always add fennel *(marathon)* to their salted
      olives,

says Hermippus (fr. 75). Philemon says: Coarse olives are
referred to as *piturides* ("bran-olives"), and black olives
are referred to as *stemphulides*.[147] Callimachus in his
Hecale (fr. 248.1) lists the types of olives:

a tree-ripened *(gergerimon)* olive and a bran-olive.

According to Didymus (p. 75 Schmidt), they called tree-
ripened olives *ischades*[148] and *gergerimoi*, and they said
simply "tree-ripened" by itself, without adding "olives."
Teleclides (fr. 40):

† Let him beg me †, after a while, to spend time
† with tree-ripened barley-cakes and chervilize[149] †.

The Athenians referred to pressed olives as *stemphula*
("olive cakes, olive pomace") and to what we call *stemphula*, that is grape pomace, as *brutea*; the word comes
from *botrus* ("grape-cluster").

Radishes *(rhaphanides)*. They are called this because
the seedlings spring up readily *(rhadiōs)*. In Attic the
word is pronounced with both a long and a short vowel.[150]

---

[148] The word is normally used of dried figs.

[149] Obscure, but perhaps a reference to Euripides, whose
mother is attacked in comedy for being a vegetable-vendor (esp.
Ar. *Ach*. 478 with Olson ad loc.).   [150] Referring to the *iota*,
which is long in Cratin. fr. 350 but short in Eup. fr. 338.1.

παρὰ Ἀττικοῖς. Κρατῖνος·

> ταῖς ῥαφανῖσι δοκεῖ, τοῖς δ᾽ ἄλλοις οὐ
> λαχάνοισιν.

Εὔπολις·

> < . . . > ῥαφανίδες ἄπλυτοι, σηπίαι.

ὅτι δὲ τὸ ἄπλυτοι ἐπὶ τῶν ῥαφανίδων ἀκούειν δεῖ, οὐκ
ἐπὶ τῶν σηπιῶν, δηλοῖ Ἀντιφάνης γράφων·

> νήττας, σχαδόνας, κάρυ᾽ ἐντραγεῖν, ᾠ᾽, ἐγκρίδας,
> ῥαφανίδας ἀπλύτους, γογγυλίδας, χόνδρον, μέλι.

f ἰδίως δ᾽ οὕτως ἐκαλοῦντο ἄπλυτοι ῥαφανίδες, | ἃς καὶ
Θασίας ὠνόμαζον. Φερεκράτης·

> ῥαφανίς τ᾽ ἄπλυτος ὑπάρχει
> καὶ θερμὰ λουτρὰ καὶ τάριχη πνικτὰ καὶ †
> κάρυα.

ὑποκοριστικῶς δ᾽ εἴρηκε Πλάτων ἐν Ὑπερβόλῳ·

> < . . . > φύλλιον ἢ ῥαφανίδιον.

Θεόφραστος δ᾽ ἐν τοῖς Περὶ Φυτῶν γένη ῥαφανίδων
φησὶν εἶναι πέντε, Κορινθίαν, Λειοθασίαν, Κλεωναί-
αν, Ἀμωρέαν, Βοιωτίαν. καλεῖσθαι δὲ ὑπό τινων τὴν
Λειοθασίαν Θρᾳκίαν· γλυκυτάτην δ᾽ εἶναι τὴν Βοιωτίαν καὶ τῷ σχήματι στρογγύλην. ἁπλῶς δέ, φησίν,
57 ὧν ἐστι λεῖα τὰ φύλλα, γλυκύτεραί εἰσι. ‖ Καλλίας δ᾽
ἐπὶ τῆς ῥαφανίδος εἴρηκε τὴν ῥάφανον. περὶ γοῦν τῆς

Cratinus (fr. 350):

> The radishes approve, but the other vegetables don't.

Eupolis (fr. 338.1):

> unwashed radishes, squid.

That the word "unwashed" is to be taken with "radishes" rather than with "squid" is made clear by Antiphanes (fr. 273), who writes:

> to eat ducks, honeycomb, nuts, eggs, honey-cakes,
> unwashed radishes, turnips, wheat porridge, honey.

The term "unwashed" was properly applied to the type of radish also called Thasian. Pherecrates (fr. 190):

> There's an unwashed radish,
> hot baths, smothered saltfish and † nuts.

Plato (fr. 186) uses the diminutive in *Hyperbolus*:

> a little leaf or a little radish.

Theophrastus in his *On Plants* (*HP* 7.4.2) says that there are five varieties of radish: Corinthian, Leiothasian, Cleonaean, Amorean, and Boeotian, but that some people refer to the Leiothasian variety as Thracian. The Boeotian variety is the sweetest and is round in shape; and as a general rule, he says, smooth-leaved radishes are sweeter. Callias (fr. 26) uses the word *rhaphanos*[151] to refer to the radish.

---

[151] Elsewhere generally "cabbage" (cf. 1.34d–e), and the argument Athenaeus offers to support the thesis that it means "radish" here is not convincing. But see 4.133d with n.

ἀρχαιότητος τῆς κωμῳδίας διεξιών φησιν·

⟨ . . . ⟩ ἔτνος, πῦρ, γογγυλίδες, ῥάφανοι,
δρυπεπεῖς, ἐλατῆρες.

ὅτι δ᾽ οὕτω τὰς ῥαφανῖδας εἴρηκε δῆλον Ἀριστοφάνης
ποιεῖ περὶ τῆς τοιαύτης ἀρχαιότητος ἐν Δαναΐσι γράφων καὶ αὐτὸς καὶ λέγων·

ὁ χορὸς δ᾽ ὠρχεῖτ᾽ ἂν ἐναψάμενος δάπιδας καὶ
στρωματόδεσμα
διαμασχαλίσας αὑτὸν σχελίσιν καὶ φύσκαις καὶ
ῥαφανῖσιν.

b   εὐτελὲς δὲ σφόδρα ἔδεσμα ἡ ῥαφανίς. | Ἄμφις·

ὅστις ἀγοράζων ὄψον ⟨ . . . ⟩
ἐξὸν ἀπολαύειν ἰχθύων ἀληθινῶν,
ῥαφανῖδας ἐπιθυμεῖ πρίασθαι, μαίνεται.

Κῶνοι. Μνησίθεος ὁ Ἀθηναῖος ἰατρὸς ἐν τῷ Περὶ
Ἐδεστῶν ὀστρακίδας καλεῖ τῶν κώνων τοὺς πυρῆνας,
ἔτι δὲ κώνους. Διοκλῆς δ᾽ ὁ Καρύστιος πιτύινα κάρυα.
ὁ δὲ Μύνδιος Ἀλέξανδρος πιτυΐνους κώνους. Θεόφραστος δὲ τὸ μὲν δένδρον πεύκην ὀνομάζει, τὸν δὲ
c   καρπὸν κῶνον. | Ἱπποκράτης δὲ ἐν τῷ Περὶ Πτισάνης,
ὃ ἐκ τοῦ ἡμίσους μὲν νοθεύεται, ὑπ᾽ ἐνίων δὲ καὶ ὅλον,
κοκκάλους· οἱ πολλοὶ δὲ πυρῆνας, ὡς καὶ Ἡρόδοτος

---

152 Quoted again at 7.277c, where the play is identified as *The
Girl from Leucas*.

When he describes the antiquity of comedy, at any rate, he says:

> pea-soup, a fire, turnips, *rhaphanoi*, tree-ripened
> olives, flat-cakes.

That the reference is to radishes is made clear by Aristophanes in *Danaids* (fr. 264), where he too writes about the antiquity of comedy and says:

> The chorus used to dress up in rugs and bedding-
> sacks and dance,
> sticking beef-ribs, sausages, and radishes under their
> arms.

The radish is very inexpensive food. Amphis (fr. 26)[152]:

> If anyone who's buying food
> has the opportunity to enjoy real fish
> but wants to purchase radishes, he's crazy.

Pine seeds. The physician Mnesitheus of Athens in his *On Edible Substances* (fr. 31 Bertier) refers to pine-cone stones as *ostrakides*[153], and also as cones. Diocles of Carystus (fr. 203 van der Eijk) refers to them as pine nuts, Alexander of Myndus as pine cones; and Theophrastus (e.g. *HP* 2.2.6) calls the tree a pine and its fruit a cone. Hippocrates in his *On Barley Gruel* (*Acut. (Sp.)* 2.456.4, 466.1 Littré), half of which is spurious, although some authorities claim that all of it is, refers to them as kernels. Many authors call them stones, as Herodotus (4.23.3) does when

---

[153] Cognate with *ostrakon*, "pot-sherd." Cf. 3.126a.

ὅταν περὶ τοῦ Ποντικοῦ καρύου λέγῃ. φησὶ γάρ·
πυρῆνα δ' ἔχει τοῦτο ἐπὰν γένηται πέπον. Δίφιλος δ' ὁ
Σίφνιός φησιν· οἱ στρόβιλοι πολύτροφοι μέν εἰσι,
λεαντικοὶ δὲ ἀρτηρίας καὶ θώρακος καθαρτικοὶ διὰ τὸ
ἔχειν παρεμπεπλεγμένον τὸ ῥητινῶδες. Μνησίθεος δέ
φησι πιαίνειν αὐτοὺς τὸ σῶμα καὶ πρὸς εὐπεψίαν
d ἀλύπους | εἶναι, ὑπάρχειν δὲ καὶ οὐρητικοὺς καὶ οὐκ
ἐφεκτικοὺς κοιλίας.

Ὠιά. Ἀναξαγόρας ἐν τοῖς Φυσικοῖς τὸ καλούμενόν
φησιν ὄρνιθος γάλα τὸ ἐν τοῖς ᾠοῖς εἶναι λευκόν.
Ἀριστοφάνης·

† τίκτει πρῶτον ὑπηνέμιον ᾠὸν Νύξ. †

Σαπφὼ δ' αὐτὸ τρισυλλάβως καλεῖ·

φαῖσι δή ποτα Λήδαν < . . . >
< . . . > ᾤον εὔρην.

καὶ πάλιν·

< . . . > ᾠίω πόλυ λευκότερον.

ᾤεα δ' ἔφη Ἐπίχαρμος·

< . . . > ᾤεα χανὸς κἀλεκτορίδων πετεηνῶν.

Σιμωνίδης ἐν δευτέρῳ Ἰάμβων·

< . . . > οἷόν τε χηνὸς ᾤεον Μαιανδρίου.

---

154 Athenaeus or his source has misdivided the clause and thus
garbled the sense.

he discusses the Pontic nut. For he says: When this is ripe, it has a stone.[154] Diphilus of Siphnos says: Pine nuts are very nutritious, and they lubricate the windpipe and cleanse the abdominal cavity because of the resinous element they contain. Mnesitheus claims that they are fattening and do not damage the digestion, and that they are also diuretic and do not inhibit the action of the bowels.

Eggs. Anaxagoras in his *Physics* (59 B 22) says that what is referred to as bird's milk[155] is actually egg-white. Aristophanes (*Av.* 695, condensed):

First did Night bring forth a wind-egg *(hupēnemion ōion).*

Sappho (fr. 166) uses a trisyllabic form of the word:

They say that Leda once
found an egg *(ōïon).*[156]

And again (fr. 167):

much whiter than an egg *(ōïon).*

Epicharmus (fr. 150) uses *ōea*:

eggs *(ōea)* of a goose and of winged hens.

Simonides in Book II of the *Iambs* (Semon. iamb. fr. 11 West[2]):

like an egg *(ōeon)* of a Maeandrian goose.

---

[155] An expression used of anything rare and delicious (e.g. Ar. V. 508; Mnesim. fr. 9.1–2).

[156] I.e. the egg from which Helen hatched. Sappho apparently followed the version of the story according to which the goddess Nemesis, rather than Leda herself, produced the egg.

e δια τεσσάρων δ' αὐτὰ | προενήνεκται Ἀναξανδρίδης ὠάρια εἰπών. καὶ Ἔφιππος·

σταμνάριά τ' οἴνου μικρὰ τοῦ Φοινικικοῦ,
ὠάρια, τοιαῦθ' ἕτερα πολλὰ παίγνια.

Ἄλεξις δὲ ἡμίτομά που ᾠῶν λέγει. ᾠὰ δὲ οὐ μόνον ἀνεμιαῖα ἐκάλουν, ἀλλὰ καὶ ὑπηνέμια. ἐκάλουν δὲ καὶ τὰ νῦν τῶν οἰκιῶν παρ' ἡμῖν καλούμενα ὑπερῷα ᾠά, φησὶ Κλέαρχος ἐν Ἐρωτικοῖς, τὴν Ἑλένην φάσκων ἐν τοιούτοις οἰκήμασι τρεφομένην δόξαν ἀπενέγκασθαι

f παρὰ | πολλοῖς ὡς ἐξ ᾠοῦ εἴη γεγεννημένη. οὐκ εὖ δὲ Νεοκλῆς ὁ Κροτωνιάτης ἔφη ἀπὸ τῆς σελήνης πεσεῖν τὸ ᾠὸν ἐξ οὗ τὴν Ἑλένην γεννηθῆναι· τὰς γὰρ σεληνίτιδας γυναῖκας ᾠοτοκεῖν καὶ τοὺς ἐκεῖ γεννωμένους πεντεκαιδεκαπλασίονας ἡμῶν εἶναι, ὡς Ἡρόδωρος ὁ Ἡρακλεώτης ἱστορεῖ. Ἴβυκος δὲ ἐν πέμπτῳ Μελῶν

58 περὶ Μολιονιδῶν φησι· ||

τούς τε λευκίππους κόρους
τέκνα Μολιόνας κτάνον,
ἅλικας ἰσοκεφάλους ἑνιγυίους
ἀμφοτέρους γεγαῶτας ἐν ὠέῳ
ἀργυρέῳ.

Ἔφιππος·

---

[157] Cf. 1.29d.   [158] Quoted in full at 2.60a.
[159] Cognate with *anemos*, "wind."   [160] Cf. Ar. *Av.* 695 (quoted above). "Wind-eggs" are normally infertile eggs, which

Anaxandrides (fr. 80) lengthened the word to four syllables, saying *ōaria* ("little eggs"). Also Ephippus (fr. 24.2–3):[157]

> and little jars of Phoenician wine,
> little eggs, many other such baubles.

Alexis (fr. 263.10)[158] somewhere mentions eggs sliced in half. They referred to wind-eggs not just as *anemiaia*[159] but as *hupēnemia*[160]. They also referred to the parts of houses we call *huperōa* ("upper floors") as *ōa* ("eggs"), according to Clearchus in his *Erotica* (fr. 35 Wehrli), where he claims that Helen was brought up in rooms of this sort and thus got a widespread reputation for having been born from an egg. Neocles of Croton was mistaken to say that the egg from which Helen was born fell from the moon; for moon-women produce eggs, but the people born there are 15 times larger than us, according to Herodorus of Heracleia (*FGrH* 31 F 21). Ibycus in Book V of the *Lyrics* (*PMG* 285) says about the Molionidae:[161]

> I killed the young men
> who rode white horses, the children of Molion,
> who were the same age and equally tall, and had a
>   single body,
> and were both born in a silver
> egg.

Ephippus (fr. 8.3–4):[162]

have seemingly been fathered by the wind rather than a rooster.

[161] Twin brothers (here Siamese twins) killed by Heracles, who must be the speaker; cf. Pi. *O.* 10.26–34; [Apollod.] *Bib.* 2.7.2.   [162] Quoted in full at 14.642e.

ἴτρια, τραγήμαθ᾽ ἧκε, πυραμοῦς, ἄμης,
ᾠῶν ἑκατόμβη. πάντα ταῦτ᾽ ἐχναύομεν.

ᾠῶν δὲ ῥοφητῶν μνημονεύει Νικόμαχος·

οὐσίδιον γὰρ καταλιπόντος τοῦ πατρός,
οὕτω συνεστρόγγυλα κἀξεκόκκισα
ἐν μησὶν ὀλίγοις ὥσπερ ᾠόν τις ῥοφῶν.

b χηνείων δ᾽ ᾠῶν Ἔριφος· |

(Α.) ᾠά. (Β.) λευκά γε
καὶ μεγάλα. χήνει᾽ ἐστίν, ὥς γ᾽ ἐμοὶ δοκεῖ.
(Α.) οὗτος δέ φησι ταῦτα τὴν Λήδαν τεκεῖν.

Ἐπαίνετος δὲ καὶ Ἡρακλείδης ὁ Συρακούσιος ἐν
Ὀψαρτυτικῷ τῶν ᾠῶν φασι πρωτεύειν τὰ τῶν ταῶν,
μεθ᾽ ἃ εἶναι τὰ χηναλωπέκεια, τρίτα καταλέγοντες τὰ
ὀρνίθεια.

Πρόπομα. τούτου, φησί, περιενεχθέντος ὁ τῶν δείπνων ταμίας Οὐλπιανὸς ἔφη, εἰ κεῖται παρά τινι τὸ
πρόπομα οὕτω καλούμενον ὡς νῦν ἡμεῖς φαμεν. καὶ
c ζητούντων πάντων, αὐτός, ἔφη, ἐγὼ ἐρῶ. | Φύλαρχος ὁ
Ἀθηναῖος ἢ Ναυκρατίτης ἐν οἷς ὁ λόγος ἐστὶν αὐτῷ
περὶ Ζηλᾶ τοῦ Βιθυνῶν βασιλέως, ὃς ἐπὶ ξένια καλέσας τοὺς τῶν Γαλατῶν ἡγεμόνας ἐπιβουλεύσας αὐτοῖς καὶ αὐτὸς διεφθάρη, φησὶν οὕτως, εἰ μνήμης

Wafer-bread came, dainties, honey-cake, milk-cake,
a hecatomb of eggs. We were nibbling on all these
  items.

Nicomachus (fr. 3) mentions eggs gulped down raw:

Because my father left me a small estate,
and I rolled it up and squeezed it dry
within a few months, like someone gulping down a
  raw egg.

Eriphus (fr. 7) mentions goose eggs:

(A.) Eggs. (B.) Big
white ones; I think they're goose eggs.
(A.) But this fellow says Leda laid them!

Epaenetus and Heracleides of Syracuse in the *Art of
Cooking* say that the best eggs are produced by peacocks;
after these come fox-goose eggs; and they list hens' eggs
third.

An appetizer plate. After this made its way around the
company, says [Athenaeus], Ulpian, who was in charge of
the dinner-party, asked if any ancient author referred to
the appetizer plate using the same word we do currently.
While everyone was considering the question, he said: I
will tell you myself. Phylarchus of Athens or Naucratis
(*FGrH* 81 F 50), in the passage that contains his story
about Zelas the king of the Bithynians, who invited the
Galatian chieftains to a party, intending to do them harm,
but was killed himself,[163] says the following, if I remember

---

[163] Jacoby dates the incident (also mentioned by Trogus) to
around 235 BCE.

εὐτυχῶ· πρόπομά τι πρὸ τοῦ δείπνου περιεφέρετο,
καθὼς εἰώθει τὸ πρῶτον. καὶ ταῦτ' εἰπὼν ὁ Οὐλπιανὸς
ᾔτει πιεῖν[37] ψυκτῆρι, ἀρέσκειν ἑαυτὸν φάσκων διὰ τὸ
ἑτοίμως ἀπεμνημονευκέναι. ἦν δὲ τῶν ἐν τοῖς προπόμασι, φησί, παρασκευαζομένων ἄλλα τε καὶ δὴ καὶ
d   ταῦτα. |

Μαλάχαι. Ἡσίοδος·

οὐδ' ὅσον ἐν μαλάχῃ τε καὶ ἀσφοδέλῳ μέγ'
    ὄνειαρ.

τοῦτο Ἀττικόν. ἐγὼ δέ, φησίν, ἐν πολλοῖς ἀντιγράφοις
εὗρον τοῦ Ἀντιφάνους Μίνωος διὰ τοῦ ō γεγραμμένον·

< . . . > τρώγοντες μολόχης ῥίζαν.

καὶ Ἐπίχαρμος·

πραΰτερος ἐγών γα μολόχας.

Φαινίας δ' ἐν τοῖς Φυτικοῖς φησι· τῆς ἡμέρου μαλά-
e   χης ὁ σπερματικὸς τύπος καλεῖται πλακοῦς, | ἐμφερὴς
ὢν αὐτῷ· τὸ μὲν γὰρ κτενῶδες ἀνάλογον καθάπερ ἡ
τοῦ πλακοῦντος κρηπίς, κατὰ μέσον δὲ τοῦ πλακουν-
τικοῦ ὄγκου τὸ κέντρον ὀμφαλικόν. καὶ περιληφθεί-
σης τῆς κρηπῖδος ὅμοιον γίνεται τοῖς θαλαττίοις
περιγεγραμμένοις ἐχίνοις. ὁ δὲ Σίφνιος Δίφιλος ἱστορεῖ ὡς ἡ μαλάχη ἐστὶν εὔχυλος, λεαντικὴ ἀρτηρίας,
τὰς ἐπιπολαίους ἀποκρίνουσα[38] δριμύτητας. ἐπιτή-

_____

[37] πιεῖν ἐν ψυκτῆρι CE   [38] κατὰς CE

rightly: Before dinner an appetizer plate went around, as was the custom at first. After he said this, Ulpian asked to drink from a wine-cooler, saying that he was pleased at how ready his memory was. The items prepared for the appetizer plates, [Athenaeus] says, included the following in particular:

Mallows. Hesiod (*Op.* 41):

> nor how great a benefit there is in mallow *(malachē)*
>   and asphodel.

Malachē is the Attic form. But, says [Athenaeus], I found the word written with an *omicron* in many copies of Antiphanes' *Minos* (fr. 156):

> eating mallow *(molochē)* root.

And Epicharmus (fr. 151):

> I am milder than a mallow *(molocha)*.

Phaenias says in his *On Plants* (fr. 44 Wehrli): The seed-pod of the domesticated mallow is referred to as a "flat-cake," since it looks like one; because the scalloped part resembles the bottom of the cake, and in the middle of the cake-like mass is a nub like a belly-button. When the bottom is removed, it is like sea urchins drawn in out-line.[164] Diphilus of Siphnos records that the mallow pro-duces good *chulē*, lubricates the windpipe, and separates out the bitterness that rises to the top of the stomach. He

---

[164] Referring to the way the individual seeds within the pod sit tight-packed against one another around the core.

δειόν τε εἶναί φησιν αὐτὴν τοῖς τῶν νεφρῶν καὶ τῆς
κύστεως ἐρεθισμοῖς εὐέκκριτόν τε εἶναι μετρίως καὶ
f τρόφιμον, κρείττω δὲ τὴν ἀγρίαν τῆς κηπευομένης. |
Ἕρμιππος δ' ὁ Καλλιμάχειος καὶ εἰς τὴν καλουμένην
φησὶν ἄλιμον προσέτι τε ἄδιψον ἐμβάλλεσθαι τὴν
μαλάχην οὖσαν χρησιμωτάτην.

Κολοκύνται. Εὐθύδημος <ὁ> Ἀθηναῖος ἐν τῷ Περὶ
Λαχάνων σικύαν Ἰνδικὴν καλεῖ τὴν κολοκύντην διὰ
τὸ κεκομίσθαι τὸ σπέρμα ἐκ τῆς Ἰνδικῆς. Μεγαλο-
πολῖται δ' αὐτὴν σικυωνίαν ὀνομάζουσι. Θεόφραστος
δὲ τῶν κολοκυντῶν φησιν οὐκ εἶναι ἐν μέρει ἰδέας,
ἀλλ' εἶναι τὰς μὲν βελτίους, τὰς δὲ χείρους. Μηνόδω-
ρος δ' ὁ Ἐρασιστράτειος, Ἱκεσίου φίλος, τῶν κολο-
59 κυντῶν, φησίν, ἡ μὲν Ἰνδική, ‖ ἢ δ'[39] αὐτὴ καὶ σικύα,
ἡ δὲ κολοκύντη· καὶ ἡ μὲν Ἰνδικὴ κατὰ τὸ πλεῖστον
ἕψεται, ἡ δὲ κολοκύντη καὶ ὀπτᾶται. ἄχρι δὲ τοῦ νῦν
λέγεσθαι παρὰ Κνιδίοις τὰς κολοκύντας Ἰνδικάς.
Ἑλλησπόντιοι δὲ σικύας μὲν τὰς μακρὰς καλοῦσι,
κολοκύντας δὲ τὰς περιφερεῖς. Διοκλῆς δὲ κολοκύντας
μὲν καλλίστας γίνεσθαι περὶ Μαγνησίαν, προσέτι τε
γογγύλην ὑπερμεγέθη γλυκεῖαν καὶ εὐστόμαχον, ἐν
Ἀντιοχείᾳ δὲ σικυόν, ἐν δὲ Σμύρνῃ καὶ Γαλατίᾳ θρί-
b δακα, πήγανον δ' ἐν Μύροις. Δίφιλος δέ φησιν· ἡ δὲ |
κολοκύντη ὀλιγότροφός ἐστι καὶ εὔφθαρτος καὶ
ὑγραντικὴ τῆς ἕξεως καὶ εὐέκκριτος, εὔχυλος. εὐστομαχωτέρα δ' ἐστὶν ἡ δι' ὕδατος καὶ ὄξους λαμβανο-

───────────────

[39] δ' Coraes: καὶ CE

says that it is useful for irritations of the kidneys and the bladder, and is fairly easily digested and nutritious, and that the wild variety is superior to the cultivated variety. Callimachus' student Hermippus (fr. 15b Wehrli) says that mallow is very useful to add to what is referred to as *alimos*, and to *adipsos*[165] as well.

Gourds.[166] Euthydemus of Athens in his *On Vegetables* refers to the gourd as an "Indian cucumber," since the seed was brought from India. The Megapolitans call it a *sikuonios*.[167] Theophrastus (*HP* 7.4.6) says that there are no specific varieties of gourd, although some are better and others worse. Menodorus the student of Erasistratus and friend of Hicesius says: There is the Indian gourd, which is also called the *sikua*, and the gourd *(kolokuntē)*. The Indian variety is generally stewed, whereas the gourd *(kolokuntē)* is baked. Up to the present day the Cnidians still refer to gourds as "Indian." The inhabitants of the Hellespont refer to long gourds as *sikuai*, and round gourds as *kolokuntai*. Diocles (fr. 201 van der Eijk) maintains that the best gourds grow in Magnesia and that this variety is moreover round, very large, sweet, and easy on the stomach; and that the best cucumbers grow in Antiocheia, the best lettuce in Smyrna and Galatia, and the best rue in Myra. Diphilus says: The gourd is not very nutritious, but is easily broken down in the stomach, adds moisture to the system, is easily excreted, and produces good *chulē*. It is easier on the stomach when eaten with water and vin-

---

[165] *Alimos* is "hunger-quenching (food)," and *adipsos* is "thirst-quenching (food)"; cf. Herodor. *FGrH* 31 F 1; Plu. *Mor.* 157d–f. [166] To be distinguished from pumpkins and squash, which are New World vegetables.

μένη, εὐχυλοτέρα δὲ ἡ ἀρτυτή. λεπτυντικωτέρα δ'
ἐστὶν ἡ μετὰ νάπυος, εὐπεπτοτέρα δὲ καὶ εὐεκκριτω-
τέρα ἡ κάθεφθος. Μνησίθεος δέ φησιν· ὅσα εὐφυῶς
διάκειται πρὸς τὴν τοῦ πυρὸς κατεργασίαν, οἷον ὅ τε
σικυὸς καὶ ἡ κολοκύντη καὶ μῆλα Κυδώνια καὶ στρουθία καὶ εἴ τι τοιοῦτο, ταῦθ᾽ ὅταν προσενεχθῇ πυρω-
c θέντα, δίδωσι τῷ σώματι τροφὴν | οὐ πολλὴν μέν,
ἄλυπον δὲ καὶ μᾶλλον ὑγράν. ἐστὶ δὲ καὶ ταῦτα τῆς
κοιλίας ἐφεκτικὰ πάντα. δεῖ δὲ αὐτὰ λαμβάνειν ἐφθὰ
μᾶλλον. Ἀττικοὶ δὲ μόνως καλοῦσιν αὐτὴν κολοκύντην. Ἕρμιππος·

> τὴν κεφαλὴν ὅσην ἔχει·
ὅσην κολοκύντην.

Φρύνιχος ὑποκοριστικῶς·

> ἢ μαζίου τι μικρὸν ἢ κολοκυντίου.

Ἐπίχαρμος·

> < . . . > ὑγιέστερόν θην ἐστὶ κολοκύντας πολύ.

d Ἐπικράτης ὁ κωμῳδιοποιός· |

> (Α.) τί Πλάτων
καὶ Σπεύσιππος καὶ Μενέδημος;

---

167 Cognate with *sikua*, "cucumber."   168 I.e. when
stewed in a vinegar sauce.   169 See 3.81a–d.

170 Speusippus son of Eurymedon of the deme Myrrhinous
(*PA* 12847) was Plato's nephew and student, and his successor in
347 BCE as head of his school; his works survive only in fragments.

egar,[168] and produces better *chulē* when seasoned. It is better for taking off weight when eaten with mustard, and is more easily digested and excreted when stewed. Mnesitheus (fr. 34 Bertier) says: Foods that respond well to the application of fire, such as cucumber, gourd, quinces, *strouthia*[169], and whatever else falls into this category, do not furnish the body with much nourishment when served cooked, but do no harm and supply a considerable amount of moisture. All these foods also inhibit the action of the bowels and are best eaten stewed. Attic authors refer to the vegetable exclusively as a *kolokuntē*. Hermippus (fr. 69):

> What a big head he has!
> As big as a gourd *(kolokuntē)*!

Phrynichus (fr. 65) uses the diminutive:

> or a little bit of a barley-cake or a small gourd
> *(kolokuntion)*.

Epicharmus (fr. 152):

> It's much healthier, I think, than a gourd *(kolokunta)*.

The comic poet Epicrates (fr. 10):

> (A.) What about Plato
> and Speusippus and Menedemus?[170]

Menedemus of Pyrrha was also one of Plato's students, and when Speusippus died in 339, some of the younger members of the Academy supported him for head. But Xenocrates was elected instead, and Menedemus withdrew to found his own school. Nothing survives of Menedemus' work, although he appears to have written Socratic dialogues.

πρὸς τίσι νυνὶ διατρίβουσιν;
ποία φροντίς, ποῖος δὲ λόγος
  διερευνᾶται παρὰ τοῖσιν;
τάδε μοι πινυτῶς, εἴ τι κατειδὼς
ἥκεις, λέξον, πρὸς Γᾶς < . . . >.
(B.) ἀλλ᾽ οἶδα λέγειν περὶ τῶνδε σαφῶς.
Παναθηναίοις γὰρ ἰδὼν ἀγέλην
< . . . > μειρακίων
ἐν γυμνασίοις Ἀκαδημείας
ἤκουσα λόγων ἀφάτων, ἀτόπων.
περὶ γὰρ φύσεως ἀφοριζόμενοι
e διεχώριζον ζῴων τε | βίον
δένδρων τε φύσιν λαχάνων τε γένη.
κᾆτ᾽ ἐν τούτοις τὴν κολοκύντην
ἐξήταζον τίνος ἐστὶ γένους.
(A.) καὶ τί ποτ᾽ ἄρ᾽ ὡρίσαντο καὶ τίνος γένους
εἶναι τὸ φυτόν; δήλωσον, εἰ κάτοισθά τι.
(B.) πρώτιστα μὲν <οὖν> πάντες ἀναυδεῖς
τότ᾽ ἐπέστησαν καὶ κύψαντες
χρόνον οὐκ ὀλίγον διεφρόντιζον.
κᾆτ᾽ ἐξαίφνης, ἔτι κυπτόντων
καὶ ζητούντων τῶν μειρακίων,
λάχανόν τις ἔφη στρογγύλον εἶναι,
ποίαν δ᾽ ἄλλος, δένδρον δ᾽ ἕτερος.
f ταῦτα δ᾽ ἀκούων | ἰατρός τις
Σικελᾶς ἀπὸ γᾶς

---

171 Where Plato's school was located.

What's occupying their time nowadays?
What deep thoughts, what sort of speculation
   is under investigation at their establishment?
Give me an insightful account of these matters,
if you've come with any knowledge of them, by
      Earth!
(B.) I know enough to give you a clear report about
      this;
because during the Panathenaic festival, I saw a herd
of young men
in the exercise grounds of the Academy,[171]
and I listened to unspeakably strange discussions.
They were producing definitions having to do with
      natural history
and trying to distinguish between animals,
trees, and vegetables;
and in the course of these discussions they attempted
      to determine
which category the gourd *(kolokuntē)* belongs to.
(A.) What definition did they settle on? And what
      category did they
put the plant into? Reveal this, if you have any
      information!
(B.) At first they all stood
silent and gazed at the ground
for a long time, thinking the matter through.
Then suddenly, while the other boys were still
staring at the ground and considering the question,
one of them said it was a round vegetable,
another a type of grass, and a third a tree.
And a Sicilian doctor,
when he heard this,

κατέπαρδ᾽ αὐτῶν ὡς ληρούντων.
(Α.) ἢ που δεινῶς ὠργίσθησαν χλευάζεσθαί τ᾽
    ἐβόησαν;
τὸ γὰρ ἐν λέσχαις τοιαῖσδε † τοιαῦτα ποιεῖν
    εὐπρεπές.
(Β.) οὐδ᾽ ἐμέλησεν τοῖς μειρακίοις.
ὁ Πλάτων δὲ παρὼν καὶ μάλα πρᾴως,
οὐδὲν ὀρινθείς, ἐπέταξ᾽ αὐτοῖς
πάλιν < . . . >
ἀφορίζεσθαι τίνος ἐστὶ γένους.
οἳ δὲ διῄρουν.

Ἄλεξις ὁ χαρίεις πρόπομα ὅλον παρατίθησι τοῖς
60 διακρίνειν δυναμένοις· ‖

ἔλαθον γενόμενος οὗ τὸ πρᾶγμ᾽ ἠβούλετο.
κατὰ χειρὸς ἐδόθη· τὴν τράπεζαν ἧκ᾽ ἔχων,
ἐφ᾽ ἧς ἐπέκειτ᾽ οὐ τυρὸς οὐδ᾽ ἐλαῶν γένη
οὐδὲ παρέχουσαι κνῖσαν ἡμῖν πλείονα
παροψίδες καὶ λῆρος, ἀλλὰ παρετέθη
ὑπερηφάνως ὄζουσα τῶν Ὡρῶν λοπάς,
τὸ τοῦ πόλου τοῦ παντὸς ἡμισφαίριον.
ἅπαντ᾽ ἐνῆν τἀκεῖ γὰρ ἐν ταύτῃ καλά,
ἰχθῦς, ἔριφοι, διέτρεχε τούτων σκορπίος,
b   ὑπέφαινεν ᾠῶν ἡμίτομα τοὺς ἀστέρας. |

---

172 An allusion to the constellations Pisces, Capricorn, and Scorpio.

farted on them for talking nonsense.
(A.) I imagine they got terribly angry and shouted
    that they were being mocked?
Because during conversations of this sort † it's
    appropriate to do something like that.
(B.) The young men paid no attention.
But Plato was there, and very gently
and with no sign of excitement he ordered them
    once again
to try to determine what category it belonged to.
And they began drawing distinctions.

The witty Alexis (fr. 263) serves a full plate of appetizers
for the discriminating:

No one noticed that I was where he wanted the
    business to take place.
Water was poured over my hands. A slave came
    carrying the table,
on which lay not just cheese or different types of
    olives
or side-dishes supplying us with more steam and
    bullshit
than anything else. Instead, a casserole-dish
was set beside us that exuded the sumptuous smell of
    the Seasons
and represented the circle of the whole sky.
Because every good thing that's up there was in it:
fish and kids, and a scorpion-fish ran between
    them;[172]
and hard-boiled eggs cut in half suggested the stars.

ἐπεβάλομεν τὰς χεῖρας. ὁ μὲν ἐμοὶ λαλῶν
ἅμα καὶ διανεύων ἠσχολεῖθ'· ὁ πᾶς δ' ἀγὼν
ἐπ' ἐμὲ κατήντα. τὸ πέρας οὐκ ἀνῆχ' ἕως
τὴν λοπάδ' ὀρύττων ἀποδέδειχα κόσκινον.

Μύκαι. Ἀριστίας·

μύκαισι[40] δ' ὠρέχθει τὸ λάινον πέδον.

Πολίοχος·

μεμαγμένην
μικρὰν μελαγχρῆ μᾶζαν ἠχυρωμένην
c   ἑκάτερος ἡμῶν εἶχε δὶς τῆς ἡμέρας |
καὶ σῦκα βαιά, καὶ μύκης τις ἐνίοτ' ἂν
ὠπτᾶτο, καὶ κοχλίας γενομένου ψακαδίου
ἠγρεύετ' ἄν. καὶ λάχανα τῶν αὐτοχθόνων
θλαστή τ' ἐλαία, καὶ πιεῖν οἰνάριον ἦν
ἀμφίβολον.

Ἀντιφάνης·

τὸ δεῖπνόν ἐστι μᾶζα κεχαρακωμένη
ἀχύροις, πρὸς εὐτέλειαν ἐξωπλισμένη,
καὶ βολβὸς εἷς <τις> καὶ παροψίδες τινές,
d   σόγχος τις ἢ μύκης τις ἢ τοιαῦθ' ἃ δὴ |
δίδωσιν ἡμῖν ὁ τόπος ἄθλι' ἀθλίοις.
τοιοῦτος ὁ βίος, ἀπύρετος, φλέγμ' οὐκ ἔχων.

*   *   *

[40] μυκαῖσι ("the sound of bellowing"; more appropriate for
tragedy) Schneidewin

We set our hands to work. The other fellow[173] was
   busy
talking to me and nodding his head; so the whole
   enterprise
devolved to me. To sum up, I didn't stop
digging at the dish until I'd made it look like a sieve.

Mushrooms. Aristias (*TrGF* 9 F 6):

The stony ground was swelling with mushrooms.

Poliochus (fr. 2):

A small,
swarthy barley-cake kneaded full of bran
was what each of us had twice a day,
and a few figs. Sometimes we roasted
a mushroom; and if there was a bit of rain,
we caught a snail. And there were wild vegetables
and a bruised olive, and a little dubious wine
to drink.

Antiphanes (fr. 225, encompassing both quotations):

Our dinner is a barley-cake bristling
with bran and cheaply made,
and a single hyacinth bulb, and some side-dishes—
a thistle or a mushroom or whatever
miserable items this spot provides for miserable us.
Such is our way of life, free of fever and heat.

*   *   *

[173] The man with whom the speaker was sharing a couch and a
table—and who was trying to behave in a decent, friendly fashion.

οὐδεὶς κρέως παρόντος ἐσθίει θύμον,
οὐδ᾽ οἱ δοκοῦντες πυθαγορίζειν.

καὶ προελθών·

τίς γὰρ † οἶδ᾽ ἡμῶν τὸ μέλλον ὅ τι παθεῖν
πέπρωθ᾽ ἑκάστῳ τῶν φίλων; ταχὺ δὴ λαβὼν
ὄπτα μύκητας πρινίνους τουσδὶ δύο.

Ὅτι Κηφισόδωρος[41] ὁ Ἰσοκράτους μαθητὴς ἐν
τοῖς Κατὰ Ἀριστοτέλους (τέσσαρα δ᾽ ἐστὶ ταῦτα
e βιβλία) | ἐπιτιμᾷ τῷ φιλοσόφῳ ὡς οὐ ποιήσαντι
λόγου ἄξιον τὸ παροιμίας ἀθροῖσαι, Ἀντιφάνους ὅλον
ποιήσαντος δρᾶμα τὸ ἐπιγραφόμενον Παροιμίαι· ἐξ
οὗ καὶ παρατίθεται τάδε·

ἐγὼ γὰρ ἂν τῶν ὑμετέρων φάγοιμί ‹τι›,
μύκητας ὠμοὺς ἂν φαγεῖν ‹ἐμοὶ› δοκῶ
καὶ στρυφνὰ μῆλα κεἴ τι πνίγει βρῶμά τι.

φύονται δὲ οἱ μύκητες γηγενεῖς καὶ εἰσιν αὐτῶν ἐδώδιμοι ὀλίγοι· οἱ γὰρ πολλοὶ ἀποπνίγουσιν. διὸ καὶ
f Ἐπίχαρμος παίζων ἔφη· |

οἱοναὶ μύκαι † ἄρ᾽ ἐπεσκληκότες πνιξεῖσθέ ‹με›.

Νίκανδρος δ᾽ ἐν Γεωργικοῖς καταλέγει καὶ τίνες αὐτῶν
εἰσιν οἱ θανάσιμοι, λέγων·

____
[41] Κηφισόδωρος Ionsius: κηφισόδοτος CE

340

No one eats garlic[174] when meat's available,
including those who pretend to be Pythagoreans.[175]

And further on:

For who † among us knows what any of our friends
is fated to suffer in the future? Hurry up and take
these two holm-oak mushrooms and roast them!

Isocrates' student Cephisodorus[176] in his *Against Aristotle* (fr. 3 Radermacher = Arist. fr. 464)—there are four
books—faults the philosopher for not treating collecting
proverbs as a worthwhile activity, even though Antiphanes
wrote an entire play entitled *Proverbs*. The following lines
(fr. 186) are cited from it:

Because if I were to eat anything that belongs to you,
I'd feel like I was eating raw mushrooms,
sour apples, and whatever food makes a person
choke.

Mushrooms grow out of the earth; few of them are edible,
because the majority cause death by choking. This is why
Epicharmus (fr. 153) jokingly says:

You're going to dry me up and choke me, just as
mushrooms † do.

Nicander in the *Georgics* (fr. 78 Schneider, encompassing
both quotations) lists the poisonous ones, saying:

---

[174] For *thumon* as a generic term for edible bulbs, see Arnott
on Alex. fr. 122.2.   [175] For Pythagorean vegetarianism, see
the texts collected at 4.160f–1f.

[176] *PAA* 568030; cf. 3.122b.

ἐχθρὰ δ' ἐλαίης
ῥοιῆς τε πρίνου τε δρυός τ' ἄπο πήματα κεῖται,

*   *   *

οἰδαλέων σύγκολλα βάρη πνιγόεντα μυκήτων.

61   φησὶ δὲ καὶ ὅτι ‖

συκέης ὁπότε στέλεχος βαθὺ κόπρῳ
κακκρύψας ὑδάτεσσιν ἀειναέεσσι νοτίζοις,
φύσονται πυθμέσσιν ἀκήριοι· ὧν σὺ μύκητα
θρεπτὸν μή τι χαμηλὸν ἀπὸ ῥίζης προτάμοιο.[42]

καί τε μύκητας ἀμανίτας τότ' ἐφεύσεις,

φησὶν ὁ αὐτὸς Νίκανδρος ἐν τῷ αὐτῷ. Ἔφιππος·

ἵν' ὥσπερ οἱ μύκητες ἀποπνίξαιμί σε.

b   Ἐπαρχίδης Εὐριπίδην φησὶ τὸν ποιητὴν ἐπιδημῆσαι |
τῇ Ἰκάρῳ καὶ γυναικός τινος μετὰ τέκνων κατὰ τοὺς
ἀγρούς, δύο μὲν ἀρρένων τελείων, μιᾶς δὲ παρθένου,
φαγούσης θανασίμους μύκητας καὶ ἀποπνιγείσης μετὰ τῶν τέκνων ποιῆσαι τουτὶ τὸ ἐπίγραμμα·

ὦ τὸν ἀγήρατον πόλον αἰθέρος, Ἥλιε, τέμνων,
ἆρ' εἶδες τοιόνδ' ὄμματι πρόσθε πάθος,
μητέρα παρθενικήν τε κόρην δισσούς τε
συναίμους
c   ἐν ταὐτῷ φέγγει μοιραδίῳ φθιμένους; |

[42] Followed by an intrusive copyist's note: τὰ δ' ἄλλα οὐκ ἦν
ἀναγνῶναι ("The rest was illegible").

342

                        Horrible pains are in store
from the olive, the pomegranate, the holm-oak, and
   the oak.

          *   *   *

the choking, clinging weight of puffy mushrooms.

He also says:

> Whenever you bury the trunk of a fig tree deep in
>   dung
> and keep it moist with constant streams of water,
> harmless mushrooms will grow on its lower parts. You
>   may cut
> any of these that grow from the root and not from the
>   ground.

Then you will cook some *amanita* mushrooms as well,

says the same Nicander in the same poem (fr. 79 Schneider). Ephippus (fr. 27):

So that I can choke you to death, like mushrooms do.

Eparchides (*FGrH* 437 F 2 = E. test. 93) says that the poet Euripides was on Icaros; and when a woman who was out in the fields with her children, two adult boys and an unmarried girl, ate poisonous mushrooms and choked to death along with her children, he wrote the following epigram (*FGE* 560–3):

> O Sun, as you cut your path through the ageless vault
>   of the upper air,
>   did your eye ever before behold such woe,
> a mother, a virgin girl, and two brothers
>   dead on a single fateful day?

Διοκλῆς ὁ Καρύστιος ἐν πρώτῳ Ὑγιεινῶν φησιν·
ἄγρια ἑψήματα τεῦτλον, μαλάχη, λάπαθον, ἀκαλήφη,
ἀνδράφαξυς, βολβοί, ὕδνα, μύκαι.

Σία. Σπεύσιππος ἐν δευτέρῳ Ὁμοίων φησὶ ἐν ὕδατι
γίνεσθαι, σελίνῳ ἐλείῳ τὸ φύλλον ἐοικός. διὸ καὶ
Πτολεμαῖος ὁ δεύτερος Εὐεργέτης Αἰγύπτου βασιλεύ-
σας παρ᾽ Ὁμήρῳ ἀξιοῖ γράφειν·

ἀμφὶ δὲ λειμῶνες μαλακοὶ σίου ἠδὲ σελίνου.[43]

σία γὰρ μετὰ σελίνου φύεσθαι, ἀλλὰ μὴ ἴα.

Δίφιλός φησι τοὺς μύκητας εἶναι εὐστομάχους[44],
d κοιλίας | διαχωρητικούς, θρεπτικούς, δυσπέπτους δὲ
καὶ φυσώδεις. τοιούτους δὲ εἶναι τοὺς ἐκ Κέω τῆς
νήσου. πολλοὶ μέντοι καὶ κτείνουσι. δοκοῦσι δὲ οἰκεῖοι
εἶναι οἱ λεπτότατοι καὶ ἁπαλοὶ καὶ εὔθρυπτοι οἱ ἐπὶ
πτελέαις καὶ πεύκαις γινόμενοι· ἀνοίκειοι δὲ οἱ μέλα-
νες καὶ πελιοὶ καὶ σκληροὶ καὶ οἱ μετὰ τὸ ἑψηθῆναι
καὶ τεθῆναι πησσόμενοι, οἵτινες λαμβανόμενοι κτείνουσι. βοηθοῦνται δ᾽ ἀπὸ ὑδρομέλιτος πόσεως καὶ
ὀξυμέλιτος, νίτρου καὶ ὄξους· μετὰ τὴν πόσιν δὲ ἐμεῖν
e δεῖ. διόπερ καὶ | δεῖ μάλιστα σκευάζειν αὐτοὺς μετὰ
ὄξους καὶ ὀξυμέλιτος ἢ μέλιτος ἢ ἁλῶν· οὕτω γὰρ
αὐτῶν τὸ πνιγῶδες ἀφαιρεῖται. Θεόφραστος δὲ ἐν τῷ

---

[43] The traditional reading is ἴου ἠδὲ σελίνου, "of violet and
celery".   [44] εὐστομάχους E: εὐστόμους C

[177] This entry interrupts the discussion of mushrooms (which

Diocles of Carystus in Book I of *On Matters of Health* (fr. 195 van der Eijk) says: Wild plants that should be stewed are beet, mallow, monk's rhubarb, nettle, orach, hyacinth bulbs, truffles, and mushrooms.

Marshwort.[177] Speusippus in Book II of *Similar Things* (fr. 6 Tarán) says that the plant grows in water and its leaf resembles marsh-celery. This is why Ptolemy Euergetes the Second, who was king of Egypt, proposes writing in Homer (*Od.* 5.72):

and round about were soft meadows of marshwort
    and celery;

because marshwort grows in the same place as celery, but violets do not.

Diphilus says that mushrooms are easy on the stomach, laxative, and nourishing, but are difficult to digest and produce gas; and that the mushrooms from the island of Ceos are like this. Many mushrooms, however, are deadly. Those that are very delicate, soft, and friable, which grow on elms and pines, appear to be fit to eat. Not fit to eat are those that are black, bruised-looking, and hard, and that become tough after being cooked and served; these kill anyone who consumes them. Drinking a mixture of honey and water, honey and vinegar, or soda ash and vinegar counteracts the poison; after drinking this, the patient should be made to vomit. This is why mushrooms are best prepared with vinegar, vinegar and honey, honey, or salt; because this removes the element that causes asphyxia-

resumes a few lines below, with the quotation from Diphilus of Siphnos); most likely it fell out of the text and was reinserted in the wrong place.

Περὶ Φυτῶν Ἱστορίας γράφει· ὑπόγεια δὲ τὰ τοιαῦτά
ἐστι καὶ ἐπίγεια, καθάπερ οὓς καλοῦσί τινες πέζιας,
ἅμα τοῖς μύκησι γινομένους· ἄριζοι γὰρ καὶ αὐτοὶ
τυγχάνουσιν. ὁ δὲ μύκης ἔχει προσφύσεως δίκην[45]
τὸν καυλὸν εἰς μῆκος, καὶ ἀποτείνουσιν ἀπ' αὐτοῦ
ῥίζαι. φησὶ δὲ καὶ ὅτι ἐν τῇ περὶ Ἡρακλέους στήλας
f θαλάσσῃ ὅταν | ὕδατα πλείω γένηται, μύκητες φύον-
ται πρὸς τῇ θαλάσσῃ, οὓς καὶ ἀπολιθοῦσθαι ὑπὸ τοῦ
ἡλίου φησί. καὶ Φαινίας δὲ ἐν πρώτῳ Περὶ Φυτῶν· τὰ
δὲ οὐδὲ φύει τὴν ἀνθήλην οὐδὲ τῆς σπερματικῆς ἴχνος
κορυνήσεως οὐδὲ σπερματώσεως, οἷον μύκης, ὕδνον,
πτέρις, ἕλιξ. ὁ αὐτός φησι· πτέρις, ἣν ἔνιοι βλάχνον
καλοῦσι. Θεόφραστος ἐν Φυτικοῖς· λειόφλοια, καθάπερ ὕδνον, μύκης, πέζις, γεράνειον.

62 Ὕδνα. ‖ γίνεται καὶ ταῦτα αὐτόματα ἀπὸ γῆς
μάλιστα περὶ τοὺς ἀμμώδεις τόπους. λέγει δὲ περὶ
αὐτῶν Θεόφραστος· τὸ ὕδνον, ὃ καλοῦσί τινες γεράνειον, καὶ εἴ τι ἄλλο ὑπόγειον. καὶ πάλιν· καὶ ἡ τῶν
ἐγγεοτόκων τούτων γένεσις ἅμα καὶ φύσις, οἷον τοῦ τε
ὕδνου καὶ τοῦ φυομένου περὶ Κυρήνην ὃ καλοῦσι
μίσυ· δοκεῖ δ' ἡδὺ σφόδρα τοῦτ' εἶναι καὶ τὴν ὀσμὴν
ἔχειν κρεώδη· καὶ τὸ ἐν τῇ Θράκῃ δὲ γενόμενον οἰτόν.

---

[45] δίκην Kaibel: ἀρχὴν CE

---

[178] Theophrastus mentions the area around the Pillars of
Heracles at *HP* 4.7.1; but at 4.7.2 the reference is actually to
mushrooms around the Red Sea.

tion. Theophrastus writes in his *Research on Plants* (fr. 399): Plants of this sort grow underground as well as above ground, as for example those some people refer to as *peziai* ("puffballs"), which belong among the mushrooms; because they too lack roots. The mushroom has a long stem that resembles a secondary growth, and the roots extend from it. He also says (*HP* 4.7.2)[178] that whenever there is more rain than usual in the sea around the Pillars of Heracles, mushrooms grow along the shore; and he claims that the sun turns them into stone. Also Phaenias in Book I of *On Plants* (fr. 37 Wehrli): Some produce no flower-tuft or trace of a seed-pod or seed-production, for example the mushroom, truffle, fern, and ivy. The same author says: the fern, which some authorities refer to as a *blachnon*. Theophrastus in *On Plants*:[179] smooth-skinned plants, such as the truffle, mushroom, puffball, and *geranion*.[180]

Truffles. These too are produced spontaneously from the earth, especially in sandy regions. Theophrastus (*HP* 1.6.9) says about them: the truffle, which some people refer to as a *geranion*, and anything else that grows underground. And again (fr. 400a):[181] The generation and growth of these plants produced within the earth are simultaneous, for example that of the truffle and the plant that grows around Cyrene, which they refer to as *misu*—it is apparently very sweet and smells like meat—and also the *oiton*[182] that grows in Thrace. Something peculiar is

---

[179] Cf. *HP* 1.6.5, although the discussion there has to do with root-systems.

[180] A type of truffle; see below.

[181] The text is difficult, and something may have been lost.

[182] Obscure, like *misu* (above).

περὶ δὲ τούτων ἴδιόν τι λέγεται· φασὶ γάρ, ὅταν ὕδατα
b μετοπωρινὰ καὶ βρονταὶ | γίνωνται σκληραί, τότε
γίνεσθαι, καὶ μᾶλλον ὅταν αἱ βρονταί, ὡς ταύτης
αἰτιωτέρας οὔσης. οὐ διετίζειν δέ, ἀλλ᾽ ἐπέτειον εἶναι·
τὴν δὲ χρείαν καὶ τὴν ἀκμὴν ἔχειν τοῦ ἦρος. οὐ μὴν
ἀλλ᾽ ἔνιοί γε ὡς σπερματικῆς οὔσης τῆς ἀρχῆς ὑπο-
λαμβάνουσιν. ἐν γοῦν τῷ αἰγιαλῷ τῶν Μιτυληναίων
οὔ φασι πρότερον εἶναι πρὶν ἢ γενομένης ἐπομβρίας
τὸ σπέρμα κατενεχθῇ ἀπὸ Τιαρῶν· τοῦτο δ᾽ ἐστὶ
χωρίον ἐν ᾧ πολλὰ γίνεται. γίνεται δὲ ἔν τε τοῖς
c αἰγιαλοῖς μάλιστα καὶ ὅπου χώρα ὕπαμμος· | καὶ γὰρ
αἱ Τίαραι[46] τοιαῦται. φύεται δὲ καὶ περὶ Λάμψακον ἐν
τῇ Ἀβαρνίδι καὶ ἐν Ἀλωπεκοννήσῳ κἂν τῇ Ἠλείων.
Λυγκεὺς ὁ Σάμιός φησιν· ἀκαλήφην ἡ θάλασσα ἀνίη-
σιν, ἡ δὲ γῆ ὕδνα. καὶ Μάτρων ὁ παρῳδὸς ἐν τῷ
Δείπνῳ·

ὄστρεά τ᾽ ἤνεικεν, Θέτιδος Νηρηίδος ὕδνα.

Δίφιλος δὲ δύσπεπτά φησιν εἶναι τὰ ὕδνα, εὔχυλα δὲ
καὶ παραλεαντικά, προσέτι δὲ διαχωρητικά, καὶ ἔνια
αὐτῶν ὁμοίως τοῖς μύκαις πνιγώδη εἶναι. Ἡγήσαν-
d δρος δ᾽ ὁ Δελφὸς ἐν Ἑλλησπόντῳ | φησὶν οὔτε ὕδνον
γίνεσθαι οὔτε γλαυκίσκον οὔτε θύμον[47]· διὸ Ναυσι-
κλείδην εἰρηκέναι μήτε ἔαρ μήτε φίλους. ὑδνόφυλλον
δέ φησι Πάμφιλος ἐν Γλώσσαις τὴν φυομένην τῶν

46 Τίαραι Schweighäuser: τι ως CE
47 θύννον (thynnum) Natalis Comes

said about these plants: they claim that they are produced whenever there are autumn rains and loud thunder, and especially when there is thunder, since this is the most significant cause. The plant is not perennial but annual; the proper time to eat it and its prime is in the spring. Some authorities nonetheless suppose that their origin involves seeds. On the coast of Mitylene, at any rate, they say, there are no truffles until a heavy rain falls and the seed is washed down from Tiara, a spot where the plant grows plentifully. It is found in particular along seashores and wherever the ground is sandy, as it is in fact in Tiara. It also grows in Abarnis near Lampsacus, in Alopeconnesus, and in Elis. Lynceus of Samos (fr. 22 Dalby) says: The sea sends up a nettle,[183] while the land sends up truffles. Also the parodist Matro in his *Dinner Party* (fr. 2 Olson–Sens = *SH* 535):

> He also brought oysters, the truffles of the Nereid
> Thetis.

Diphilus claims that truffles are hard to digest but produce good *chulē* and are soothing, as well as laxative, and that some of them cause death by choking in the same way mushrooms do. Hegesander of Delphi (fr. 35, *FHG* iv.420) says that no truffles, *glaukiskoi*[184], or thyme are found in the Hellespont, and that Nausicleides[185] therefore claimed that there was no spring and he had no friends there. Pamphilus in the *Glossary* (fr. XXXVI Schmidt) reports

183 Probably a riddling reference to the sea-urchin.
184 An unidentified fish, also referred to at 3.102b, 103d.
185 Otherwise unknown.

ὕδνων ὕπερθε πόαν, ἀφ' ἧς τὸ ὕδνον γινώσκεσθαι.

Ἀκαλήφη. λέγεται παρὰ τοῖς Ἀττικοῖς οὕτως καὶ τὸ βοτανῶδες καὶ ⟨τὸ⟩ κνησμοῦ αἴτιον. Ἀριστοφάνης Φοινίσσαις·

πρῶτον ἁπάντων ἴφυα φῦναι.

εἶθ' ἑξῆς·

τὰς κραναὰς ἀκαλήφας.

e   Ἀσπάραγοι. οὗτοι καὶ ἔλειοι καὶ ὄρειοι | καλοῦνται. ὧν οἱ κάλλιστοι οὐ σπείρονται, πάντων ὄντες τῶν ἐντὸς θεραπευτικοί. οἱ δὲ σπαρτοὶ καὶ σφόδρα ὑπερμεγέθεις γίνονται. ἐν Λιβύῃ δέ φασιν ἐν Γαιτουλίᾳ γίνεσθαι πάχος μὲν Κυπρίου καλάμου, μῆκος δὲ ποδῶν δώδεκα· ἐν δὲ τῇ ὀρεινῇ καὶ παρωκεανίτιδι πάχος μὲν μεγάλων ναρθήκων, μῆκος δὲ περὶ τοὺς εἴκοσι πήχεις. Κρατῖνος δὲ διὰ τοῦ φ ἀσφάραγον ὀνομάζει. καὶ Θεόπομπος·

f   κἄπειτ' ἰδὼν ἀσφάραγον ἐν θάμνῳ τινί. |

Ἀμειψίας·

οὐ σχῖνος οὐδ' ἀσφάραγος, οὐ δάφνης κλάδοι.

Δίφιλος δέ φησιν ὡς ὁ τῆς κράμβης ἀσφάραγος λεγόμενος ἰδίως ὅρμενος εὐστομαχώτερός ἐστι καὶ εὐεκκριτώτερος, ὄψεων δὲ βλαπτικός. ἐστὶ δὲ δριμὺς

that the grass that grows above truffles and allows them to be detected is called *hydnophullon* ("truffle-foliage").

Nettle. Attic authors use this word to refer to both the herb-like plant and the one that produces stings. Aristophanes in *Phoenician Women* (fr. 572.2–3, encompassing both verses)[186]:

first of all grows spike-lavender;

then right after that:

the rugged nettles.

Asparagus. Both marsh-asparagus and mountain-asparagus are referred to. The best asparagus is not grown from seed; and it helps cure all internal disorders. The sown varieties grow very large. They say that in Gaetulia in Libya the asparagus grows as thick as Cyprus reed and 12 feet tall; and in the mountainous country and along the sea-coast it grows as thick as giant fennel and about 20 cubits[187] high. Cratinus (fr. 363.2) refers to it as *aspharagos* with a *phi*. Also Theopompus (fr. 69):

and then, when he saw *aspharagos* in a thicket.

Amipsias (fr. 24):

no squill or *aspharagos*, no laurel branches.

Diphilus says that what is called "cabbage-asparagus," properly *ormenos*, is easier on the stomach and more easily digested, but bad for one's vision. It is bitter and diu-

---

[186] Quoted in a slightly more complete form at 3.90a, where the fragment is assigned to *Phoenician Women*.
[187] About 30 feet; see 2.50b n.

καὶ οὐρητικὸς καὶ ἀδικεῖ νεφροὺς καὶ κύστιν. Ἀττικοὶ
δ᾽ εἰσὶν οἱ λέγοντες ὅρμενον τὸν ἀπὸ τῆς κράμβης
ἐξηνθηκότα. Σοφοκλῆς Ἰχνευταῖς·

63   κἀξορμενίζει κοὐκέτι σχολάζεται ‖
     βλάστῃ.

παρὰ τὸ ἐξορούειν καὶ βλαστάνειν. Ἀντιφάνης δὲ διὰ
τοῦ π̄ φησὶν ἀσπάραγον·

    ἀσπάραγος † ἠγλάιζεν, ὠχρὸς ἐξήνθηκέ τις.

Ἀριστοφῶν·

         κάππαριν, βληχώ, θύμον,
    ἀσπάραγον, † πίτταν, ῥάμνον, σφάκελον,
    τύμπανον †.

Κοχλίας. Φιλύλλιος·

    οὔκ εἰμι τέττιξ οὐδὲ κοχλίας, ὦ γύναι.

καὶ πάλιν·

    μαινίδες, < . . . > σκόμβροι, κοχλίαι, κορακῖνοι.

Ἡσίοδος δὲ τὸν κοχλίαν φερέοικον καλεῖ. καὶ Ἀνα-
b ξίλας δέ· |

    ἀπιστότερος εἶ τῶν κοχλιῶν πολλῷ πάνυ,
    οἳ περιφέρουσ᾽ ὑπ᾽ ἀπιστίας τὰς οἰκίας.

Ἀχαιός·

retic, and damages the kidneys and the bladder. It is Attic authors who refer to the flower-stalk of the cabbage as *ormenos*. Sophocles in *Trackers* (fr. 314.281–2):

> and the shoot *(blastē)* sprouts up *(exormenizei)* and no longer
> loiters,

in reference to the notion that it leaps forth *(exorouein)* and sprouts *(blastanein)*. But Antiphanes (fr. 294) says *asparagos* with a *pi*:

> *Asparagos* † was glorious, and some bird's pease was in bloom.

Aristophon (fr. 15):

> a caper, pennyroyal, thyme,
> *asparagos*, † pitch, thorn, sage, a drum †.

Snail. Philyllius (fr. 20):

> I'm not a cicada or a snail, woman!

And again (fr. 26):

> small-fry, mackerel, snails, raven-fish.

Hesiod (*Op.* 571) refers to the snail as a "house-carrier." Likewise Anaxilas (fr. 33):

> You're much more suspicious than snails,
> which are so mistrustful that they carry their houses around with them.

Achaeus (*TrGF* 20 F 42):

ἢ τοσούσδ᾽ Αἴτνη τρέφει
κοχλίας κεράστας;

προβάλλεται δὲ κἀν τοῖς συμποσίοις γρίφου τάξιν
ἔχον περὶ τῶν κοχλιῶν οὕτως·

ὑλογενής, ἀνάκανθος, ἀναίματος, ὑγροκέλευθος.

Ἀριστοτέλης δὲ ἐν πέμπτῳ Περὶ Ζῴων Μορίων φησίν·
οἱ κοχλίαι φαίνονται κύοντες ἐν τῷ μετοπώρῳ καὶ τοῦ
ἔαρος· μόνοι τε οὗτοι τῶν ὀστρακοδέρμων συνδυα-
c ζόμενοι ὤφθησαν. Θεόφραστος | δὲ ἐν τῷ Περὶ Φω-
λευόντων, οἱ κοχλίαι, φησί, φωλεύουσι μὲν καὶ τοῦ
χειμῶνος, μᾶλλον δὲ τοῦ θέρους. διὸ καὶ πλεῖστοι
φαίνονται τοῖς μετοπωρινοῖς ὕδασιν. ἡ δὲ φωλεία τοῦ
θέρους καὶ ἐπὶ τῆς γῆς καὶ ἐπὶ τῶν δένδρων. λέγονται
δέ τινες τῶν κοχλιῶν καὶ σέσιλοι. Ἐπίχαρμος·

(Α.) τούτων ἁπάντων ἀκρίδας ἀνταλλάσσομαι,
κόγχων δὲ τὸν σέσιλον. (Β.) ἄπαγ᾽ ἐς τὸν
φθόρον.

Ἀπολλᾶς[48] δὲ Λακεδαιμονίους φησὶ σέμελον τὸν κοχλίαν λέγειν. Ἀπολλόδωρος δὲ ἐν δευτέρῳ Ἐτυμο-

----

[48] ἀπελλᾶς CE; cf. 9.369a

Does Aetna nourish horned
snails as big as this?[188]

Something along the lines of a riddle about snails is posed
at symposia and runs thus:[189]

Born in the woods, spineless and bloodless, leaving a
moist trail.[190]

Aristotle in Book V of *Parts of Animals* says:[191] Snails apparently conceive in the fall and during the spring; they
are the only testaceans that have been seen copulating.
Theophrastus in his *On Animals that Live in Holes* (fr. 366)
says: Snails remain in their holes during the winter and
even more so during the summer. This is why large numbers of them appear during the autumn rains. During the
summer their holes are both in the ground and in trees.
Some snails are called *sesiloi*. Epicharmus (fr. 154):

(A.) I'll trade you all this for some locusts,
and the *sesilos* for some mussels. (B.) Go to hell!

Apollas (fr. 5, *FHG* iv.307) says that the Spartans call the
snail a *semelos*. And Apollodorus in Book II of the *Etymol-*

---

[188] Mount Aetna in Sicily was believed to be home to an extraordinarily large species of beetle (Ar. *Pax* 73 with Olson ad
loc.), an idea extended here to snails.

[189] For the use of riddles at symposia, cf. 10.457c–9b.

[190] Cf. 10.455e. Cicero cites a Latin version of Athenaeus'
riddle at *de Div.* 2.133: *terrigenam, herbigradam, domiportam,
sanguine cassam.*

[191] The first clause is a crude summary of the sense of *HA*
544a16–24, while the second is drawn from *GA* 762a32–3.

d λογιῶν | τῶν κοχλιῶν φησί τινας καλεῖσθαι κωλυσι-
δείπνους.

Βολβοί. τούτων Ἡρακλῆς ἐσθίειν παραιτεῖται ἐν
Ἀμαλθείᾳ Εὐβούλου λέγων·

θερμότερον ἢ κραυρότερον ἢ μέσως ἔχον,
τοῦτ' ἔσθ' ἑκάστῳ μεῖζον ἢ Τροίαν ἑλεῖν.
κἀγὼ γὰρ οὐ καυλοῖσιν οὐδὲ σιλφίῳ
οὐδ' ἱεροσύλοις καὶ πικραῖς παροψίσι
βολβοῖς τ' ἐμαυτὸν χορτάσων ἐλήλυθα.

e ἃ δ' εἴς τ' ἐδωδὴν πρῶτα καὶ ῥώμης ἀκμὴν |
καὶ πρὸς ὑγίειαν, πάντα ταῦτ' ἐδαινύμην,
κρέας βόειον ἑφθὸν ἀσόλοικον μέγα,
ἀκροκώλιόν τε γεννικόν, † ὀπτὰ δελφάκι'
ἁλίπαστα τρία.

Ἄλεξις ἐμφανίζων τὴν τῶν βολβῶν πρὸς τὰ ἀφροδίσια δύναμίν φησι·

πίννας, κάραβον,
βολβούς, κοχλίας, κήρυκας, ᾦ', ἀκρωκώλια,
f τοσαῦτα· τούτων ἄν τις εὕρῃ φάρμακα |
ἐρῶν ἑταίρας ἕτερα χρησιμώτερα.

---

192 The original point (confused either by Apollodorus, Athenaeus, or the Epitomator) was presumably that snails move very
slowly and that individuals who come late to dinner, keeping the
rest of the company from beginning the meal, are thus both
"snails" and "dinner-hinderers"; cf. Plu. *Mor.* 725f–6a.

ogies (*FGrH* 244 F 223) says that some snails are referred to as *kōlusideipnoi* ("dinner-hinderers").[192]

Hyacinth bulb. Heracles refuses to eat this in Eubulus' *Amaltheia* (fr. 6), saying:

> Whether it's a bit hot, or a bit dry, or perfectly done
> is more important to each of us than sacking Troy.[193]
> Because I haven't come to stuff myself
> with silphium stalk or silphium juice or
> filthy, bitter side-dishes and hyacinth bulbs.
> Whatever's best for eating and building one's strength
> and staying healthy, all that's what I'm used to eating:
> a big chunk of boiled beef that hasn't gone bad,
> a nice pig's trotter, three slices of † roast piglet
> sprinkled with salt.

Alexis (fr. 281) alludes to the aphrodisiac properties of hyacinth bulbs, saying:[194]

> pinnas, a crayfish,
> hyacinth bulbs, snails, trumpet-shells, eggs, pigs'
>   trotters,
> things like that. If anyone who's in love with a
>   courtesan
> finds other drugs more useful than these . . .

[193] The verse is a quotation of E. *Andr.* 369.

[194] For hyacinth bulbs and octopi (referred to in the fragment of Xenarchus quoted below) as aphrodisiacs, see Pl. Com. fr. 189.9–10, 17–19 (quoted at 1.5c–d).

Ξέναρχος <ἐν Βουταλίωνι>⁴⁹·

φθίνει δόμος
ἀσυντάτοισι δεσποτῶν κεχρημένος
τύχαις, ἀλάστωρ τ᾽ εἰσπέπαικε Πελοπιδῶν.
ἄστυτος οἶκος κοὐδὲ βυσαύχην θεᾶς
Δηοῦς σύνοικος, γηγενὴς βολβός, φίλοις
ἐφθὸς βοηθῶν δυνατός ἐστ᾽ ἐπαρκέσαι·
μάτην δὲ πόντου κυανέαις δίναις τραφεὶς ‖
φλεβὸς τροπωτὴρ πουλύπους, ἁλοὺς βρόχων
πλεκταῖς ἀνάγκαις, τῆς τροχηλάτου κόρης
πίμπλησι λοπάδος στερροσώματον κύτος.

64

Ἀρχέστρατος·

βολβῶν καὶ καυλῶν χαίρειν λέγω ὀξυβάφοισι
ταῖς τ᾽ ἄλλαις πάσῃσι παροψίσι.

Ἡρακλείδης ὁ Ταραντῖνος ἐν Συμποσίῳ· βολβὸς καὶ κοχλίας καὶ ᾠὸν καὶ τὰ ὅμοια δοκεῖ σπέρματος εἶναι ποιητικά, οὐ διὰ τὸ πολύτροφα εἶναι, ἀλλὰ διὰ τὸ ὁμοειδεῖς ἔχειν τὰς πρώτας φύσεις αὐτὰς τὰς δυνά- μεις τῷ σπέρματι. Δίφιλος· | οἱ βολβοὶ δύσπεπτοι μέν

b

⁴⁹ from Suda ξ 22

---

¹⁹⁵ Suda ξ 22 reports that Athenaeus in Book II referred to *Boutalion* as one of Xenarchus' plays, and since this is the only ref- erence to the poet in Book II, the title can be restored.

¹⁹⁶ Referring to Orestes, who killed Aegisthus, the murderer

Xenarchus ‹in *Boutalion*› (fr. *1):[195]

> A house wanes
> when the fortunes of the masters upon which it
>   depends
> are not taut and hard, and the Pelopid avenger[196] has
>   fallen upon it.
> Impotent is the household; and the short-necked
>   associate
> of the goddess Deo, the earth-born hyacinth bulb,
>   who aids
> his friends when stewed, is unable to lend assistance.
> In vain does an octopus, rouser of a man's vein, after
>   growing up
> in the dark eddies of the sea and being caught in the
>   woven
> compulsions of the net's mesh, fill the solid-bodied
> hollow of the wheel-formed maiden, the casserole-
>   dish.

Archestratus (fr. 9 Olson–Sens = *SH* 137):

> I say to hell with sauce-plates full of hyacinth bulbs,
>   silphium stalks,
> and all other side-dishes.

Heracleides of Tarentum in the *Symposium* (fr. 65 Guardasole): Hyacinth bulbs, snails, eggs, and the like have a reputation for producing sperm not because they are nutritious, but because their primary natures, in and of themselves, have capacities similar to sperm. Diphilus:

of his father Agamemnon, although the exact point of the allusion is unclear.

359

εἰσι, πολύτροφοι δὲ καὶ εὐστόμαχοι, ἔτι δὲ σμηκτικοὶ
καὶ ἀμβλυντικοὶ ὄψεως, διεγερτικοὶ δ' ἀφροδισίων. ἡ
δὲ παροιμία φησίν·

οὐδέν σ' ὀνήσει βολβός, ἂν μὴ νεῦρ' ἔχῃς.

διεγείρουσι δ' ὄντως αὐτῶν πρὸς ἀφροδίσια οἱ βασι-
λικοὶ λεγόμενοι, οἳ καὶ κρείσσονες τῶν ἄλλων εἰσί·
μεθ' οὓς οἱ πυρροί. οἱ δὲ λευκοὶ καὶ Λιβυκοὶ σκιλ-
λώδεις· χείρονες δὲ πάντων οἱ Αἰγύπτιοι. αἱ δὲ βολβῖ-
ναι καλούμεναι εὐχυλότεραι μέν εἰσι τῶν βολβῶν, οὐ
μὴν οὕτως εὐστόμαχοι διὰ τὸ γλυκάζον ἔχειν ⟨τι⟩·
c παχυντικαί τε[50] ἱκανῶς εἰσι διὰ | τὴν πολλὴν σκληρό-
τητα καὶ εὐέκκριτοι. μνημονεύει δὲ βολβίνης Μάτρων
ἐν παρῳδίαις·

σόγκους δ' οὐκ ἂν ἐγὼ μυθήσομαι οὐδ' ὀνομήνω,
μυελόεν βλάστημα, καρηκομόωντας ἀκάνθαις,
βολβίνας θ', αἳ Ζῆνος Ὀλυμπίου εἰσὶν ἀοιδοί,
ἃς ἐν χέρσῳ θρέψε Διὸς παῖς ἄσπετος Ὄμβρος,
λευκοτέρας χιόνος, ἰδέειν ἀμύλοισιν ὁμοίας·
d τάων φυομένων ἠράσσατο πότνια Γαστήρ. |

Ὅτι Νίκανδρος Μεγαρῆας βολβοὺς ἐπαινεῖ. Θεό-

---

[50] ἔχειν τι· παχυντικαί τε Madvig, Kaibel: ἔχειν παχύ τι·
καί γε CE

Hyacinth bulbs are difficult to digest, but are nutritious and easy on the stomach. They are also purgative and dull the eyesight, and stimulate sexual desire. The proverb says:

> A hyacinth bulb won't do you any good if you don't
>   have a male muscle.[197]

What are called "royal" hyacinth bulbs do indeed arouse sexual desire and are superior to the other varieties; after them come the red ones. The white and Libyan varieties resemble squill; and the Egyptian variety are the worst of all. The so-called *bolbinai* produce better *chulē* than hyacinth bulbs do, but are not as easy on the stomach, since they have a somewhat sweet character. They are also quite fattening because they are so hard, and are easily excreted. Matro mentions *bolbinai* in his parodies (fr. 3 Olson–Sens = *SH* 536):

> I could not mention or name the sow-thistles,
> a marrowy growth, with their long, spiny hair,
> and the *bolbinai*, which are the singers of Olympian
>   Zeus,
> and which the child of Zeus, the endless Rain, raised
>   on the mainland,
> whiter than snow, like wheat-paste cakes in
>   appearance.
> My lady Belly fell in love with them as they were
>   growing.

Nicander (fr. 88 Schneider) recommends Megarian hy-

---

[197] For *neuron* in this sense, cf. Pl. Com. fr. 189.20, quoted at 1.5d.

φραστος δ' ἐν ἑβδόμῳ Φυτικῶν, ἐνιαχοῦ, φησίν, οὕτω
γλυκεῖς εἰσιν οἱ βολβοὶ ὥστε καὶ ὠμοὺς ἐσθίεσθαι,
ὥσπερ ἐν τῇ Ταυρικῇ Χερρονήσῳ. τὰ αὐτὰ ἱστορεῖ
καὶ Φαινίας. ἔστι δὲ καὶ γένος, φησί, βολβῶν[51] ἐριο-
φόρων, ὃ φύεται ἐν αἰγιαλοῖς, ἔχει δὲ τὸ ἔριον ὑπὸ
τοὺς πρώτους χιτῶνας, ὥστε ἀνὰ μέσον εἶναι τοῦ
ἐδωδίμου τοῦ ἐντὸς καὶ τοῦ ἔξω. ὑφαίνεται δ' ἐξ αὐτοῦ
καὶ πόδεια καὶ ἄλλα ἱμάτια, ὡς καὶ Φαινίας φησί, τὸ
e   δὲ ἐν Ἰνδοῖς τριχῶδές ἐστι. περὶ δὲ | τῆς τῶν βολβῶν
σκευασίας Φιλήμων φησί·

          τὸν βολβόν, εἰ βούλει, σκόπει
     ὅσα δαπανήσας εὐδοκιμεῖ, τυρόν, μέλι,
     σήσαμον, ἔλαιον, κρόμυον, ὄξος, σίλφιον.
     αὐτὸς δ' ἐφ' αὑτοῦ 'στιν πονηρὸς καὶ πικρός.

Ἡρακλείδης δ' ὁ Ταραντῖνος τοῦ συμποσίου περι-
γράφων τοὺς βολβούς φησι· περιγράφειν δεῖ τὴν
πολλὴν βρῶσιν καὶ μάλιστα τῶν ἐχόντων ὁλκιμόν τι
καὶ γλίσχρον, οἷον ᾠῶν, βολβῶν, ἀκροκωλίων,
κοχλιῶν καὶ τῶν ὁμοίων. ἐπιμένει γὰρ τῇ κοιλίᾳ
f   πλείονας χρόνους | καὶ ἐμπλεκόμενα παρακατέχει τὰ
ὑγρά.
     Κίχλαι. καὶ τούτων ἦσαν καὶ ἄλλων ὀρνίθων ἀγέ-
λαι ἐν τοῖς προπόμασι. Τηλεκλείδης·

51 βολβῶν, Θεόφραστος, CE

362

acinth bulbs. Theophrastus in Book VII (13.8) of *On Plants* says: In some places the hyacinth bulbs are so sweet that they can be eaten raw, as for example in the Tauric Chersonese. Phaenias (fr. 45 Wehrli) records the same fact. Theophrastus says that there is also a wool-bearing variety of hyacinth bulb, which grows on sea-shores. Its wool is under its outer layers and is thus between the edible interior and the skin. Socks and other items of clothing are woven from it, as Phaenias reports; and the Indian variety is hairy. As for how hyacinth bulbs are prepared, Philemon (fr. 113) says:

> Consider, if you please, how much expense
> the hyacinth bulb goes to in order to win a good
>   reputation: cheese, honey,
> sesame seed, oil, onion, vinegar, silphium juice.
> But on its own it's nasty and bitter.

Heracleides of Tarentum (fr. 66 Guardasole) restricts the consumption of hyacinth bulbs at symposia, saying: There ought to be a restriction on eating large amounts of food, especially those with a sticky, glutinous character, such as eggs, hyacinth bulbs, pigs' trotters, snails, and the like. For such foods remain in the belly for a long time, and become entangled with the moist elements there and prevent them from moving.

Thrushes. There were flocks of these and of other birds on the appetizer plates. Teleclides (fr. 1.12):[198]

---

[198] Quoted in full at 6.268a.

ὀπταὶ δὲ κίχλαι μετ᾽ ἀμητίσκων ἐς τὸν φάρυγ᾽
εἰσεπέτοντο.

Συρακούσιοι δὲ τὰς κίχλας κιχήλας λέγουσιν. Ἐπί-
χαρμος·

< . . . > τάς τ᾽ ἐλαιοφιλοφάγους κιχήλας.

μέμνηται τούτων καὶ Ἀριστοφάνης ἐν Νεφέλαις. τρία
65 δὲ γένη κιχλῶν Ἀριστοτέλης εἶναι ἱστορεῖ, ‖ ὧν τὴν
πρώτην καὶ μεγίστην κίσσῃ πάρισον εἶναι, ἣν καὶ
καλεῖσθαι ἰξοφάγον, ἐπειδὴ ἰξὸν ἐσθίει· τὴν δὲ τῷ
κοσσύφῳ ἴσην, ἣν ὀνομάζεσθαι τριχάδα· τὴν δὲ τρίτην ἐλαχίστην τῶν προειρημένων οὖσαν ἰλλάδα ὀνομάζεσθαι. οἱ δὲ τυλάδα λέγουσιν, ὡς Ἀλέξανδρος
ἱστορεῖ ὁ Μύνδιος· ἣν καὶ συναγελαστικὴν εἶναι καὶ
νεοττεύειν ὡς καὶ τὰς χελιδόνας.

b Ὅτι | τὸ εἰς Ὅμηρον ἀναφερόμενον ἐπύλλιον, ἐπι-
γραφόμενον δὲ Ἐπικιχλίδες, ἔτυχε ταύτης τῆς προσηγορίας διὰ τὸ τὸν Ὅμηρον ᾄδοντα αὐτὸ τοῖς παισὶ
κίχλας δῶρον λαμβάνειν, ἱστορεῖ Μέναιχμος ἐν τῷ
Περὶ Τεχνιτῶν.

Συκαλίδες. Ἀλέξανδρος ὁ Μύνδιος ἱστορεῖ· ἄτερος
τῶν αἰγιθαλῶν ὑφ᾽ ὧν μὲν ἔλαιον καλεῖται, ὑπὸ δέ
τινων πυρρίας· συκαλὶς δ᾽, ὅταν ἀκμάζῃ τὰ σῦκα. δύο

---

199 See 14.639a.
200 "A Beccafico, Lat. *ficedula*, that is to say a small bird of the
gardens and orchards. . . . The Beccafico *par excellence* is *Sylvia*

Roast thrushes accompanied by milk-cakes flew into
their gullets.

The Syracusans call thrushes *(kichlai) kichēlai*. Epicharmus (fr. 155):

and thrushes *(kichēlas)* that love to eat olives.

Aristophanes also mentions them in *Clouds* (339). Aristotle (fr. 181) records that there are three varieties of
thrush. The first and largest is the size of a jay and is referred to as an *ixophagos* ("mistletoe-eater"), because it
eats mistletoe-berries *(ixos)*. The second is the size of a
blackbird and is called a *trichas* ("hairy [thrush]"). The
third is the smallest of the birds mentioned above and is
called an *illas*, although according to Alexander of Myndus
(fr. I.4 Wellmann) some people refer to it as a *tulas*. It
forms flocks and builds its nest in the same way swal-
lows do.

The short epic poem attributed to Homer and entitled
Epikichlides ("For Thrushes")[199] got this name, according
to Menaechmus in his *On Artists (FGrH* 131 F 3), because
when Homer sang it to the children, they would give him
thrushes.

Warblers.[200] Alexander of Myndus (fr. I.5 Wellmann)
reports: The other titmouse is called the *elaios* by some
authorities, and the *purrhias* ("redhead") by others. It is
called *sukalis* whenever the figs *(suka)* are ripe. There are

atricapilla, the Blackcap Warbler, which, both in Greece and Italy,
comes down into the plains in autumn and is caught in multitudes
among the fig-trees" (D. W. Thompson, *A Glossary of Greek Birds*
[Oxford, 1936] 274).

δ᾽ εἶναι γένη αὐτοῦ συκαλίδα καὶ μελαγκόρυφον.
Ἐπίχαρμος·

< . . . > ἀγλαὰς συκαλλίδας.

καὶ πάλιν·

ἦν δ᾽ ἐρῳδιοὶ < . . . > μακροκαμπυλαύχενες
c   τέτραγές τε σπερματολόγοι κἀγλααὶ συκαλλίδες. |

ἁλίσκονται δ᾽ αὗται τῷ τῶν σύκων καιρῷ. διὸ βέλτιον
ὀνομάζοιτ᾽ ἂν δι᾽ ἑνὸς λ· διὰ δὲ τὸ μέτρον Ἐπίχαρμος
διὰ δυεῖν εἴρηκεν.

Σπίνοι. Εὔβουλος·

Ἀμφιδρομίων ὄντων, ἐν οἷς νομίζεται
ὀπτᾶν τε τυροῦ Χερρονησίτου τόμον
ἕψειν τ᾽ ἐλαίῳ ῥάφανον ἠγλαϊσμένην
πνίγειν τε παχέων ἀρνίων στηθύνια
d   τίλλειν τε φάττας καὶ κίχλας ὁμοῦ σπίνοις |
ὁμοῦ τε χναύειν μαινίσιν σηπίδια
πιλοῦν τε πολλὰς πλεκτάνας ἐπιστρεφῶς
πίνειν τε πολλὰς κύλικας εὐζωρεστέρας.

---

201 Quoted in full at 9.398d.

202 Quoted in a more complete form at 9.398d.

203 For the disputed identification of this bird, see 9.398b–f.

204 At 9.370c–d these lines are assigned to Ephippus, and most
likely a quotation and a lemma have dropped out of the text at one
place or the other.

two varieties of the bird: the *sukalis* and the *melanko-ruphos* ("blackcap"). Epicharmus (fr. 42.3):[201]

colorful warblers.

And again (fr. 85):[202]

There were herons with long curved necks
and seed-gathering grouse[203] and colorful warblers
(sukallides).

These birds are caught *(haliskontai)* during fig season. The name is therefore better spelled with one *lambda*; but Epicharmus pronounces it with two for the sake of the meter.

Chaffinches. Eubulus (fr. dub. 148):[204]

When the Amphidromia[205] is going on, where it's
customary
to roast a slice of Chersonesian cheese
and stew cabbage shimmering with oil
and bake fat lambs' breasts
and pluck ringdoves and thrushes, as well as finches,
and nibble on cuttlefish and small-fry together
and vigorously pound numerous octopus tentacles[206]
and drink many cups of strong wine.

[205] A ritual celebrated a few days after the birth of a child, at which it was formally introduced to the household and the family's friends.

[206] To make them soft enough to eat.

Κόψιχοι. Νικόστρατος ἢ Φιλέταιρος <ἐν Ἀντύλ-
λῳ>[52].

                 (Α.) τί οὖν ἀγοράζω; φράζε γάρ.
(Β.) μὴ πολυτελῶς, ἀλλὰ καθαρείως δασύποδα,
ἐὰν περιτύχῃς, ἀγόρασον καὶ νηττία,
ὁπόσα σὺ βούλει, καὶ κίχλας καὶ κοψίχους,
ὀρνιθάριά τε τῶν ἀγρίων τούτων συχνά.
e   (Α.) χάριεν. |

Ἀντιφάνης δὲ καὶ ψᾶρας ἐν τοῖς βρώμασι καταλέγει·

               μέλι, πέρδικες,
φάτται, νῆτται, χῆνες, ψᾶρες,
κίττα, κολοιός, κόψιχος, ὄρτυξ,
ὄρνις θήλεια.

Πάντων ἡμᾶς λόγον ἀπαιτεῖς καὶ οὐδ᾽ ὁτιοῦν ἔξ-
εστιν εἰπεῖν ἀνυπεύθυνον.

Ὅτι τὸ στρουθάριον παρ᾽ ἄλλοις τε καὶ δὴ καὶ
παρ᾽ Εὐβούλῳ·

                              περδίκια
λαβὲ τέτταρ᾽ ἢ καὶ πέντε, δασύποδας <δὲ> τρεῖς,
στρουθάριά θ᾽ οἷον ἐντραγεῖν † ἀκανθυλλίδας,
βιττάκους, σπινία, κερχνῇδας,
f   τά τ᾽ | ἄλλ᾽ ἅττ᾽ ἂν ἐπιτύχῃς †.

[52] <ἐν Ἀντύλλῳ> Schweighäuser

Blackbirds. Nicostratus (fr. *4) or Philetaerus ⟨in *Antylla*⟩:[207]

> (A.) What should I buy, then? Tell me!
> (B.) Don't be extravagant; keep it simple. Buy
> some hares, if you happen on any, and as many ducks
> as you like, and thrushes and blackbirds,
> and a lot of these little wild birds.
> (A.) Nice!

Antiphanes (fr. 295) also includes starlings in a list of food:

> honey, partridges,
> ringdoves, ducks, geese, starlings,
> a jay, a jackdaw, a blackbird, a quail,
> a hen.

You ask us to give an account of everything, and it is impossible to say a word without being cross-examined.[208]

The sparrow is mentioned by a number of authors, including Eubulus (fr. 120):

> Get
> four or even five partridges, three hares,
> and sparrows such as to nibble on † siskins,
> parrots, chaffinches, kestrel-hawks,
> and whatever else you happen on †.

---

[207] At 3.108c, 118e, Athenaeus expresses doubt as to whether *Antylla* ought to be assigned to Nicostratus or Philetaeurus; as this is the only play he refers to in this way, it must be the one quoted here.

[208] A complaint by a member of the company, doubtless addressed to Ulpian.

Ἐγκέφαλοι χοίρειοι. τούτων ἡμᾶς ἐσθίειν οὐκ εἴων
οἱ φιλόσοφοι φάσκοντες τοὺς αὐτῶν μεταλαμβάνον-
τας ἶσον καὶ κυάμων τρώγειν κεφαλῶν τε οὐ τοκήων
μόνον, ἀλλὰ καὶ τῶν ἄλλων βεβήλων. οὐδένα γοῦν
τῶν ἀρχαίων βεβρωκέναι διὰ τὸ τὰς αἰσθήσεις ἁπά-
σας σχεδὸν ἐν αὐτῷ εἶναι. Ἀπολλόδωρος δ᾽ ὁ Ἀθηναῖος οὐδ᾽ ὀνομάζειν τινὰ τῶν παλαιῶν φησιν ἐγκέφα-
66   λον· ‖ καὶ Σοφοκλέα γοῦν ἐν Τραχινίαις ποιήσαντα
τὸν Ἡρακλέα ῥιπτοῦντα τὸν Λίχαν ἐς θάλασσαν οὐκ
ὀνομάσαι ἐγκέφαλον, ἀλλὰ λευκὸν μυελόν, ἐκκλίνοντα
τὸ μὴ ὀνομαζόμενον·

κόμης δὲ λευκὸν μυελὸν ἐκραίνει, μέσου
κρατὸς διασπαρέντος αἵματός θ᾽ ὁμοῦ,

καίτοι τἆλλα διαρρήδην ὀνομάσαντα. καὶ Εὐριπίδης
δὲ τὴν Ἑκάβην θρηνοῦσαν εἰσαγαγὼν τὸν Ἀστυά-
νακτα ὑπὸ τῶν Ἑλλήνων ῥιφέντα φησί·

b   δύστηνε, κρατὸς ὥς σ᾽ ἔκειρεν ἀθλίως |
τείχη πατρῷα, Λοξίου πυργώματα,
ὃν πόλλ᾽ ἐκήπευσ᾽ ἡ τεκοῦσα βόστρυχον
φιλήμασίν τ᾽ ἔδωκεν, ἔνθεν ἐκγελᾷ
ὀστέων ῥαγέντων φόνος, ἵν᾽ αἰσχρὰ μὴ λέγω⁵³.

---

⁵³ στέγω Diggle

Pigs' brains. The philosophers did not permit us to eat these, saying about those who partake of them that eating fava beans is equivalent to eating not just the heads of one's parents, but the heads of anything polluted.[209] None of the ancients, at any rate, ate pigs' brains, because they contain almost all the senses. Apollodorus of Athens (*FGrH* 244 F 246) denies that any ancient author even uses the word "brain." Sophocles, for example, when he describes Heracles throwing Lichas into the sea in *Trachiniae* (781–2), does not use the word "brain," but says "white marrow," avoiding a term that is not used:

> He made the white marrow ooze out of his hair, as
> his head was split in two, and the blood along with it.

But he describes everything else explicitly. So too Euripides (*Tr.* 1173–7) brings Hecabe onstage mourning for Astyanax, who was thrown from the walls by the Greeks, and says:

> Poor thing, how cruelly your paternal walls,
> the battlements erected by Loxias, sheared from your
>   head
> the locks of hair your mother often tended
> and kissed, whence from your shattered bones
> shines forth the gore—my purpose being to avoid
>   shameful words.

[209] A reference to the Pythagorean prohibition against eating beans: "Eating beans is no different from eating your parents' heads." Athenaeus' (illogical) argument is apparently that, if one cannot eat one's parents' heads, one certainly cannot eat the heads of other obviously unclean creatures; and that the fact that the ancients did not eat pigs' heads proves that they understood this.

ἔχει δὲ ἐπίστασιν ἡ τῶν ποιημάτων τούτων ἐκδοχή. καὶ γὰρ Φιλοκλῆς τε ἐγκέφαλόν φησιν·

< . . . > οὐδ᾽ ἂν ἐγκέφαλον ἔσθων λίποι.

καὶ Ἀριστοφάνης·

< . . . > ἀπολέσαιμ᾽ ἂν ἐγκεφάλου θρίω δύο,

c καὶ ἄλλοι. λευκὸν οὖν ἂν εἴη μυελὸν εἰρηκὼς | Σοφο-
κλῆς ποιητικῶς, Εὐριπίδης δὲ τὸ τῆς προσόψεως εἰ-
δεχθὲς καὶ αἰσχρὸν οὐχ αἱρούμενος ἐναργῶς ἐμφανί-
σαι ἐδήλωσεν ὡς ἐβούλετο. ὅτι δ᾽ ἱερὸν ἐνόμιζον τὴν
κεφαλὴν δῆλον ἐκ τοῦ καὶ κατ᾽ αὐτῆς ὀμνύειν καὶ τοὺς
γινομένους ἀπ᾽ αὐτῆς πταρμοὺς προσκυνεῖν ὡς ἱε-
ρούς. ἀλλὰ μὴν καὶ τὰς συγκαταθέσεις βεβαιοῦμεν τῇ
ταύτης ἐπινεύσει, ὡς καὶ ὁ Ὁμηρικὸς Ζεύς φησιν·

εἰ δ᾽ ἄγε τοι κεφαλῇ ἐπινεύσομαι.[54]

Ὅτι εἰς τὸ πρόπομα καὶ ταῦτα ἐνεβάλλοντο, πέ-
d περι, | φυλλίς, σμύρνα, κύπειρον, μύρον Αἰγύπτιον.
Ἀντιφάνης·

ἂν μὲν ἄρα πέπερι πριάμενός τις εἰσφέρῃ,
στρεβλοῦν γράφουσι τοῦτον ὡς κατάσκοπον.

πάλιν·

[54] Most witnesses have κατανεύσομαι, but Athenaeus᾽ ἐπι- is
attested elsewhere.

The interpretation of these verses involves some difficulty; because Philocles (*TrGF* 24 F 5) does use the word "brain":

He wouldn't stop eating brain.

Also Aristophanes (*Ra.* 134):

I'd be wasting two brain croquettes.

And other authors as well. Sophocles must therefore have said "white marrow" for poetic effect, while Euripides chose not to put an ugly, shameful sight on open display, but made the matter clear in a way that suited him. That they regarded the head as sacred is clear from the fact that they swore by it and treated the sneezes it produced as holy.[210] Indeed, we confirm agreements by nodding our head, as the Homeric Zeus says (*Il.* 1.524):

Come now, I will nod my head in assent.

The following items were also placed on the appetizer plate: pepper, greens, myrrh, galingale, and Egyptian perfume. Antiphanes (fr. 274):

If someone buys some pepper and takes it home,
they put him on the list for torture, on the ground
    that he's a spy.

Again (fr. 275):

[210] Sneezes are treated as omens at e.g. *Od.* 17.541–7; Men. fr. 844.9. See Pease, *CP* 6 (1911) 429–43.

νῦν δεῖ περιόντα πέπερι καὶ καρπὸν βλίτου
ζητεῖν.

Εὔβουλος·

κόκκον λαβοῦσα Κνίδιον ἢ τοῦ πεπέριδος
τρίψασ' ὁμοῦ σμύρνῃ διάπαττε τὴν ὁδόν.

Ὠφελίων·

e † Λιβυκὸν πέπερι θυμίαμα καὶ βιβλίον |
Πλάτωνος ἐμβρόντητον.

Νίκανδρος Θηριακοῖς·

ἢ καὶ λεπτοθρίοιο πολύχνοα φύλλα κονύζης.
πολλάκι δ' ἢ πέπεριν κόψας νέον ἢ ἀπὸ Μήδων
κάρδαμον.

Θεόφραστος ἐν Φυτῶν Ἱστορίᾳ· τὸ πέπερι καρπὸς μέν
ἐστι, διττὸν δὲ αὐτοῦ τὸ γένος· τὸ μὲν στρογγύλον
ὥσπερ ὄροβος, κέλυφος ⟨ἔχον⟩ ὑπέρυθρον, τὸ δὲ
πρόμηκες, μέλαν, σπερμάτια μηκωνικὰ ἔχον. ἰσχυρό-
τερον δὲ πολὺ τοῦτο θατέρου, θερμαντικὰ δὲ ἄμφω·
διὸ καὶ πρὸς τὸ κώνειον βοηθεῖ ταῦτα. ἐν δὲ τῷ Περὶ
f Πνιγμοῦ γράφει· ἡ δὲ τούτων | ἀνάκτησις ὄξους ἐγχύ-
σει καὶ πεπέριδος ἢ κνίδης καρπῷ τριφθείσης. τοῦτο
δ' ἡμᾶς τηρῆσαι δεῖ ὅτι οὐδέτερον ὄνομα οὐδέν ἐστι
παρὰ τοῖς Ἕλλησιν εἰς ι λῆγον, εἰ μὴ μόνον τὸ μέλι·

211 At 3.126b these verses are said to have been quoted by
Ulpian.

Now I have to go around and look for pepper
and blite-berry.

Eubulus (fr. 125):

Get some Cnidian bay-seed or some pepper,
grind it up with myrrh, and sprinkle the path with it!

Ophelio (fr. 3):

† Libyan pepper, incense, and a crazy
book by Plato.

Nicander in the *Theriaca* (875–7):[211]

or even the downy foliage of the fine-leaved fleabane.
And often too, after cutting some fresh pepper or
    Persian
garden-cress . . .

Theophrastus in *Research on Plants* (*HP* 9.20.2): Pepper is
a fruit, of which there are two varieties. One is round like
bitter vetch and has a reddish case. The other is elongated
and black and has poppy-like seeds; it is much stronger
than the other kind, although both are heating. This is why
they can be used as antidotes for hemlock.[212] In his *On Suf-
focation* (fr. 347a) he writes: They can be resuscitated by
pouring a mixture of vinegar and pepper or ground nettle-
seed into them. We should note that the Greeks have
no neuter noun that ends in *iota* except *meli* ("honey");
because *peperi* ("pepper"), *kommi* ("gum"), and *koiphi* (a

---

[212] For the cooling effect of hemlock, cf. Ar. *Ra*. 124–5; Pl.
Phd. 117e–18a.

τὸ γὰρ πέπερι καὶ κόμμι καὶ κοῖφι ξενικά.

Ἔλαιον. Σαμιακοῦ ἐλαίου μνημονεύει Ἀντιφάνης ἢ Ἄλεξις·

                    οὑτοσὶ δέ σοι
τοῦ λευκοτάτου πάντων ἐλαίου Σαμιακοῦ
ἔστιν μετρητής.

67 Καρικοῦ δὲ Ὠφελίων· ‖

                    ἐλαίῳ Καρικῷ
ἀλείφεται.

Ἀμύντας ἐν Σταθμοῖς Περσικοῖς φησι· φέρει τὰ ὄρη τέρμινθον καὶ σχῖνον καὶ κάρυα τὰ Περσικά, ἀφ' ὧν ποιοῦσι τῷ βασιλεῖ ἔλαιον πολύ. Κτησίας δ' ἐν Καρμανίᾳ φησὶ γίνεσθαι ἔλαιον ἀκάνθινον, ᾧ χρῆσθαι βασιλέα· ὃς καὶ καταλέγων ἐν τῷ Περὶ τῶν Κατὰ τὴν Ἀσίαν Φόρων[55] πάντα τὰ τῷ βασιλεῖ παρασκευαζόμενα ἐπὶ τὸ δεῖπνον οὔτε πεπέρεως μέμνηται οὔτε ὄξους,

ὃ μόνον ἄριστόν ἐστι τῶν ἡδυσμάτων.

b ἀλλὰ μὴν οὐδὲ Δείνων ἐν τῇ | Περσικῇ Πραγματείᾳ, ὅς γέ φησι καὶ ἅλας Ἀμμωνιακὸν ἀπ' Αἰγύπτου ἀνα-

_____

[55] φόρων τούτῳ βιβλίῳ CE: φόρων τρίτῳ βιβλίῳ Musurus

_____

[213] Sinapi ("mustard") is omitted because Athenaeus habitually spells it sinapu. But he or his source also ignores e.g. alphi

type of Egyptian incense) are foreign loan-words.[213]

Oil. Antiphanes (fr. *212)[214] or Alexis mentions Samian oil:

> Here you have
> an amphora-ful of Samian oil,
> which is the clearest of all.

Ophelio (fr. 5) mentions Carian oil:

> He anoints himself
> with Carian oil.

Amyntas in *Stations on the Persian Royal Road* (*FGrH* 122 F 4) says: The mountains produce turpentine, squill, and Persian nuts, from which they make a large amount of oil for the King. Ctesias (*FGrH* 688 F 38) says that thorn-tree oil is produced in Carmania and used by the King. When he offers a list in his book *On the Tributes Paid throughout Asia* (*FGrH* 688 F 53) of everything prepared for the King's dinner, he does not mention pepper or vinegar,

> which is the single best seasoning. (adesp. com. fr. *104)

Nor indeed does Deinon in his *Study of Persia* (*FGrH* 690 F 23a), although he does note that Ammoniac salt and wa-

---

("barley-groats"), *kiki* ("castor oil"; an Egyptian loan-word) and *sesili* ("hartwort"; also Egyptian?). *Peperi* is in fact originally a Sanskrit word, while *kommi* is Egyptian.

[214] Probably from *Aleiptria*, *Anteia*, or *Sleep*, the authorship of all of which, Athenaeus reports at various points, was disputed between Antiphanes and Alexis.

πέμπεσθαι βασιλεῖ καὶ ὕδωρ ἐκ τοῦ Νείλου. ἐλαίου δὲ
τοῦ ὠμοτριβοῦς καλουμένου μέμνηται Θεόφραστος ἐν
τῷ Περὶ Ὀδμῶν φάσκων αὐτὸ γίνεσθαι ἐκ τῶν φαυ-
λιῶν ἐλαιῶν καὶ ἐξ ἀμυγδάλων. τοῦ δὲ ἐν Θουρίοις
γινομένου ἐλαίου ὡς διαφόρου μνημονεύει Ἄμφις·

ἐν Θουρίοις τοὔλαιον, ἐν Γέλᾳ φακῆ.

c Γάρος. Κρατῖνος· |

ὁ τάλαρος ὑμῖν διάπλεως ἔσται γάρου.

Φερεκράτης·

< . . . > ἀνεμολύνθη τὴν ὑπήνην τῷ γάρῳ.

Σοφοκλῆς Τριπτολέμῳ·

< . . . > τοῦ ταριχηροῦ γάρου.

Πλάτων·

ἐν σαπρῷ γάρῳ
βάπτοντες ἀποπνίξουσί με.

ὅτι δ᾽ ἀρσενικόν ἐστι τοὔνομα Αἰσχύλος δηλοῖ εἰπών·

< . . . > καὶ τὸν ἰχθύων γάρον.

Ὄξος. τοῦτο μόνον Ἀττικοὶ τῶν ἡδυσμάτων ἡδὸς
καλοῦσι. κάλλιστον δ᾽ ὄξος εἶναί φησι Χρύσιππος ὁ

---

[215] Cited in a slightly different form (and with the verse that
follows) at 1.30b.

378

ter from the Nile are imported from Egypt for the King. Theophrastus mentions what is called "raw-pressed" oil in his *On Odors* (15–16), and says that it is made from low-quality olives and from almonds. Amphis (fr. 40.1)[215] notes that the oil produced in Thurii is particularly good:

the oil in Thurii, lentil soup in Gela.

Fermented fish-sauce. Cratinus (fr. 312):

Your basket will be full of fish-sauce.

Pherecrates (fr. 188):

He got his beard dirty with the fish-sauce.

Sophocles in *Triptolemus* (fr. 606):

of sauce made of preserved fish.

Plato (fr. 215):

They're going to choke me to death
by dipping me in rotten fish-sauce.

Aeschylus (fr. 211) shows that the word is masculine, when he says:[216]

and the fish-sauce.

Vinegar. Attic authors refer to this seasoning alone as "a delight."[217] The philosopher Chrysippus (xxviii fr. 14, *SVF*

[216] Identified by Herodian as coming from the satyr play *Proteus*. In all the passages quoted above, the masculine forms could be emended to feminine. But here the masculine definite article is metrically guaranteed.

[217] Cf. Antiph. fr. 132.4–6 (quoted at 9.366c) with K–A ad loc.

φιλόσοφος τό τε Αἰγύπτιον καὶ τὸ Κνίδιον. Ἀριστο-
d φάνης | δὲ ἐν Πλούτῳ φησίν·

< . . . > ὄξει διέμενος Σφηττίῳ.

Δίδυμος δ' ἐξηγούμενος τὸ ἰαμβεῖον φησιν· ἴσως
διότι οἱ Σφήττιοι ὀξεῖς. μνημονεύει δέ που καὶ τοῦ ἐκ
Κλεωνῶν ὄξους ὡς διαφόρου·

< . . . > ἐν δὲ Κλεωναῖς ὀξίδες εἰσί.

καὶ Δίφιλος·

(Α.) δειπνεῖ τε καταδύς, πῶς δοκεῖς, Λακωνικῶς,
ὄξους δὲ κοτύλην. (Β.) πάξ. (Α.) τί πάξ; ὀξὶς
    μέτρον
χωρεῖ τοσοῦτο τῶν Κλεωναίων.

Φιλωνίδης·

                    τὰ καταχύσματα
e αὐτοῖσιν ὄξος οὐκ ἔχει. |

ὁ δὲ Ταραντῖνος Ἡρακλείδης ἐν τῷ Συμποσίῳ φησί·
τὸ ὄξος τινὰ τῶν ἐκτὸς συνιστάνει, παραπλησίως δὲ
καὶ τὰ ἐν κοιλίᾳ, τὰ <δ'> ἐν τῷ ὄγκῳ διαλύει, διὰ τὸ
δηλονότι διαφόρους ἐν ἡμῖν μίγνυσθαι χυμούς. ἐθαυμάζετο δὲ καὶ τὸ Δεκελεικὸν ὄξος. Ἄλεξις·

---

218 *oxos* can refer to both vinegar and cheap, vinegarish wine;
here (as in Alex. fr. 286, below) it clearly means the latter.

iii.200) maintains that the best vinegar comes from Egypt and Cnidus. Aristophanes says in *Wealth* (720):

> drenched in Sphettian vinegar *(oxos)*.

Didymus (p. 76 Schmidt) explains the verse by saying: Perhaps because the Sphettians are sharp-tempered *(oxeis)*. Aristophanes (fr. 709) also notes somewhere that the vinegar from Cleonae is particularly good:

> There are vinegar cruets in Cleonae.

Also Diphilus (fr. 96):

> (A.) He went down and is dining—can you
>   imagine?—in Spartan style
> on a cup of cheap wine[218]. (B.) That's enough!
>   (A.) What do you mean, "That's enough"?
> A Cleonaean vinegar cruet holds exactly this
>   much!

Philonides (fr. 9):

>   Their sauces
> lack vinegar.

Heracleides of Tarentum in his *Symposium* (fr. 67 Guardasole) says: Vinegar curdles some substances outside the body, just as it does the contents of the belly; but it breaks up solid tissue, because of the fact that various humours are obviously mixed together inside us. Deceleian vinegar was also highly regarded. Alexis (fr. 286):[219]

---

[219] Athenaeus (or his source) has missed the point: the speaker is unhappy about having been forced to drink Deceleian wine.

κοτύλας τέτταρας

ἀναγκάσας με † μεστὰς αὐτοῦ † σπάσαι

ὄξους Δεκελεικοῦ δι᾽ ἀγορᾶς μέσης ἄγεις.

f λεκτέον δὲ ὀξύγαρον⁵⁶ διὰ τοῦ υ καὶ τὸ δεχόμενον |
αὐτὸ ἀγγεῖον ὀξύβαφον· ἐπεὶ καὶ Λυσίας ἐν τῷ Κατὰ
Θεοπόμπου Αἰκίας εἴρηκεν· ἐγὼ δ᾽ ὀξύμελι πίνω. οὕτως οὖν ἐροῦμεν καὶ ὀξυρόδινον.

῞Οτι ἀρτύματα εὕρηται παρὰ Σοφοκλεῖ⁵⁷·

< . . . > καὶ βορᾶς ἀρτύματα.

καὶ παρ᾽ Αἰσχύλῳ·

< . . . > διαβρέχεις τἀρτύματα.

καὶ Θεόπομπος δέ φησι· πολλοὶ μὲν ἀρτυμάτων μέ-
διμνοι, πολλοὶ δὲ σάκκοι καὶ θύλακοι βιβλίων καὶ τῶν
ἄλλων ἁπάντων τῶν χρησίμων πρὸς τὸν βίον. τὸ δὲ
68 ῥῆμα κεῖται παρὰ Σοφοκλεῖ· ‖

< . . . > ἐγὼ μάγειρος ἀρτύσω σοφῶς.

Κρατῖνος·

⁵⁶ ὀξύγαρον Levinius: ὀξύ γὰρ E: ὅτι γὰρ C
⁵⁷ Σωφίλῳ ἐν ᾽Ανδροκλεῖ Valckenaer

382

After forcing me
to drain four cups † full of it † of cheap Deceleian
   wine,
you're dragging me through the middle of the
   marketplace.

Oxugaron ("vinegar-fish-sauce") ought to be pronounced
with an *upsilon*;[220] the vessel that holds it should be
pronounced *oxubaphon*. For Lysias in his *Against Theopompus for Assault* (fr. 154 Carey) says: I drink *oxumeli*
("cheap wine or vinegar sweetened with honey"). In the
same way, therefore, we will also say *oxurhodinon* ("cheap
wine or vinegar flavored with roses").

The word "seasonings" is found in Sophocles (fr. *675):

and seasonings for food.

Also in Aeschylus (fr. 306):

You're soaking the seasonings.

Theopompus (*FGrH* 115 F 263b) too says: Many
medimnoi[221] of seasonings, and many sacks and bags full of
books and all the other necessities of life. The verb is attested in Sophocles (fr. dub. 1122):

I the cook will season it skilfully.

Cratinus (fr. 336):

[220] Rather than with an *iota*, *oxigaron*. So too in the next
clause, the pronunciation *oxubaphon* is implicitly contrasted
with *oxibaphon*.
[221] A *medimnos* is a dry measure equivalent to about eight
American bushels.

γλαῦκον οὐ πρὸς παντὸς ⟨ἀνδρός⟩ ἐστιν ἀρτῦσαι
καλῶς.

Εὔπολις·

ὄψῳ πονηρῷ πολυτελῶς ἠρτυμένῳ.

Ὅτι ἀρτύματα ταῦτα καταλέγει που Ἀντιφάνης·

ἀσταφίδος, ἁλῶν, σιραίου, σιλφίου, τυροῦ,
   θύμου,
σησάμου, λίτρου, κυμίνου, ⟨ . . . ⟩[58] ὀριγάνου,
βοτανίων, ὄξους, ἐλαῶν, εἰς ἀβυρτάκην χλόης,
καππάριδος, ᾠῶν, ταρίχους, καρδάμων, θρίων,
   ὀποῦ. |

b

Ὅτι οἴδασιν οἱ παλαιοὶ τὸ Αἰθιοπικὸν καλούμενον
κύμινον.

Ὅτι εἴρηται ἀρσενικῶς ὁ θύμος καὶ ὁ ὀρίγανος.
Ἀναξανδρίδης·

ἀσφάραγον σχῖνόν τε τεμὼν καὶ ὀρίγανον, ὃς δὴ
σεμνύνει τὸ τάριχος ὁμοῦ μιχθεὶς κοριάννῳ.

Ἴων·

αὐτὰρ ὅ γ᾽ ἐμμαπέως τὸν ὀρίγανον ἐν χερὶ
   κεύθει.

[58] ῥοῦ, μέλιτος Poll. 6.66

Not every man can do a good job seasoning
  glaukos.[222]

Eupolis (fr. 365):

nasty food expensively seasoned.

Antiphanes (fr. 140) somewhere[223] lists the following
seasonings:

a raisin, salt, grape-syrup, silphium, cheese, thyme,
sesame, soda ash, cumin, oregano,
chopped herbs, vinegar, olives, greens for a sour
    sauce,
a caper, eggs, preserved fish, cress, fig leaves, rennet.

The ancients were familiar with what is referred to as
Ethiopian cumin.
"Thyme" and "oregano" are found as masculine
nouns.[224] Anaxandrides (fr. 51):

cutting up asparagus, squill, and oregano, which
makes the preserved fish magnificent when mixed
    with coriander.

Ion (eleg. fr. 28 West²):

But he quickly conceals the oregano in his hand.

---

[222] Unidentified, but apparently a large, sharklike fish; see
Olson–Sens on Archestr. fr. 21.1.
[223] Pollux 6.66 quotes the second and third verses in a more
complete form and identifies the play as *The Girl from Leucas*.
[224] In Anaxandr. fr. 51, the gender of the noun is metrically
guaranteed. In Ion eleg. fr. 28 West², on the other hand, Athenaeus' masculine could easily be emended to neuter.

θηλυκῶς δὲ Πλάτων ἢ Κάνθαρος ⟨ἐν Συμμαχίᾳ⟩[59].

ἢ 'ξ Ἀρκαδίας † οὕτω † δριμυτάτην ὀρίγανον.

οὐδετέρως δ' Ἐπίχαρμος καὶ Ἀμειψίας. τὸν δὲ θύμον

c ἀρσενικῶς | Νίκανδρος ἐν Μελισσουργικοῖς.

Ὅτι τοὺς πέπονας Κρατῖνος μὲν σικυοὺς σπερματίας κέκληκεν ἐν Ὀδυσσεῦσι·

(A.) ποῦ ποτ' εἶδές μοι τὸν ἄνδρα, παῖδα Λαέρτα φίλον;

(B.) ἐν Πάρῳ, σικυὸν μέγιστον σπερματίαν ὠνούμενον.

Πλάτων Λαίῳ·

οὐχ ὁρᾷς ὅτι
ὁ μὲν Λέαγρος, Γλαύκωνος ὢν μεγάλου γένους,
d ⟨ἀβελτερο⟩κόκκυξ ἠλίθιος περιέρχεται |
σικυοῦ πέπονος εὐνουχίου κνήμας ἔχων;

Ἀναξίλας·

τὰ δὲ σφύρ' ᾦδει μᾶλλον ἢ σικυὸς πέπων.

Θεόπομπος·

[59] ἐν Συμμαχίᾳ add. Olson

---

[225] At 7.312c, 314a, Athenaeus expresses uncertainty as to whether *The Alliance* was written by Plato or Cantharus, and this must be the play referred to here.

But Plato (fr. *169) or Cantharus ⟨in *The Alliance*⟩[225] makes it feminine:

> or very pungent † as this † oregano from Arcadia.

Whereas Epicharmus (fr. 15) and Amipsias (fr. 36) make it neuter. Nicander in *Beekeeping* (fr. 92 Schneider) makes the word "thyme" masculine.[226]

Cratinus in *Odysseuses* (fr. 147) refers to melons as seed-filled cucumbers:

> (A.) Where did you, please, see my husband, the
>   beloved son of Laertes?
> (B.) On Paros, where he was buying a huge seed-
>   filled cucumber.

Plato in *Laius* (fr. 65.1–4):

>   Don't you see
> that Leagrus,[227] although he's from the distinguished
>   family of Glaucon,
> wanders around like a senseless simpleton,
> with shins the size of a sterile melon?

Anaxilas (fr. 35):

> His ankles were swollen up larger than a melon.

Theopompus (fr. 76):

---

[226] It is more often neuter (e.g. Eup. fr. 13.5; Thphr. *HP* 3.1.3).

[227] Nothing else is known of this Leagrus (*PAA* 602660), but the family was old and important; see J.K. Davies, *Athenian Propertied Families 600–300* B.C. (Oxford, 1971) 90–2.

μαλθακωτέρα
πέπονος σικυοῦ μοι γέγονε.

Φαινίας· βρωτὰ μὲν ἁπαλὰ τῷ περικαρπίῳ σικυὸς καὶ
πέπων ἄνευ τοῦ σπέρματος, πεττόμενον δὲ τὸ περικάρπιον μόνον. κολοκύντη δὲ ὠμὴ μὲν ἄβρωτος, ἑφθὴ δὲ
καὶ ὀπτὴ βρωτή. Διοκλῆς δ' ὁ Καρύστιος ἐν πρώτῳ
Ὑγιεινῶν φησιν ἑψανὰ ἄγρια εἶναι θρίδακα (ταύτης
e κρατίστην | τὴν μέλαιναν), κάρδαμον, κορίαννον⁶⁰,
σίναπυ, κρόμμυον (τούτου εἶδος ἀσκαλώνιον καὶ γή-
τειον), σκόροδον, φύσιγγες, σικυός, πέπων, μήκων.
καὶ μετ' ὀλίγα· ὁ πέπων δ' ἐστὶν εὐκαρδιώτερος καὶ
εὐπεπτότερος. ἑφθὸς δ' ὁ σικυὸς ἁπαλὸς ἄλυπος, οὐ-
ρητικός. ὁ δὲ πέπων ἑψηθεὶς ἐν μελικράτῳ διαχωρητι-
κώτερος. Σπεύσιππος δ' ἐν τοῖς Ὁμοίοις τὸν πέπονα
καλεῖ σικύαν, Διοκλῆς δὲ πέπονα ὀνομάσας οὐκ ἔτι
καλεῖ σικύαν, καὶ ὁ Σπεύσιππος δὲ σικύαν εἰπὼν
f πέπονα οὐκ ὀνομάζει. | Δίφιλος δέ φησιν· ὁ πέπων
εὐχυλότερός ἐστι καὶ ἐπικρατητικὸς . . . κακοχυλό-
τερος δέ, ὀλιγότροφος δὲ καὶ εὔφθαρτος καὶ εὐεκκριτώτερος.

Θρίδαξ. ταύτην Ἀττικοὶ θριδακίνην καλοῦσιν.
Ἐπίχαρμος·

< . . . > θρίδακος ἀπολελεμμένας τὸν καυλόν.

⁶⁰ κορίαννον Casaubon: ἀδριανόν CE

388

She's become
softer than a melon to me.

Phaenias (fr. 46 Wehrli): Cucumbers and melons are edible, except for the seeds, once the flesh is soft; the flesh is the only part that is cooked. Gourds are inedible when raw, but are edible if stewed or baked. Diocles of Carystus in Book I of *On Matters of Health* (fr. 196 van der Eijk) says that the wild plants fit for stewing are lettuce (the dark variety is best), cress, coriander, mustard, onions (the scallion and the leek are onion-varieties), garlic, *phusinkes*[228], cucumber, melon, and poppy. And shortly after this: The melon is better for the heart and more easily digested.[229] When stewed, the cucumber is soft, innocuous, and diuretic; but the melon is more laxative when stewed in a honey sauce. Speusippus in his *On Similar Things* (fr. 7 Tarán) refers to the melon as a *sikua*. Diocles uses the word "melon" but then never refers to a *sikua*; whereas Speusippus uses the word *sikua* but never mentions a "melon." Diphilus says: The melon produces better *chulē* and is more astringent[230] . . . but produces inferior *chulē*, provides little nourishment, and is easily broken down in the stomach and more easily excreted.

Lettuce *(thridax)*. Attic authors refer to this as *thridakinē*. Epicharmus (fr. 156):

lettuce *(thridax)* stripped of its stem.

[228] Apparently a garlic-variety.
[229] Sc. than the cucumber, as what follows makes clear.
[230] The Supplement to LSJ wrongly calls for the deletion of this adjective from the lexicon.

69   θριδακινίδας δ' εἴρηκε Στράττις· ||

πρασοκουρίδες, αἱ καταφύλλους
ἀνὰ κήπους πεντήκοντα ποδῶν
ἴχνεσι βαίνετ', ἐφαπτόμεναι
ποδοῖν σατυριδίων μακροκέρκων,
χοροὺς ἑλίσσουσαι παρ' ὠκίμων
πέταλα καὶ θριδακινίδων
εὐόσμων τε σελίνων.

Θεόφραστος δέ φησι· τῆς θριδακίνης ἡ λευκὴ γλυκυ-
τέρα καὶ ἁπαλωτέρα. γένη δ' αὐτῆς τρία, τὸ πλατύ-
καυλον καὶ στρογγυλόκαυλον καὶ τρίτον τὸ Λακωνι-
κόν. αὕτη δ' ἔχει τὸ μὲν φύλλον σκολυμῶδες, ὀρθὴ δὲ
καὶ εὐαυξὴς ⟨καὶ⟩ ἀπαράβλαστός ἐστιν ἐκ τοῦ καυ-
b   λοῦ. | τῶν δὲ πλατειῶν οὕτω τινὲς γίνονται πλατύκαυ-
λοι ὥστ' ἐνίους καὶ θύραις χρῆσθαι κηπουρικαῖς. τῶν
δὲ καυλῶν φησι κολουσθέντων ἡδίους τοὺς παλιμ-
βλαστεῖς εἶναι.

Νίκανδρος δ' ὁ Κολοφώνιος ἐν δευτέρῳ Γλωσσῶν
βρένθιν λέγεσθαί φησι παρὰ Κυπρίοις θρίδακα, οὗ ὁ
Ἄδωνις καταφυγὼν ὑπὸ τοῦ κάπρου διεφθάρη. Ἄμφις
τε ἐν Ἰαλέμῳ φησίν·

ἐν ταῖς θριδακίναις ταῖς κάκιστ' ἀπολουμέναις,
c   ἃς εἰ φάγοι τις ἐντὸς ἑξήκοντ' ἐτῶν, |
ὁπότε γυναικὸς λαμβάνοι κοινωνίαν,

Whereas Strattis (fr. 71) uses *thridakinidē*:

> leek-caterpillars, you who travel
> through leafy gardens on tracks
> made by your 50 feet, laying hold
> of the long-tailed little orchids (?) with your feet,
> setting your dances twisting through the leaves
> of basil and lettuce *(thridakinidē)*
> > and fragrant celery.

Theophrastus (*HP* 7.4.5) says: Pale lettuce *(thridakinē)* is sweeter and softer. There are three varieties: the flat-stemmed, the round-stemmed, and, third, the Spartan. The Spartan variety has a leaf that resembles the golden thistle's; it grows erect and vigorously, and has no side-shoots from the stem. Some types of the flat variety have such flat stems that people use them to make garden gates. He also says (*HP* 7.2.4) that if the stems are docked, the new shoots are sweeter.

Nicander of Colophon in Book II of the *Glossary* (fr. 120 Schneider) says that the Cyprians use the word *brenthis* for lettuce; it was lettuce that Adonis took refuge in when the boar killed him.[231] And Amphis says in *Lamentation* (fr. 20):

> in the damned lettuce!
> If anyone under 60 years old eats it,
> if he ever gets some time with a woman,

---

[231] Adonis was Aphrodite's mortal lover (Bion *Adonis*; [Apollod.] *Bib*. 3.14.4; Ov. *Met*. 10.519–52, 708–39 with Bömer ad loc.), and Athenian women commemorated his death by growing short-lived "gardens of Adonis"; cf. Olson on Ar. *Pax* 420.

στρέφοιθ' ὅλην τὴν νύκτ' ἂν οὐδὲ ἓν πλέον
ὧν βούλεται δρῶν, ἀντὶ τῆς ὑπουργίας
τῇ χειρὶ τρίβων τὴν ἀναγκαίαν τύχην.

καὶ Καλλίμαχος δέ φησιν ὅτι ἡ Ἀφροδίτη τὸν Ἄδωνιν ἐν θριδακίνῃ κρύψειεν, ἀλληγορούντων τῶν ποιητῶν ὅτι ἀσθενεῖς εἰσι πρὸς ἀφροδίσια οἱ συνεχῶς
χρώμενοι θρίδαξι. καὶ Εὔβουλος δ' ἐν Ἀστύτοις φησί·

d † μὴ παρατίθει μοι † θριδακίνας, ὦ γύναι, |
ἐπὶ τὴν τράπεζαν, ἢ σεαυτὴν αἰτιῶ.
ἐν τῷ λαχάνῳ τούτῳ γάρ, ὡς λόγος, ποτὲ
τὸν Ἄδωνιν ἀποθανόντα προὔθηκεν Κύπρις·
ὥστ' ἐστὶ νεκύων βρῶμα.

Κρατῖνος δέ φησι Φάωνος ἐρασθεῖσαν τὴν Ἀφροδίτην ἐν καλαῖς θριδακίναις αὐτὸν ἀποκρύψαι, Μαρ-
σύας δ' ὁ νεώτερος ἐν χλόῃ κριθῶν. Ἱππώνακτα δὲ
τετρακίνην τὴν θρίδακα καλεῖν Πάμφιλος ἐν Γλώσσαις φησί, Κλείταρχος δὲ Φρύγας οὕτω καλεῖν. Λύ-
e κος[61] δ' ὁ Πυθαγόρειος | τὴν ἐκ γενέσεώς φησι θρίδα-
κα πλατύφυλλον τετανὴν ἄκαυλον ὑπὸ μὲν τῶν
Πυθαγορείων λέγεσθαι εὐνοῦχον, ὑπὸ δὲ τῶν γυναικῶν ἀστύτιδα· διουρητικοὺς γὰρ παρασκευάζει καὶ
ἐκλύτους πρὸς τὰ ἀφροδίσια· ἐστὶ δὲ κρατίστη ἐσθίεσθαι. Δίφιλος δέ φησιν ὡς ὁ τῆς θρίδακος καυλὸς
πολύτροφός ἐστι καὶ δυσέκκριτος μᾶλλον τῶν φύλ-

---

[61] Λύκος Valckenaer (cf. 10.418e): ἴβυκος CE

he can twist and turn all night long without making
   any progress
on what he wants to do. Instead of getting help,
he uses his hand to massage his inescapable fate.

Callimachus (fr. 478) as well claims that Aphrodite hid
Adonis in a bed of lettuce, which is the poets' way of saying
allegorically that men who eat too much of it lose their sexual powers. Eubulus too says in *Impotents* (fr. 13):

† Don't serve me † lettuce on the dinner table,
woman, or you'll have only yourself to blame.
Because the story goes that it was in this vegetable,
   once upon a time,
that Cypris laid Adonis after he died;
so this is dead men's food.

Cratinus (fr. 370) says that after Aphrodite fell in love with
Phaon,[232] she hid him in a beautiful bed of lettuce; whereas
Marsyas the Younger (*FGrH* 135–6 F 9) claims that it was
in a field of unripe barley. According to Pamphilus in the
Glossary (fr. XXXIV Schmidt), Hipponax (fr. 178 Degani)
refers to lettuce as *tetrakinē*; and Cleitarchus says that this
is a Phrygian word. Lycus the Pythagorean (57.2 D–K) reports that lettuce that is naturally flat-leafed, smooth, and
stemless is called "eunuch-lettuce" by the Pythagoreans,
but "impotent lettuce" by the women; for it makes people
need to urinate and diminishes sexual desire. But it is the
best kind to eat. Diphilus says that lettuce stem is full of
nutrition and more difficult to excrete than the leaves;

[232] See 1.5b n.

λων· ταῦτα δὲ πνευματικώτερά ἐστι καὶ τροφιμώτερα
καὶ εὐεκκριτώτερα. κοινῶς μέντοι ἡ θρίδαξ εὐστόμα-
f χος, ψυκτική, εὐκοίλιος, ὑπνωτική, εὔχυλος, ἐφεκτικὴ |
τῆς πρὸς τὰ ἀφροδίσια ὁρμῆς. ἡ δὲ τρυφερωτέρα
θρίδαξ εὐστομαχωτέρα καὶ μᾶλλον ὕπνον ποιοῦσα. ἡ
δὲ σκληροτέρα καὶ ψαθυρὰ ἧττόν ἐστι καὶ εὐστόμαχος καὶ εὐκοίλιος, ὕπνον τε ποιεῖ. ἡ δὲ μέλαινα θρίδαξ
ψύχει μᾶλλον εὐκοίλιός τέ ἐστι. καὶ αἱ μὲν θεριναὶ
εὐχυλότεραι καὶ τροφιμώτεραι, αἱ δὲ φθινοπωριναὶ
ἄτροφοι καὶ ἀχυλότεραι. ὁ δὲ καυλὸς τῆς θρίδακος
ἄδιψος εἶναι δοκεῖ. θρίδαξ δ' ἑψομένη ὁμοίως τῷ ἀπὸ
κράμβης ἀσπαράγῳ ἐν λοπάδι, ὡς Γλαυκίδης ἱστορεῖ, κρείττων τῶν ἄλλων ἑψητῶν λαχάνων. ἐν ἄλλοις
70 δὲ Θεόφραστος ‖ ἐπίσπορά φησι καλεῖσθαι τευτλίον,
θριδακίνην, εὔζωμον, νᾶπυ, λάπαθον, κορίαννον, ἄνη-
θον, κάρδαμον. Δίφιλος δὲ κοινῶς φησιν εἶναι πάντα
τὰ λάχανα ἄτροφα καὶ λεπτυντικὰ καὶ κακόχυλα ἔτι
τε ἐπιπολαστικὰ καὶ δυσοικονόμητα. θερινῶν δὲ λαχάνων Ἐπίχαρμος μέμνηται.

Κινάρα. ταύτην Σοφοκλῆς ἐν Κολχίσι κυνάραν
καλεῖ, ἐν δὲ Φοίνικι·

κύναρος ἄκανθα πάντα πληθύει γύην.

b Ἑκαταῖος δ' ὁ Μιλήσιος ἐν Ἀσίας Περιηγήσει, εἰ |

---

233 Cf. 2.62f.
234 Cardoon (or artichoke thistle) is the wild progenitor of the

they, on the other hand, produce more gas and are more nourishing and easier to excrete. In general, however, lettuce is easy on the stomach, cooling, and easy on the bowels; produces drowsiness and good *chulē*; and checks sexual desire. The tenderer lettuce is, the easier it is on the stomach and the more pronounced its tendency to produce drowsiness. Tougher and crunchier lettuce is harder on the stomach and the bowels, but does nonetheless put one to sleep. Dark lettuce has more of a cooling effect and is easy on the bowels. Lettuce grown in the summer produces better *chulē* and is more nourishing, whereas fall lettuce is not nourishing and produces less *chulē*. Lettuce stem has a reputation for satisfying thirst. According to Glaucias (fr. 162 Deichgräber), when lettuce is stewed like cabbage-asparagus[233] in a casserole-dish, it is better than any other stewed vegetable. Theophrastus (*HP* 7.1.2) says elsewhere that the term *episporos* ("secondary crop") is used of: beet, lettuce, arugula, mustard, sorrel, coriander, anise, and cress. Diphilus says that in general all vegetables have little nutritional value, do not help one put on weight, produce bad *chulē*, and also rise to the top of the stomach and are difficult to digest. Epicharmus (fr. 157) mentions summer vegetables.

Cardoon *(kinara)*.[234] Sophocles in *Colchian Women* (fr. 348) refers to this plant as a *kunara*. But in *Phoenix* (fr. 718) he says:

Cardoon-thorn *(kinara akantha)* fills the whole area.

Hecataeus of Miletus in the *Tour of Asia* (*FGrH* 1 F 291)—

artichoke; the tender leaves and undeveloped flower stalks are edible.

γνήσιον τοῦ συγγραφέως τὸ βιβλίον· Καλλίμαχος γὰρ Νησιώτου αὐτὸ ἀναγράφει. ὅστις οὖν ἐστιν ὁ ποιήσας, λέγει οὕτως· περὶ τὴν Ὑρκανίην θάλασσαν καλεομένην οὔρεα ὑψηλὰ καὶ δασέα ὕλησιν, ἐπὶ δὲ τοῖσιν οὔρεσιν ἄκανθα κυνάρα. καὶ ἑξῆς· Πάρθων πρὸς ἥλιον ἀνίσχοντα Χοράσμιοι οἰκοῦσι γῆν, ἔχοντες καὶ πεδία καὶ οὔρεα· ἐν δὲ τοῖσιν οὔρεσι δένδρεα ἔνι ἄγρια, ἄκανθα κυνάρα, ἰτέα, μυρίκη. καὶ περὶ τὸν Ἰνδὸν δέ φησι ποταμὸν γίνεσθαι τὴν Κυνάραν. καὶ Σκύλαξ δὲ ἢ Πολέμων γράφει· εἶναι δὲ τὴν γῆν c ὑδρηλὴν | κρήνῃσι καὶ ὀχετοῖσιν, ἐν δὲ τοῖς οὔρεσι πέφυκε κυνάρα καὶ βοτάνη ἄλλη. καὶ ἐν τοῖς ἑξῆς· ἐντεῦθεν δὲ ὄρος παρέτεινε τοῦ ποταμοῦ τοῦ Ἰνδοῦ καὶ ἔνθεν καὶ ἔνθεν ὑψηλόν τε καὶ δασὺ ἀγρίῃ ὕλῃ καὶ ἀκάνθῃ κυνάρα. Δίδυμος δ᾽ ὁ γραμματικὸς ἐξηγούμενος παρὰ τῷ Σοφοκλεῖ τὸ κύναρος ἄκανθα, μήποτε, φησί, τὴν κυνόσβατον λέγει διὰ τὸ ἀκανθῶδες καὶ τραχὺ εἶναι τὸ φυτόν. καὶ γὰρ ἡ Πυθία ξυλίνην κύνα αὐτὸ εἶπεν, καὶ ὁ Λοκρὸς χρησμὸν λαβὼν ἐκεῖ πόλιν d οἰκίζειν ὅπου ἂν ὑπὸ ξυλίνης | κυνὸς δηχθῇ, καταμυχθεὶς τὴν κνήμην ὑπὸ κυνοσβάτου ἔκτισε τὴν πόλιν. ἐστὶ δὲ ὁ κυνόσβατος μεταξὺ θάμνου καὶ δένδρου, ὥς φησι Θεόφραστος, καὶ τὸν καρπὸν ἔχει ἐρυθρόν, παραπλήσιον τῇ ῥοιᾷ. ἔχει δὲ καὶ τὸ φύλλον ἀγνῶδες.

Φαινίας δ᾽ ἐν πέμπτῳ Περὶ Φυτῶν κάκτον Σικελι-

---

235 Unidentified. Cf. 9.410e for similar doubts about the authorship of the work.

if the book is actually his; because Callimachus (fr. 437) ascribes it to Nesiotes.[235] Whoever the author is, therefore, he says the following: Around the so-called Hyrcanean Sea[236] are high mountains covered with thick woods, and cardoon-thorn grows on the mountains. And immediately after this: The territory east of the Parthians belongs to the Chorasmioi, who inhabit both the plains and the mountains. In the mountains are wild trees, cardoon-thorn, willow, and tamarisk. He says that cardoons also grow around the Indus River. Scylax or Polemon (fr. 92 Preller) as well writes: The land is watered by springs and irrigation channels, and cardoons and other foliage grow in the mountains. And in the section immediately after this: The mountain range extends from here along both sides of the Indus River, and is high and thickly covered by wild trees and bushes and cardoon-thorn. The grammarian Didymus (p. 242 Schmidt) explains the words "cardoon-thorn" in Sophocles (fr. 718, above) by saying: Perhaps he is referring to the wild rose, since the plant is thorny and rough. The Pythia, in fact, referred to it as a "wooden dog" (Delphi oracle L83 Fontenrose); and after Locrus received an oracle telling him to plant a city in a place where he was bitten by a wooden dog, he founded it when his shin was scratched by a wild rose.[237] According to Theophrastus (*HP* 3.18.4), the wild rose is something between a bush and a tree, and has red fruit that resembles a pomegranate. It also has a spiny leaf.

Phaenias in Book V of *On Plants* (fr. 38 Wehrli) men-

---

[236] The Caspian.

[237] The city in question is Ozolian Locris; cf. Plu. *Mor.* 294d–f.

κήν τινα καλεῖ, ἀκανθῶδες φυτόν, ὡς καὶ Θεόφραστος
ἐν ἕκτῳ Περὶ Φυτῶν· ἡ δὲ κάκτος καλουμένη περὶ
Σικελίαν μόνον, ἐν τῇ Ἑλλάδι δ' οὐκ ἔστι. ἀφίησι δ'
εὐθὺς ἀπὸ[62] τῆς ῥίζης καυλοὺς ἐπιγείους· τὸ δὲ φύλ-
e λον ἔχει πλατὺ | καὶ ἀκανθῶδες· καυλοὺς δὲ τοὺς
καλουμένους κάκτους. ἐδώδιμοι δ' εἰσὶ περιλεπόμενοι
καὶ μικρὸν ὑπόπικροι, καὶ ἀποθησαυρίζουσιν αὐτοὺς
ἐν ἅλμῃ. ἕτερον δὲ καυλὸν ὀρθὸν ἀφίησιν, ὃν καλοῦσι
πτέρνικα, καὶ τοῦτον ἐδώδιμον. τὸ δὲ περικάρπιον
ἀφαιρεθέντων τῶν παππωδῶν ἐμφερὲς τῷ τοῦ φοίνικος ἐγκεφάλῳ, ἐδώδιμον καὶ τοῦτο· καλοῦσι δ' αὐτὸ
ἀσκάληρον. τίς δὲ τούτοις οὐχὶ πειθόμενος θαρρῶν ἂν
εἴποι τὴν κάκτον εἶναι ταύτην τὴν ὑπὸ Ῥωμαίων μὲν
f καλουμένην κάρδον, οὐ μακρὰν ὄντων | τῆς Σικελίας,
περιφανῶς δ' ὑπὸ τῶν Ἑλλήνων κινάραν ὀνομαζομέ-
νην; ἀλλαγῇ γὰρ δύο γραμμάτων κάρδος καὶ κάκτος
ταὐτὸν ἂν εἴη. σαφῶς δ' ἡμᾶς διδάσκει καὶ Ἐπίχαρμος μετὰ τῶν ἐδωδίμων λαχάνων καὶ τὴν κάκτον
καταλέγων οὕτως·

μακωνίδες,
μάραθα, τραχέες τε κάκτοι, τοὶ σὺν ἄλλοις μὲν
φαγεῖν
ἐντὶ λαχάνοις † εἰς τοπιον †.

εἶτα προϊών·

<hr>

[62] ἀπὸ Thphr.: πρὸ CE

tions a Sicilian cactus *(kaktos),* which is a spiny plant. Likewise Theophrastus in Book VI of *On Plants (HP* 6.4.10–11): The so-called *kaktos* is found only around Sicily, and not in Greece. It sends out stalks that spread out on the ground straight up from the root. It has a flat, spiny leaf; the term *kaktos* is properly applied to the stalks. They are edible when peeled, and are slightly bitter; and they preserve them in brine. Another type sends up an erect stalk, which they refer to as a *pternix;* this too is edible. After the downy parts[238] have been removed, the flesh resembles palm heart. This too is edible, and their name for it is *askalēron.*[239] Can anyone accept this evidence but lack the courage to say that this *kaktos* is what the Romans, who are not located far from Sicily, call *kardos*[240] and what the Greeks patently refer to as *kinara* ("cardoon")? Because if two letters were changed, *kardos* and *kaktos* would be the same word. Epicharmus (fr. 158, encompassing all four quotations) as well manifestly teaches us this when he includes the cactus in a list of edible vegetables, as follows:

> poppy,
> fennel, and rough cacti, which are there to eat
> among the other vegetables † to a little spot †.

Then he continues:

[238] The spines or bristles.

[239] Our manuscripts of Theophrastus (seemingly inferior to those Athenaeus knew) offer *skalian* here; but Plin. *Nat.* 21.97 (drawing on Theophrastus) has *ascalian.*

[240] Latin *carduus/cardus* ("thistle"), whence ultimately English "cardoon."

αἴ κα τις ἐκτρίψας καλῶς
παρατιθῇ νιν, ἁδύς ἐστ'· αὐτὸς δ' ἐπ' αὐτοῦ
χαιρέτω.

71 καὶ πάλιν· ‖

θρίδακας, ἐλάταν, σχῖνον, < . . . > ῥαφανίδας,
κάκτους < . . . >.

καὶ πάλιν·

ὁ δέ τις ἄγροθεν ἔοικε μάραθα καὶ κάκτους
φέρειν,
ἴφυον, λάπαθον, † ὀτόστυλλον, σκόλιον, † σερίδ',
ἀτράκτυλον.
πτέριν, † κάκτον ὀνόπορδον.

καὶ Φιλητᾶς ὁ Κῷος·

γηρύσαιτο δὲ νεβρὸς ἀπὸ ψυχὴν ὀλέσασα,
ὀξείης κάκτου τύμμα φυλαξαμένη.

Ἀλλὰ μὴν καὶ κινάραν ὠνόμασε παραπλησίως
b ἡμῖν Σώπατρος ὁ Πάφιος γεγονὼς τοῖς χρόνοις | κατ'
Ἀλέξανδρον τὸν Φιλίππου, ἐπιβιοὺς δὲ καὶ ἕως τοῦ
δευτέρου τῆς Αἰγύπτου βασιλέως, ὡς αὐτὸς ἐμφανίζει
ἔν τινι τῶν συγγραμμάτων αὐτοῦ. Πτολεμαῖος δ' ὁ
Εὐεργέτης βασιλεὺς Αἰγύπτου, εἷς ὢν τῶν Ἀριστάρ-
χου τοῦ γραμματικοῦ μαθητῶν, ἐν δευτέρῳ Ὑπομνημάτων γράφει οὕτως· περὶ Βερενίκην τῆς Λιβύης
Λήθων ποτάμιον, ἐν ᾧ γίνεται ἰχθὺς λάβραξ καὶ

> If someone scrubs it nice and smooth
> and serves it, it's quite pleasant. But all by itself—to
> hell with it.

And again:

> lettuce, *elata*, squill, radishes, cacti.

And again:

> One fellow is likely to bring from his field fennel and
> cacti,
> spike-lavender, sorrel † *otostullon skolion* † chicory,
> spindle-thistle,
> fern, † cactus, bindweed.

Also Philetas of Cos (fr. 16, p. 93 Powell = fr. 18 Sbardella):

> a fawn cries out as it expires,
> hiding within sharp cactus spines.

And yet Sopater of Paphos (fr. 21) referred to it as *kinara*, just as we do; he (test. 1) was born in the time of Alexander son of Philip[241] and survived into the reign of the second king of Egypt,[242] as he himself indicates in one of his treatises. Ptolemy Euergetes (*FGrH* 234 T 1), who was king of Egypt and one of the students of the grammarian Aristarchus, writes as follows in Book II of the *Memoirs* (*FGrH* 234 F 1): Around Berenice in Libya is a small river called the Lethon. In the river are bass, giltheads, and

[241] Alexander the Great (356–323 BCE).
[242] Ptolemy II, whose reign began in 285 BCE.

χρύσοφρυς καὶ ἐγχέλεων πλῆθος τῶν καλουμένων
βασιλικῶν, αἱ τῶν τε ἐκ Μακεδονίας καὶ τῆς Κω-
c παΐδος λίμνης τὸ ǀ μέγεθός εἰσιν ἡμιόλιαι, πᾶν τε τὸ
ῥεῖθρον αὐτοῦ ἰχθύων ποικίλων ἐστὶ πλῆρες. πολλῆς
δ' ἐν τοῖς τόποις κινάρας φυομένης οἵ τε συνακολου-
θοῦντες ἡμῖν στρατιῶται πάντες δρεπόμενοι συν-
εχρῶντο καὶ ἡμῖν προσέφερον ψιλοῦντες τῶν ἀκαν-
θῶν. οἶδα δὲ καὶ Κίναρον καλουμένην νῆσον, ἧς
μνημονεύει Σῆμος.

Ἐγκέφαλος φοίνικος. Θεόφραστος περὶ φοίνικος
τοῦ φυτοῦ εἰπὼν ἐπιφέρει· ἡ μὲν οὖν ἀπὸ τῶν καρπῶν
d φυτεία τοιαύτη τις· ἡ δ' ἀπ' αὐτοῦ, ὅταν ἀφέλωσι τὸ ǀ
ἄνω ἐν ᾧπερ ὁ ἐγκέφαλος. καὶ Ξενοφῶν ἐν δευτέρῳ
Ἀναβάσεως γράφει τάδε· ἐνταῦθα καὶ τὸν ἐγκέφαλον
τοῦ φοίνικος πρῶτον ἔφαγον οἱ στρατιῶται· καὶ οἱ
πολλοὶ ἐθαύμαζον τό τε εἶδος καὶ τὴν ἰδιότητα τῆς
ἡδονῆς· ἦν δὲ σφόδρα καὶ τοῦτο κεφαλαλγές. ὁ δὲ
φοῖνιξ, ὅταν ἐξαιρεθῇ ὁ ἐγκέφαλος, ὅλος ἐξαυαίνεται.
Νίκανδρος Γεωργικοῖς·

συν καὶ φοίνικος παραφυάδας ἐκκόπτοντες
e ἐγκέφαλον φορέουσι νέοις ἀσπαστὸν ἔδεσμα. ǀ

Δίφιλος δ' ὁ Σίφνιος ἱστορεῖ· οἱ τῶν φοινίκων ἐγκέφαλοι πλήσμιοι καὶ πολύτροφοι, ἔτι δὲ βαρεῖς καὶ δυ-
σοικονόμητοι διψώδεις τε καὶ στατικοὶ κοιλίας.

---

243 Lake Copais in Boeotia was a famous source of eels; cf. the
material collected at 7.297c–d, 298f–9b, 300c.

large numbers of what are referred to as royal eels, which are half again as big as the eels in Macedon and Lake Copais;[243] and its entire stream is full of fish of various types. Cardoons grow widely throughout the region, and all the soldiers accompanying us picked and ate them, and stripped off the thorns and brought them to us. I also know of an island called Cinarus, which is mentioned by Semus (*FGrH* 396 F 17).

Palm brain.[244] After describing the palm tree, Theophrastus (*HP* 2.6.2) continues: Such, then, is the method of growing the plant from seed. The other method is by propagation, when they remove the upper portion of the tree, which contains the brain. And Xenophon in Book II (3.16) of the *Anabasis* writes as follows: Here the soldiers ate palm brain for the first time, and many of them were surprised at its appearance and the peculiar flavor. But it was very apt to cause headaches. When the brain is removed, the whole palm tree withers up. Nicander in the *Georgics* (fr. 80 Schneider):

At the same time they cut off the palm tree's side-
     growths[245]
and take away the brain, a food children relish.

Diphilus of Siphnos records: Palm brains are filling and full of nourishment, but are also heavy and difficult to digest, produce thirst, and arrest the movement of the bowels.

[244] The terminal bud of the palm tree, commonly referred to as palm heart.
[245] The fronds.

Ἡμεῖς δέ, φησὶν οὗτος, ἑταῖρε Τιμόκρατες, δόξο-
μεν ἐγκέφαλον ἔχειν μέχρι τοῦ τέλους, εἰ καταπαύ-
σομεν ἐνταῦθα καὶ τήνδε τὴν συναγωγήν.

ἔργον εἰς τρίκλινον συγγενείας εἰσπεσεῖν.
οὗ λαβὼν τὴν κύλικα πρῶτος ἄρχεται λόγου
    πατὴρ
καὶ παραινέσας πέπωκεν, εἶτα μήτηρ δευτέρα,
εἶτα τηθὶς παραλαλεῖ τις, εἶτα βαρύφωνος
    γέρων,
τηθίδος πατήρ, ἔπειτα γραῦς καλοῦσα φίλτατον.
ὁ δ' ἐπινεύει πᾶσι τούτοις,

φησὶ Μένανδρος. πάλιν·

                    τῆς σκιᾶς τὴν πορφύραν
πρῶτον ἐνυφαίνουσ', εἶτα μετὰ τὴν πορφύραν
τοῦτ' ἔστιν οὔτε λευκὸν οὔτε πορφύρα,
ἀλλ' ὥσπερ αὐγὴ τῆς κρόκης κεκραμένη.

Ἀντιφάνης·

τί φής; † ἐνθάδ' οἴσεις τι † καταφαγεῖν
ἐπὶ τὴν θύραν, εἶθ' ὥσπερ οἱ πτωχοὶ χαμαὶ

---

246 The narrator, the character Athenaeus.

247 The material that follows is preserved in C at the end of
Book XIII, and in E at the end of Book XV. It apparently represents quotations that fell out of the text and were inserted in the
margin, and that were then swept up together into a single omni-

But as for us, my friend Timocrates, this fellow[246] says,
we will seem to have the maximum amount of brains if we
put an end to our collection of material at this point.[247]

> It's hard work to be thrown into a family
>   dinner party.
> The father picks up the cup and makes the first
>   speech,
> and after giving some advice, has a drink; the
>   mother's second;
> then an aunt rambles on, followed by a deep-voiced
>   old man,
> who's the aunt's father; then comes an old woman
>   who calls him "dearest."
> And he nods his head, agreeing with them all,

says Menander (fr. *186). Again (fr. 435):

> First they weave in
> the purple, for the shadow; then after the purple
> comes this part, which is neither white nor purple,
> but is like a beam of light mixed into the woof.

Antiphanes (fr. 242):

> What are you saying? † Will you bring me something
>   here † to eat
> at the door? In that case, I'll sit on the ground here

bus supplementary section. Cratinus fr. 334 appears complete between Men. fr. 435 and Antiph. fr. 242, but has been printed at
2.49a, where it is preserved in battered form in the manuscripts;
it thus seems likely that the Menander fragments come from earlier in the Book than this (fr. 435 probably at 2.48c), and the
Antiphanes fragments from later (fr. 243 most likely at 2.49c).

ἐνθάδ᾽ ἔδομαι < . . . > καί τις ὄψεται.

ὁ αὐτός·

εὐτρέπιζε < . . . >

ψυκτῆρα, λεκάνην, τριπόδιον, ποτήριον,
χύτραν, θυείαν, κάκκαβον, ζωμήρυσιν.

to eat, as beggars do, and someone will see.

The same author (fr. 243):

Prepare

a cooler, a basin, a little table, a cup,
a cookpot, a mortar, a three-footed pot, a soup-ladle.

ΕΚ ΤΟΥ ΤΡΙΤΟΥ ΒΙΒΛΙΟΥ

72 Ὅτι Καλλίμαχος ὁ γραμματικὸς τὸ μέγα βιβλίον ἴσον ἔλεγεν εἶναι τῷ μεγάλῳ κακῷ.

Κιβώρια. Νίκανδρος ἐν Γεωργικοῖς·

> σπείρειας κυάμων Αἰγύπτιον, ὄφρα θερείης
> ἀνθέων μὲν στεφάνους ἀνύσῃς, τὰ δὲ πεπτηῶτα

b ἀκμαίου καρποῖο κιβώρια δαινυμένοισιν |
> ἐς χέρας ἠιθέοισι πάλαι ποθέουσιν ὀρέξῃς.
> ῥίζας δ᾽ ἐν θοίνῃσιν ἀφεψήσας προτίθημι.

ῥίζας δὲ λέγει Νίκανδρος τὰ ὑπ᾽ Ἀλεξανδρέων κολοκάσια καλούμενα· ὡς ὁ αὐτός·

> κυάμου λέψας κολοκάσιον ἐντμήξας τε.

ἐστὶ δ᾽ ἐν Σικυῶνι Κολοκασίας Ἀθηνᾶς ἱερόν. Ἐστὶ δὲ καὶ κιβώριον εἶδος ποτηρίου.

c Θεόφραστος δ᾽ ἐν τῷ | Περὶ Φυτῶν οὕτω γράφει· ὁ κύαμος ἐν Αἰγύπτῳ φύεται μὲν ἐν ἔλεσι καὶ λίμναις. καυλὸς δ᾽ αὐτοῦ μῆκος μὲν ὁ μακρότατος εἰς τέτταρας

---

[1] Probably a self-effacing comment by the narrator Athenaeus before he launches into the next section of his report to Timocrates. [2] Cf. 11.477e–f.

FROM BOOK III

The grammarian Callimachus (fr. 465) used to say that a big book is equivalent to a big evil.[1]

Lotus pods *(kibōria)*. Nicander in the *Georgics* (fr. 81 Schneider):

> Sow the Egyptian variety of bean, so that in the
>   summer
> you can produce garlands from its flowers and, when
>   the pods
> full of ripe fruit have fallen, put them into the hands
> of young men who are dining and have long been
>   desiring them.
> As for the roots, I boil them and serve them at
>   banquets.

Nicander uses the term "roots" for what the Alexandrians refer to as *kolokasia*. As he himself says (fr. 82 Schneider):

> after stripping the *kolokasion* from the bean and
>   cutting it up.

In Sicyon there is a temple of Athena Kolokasia.

There is also a type of drinking vessel known as a *kibōrion*.[2]

Theophrastus in his *On Plants* (*HP* 4.8.7–8) writes as follows: The bean grows in Egypt in swamps and marshes. Its stalk is a maximum of four cubits long and one finger

πήχεις, πάχος δὲ δακτυλιαῖος, ὅμοιος καλάμῳ μακρῷ
ἀγονάτῳ· διαφύσεις δ᾽ ἔνδοθεν ἔχει δι᾽ ὅλου διειλημ-
μένας ὁμοίας τοῖς κηρίοις. ἐπὶ τούτῳ δ᾽ ἡ κωδύα καὶ τὸ
ἄνθος διπλάσιον ἢ μήκωνος· χρῶμα δ᾽ ὅμοιον ῥόδῳ
d κατακορές. παραφύεται δὲ φύλλα μεγάλα. | ἡ δὲ ῥίζα
παχυτέρα καλάμου τοῦ παχυτάτου καὶ διαφύσεις
ὁμοίας ἔχουσα τῷ καυλῷ. ἐσθίουσι δ᾽ αὐτὴν καὶ
ἑφθὴν καὶ ὠμὴν καὶ ὀπτήν, καὶ οἱ περὶ τὰ ἕλη τούτῳ
σίτῳ χρῶνται. γίνεται δὲ καὶ ἐν Συρίᾳ καὶ ⟨κατὰ⟩
Κιλικίαν, ἀλλ᾽ οὐκ ἐκπέττουσιν αἱ χῶραι· καὶ περὶ
Τορώνην τῆς Χαλκιδικῆς ἐν λίμνῃ τινὶ μετρίᾳ τῷ
μεγέθει, καὶ αὕτη πέττεται καὶ τελεοκαρπεῖ. Δίφιλος
δὲ ὁ Σίφνιός φησιν· ἡ τοῦ κυάμου τοῦ Αἰγυπτίου ῥίζα,
73 ‖ ἥτις λέγεται κολοκάσιον, εὔστομός τέ ἐστι καὶ
τρόφιμος, δυσέκκριτος ⟨δὲ⟩ διὰ τὸ παραστύφειν·
κρεῖττον δ᾽ ἐστὶ τὸ ἥκιστα ἐριῶδες. οἱ δὲ γινόμενοι,
φησί, κύαμοι ἐκ τῶν κιβωρίων χλωροὶ μέν εἰσι δύσπεπτοι, ὀλιγότροφοι, διαχωρητικοί, πνευματικώτα-
τοι, ξηρανθέντες δὲ ἧττον πνευματοῦσι. γίνεται δὲ
ὄντως ἐκ τῶν κιβωρίων καὶ ἄνθος στεφανωτικόν. καλοῦσι δ᾽ Αἰγύπτιοι μὲν αὐτὸ λωτόν, Ναυκρατῖται δὲ οἱ
ἐμοί, λέγει οὗτος ὁ Ἀθήναιος, μελίλωτον· ἀφ᾽ οὗ καὶ
b μελιλώτινοι στέφανοι | πάνυ εὐώδεις καὶ καύσωνος
ὥρᾳ ψυκτικώτατοι.

Φύλαρχος δέ φησιν· οὐδέποτε πρότερον ἐν οὐδενὶ
τόπῳ κυάμων Αἰγυπτίων οὔτε σπαρέντων οὔτ᾽ εἰ σπεί-
ρειέ τις τικτομένων εἰ μὴ κατὰ Αἴγυπτον, ἐπὶ τοῦ
βασιλέως Ἀλεξάνδρου τοῦ Πύρρου παρὰ τὸν Θύαμιν

wide, and resembles a large jointless reed; inside are separate tubes that run the length of the plant and resemble honeycombs.[3] On the stalk are set the head and the flower, which is twice as large as a poppy and a deep, rose-like color. Large leaves grow along the sides. The root is thicker than the thickest reed and contains tubes that resemble the stalk. They eat it stewed, raw, and baked; and the people who live around the marshes use it for food. It grows in Syria and throughout Cilicia as well, but does not reach maturity there. It is also found in a fairly large marsh near Torone, in the Chalcidic peninsula, where it ripens completely and bears fruit. Diphilus of Siphnos says: The Egyptian bean's root, called a *kolokasion*, is tasty and nourishing, but is difficult to digest because it is rather astringent. The least wooly variety is the best. He says that the beans produced within the pods, when green, are difficult to digest, contain little nutrition, are laxative, and produce a great deal of gas; but after they dry, they produce less gas. A flower used to make garlands is also produced by the pods. The Egyptians refer to it as a *lōtos*;[4] but my people, in the city of Naucratis, says our Athenaeus, call it *melilōtos* ("honey-*lōtos*"). This is the source of honey-*lōtos* garlands, which are quite fragrant and very cooling in the hot season.[5]

Phylarchus (*FGrH* 81 F 65) says: Although Egyptian beans had never been planted anywhere other than Egypt, or if they were planted, did not sprout, in the time of King Alexander son of Pyrrhus[6] some happened to grow in a

---

[3] *Viz.* in cross-section.

[4] Cf. 15.677d–e.   [5] Cf. 15.678c.

[6] King of Molossia 272–*c*.240 BCE.

ποταμὸν τῆς ἐν Ἠπείρῳ Θεσπρωτίας ἐν ἕλει τινὶ
συνέβη φυῆναι. δύο μὲν οὖν ἤνεγκέ πως ἔτη καρπὸν
ἐκτενῶς καὶ ηὔξησε· τοῦ δ᾿ Ἀλεξάνδρου φυλακὴν
c ἐπιστήσαντος καὶ κωλύοντος οὐχ ὅτι λαμβάνειν τὸν |
βουλόμενον, ἀλλὰ μηδὲ προσέρχεσθαι πρὸς τὸν τόπον, ἀνεξηράνθη τὸ ἕλος καὶ τὸ λοιπὸν οὐχ ὅτι τὸν
προειρημένον ἤνεγκε καρπόν, ἀλλ᾿ οὐδὲ ὕδωρ εἴ ποτε
ἔσχε φαίνεται. τὸ παραπλήσιον ἐγένετο καὶ ἐν Αἰδη-
ψῷ. χωρὶς γὰρ τῶν ἄλλων ὑδάτων ναμάτιόν τι ἐφάνη
ψυχρὸν ὕδωρ προϊέμενον οὐ πόρρω τῆς θαλάσσης.
τούτου πίνοντες οἱ ἀρρωστοῦντες τὰ μέγιστα ὠφε-
λοῦντο· διὸ πολλοὶ παρεγίνοντο καὶ μακρόθεν τῷ
ὕδατι χρησόμενοι. οἱ οὖν τοῦ βασιλέως Ἀντιγόνου
d στρατηγοὶ | βουλόμενοι οἰκονομικώτεροι εἶναι διάφο-
ρόν τι ἔταξαν διδόναι τοῖς πίνουσι, καὶ ἐκ τούτου
ἀπεξηράνθη τὸ νᾶμα. καὶ ἐν Τρῳάδι δὲ ἐξουσίαν εἶχον
οἱ βουλόμενοι τὸν πρὸ τοῦ χρόνον τὸν Τραγασαῖον
ἅλα λαμβάνειν· Λυσιμάχου δὲ τέλος ἐπιβαλόντος
ἠφανίσθη. θαυμάσαντος δὲ καὶ ἀφέντος τὸν τόπον
ἀτελῆ πάλιν ηὐξήθη.

Σικυός. παροιμία·

σικυὸν τρώγουσα, γύναι, τὴν χλαῖναν ὕφαινε.

e Μάτρων ἐν παρῳδίαις· |

καὶ σικυὸν εἶδον, γαίης ἐρικυδέος υἱόν,
κείμενον ἐν λαχάνοις· ὁ δ᾿ ἐπ᾿ ἐννέα κεῖτο
τραπέζας.

swamp near the Thyamis river in Thesprotia, which is a region in Epirus. For two years, in fact, the plant somehow produced fruit vigorously and flourished. But when Alexander set a guard over it and prevented anyone who wanted from taking some or even approaching the place, the swamp dried up; after that, not only did it not produce the crop mentioned above, but it was not even apparent that there had ever been any water there. Something similar happened in Aedepsus. A small spring, unconnected with the other water-sources there, appeared not far from the sea and emitted cold water. When sick people drank from it, it helped them immensely; as a result large numbers of them came, even from far away, to drink the water. King Antigonus'[7] generals wanted to get as much profit as they could from the situation and therefore ordered that those who drank the water would have to pay a fee; after this, the spring dried up. Likewise in the Troad, before this time anyone who wanted to gather salt at Tragasae was free to do so. But when Lysimachus[8] imposed a tax on it, the salt disappeared; when he was surprised and made the place free of taxation, the salt accumulated again.

Cucumber. A proverb:

Eat a cucumber, woman, and weave your cloak![9]

Matro in his parodies (fr. 4 Olson–Sens = *SH* 537):

And I saw a cucumber, the son of famous earth,
lying among the vegetables; he lay over nine tables.

---

[7] Antigonus Gonatas; see 2.44b n.
[8] See 2.51a n.
[9] I.e. "Do your work and keep quiet!"

καὶ Διεύχης[1]·

ὡς δ᾽ ὅτ᾽ ἀέξηται σικυὸς δροσερῷ ἐνὶ χώρῳ.

Ἀττικοὶ μὲν οὖν ἀεὶ τρισυλλάβως, Ἀλκαῖος δὲ

< . . . > δάκη (φησί) τὼ σίκυος,

ἀπὸ εὐθείας τῆς σίκυς, ὡς στάχυς στάχυος.

Γ

74   † Στελεω ῥαφανίδας, σικυοὺς τέτταρας. † σικύδιον
δ᾽ ὑποκοριστικῶς εἴρηκε Φρύνιχος ἐν Μονοτρόπῳ·

< . . . > κἀντραγεῖν σικύδιον.

Θεόφραστος δέ φησι σικυῶν τρία εἶναι γένη, Λα-
κωνικόν, σκυταλίαν, Βοιώτιον· καὶ τούτων τὸν μὲν
Λακωνικὸν ὑδρευόμενον βελτίω γίνεσθαι, τοὺς δ᾽ ἄλλους ἀνύδρους. γίνονται δέ, φησί, καὶ εὐχυλότεροι[2] οἱ
σικυοί, ἐὰν τὸ σπέρμα ἐν γάλακτι βραχὲν σπαρῇ ἢ ἐν
μελικράτῳ· ἱστορεῖ δὲ ταῦτα ἐν Φυτικοῖς Αἰτίοις. θᾶτ-
b   τον αὔξεσθαι, κἂν ἐν ὕδατι κἂν ἐν γάλακτι πρότερον |
ἢ εἰς τὴν γῆν κατατεθῆναι βραχῇ. Εὐθύδημος δ᾽ ἐν τῷ
Περὶ Λαχάνων εἶδος σικυῶν εἶναι τοὺς προσαγο-
ρευομένους δρακοντίας. ὠνομάσθαι δὲ σικυούς φησι

---

[1] Διεύχης Kaibel: λεύχης C: λάχης E
[2] The traditional text of Theophrastus reads γλυκύτεροι
("sweeter").

BOOK III

Also Dieuches (*SH* 379):[10]

> as when a cucumber grows large in a moist place.

Attic authors always use the trisyllabic form.[11] But Alcaeus (fr. 401A) says:

> may bite the cucumber *(sikuos),*

deriving the word from the nominative form *sikus*, like *stachus* (nominative), *stachuos* (genitive).

BOOK III[12]

> † a rolling pin, radishes, four cucumbers † (adesp. com. fr. *105, unmetrical). Phrynichus uses the diminutive form *sikudion* in *The Recluse* (fr. 26):

> and to eat a gherkin *(sikudion).*

Theophrastus (*HP* 7.4.6) says that there are three varieties of cucumber: the Spartan, the club-shaped, and the Boeotian. Of these, the Spartan variety is better if it is watered, whereas the other varieties are better if not watered. Cucumbers produce better *chulē*, he claims, if the seed is soaked in milk or honey-water before sowing; he records this in his *Causes of Plants* (2.14.3). (*HP* 7.1.6) It grows more rapidly if it is soaked in either water or milk before being put in the ground. Euthydemus in his *On Vegetables* claims that what are called *drakontiai* are a type of cu-

---

[10] For Dieuches, see 1.5b; but perhaps a different name should be restored.   [11] *sikuos*.

[12] Manuscript A (which preserves the unepitomized version of the text) begins at this point.

Δημήτριος ὁ Ἰξίων ἐν πρώτῳ Ἐτυμολογουμένων ἀπὸ
τοῦ σεύεσθαι καὶ κίειν· ὁρμητικὸν γὰρ ὑπάρχειν.
Ἡρακλείδης δ᾽ ὁ Ταραντῖνος ἐν τῷ Συμποσίῳ ἡδύ-
γαιον καλεῖ τὸν σικυόν. Διοκλῆς δ᾽ ὁ Καρύστιος τὸν
σικυόν φησι μετὰ σίων ἐν πρώτοις λαμβανόμενον
ἐνοχλεῖν· φέρεσθαι γὰρ ἄνω καθάπερ τὴν ῥάφανον.
c τελευταῖον | δὲ λαμβανόμενον ἀλυπότερον εἶναι καὶ
εὐπεπτότερον· ἑφθὸν δὲ καὶ διουρητικὸν μετρίως ὑπάρχειν. Δίφιλος δέ φησιν· ὁ σικυὸς ψυκτικὸς ὑπάρχων
δυσοικονόμητός ἐστι καὶ δυσυποβίβαστος, ἔτι δὲ φρι-
κοποιὸς καὶ γεννητικὸς χολῆς ἀφροδισίων τε ἐφεκτι-
κός. αὔξονται δ᾽ ἐν τοῖς κήποις οἱ σικυοὶ κατὰ τὰς
πανσελήνους καὶ φανερὰν ἴσχουσι τὴν ἐπίδοσιν, καθάπερ καὶ οἱ θαλάττιοι ἐχῖνοι.

Σῦκα. ἡ συκῆ, φησὶν ὁ Μάγνος· οὐδενὶ γὰρ τῶν
περὶ σύκων λογίων[3] παραχωρήσαιμι ⟨ἄν⟩, κἂν ἀπὸ
d κράδης ἀποκρέμασθαι | δέῃ. φιλόσυκος γάρ εἰμι δαι-
μονίως· λέξω τά μοι προσπίπτοντα—ἡ συκῆ, ἄνδρες
φίλοι, ἡγεμὼν τοῦ καθαρείου βίου τοῖς ἀνθρώποις
ἐγένετο. δῆλον δὲ τοῦτο ἐκ τοῦ καλεῖν τοὺς Ἀθηναίους
ἱερὰν μὲν συκῆν τὸν τόπον ἐν ᾧ πρῶτον εὑρέθη, τὸν δ᾽
ἀπ᾽ αὐτῆς καρπὸν ἡγητηρίαν διὰ τὸ πρῶτον εὑρεθῆναι
τῆς ἡμέρου τροφῆς. τῶν δὲ σύκων ἐστὶ γένη πλείονα·

---

3 λογίων Olson: λόγων ACE

---

13 Cf. 3.88c.
14 This is most likely the beginning of Magnus' speech.

cumber. Demetrius Ixion in Book I of the *Etymologies* (fr.
41 Staesche) says that cucumbers *(sikuoi)* get their name
from the verbs *seuomai* ("rush") and *kiō* ("go"), because
they are a stimulant. Heracleides of Tarentum in his *Symposium* (fr. 70 Guardasole) refers to the cucumber as
hēdugaios ("from sweet soil"). Diocles of Carystus (fr. 197
van der Eijk) says that when the cucumber is eaten along
with marshwort at the beginning of a meal, it causes trouble, because it moves upward in the stomach, just as cabbage does. But if it is eaten last, it does less damage and is
more easily digested; when stewed, it is moderately diuretic. Diphilus says: Because the cucumber is cooling, it
is hard to digest and to purge from one's system. It also
causes chills, produces bile, and checks sexual desire. Cucumbers increase in size in gardens during full moons,
and the growth is noticeable, as is also the case with sea-
urchins.[13]

Figs. The fig-tree, says Magnus[14]—for I would yield to
none of those who claim expertise in regard to figs, even if I
must be hung from a fig-branch, since I am extraordinarily
fond of figs; I will tell you what occurs to me—the fig-tree,
my friends, was mankind's guide to the refined way of life.
This is clear from the fact that the Athenians refer to the
place where it was first discovered as "Sacred Fig-Tree"[15]
and to the fruit that comes from it as "Leader"[16], because it
was the first domesticated food to be discovered. There are
many varieties of figs, such as the Attic, which Antiphanes

[15] Near Eleusis; see *IG* I[3] 386.163; Paus. 1.37.2.
[16] The name of a fig-cake carried in the procession at the
Plyntheria festival (Hsch. η 68; Phot. η 37).

Ἀττικὸν μέν, οὗ μνημονεύει Ἀντιφάνης ἐν Ὁμωνύ-
μοις· ἐπαινῶν δὲ τὴν χώραν τὴν Ἀττικὴν τάδε λέγει·

e   (A.) οἶα δ᾽ ἡ χώρα | φέρει
διαφέροντα † πάσης, Ἱππόνικε, τῆς οἰκουμένης,
τὸ μέλι, τοὺς ἄρτους, τὰ σῦκα. (B.) σῦκα μέν, νὴ
      τὸν Δία,
πάνυ φέρει.

Ἴστρος δ᾽ ἐν τοῖς Ἀττικοῖς οὐδ᾽ ἐξάγεσθαί φησι τῆς
Ἀττικῆς τὰς ἀπ᾽ αὐτῶν γινομένας ἰσχάδας, ἵνα μόνοι
ἀπολαύοιεν οἱ κατοικοῦντες· καὶ ἐπεὶ πολλοὶ ἐνεφανί-
ζοντο διακλέπτοντες, οἱ τούτους μηνύοντες τοῖς δικα-
σταῖς ἐκλήθησαν τότε πρῶτον συκοφάνται. Ἄλεξις δ᾽
ἐν Ποιητῇ φησιν·

f   ὁ συκοφάντης οὐ δικαίως τοὔνομα |
ἐν τοῖσι μοχθηροῖσίν ἐστι κείμενον.
ἔδει γάρ, ὅστις χρηστὸς ἦν ἡδύς τ᾽ ἀνήρ,
τὰ σῦκα προστεθέντα δηλοῦν τὸν τρόπον·
νυνὶ δὲ πρὸς μοχθηρὸν ἡδὺ προστεθὲν
ἀπορεῖν πεπόηκε διὰ τί τοῦθ᾽ οὕτως ἔχει.

Φιλόμνηστος δ᾽ ἐν τῷ Περὶ τῶν ἐν Ῥόδῳ Σμινθείων
φησίν· ἐπεὶ καὶ ὁ συκοφάντης ἐντεῦθεν προσηγο-

---

[17] Quoted in more complete form at 2.43b.

[18] A cynical allusion to the country's abundance of sycophants
(allegedly cognate with *sukon*, "fig"; see below).

[19] Here understood "fig-revealers," as if from *sukon* +
phainizō; cf. Philomnestus, below.

418

(fr. 177.1–4) mentions in *Men Who Shared a Name*. In praise of the land of Attica he says the following:[17]

> (A.) The products of this country,
> Hipponicus, better than those in the † whole
>   inhabited world!
> Honey! bread! figs! (B.) By Zeus, it certainly
>   produces
> figs.[18]

Istrus in his *Attic History* (*FGrH* 334 F 12) says that the dried figs produced by these trees were not exported from Attica, in order that only the inhabitants of the country could enjoy them. When many people were found (*enephanizonto*) to be evading the law, those who informed the jurors about them were then for the first time referred to as sycophants.[19] Alexis says in *The Poet* (fr. 187):[20]

> It's not right that the name "sycophant"
> is bestowed on scoundrels.
> For it should have been the case that, if someone was
>   a decent, pleasant man,
> figs were attached to him and revealed his character.
> But as it is, attaching something pleasant to a
>   scoundrel
> makes one wonder why this is so.

Philomnestus says in his *On the Smintheian Festival in Rhodes* (*FGrH* 527 F 1)[21]: Since the sycophant got his

---

[20] Called *The Poets* at 6.241d.

[21] *Smintheus* was a epithet of Apollo (e.g. *Il.* 1.39), and *Sminthios* was the name of one of the months in Rhodes.

ρεύθη, διὰ τὸ εἶναι τότε τὰ ἐπιζήμια καὶ τὰς εἰσφορὰς
75 σῦκα καὶ οἶνον καὶ ἔλαιον, ‖ ἀφ᾽ ὧν τὰ κοινὰ διῴκουν,
καὶ τοὺς ταῦτα εἰσπράττοντας καὶ φαίνοντας[4] ἐκάλουν, ὡς ἔοικε, συκοφάντας, αἱρούμενοι τοὺς ἀξιοπι-
στοτάτους τῶν πολιτῶν.

Λακωνικοῦ δὲ σύκου μνημονεύει ἐν Γεωργοῖς Ἀριστοφάνης ταδὶ λέγων·

συκᾶς φυτεύω πάντα πλὴν Λακωνικῆς·
τοῦτο γὰρ τὸ σῦκον ἐχθρόν ἐστι καὶ τυραννικόν.
οὐ γὰρ ἦν ἂν μικρόν, εἰ μὴ μισόδημον ἦν
σφόδρα.

μικρὸν δὲ αὐτὸ εἶπε διὰ τὸ μὴ μέγα εἶναι φυτόν.
b Ἄλεξις δ᾽ ἐν Ὀλυνθίῳ Φρυγίων σύκων | μνημονεύων
φησί·

τό τε θειοπαγὲς μητρῷον ἐμοὶ
μελέδημ᾽ ἰσχάς,
Φρυγίας εὑρήματα συκῆς.

τῶν δὲ καλουμένων φιβάλεων σύκων πολλοὶ μὲν μέμνηνται τῶν κωμῳδιοποιῶν, ἀτὰρ καὶ Φερεκράτης ἐν
Κραπατάλλοις·

ὦ δαιμόνιε, πύρεττε μηδὲν φροντίσας
καὶ τῶν φιβάλεων τρῶγε σύκων τοῦ θέρους
κἀμπιμπλάμενος κάθευδε τῆς μεσημβρίας,

---

[4] εἰσπράττοντας καὶ φαίνοντας Kaibel: πράττοντας καὶ
εἰσφαίνοντας ACE

name from this source; because in those days the fines and
levies were figs, wine, and oil,[22] and they administered the
state with these. They referred to the people who made
these assessments or publicized *(phainontas)* them, so it
seems, as sycophants, and they selected the most trust-
worthy citizens.

Aristophanes (fr. 110) mentions a Laconian fig in
Farmers, saying the following:

> I grow every sort of fig tree except the Laconian
>   variety,
> because this fig is hostile and tyrannical;
> for it wouldn't be small, if it weren't a great enemy of
>   the common people.

He calls it "small" because it is not a large plant. Alexis in
The Man from Olynthus (fr. 167.14–16)[23] mentions Phrygian figs and says:

> and the divinely-planted, maternal
> object of my care, a dried fig,
>   invention of a Phrygian fig tree.

Many comic poets mention the so-called phibalian figs, in
particular Pherecrates in *Small Change* (fr. 85):

> My good sir—don't worry about it. Have a fever;
> eat some phibalian figs in the summer;
> after you're full of them, take a nap at noon;

[22] The point is that money was not yet in use.
[23] Quoted in more complete form at 2.54f–5a, where see n.

c   κᾆτα σφακέλιζε καὶ πέπρησο καὶ βόα. |

Τηλεκλείδης δ' ἐν Ἀμφικτύοσι·

   ⟨ . . . ⟩ ὡς καλοὶ καὶ φιβάλεῳ.

καὶ τὰς μυρρίνας δὲ φιβάλεας λέγουσιν, ὡς Ἀπολλοφάνης[5] ἐν Κρησί·

               πρώτιστα δὲ
τῶν μυρρινῶν ἐπὶ τὴν τράπεζαν βούλομαι,
ἃς διαμασῶμ' ὅταν τι βουλεύειν δέῃ,
† τὰς δὲ φιβάλεως † πάνυ καλὰς στεφανωτρίδας.

χελιδονείων δὲ σύκων μνημονεύει Ἐπιγένης ἐν Βακ-
d χίδι[6]. |

               εἶτ' ἔρχεται
χελιδονείων μετ' ὀλίγον σκληρῶν ἁδρὸς
πινακίσκος.

Ἀνδροτίων δὲ ἢ Φίλιππος ἢ Ἡγήμων ἐν τῷ Γεωργικῷ
γένη συκῶν τάδε ἀναγράφει οὕτως· ἐν μὲν οὖν τῷ
πεδίῳ φυτεύειν χρὴ χελιδόνεων, ἐρινεῶν, λευκερινεῶν,
φιβάλεων· ὀπωροβασιλίδας δὲ πανταχοῦ. ἔχει γάρ τι
χρήσιμον ἕκαστον τὸ γένος· ἐπὶ δὲ τὸ πλεῖστον αἱ
κόλουροι καὶ φορμύνιοι καὶ δίφοροι καὶ Μεγαρικαὶ
καὶ Λακωνικαὶ συμφέρουσιν, ἐὰν ἔχωσιν ὕδωρ.

e   Τῶν δὲ ἐν Ῥόδῳ γινομένων σύκων | μνημονεύει

---

[5] Ἀπολλοφάνης Porson: Ἀντιφάνης ACE

and then have spasms and feel like you're on fire and
scream!

And Teleclides in *Amphictyons* (fr. 6):

How fine and phibalian!

They also call myrtle-berries "phibalian," as Apollophanes
does in *Cretans* (fr. 5):

first and foremost,
I want some myrtle-berries on my dinner table,
so that I can chew them whenever I need to make a
decision—
† the phibalian variety †, very fine and fit for
garlands.

Epigenes in *Bacchis* (fr. 1) mentions swallow-figs:

then after a little while
comes a small platter full of hard
swallow-figs.

Androtion (*FGrH* 324 F 75) or Philip or Hegemon in his
On Agriculture lists the following types of fig trees: On
level ground one should plant swallow-figs, wild figs,
white-figs, and phibalian figs, whereas autumn-queens can
be planted anywhere. For each type is useful for something; but the most profitable are the dwarves, *phor-
munioi*, double-bearing, Megarian, and Laconian varieties, provided they have water.

Lynceus in his *Letters* (fr. 12 Dalby) mentions the figs

---

6 Βακχίδι Kock: Βραχχίᾳ A: Βακχίῳ Kaibel: cf. 9.384a
Βάχχαις; 11.498e Βαχχίᾳ

Λυγκεὺς ἐν Ἐπιστολαῖς σύγκρισιν ποιούμενος τῶν
Ἀθήνησι γινομένων καλλίστων πρὸς τὰ Ῥοδιακά.
γράφει δὲ οὕτως· τὰ δὲ ἐρινεὰ τοῖς Λακωνικοῖς ὥστε
συκάμινα σύκοις δοκεῖν ἐρίζειν. καὶ ταῦτ᾽ οὐκ ἀπὸ
δείπνου καθάπερ ἐκεῖ διεστραμμένης ἤδη διὰ τὴν
πλησμονὴν τῆς γεύσεως, ἀλλ᾽ ἀθίκτου τῆς ἐπιθυμίας
οὔσης πρὸ δείπνου παρατέθεικα. τῶν δ᾽ ἐν τῇ καλῇ
Ῥώμῃ καλλιστρουθίων καλουμένων σύκων εἰ ὁ Λυγκεὺς ἐγεύσατο ὥσπερ ἐγώ, ὀξυωπέστερος ἂν ἐγεγόνει
f παρὰ πολὺ τοῦ ὁμωνύμου· | τοσαύτην ὑπεροχὴν ἔχει
ταῦτα τὰ σῦκα πρὸς τὰ ἐν τῇ πάσῃ οἰκουμένῃ γινόμενα. ἐπαινεῖται δὲ καὶ ἄλλα σύκων γένη κατὰ τὴν
Ῥώμην γινόμενα, τά τε καλούμενα Χῖα καὶ τὰ Λι-
βιανά, ἔτι δὲ καὶ τὰ Χαλκιδικὰ ὀνομαζόμενα καὶ τὰ
Ἀφρικανά, ὡς καὶ Ἡρόδοτος ὁ Λύκιος μαρτυρεῖ ἐν τῷ
Περὶ Σύκων συγγράμματι.

Παρμένων δ᾽ ὁ Βυζάντιος ἐν τοῖς Ἰάμβοις τὰ ἀπὸ
Κανῶν τῆς Αἰολικῆς πόλεως ὡς διάφορα ἐπαινῶν
76 φησιν· ‖

ἦλθον μακρὴν θάλασσαν, οὐκ ἄγων σῦκα
Καναῖα φόρτον.

ὅτι δὲ καὶ τὰ ἀπὸ Καύνου τῆς Καρίας ἐπαινεῖται
κοινόν. ὀξαλέων δὲ σύκων οὕτως καλουμένων μνημονεύει Ἡρακλέων ὁ Ἐφέσιος καὶ Νίκανδρος ὁ Θυατειρηνὸς παρατιθέμενοι Ἀπολλοδώρου τοῦ Καρυστίου ἐκ
δράματος Προικιζομένης ⟨ἢ⟩ Ἱματιοπώλιδος τάδε·

produced on Rhodes, comparing the Rhodian figs to the best that grow in Athens. He writes as follows: But the wild figs appear to compare with Laconian figs as mulberries compare to figs generally. I have served them not after dinner, as they do there, when the sense of taste has already been distorted by satiety, but when the appetite is unspoiled, before dinner. But if Lynceus had tasted the so-called fair-swallow-figs in our lovely Rome, as I have, he would have become far more keen-sighted than his namesake,[24] so superior are these figs to those that grow in all the rest of the inhabited world. Other types of figs produced around Rome are also praised: the so-called Chian and Livian varieties, as well as those called Chalcidian and African, as Herodotus of Lycia attests in his treatise on figs.

Parmenon of Byzantium in his *Iambs* (fr. 2, p. 237 Powell), praising the products of the Aeolian city of Canae as excellent, says:

> I journeyed far over the sea, with no freight
> of Canaean figs.

That those from Carian Caunus are acclaimed is a commonplace. Heracleon of Ephesus and Nicander of Thyateira (*FGrH* 343 F 8) mention the so-called sour figs, citing the following lines from Apollodorus of Carystus' play *The Girl with a Dowry or The Clothing Vendor* (fr. 30):

---

[24] The "lynx-eyed" Lynceus of the Argonauts (e.g. Pi. *N.* 10.61–3; Ar. *Pl.* 210; Pl. *Epist.* 7 344a).

425

πλὴν τό ‹γ᾽› οἰνάριον πάνυ

ἦν ὀξὺ καὶ πονηρόν, ὥστ᾽ ἠσχυνόμην.

b τὰ λοιπὰ μὲν γὰρ ὀξαλείους χωρία |
συκᾶς φέρει, τοὐμὸν δὲ καὶ τὰς ἀμπέλους.

τῶν δ᾽ ἐν Πάρῳ τῇ νήσῳ—διάφορα γὰρ κἀνταῦθα
γίνεται σῦκα τὰ καλούμενα παρὰ τοῖς Παρίοις αἰμώ-
νια, ταὐτὰ ὄντα τοῖς Λυδίοις καλουμένοις, ἅπερ διὰ τὸ
ἐρυθρῶδες καὶ τῆς προσηγορίας ταύτης ἔτυχεν—Ἀρχίλοχος μνημονεύει λέγων οὕτως·

ἔα Πάρον καὶ σῦκα κεῖνα καὶ θαλάσσιον βίον.

τὰ δὲ σῦκα ταῦτα τοσαύτην ἔχει παραλλαγὴν πρὸς τὰ
c ἀλλαχοῦ[7] γινόμενα ὡς τὸ τοῦ | ἀγρίου συὸς κρέας
πρὸς τὰ ἄλλα[8].

Λευκερινεὼς δέ τι εἶδός ἐστι συκῆς, καὶ ἴσως αὕτη
ἐστὶν ἡ τὰ λευκὰ σῦκα φέρουσα. μνημονεύει δ᾽ αὐτῆς
Ἕρμιππος ἐν Ἰάμβοις οὕτως·

‹ . . . › τὰς λευκερινεὼς δὲ χωρὶς ἰσχάδας.

τῶν δ᾽ ἐρινῶν σύκων Εὐριπίδης ἐν Σκίρωνι·

ἢ προσπηγνύναι
κράδαις ἐριναῖς.

καὶ Ἐπίχαρμος ἐν Σφιγγί·

(Α.) ἀλλ᾽ οὐχ ὅμοια ‹τάδε› γ᾽ ἐρινοῖς. (Β.)
οὐδαμῶς.

except that the wine was
quite acidic and bad, so that I was ashamed.
Because the other farms produce
sour-fig trees; but mine produces sour vines as well.

As for those on the island of Paros—excellent figs grow
there too, which the Parians refer to as blood-figs and
which are the same as the so-called Lydian figs; they got
this name because of their reddish color—Archilochus (fr.
116 West[2]) mentions them, saying the following:

Farewell to Paros and its famous figs and its seafaring
   way of life—

these figs are as different from those grown elsewhere as
the meat of a wild boar is from other meats.

There is a white-fig variety of fig tree, which is perhaps
the one that bears white figs. Hermippus mentions it in his
Iambs (iamb. fr. 2 West[2]), as follows:

apart from the dried white-figs.

Euripides mentions wild figs in *Sciron* (fr. 679):

   or to impale him
on wild-fig branches.

Also Epicharmus in *Sphinx* (fr. 126):

(A.) But these aren't like wild figs. (B.) Not at all!

---

7 ἀλλαχοῦ Coraes: πολλαχοῦ ACE

8 τὰ ἄλλα τὰ μὴ τῶν ἀγρίων χοίρων κρέα A: τὰ τῶν μὴ
ἀγρίων CE

Σοφοκλῆς δ᾽ ἐν Ἑλένης Γάμῳ τροπικῶς τῷ τοῦ δέν-
d δρου ὀνόματι τὸν καρπὸν ἐκάλεσεν | εἰπών·

πέπων ἐρινὸς < . . . > ἀχρεῖος ὢν
ἐς βρῶσιν ἄλλους ἐξερινάζεις λόγῳ.

πέπων δ᾽ ἐρινὸς εἴρηκεν ἀντὶ τοῦ πέπον ἐρινόν. καὶ
Ἄλεξις ἐν Λέβητι·

                    καὶ τί δεῖ
λέγειν ἔθ᾽ ἡμᾶς τοὺς τὰ σῦχ᾽ ἑκάστοτε
ἐν τοῖς συρίχοις πωλοῦντας; οἳ κάτωθε μὲν
τὰ σκληρὰ καὶ μοχθηρὰ τῶν σύκων ἀεὶ
e τιθέασιν, ἐπιπολῆς δὲ πέπονα καὶ καλά. |
εἶθ᾽ ὁ μὲν ἔδωκεν ὡς τοιαῦτ᾽ ὠνούμενος
τιμήν, ὁ δ᾽ ἐγκάψας τὸ κέρμ᾽ εἰς τὴν γνάθον
ἐρίν᾽ ἀπέδοτο σῦκα πωλεῖν ὀμνύων.

τὸ δὲ δένδρον ἡ ἀγρία συκῆ, ἐξ ἧς τὰ ἐρινά, ἐρινὸς
κατὰ τὸ ἄρρεν λέγεται. Στράττις Τρωίλῳ·

          ἐρινὸν οὖν τιν᾽ αὐτῆς πλησίον
νενόηκας ὄντα;

καὶ Ὅμηρος·

τῷ δ᾽ ἐν ἐρινεός ἐστι μέγας, φύλλοισι τεθηλώς.

Ἀμερίας δ᾽ ἐρινάδας καλεῖσθαι τοὺς ὀλόνθους.

Sophocles in *The Marriage of Helen* (fr. 181) referred to
the fruit figuratively by the name of the tree, saying:

> a ripe wild-fig tree, . . . although worthless
> for food, you fertilize others with your talk.

He said "ripe wild-fig tree" in place of "ripe wild fig." Also
Alexis in *The Cauldron* (fr. 133):

> And why
> should we, moreover, mention those who always sell
> figs in baskets? They routinely
> put the hard, bad figs on the bottom
> and the nice, ripe ones on top.
> Then a fellow pays what's asked, thinking he's being
>   sold good ones;
> and the vendor pops the coin into his mouth[25]
> and sells wild figs, while swearing he's selling the
>   domesticated variety.

The wild-fig tree, from which wild figs come, is called an
erinos in the masculine. Thus Strattis in *Troilus* (fr. 43):

> Have you noticed a wild-fig tree *(erinon)*,
> then, close to it?

And Homer (*Od.* 12.103):

> and on it is a large wild-fig tree *(erineos)*, full of
>   leaves.

Amerias (p. 13 Hoffmann) says that wild figs are referred
to as *erinades*.

---

[25] The normal place to store money temporarily, since Greek
clothing lacked pockets.

f   Ἑρμῶναξ δ' ἐν Γλώτταις Κρητικαῖς σύκων γένη |
ἀναγράφει ἀμάδεα καὶ νικύλεα. Φιλήμων δ' ἐν Ἀττι-
καῖς Λέξεσι καλεῖσθαί φησί τινα σῦκα βασίλεια, ἀφ'
ὧν καλεῖσθαι καὶ τὰς βασιλίδας ἰσχάδας, προσιστο-
ρῶν ὅτι κόλυθρα καλεῖται τὰ πέπονα σῦκα. Σέλευκος
δ' ἐν ταῖς Γλώσσαις καὶ γλυκυσίδην τινὰ καλεῖσθαί
φησι σύκῳ τὴν μορφὴν μάλιστα ἐοικυῖαν, φυλάσ-
σεσθαι δὲ τὰς γυναῖκας ἐσθίειν διὰ τὸ ποιεῖν μαται-
σμούς, ὡς καὶ Πλάτων ὁ κωμῳδιοποιός φησιν ἐν
77 Κλεοφῶντι. ‖ τὰ δὲ χειμερινὰ σῦκα Πάμφιλος καλεῖσθαί φησιν κωδωναῖα ὑπὸ Ἀχαιῶν,[9] τοῦτο λέγων
Ἀριστοφάνην εἰρηκέναι ἐν Λακωνικαῖς Γλώσσαις. κο-
ράκεων δὲ σύκων εἶδος Ἕρμιππος ἐν Στρατιώταις
παραδίδωσι διὰ τούτων·

> τῶν φιβάλεων μάλιστ' ἂν ἦ τῶν κοράκεων.

Θεόφραστος δ' ἐν δευτέρῳ Φυτῶν Ἱστορίας συκῶν
φησι γένος τοιοῦτόν τι εἶναι οἷον ἡ Ἀράτειος[10] καλουμένη. ἐν δὲ τῷ τρίτῳ περὶ τὴν Τρωικήν φησιν Ἴδην
b γίνεσθαι συκῆν θαμνώδη, φύλλον ὅμοιον | ἔχουσαν
τῷ τῆς φιλύρας· φέρειν δὲ σῦκα ἐρυθρὰ ἡλίκα ἐλαία
τὸ μέγεθος, στρογγυλώτερα <δέ>, εἶναι δὲ τὴν γεῦσιν
μεσπιλώδη. περὶ δὲ τῆς ἐν Κρήτῃ καλουμένης Κυ-
πρίας συκῆς ὁ αὐτὸς Θεόφραστος ἐν τῷ τετάρτῳ τῆς
Φυτικῆς Ἱστορίας τάδε γράφει· ἡ ἐν Κρήτῃ καλου-

---

[9] Cf. Hsch. κ 3211 κοδώνεα· σῦκα χειμερινά. But it is impossible to know which text is corrupt.

Hermonax in *Cretan Vocabulary* lists as varieties of figs the *hamadea* and the *nikulea*. Philemon in the *Attic Lexicon* says that certain figs are referred to as "royal," and that the dried queen-figs get their name from them; he adds that ripe figs are referred to as *koluthra*. Seleucus in his *Glossary* (fr. 45 Müller) claims that something referred to as a *glukusidē* is much like the fig in shape, but that women are careful not to eat it, because it produces an unfortunate noise, as the comic poet Plato says in *Cleophon* (fr. 62).[26] Pamphilus (fr. XVIII Schmidt) says that the Achaeans refer to winter figs as *kōdōnaia*; he reports that Aristophanes asserts this in *Spartan Vocabulary* (Ar. Byz. fr. 352 Slater). Hermippus in *Soldiers* (fr. 53) informs us about a type of figs known as ravens in the following words:

preferably some phibalian or raven-figs.

Theophrastus in Book II of *Inquiry into Plants* (fr. 392) says that there is a type of fig tree that resembles the so-called Aratean variety. And in Book III (*HP* 3.17.4–5) he asserts that a shrub-like fig tree grows around the Trojan Mount Ida and that its leaf is similar to the lime tree's. It produces red figs that are as big as an olive but rounder and taste like a medlar. Concerning the so-called Cyprian fig tree on Crete, the same Theophrastus writes the following in Book IV (2.3) of *Inquiry into Plants*: The so-called

---

[26] The word *mataismos* is attested nowhere else and must be a colloquial term for a fart, a queef, or the like.

---

[10] ἡ χαρίτιος Ἀράτειος Α

μένη Κυπρία συκῆ φέρει τὸν καρπὸν ἐκ τοῦ στελέχους καὶ τῶν παχυτάτων ἀκρεμόνων, βλαστὸν δέ τινα ἀφίησι μικρὸν ἄφυλλον ὥσπερ ῥίζιον, πρὸς ᾧ ὁ καρπός. τὸ δὲ στέλεχος μέγα καὶ παρόμοιον τῇ λεύκῃ, φύλλον
c δὲ τῇ πτελέᾳ. πεπαίνει | δὲ τέτταρας καρπούς, ὅσαιπερ αὐτοῦ καὶ αἱ βλαστήσεις. ἡ δὲ γλυκύτης προσεμφερὴς τῷ σύκῳ καὶ ⟨τὰ⟩ ἔσωθεν τοῖς ἐρινοῖς· μέγεθος δὲ ἡλίκον κοκκύμηλον.

Τῶν δὲ προδρόμων καλουμένων σύκων ὁ αὐτὸς Θεόφραστος μνημονεύει ἐν πέμπτῳ Φυτικῶν Αἰτίων οὕτως· τῇ συκῇ ὅταν ἀὴρ ἐπιγένηται μαλακὸς καὶ ὑγρὸς καὶ θερμός, ἐξεκαλέσατο τὴν βλάστησιν· ὅθεν καὶ οἱ πρόδρομοι. καὶ προελθὼν τάδε λέγει· πάλιν δὲ τοὺς προδρόμους αἱ μὲν φέρουσιν, ἥ τε Λακωνικὴ καὶ
d ἡ λευκομφάλιος καὶ ἕτεραι | πλείους, αἱ δ' οὐ φέρουσι. Σέλευκος δ' ἐν Γλώσσαις πρωτερικήν φησι καλεῖσθαι γένος τι συκῆς, ἥτις φέρει πρώϊον τὸν καρπόν. διφόρου δὲ συκῆς μνημονεύει καὶ Ἀριστοφάνης ἐν Ἐκκλησιαζούσαις·

> ὑμᾶς δὲ τέως θρῖα λαβόντας
> διφόρου συκῆς.

καὶ Ἀντιφάνης ἐν Σκληρίαις·

> ἔστιν παρ' αὐτὴν τὴν δίφορον συκῆν κάτω.

Cyprian fig tree on Crete produces its fruit on the stem and the thickest branches, and sends out a small, leafless shoot that resembles a tiny root, to which the fruit is attached. The stem is large and resembles the white poplar's, whereas the leaf resembles the elm's. It produces four crops a year, which is also the number of periods of growth it has. The sweetness of the fruit resembles the fig; its interior resembles the wild fig; and it is the size of a plum.

The same Theophrastus mentions the so-called forerunner figs[27] in Book V (1.4–5) of *Causes of Plants*, in the following words: As for the fig tree, whenever mild, moist, warm weather follows, it encourages sprouting; this is the source of forerunners. And further on he says the following (*CP* 5.1.8): Some trees bear forerunners, such as the Spartan and the white-navel varieties, and many others; but some do not. Seleucus in the *Glossary* (fr. 63 Müller) claims that there is a type of fig tree referred to as a *prōterikē* ("early"), which bears its fruit early. Aristophanes in *Ecclesiazusae* (707–8) mentions a double-bearing fig tree:[28]

and you in the meantime, taking hold of the leaves
of a double-bearing fig tree.

Also Antiphanes in *Hard Times* (fr. 196):

It's down below, right beside the double-bearing fig
tree.

[27] The breba crop, produced in the spring on the previous year's growth.   [28] An obscene double-entendre: the two "figs" are the testicles, and the addressees are being told to masturbate. Antiphanes fr. 196 (below) may have a similar point.

ὁ Θεόπομπος δὲ ἐν τῇ πεντηκοστῇ τετάρτῃ τῶν Ἱστοριῶν κατὰ τὴν Φιλίππου φησὶν ἀρχὴν περὶ τὴν Βι-
σαλτίαν καὶ Ἀμφίπολιν καὶ Γραστωνίαν τῆς Μακεδο-
e νίας | ἔαρος μεσοῦντος τὰς μὲν συκᾶς σῦκα, τὰς δ'
ἀμπέλους βότρυς, τὰς δ' ἐλαίας ἐν ᾧ χρόνῳ βρύειν
εἰκὸς ἦν αὐτὰς ἐλαίας ἐνεγκεῖν, καὶ εὐτυχῆσαι πάντα
Φίλιππον. ἐν δὲ τῷ δευτέρῳ Περὶ Φυτῶν ὁ Θεόφραστος καὶ τὸν ἐρινεὸν εἶναί φησι δίφορον· οἱ δὲ καὶ
τρίφορον, ὥσπερ ἐν Κέῳ. λέγει δὲ καὶ τὴν συκῆν ἐὰν
ἐν σκίλλῃ φυτευθῇ θᾶττον παραγίνεσθαι καὶ ὑπὸ
σκωλήκων μὴ διαφθείρεσθαι· καὶ πάντα δὲ τὰ ἐν
σκίλλῃ φυτευθέντα καὶ θᾶττον αὐξάνεσθαι καὶ εὐ-
f βλαστῆ γίγνεσθαι. πάλιν δὲ ὁ Θεόφραστος | ἐν τῷ
δευτέρῳ τῶν Αἰτίων, ἡ Ἰνδική, φησί, συκῆ καλουμένη
θαυμαστὴ οὖσα τῷ μεγέθει μικρὸν ἔχει τὸν καρπὸν
καὶ ὀλίγον, ὡς ἂν εἰς τὴν βλάστησιν ἐξαναλίσκουσα
ἅπασαν τὴν τροφήν. ἐν δὲ τῷ δευτέρῳ τῆς Φυτικῆς
Ἱστορίας ὁ φιλόσοφός φησιν· ἔστι καὶ ἄλλο γένος
συκῆς ἔν τε τῇ Ἑλλάδι καὶ περὶ Κιλικίαν καὶ Κύπρον
ὀλονθοφόρον, ὃ τὸ μὲν σῦκον ἔμπροσθε φέρει τοῦ
θρίου[11], τὸν δὲ ὄλονθον ἐξόπισθεν. αἱ δὲ ὅλως ἐκ τοῦ
ἔνου βλαστοῦ καὶ οὐκ ἐκ τοῦ νέου. πρῶτον δὲ τοῦτο
τῶν σύκων πέπονά τε καὶ γλυκὺν ἔχει καὶ οὐχ ὥσπερ
78 τὸν παρ' ἡμῖν. ‖ γίνεται δὲ καὶ μείζων οὗτος πολὺ τῶν
σύκων· ἡ δ' ὥρα μετὰ τὴν βλάστησιν οὐ πολύ.

Οἶδα δὲ καὶ ἄλλα σύκων ὀνόματα λεγόμενα· βασίλεια, συκοβασίλεια, κιρροκοιλάδια[12], σαρκελάφεια,

Theopompus in Book LIV of his *Histories* (*FGrH* 115 F 237a) says that in Philip's domain around Bisaltia, Amphipolis, and Macedonian Grastonia, the fig trees produced figs in mid-spring and the vines produced grape clusters, and the olive trees produced olives at a time of year when they should have been budding; he claims that Philip was lucky in everything. In Book II of *On Plants* (fr. 393) Theophrastus says that the wild-fig tree bears fruit twice a year; some authorities report that it bears three times a year, as it does on Ceos. He also asserts (*HP* 2.5.5) that if the fig tree is planted in a squill bulb, it matures more rapidly and is not damaged by worms. In fact, anything planted in a squill bulb grows more rapidly and becomes sturdy. Again, Theophrastus says in Book II of his *Causes* (*CP* 2.10.2): The so-called Indian fig tree, although amazingly large, bears small fruit in limited quantities, as if it used up all its nourishment on its growth. In Book II of his *Inquiry into Plants* (fr. 394) the philosopher says: There is another type of fig tree in Greece and around Cilicia and Cyprus that bears *olonthoi*; it bears its fig in front of the leaf, but the *olonthos* behind it. These trees generally bear their crop from the previous year's growth and not from the new growth. They bear the *olonthos* first, before the figs; it is ripe and sweet, unlike the *olonthos* we know. This fig also grows much larger than others do, and is ripe not long after it sprouts.

I also know other names given to figs: royal figs, fig-royal figs, yellow-bellied figs, venison-figs, crackle-figs, bit-

---

11 θρίον Meineke (cf. Thphr. *CP* 5.1.8; Plin. *Nat.* 16.113): φυτοῦ A: καρποῦ CE

12 κιρροκοιλάδια καὶ ὑλάδια A: κιρροκοιλάδια ὑλάδια CE

καπύρια, πικρίδια, δρακόντια, λευκόφαια, μελανό-
φαια, κρήνεια, μυλαικά, ἀσκαλώνια.

Περὶ δὲ τῆς προσηγορίας τῶν σύκων λέγων Τρύφων ἐν δευτέρῳ Φυτῶν Ἱστορίας Ἀνδροτίωνά[13] φησιν
ἐν Γεωργικῷ ἱστορεῖν Συκέα ἕνα τινὰ τῶν Τιτάνων
διωκόμενον ὑπὸ Διὸς τὴν μητέρα Γῆν ὑποδέξασθαι
b καὶ ἀνεῖναι τὸ φυτὸν | εἰς διατριβὴν τῷ παιδί, ἀφ' οὗ
καὶ Συκέαν πόλιν εἶναι ἐν Κιλικίᾳ. Φερένικος δ' ὁ
ἐποποιός, Ἡρακλεώτης δὲ γένος, ἀπὸ Συκῆς τῆς Ὀξύ-
λου θυγατρὸς προσαγορευθῆναι· Ὄξυλον γὰρ τὸν
Ὀρείου Ἁμαδρυάδι τῇ ἀδελφῇ μιγέντα μετ' ἄλλων
γεννῆσαι Καρύαν, Βάλανον, Κράνειαν, Μορέαν, Αἴ-
γειρον, Πτελέαν, Ἄμπελον, Συκῆν· καὶ ταύτας Ἁμα-
δρυάδας νύμφας καλεῖσθαι καὶ ἀπ' αὐτῶν πολλὰ τῶν
δένδρων προσαγορεύεσθαι. ὅθεν καὶ τὸν Ἱππώνακτα
c φάναι· |

συκῆν μέλαιναν, ἀμπέλου κασιγνήτην.

Σωσίβιος δ' ὁ Λάκων ἀποδεικνὺς εὕρημα Διονύσου
τὴν συκῆν διὰ τοῦτό φησι καὶ Λακεδαιμονίους Συκί-
την Διόνυσον τιμᾶν. Νάξιοι δέ, ὡς Ἀνδρίσκος, ἔτι δ'
Ἀγλαοσθένης[14] ἱστοροῦσι, Μειλίχιον καλεῖσθαι τὸν
Διόνυσον διὰ τὴν τοῦ συκίνου καρποῦ παράδοσιν. διὸ

[13] Ἀνδροτίωνα Kaibel: δωρίωνα A: δωρίων (nom.) CE
[14] Ἀγλαοσθένης Schweighäuser: ἀγασθένης A

ter figs, dragon-figs, whitish-gray and dark-gray figs, fountain-figs, mill-figs, and scallion-figs.

In his discussion of the names of figs *(sukai)* in Book II of *Inquiry into Plants*, Tryphon (fr. 119 Velsen) says that Androtion in his *On Agriculture* (*FGrH* 324 F *76) records that when Syceas, who was one of the Titans, was being pursued by Zeus,[29] his mother Earth protected him and made the plant grow up to entertain her child, who also gave his name to the city of Sycea in Cilicia. But the epic poet Pherenicus (*SH* 672), who was a Heracleot by birth, claims that the name came from Sycē ("Fig Tree") the daughter of Oxylus. For Oxylus son of Oreius had sex with his sister Hamadryas and begot, among others, daughters named Nut-tree, Oak, Cornel-cherry, Mulberry, Poplar, Elm, Grapevine, and Fig-tree. They were referred to as the Hamadryad[30] nymphs, and many trees got their names from them. Hipponax (fr. 52 Degani) as well, therefore, says:

a dark fig tree, sister of a grapevine.

Sosibius of Sparta (*FGrH* 595 F 10), in the course of demonstrating that Dionysus discovered the fig tree, says that this is why the Spartans worship Dionysus Sukitēs ("of the fig"). According to Andriscus (*FGrH* 500 F 3), as well as Aglaosthenes (*FGrH* 499 F *4), the Naxians refer to Dionysus as Meilichios ("Gentle") because he gave us the fruit

[29] *Viz.* during the Titanomachy; but the incident seems more appropriate for the Gigantomachy, with which the Titanomachy was sometimes confounded. [30] Literally "Simultaneous with a Tree," the point of the name being that the nymph lived as long as the tree with which she was associated.

καὶ τὸ πρόσωπον τοῦ θεοῦ παρὰ τοῖς Ναξίοις τὸ μὲν
τοῦ Βακχέως Διονύσου καλουμένου εἶναι ἀμπέλινον,
τὸ δὲ τοῦ Μειλιχίου σύκινον· τὰ γὰρ σῦκα μείλιχα
καλεῖσθαι.

d   Ὅτι δὲ πάντων τῶν καλουμένων | ξυλίνων καρπῶν
ὠφελιμότερά ἐστι τοῖς ἀνθρώποις τὰ σῦκα ἱκανῶς
Ἡρόδοτος ὁ Λύκιος διὰ πολλῶν ἀποδείκνυσιν ἐν τῷ
περὶ σύκων συγγράμματι, εὐτραφῆ λέγων γίνεσθαι
τὰ νεογνὰ τῶν παιδίων, ἐν τῷ χυλῷ τῶν σύκων εἰ
διατρέφοιτο. Φερεκράτης δὲ ἢ ὁ πεποιηκὼς τοὺς Πέρσας φησίν·

   ἢν δ᾽ ἡμῶν σύκόν τις ἴδῃ διὰ χρόνου νέον ποτέ,
   τὠφθαλμὼ τούτῳ περιμάττομεν ⟨τὼ⟩ τῶν
      παιδίων,

ὡς καὶ ἰάματος οὐ τοῦ τυχόντος τῶν σύκων ὑπαρ-
e χόντων. ὁ δὲ θαυμασιώτατος καὶ μελίγηρυς | Ἡρό-
δοτος ἐν τῇ πρώτῃ τῶν Ἱστοριῶν καὶ μέγα ἀγαθὸν
φησιν εἶναι τὰ σῦκα οὑτωσὶ λέγων· βασιλεῦ, σὺ δ᾽ ἐπ᾽
ἄνδρας τοιούτους παρασκευάζεαι στρατεύεσθαι, οἳ
σκυτίνας μὲν ἀναξυρίδας, σκυτίνην δὲ τὴν ἄλλην
ἐσθῆτα φορέουσι, σιτέονταί τ᾽ οὐχ ὅσα ἐθέλουσιν,
ἀλλ᾽ ὅσα ἔχουσι, χώρην ἔχοντες τρηχείην· πρὸς δὲ
οὐκ οἴνῳ διαχρέονται, ἀλλ᾽ ὑδροποτέουσιν· οὐ σῦκα
ἔχουσι τρώγειν, οὐκ ἄλλο οὐθὲν ἀγαθόν. Πολύβιος δ᾽
f ὁ Μεγαλοπολίτης ἐν τῇ ἑξκαιδεκάτῃ τῶν ἱστοριῶν, |
Φίλιππος, φησίν, ὁ Περσέως πατὴρ ὅτε τὴν Ἀσίαν
κατέτρεχεν ἀπορῶν τροφῶν τοῖς στρατιώταις παρὰ

of the fig tree. This is why on Naxos the face of the god referred to as Dionysus Baccheus is made of vine-wood, while the face of Dionysus Meilichios is made of fig-wood; because figs are called *meilicha*.

Herodotus of Lycia in his treatise on figs uses many arguments to prove that figs benefit mankind more than all the other so-called "tree fruits," saying that newborn infants thrive if fed fig juice. Pherecrates (fr. 139) or whoever wrote *Persians*[31] says:

If one of us ever spies a fresh fig,
we smear our children's eyes with it,

as if figs were unusually fine medicine. The admirable, sweet-voiced Herodotus in Book I (71.2–3) of his *Histories* claims that figs are a very good food in the following words: O King, you are preparing to mount an expedition against men who wear leather pants, and whose other clothing is leather as well; who do not eat as much as they want but as much as they have; and who inhabit a rough country. Furthermore, they drink not wine but water, and have no figs to eat or anything else that is good. Polybius of Megalopolis in Book XVI (24.9) of his *Histories* says: When Philip the father of Perseus[32] overran Asia and was short of food for his soldiers, he accepted figs from the Magnesians, since

---

31 For Athenaeus' doubts about the authorship of *Persians*, cf. 11.502a; 15.685a. Pherecrates is supposed to have written 17 or 18 comedies (test. 1, 3), but 19 titles are preserved, and ancient scholars were concerned to identify the spurious play or plays.

32 Philip V, King of Macedon (reigned 222–179 BCE). The events referred to here took place in 201.

Μαγνήτων, ἐπεὶ σῖτον οὐκ εἶχον, σῦκα ἔλαβε. διὸ καὶ
Μυοῦντος κυριεύσας τοῖς Μάγνησιν ἐχαρίσατο τὸ
χωρίον ἀντὶ τῶν σύκων. καὶ Ἀνάνιος δ' ὁ ἰαμβοποιὸς
ἔφη·

εἴ τις καθείρξαι χρυσὸν ἐν δόμοις πολὺν
καὶ σῦκα βαιὰ καὶ δύ᾽ ἢ τρεῖς ἀνθρώπους,
γνοίη χ᾽ ὅσῳ τὰ σῦκα τοῦ χρυσοῦ κρέσσω. ‖

79

Τοσαῦτα τοῦ Μάγνου συκολογήσαντος Δάφνος ὁ
ἰατρὸς ἔφη· Φυλότιμος ἐν τρίτῳ Περὶ Τροφῆς, τὰ
ἀπαλά, φησί, σῦκα διαφορὰς μὲν ἔχει πλείους πρὸς
ἄλληλα καὶ τοῖς γένεσι καὶ τοῖς χρόνοις ἐν οἷς ἕκα-
στα γίγνεται καὶ ταῖς δυνάμεσιν, οὐ μὴν ἀλλὰ καθόλου εἰπεῖν τά τε ὑγρὰ τὰ πεπεμμένα καὶ μάλιστα
αὐτῶν διαλύεται ταχέως καὶ κατεργάζεται μᾶλλον τῆς
ἄλλης ὀπώρας καὶ τὴν λοιπὴν τροφὴν οὐ κωλύει
κατεργάζεσθαι. δυνάμεις δ' ἔχει τῶν ὑγρῶν κολλώδεις
b | τε καὶ γλυκείας ὑπονιτρώδεις τε, καὶ τὴν διαχώρησιν
ἀθρουστέραν καὶ διακεχυμένην καὶ θάττω καὶ λίαν
ἄλυπον παρασκευάζει. χυλὸν δ' ἁλυκὸν δριμύτητα
ἔχοντα ἀναδίδωσι μεθ᾽ ἁλῶν καταπινόμενα. διαλύεται
μὲν οὖν ταχέως, διότι πολλῶν καὶ μεγάλων ὄγκων
εἰσενεχθέντων μετὰ μικρὸν χρόνον λαγαροὶ γινόμεθα
καθ᾽ ὑπερβολήν· ἀδύνατον δ' ἦν ⟨ἂν⟩[15] τοῦτο συμ-
βαίνειν διαμενόντων καὶ μὴ ταχὺ διαλυομένων τῶν
c σωμάτων[16]. κατεργάζεται δὲ μᾶλλον | τῆς ἄλλης οὐ
μόνον ὅτι πολλαπλασίονα λαμβάνοντες αὐτὴν τῆς
λοιπῆς ὀπώρας ἀλύπως διάγομεν, ἀλλ᾽ οὐδὲ τὴν εἰ-

they had no grain. After he got control of Myus, therefore, he gave the place to the Magnesians in return for the figs. And the iambic poet Ananius (fr. 3 West²) says:

If someone were to shut up a lot of gold, a few figs,
and three or four people in a house,
    he would find out how much better figs are than gold.

This was the extent of Magnus' fig-harvest, and after it the physician Daphnus said: Phylotimus in Book III of *On Food* (fr. 9 Steckerl) says that ripe figs differ greatly from one another in their varieties, the time when each of them is produced, and their qualities. But in any case, speaking generally, juicy, ripe figs dissolve the most rapidly, are more easily digested than other fruit, and do not prevent the rest of one's food from being digested. They have the sticky, sweet, and somewhat alkaline qualities of moist foods; and they produce larger, looser, faster, and quite painless bowel movements. When consumed with salty foods, they yield a salty, bitter *chulē*. They are broken down quickly, the evidence being that when we consume them in large quantities, after a little while our bowels become extraordinarily loose; this would be impossible if they maintained their form and were not quickly broken down. They are more easily digested than other food; the evidence is not only that when we eat many times more of this type of food than of any other, we suffer no discomfort, but also that we have no trouble if we eat our normal food

---

15 ἄν add. Olson
16 τῶν σωμάτων A: τῶν σύκων CE

ωθυῖαν τροφὴν ἴσην λαμβάνοντες τούτων προχειρι-
σθέντων οὐθὲν ἐνοχλούμεθα. δῆλον οὖν ὡς εἰ κρατοῦ-
μεν ἀμφοτέρων, ταῦτά τε πέττεται μᾶλλον καὶ τὴν
λοιπὴν οὐ κωλύει κατεργάζεσθαι τροφήν. τὰς δὲ δυνάμεις ἔχει τὰς λεγομένας· τὴν μὲν κολλώδη τε καὶ
τὴν ἁλυκὴν ἐκ τοῦ κολλᾶν τε καὶ ῥύπτειν τὰς χεῖρας,
d τὴν δὲ γλυκεῖαν ἐν | τῷ στόματι γινομένην ὁρῶμεν.
τὴν δὲ διαχώρησιν ἄνευ στρόφων τε καὶ ταραχῆς καὶ
πλείω καὶ θᾶττω καὶ μαλακωτέραν ὅτι παρασκευάζει,
λόγου προσδεῖν οὐθὲν νομίζομεν. ἀλλοιοῦται δ' οὐ
λίαν, οὐ διὰ τὸ δύσπεπτον αὐτῶν, ἀλλ' ὅτι καταπίνο-
μέν τε ταχέως οὐ λεάναντες καὶ τὴν διέξοδον διότι
ταχεῖαν ποιεῖται. χυμὸν δ' ἁλυκὸν ἀναδίδωσι, διότι τὸ
μὲν νιτρῶδες ἀπεδείχθη τὰ σῦκα ἔχοντα, ἁλυκώτερον
δὲ ποιήσει ἢ δριμύν, ἐκ τῶν ἐπιπινομένων. οἱ μὲν γὰρ
e ἅλες | τὸν ἁλυκόν, τὸ δ' ὄξος καὶ τὸ θύμον τὸν δριμὺν
αὔξει χυμόν.

Ἡρακλείδης δ' ὁ Ταραντῖνος ἐν τῷ Συμποσίῳ ζητεῖ
πότερον ἐπιλαμβάνειν δεῖ μετὰ τὴν τῶν σύκων
προσφορὰν θερμὸν ὕδωρ ἢ ψυχρόν. καὶ τοὺς μὲν
λέγοντας θερμὸν δεῖν ἐπιλαμβάνειν προορῶντας τὸ
τοιοῦτο παρακελεύεσθαι, διότι καὶ τὰς χεῖρας ταχέως
τὸ θερμὸν ῥύπτει· διὸ πιθανὸν εἶναι καὶ ἐν κοιλίᾳ
συντόμως αὐτὰ τῷ θερμῷ διαλύεσθαι. καὶ ἐπὶ τῶν
f ἐκτὸς δὲ ⟨τῶν⟩ σύκων τὸ θερμὸν διαλύει | τὴν συν-
έχειαν αὐτῶν καὶ εἰς λεπτομερεῖς τόμους ἄγει, τὸ δὲ
ψυχρὸν συνίστησιν. οἱ δὲ ψυχρὸν λέγοντες προσφέρεσθαι, ἢ τοῦ ψυχροῦ, φασί, πόματος λῆψις τὰ ἐπὶ τοῦ

in the ordinary quantity, even though we have eaten figs earlier. It is thus clear that, if we can manage both of these, figs are very easily digested and do not hinder the digestion of the rest of our food. They have the qualities mentioned: the stickiness and the saltiness are apparent from the way they stick to our hands and remove dirt from them, and the sweetness reveals itself in our mouths. As for their producing larger, softer bowel movements more rapidly and without cramps or indigestion, we believe this requires no argument. Figs do not change much,[33] not because they are difficult to digest, but because we swallow them quickly without much chewing and they pass rapidly out of the body. They yield a salty humour on account of the fact that, as shown, figs have an alkaline character. They will produce a saltier or more bitter humour depending on what is eaten after them; for salty food will increase the salty humour, whereas vinegar and thyme will increase the bitter humour.

Heracleides of Tarentum in his *Symposium* (fr. 68 Guardasole) raises the question of whether one ought to consume warm water or cold water after eating figs. Those who say one ought to consume warm water base their advice on the observation that warm water rapidly removes dirt from our hands; it is therefore a reasonable expectation that figs are rapidly broken down inside the belly by warm water. And when warm water is applied to figs outside the body, it breaks down their structure and reduces them to small pieces, whereas cold water firms them up.

---

[33] *Viz.* as they pass through the body.

στομάχου καθήμενα τῷ βάρει καταφέρει· τὰ γὰρ
σῦκα οὐκ ἀστείως διατίθησι τὸν στόμαχον, καυσώδη
καὶ ἀτονώτερον αὐτὸν ποιοῦντα· διόπερ τινὲς καὶ τὸν
ἄκρατον συνεχῶς προσφέρονται. μετὰ δὲ ταῦτα ἑτοί-
80 μως καὶ τὰ ἐν τῇ κοιλίᾳ προωθεῖ. ‖ δεῖ δὲ πλέονι καὶ
ἀθρουστέρῳ χρῆσθαι τῷ πόματι μετὰ τὴν τῶν σύκων
προσφορὰν ἕνεκα τοῦ μὴ ὑπομένειν αὐτὰ ἐν κοιλίᾳ,
φέρεσθαι δὲ εἰς τὰ κάτω μέρη τῶν ἐντέρων.

Ἄλλοι δέ φασιν ὅτι μὴ δεῖ σῦκα προσφέρεσθαι
μεσημβρίας· νοσώδη γὰρ εἶναι τότε, ὡς καὶ Φερεκράτης ἐν Κραπατάλλοις εἴρηκεν. Ἀριστοφάνης δ᾽ ἐν
Προαγῶνι·

κάμνοντα δ᾽ αὐτὸν τοῦ θέρους ἰδών ποτε
ἔτρωγ᾽, ἵνα κάμνοι, σῦκα τῆς μεσημβρίας.

b καὶ Εὔβουλος ἐν Σφιγγοκαρίωνι· |

νὴ τὸν Δί᾽, ἠσθένουν γάρ, ὦ βέλτιστε σύ,
φαγοῦσα πρῴην σῦκα τῆς μεσημβρίας.

Νικοφῶν δ᾽ ἐν Σειρῆσιν·

ἐὰν δέ γ᾽ ἡμῶν σῦκά τις μεσημβρίας
τραγὼν καθεύδῃ χλωρά, πυρετὸς εὐθέως
ἥκει τρέχων οὐκ ἄξιος τριωβόλου·
κᾆθ᾽ οὗτος ἐπιπεσὼν ἐμεῖν ποιεῖ χολήν.

Δίφιλος δ᾽ ὁ Σίφνιός φησι τῶν σύκων εἶναι τὰ μὲν

But those who argue for drinking cold water say: When cold water is consumed, its weight[34] forces whatever is sitting in the stomach downward. For figs do not have a gentle effect on the stomach, but make it dry and less elastic; this is why some people constantly consume unmixed wine. But after this, the belly's contents move readily forward. One should drink a lot at one time after one eats figs, to prevent them from lingering in the belly and to keep them moving toward the lower portions of one's guts.

Other authorities say that one should not eat figs at midday, because they cause sickness then, as Pherecrates says in *Small Change* (fr. 85).[35] Aristophanes in *The Proagon* (fr. 479):

> Once in the summer, when he saw this fellow was sick,
> he ate some figs at midday so that *he* would get sick.

Also Eubulus in *Sphinx-Carion* (fr. 105):

> Yes, by Zeus, my dear friend—because I was sick,
> since I'd eaten some figs the day before yesterday at midday.

Nicophon in *Sirens* (fr. 20):

> If one of us eats some unripe figs
> at midday and falls asleep, a lousy
> fever immediately comes on the run;
> and then it attacks him and makes him vomit bile.

Diphilus of Siphnos says that ripe figs provide little

---

[34] For cold water as heavier than warm water, see 2.42a–b.
[35] Quoted at 3.75b.

ἁπαλὰ ὀλιγότροφα καὶ κακόχυλα, εὐέκκριτα δὲ καὶ
c ἐπιπολαστικὰ εὐοικονομητότερά | τε τῶν ξηρῶν. τὰ δὲ
πρὸς τῷ χειμῶνι γινόμενα βίᾳ πεπαινόμενα χείρονα
τυγχάνει· τὰ δ᾽ ἐν τῇ ἀκμῇ τῶν ὡρῶν κρείττονα ὡς ἂν
κατὰ φύσιν πεπαινόμενα. τὰ δὲ πολὺν ὀπὸν ἔχοντα,
καὶ τὰ σπάνυδρα δ᾽ εὐστομαχώτερα[17] μέν, βαρύτερα
δέ. τὰ δὲ Τραλλιανὰ ἀναλογεῖ τοῖς Ῥοδίοις, τὰ δὲ Χῖα
καὶ τἆλλα πάντα τούτων εἶναι κακοχυλότερα. Μνησίθεος δ᾽ ὁ Ἀθηναῖος ἐν τῷ Περὶ Ἐδεστῶν φησιν· ὅσα
δὲ ὠμὰ προσφέρεται τῶν τοιούτων, οἷον ἄπιοι καὶ
d σῦκα καὶ μῆλα Δελφικὰ καὶ τὰ τοιαῦτα, | δεῖ παρα-
φυλάττειν τὸν καιρὸν ἐν ᾧ τοὺς χυλοὺς τοὺς ἐν αὐτοῖς
μήτε ἀπέπτους μήτε σαπροὺς μήτε κατεξηραμμένους
λίαν ὑπὸ τῆς ὥρας ἕξει. Δημήτριος δ᾽ ὁ Σκήψιος ἐν τῷ
πεντεκαιδεκάτῳ τοῦ Τρωικοῦ Διακόσμου εὐφώνους
φησὶ γίνεσθαι τοὺς μὴ σύκων ἐσθίοντας. Ἡγησιά-
νακτα γοῦν τὸν Ἀλεξανδρέα τὸν τὰς ἱστορίας γρά-
ψαντα κατ᾽ ἀρχὰς ὄντα πένητα καὶ τραγῳδὸν φησι
γενέσθαι καὶ ὑποκριτικὸν καὶ εὔηχον, ὀκτωκαίδεκα
ἔτη σύκων μὴ γευσάμενον. καὶ παροιμίας δὲ οἶδα περὶ
e | σύκων λεγομένας τοιάσδε·

σῦκον μετ᾽ ἰχθύν, ὄσπρεον μετὰ κρέα.
σῦκα φίλ᾽ ὀρνίθεσσι, φυτεύειν δ᾽ οὐκ ἐθέλουσι.

Μῆλα. ταῦτα Μνησίθεος ὁ Ἀθηναῖος ἐν τῷ Περὶ
Ἐδεστῶν μῆλα Δελφικὰ καλεῖ. Δίφιλος δέ φησι τῶν

---

[17] εὐστομώτερα Kaibel

nourishment and produce bad *chulē*, but are easily excreted, rise to the top of the stomach, and are more easily absorbed than the dried ones. Those produced when it is almost winter and force-ripened are inferior, while those produced at peak season are better, since they have ripened naturally. Those that have a large amount of juice and those that contain little water are harder on the stomach, although heavier. Figs from Tralles are comparable to Rhodian figs; but Chian figs and all other varieties produce worse *chulē* than these do. Mnesitheus of Athens in his *On Edible Substances* (fr. 32 Bertier) says: As for the foods of this type that are eaten raw, such as pears, figs, Delphic apples[36], and the like, one should watch for the time when they are likely to contain juices that are neither uncon- cocted nor putrid nor excessively dried up because they are so ripe. Demetrius of Scepsis in Book XV of his *Trojan Battle-Order* (fr. 9 Gaede) claims that people who avoid eating figs have good voices. The historian Hegesianax of Alexandria (*FGrH* 45 T 2), for example, although origi- nally a pauper, says that he became a tragic poet and an ac- tor with a beautiful voice after not tasting figs for 18 years. I also know proverbs such as the following (Apostol. 15.70a– b) that are recited about figs:

A fig after fish, a pea after meat.
Birds love figs, but are unwilling to plant them.[37]

Apples. Mnesitheus of Athens in his *On Edible Sub- stances* (fr. 33 Bertier) refers to these as Delphic apples.[38]

---

36 See 3.80e.   37 I.e. "Everything in its time" and "He who pays the piper calls the tune."

38 The passage is quoted at 3.80c–d, above.

μήλων τὰ χλωρὰ καὶ μηδέπω πέπονα κακόχυλα εἶναι
καὶ κακοστόμαχα ἐπιπολαστικά τε καὶ χολῆς γεν-
νητικὰ νοσοποιά τε καὶ φρίκης παραίτια. τῶν δὲ

f πεπόνων εὐχυλότερα μὲν | εἶναι τὰ γλυκέα καὶ εὐεκ-
κριτότερα διὰ τὸ στύψιν μὴ ἔχειν, κακοχυλότερα δὲ
εἶναι τὰ ὀξέα καὶ στατικώτερα. τὰ δὲ τῆς γλυκύτητος
ὑφειμένα, προσλαμβάνοντα δ᾽ εὐστομεῖν διὰ τὴν πο-
σὴν στύψιν εὐστομαχώτερα. εἶναι δὲ αὐτῶν τὰ μὲν
θερινὰ κακοχυλότερα, τὰ δὲ φθινοπωρινὰ εὐχυλότερα.
τὰ δὲ καλούμενα ὀρβικλᾶτα μετὰ στύψεως ἡδείας

81 ἔχοντα καὶ γλυκύτητα εὐστόμαχα εἶναι. ‖ τὰ δὲ ση-
τάνια λεγόμενα, προσέτι δὲ ⟨τὰ⟩ πλατάνια εὔχυλα
μὲν καὶ εὐέκκριτα, οὐκ εὐστόμαχα δέ. τὰ δὲ Μορδιανὰ
καλούμενα γίνεται μὲν κάλλιστα ἐν Ἀπολλωνίᾳ τῇ
Μορδίῳ λεγομένῃ, ἀναλογεῖ δὲ τοῖς ὀρβικλάτοις. τὰ
δὲ κυδώνια, ὧν ἔνια καὶ στρουθία λέγεται, κοινῶς
ἁπάντων ἐστὶ τῶν μήλων εὐστομαχώτατα καὶ μάλιστα τὰ πέπονα. Γλαυκίδης δέ φησιν ἄριστα τῶν
ἀκροδρύων εἶναι μῆλα κυδώνια, φαύλια, στρουθία.

b Φυλότιμος δ᾽ ἐν τρίτῳ καὶ δεκάτῳ Περὶ | Τροφῆς, τὰ
μῆλα, φησί, τὰ μὲν ἐαρινὰ δυσπεπτότερα πολὺ τῶν
ἀπίων καὶ τὰ ὠμὰ τῶν ὠμῶν καὶ τὰ πέπονα τῶν
πεπόνων. τὰς δὲ δυνάμεις ἔχει τῶν ὑγρῶν τὰ μὲν ὀξέα
καὶ μήπω πέπονα στρυφνοτέρας καὶ ποσῶς ὀξείας
χυμόν τε ἀναδίδωσιν εἰς τὸ σῶμα τὸν καλούμενον

---

39 ~ Latin *orbiculata* ("round"); Diphilus is unlikely to have
used the term.

Diphilus says that green apples that are not yet ripe produce bad *chulē*, are hard on the stomach and rise to the top of it, generate bile, and are a cause of sickness and chills. As for ripe apples, the sweet ones produce better *chulē* and are more easily excreted, because they are not astringent; whereas the acidic ones produce worse *chulē* and have more of a tendency to slow down the bowels. Those that are not very sweet but nonetheless taste good are easier on the stomach, because they are somewhat astringent. Summer apples produce worse *chulē*, whereas fall apples produce better *chulē*. The so-called *orbiklata*[39] combine a pleasant astringency with sweetness and are easy on the stomach. Those called *sētania*[40], as well as *platania* apples, produce good *chulē* and are easily excreted, but are not easy on the stomach. The so-called Mordian apples grow best in Apollonia (also referred to as Mordia) and are comparable to *orbiklata*. Quinces[41], some of which are also referred to as *strouthia*, are in general the easiest of all apples on the stomach, especially when ripe. Glaucides (Glaucias fr. dub. 163 Deichgräber) says that the best tree-fruits are quinces, *phaulia*, and *strouthia*.[42] Phylotimus in Books III and X of *On Food* (fr. 11 Steckerl) says: Spring apples are far more difficult to digest than pears, regardless of whether unripe apples and unripe pears or ripe apples and ripe pears are compared. Those that are sour and not yet ripe have the qualities of moist foods, but with more astringency and some sourness, and in the body they

[40] Literally "this year's crop"; the adjective is most often used of winter wheat.   [41] Literally "Cydonian apples."

[42] For *phaulia* and *strouthia*, see 3.82b–c. The adjective *phaulios* is applied to olives at 2.56c.

ξυστικόν. καθόλου τε τὰ μῆλα τῶν ἀπίων δυσπεπτότερα εἶναι, διότι τὰ μὲν ἐλάττω φαγόντες ἧττον, τὰς δὲ
πλείους προσαράμενοι μᾶλλον πέττομεν. ξυστικὸς δὲ
c γίνεται χυμὸς ἐξ αὐτῶν ὁ | λεγόμενος ὑπὸ Πραξαγό-
ρου ⟨ὑαλώδης⟩[18], διότι τὰ μὴ κατεργαζόμενα παχυτέρους ἕξει τοὺς χυμούς· ἀπεδείχθη δὲ καθόλου τὰ μῆλα
δυσκατεργαστότερα τῶν ἀπίων, καὶ ὅτι τὰ στρυφνὰ
μᾶλλον ἔτι παχυτέρους παρασκευάζειν εἴωθεν αὐτούς.
τὰ δὲ χειμερινὰ τῶν μήλων τὰ μὲν κυδώνια στρυφνοτέρους, τὰ δὲ στρουθία τοὺς χυμοὺς ἐλάττους ἀναδίδωσι καὶ στρυφνοτέρους ἧττον πέττεσθαί τε μᾶλλον
δύναται.

Νίκανδρος δ᾿ ὁ Θυατειρηνὸς τὰ κυδώνια μῆλα
d στρουθία φησὶ καλεῖσθαι | ἀγνοῶν· Γλαυκίδης γὰρ
ἱστορεῖ ἄριστα λέγων τῶν ἀκροδρύων εἶναι μῆλα
κυδώνια, φαύλια, στρουθία. κυδωνίων δὲ μήλων μνημονεύει Στησίχορος ἐν Ἑλένῃ οὕτως·

πολλὰ μὲν κυδώνια μᾶλα ποτερρίπτουν ποτὶ
    δίφρον ἄνακτι,
πολλὰ δὲ μύρσινα φύλλα
καὶ ῥοδίνους στεφάνους ἴων τε κορωνίδας οὔλας.

καὶ Ἀλκμάν. ἔτι δὲ Κάνθαρος ἐν Τηρεῖ·

κυδωνίοις μήλοισιν εἰς τὰ τιτθία.

καὶ Φιλήμων δ᾿ ἐν Ἀγροίκῳ τὰ κυδώνια μῆλα στρου-

[18] add. Coraes

produce the so-called corrosive humour. In general apples are more difficult to digest than pears, the proof being that even if we eat less of the former, we digest them less effectively, whereas if we eat more of the latter, we digest them more effectively. The corrosive humour they produce is what Praxagoras calls the glassy humour,[43] the proof being that whatever foods are not digested will have thicker humours; and it was demonstrated that apples are in general more difficult to digest than pears, and that astringent foods tend to produce humours that are even thicker. As for winter apples, quinces produce more astringent humours, whereas *strouthia* produce less astringent humours in smaller quantities, and are more capable of being digested.

Nicander of Thyateira (*FGrH* 343 F 9) asserts that quinces are called *strouthia*, but he is in error; for Glaucides (above) records that the best tree-fruits are quinces, *phaulia*, and *strouthia*. Stesichorus mentions quinces in *Helen* (*PMG* 187), in the following words:

> They threw many quinces toward the king's chariot, and many myrtle leaves
> and garlands of roses and twisted wreaths made of violets.

Also Alcman (*PMG* 99). And Cantharus as well, in *Tereus* (fr. 6):

> with quinces to her titties.

Philemon in *The Rustic* (fr. 1) also refers to quinces as

[43] Praxagoras was Phylotimus' teacher.

e θία καλεῖ. Φύλαρχος δ' ἐν | τῇ ἕκτῃ τῶν Ἱστοριῶν τὰ
κυδώνιά φησι μῆλα τῇ εὐωδίᾳ καὶ τὰς τῶν θανασίμων
φαρμάκων δυνάμεις ἀπαμβλύνειν. τὸ γοῦν Φαριακὸν
φάρμακον ἐμβληθέν φησιν εἰς ῥίσκον ἔτι ὀδωδότα
ἀπὸ τῆς τῶν μήλων τούτων συνθέσεως ἐξίτηλον γενέσθαι μὴ τηρῆσαν τὴν ἰδίαν δύναμιν· κερασθὲν οὖν[19]
καὶ δοθὲν πιεῖν τοῖς εἰς τοῦτο ἐνεδρευθεῖσιν ἀπαθεῖς
αὐτοὺς διατηρῆσαι. ἐπιγνωσθῆναι δὲ τοῦτο ὕστερον
f ἐξ ἀνακρίσεως τοῦ τὸ φάρμακον πωλήσαντος καὶ |
ἐπιγνόντος τὸ γενόμενον ἐκ τῆς τῶν μήλων συνθέσεως. Ἕρμων δ' ἐν Κρητικαῖς Γλώσσαις κοδύμαλα
καλεῖσθαί φησι τὰ κυδώνια μῆλα. Πολέμων δ' ἐν
πέμπτῳ τῶν Πρὸς Τίμαιον ἄνθους γένος τὸ κοδύμαλον εἶναί τινας ἱστορεῖν. Ἀλκμὰν δὲ τὸ στρουθίον
μῆλον, ὅταν λέγῃ·

   < . . . > μεῖον ἢ κοδύμαλον.

Ἀπολλόδωρος δὲ καὶ Σωσίβιος τὸ κυδώνιον μῆλον
ἀκούουσιν. ὅτι δὲ διαφέρει τὸ κυδώνιον μῆλον τοῦ
82 στρουθίου ‖ σαφῶς εἴρηκε Θεόφραστος ἐν δευτέρῳ
τῆς Ἱστορίας.

   Διάφορα δὲ μῆλα γίνεται ἐν Σιδοῦντι. κώμη δ'
ἐστὶν αὕτη Κορίνθου, ὡς Εὐφορίων ἢ Ἀρχύτας ἐν
Γεράνῳ φησίν·

   ὥριον οἷά τε μῆλον, ὅ τ' ἀργιλώδεσιν ὄχθαις
   πορφύρεον ἐλαχείη ἐνιτρέφεται Σιδόεντι.

μνημονεύει δ' αὐτῶν καὶ Νίκανδρος ἐν Ἑτεροιουμέ-

strouthia. Phylarchus in Book VI of his *Histories* (*FGrH* 81 F 10) says that the pleasant smell of quinces blunts the effect of deadly poisons. For example, he says, when Phariac poison was put in a chest that still had the smell of quinces, which had been stored there, it failed to retain its proper character and lost its effect; so that when it was mixed with wine and given to the victims of the plot to drink, it left them unscathed. That this was the case was recognized afterwards, when the man who had sold the poison was interrogated and recognized what had happened as a result of storing the quinces in the chest. Hermon in *Cretan Vocabulary* says that quinces are referred to as *kodumala*. But Polemon in Book V of his *Response to Timaeus* (fr. 43 Preller) says that other authorities record that the *kodumalon* is a type of flower. Alcman (*PMG* 100) is referring to the *strouthian* apple when he says:

> smaller than a *kodumalon*.

But Apollodorus (*FGrH* 244 F 252) and Sosibius (*FGrH* 595 F 11) take this to refer to the quince. Theophrastus in Book II of his *Inquiry* (*HP* 2.2.5) says explicitly that the quince is different from the *strouthion*.

Exceptional apples grow in Sidous, which is a village that belongs to Corinth, according to Euphorion (fr. 11, p. 32 Powell = fr. 188 van Groningen) or Archytas in *The Crane*:

> Like a ripe apple, which grows dark red
> on the hills of clay in little Sidous.

Nicander also mentions them in his *Metamorphoses* (fr. 50

---

[19] οὖν Olson: γοῦν ACE

νοις οὕτως·

    αὐτίχ᾽ ὅγ᾽ ἢ Σιδόεντος ἠὲ Πλείστου ἀπὸ κήπων

b   μῆλα ταμὼν χνοάοντα τύπους ἐνεμάσσετο |
      Κάδμου.

ὅτι δ᾽ ἡ Σιδοῦς τῆς Κορίνθου ἐστὶ κώμη Ῥιανὸς
εἴρηκεν ἐν πρώτῳ Ἡρακλείας καὶ Ἀπολλόδωρος ὁ
Ἀθηναῖος ἐν πέμπτῳ Περὶ Νεῶν Καταλόγου. Ἀντίγονος δ᾽ ὁ Καρύστιος ἐν Ἀντιπάτρῳ φησίν·

    ἧχι μοι ὡραίων πολὺ φίλτερον εἴαρι μῆλον
    πορφυρέων, Ἐφύρῃ τά τ᾽ ἀέξεται ἠνεμοέσσῃ.

    Φαυλίων δὲ μήλων μνημονεύει Τηλεκλείδης ἐν Ἀμ-
φικτύοσιν οὕτως·

    ὦ τὰ μὲν κομψοί, τὰ δὲ φαυλότεροι

c   φαυλίων | μήλων.

καὶ Θεόπομπος ἐν Θησεῖ. Ἀνδροτίων δ᾽ ἐν τῷ Γεωργικῷ, τὰς δὲ μηλέας, φησί, φαυλίας καὶ στρουθίας· οὐ
γὰρ ἀπορρεῖ τὸ μῆλον ἀπὸ τοῦ μίσχου τῶν στρου-
θιῶν· τὰς δὲ ἠρινὰς ἢ Λακωνικὰς ἢ Σιδουντίας ἢ
χνοωδίας. ἐγὼ δ᾽, ἄνδρες φίλοι, πάντων μάλιστα τε-
θαύμακα τὰ ⟨κατὰ⟩ τὴν Ῥώμην πιπρασκόμενα μῆλα
τὰ Ματιανὰ καλούμενα, ἅπερ κομίζεσθαι λέγεται ἀπό
τινος κώμης ἱδρυμένης ἐπὶ τῶν πρὸς Ἀκυληΐᾳ Ἄλ-
πεων. τούτων δ᾽ οὐ πολὺ ἀπολείπεται τὰ ἐν Γάγγροις

44 Letters (the alphabet having supposedly been invented by

Schneider), as follows:

> At once he cut downy apples from the orchards
> of Sidous or Pleistus, pressing Cadmaean characters[44]
>   into them.

That Sidous is a village that belongs to Corinth is asserted by Rhianus in Book I of the *Heracleia* (*FGrH* 265 F 47) and by Apollodorus of Athens in Book V of *On the Catalogue of Ships* (*FGrH* 244 F 159). Antigonus of Carystus says in *Antipater* (p. 170 Wilamowitz = *SH* 47):

> where is an apple far dearer to me in springtime than
>   the ripe,
> dark red fruit that grows in windy Ephyra.

Teleclides mentions *phaulian* apples in *Amphictyonies* (fr. 4), as follows:

> O you who are sometimes smart, but at other times
>   worse *(phauloteroi)*
> than *phaulian* apples.

Also Theopompus in *Theseus* (fr. 20). Androtion in his *On Agriculture* (*FGrH* 324 F 77) says: As for apple trees, *phaulians* and *strouthians*; because the apple does not fall off the stem of the *strouthians*. As for spring apples, either Spartans or Sidountians or the downy variety. But I, my friends, am most impressed by the so-called Matian apples that are sold in Rome and said to be imported from a village situated in the Alps near Aquileia; although the apples in the Paphlagonian city of Gangra are not much inferior to

Cadmus), which formed a love-vow Ctesilla was bound by after she read it aloud.

d πόλει Παφλαγονικῇ. | ὅτι δὲ καὶ τῶν μήλων εὑρετής
ἐστι Διόνυσος μαρτυρεῖ Θεόκριτος ὁ Συρακόσιος οὑ-
τωσί πως λέγων·

μᾶλα μὲν ἐν κόλποισι Διωνύσοιο φυλάσσων,
κρατὶ δ᾽ ἔχων λεύκαν, Ἡρακλέος ἱερὸν ἔρνος.

Νεοπτόλεμος δ᾽ ὁ Παριανὸς ἐν τῇ Διονυσιάδι καὶ
αὐτὸς ἱστορεῖ ὡς ὑπὸ Διονύσου εὑρεθέντων τῶν μήλων, καθάπερ καὶ τῶν ἄλλων ἀκροδρύων. ἐπιμηλὶς δὲ
καλεῖται, φησὶ Πάμφιλος, τῶν ἀπίων τι γένος. Ἑσπερίδων δὲ μῆλα οὕτως καλεῖσθαί τινά φησι Τιμαχίδας
e | ἐν τῷ τετάρτῳ Δείπνων. καὶ ἐν Λακεδαίμονι δὲ παρα-
τίθεσθαι τοῖς θεοῖς φησι Πάμφιλος ταῦτα· εὔοσμα δὲ
εἶναι καὶ ἄβρωτα, καλεῖσθαι δ᾽ Ἑσπερίδων μῆλα.
Ἀριστοκράτης γοῦν ἐν τετάρτῃ Λακωνικῶν· ἔτι δὲ
μῆλα καὶ ⟨μηλέας⟩ τὰς λεγομένας Ἑσπερίδας.

Περσικά. Θεόφραστος ἐν δευτέρῳ Περὶ Φυτῶν
Ἱστορίας λέγων περὶ ὧν ὁ καρπὸς οὐ φανερός, γράφει
καὶ τάδε· ἐπεὶ τῶν γε μειζόνων φανερὰ πάντων ἡ
ἀρχή, καθάπερ ἀμυγδαλῆς, καρύου, βαλάνου, τῶν
f ἄλλων ὅσα τοιαῦτα πλὴν τοῦ Περσικοῦ, | τούτου δ᾽
ἥκιστα· καὶ πάλιν ῥόας, ἀπίου, μηλέας. Δίφιλος δ᾽ ὁ
Σίφνιος ἐν τῷ Περὶ τῶν Προσφερομένων τοῖς Νοσοῦ-
σι καὶ τοῖς Ὑγιαίνουσίν φησι· τὰ δὲ Περσικὰ λεγόμενα μῆλα, ὑπό τινων δὲ Περσικὰ κοκκύμηλα, μέσως
ἐστὶν εὔχυλα, θρεπτικώτερα δὲ τῶν μήλων. Φυλότιμος

them. Theocritus of Syracuse (2.120–1) bears witness to the fact that Dionysus discovered apples, saying something more or less like this:

> keeping apples of Dionysus in my bosom,
> and wearing white poplar, the holy shoot of Heracles,
>   on my head.

Neoptolemus of Paros in his *Dionysiad* (*FGrH* 702 F 3 = fr. 1 Mette) also records that apples, like the other tree-fruit, were discovered by Dionysus. According to Pamphilus (fr. V Schmidt), the word *epimēlis* is used for a variety of pear. Timachidas says in Book IV of the *Dinner Parties* (*SH* 771) that certain apples are referred to as apples of the Hesperides. Pamphilus says that in Sparta these are served to the gods; they are sweet-smelling but inedible, and are referred to as apples of the Hesperides. Aristocrates, at any rate, says in Book IV of the *History of Sparta* (*FGrH* 591 F 1): also apples and what are called the apple trees of the Hesperides.

  Peaches.[45] Theophrastus in Book II of *Research on Plants* (fr. 397), in his discussion of plants whose fruit is not apparent, writes as follows: Since for all the larger ones the growth is apparent from the very first, as for example the almond, the nut *(karuon)*, the acorn, and the rest of this type except the Persian nut (of which this is emphatically not true). And again the pomegranate, the pear, and the apple tree. Diphilus of Siphnos says in his *On Food for the Sick and the Healthy*: The so-called Persian apples, referred to by some authorities as Persian plums, produce moderately good *chulē* and are more nourishing than ap-

---

[45] Literally "Persian (apples)."

δ' ἐν τῷ τρίτῳ Περὶ Τροφῆς τὸ Περσικόν φησι λιπα-
ρώτερον καὶ κεγχρῶδες εἶναι, χαυνότερον δ' ὑπάρχειν
83 καὶ πιεζόμενον πλεῖστον ἔλαιον ἀνιέναι. ‖ Ἀριστοφάνης δ' ὁ γραμματικὸς ἐν Λακωνικαῖς Γλώσσαις τὰ
κοκκύμηλά φησι τοὺς Λάκωνας καλεῖν ὀξύμαλα Περσικά, ἅ τινες ἄδρυα.

Κιτρίον. περὶ τούτου πολλὴ ζήτησις ἐνέπεσε τοῖς
δειπνοσοφισταῖς, εἴ τίς ἐστιν αὐτοῦ μνήμη παρὰ τοῖς
παλαιοῖς. Μυρτίλος μὲν γὰρ ἔφασκεν, ὥσπερ εἰς αἶ-
γας ἡμᾶς ἀγρίας ἀποπέμπων τοὺς ζητοῦντας, Ἡγήσανδρον τὸν Δελφὸν ἐν τοῖς Ὑπομνήμασιν αὐτοῦ
μνημονεύειν, τῆς ⟨δὲ⟩ λέξεως τὰ νῦν οὐ μεμνῆσθαι.
πρὸς ὃν ἀντιλέγων ὁ Πλούταρχος· ἀλλὰ μὴν ἔγωγε,
b φησί, ‖ διορίζομαι μηδ' ὅλως τὸν Ἡγήσανδρον τοῦτο
εἰρηκέναι, δι' αὐτὸ τοῦτ' ἐξαναγνοὺς αὐτοῦ πάντα τὰ
Ὑπομνήματα, ἐπεὶ καὶ ἄλλος τις τῶν ἑταίρων τοῦτ'
ἔχειν οὕτω διεβεβαιοῦτο, ὁρμώμενος ἔκ τινων σχολι-
κῶν ὑπομνημάτων ἀνδρὸς οὐκ ἀδόξου· ὥστε ὥρα σοι,
φίλε Μυρτίλε, ἄλλον ζητεῖν μάρτυρα. Αἰμιλιανὸς δὲ
ἔλεγεν Ἰόβαν τὸν Μαυρουσίων βασιλέα, ἄνδρα πολυ-
μαθέστατον, ἐν τοῖς περὶ Λιβύης συγγράμμασι μνη-
μονεύοντα τοῦ κιτρίου καλεῖσθαι φάσκειν αὐτὸ παρὰ
c τοῖς Λίβυσι μῆλον Ἑσπερικόν, ‖ ἀφ' ὧν καὶ Ἡρακλέα
κομίσαι εἰς τὴν Ἑλλάδα τὰ χρύσεα διὰ τὴν ἰδέαν
λεγόμενα μῆλα. τὰ δὲ τῶν Ἑσπερίδων λεγόμενα μῆλα

---

46 Sc. than the apple. The oil referred to below presumably
comes from pressing the pits.

ples. Phylotimus in Book III of *On Food* (fr. 10 Steckerl) says that the peach is oilier[46], mealy, and spongier, and releases a large amount of oil when pressed. The grammarian Aristophanes in *Spartan Vocabulary* (fr. 350 Slater) says that the Spartans refer to plums as Persian sour apples, which some authorities call *adrua*.[47]

Citron. Considerable discussion arose among the learned banqueters as to whether the ancients mentioned this anywhere. For Myrtilus asserted, as it were sending us off to the wild goats[48] in our inquiries, that Hegesander of Delphi refers to the fruit in his *Commentaries*, although he was momentarily unable to remember the exact words. Plutarch contradicts him and says: No, I myself am certain that Hegesander never uses this word at all, since I read all his *Commentaries* for precisely this reason. For another friend of mine was sure that this was so, having been encouraged by certain scholarly essays produced by a not undistinguished gentleman. And so, my dear Myrtilus, it is time for you to look for another witness to the word. Aemilianus claimed that Juba the king of the Mauretanians, a very learned man, mentioned the citron in his treatise on Libya (*FGrH* 275 F 6) and asserted that the Libyans referred to it as an apple of Hesperia and that Heracles brought some of these, which were called golden apples because of their appearance, to Greece.[49] As for what are called apples of the Hesperides, Asclepiades in Book LX of

---

[47] Hsch. α 1210 identifies this as a Sicel (i.e. Sicilian) term.

[48] I.e. to the furthest and most inaccessible places.

[49] As one of his final labors.

459

ὅτι ἐς τοὺς Διὸς καὶ Ἥρας λεγομένους γάμους ἀνῆκεν
ἡ γῆ Ἀσκληπιάδης εἴρηκεν ἐν ἑξηκοστῇ Αἰγυπτια-
κῶν. πρὸς τούτους ἀποβλέψας ὁ Δημόκριτος ἔφη· εἰ
μέν τι τούτων Ἰόβας ἱστορεῖ, χαιρέτω Λιβυκαῖσι
βίβλοις ἔτι τε ταῖς Ἄννωνος πλάναις. ἐγὼ δὲ τὸ μὲν
ὄνομα οὔ φημι κεῖσθαι[20] παρὰ τοῖς παλαιοῖς τοῦτο, τὸ
δὲ πρᾶγμα ὑπὸ τοῦ Ἐρεσίου Θεοφράστου οὕτως λεγό-
d μενον ἐν τῇ Περὶ Φυτῶν Ἱστορίᾳ ἀναγκάζει | με ἐπὶ
τῶν κιτρίων ἀκούειν τὰ σημαινόμενα. φησὶ γὰρ ὁ
φιλόσοφος ἐν τῷ τετάρτῳ τῆς Περὶ Φυτῶν Ἱστορίας
οὕτως· ἡ δὲ Μηδία χώρα καὶ ἡ Περσὶς ἄλλα τε ἔχει
πλείω καὶ τὸ μῆλον τὸ Περσικὸν ἢ Μηδικὸν καλούμενον. ἔχει δὲ τὸ δένδρον τοῦτο φύλλον μὲν ὅμοιον καὶ
σχεδὸν ἴσον τῷ τῆς ἀνδράχλης[21] καὶ καρύας, ἀκάνθας
δ᾽ οἵας ἄπιος ἢ ὀξυάκανθος, λείας δὲ καὶ ὀξείας
σφόδρα καὶ ἰσχυράς. τὸ δὲ μῆλον οὐκ ἐσθίεται μέν,
εὔοσμον δὲ πάνυ καὶ αὐτὸ καὶ τὰ φύλλα τοῦ δένδρου·
e κἂν εἰς ἱμάτια | τεθῇ τὸ μῆλον, ἄκοπα διατηρεῖ.
χρήσιμον δὲ ἐπειδὰν καὶ τύχῃ τις πεπωκὼς θανάσι-
μον φάρμακον· δοθὲν γὰρ ἐν οἴνῳ διακόπτει τὴν
κοιλίαν καὶ ἐξάγει τὸ φάρμακον, καὶ πρὸς στόματος
εὐωδίαν· ἐὰν γάρ τις ἑψήσῃ ἐν ζωμῷ ἢ ἐν ἄλλῳ τινὶ τὸ
εἴσω τοῦ μήλου ἐκπιέσῃ τε εἰς τὸ στόμα καὶ καταρ-
ροφήσῃ, ποιεῖ τὴν ὀσμὴν ἡδεῖαν. σπείρεται δὲ τοῦ

[20] κεῖσθαι τοῦ κιτρίου ACE
[21] τῆς δαφνῆς ἀνδράχλης ACE

460

the *History of Egypt* (fr. 1, *FHG* iii.306) says that the earth sent them up in response to what is referred to as the "wedding of Zeus and Hera."[50] Democritus gave them a look and said: If Juba records any of this, to hell with Libyan books and Hanno's wanderings as well.[51] I deny that this word is attested in the ancients; but the thing itself, which is discussed by Theophrastus of Eresus in his *Research on Plants*, as follows, compels me to take the description to refer to citrons. For in Book IV of his *Research on Plants* (*HP* 4.4.2–3) the philosopher says the following: Media and Persia contain, among many other things, what is referred to as the Persian or Median apple. This tree has a leaf that resembles and is nearly the same size as that of the arbutus and the nut-tree,[52] and has spines like the pear tree's or the white-thorn's, which are smooth and extremely sharp and strong. Its apple is not eaten, but it and the tree's leaves are both very fragrant; if the apple is placed among clothes, it keeps them free of moths. It is also useful when someone has drunk a deadly poison, since when administered mixed in wine, it upsets the stomach and brings up the poison, as well as for sweetening your breath. For if you stew the interior of the apple in meat-broth or something else, squeeze it into your mouth, and swallow it down, it makes your breath smell sweet. The seed is extracted and sown in

---

[50] Cf. *Il.* 14.346–9, where flowers spring up from the earth as Zeus and Hera make love.   [51] The Phoenician Hanno supposedly wrote an account of his journey along the Atlantic coast of Morocco early in the 5th century, and this account was believed to have been translated into Greek. For the fragments, see *GGM* i.1–14.   [52] *karua*; cf. 2.52a–b. Only the arbutus is mentioned in the traditional text of Theophrastus.

ἦρος εἰς πρασιὰς ἐξαιρεθὲν τὸ σπέρμα διειργασμένας
ἐπιμελῶς· εἶτ᾽ ἄρδεται διὰ τετάρτης ἢ πέμπτης ἡμέ-
f ρας. ὅταν δὲ ἁδρὸν ᾖ, διαφυτεύεται πάλιν | τοῦ ἔαρος
εἰς χωρίον μαλακὸν καὶ ἔφυδρον καὶ οὐ λίαν λεπτόν.
φέρει δὲ τὰ μῆλα πᾶσαν ὥραν· τὰ μὲν γὰρ ἀφήρηται,
τὰ δ᾽ ἀνθεῖ, τὰ δ᾽ ἐκπέττει. τῶν δ᾽ ἀνθῶν ὅσα ἔχει
καθάπερ ἠλακάτην ἐκ μέσου τινὰ ἐξέχουσαν, ταῦτά
ἐστι γόνιμα· ὅσα δὲ μή, ἄγονα. κἂν τῷ πρώτῳ δὲ τῆς
αὐτῆς πραγματείας τὰ περὶ τῆς ἠλακάτης καὶ τῶν
γονίμων εἴρηκεν. ἐκ τούτων ἐγὼ κινούμενος, ὦ ἑταῖροι,
ὧν φησιν ὁ Θεόφραστος περὶ χρόας, περὶ ὀδμῆς, περὶ
φύλλων τὸ κιτρίον λέγεσθαι πεπίστευκα, καὶ μηδεὶς
84 ὑμῶν θαυμαζέτω εἰ φησιν μὴ ἐσθίεσθαι αὐτό, ‖ ὁπότε
γε καὶ μέχρι τῶν κατὰ τοὺς πάππους ἡμῶν χρόνων
οὐδεὶς ἤσθιεν, ἀλλ᾽ ὥς τι μέγα κειμήλιον ἀπετίθεντο
ἐν ταῖς κιβωτοῖς μετὰ τῶν ἱματίων. ὅτι δ᾽ ὄντως ἐκ τῆς
ἄνω χώρας ἐκείνης κατέβη εἰς τοὺς Ἕλληνας τὸ
φυτὸν τοῦτο, ἔστιν εὑρεῖν λεγόμενον καὶ παρὰ τοῖς
τῆς κωμῳδίας ποιηταῖς, οἳ καὶ περὶ μεγέθους αὐτῶν τι
λέγοντες τῶν κιτρίων μνημονεύειν φαίνονται. Ἀντιφάνης μὲν ἐν Βοιωτίῳ·

(Α.) καὶ περὶ μὲν ὄψου γ᾽ ἠλίθιον τὸ καὶ λέγειν
b ὥσπερ πρὸς ἀπλήστους. ἀλλὰ ταυτὶ λάμβανε, |
παρθένε, τὰ μῆλα. (Β.) καλά γε. (Α.) καλὰ δῆτ᾽,
    ὦ θεοί·
νεωστὶ γὰρ τὸ σπέρμα τοῦτ᾽ ἀφιγμένον
εἰς τὰς Ἀθήνας ἐστὶ παρὰ τοῦ βασιλέως.

the spring in carefully prepared garden beds, and is then watered every fourth or fifth day. Once it is well-established, it is transplanted again in the spring to a soft, well-watered spot where the soil is not too thin. It bears fruit in every season; for when some have already been picked, others are in bloom or are growing ripe. The flowers that have what looks like a distaff sticking out of the middle are fertile, while those that do not are sterile. He also discusses the distaff and the fertile flowers in Book I of the same work (*HP* 1.13.4). I, my friends, am influenced by what Theophrastus says about the color, smell, and leaves, and am convinced that the citron is being referred to. Nor should any of you be surprised if he denies that it is eaten, given that as recently as our grandfathers' times no one ate it, but they stored it away like a great treasure in their chests along with their clothes.[53] That this plant in fact made its way to the Greeks from the upper country[54] can also be found asserted by the comic poets who, when they refer to their size, are patently thinking of citrons. Antiphanes in *The Boeotian*[55] (fr. 59):

(A.) It's foolish to talk about fine food
with people who are almost insatiable. But take these
apples, my girl. (B.) They're lovely! (A.) They ought
    to be, by the gods!
For this seed has come only recently
to Athens from the King.[56]

[53] Cf. Ar. *V.* 1056 with MacDowell ad loc.
[54] The interior of Asia.   [55] Athenaeus also refers to the play as *The Boeotian* at 9.367f, but calls it *The Boeotian Woman* at 11.474e; 14.650e.   [56] Sc. of Persia.

(B.) παρ' Ἑσπερίδων ᾤμην γε. (Α.) νὴ τὴν
 Φωσφόρον,
φησὶν τὰ χρυσᾶ μῆλα ταῦτ' εἶναι. (Β.) τρία
μόνον ἐστίν. (Α.) ὀλίγον τὸ καλόν ἐστι πανταχοῦ
καὶ τίμιον.

Ἔριφος δ' ἐν Μελιβοίᾳ αὐτὰ ταῦτα τὰ ἰαμβεῖα προθεὶς ὡς ἴδια²² ἐπιφέρει·

 (B.) παρ' Ἑσπερίδων ᾤμην γε. (Α.) νὴ τὴν
c Ἄρτεμιν, |
φησὶν τὰ χρυσᾶ μῆλα ταῦτ' εἶναι. (Β.) τρία
μόνον ἐστίν. (Α.) ὀλίγον τὸ καλόν ἐστι πανταχοῦ
καὶ τίμιον. (Β.) τούτων μὲν ὀβολόν, εἰ πολύ,
τίθημι· λογιοῦμαι γάρ. (Α.) αὗται δὲ ῥόαι.
(Β.) ὡς εὐγενεῖς. (Α.) τὴν γὰρ Ἀφροδίτην ἐν
 Κύπρῳ
δένδρον φυτεῦσαι τοῦτό φασιν ἓν μόνον.
(Β.) † βέρβεαι † πολυτίμητε· κᾆτα τρεῖς μόνας
καὶ τάσδ' ἐκόμισας; (Α.) οὐ γὰρ εἶχον πλείονας.

τούτοις εἴ τις ἀντιλέγειν ἔχει ὅτι μὴ τὸ νῦν κιτρίον
d λεγόμενον σημαίνεται, σαφέστερα μαρτύρια | παρα-
τιθέσθω· καίτοι καὶ Φαινίου τοῦ Ἐρεσίου ἔννοιαν
ἡμῖν διδόντος μήποτε ἀπὸ τῆς κέδρου τὸ κεδρίον

²² ἴδια τὰ τοῦ Ἀντιφάνους A

---

⁵⁷ I.e. Hecate, an underworld goddess often identified with
Artemis; cf. Eriph. fr. 2.1, below.

(B.) I was thinking they came from the Hesperides!
    (A.) By the light-bearer,[57]
he claims that these are the golden apples. (B.) There
    are
only three of them. (A.) Anything good is rare and
    expensive
everywhere.

Eriphus in *Meliboea* (fr. 2) begins with these same iambic
lines, as if they were his own, but continues:

(B.) I was thinking they came from the Hesperides!
    (A.) By Artemis,
he claims that these are the golden apples. (B.) There
    are
only three of them. (A.) Anything good is rare and
    expensive
everywhere. (B.) I'm setting their price at an obol,
    even though that's
a lot; because I'm going to calculate the cost. (A.)
    Here are pomegranates.
(B.) How nice they are! (A.) Of course—for they say
    that
Aphrodite planted only this one tree on Cyprus.
(B.) By much-honored † Berbeia †! So you only
    brought
these three? (A.) Because they didn't have any more!

If anyone wishes to object to these arguments that what is
today called the citron is not being referred to, he should
provide evidence clearer than this, although Phaenias of
Eresus offers us the hypothesis that perhaps the juniper
berry *(kedrion)* produced by the juniper tree is what is be-

ὠνόμασται. καὶ γὰρ τὴν κέδρον φησὶν ἐν πέμπτῳ
Περὶ Φυτῶν ἀκάνθας ἔχειν περὶ τὰ φύλλα. ὅτι δὲ τὸ
αὐτὸ τοῦτο καὶ περὶ τὸ κιτρίον ἐστὶ παντὶ δῆλον.

Ὅτι δὲ καὶ προλαμβανόμενον τὸ κιτρίον πάσης
τροφῆς ξηρᾶς τε καὶ ὑγρᾶς ἀντιφάρμακόν ἐστι παντὸς δηλητηρίου εὖ οἶδα, μαθὼν παρὰ πολίτου ἐμοῦ
πιστευθέντος τὴν τῆς Αἰγύπτου ἀρχήν. οὗτος κατεδί-
e κασέ τινας | γενέσθαι θηρίων βορὰν κακούργους
εὑρεθέντας·[23] εἰσιοῦσι δὲ αὐτοῖς εἰς τὸ[24] εἰς τιμωρίαν
ἀποδεδειγμένον θέατρον κατὰ τὴν ὁδὸν κάπηλίς τις
γυνὴ κατ᾽ ἔλεον ἔδωκεν οὗ μετὰ χεῖρας εἶχεν ἐσθί-
ουσα κιτρίου. καὶ λαβόντες ἔφαγον καὶ μετ᾽ οὐ πολὺ
παραβληθέντες ταῖς ἀσπίσι[25] δηχθέντες οὐδὲν ἔπα-
θον. ἀπορία δὲ κατέσχε τὸν ἄρχοντα. καὶ τὸ τελευ-
f ταῖον ἀνακρίνων τὸν αὐτοὺς φυλάττοντα | στρατιώτην
εἴ τι ἔφαγον ἢ ἔπιον, ὡς ἔμαθε[26] τὸ κιτρίον δεδομένον,
τῇ ἐπιούσῃ τῶν ἡμερῶν τῷ μὲν πάλιν ἐκέλευσε δοθῆ-
ναι κιτρίου, τῷ δ᾽ οὔ· καὶ ὁ μὲν φαγὼν δηχθεὶς οὐδὲν
ἔπαθεν, ὁ δὲ παραυτίκα πληγεὶς ἀπέθανε. δοκιμα-
σθέντος οὖν διὰ πολλῶν τοῦ τοιούτου εὑρέθη τὸ κιτρίον ἀντιφάρμακον ⟨ὂν⟩ παντὸς δηλητηρίου φαρμά-
85 κου. ‖ ἐὰν δέ τις ἐν μέλιτι Ἀττικῷ ὅλον κιτρίον ὡς ἔχει
φύσεως συνεψήσῃ μετὰ τοῦ σπέρματος, διαλύεται μὲν
ἐν τῷ μέλιτι, καὶ ὁ ἀπ᾽ αὐτοῦ λαμβάνων ἕωθεν δύο ἢ

---

[23] εὑρεθέντας, καὶ ἔδει αὐτοὺς ἀποσίτοις (ἅπασι CE)
ζῴοις παραβληθῆναι ACE
[24] τὸ τοῖς λῃσταῖς ACE

ing discussed. For he says in Book V of *On Plants* (fr. 47a
Wehrli) that the leaves of the juniper tree are surrounded
by spines; that the same is true of the citron is absolutely
clear.

I am also well aware that if a citron is eaten before any
other dry or liquid food, it serves as an antidote against
all dangerous substances. I learned this from a fellow-
citizen of mine who was entrusted with the governorship
of Egypt.[58] He condemned some convicted criminals to be
fed to wild beasts; but as they were entering the theater
assigned for their punishment, a peddler-woman in the
street felt pity for them and gave them part of a citron she
had in her hands and was eating. They took and ate it; and a
little later, when they were thrown to the asps and bitten,
nothing happened to them. The governor was perplexed.
Finally he questioned the soldier who was guarding them
as to whether they had eaten or drunk anything; when he
learned that they had been given a citron, he ordered that
the next day a piece of citron should be given to one man,
but not the other. The man who ate the citron was bitten,
but nothing happened to him, whereas the other man died
immediately when he was struck. When similar results
were obtained repeatedly, therefore, the citron was discovered to be an antidote for poisonous drugs of all sorts. If
one stews a whole citron just as it is, seeds and all, in Attic
honey, it dissolves in the honey; anyone who drinks two or

[58] The text of the story that follows appears to be disturbed.

---

25 πελωρίοις καὶ ἀγριωτάτοις ζῴοις ταῖς ἀσπίσι ACE
26 ὡς ἔμαθε κατὰ τὸ αὐτὸν ἐξ ἀκεραίου ACE

τρεῖς δακτύλους οὐδ᾽ ὁτιοῦν ὑπὸ φαρμάκου πείσεται.
τούτοις εἴ τις ἀπιστεῖ, μαθέτω καὶ παρὰ Θεοπόμπου
τοῦ Χίου, ἀνδρὸς φιλαλήθους καὶ πολλὰ χρήματα
καταναλώσαντος εἰς τὴν περὶ τῆς ἱστορίας ἐξέτασιν
ἀκριβῆ. φησὶ γὰρ οὗτος ἐν τῇ ὀγδόῃ καὶ τριακοστῇ
τῶν Ἱστοριῶν περὶ Κλεάρχου διηγούμενος τοῦ Ἡρα-
b κλεωτῶν | τῶν ἐν τῷ Πόντῳ τυράννου, ὡς βιαίως
ἀνῄρει πολλοὺς καὶ ὡς τοῖς πλείστοις ἐδίδου ἀκόνι-
τον²⁷ πιεῖν· ἐπειδὴ οὖν, φησί, πάντες ἔγνωσαν τὴν τοῦ
φαρμάκου ταύτην φιλοτησίαν, οὐ προῄεσαν τῶν οἰκιῶν πρὶν φαγεῖν πήγανον· τοῦτο γὰρ τοὺς προφαγόν-
τας μηδὲν πάσχειν πίνοντας τὸ ἀκόνιτον· ὃ καὶ κληθῆναί φησι διὰ τὸ φύεσθαι ἐν τόπῳ Ἀκόναις καλουμένῳ
ὄντι περὶ τὴν Ἡράκλειαν.

Ταῦτ᾽ εἰπόντος τοῦ Δημοκρίτου θαυμάσαντες οἱ
c πολλοὶ τὴν τοῦ κιτρίου δύναμιν ἀπήσθιον | ὡς μὴ
πρότερον φαγόντες ἢ πιόντες τι. Πάμφιλος δ᾽ ἐν ταῖς
Γλώσσαις Ῥωμαίους φησὶν αὐτὸ κίτρον²⁸ καλεῖν.

Ἑξῆς δὲ τοῖς προειρημένοις κατ᾽ ἰδίαν ἐπεισεν-
εχθέντων ἡμῖν πολλῶν ὀστρέων καὶ τῶν ἄλλων
ὀστρακοδέρμων σχεδὸν τὰ πλεῖστα αὐτῶν μνήμης
ἠξιωμένα παρ᾽ Ἐπιχάρμῳ ἐν Ἥβας Γάμῳ εὑρίσκω
διὰ τούτων·

ἄγει δὲ παντοδαπὰ κογχύλια,

---

²⁷ κώνιον AE: κώνειον C
²⁸ κίτρον Musurus: κρίτον ACE

three fingers of the compound first thing in the morning
will not suffer any harm from poison. If anyone does not
believe this, he can learn it from Theopompus of Chios
(*FGrH* 115 T 28a), a man who was devoted to the truth
and spent a great deal of money on the accurate investigation of history. In his description of Clearchus the tyrant
of Heraclea Pontica[59] in Book XXXVIII of his *Histories*
(*FGrH* 115 F 181a), he says that Clearchus murdered
many people violently and gave most of them aconite to
drink. So after everyone became aware of his fondness for
the poison, he claims, they did not leave their houses until
they ate some rue; because this plant keeps those who eat
it ahead of time from being injured if they drink aconite.
He says that it gets its name from the fact that it grows in a
place called Aconae, which is near Heraclea.

After Democritus made these remarks, most of the
group was astonished at the citron's power, and they ate it
up as if they had eaten and drunk nothing before this.
Pamphilus in his *Glossary* (fr. XIV Schmidt) says that the
Romans refer to it as a *kitros*.[60]

Immediately after the items described above, large
quantities of oysters and other shellfish were brought in on
separate platters. Nearly all of these, I find, were deemed
worthy of mention in Epicharmus' *The Wedding of Hebe*,
in the following passage (fr. 40):

> And he brings shellfish of every sort:

[59] Clearchus reigned *c*.364/3–353/2 BCE.
[60] Latin *citrus*.

λεπάδας, ἀσπέδους, κραβύζους, κικιβάλους,
τηθύνια,
κτένια, βαλάνους, πορφύρας, ὄστρεια
d συμμεμυκότα, |
τὰ διελεῖν μέν ἐντι χαλεπά, καταφαγῆμεν δ᾽
εὐμαρέα·
μύας ἀναρίτας τε κάρυκάς τε καὶ σκιφύδρια,
τὰ γλυκέα μέν ἐντ᾽ ἐπέσθειν, ἐμπαγῆμεν δ᾽ ὀξέα,
τούς τε μακρογογγύλους σωλῆνας· ἁ μέλαινά τε
κόγχος, ἅπερ κογχοθηρᾶν παισὶν † εστρισώνια †·
θάτεραι δὲ γάιαι κόγχοι τε κἀμαθίτιδες,
e ταὶ κακοδόκιμοι τε κηῶνοι, | τὰς ἀνδροφυκτίδας
πάντες ἄνθρωποι καλέονθ᾽, ἁμὲς δὲ λεύκας τοὶ
θεοί.

ἐν δὲ Μούσαις γράφεται ἀντὶ τοῦ

<κόγχος, ἅπερ κογχοθηρᾶν παισίν † εστρισώνια †>,

κόγχος, ἂν τέλλιν καλέομες· ἐστὶ δ᾽ ἄδιστον
κρέας.

τὴν τελλίναν δὲ λεγομένην ἴσως δηλοῖ, ἢν Ῥωμαῖοι
μίτλον ὀνομάζουσι. μνημονεύων δ᾽ αὐτῆς Ἀριστοφάνης ὁ γραμματικὸς ἐν τῷ Περὶ τῆς Ἀχνυμένης
Σκυτάλης συγγράμματι ὁμοίας φησὶν εἶναι τὰς λεπάδας ταῖς καλουμέναις τελλίναις. Καλλίας δ᾽ ὁ Μι-

limpets, *aspendoi*, *krabuzoi*, *kikibaloi*[61], sea-squirts,
scallops, barnacles, purple shellfish, tightly closed
  oysters,
which are difficult to pry open but easily gobbled
  down;
mussels, *anaritai*, whelks, and sword-shells,
which are sweet to feast upon but sharp to be
  impaled on;
and the cylindrical razor-shells. Also the black
conch, which is [corrupt] for children of fishermen;
and others that live on land, both conchs and sand-
  dwellers,
which have a bad reputation and are inexpensive, and
  which all human beings
refer to as *androphuktides*, although we gods call
  them white conchs.

In *Muses* he replaces the line

  ‹conch, which is [corrupt] for children of fishermen›

with (fr. 84):

  conch, which we refer to as a *tellis*; the meat is the
    sweetest there is.

Perhaps he is talking about what is called a *tellina*, for
which the Romans use the name *mitlos*.[62] The grammarian
Aristophanes mentions it in his treatise *On the Mournful
Message-Staff* (fr. 367 Slater) and says that limpets resemble the so-called *tellinai*. Callias of Mitylene in his *On the*

---

[61] All probably local Sicilian names.
[62] Latin *mitulus* ("mussel").

f τυληναῖος | ἐν τῷ Περὶ τῆς Παρ' Ἀλκαίῳ Λεπάδος
παρὰ τῷ Ἀλκαίῳ φησὶν εἶναι ᾠδὴν ἧς ἡ ἀρχή·

    πέτρας καὶ πολιᾶς θαλάσ-
      σας τέκνον,

ἧς ἐπὶ τέλει γεγράφθαι·

           ἐκ δὲ παί-
    δων χαύνως φρένας, ἁ θαλασσία λεπάς.

ὁ δ' Ἀριστοφάνης γράφει ἀντὶ τοῦ λεπὰς "χέλυς" καί
φησιν οὐκ εὖ Δικαίαρχον ἐκδεξάμενον λέγειν τὰς
λεπάδας· τὰ παιδάρια δὲ ἡνίκ' ἂν εἰς τὸ στόμα λάβω-
σιν, αὐλεῖν ἐν ταύταις καὶ παίζειν, καθάπερ καὶ παρ'
ἡμῖν τὰ σπερμολόγα τῶν παιδαρίων ταῖς καλουμέναις
86 τελλίναις, ‖ ὡς καὶ Σώπατρός φησιν ὁ φλυακογράφος
ἐν τῷ ἐπιγραφομένῳ δράματι Εὐβουλοθεομβρότῳ·

    ἀλλ' ἴσχε· τελλίνης γὰρ ἐξαίφνης μέ τις
    ἀκοὰς μελῳδὸς ἦχος εἰς ἐμὰς ἔβη.

πάλιν δ' ὁ Ἐπίχαρμος ἐν Πύρρᾳ καὶ Προμαθεῖ φησι·

    τὰν τελλίναν, τὸν ἀναρίταν, θᾶσαι δή, καὶ λεπὰς
      ὄσσα.

παρὰ Σώφρονι δὲ κόγχοι μελαινίδες λέγονται· μελαινίδες γάρ τοι νισοῦντι ἐμὶν ἐκ τοῦ μικροῦ λιμένος. ἐν
b δὲ τῷ ἐπιγραφομένῳ Ὡλιεὺς τὸν | Ἀγροιώταν χη-
ράμβας ὀνομάζει. καὶ Ἀρχίλοχος δὲ τῆς χηράμβης
μέμνηται, τοῦ δ' ἀναρίτου Ἴβυκος. καλεῖται δ' ὁ

472

Limpet in Alcaeus says that one of Alcaeus' songs begins (fr. 359, encompassing both quotations):

> child of the rock
>   and the gray sea,

and the end of the text runs:

>   may you puff up
> the minds of children, sea-limpet.

But Aristophanes writes "tortoise" in place of "limpet," and says that Dicaearchus (fr. 99 Wehrli) was wrong to accept the reading and discuss limpets here: When children put limpets into their mouths, they blow into them and make music, just as street-children do among us with the so-called *tellinai*, as the *phlyax*-author Sopater says in his play entitled *Eubulus the Demigod* (fr. 7):

> But wait! For a melodious sound
> of a *tellinē* came suddenly to my ears.

Again, Epicharmus says in *Pyrrha and Promatheus* (fr. 114):

> Look how big the *tellinē*, the *anarita*, and the limpet
> are!

Melainides conchs[63] are mentioned in Sophron (fr. 96): Because *melainides* are coming to us from the little harbor. And in the mime entitled *The Fisherman and the Farmer* (fr. 43) he refers to *chērambai*. Archilochus (fr. 285 West²) as well mentions the *chērambē*, and Ibycus (*PMG* 321.3)

---

[63] Mussels?

ἀναρίτης καὶ ἀνάρτας. κοχλιῶδες δὲ ὂν τὸ ὄστρεον
προσέχεται ταῖς πέτραις ὥσπερ αἱ λεπάδες. Ἡρώνδας δ᾽ ἐν Συνεργαζομέναις·

προσφὺς ὅκως τις χοιράδων ἀναρίτης.

Αἰσχύλος δ᾽ ἐν † Πέρσαις τις ἀνῄρει † τοὺς νήσους

νηριτοτρόφους

εἴρηκεν. Ὅμηρος δὲ τῶν τηθέων μέμνηται.

Διοκλῆς δ᾽ ὁ Καρύστιος ἐν τοῖς Ὑγιεινοῖς κράτιστά φησιν εἶναι τῶν κογχυλίων πρὸς διαχώρησιν καὶ οὔρησιν μύας, ὄστρεα, κτένας, χήμας. Ἄρχιππος δ᾽ ἐν Ἰχθύσι·

λεπάσιν, ἐχίνοις, ἐσχάραις, βαλάνοις τε τοῖς
κτεσίν τε·

ῥωμαλεώτατα[29] δὲ τῶν κογχυλίων φησὶν εἶναι ὁ Διοκλῆς κόγχας, πορφύρας, κήρυκας. περὶ δὲ τῶν κηρύκων ὁ Ἄρχιππος τάδε λέγει·

< . . . > κῆρυξ θαλάσσης τρόφιμος, υἱὸς
πορφύρας.

Σπεύσιππος δ᾽ ἐν δευτέρῳ Ὁμοίων παραπλήσια εἶναι κήρυκας, πορφύρας, στραβήλους, κόγχους. τῶν στραβήλων μνημονεύει καὶ Σοφοκλῆς ἐν Καμικοῖς οὕτως·

---

[29] ῥωμαλεώτατα Meineke: ῥωμαλεώτερα A: ῥωμαλέα CE

---

[64] The corruption probably conceals the word *nēritēs*, which

mentions the *anaritēs*. The *anaritēs* is also referred to as an *anartas*. The oyster is a snail-like creature that clings to the rocks just like limpets do. Herondas in *Women Working Together* (fr. 11 Cunningham):

> clinging just like an *anaritēs* to the reefs.

Aeschylus says in † *Persians* (fr. 285) [corrupt][64] † the islands

> that nourish *nēritai*.

Homer mentions sea-squirts (*Il.* 16.747).

Diocles of Carystus in his *On Matters of Health* (fr. 223 van der Eijk) says that the best shellfish for encouraging bowel movements and urination are mussels, oysters, scallops, and clams. Archippus in *Fish* (fr. 24):[65]

> limpets, sea-urchins, *escharai*, and barnacles and the scallops.

Diocles says that the shellfish that increase one's strength the most are conchs, purple shellfish, and trumpet-shells. Archippus (fr. 25) says the following about trumpet-shells:

> a trumpet-shell, nursling of the sea, son of a purple shellfish.

Speusippus in Book II of *Similar Things* (fr. 8 Tarán) says that trumpet-shells, purple shellfish, whelks, and conchs are very much alike. Sophocles mentions whelks in *Camicians* (fr. 324), as follows:

was most likely identified as a variant form of *anaritēs*. These words are not found in our text of *Persians*.

[65] Quoted again at 3.90f.

475

ἀλίας στραβήλου τῆσδε, τέκνον, εἴ τινα
δυναίμεθ᾽ εὑρεῖν.

ἔτι ὁ Σπεύσιππος ἑξῆς πάλιν ἰδίᾳ καταριθμεῖται
κόγχους, κτένας, μῦς, πίννας, σωλῆνας, καὶ ἐν ἄλλῳ
μέρει ὄστρεα, λεπάδας. Ἀραρὼς δὲ Καμπυλίωνί φησι·

τὰ κομψὰ ⟨μὲν⟩[30] δὴ ταῦτα νωγαλεύματα,
κόγχαι τε καὶ σωλῆνες αἵ τε καμπύλαι
καρῖδες ἐξήλλοντο δελφίνων δίκην.

e Σώφρων δ᾽ ἐν Μίμοις· | (Α.) τίνες δέ ἐντί ποκα, φίλα,
τοίδε τοὶ μακροὶ κόγχοι; (Β.) σωλῆνές θην τουτοί γα,
γλυκύκρεον κογχύλιον, χηρᾶν γυναικῶν λίχνευμα.
τῶν δὲ πιννῶν μνημονεύει Κρατῖνος ἐν Ἀρχιλόχοις·

ἢ μὲν δὴ πίννῃσι καὶ ὀστρείοισιν ὁμοίη.

Φιλύλλιος δ᾽ ἢ Εὔνικος[31] ἢ Ἀριστοφάνης ἐν Πόλεσι·

πουλυπόδειον, σηπιδάριον, κάραβον, ἀστακόν,
  ὄστρειον,
χήμας, λεπάδας, σωλῆνας, μῦς, πίννας, κτένας
f   ἐκ Μιτυλήνης· |
  † αἴρετ᾽ ἀνθρακίδας † τρίγλη, σαργός, κεστρεύς,
  πέρκη, κορακῖνοι.

Ἀγίας δὲ καὶ Δερκύλος ἐν Ἀργολικοῖς τοὺς στραβήλους ἀστραβήλους ὀνομάζουσι, μνημονεύοντες αὐτῶν ὡς ἐπιτηδείων ὄντων εἰς τὸ σαλπίζειν. τὰς δὲ

---

[30] cf. 2.47d   [31] Εὔνικος Schweighäuser: δύνικος A

of this sea-whelk, my child, if we
could find any . . .

Furthermore, Speusippus (fr. 8 Tarán, continued) again
lists individually in order conchs, scallops, mussels, pinnas,
and razor-shells; and in another class oysters and limpets.
Araros says in *Campulion* (fr. 8.1–3):[66]

these elegant dainties,
and snails and razor-shells and curved
shrimp, leapt out like dolphins.

Sophron in the *Mimes* (fr. 23): (A.) What in the world, my
dear, are these big conchs? (B.) These are razor-shells, a
sweet-fleshed little shellfish and a delicacy for widows.
Cratinus mentions pinnas in *Archilochuses* (fr. 8):

certainly [a woman] resembling pinnas and oysters.

Philyllius (fr. 12) or Eunicus or Aristophanes in *Cities*:

a little octopus, a little squid, a crayfish, a lobster, an
     oyster,
clams, limpets, razor-shells, mussels, pinnas,
     Mytilenean scallops.
† Hand me small-fry † a red mullet, a sargue, a grey
     mullet, a perch, a crow-fish.

Agias and Dercylus in the *History of Argos* (*FGrH* 305 F 3)
call whelks (*strabēloi*) *astrabēloi* and mention that they are
useful for trumpeting. The word "conch" can be found in

66 Other portions of the fragment are quoted at 2.47d; 3.105e.

κόγχας ἔστιν εὑρεῖν λεγομένας καὶ θηλυκῶς καὶ ἀρσενικῶς. Ἀριστοφάνης Βαβυλωνίοις·

87   ἀνέχασκον εἷς ἕκαστος ἐμφερέστατα ‖
       ὀπτωμέναις κόγχαισιν ἐπὶ τῶν ἀνθράκων.

Τηλεκλείδης δ' ἐν Ἡσιόδοις, κόγχη, φησί, διελεῖν. καὶ Σώφρων Γυναικείοις· ταί γα μὰν κόγχαι, ὥσπερ αἴ κ' ἐξ ἑνὸς κελεύματος κεχάναντι ἁμὶν πᾶσαι, τὸ δὲ κρῆς ἑκάστας ἐξέχει. ἀρσενικῶς δ' Αἰσχύλος ἐν Ποντίῳ Γλαύκῳ·

       κόγχοι, μύες κὤστρεια.

Ἀριστώνυμος Θησεῖ· † κόγχος ἦν βάπτων ἄλλων
b   ὁμοίως †. | παραπλησίως δ' εἴρηκε καὶ Φρύνιχος Σατύροις.

   Ἱκέσιος δὲ ὁ Ἐρασιστράτειος τῶν χημῶν φησι τὰς μὲν τραχείας λέγεσθαι, τὰς δὲ ‹λείας› βασιλικάς. καὶ τὰς μὲν τραχείας[32] κακοχύλους εἶναι, ὀλιγοτρόφους, εὐεκκρίτους, χρῆσθαι δὲ αὐταῖς καὶ δελέασι τοὺς πορφυρευομένους· τῶν δὲ λείων κατὰ τὰ μεγέθη καὶ τὰς διαφορὰς εἶναι κρατίστας. Ἡγήσανδρος δ' ἐν Ὑπομνήμασι τὰς τραχείας φησὶ κόγχας ὑπὸ μὲν Μακεδόνων κωρύκους καλεῖσθαι, ὑπὸ δὲ Ἀθηναίων
c   κριούς. τὰς δὲ λεπάδας | ὁ Ἱκέσιος τῶν προειρημένων

   [32] τραχείας καὶ ACE

both the masculine and the feminine.[67] Aristophanes in *Babylonians* (fr. 67):

> They all had their mouths wide open, as if they were conchs (fem.) roasting on the coals.

Teleclides says in *Hesiods* (fr. 20, unmetrical): a conch to pry open. Also Sophron in the *Women's Mimes* (fr. 24): Indeed, the conchs (fem.), as if at one command, have all opened wide for us, and the flesh of every one is sticking out. But Aeschylus has the word in the masculine in *Glaucus of the Sea* (fr. 34):

> conchs, mussels, and oysters.

Aristonymus in *Theseus* (fr. 1, unmetrical): † a conch (masc.) was dipping of others simultaneously †. Phrynichus says something similar in *Satyrs* (fr. 51).

Erasistratus' student Hicesius says that some clams are called "rough," while the smooth ones are called "royal." The rough ones produce bad *chulē*, are not very nourishing, are easily excreted, and are used as bait by fishermen trying to catch purple shellfish; as for the smooth variety, the larger they are, the more pronounced their outstanding characteristics. Hegesander in his *Commentaries* (fr. 36, *FHG* iv.420) says that the Macedonians refer to rough conchs as *kōrukoi* (literally "bags, pouchs"), whereas the Athenians refer to them as *krioi* (literally "rams"). Hicesius

---

[67] In the quotations from Teleclides and Aeschylus, the gender of the word is in fact impossible to determine, although in the first case it is certainly 1st-declension (and thus most likely feminine), while in the second it is 2nd-declension (and thus most likely masculine).

εὐεκκρίτους μᾶλλον εἶναι, τὰ δ᾽ ὄστρεα ἀτροφώτερά τε τούτων καὶ πλήσμια εὐεκκριτώτερά τε[33]. οἱ δὲ κτένες τροφιμώτεροι μέν εἰσι, κακοχυλότεροι δὲ καὶ δυσεκκριτώτεροι. τῶν δὲ μυῶν οἱ μὲν Ἐφέσιοι καὶ οἱ τούτοις ὅμοιοι τῇ εὐχυλίᾳ τῶν μὲν κτενῶν βελτίονες, τῶν δὲ χημῶν λειπόμενοι· οὐρητικώτεροι δὲ μᾶλλον ἢ ἐπὶ τὴν κοιλίαν φερόμενοι. εἰσὶ δ᾽ αὐτῶν ἔνιοι καὶ σκιλλώδεις d κακόχυλοί τε καὶ πρὸς τὴν γεῦσιν ἀπειθεῖς. | οἱ δ᾽ ἐλάσσονες τούτων καὶ δασεῖς ἔξωθεν οὐρητικώτεροι μέν εἰσι καὶ εὐχυλότεροι τῶν σκιλλωδῶν, ἀτροφώτεροι δέ, διά τε τὸ μέγεθος καὶ τῷ γένει ὄντες τοιοῦτοι. οἱ δὲ τῶν κηρύκων τράχηλοι εὐστόμαχοί τέ εἰσι καὶ ἀτροφώτεροι μυῶν τε καὶ χημῶν καὶ κτενῶν· τοῖς δ᾽ ἀσθενῆ τὸν στόμαχον ἔχουσι καὶ μὴ ῥᾳδίως ἀποδιωθοῦσι τὴν τροφὴν εἰς τὸ κύτος τῆς κοιλίας χρήσιμοι, δύσφθαρτοί τε ὄντες. τὰ γὰρ ὁμολογουμένως εὔπεπτα e κατὰ τοὐναντίον ἀλλότρια | τῆς διαθέσεως ταύτης ἐστίν, εὐχερῶς διαφθειρόμενα διὰ τὸ ἁπαλὰ καὶ εὐδιάλυτα εἶναι. ὅθεν αἱ μήκωνες αὐτῶν πρὸς μὲν τὰς τῶν στομάχων εὐτονίας οὐκ εὐθετοῦσι, πρὸς δὲ τὴν τῆς κοιλίας ἀσθένειαν χρήσιμοι. τροφιμώτεραι δὲ τούτων εἰσὶ καὶ ἀπολαυστικώτεραι αἱ τῆς πορφύρας μήκωνες, πλὴν σκιλλωδέστεραι ὑπάρχουσι· καὶ γὰρ ὅλον τὸ κογχύλιον τοιοῦτόν ἐστιν. ἴδιον δὲ καὶ ταύταις καὶ τοῖς σωλῆσι παρέπεται τὸ ἑψομέναις παχὺν ποιεῖν f τὸν ζωμόν. ἑψόμενοι δὲ | τὸ καθ᾽ ἑαυτοὺς καὶ οἱ τράχηλοι τῶν πορφυρῶν εὐθετοῦσι πρὸς τὰς τῶν στομάχων διαθέσεις. μνημονεύει δ᾽ αὐτῶν Ποσείδιππος

says that limpets are more easily excreted than the creatures discussed above, and that oysters are less nourishing than limpets, filling, and more easily excreted. Scallops are more nourishing, but produce inferior *chulē* and are not as easily excreted. Ephesian mussels and the other varieties that resemble them produce better *chulē* than scallops do, but are inferior to clams; they promote urination rather than bowel movements. Some are squill-like, produce bad *chulē*, and have an uninviting taste. The smaller ones that are rough on the outside are more diuretic and produce better *chulē* than the squill-like variety, but are less nourishing, both because of their size and because this is their nature. Trumpet-shell "necks" are easy on the stomach and less nourishing than mussels, clams, and scallops. They are useful for individuals with weak stomachs who have difficulty moving their food into their digestive tract, although they are also prone to corruption; for foods that are generally acknowledged to be easily digested are, on the principle of opposition, inimical to this condition, since they are easily corrupted due to being soft and easily broken down. This is why their "livers" are inappropriate for stomachs that are in good condition, but useful for weak bowels. The "livers" of purple shellfish are more nourishing and more enjoyable than those of trumpet-shells, except that they are more squill-like; in fact the entire creature is like this. A unique characteristic of purple shellfish and razor-shells is that they thicken the broth they are stewed in. The "necks" of purple shellfish stewed by themselves are appropriate for stomach conditions. Posidippus

---

[33] τε τούτων ACE ("alterum utrum τούτων delendum" Kaibel)

ἐν Λοκρίσιν οὕτως·

> ὥρα περαίνειν· ἐγχέλεια, καράβους,
> κόγχας, ἐχίνους προσφάτους, μηκώνια,
> πίνας, τραχήλους, μύας.

αἱ βάλανοι δ᾽ εἰ μείζονες, εὐέκκριτοι καὶ εὐστόμαχοι[34]. τὰ δ᾽ ὠτάρια—γίνεται δὲ ταῦτα κἄν τῇ κατὰ τὴν Ἀλεξάνδρειαν λεγομένη Φάρῳ νήσῳ— ‖ τροφιμώτερα τῶν προειρημένων ἁπάντων, οὐκ εὐέκκριτα δέ. Ἀντίγονος δ᾽ ὁ Καρύστιος ἐν τῷ Περὶ Λέξεως τὸ ὄστρεον τοῦτο ὑπὸ Αἰολέων καλεῖσθαι οὓς Ἀφροδίτης. αἱ δὲ φωλάδες πολυτροφώτεραι, βρομώδεις δέ· τὰ δὲ τήθη παραπλήσια τοῖς προειρημένοις καὶ πολυτροφώτερα. γίνεται δέ τινα καὶ ἄγρια λεγόμενα ὄστρεα· πολύτροφα δ᾽ ἐστὶ καὶ βρομώδη προσέτι τε εὐτελῆ κατὰ τὴν γεῦσιν. Ἀριστοτέλης δ᾽ ἐν τῷ Περὶ Ζῴων, ὄστρεα, φησίν, πίνα, ὄστρεον, μῦς, ǀ κτείς, σωλήν, κόγχη, λεπάς, τῆθος, βάλανος. πορευτικὰ δὲ κῆρυξ, πορφύρα, ἡδυπορφύρα, ἐχῖνος, στράβηλος. ἐστὶ δ᾽ ὁ μὲν κτεὶς τραχυόστρακος, ῥαβδωτός, τὸ δὲ τῆθος ἀράβδωτον, λειόστρακον, ἡ δὲ πίνη λεπτόστομον, τὸ δὲ ὄστρεον παχύστομον, δίθυρον[35] δὲ καὶ λειόστρακον, λεπὰς δὲ μονόθυρον[36] καὶ λειόστρακον, συμφυὲς δὲ μῦς, μονοφυὲς δὲ καὶ λειόστρακον σωλὴν καὶ βάλανος, κοινὸν δ᾽ ἐξ ἀμφοῖν κόγχη. τὸ δ᾽ ἐντὸς τῆς πίνης Ἐπαίνετος ǀ ἐν Ὀψαρτυτικῷ καλεῖσθαί φησι μήκωνα. ἐν δὲ πέμ-

---

[34] εὐστόμαχοι CE: εὔστομοι A

mentions them in *Locrian Women* (fr. 15), as follows:

> It's time to conclude: eels, crayfish,
> conchs, fresh-caught sea-urchins, "livers,"
> pinnas, "necks," mussels.

Large barnacles are easily excreted and easy on the stomach. Ormers—they are also produced on the island called Pharos in Alexandria—are more nourishing than any of the creatures discussed above, but are not easily excreted. Antigonus of Carystus in his *On Diction* (p. 174 Wilamowitz) says that the Aeolians call this shellfish an "Ear of Aphrodite." *Phōlades* (literally "hole-dwellers") are more nourishing, but have a nasty smell. Sea-squirts resemble the creatures discussed above and are more nourishing. There are also certain so-called "wild" shellfish; they are very nourishing and have a nasty smell, as well as a poor flavor. Aristotle says in his *Zoology* (fr. 182): Shellfish: pinna, oyster, mussel, scallop, razor-shell, conch, limpet, sea-squirt, barnacle. Those that move: trumpet-shells, purple shellfish, sweet purple shellfish, sea-urchin, whelk. The scallop has a rough, ribbed shell; the sea-squirt has a smooth, ribless shell; the pinna has a small mouth; the oyster has a wide mouth and a smooth, bivalve shell; the limpet has a single smooth shell; the mussel has an attached shell; the razor-shell and the barnacle have a single smooth shell; and the conch shares properties of both. Epaenetus in the *Art of Cooking* says that the interior of the pinna

---

35 δίθυρον Gesner: μονόθυρον A
36 μονόθυρον Gesner: δίθυρον A

πτω Ζῴων Μορίων ὁ Ἀριστοτέλης, γίνονται, φησίν, αἱ
μὲν πορφύραι περὶ τὸ ἔαρ, οἱ δὲ κήρυκες λήγοντος τοῦ
χειμῶνος. ὅλως δέ, φησί, τὰ ὀστρακόδερμα ἐν τῷ ἔαρι
φαίνεται ἔχοντα τὰ καλούμενα ᾠά, κἂν τῷ μετοπώρῳ
δὲ πλὴν τῶν ἐχίνων τῶν ἐδωδίμων. οὗτοι δὲ μάλιστα
μὲν ἐν ταύταις ταῖς ὥραις αἰεί τε ἰσχύουσι καὶ τὸ
πλέον ἐν ταῖς πανσελήνοις καὶ ταῖς ἀλεειναῖς ἡμέραις
d πλὴν τῶν ἐν τῷ Εὐρίπῳ τῶν Πυρραίων· | ἐκεῖνοι δ᾽
ἀμείνονες τοῦ χειμῶνος καί εἰσι μικροί, πλήρεις δὲ
ᾠῶν. κύοντες δὲ φαίνονται καὶ οἱ κοχλίαι πάντες
ὁμοίως τὴν αὐτὴν ὥραν[37]. προελθὼν δὲ πάλιν φησὶν ὁ
φιλόσοφος· αἱ μὲν οὖν πορφύραι τοῦ ἔαρος συναθροι-
ζόμεναι εἰς τὸ αὐτὸ ποιοῦσι τὴν καλουμένην μελίκη-
ραν, ἀλλ᾽ οὐχ οὕτως γλαφυρόν, ὥσπερ ἂν εἰ ἐκ λεπύ-
ρων ἐρεβίνθων λευκῶν πολλὰ συμπαγείη. ἔχει δὲ
e ἀνεῳγμένον οὐδὲν τούτων, οὐδὲ γίνονται ἐκ | τούτων αἱ
πορφύραι, ἀλλὰ φύονται αὗται καὶ τὰ ἄλλα ὀστρακόδερμα ἐξ ἰλύος καὶ σήψεως. τοῦτο δὲ συμβαίνει ὥσπερ
ἀποκάθαρμα καὶ ταύταις καὶ τοῖς κήρυξι· κηριάζουσι
γὰρ καὶ οὗτοι. ἀφιᾶσι δ᾽ ἀρχόμεναι κηριάζειν γλι-
σχρότητα μυξώδη, ἐξ ὧν τὰ λεπυρώδη συνίσταται.
ταῦτα μὲν οὖν ἅπαντα διαχεῖται, ἀφιᾶσι δ᾽ ἰχῶρα εἰς
τὴν γῆν· καὶ ἐν τούτῳ τῷ τόπῳ γίνεται ἐν τῇ γῇ
συστάντα πορφύρια μικρά, ἃ ἔχουσαι ἁλίσκονται αἱ
f πορφύραι. ἐὰν δὲ πρὶν ἐκτεκεῖν ἁλῶσιν, ἐνίοτε | ἐν ταῖς
φορμίσιν, εἰς δὲ ταὐτὸ συνιοῦσαι ἐκτίκτουσι, καὶ γίνε-

---

[37] ὥραν Aristotle: ὥ A

is referred to as the "liver." In Book V of *Parts of Animals* Aristotle (*HA* 544ᵃ15–24) says: Purple shellfish come into being around springtime, while trumpet-shells do so at the end of winter. In general, he says, the testacea are observed carrying their so-called eggs in the spring, as well as in the fall. The exception is the edible sea-urchin, which carries the most eggs at these seasons, but always has some, especially during full moons and on sunny days; those in the Strait of Pyrrha are an exception. Sea-urchins are better in the winter, when they are small but full of eggs. Snails too are all observed to be pregnant at the same time. And further on the philosopher says again (*HA* 546ᵇ18–547ᵃ13): The purple shellfish, then, gather together in one spot in the spring and produce the so-called honeycomb, which is not, however, as smooth as honeycomb, but more like a large number of white chickpea-husks compacted together. None of the cells has an opening, and the purple shellfish do not come into being out of them; instead, they and the other testacea are produced from slime and putrefying matter. The honeycomb is like something excreted by purple shellfish and trumpet-shells; for trumpet-shells produce it too. They begin the process of honeycombing by emitting a sticky mucous substance, from which the husk-like material congeals. This substance, then, all pours out, and they emit a fluid into the earth; in this spot tiny purple shellfish form in the earth. These are what the adults are carrying when they are caught. If they are caught before spawning occurs, they sometimes gather together and spawn in the fish-baskets, and something resembling a grape-cluster is produced.

ται οἱονεὶ βότρυς. ἐστὶ δὲ τῶν πορφυρῶν γένη πλείο-
να· καὶ ἔνιαι μὲν μεγάλαι, οἷον αἱ περὶ τὸ Σίγειον καὶ
τὸ Λεκτόν, αἱ δὲ μικραί, οἷον ἐν τῷ Εὐρίπῳ καὶ περὶ
Καρίαν. καὶ αἱ μὲν ἐν τοῖς κόλποις μεγάλαι καὶ
89 τραχεῖαι, ‖ καὶ τὸ ἄνθος αἱ μὲν πλεῖσται μέλαν
ἔχουσιν, ἔνιαι δ᾽ ἐρυθρὸν μικρόν. γίνονται δ᾽ ἔνιαι τῶν
μεγάλων καὶ μναῖαι. αἱ δ᾽ ἐν τοῖς αἰγιαλοῖς καὶ περὶ
τὰς ἀκτὰς τὸ μὲν μέγεθός εἰσι μικραί, τὸ δὲ ἄνθος
ἐρυθρὸν ἔχουσιν. ἔτι δ᾽ ἐν μὲν τοῖς προσβόρροις
μέλαιναι, ἐν δὲ τοῖς νοτίοις ἐρυθραὶ ὡς ἐπὶ τὸ πλεῖστον. Ἀπολλόδωρος δ᾽ ὁ Ἀθηναῖος ἐν τοῖς Περὶ Σώ-
φρονος προθεὶς τὸ[38] "λιχνοτέρα τᾶν προφυρᾶν" φησὶν
ὅτι παροιμία ἐστὶν καὶ λέγει, ὡς μέν τινες, ἀπὸ τοῦ
b βάμματος· οὗ γὰρ ἂν | προσψαύσῃ ἕλκει ἐφ᾽ ἑαυτὸ καὶ
τοῖς προσπαρατεθειμένοις ἐμποιεῖ χρώματος αὐγήν·
ἄλλοι δ᾽ ἀπὸ τοῦ ζῴου. ἁλίσκονται δέ, φησὶν ὁ Ἀριστοτέλης, τοῦ ἔαρος, ὑπὸ κύνα δ᾽ οὐχ ἁλίσκονται· οὐ
γὰρ νέμονται, ἀλλὰ κρύπτουσιν ἑαυτὰς καὶ φωλεύουσι. τὸ δὲ ἄνθος ἔχουσιν ἀνὰ μέσον τῆς μήκωνος καὶ
τοῦ τραχήλου. ἔχει δὲ καὶ αὐτὴ καὶ ὁ κῆρυξ τὰ
ἐπικαλύμματα κατὰ τὰ αὐτὰ καὶ τὰ ἄλλα τὰ στρομ-
βώδη, ἐκ γενετῆς πάντα. νέμονται δ᾽ ἐξείροντα τὴν
c καλουμένην | γλῶτταν ὑπὸ τὸ κάλυμμα. τὸ δὲ μέγεθος
τῆς γλώσσης ἔχει ἡ πορφύρα μεῖζον δακτύλου, ᾧ
νέμεται καὶ διατρυπᾷ καὶ τὰ κογχύλια καὶ τὸ ἑαυτῆς
ὄστρακον. μακρόβια δ᾽ ἐστὶν καὶ ἡ πορφύρα καὶ ὁ

___

[38] τὸ Musurus: τὰ A

There are many varieties of purple shellfish. Some are large, such as those around Sigeum and Lectum; others are small, such as those found in the Euripus and on the Carian coast. Those found in bays are large and rough, and most have a dark "flower,"[68] although in some it is small and red. Some of the large ones weigh a mina.[69] Those found on beachs and along headlands are small in size and have a red "flower." Furthermore, those found in areas that face north are dark-colored, whereas in places that face south they are generally red. Apollodorus of Athens in his *On Sophron* (*FGrH* 244 F 216) gives the lemma "greedier than purple shellfish" (Sophr. fr. 62) and says that this is a proverb according to some authorities drawn from dyeing; because dye attracts whatever it touches and infects anything set next to it with a sheen of color. But other authorities say that the allusion is to the animal. Aristotle (*HA* 547ª13–16, ᵇ3–18) says: They are caught in the spring, but not when the dog-star has risen,[70] because they do not feed then and instead hide themselves away in holes. Their "flower" is located between the "liver" and the "neck." Both the purple shellfish and the trumpet-shell have the same sort of opercula as other spiral-shelled creatures, and have them all from the time they are generated. They feed by extending their so-called tongue under the operculum. As for the size of the tongue, the purple shellfish has one that is larger than a man's finger; it uses it to feed and to bore into other shellfish, including its own kind. The purple shellfish and the trumpet-shell are both long-lived and

---

[68] The part of the creature that contains the dye.

[69] About one pound.

[70] I.e. at mid-summer.

κῆρυξ καὶ ζῇ περὶ ἔτη ἕξ. φανερὰ δὲ ἡ αὔξησις ἐκ τῆς
ἐν τῷ ὀστράκῳ ἕλικος. αἱ δὲ κόγχαι καὶ χῆμαι καὶ
σωλῆνες καὶ κτένες ἐν τοῖς ἀμμώδεσι λαμβάνουσι τὴν
σύστασιν. αἱ δὲ πίναι ὀρθαὶ φύονται ἐκ τοῦ βυθοῦ
d ἔχουσί τε ἐν αὐταῖς τὸν πινοφύλακα | αἱ μὲν καρίδιον,
αἱ δὲ καρκίνιον· οὗ στερόμεναι θᾶττον διαφθείρονται.
τοῦτο δὲ Πάμφιλος ὁ Ἀλεξανδρεὺς ἐν τοῖς Περὶ Ὀνομάτων συμπεφυκέναι φησὶν αὐταῖς. Χρύσιππος δ᾽ ὁ
Σολεὺς ἐκ τοῦ πέμπτου Περὶ τοῦ Καλοῦ καὶ τῆς
Ἡδονῆς· ἡ πίννη, φησίν, καὶ ὁ πιννοτήρης συνεργὰ
ἀλλήλοις, κατ᾽ ἰδίαν οὐ δυνάμενα συμμένειν. ἡ μὲν
e οὖν πίννη ὄστρεόν ἐστιν, ὁ | δὲ πιννοτήρης καρκίνος
μικρός. καὶ ἡ πίννη διαστήσασα τὸ ὄστρακον ἡσυ-
χάζει τηροῦσα τὰ ἐπεισιόντα ἰχθύδια, ὁ δὲ πιννοτήρης παρεστὼς ὅταν εἰσέλθῃ τι δάκνει αὐτὴν ὥσπερ
σημαίνων, ἡ δὲ δηχθεῖσα συμμύει. καὶ οὕτως τὸ
ἀποληφθὲν ἔνδον κατεσθίουσι κοινῇ. φασὶ δέ τινες
καὶ συγγεννᾶσθαι αὐτὰ αὑτοῖς καὶ ὡς ἂν ἐξ ἑνὸς
σπέρματος γίνεσθαι. πάλιν δὲ ὁ Ἀριστοτέλης φησί·
πάντα δὲ τὰ ὀστρακώδη γίνεται καὶ ἐν τῇ ἰλύι, ἐν μὲν
τῇ βορβορώδει τὰ ὄστρεα, ἐν δὲ τῇ ἀμμώδει κόγχαι
καὶ τὰ ῥηθέντα, περὶ δὲ τὰς σήραγγας τῶν πετρῶν
τήθεα καὶ βάλανοι καὶ τὰ ἐπιπολάζοντα, οἷον λεπάδες
f | καὶ νηρῖται. τὸν αὐτὸν δὲ τρόπον γίνεται τοῖς ὀστρα-
κοδέρμοις καὶ τὰ μὴ ἔχοντα ὄστρακα, καθάπερ αἵ τε
κνίδαι καὶ οἱ σπόγγοι ἐν ταῖς σήραγξι τῶν πετρῶν.
ἐστὶ δὲ τῶν κνιδῶν δύο γένη· αἱ μὲν γὰρ ἐν τοῖς
κοίλοις οὐκ ἀπολύονται τῶν πετρῶν, αἱ δ᾽ ἐν τοῖς

live for about six years. Their growth is discernible from the spiral of their shells. Conchs, clams, razor-shells, and scallops form in sandy places. Pinnas grow upright from the sea-floor and have inside them the pinna-guard, which may be a small shrimp or a small crab; if they are deprived of it, they quickly die. Pamphilus of Alexandria in his *On Names* (fr. XXVII Schmidt) says that the pinna-guard is generated along with the pinna. Chrysippus of Soli, from Book V of *On the Good and Pleasure* (fr. 728 Casevitz): The pinna, he says, and the pinna-guard cooperate with one another and cannot survive separately. The pinna is a testacean, whereas the pinna-guard is a small crab. The pinna opens its shell and remains still, waiting for small fish to approach; the pinna-guard stands by and nips it, as if giving it a signal, when something goes in; and after the pinna is nipped, it closes. In this way they consume whatever is caught inside together. Some authorities say that they are born together, as if from a single seed. Aristotle (*HA* 547^{b}18–23, 548^{a}24–7) again says: All testacea are generated in slime; oysters in muddy slime, conchs and the other creatures mentioned in sandy slime, and sea-squirts, barnacles, and the more common types, such as limpets and *nēritai*, in hollows in the rocks. The creatures that lack shells are generated in the same way as testacea, as for example sea-anemones and sponges in hollows in the rocks. There are two varieties of sea-anemone. Some are found in hollow places and cling to the rocks, whereas others are

λείοις καὶ πλαταμώδεσιν ἀπολυόμεναι μεταχωροῦσι.
τὰς δὲ κνίδας ὁ Εὔπολις ἐν Αὐτολύκῳ ἀκαλήφας
90 ὀνομάζει ‖ ἔτι τε Ἀριστοφάνης ἐν Φοινίσσαις οὕτως·

ἔχε τὸν[39]
πρῶτον ἁπάντων ἴφυα φῦναι.

εἶθ᾽ ἑξῆς·

< . . . > τὰς κραναὰς ἀκαλήφας.

καὶ ἐν Σφηξί. Φερεκράτης δ᾽ ἐν Αὐτομόλοις·

< . . . > κἂν ἀκαλήφαις τὸν ἴσον χρόνον
ἐστεφανῶσθαι.

Δίφιλος δ᾽ ὁ Σίφνιος ἰατρός, ἡ δὲ ἀκαλήφη, φησίν,
ἐστὶν εὐκοίλιος, οὐρητική, εὐστόμαχος· κνησμὸν δὲ
ποιεῖ τοῖς συνάγουσιν, ἐπειδὰν μὴ προαλείψωνται.
ὄντως γὰρ ἀνιᾷ τοὺς θηρεύοντας αὐτήν· ὑφ᾽ ὧν κατὰ
παραφθορὰν νῦν ἀκαλήφη ὀνομάζεται· τάχα δὲ ἴσως
b διὰ | ταύτην καὶ ἡ βοτάνη· κατ᾽ εὐφημισμὸν γὰρ τῆς
ἀντιφράσεως ὠνόμασται· οὐ γὰρ πραεῖά ἐστιν καὶ
ἀκαλὴ[40] τῇ ἁφῇ, τραχεῖα δὲ καὶ ἀηδής. τῆς μέντοι
θαλασσίας ἀκαλήφης μνημονεύει καὶ Φιλιππίδης ἐν
Ἀμφιαράῳ οὕτως·

[39] All other witnesses have εἰκὸς δήπου.
[40] ἀκαλὴ Kaibel: ἁπαλὴ A

490

found in smooth, level spots, and let go and move around.
Eupolis refers to sea-anemones as nettles *(akalēphai)* in
Autolycus (fr. 68), as does Aristophanes in *Phoenician
Women* (fr. 572.1–2), as follows:

> Understand that
> the first plant to grow was spike-lavender.

Then immediately after that (fr. 572.3):

> the rough *akalēphai*.[71]

Likewise in *Wasps* (884). Pherecrates in *Deserters* (fr.
29.2):

> even to be garlanded with *akalēphai* for an equal
> amount of time.

The physician Diphilus of Siphnos says: The sea-anemone
(akalēphē) is easy on the bowels, diuretic, and easy on the
stomach. It irritates the skin of those who gather it, unless
they oil themselves beforehand. The sea-anemone does in
fact injure those who hunt it, and they refer to it today as an
akalēphē through a process of corruption; it may be that
the plant too gets its name this way. It got its name via a eu-
phemism, in which a term is replaced by its opposite; because it is not soft and peaceful to the touch[72], but rough
and unpleasant. Philippides, moreover, mentions the sea-
akalēphē in *Amphiaraus* (fr. 4), as follows:

---

[71] Despite Athenaeus, the word most likely means "nettles"
rather than "sea-anemones" here, as also in the fragment of
Pherecrates quoted below.

[72] *akalē tēi haphēi*, whence supposedly the name *akalēphē*.

ὄστρε᾽, ἀκαλήφας ⟨καὶ⟩ λεπάδας παρέθηκέ μοι.

τὸ δ᾽ ἐν Λυσιστράτῃ Ἀριστοφάνους πέπαικται·

ἀλλ᾽ ὦ τηθῶν ἀνδρειοτάτη καὶ μητριδίων
ἀκαληφῶν.

c ἐπεὶ τήθεα τὰ ὄστρεα· μέμικται γὰρ κωμῳδικῶς | πρὸς
τὴν τήθην καὶ μητέρα. καὶ περὶ τῶν ἄλλων ὀστρέων ὁ
Δίφιλος τάδε φησί· χημῶν δὲ τῶν τραχειῶν αἱ μικραὶ
καὶ λεπτὴν ἔχουσαι τὴν σάρκα ὄστρεα λέγονται καὶ
εὐστόμαχοί εἰσι καὶ εὐέκκριτοι· αἱ δὲ λεῖαι[41], βασιλικαὶ δὲ πρός τινων καλούμεναι πελώριαί τε λεγόμεναι,
τρόφιμοι, δυσέκκριτοι, εὔχυλοι, εὐστόμαχοι, καὶ μάλιστα αἱ μείζους. τελλῖναι γίνονται μὲν ἐν Κανώβῳ
πολλαὶ καὶ ὑπὸ τὴν τοῦ Νείλου ἀνάβασιν πληθύ-
ουσιν. ὧν λεπτότεραι μέν εἰσιν αἱ βασιλικαὶ διαχω-
d ρητικαί | τε καὶ κοῦφαι, ἔτι δὲ καὶ τρόφιμοι, αἱ δὲ
ποτάμιαι γλυκύτεραι. οἱ δὲ μύες μέσως εἰσὶ τρόφιμοι,
διαχωρητικοί, οὐρητικοί· κράτιστοι δὲ οἱ Ἐφέσιοι καὶ
τούτων οἱ φθινοπωρινοί. αἱ δὲ μύϊσκαι τῶν μυῶν
οὖσαι μικρότεραι γλυκεῖαί τε καὶ εὔχυλοί εἰσι προσέτι τε καὶ τρόφιμοι. οἱ δὲ σωλῆνες μὲν πρός τινων
καλούμενοι, πρός τινων δὲ αὐλοὶ καὶ δόνακες καὶ
ὄνυχες, πολύχυλοι καὶ κακόχυλοι, κολλώδεις. καὶ οἱ

[41] λεῖαι Schneider: παχεῖαι ACE

BOOK III

He served me oysters, sea-anemones *(akalēphas)*, and
limpets.

The passage in Aristophanes' *Lysistrata* (549) represents a
play on words:

O most manly of sea-squirts *(tēthea)* and nettle-
mommies *(mētridia);*

since sea-squirts are a type of shellfish, and he has created
a comic jumble involving the words *tēthē* ("grandmother")
and *mētēr* ("mother"). Concerning the other types of shellfish, Diphilus says the following: Small, rough clams with
delicate flesh are called oysters and are easy on the stomach and easily excreted. Smooth clams, which are referred
to as royal clams by some authorities and are also called giant *(pelōriai)*[73] clams, are nourishing, difficult to excrete,
productive of good *chulē*, and easy on the stomach; this is
particularly true of the larger ones. *Tellinai* are found in
large numbers in Canobus and are abundant when the
Nile is rising. Royal clams are more delicate than these,
encourage bowel movements, and are light but also nourishing, whereas river-clams are sweeter. Mussels are moderately nourishing, encourage bowel movements, and are
diuretic. The ones from Ephesus are best, particularly
those gathered in the fall. *Muiskai*[74] are smaller than mussels and are sweet and productive of good *chulē*, as well
as nourishing. What are referred to as *sōlēnes* ("razor-
clams") by some authorities, but as *auloi* ("pipes"),
donakes ("reeds"), or *onuches* ("fingernails") by others,
produce a great deal of bad *chulē* and are glutinous. Male

[73] Cf. 3.92f *pelōrides*.   [74] Diminutive of *mus* ("mussel").

μὲν ἄρρενες αὐτῶν ῥαβδωτοί εἰσι καὶ οὐ μονοχρώ-
e ματοι· εἰσὶ δὲ τοῖς λιθιῶσι | καὶ ἄλλοις δυσουροῦσιν
εὔθετοι. οἱ δὲ θήλεις μονοχρώματοί τέ εἰσι καὶ γλυκύτεροι. λαμβάνονται δὲ ἐφθοὶ καὶ τηγανιστοί· κρείτ-
τονες δ᾽ εἰσὶν οἱ μέχρι τοῦ χανεῖν ἐπ᾽ ἀνθράκων
ὀπτώμενοι. σωληνισταὶ δ᾽ ἐκαλοῦντο οἱ συνάγοντες
τὰ ὄστρεα ταῦτα, ὡς ἱστορεῖ Φαινίας ὁ Ἐρέσιος ἐν
τῷ ἀπιγραφομᾱνῳ Τυράννων Ἀναίρεσις Ἐκ Τιμωρίας
γράφων οὕτως· Φιλόξενος ὁ καλούμενος σωληνιστὴς
ἐκ δημαγωγοῦ τύραννος ἀνεφάνη, ζῶν τὸ μὲν ἐξ ἀρ-
f χῆς ἁλιευόμενος καὶ σωληνοθήρας | ὦν· ἀφορμῆς δὲ
λαβόμενος καὶ ἐμπορευσάμενος βίον ἐκτήσατο. τῶν
δὲ κτενῶν ἁπαλώτεροι μέν εἰσιν οἱ λευκοί· ἄβρομοι
γὰρ καὶ εὐκοίλιοι. τῶν δὲ μελάνων καὶ πυρρῶν οἱ
μείζονες καὶ εὔσαρκοι, εὔστομοι. κοινῶς δὲ πάντες
εὐστόμαχοι, εὔπεπτοι, εὐκοίλιοι λαμβανόμενοι μετὰ
κυμίνου καὶ πεπέρεως. μνημονεύει δ᾽ αὐτῶν καὶ Ἄρχιππος ἐν Ἰχθύσι·

   λεπάσιν, ἐχίνοις, ἐσχάραις, βαλάνοις τε τοῖς
91   κτεσίν τε. ‖

αἱ δὲ βάλανοι καλούμεναι ἀπὸ τῆς πρὸς τὰς δρυΐνας
ὁμοιότητος διαφέρουσι παρὰ τοὺς τόπους. αἱ μὲν γὰρ
Αἰγύπτιαι γλυκεῖαι, ἁπαλαί, εὔστομοι, θρεπτικαί, πολύχυλοι, οὐρητικαί, εὐκοίλιοι, αἱ δὲ ἄλλαι ἁλυκώτεραι.

---

[75] Otherwise unknown.

razor-shells are striped and of several colors, and are appropriate for individuals with stones and other urinary problems. Female razor-shells, on the other hand, are of only one color and sweeter. They are eaten stewed and fried, but are best when roasted on coals until their shells open. According to Phaenias of Eresus in his work entitled *Revenge-Killings of Tyrants* (fr. 15 Wehrli), the men who collect shellfish of this sort were referred to as *sōlēnistai*. He writes as follows: Philoxenus, nicknamed *Sōlēnistēs*,[75] emerged as tyrant after having been a demagogue. He originally made his living by fishing and hunting for razor-shells; but after he accumulated capital and made a business of it, he became wealthy. White scallops are the tenderest; they have no smell and are easily digested.[76] Of the dark, reddish type, those that are large and full of flesh have a good flavor. They are all in general easy on the stomach, easily digested and easy on the bowels when eaten with cumin and pepper. Archippus mentions them in *Fish* (fr. 24):[77]

> limpets, sea-urchins, *escharai,* and barnacles and the
> scallops.

Barnacles,[78] which get their name from their resemblance to acorns, vary from place to place. The Egyptian variety are sweet and tender, have a pleasant flavor, are nourishing, full of *chulē*, diuretic, and easy on the bowels, whereas the other varieties are saltier. Ormers are difficult to di-

[76] This material (except for the quotation from Archippus) must come once again from Diphilus.

[77] Also quoted at 3.86c.   [78] Literally "acorns"; exactly what creature is being referred to is uncertain.

τὰ δὲ ὠτία δύσπεπτα, τρόφιμα δὲ μᾶλλον τηγανιζό-
μενα. αἱ δὲ φωλάδες εὔστομοι, βρομώδεις δὲ καὶ
κακόχυλοι. ἐχῖνοι δὲ ἁπαλοὶ μέν, εὔχυλοι, βρομώδεις,
πλήσμιοι, εὔφθαρτοι, μετὰ δὲ ὀξυμέλιτος λαμβανόμενοι καὶ σελίνου καὶ ἡδυόσμου εὐστόμαχοι, γλυκεῖς
b τε καὶ εὐκοίλιοι[42]. προσηνέστεροι ‖ δ᾽ αὐτῶν οἱ ἐρυθροὶ
καὶ οἱ μήλινοι καὶ οἱ παχύτεροι καὶ οἱ ἐν τῷ ξύεσθαι
τὴν σάρκα γαλακτῶδες ἀνιέντες. οἱ δὲ περὶ τὴν Κε-
φαλληνίαν γινόμενοι καὶ περὶ τὴν Ἰκαρίαν καὶ τὸν
Ἀδρίαν < . . . > τινὲς αὐτῶν καὶ ὑπόπικροί εἰσιν· οἱ δ᾽
ἐπὶ τοῦ † σκοπέλου † τῆς Σικελίας κοιλίας λυτικοί.
Ἀριστοτέλης δέ φησι τῶν ἐχίνων πλείω γένη εἶναι· ἓν
μὲν τὸ ἐσθιόμενον, ἐν ᾧ τὰ καλούμενά ἐστιν ᾠά, ἄλλα
δὲ δύο τό τε τῶν σπαταγγῶν καὶ τὸ τῶν καλουμένων
βρυσῶν. μνημονεύει τῶν σπαταγγῶν καὶ Σώφρων καὶ
c Ἀριστοφάνης ἐν Ὁλκάσιν ‖ οὕτως·

δαρδάπτοντα, μιστύλλοντα, διαλείχοντά μου
τὸν κάτω σπατάγγην.

καὶ Ἐπίχαρμος δὲ ἐν Ἥβας Γάμῳ περὶ τῶν ἐχίνων
φησί·

καρκίνοι θ᾽ ἵκοντ᾽ ἐχῖνοί θ᾽, οἳ καθ᾽ ἁλμυρὰν ἅλα
νεῖν μὲν οὐκ ἴσαντι, πεζᾷ δ᾽ ἐμπορεύονται μόνοι.

Δημήτριος δ᾽ ὁ Σκήψιος ἐν ἕκτῳ καὶ εἰκοστῷ τοῦ
Τρωικοῦ Διακόσμου Λάκωνά φησί τινα κληθέντα ἐπὶ

____

42 εὐκοίλιοι Meineke: εὔχυλοι ACE

gest, but are more nourishing when fried. *Phōlades* taste
good, but have a nasty smell and produce bad *chulē*. Sea-
urchins are tender, produce good *chulē*, have a nasty smell,
are filling, spoil easily, are easy on the stomach when eaten
with honey-vinegar sauce, celery and mint, and are sweet
and easy on the bowels. Those that are red, quince-
colored, or fatter, or that emit a milky fluid when their
flesh is scraped, are more pleasant. Those found around
Cephallenia and around Icaria and the Adriatic . . . some of
them are also slightly bitter; but those found on the Sicilian
† promontory † tend to relax the bowels. Aristotle (*HA*
530^{a}34–^{b}5) claims that there are many types of sea-urchins. One is the edible variety, which contains the so-
called eggs; the other two are the *spatangē* variety and the
so-called *brusai*. Sophron (fr. 97) mentions the *spatangai*,
as does Aristophanes in *Merchantships* (fr. 425), as follows:

> devouring me, mincing me up, and giving a
>   thorough licking
> to my sea-urchin *(spatangē)* down below.[79]

And Epicharmus in *The Wedding of Hebe* (fr. 47) says concerning sea-urchins:

> Crabs have come and sea-urchins, which do not know
>   how to swim
> through the salty sea, but are the only creatures to
>   travel through it by foot.

Demetrius of Scepsis in Book XXVI of his *Trojan Battle-
Order* (fr. 15 Gaede) says that a Spartan was once invited to

---

[79] "Sea-urchin" is used here to refer to the female genitalia.

θοῖναν παρατεθέντων ἐπὶ τὴν τράπεζαν θαλαττίων
ἐχίνων ἐπιλαβέσθαι ἑνός, οὐκ εἰδότα τὴν χρῆσιν τοῦ
ἐδέσματος, ἀλλ᾽ οὐδὲ προσέχοντα τοῖς συνδειπνοῦσι
d πῶς | ἀναλίσκουσιν· ἐνθέντα δὲ εἰς τὸ στόμα σὺν τῷ
κελύφει βρύκειν τοῖς ὀδοῦσι τὸν ἐχῖνον. δυσχρηστού-
μενον οὖν τῇ βρώσει καὶ οὐ συνιέντα τὴν ἀντιτυπίαν
τῆς τραχύτητος εἰπεῖν· "ὦ φάγημα μιαρόν, οὔτε μὴ
νῦν σε ἀφέω μαλθακισθεὶς οὔτ᾽ αὖτις ἔτι <κα> λάβοι-
μι." ὅτι δὲ οἱ ἐχῖνοι, λέγω δὲ καὶ τοὺς χερσαίους καὶ
τοὺς θαλαττίους, καὶ ἑαυτῶν εἰσι φυλακτικοὶ πρὸς
τοὺς θηρῶντας, προβαλλόμενοι τὰς ἀκάνθας ὥσπερ τι
χαράκωμα, Ἴων ὁ Χῖος μαρτυρεῖ ἐν Φοίνικι ἢ Καινεῖ[43] λέγων οὕτως·

e   ἀλλ᾽ ἔν τε χέρσῳ τὰς λέοντος ᾔνεσα |
    ἢ τὰς ἐχίνου μᾶλλον οἰζυρὰς τέχνας·
    ὃς εὖτ᾽ ἂν ἄλλων κρεισσόνων ὁρμὴν μάθῃ,
    στρόβιλος ἀμφ᾽ ἄκανθον εἱλίξας δέμας
    κεῖται δακεῖν τε καὶ θιγεῖν ἀμήχανος.

    Τῶν δὲ λεπάδων, φησὶν ὁ Δίφιλος, τινὲς μέν εἰσι
μικραί, τινὲς δὲ καὶ ὀστρέοις ἐοικυῖαι. εἰσὶ δὲ σκληραὶ
καὶ ὀλιγόχυλοι καὶ οὐκ ἄγαν δριμεῖαι, εὔστομοί τε[44]
καὶ εὐκατέργαστοι, ἐφθαὶ δὲ ποσῶς εὐστόμαχοι[45]. αἱ
δὲ πίνναι οὐρητικαί, τρόφιμοι, δύσπεπτοι, δυσανάδο-
f τοι. ἐοίκασι δ᾽ αὐταῖς καὶ οἱ κήρυκες· ὧν | οἱ μὲν

_____

43 ἢ Καινεῖ Dalechamp: καινη A   44 τε Coraes: δὲ
ACE   45 εὐστόμαχοι Coraes: εὔστομοι ACE

a feast, and when sea-urchins were set on the table, he took one. He did not know how to eat it and was not paying attention to how the other guests were disposing of the creature; so he put it into his mouth, shell and all, and tried to bite it with his teeth. He had a bad time with the food and could not understand why it was so rough and resistant, and said: "Dirty food! I'm not going to give up now and let you go; but I'll never eat one of these again, either!" That urchins (I am referring to both the terrestrial[80] and the marine varieties) protect themselves against hunters by sticking their spines out like a palisade is attested by Ion of Chios in *The Phoenician or Caineus* (*TrGF* 19 F 38), in the following words:

> But on the mainland I have more praise for lions'
> ways
> than for the dreary tricks of the hedgehog.
> When it realizes it is being attacked by other,
> stronger creatures,
> it twists its prickly body around in a ball
> and lies there, immune to being bitten or touched.

Some limpets, says Diphilus, are small, whereas others resemble oysters. They are tough, produce little *chulē*, and do not have much of a tang. But they taste good and are easily digested; when stewed, they are fairly easy on the stomach. Pinnas are diuretic, nourishing, and difficult to digest and assimilate. Trumpet-shells resemble them;

---

[80] Hedgehogs, which are also referred to as *echinoi*.

τράχηλοι εὐστόμαχοι, δυσκατέργαστοι δέ· διὸ τοῖς
ἀσθενοῦσι τὸν στόμαχον οἰκεῖοι· δυσέκκριτοί τε καὶ
μέσως τρόφιμοι. τούτων δὲ αἱ μήκωνες λεγόμεναι
πρὸς τοῖς πυθμέσιν ἁπαλαί, εὔφθαρτοι· διὸ τοῖς τὴν
γαστέρα ἀσθενοῦσιν οἰκεῖαι. αἱ δὲ πορφύραι μεταξὺ
πίννης εἰσὶ καὶ κήρυκος· ὧν οἱ μὲν τράχηλοι πολύχυλοι, εὔστομοι, τὸ δὲ λοιπὸν αὐτῶν ἁλυκὸν καὶ γλυκὺ
92 καὶ εὐανάδοτον εἰς ἐπίκρασίν τ᾽ ἐπιτήδειον. ‖ τὰ δὲ
ὄστρεα γεννᾶται μὲν καὶ ἐν ποταμοῖς καὶ ἐν λίμναις
καὶ ἐν θαλάσσῃ. κράτιστα δὲ τὰ θαλάττια, ὅταν λίμνη
ἢ ποταμὸς παρακέηται· γίνεται γὰρ εὔχυλα καὶ μεί-
ζονα καὶ γλυκύτερα. τὰ δὲ πρὸς ἠόσι καὶ πέτραις
ἰλύος καὶ ⟨γλυκέος⟩ ὕδατος ἀμιγῆ μικρά, σκληρά,
δηκτικά. τὰ δὲ ἐαρινὰ ὄστρεα καὶ τὰ κατὰ τὴν τοῦ
θέρους ἀρχὴν κρείσσονα, πλήρη, θαλασσίζοντα μετὰ
γλυκύτητος, εὐστόμαχα, εὐέκκριτα. τὰ δὲ συνεψόμενα
μαλάχῃ ἢ λαπάθῳ ἢ ἰχθύσιν ⟨μᾶλλον⟩[46] ἢ καθ᾽ αὑτὰ
τρόφιμα καὶ εὐκοίλια. Μνησίθεος δ᾽ ὁ Ἀθηναῖος ἐν τῷ
b ‖ Περὶ Ἐδεστῶν φησιν· ὄστρεα καὶ κόγχαι καὶ μύες
καὶ τὰ ὅμοια τὴν μὲν σάρκα δυσκατέργαστά ἐστι διὰ
τὴν ὑγρότητα τὴν ἐν αὐτοῖς ἁλυκήν· διόπερ ὠμὰ μὲν
ἐσθιόμενα κοιλίας ἐστὶν ὑπακτικὰ διὰ τὴν ἁλυκότητα,
τὰ δὲ ἑψόμενα ἀφίησιν ἤτοι πᾶσαν ἢ τὴν πλείστην
ἅλμην εἰς τὴν συνέψουσαν αὐτοῖς ὑγρότητα. διόπερ αἱ
μὲν ὑγρότητες, ἐν αἷς ἂν ἑψηθῇ τι τῶν ὀστρέων,
ταρακτικαὶ καὶ ὑπακτικαὶ κοιλίας εἰσίν, αἱ δὲ σάρκες
τῶν ἑψομένων ὀστρέων ψόφους ποιοῦσιν ἐστερημέναι

their "necks" are easy on the stomach but difficult to digest, and they are therefore appropriate for individuals with stomach problems. They are also difficult to excrete and moderately nourishing. What are referred to as their "livers" are tender at the fundus and easily broken down; they are therefore appropriate for individuals with stomach problems. Purple shellfish fall between a pinna and a trumpet-shell; their "necks" produce a great deal of *chulē* and taste good, whereas the rest of them is salty, sweet, easily assimilated, and useful for tempering humours. Oysters are produced in rivers, marshes, and the sea. The best ones come from the sea, provided a marsh or river is nearby; for they produce good *chulē* and are larger and sweeter. Those found along beaches and on rocks, and that have no contact with muck and fresh water, are small and tough and have a sharp taste. Oysters gathered in the spring and early summer are larger, full of meat, have the taste of the sea but are simultaneously sweet, and are easy on the stomach and easily digested. When stewed with mallow, sorrel, or fish, they are more nourishing and easier on the bowels than when stewed alone. Mnesitheus of Athens says in his *On Edible Substances* (fr. 36 Bertier): The flesh of oysters, conchs, mussels, and the like is difficult to digest because of the salty fluid they contain. When eaten raw, therefore, they evacuate the bowels because of their saltiness, whereas if stewed, they release all or most of the brine into the stewing liquid. The liquid in which shellfish of any kind are stewed therefore disturbs and evacuates the bowels; and the flesh of the shellfish being stewed pro-

---

[46] add. Kaibel

c τῶν ὑγρῶν. τὰ δὲ ὀπτὰ τῶν ὀστρέων, ἐάν τις | αὐτὰ
καλῶς ὀπτήσῃ, ἀλυποτάτην ἔχει διάθεσιν· πεπύρωται
γάρ· διὸ οὐχ ὁμοίως τοῖς ὠμοῖς ἐστι δύσπεπτα καὶ τὰς
ὑγρότητας ἐν αὐτοῖς ἔχει κατεξηραμμένας, δι᾽ ὧν
ἔκλυτος ἡ κοιλία γίνεται. τροφήν τε δίδωσιν ὑγράν τε
καὶ δύσπεπτον ἅπαν ὄστρεον καὶ πρὸς τὰς οὐρήσεις
ἐστὶν οὐκ εὔοδα. ἀκαλήφη δὲ καὶ ἐχίνων ᾠὰ καὶ τὰ
τοιαῦτα τροφὴν μὲν δίδωσιν ὑγρὰν καὶ μικράν, τῆς δὲ
κοιλίας ἐστὶν λυτικὰ καὶ οὐρήσεως κινητικά.

Νίκανδρος δ᾽ ὁ Κολοφώνιος ἐν Γεωργικοῖς τάδε
d τῶν ὀστρέων καταλέγει· |

  ἠὲ καὶ ὄστρεα τόσσα βυθοὺς ἅ τε βόσκεται
      ἅλμης,
  νηρῖται στρόμβοι τε πελωριάδες τε μύες τε,
  γλίσχρ᾽ ἁλοσύδνης τέκνα, καὶ αὐτῆς φωλεὰ
      πίνης.

καὶ Ἀρχέστρατος δ᾽ ἐν Γαστρονομίᾳ φησί·

  τοὺς μῦς Αἶνος ἔχει μεγάλους, ὄστρεια δ᾽
      Ἄβυδος,
  τὰς ἄρκτους Πάριον, τοὺς δὲ κτένας ἡ Μιτυλήνη·
  πλείστους δ᾽ Ἀμβρακία παρέχει καὶ ἄπλατα μετ᾽
      αὐτῶν

              *   *   *

e Μεσσήνη δὲ πελωριάδας στενοπορθμίδι κόγχας |
  κἀν Ἐφέσῳ λήψει τὰς λείας οὔ τι πονηράς.

duces noises[81] after losing its fluid. Roasted shellfish cause the least trouble, provided one roasts them properly, because of the action of the fire. They are therefore not as difficult to digest as the raw ones; and the moisture they contain, which loosens the bowels, is dried up. Shellfish of all sorts provide nourishment that is moist and difficult to digest and does not encourage urination. Sea-urchins (*akalēphē*), sea-urchin *(echinos)* eggs, and the like provide moist nourishment in small quantities and tend to relax the bowels and encourage urination.

Nicander of Colophon in the *Georgics* (fr. 83 Schneider) lists the following shellfish:

> or however many shellfish feed in the briny depths,
> *nēritai*, whelks, giant clams, and mussels,
> clinging children of the sea-goddess; and the den of
>   the pinna itself.

Archestratus as well says in the *Gastronomy* (fr. 7 Olson–Sens = *SH* 187):

> Aenus has large mussels, Abydus oysters,
> Parion bear-crabs, and Mitylene scallops.
> But Ambracia supplies the largest number of these
>   and, along with them, boundless . . .

> *   *   *

> You shall buy giant clams in Messene, where the sea's
>   strait is narrow,
> and excellent smooth-shelled ones in Ephesus.

---

[81] *Viz.* in the bowels after it has been consumed.

τήθεα Καλχηδών, τοὺς κήρυκας δ' ἐπιτρίψαι
ὁ Ζεύς, τούς τε θαλασσογενεῖς καὶ τοὺς
   ἀγοραίους,
πλὴν ἑνὸς ἀνθρώπου· κεῖνος δέ μοί ἐστιν ἑταῖρος
Λέσβον ἐριστάφυλον ναίων, Ἀγάθων δὲ
   καλεῖται.

καὶ Φιλύλλιος δὲ ἢ ὅστις ἐστὶν ὁ ποιήσας τὰς Πόλεις
φησί·

χήμας, λεπάδας, σωλῆνας, μῦς, πίννας, κτένας
   ἐκ Μυτιλήνης.[47]

f ὄστρεια δὲ μόνως οὕτως | ἔλεγον οἱ ἀρχαῖοι. Κρατῖνος
Ἀρχιλόχοις·

   < . . . > πίννῃσι καὶ ὀστρείοισιν ὁμοίη.

καὶ Ἐπίχαρμος ἐν Ἥβας Γάμῳ·

   < . . . > ὄστρεια συμμεμυκότα.[48]

ὄστρεον δὲ ὡς ὄρνεον Πλάτων ἐν Φαίδρῳ· ὀστρέου
τρόπον, φησί, δεδεσμευμένοι, καὶ ἐν Τιμαίῳ· τὸ τῶν
ὀστρέων γένος συμπάντων.[49] ἐν δὲ τῷ τῆς Πολιτείας
δεκάτῳ ὄστρεα εἶπε· συμπεφυκέναι ὄστρειά τε καὶ
φυκία. αἱ δὲ πελωρίδες ὠνομάσθησαν παρὰ τὸ πελώ-

[47] Μυτιλήνης 3.86e: Μηθύμνης ACE   [48] συμμεμυκότα
3.85c: συμπεφυκότα A   [49] A garbled excerpt from the text:
συμπάντων does not go with ὀστρέων but with the words that
follow (omitted by Athenaeus).

Calchedon has sea-squirts, and as for trumpet-
    shells[82]—may Zeus
destroy both those born in the sea and those who
    frequent marketplaces,
except for one man; he is a comrade of mine
who inhabits Lesbos rich in grapevines and is named
    Agathon.

Likewise Philyllius (fr. 12.2)[83] or whoever the author of
Cities is says:

clams, limpets, razor-shells, mussels, pinnas,
    Mitylenean scallops.

The ancients used the form *ostreia* ("oyster, shellfish") exclusively. Cratinus in *Archilochuses* (fr. 8.1):[84]

[a woman] resembling pinnas and oysters (*ostreia*).

Also Epicharmus in *The Wedding of Hebe* (fr. 40.3):[85]

tightly closed oysters (*ostreia*).

But Plato in the *Phaedrus* (250c) uses *ostreon*, like *orneon*
("bird"). He says: imprisoned like an *ostreon*. Also in the
Timaeus (92b): the entire family of *ostrea*. But in Book X of
his *Republic* (611d): *ostreia* and seaweed have joined to-

---

[82] Literally "heralds," hence the joke in the next line.

[83] Quoted in a more complete form at 3.86e (with the names
of several other playwrights to whom the comedy might be attributed; cf. 4.140a). [84] Quoted in a more complete form at
3.86e. [85] Quoted in a more complete form at 3.85c.

[86] The traditional text of Plato has *ostrea*, as well as *pros-
pephukenai*, "have attached themselves to him," rather than Athenaeus' *sumpephukenai*, "have joined together."

93 ριον· μεῖζον γάρ ἐστι χήμης καὶ παρηλλαγμένον. ||
Ἀριστοτέλης δέ φησι καὶ ἐν ἄμμῳ αὐτὰς γίνεσθαι.
τῶν δὲ χημῶν μνημονεύει Ἴων ὁ Χῖος ἐν Ἐπιδημίαις.
καὶ ἴσως οὕτως ὠνόμασται τὰ κογχύλια παρὰ τὸ
κεχηνέναι.[50]

Περὶ δὲ τῶν κατὰ τὴν Ἰνδικὴν γινομένων ὀστρέων—οὐ γὰρ ἄκαιρον καὶ τούτων μνησθῆναι διὰ τὴν
τῶν μαργαριτῶν χρῆσιν—Θεόφραστος μὲν ἐν τῷ Περὶ
Λίθων γράφει οὕτως· τῶν θαυμαζομένων δὲ λίθων
ἐστὶν καὶ ὁ μαργαρίτης καλούμενος, διαφανὴς μὲν τῇ
φύσει· ποιοῦσι δ' ἐξ αὐτοῦ τοὺς πολυτελεῖς ὅρμους.
b γίνεται δὲ ἐν ὀστρέῳ τινὶ παραπλησίῳ ταῖς πίνναις, |
πλὴν ἐλάττονι. μέγεθος δὲ ἡλίκον ἰχθύος ὀφθαλμὸς
εὐμεγέθης. Ἀνδροσθένης δ' ἐν τῷ τῆς Ἰνδικῆς Παρά-
πλῳ γράφει οὕτως· τῶν δὲ στρόμβων καὶ χοιρίνων καὶ
τῶν λοιπῶν κογχυλίων ποικίλαι αἱ ἰδέαι[51] καὶ πολὺ
διάφοροι τῶν παρ' ἡμῖν. γίνονται δὲ πορφύραι τε καὶ
ὀστρέων πολὺ πλῆθος τῶν λοιπῶν· ἐν δὲ ἴδιον ὃ
καλοῦσιν ἐκεῖνοι βέρβερι, ἐξ οὗ ἡ μαργαρῖτις λίθος
γίνεται. αὕτη δ' ἐστὶ πολυτελὴς κατὰ τὴν Ἀσίαν καὶ
πωλεῖται περὶ Πέρσας τε καὶ τοὺς ἄνω τόπους πρὸς
c χρυσίον. ἔστι δ' ἡ μὲν τοῦ ὀστρέου ὄψις παραπλησία |
τῷ κτενί, οὐ διέγλυπται δὲ ἀλλὰ λεῖον τὸ ὄστρακον
ἔχει καὶ δασύ, οὐδὲ ὦτα ἔχει δύο ὥσπερ ὁ κτεὶς ἀλλὰ
ἕν. ἡ δὲ λίθος γίνεται ἐν τῇ σαρκὶ τοῦ ὀστρέου, ὥσπερ

---

[50] καὶ ἴσως κτλ.] χήμαι δέ φησι παρὰ τὸ κεχηνέναι ἴσως
CE   [51] ποικίλαι αἱ ἰδέαι Coraes: αἱ ποικίλαι ἡδεῖαι ACE

gether.[86] Giant clams *(pelōrides)* got their name from the word *pelōrion* ("huge"); for they are larger than ordinary clams, immensely so. Aristotle (fr. 186) says that they are generated in sand. Ion of Chios mentions clams in the *Travels* (FGrH 392 F 4). *Konchulia* ("shellfish") perhaps got their name from the verb *kechēna* ("gape, yawn").[87]

As regards the shellfish found in India—for some mention of them as well is not untimely, given the fashion for pearls—Theophrastus in his *On Stones* (36)[88] writes as follows: Among the most admired stones is the so-called *margaritēs* ("pearl"), which is naturally translucent; they use it to make expensive necklaces. The pearl is found in a shellfish that resembles the pinna but is smaller; it is the size of a large fish-eye. Androsthenes in his *Voyage along the Indian Coast* (FGrH 711 F 1) writes as follows: There are many types of whelks, cowries, and other shellfish, which are very different from those we know; purple shellfish and large quantities of the other types of shellfish are also found. One unusual type, which they refer to as the *berberi*, is the source of the *margaritis*-stone, which is very expensive throughout Asia and is sold in Persia and other inland regions for its weight in gold. The shellfish looks like a scallop, but is not striated and instead has a smooth, thick shell; and it does not have two "ears," like the scallop, but

[87] The paraphrase of this sentence in CE uses *kechēna* to explain the origin of the word *chēmai* ("clam") rather than *konchulia*, and Athenaeus may well have cited both words.

[88] Athenaeus' quotation includes material not found in the traditional version of the text.

ἐν τοῖς συείοις ἡ χάλαζα, καί ἐστιν ἡ μὲν χρυσοειδὴς
σφόδρα, ὥστε μὴ ῥᾳδίως διαγνῶναι ὅταν παρατεθῇ
παρὰ τὸ χρυσίον, ἡ δὲ ἀργυροειδής, ἡ δὲ τελέως
λευκή, ὁμοία τοῖς ὀφθαλμοῖς τῶν ἰχθύων. Χάρης δ᾽ ὁ
Μιτυληναῖος ἐν ἑβδόμῃ τῶν Περὶ Ἀλέξανδρον Ἱστοριῶν φησι· θηρεύεται δὲ κατὰ τὴν Ἰνδικὴν θάλασσαν,
d ὡσαύτως δὲ καὶ κατὰ τὴν | Ἀρμενίαν καὶ Περσικὴν
καὶ Σουσιανὴν καὶ Βαβυλωνίαν, παρόμοιον ὀστρέῳ·
τὸ δ᾽ ἐστὶν ἀδρὸν καὶ πρόμηκες, ἔχον ἐν αὐτῷ σάρκα
καὶ μεγάλην καὶ λευκήν, εὐώδη σφόδρα. ἐξ ὧν ἐξαι-
ροῦντες ὀστᾶ λευκὰ προσαγορεύουσι μὲν μαργαρί-
τας, κατασκευάζουσι δ᾽ ἐξ αὐτῶν ὁρμίσκους τε καὶ
ψέλια περὶ τὰς χεῖρας καὶ τοὺς πόδας· περὶ ἃ σπου-
δάζουσιν Πέρσαι καὶ Μῆδοι καὶ πάντες Ἀσιανοὶ πολὺ
μᾶλλον τῶν ἐκ χρυσίου γεγενημένων. Ἰσίδωρος δ᾽ ὁ
Χαρακηνὸς ἐν τῷ τῆς Παρθίας Περιηγητικῷ κατὰ τὸ
e Περσικὸν | πέλαγος νῆσόν φησιν εἶναί τινα, ἔνθα
πλείστην μαργαρῖτιν εὑρίσκεσθαι. διόπερ σχεδίας
καλαμίνας πέριξ εἶναι τῆς νήσου, ἐξ ὧν καθαλλομέ-
νους εἰς τὴν θάλασσαν ἐπ᾽ ὀργυιὰς εἴκοσιν ἀναφέρειν
διπλοῦς κόγχους. φασὶ δ᾽ ὅταν βρονταὶ συνεχεῖς ὦσι
καὶ ὄμβρων ἐκχύσεις, τότε μᾶλλον τὴν πίνναν κύειν,
καὶ πλείστην γίγνεσθαι μαργαρῖτιν καὶ εὐμεγέθη. τοῦ
δὲ χειμῶνος εἰς τὰς ἐμβυθίους θαλάμας δύνειν εἰώθα-
σιν αἱ πίνναι· θέρους δὲ τὰς μὲν νύκτας κεχήνασι
f διανηχόμεναι, ἡμέρας | δὲ μύουσιν. ὅσαι δ᾽ ἂν πέτραις
ἢ σπιλάσι προσφύωσι, ῥιζοβολοῦσι κἀνταῦθα μένου-
σαι τὴν μαργαρῖτιν γεννῶσι. ζῳογονοῦνται δὲ καὶ

one. The stone is found in the creature's flesh, like a tubercle in a pig's flesh. Sometimes it looks very much like gold, to the extent that it can be difficult to tell them apart when they are set side by side, while at other times it looks like silver or is perfectly white and resembles fish-eyes. Chares of Mitylene says in Book VII of his *Tales about Alexander* (*FGrH* 125 F 3): In the Indian sea, as also along the coast of Armenia, Persia, Susa, and Babylon, a creature that resembles an oyster is caught. It is large and oblong, and contains a substantial amount of white flesh that is very fragrant. They extract white bones, which they call *margaritai*, from it, and use them to produce necklaces, bracelets, and ankle bracelets. The Persians, the Medes, and all the inhabitants of Asia are more interested in these than in jewelry made of gold. Isidorus of Charax claims in his *Journey through Parthia* (*FGrH* 781 F 1) that there is an island in the Persian Sea where large numbers of pearls are found. The island is therefore surrounded by rafts made of reeds; they dive 20 fathoms down into the sea from them and bring up bivalve shellfish. They say that when there is constant thunder and downpours of rain, the pinnas[89] reproduce most and the pearls are the most numerous and largest. During the winter the pinnas tend to go down into their hiding-places deep in the sea; whereas in the summer they swim around with their shells open at night, but close up during the day. Those that cling to rocks or reefs put

---

[89] The word is seemingly used here to refer to pearl-oysters, although the reference to the *pinophulax* (cf. 3.89c–e) below suggests that Isidorus is thinking of the pinna itself.

τρέφονται διὰ τοῦ προσπεφυκότος τῇ σαρκὶ μέρους.
τοῦτο δὲ συμπέφυκε τῷ τοῦ κόγχου στόματι χηλὰς
ἔχον καὶ νομὴν εἰσφέρον. ὃ δή ἐστιν ἐοικὸς καρκίνῳ
μικρῷ καλούμενον πινοφύλαξ. διήκει δ᾽ ἐκ τούτου ἡ
σὰρξ μέχρι μέσου τοῦ κόγχου οἱονεὶ ῥίζα, παρ᾽ ἣν ἡ
μαργαρῖτις γεννωμένη αὔξεται διὰ τοῦ στερεοῦ τῆς
κόγχης καὶ τρέφεται ὅσον ἂν ᾖ προσπεφυκυῖα χρό-
94 νον. ‖ ἐπειδὰν δὲ παρὰ τὴν ἔκφυσιν ὑποδυομένη ἡ
σὰρξ καὶ μαλακῶς ἐντέμνουσα χωρίσῃ τὴν μαργαρῖτιν ἀπὸ τοῦ κόγχου, ἀμπέχουσα μὲν οὐκέτι τρέφει,
λειοτέραν δ᾽ αὐτὴν καὶ διαυγεστέραν ποιεῖ καὶ καθα-
ρωτέραν. ἡ μὲν οὖν ἐμβύθιος πίννα διαυγεστάτην καὶ
καθαρωτάτην καὶ μεγάλην γεννᾷ μαργαρῖτιν, ἡ δὲ
ἐπιπολάζουσα καὶ ἀνωφερὴς διὰ τὸ ὑπὸ τοῦ ἡλίου
ἀκτινοβολεῖσθαι δύσχρους καὶ ἥσσων. κινδυνεύουσι
b   δ᾽ οἱ θηρῶντες τοὺς μαργαρίτας, ὅταν εἰς κεχηνότα |
κόγχον κατ᾽ εὐθὺ ἐκτείνωσι τὴν χεῖρα· μύει γὰρ τότε,
καὶ πολλάκις οἱ δάκτυλοι αὐτῶν ἀποπρίονται· ἔνιοι δὲ
καὶ παραχρῆμα ἀποθνήσκουσιν. ὅσοι δ᾽ ἂν ἐκ πλα-
γίου ὑποθέντες τὴν χεῖρα τύχωσι, ῥᾳδίως τοὺς κόγχους ἀπὸ τοῦ λίθου ἀποσπῶσιν. μαράγδων δὲ μνημονεύει Μένανδρος ἐν Παιδίῳ·

μάραγδον εἶναι ταῦτ᾽ ἔδει καὶ σάρδια.

ἄνευ δὲ τοῦ ξ̄ λεκτέον· παρὰ γὰρ τὸ μαρμαίρειν ὠνό-

---

[90] Sc. to pluck out a pearl.

down roots and stay there and produce pearls. They bear their young and feed through the part that is attached to their flesh. This part grows by the shell's mouth and has claws and introduces food into it; in fact, it resembles a small crab and is referred to as the *pinophulax*. The flesh extends from here to the middle of the shell, like a root; after the pearl has been generated next to this, it gets bigger with the help of the hard part of the shell, and receives nourishment as long as it is in contact with it. But when the flesh makes its way under this growth and gently cuts the pearl away and separates it from the shell, it enfolds it and no longer gives it any nourishment, but makes it smoother, more translucent, and purer. Pinnas found deep in the sea produce pearls that are more translucent, purer, and larger, whereas those that move upward toward the surface, because they are affected by the sun's rays, are of an inferior color and smaller. Pearl-fishers run a risk when they stick their hand straight into an open shell.[90] For then it closes, and their fingers are often sheared off; some of them even die then and there. But if they manage to get their hand sideways underneath the shells, they can easily pull them away from the rock. Menander mentions emeralds (*maragdoi*)[91] in *The Child* (fr. 276):

These ought to be an emerald and a carnelian.

[91] The word in fact appears to be used of various stones with a pronounced green color; see Caley–Richards on Thphr. *Lap*. 23–4.

[92] I.e. *maragdos* rather than *smaragdos*. The form without the *sigma* may in fact be original; but the etymology offered is incorrect, and this is very clearly an Eastern loan-word.

c μασται τῷ διαυγὴς ὑπάρχειν. |

Μετὰ ταῦτα περιηνέχθησαν πίνακες ἔχοντες τῶν
ἐκ ὕδατος κρεῶν πολλά, πόδας καὶ κεφαλὰς καὶ ὠτία
καὶ σιαγόνας, ἔτι δὲ καὶ χορδὰς καὶ κοιλίας καὶ
γλώσσας, ὥσπερ ἔθος ἐστὶν ἐν τοῖς κατὰ τὴν Ἀλεξάνδρειαν λεγομένοις ἐφθοπωλίοις. εἴρηται γάρ, Οὐλπιανέ, καὶ τὸ ἐφθοπώλιον παρὰ Ποσειδίππῳ ἐν Παιδίῳ.
καὶ πάλιν ζητούντων τοὺς ὀνομάσαντάς τι τούτων ὁ
μέν τις ἔλεγε· τῶν ἐδωδίμων κοιλιῶν μνημονεύει Ἀρι-
d στοφάνης ἐν Ἱππεῦσι· | † φήσω σε ἀδεκατεύτους κοι-
λίας πωλεῖν †. καὶ ἑξῆς·

> τί μ᾽, ὦγάθ᾽, οὐ πλύνειν ἐᾷς τὰς κοιλίας
> πωλεῖν τε τοὺς ἀλλᾶντας, ἀλλὰ καταγελᾷς;

καὶ πάλιν·

> ἐγὼ δέ γ᾽ ἤνυστρον βοὸς καὶ κοιλίαν ὑείαν
> καταβροχθίσας κᾆτ᾽ ἄπιπι ν τὰν ζωμὰν
>   ναπῶνιπτος
> λαρυγγιῶ τοὺς ῥήτορας καὶ Νικίαν ταράξω.

e καὶ πάλιν· |

> ἡ δ᾽ Ὀβριμοπάτρα γ᾽ ἐφθὸν ἐκ ζωμοῦ κρέας
> καὶ χόλικος ἠνύστρου τε καὶ γαστρὸς τόμον.

σιαγόνος δὲ Κρατῖνος Πλούτοις·

---

93 A garbled, unmetrical recollection of the passage; and the

The word should be pronounced without a *sigma*[92], since the name came from the verb *marmairein* ("to flash, sparkle"), because the stone is translucent.

After this, platters were carried around loaded with many types of boiled meat: feet, heads, ears, jawbones, and also tripe, intestines, and tongues, as is customary in what are called the boil-shops in Alexandria. For the word "boil-shop," Ulpian, is used by Posidippus in *The Child* (fr. 22). While they were again trying to discover who had mentioned any of these items, one of them said: Aristophanes mentions edible tripe in *Knights* (300–2)[93]: I'm going to denounce you for selling tripe on which no tithe has been paid! And immediately after this (*Eq.* 160–1):

Look, mister; why don't you let me soak my tripe
and sell my sausages, instead of making fun of me?

And again (*Eq.* 356–8):

But I'll gobble down cow-belly and hog-tripe,
and drink up the broth; and then, without washing
my hands,
I'll throttle the politicians and harass Nicias.

And again (*Eq.* 1178–9):

Athena Strong-like-her-Father gave you meat stewed
in broth
and a cut of fourth-stomach tripe and paunch.

quote that follows does not come "immediately after" it, although a reader without access to the complete text of the play could easily mistake the second excerpt for a response to the threat made in the first.

< . . . > περὶ σιαγόνος βοείας μαχόμενος.

καὶ Σοφοκλῆς Ἀμύκῳ·

σιαγόνας τε δὴ
μαλθακὰς τίθησι.

Πλάτων δ᾽ ἐν Τιμαίῳ γράφει· καὶ τὰς σιαγόνας ἄκρας
αὐτοῖς συνέδησεν ὑπὸ τὴν φύσιν τοῦ προσώπου. καὶ
Ξενοφῶν ἐν τῷ Περὶ Ἱππικῆς· σιαγόνα μικρὰν συν-
f εσταλμένην. οἱ δὲ διὰ | τοῦ ῦ στοιχείου ἐκφέροντες
κατ᾽ ἀναλογίαν λέγουσιν ἀπὸ τοῦ συός[52]. χορδῶν τε
μέμνηται Ἐπίχαρμος, ἃς ὀρύας ὀνομάζει, ἐπιγράψας
τι καὶ τῶν δραμάτων Ὀρύαν. Ἀριστοφάνης ἐν Νε-
φέλαις·

ἔκ μου χορδὴν
τοῖς φροντισταῖς παραθέντων.

Κρατῖνος ἐν Πυτίνῃ·

ὡς λεπτός, ἦ δ᾽ ὅς, ἔσθ᾽ ὁ τῆς χορδῆς τόμος.

καὶ Εὔπολις ἐν Αἰξίν. Ἄλεξις δ᾽ ἐν Λευκαδίᾳ ἢ Δρα-
95 πέταις· ‖

χορδαρίου τόμος ἧκεν καὶ περικομμάτιον.

Ἀντιφάνης ἐν Γάμοις·

< . . . > ἐκτεμὼν χορδῆς μεσαῖον.

[52] συός Kaibel: ὑός A

514

Cratinus mentions a jawbone in *Gods of Wealth* (fr. 174):

fighting over a jawbone of an ox.

Also Sophocles in *Amycus* (fr. 112):

He makes
jawbones soft.

Plato writes in the *Timaeus* (75d): With those he attached the ends of the jawbones under the substance of the face. Also Xenophon in his *On Horsemanship* (cf. 1.8): a small, compact jawbone. Others pronounce the word with the letter *upsilon*[94] and claim that it is formed on analogy with *sus* ("pig"). Epicharmus mentions guts, which he calls *oruai*, and entitles one of his plays *Orua*.[95] Aristophanes in *Clouds* (455–6):

Let them make me into sausage
and serve it to the thinkers!

Cratinus in *Wineflask* (fr. 205):

How thin, he said, this slice of sausage is!

Also Eupolis in *Nanny-Goats* (fr. 34). Alexis in *The Girl from Leucas or Runaways* (fr. 137):

A slice of sausage has arrived, and some mincemeat.

Antiphanes in *The Wedding Feast*[96] (fr. 73):

---

94 I.e. *suagōn* rather *siagōn*.
95 Otherwise unattested.
96 Called *The Wedding* at 4.160d, 169d.

Ποδῶν δὲ καὶ ὠτίων, ἔτι δὲ ῥύγχους Ἄλεξις ἐν
Κρατείᾳ ἢ Φαρμακοπώλῃ· τὸ δὲ μαρτύριον ὀλίγον
ὕστερον ἐκθήσομαι, πολλὰ ἔχον τῶν ζητουμένων ὀνομάτων. Θεόφιλος Παγκρατιαστῇ·

(Α.) ἐφθῶν μὲν σχεδὸν
τρεῖς μνᾶς— (Β.) λέγ᾽ ἄλλο. (Α.) ῥυγχίον,
b κωλῆν, πόδας |
τέτταρας ὑείους— (Β.) Ἡράκλεις. (Α.) βοὸς δὲ
τρεῖς.

Ἀναξίλας Μαγείροις·

(Α.) τῶν Αἰσχύλου πολὺ μᾶλλον εἶναί μοι δοκεῖ
ἰχθύδι᾽ ὀπτᾶν. (Β.) τί σὺ λέγεις; ἰχθύδια;
συσσίτιον μέλλεις νοσηλεύειν. ὅσον
ἀκροκώλι᾽ ἕψειν < . . . > ῥύγχη, πόδας.

Ἀναξίλας δ᾽ ἐν Κίρκῃ·

δεινὸν μὲν γὰρ ἔχονθ᾽ ὑὸς
ῥύγχος, ὦ φίλε, κνισιᾶν.

c καὶ ἐν Καλυψοῖ· |

ῥύγχος φορῶν ὕειον ᾐσθόμην τότε.

ὠτάρια δ᾽ ὠνόμασε καὶ Ἀναξανδρίδης ἐν Σατυρίᾳ.
Ἀξιόνικος δὲ ἐν Χαλκιδικῷ φησιν·

ζωμὸν πσῶ
θερμὸν ἰχθὺν ἐπαναπλάττων, ἡμίβρωτα λείψανα

after cutting a slice out of the middle of the sausage.

Alexis mentions feet and ears, as well as snouts, in *Crateia or The Pharmacist*; I will quote his testimony, which includes many of the words under discussion, a little later.[97] Theophilus in *The Pancratiast* (fr. 8.1–3):[98]

> (A.) Almost three minas[99]
> of stewed meat— (B.) Keep going. (A.) a little snout,
>   a ham, four
> pigs' feet— (B.) Heracles! (A.) and three cows' feet.

Anaxilas in *Cooks* (fr. 19):

> (A.) I much prefer roasting little fish
> to Aeschylus' plays. (B.) What are you talking about?
>   Little fish?
> You'll soon be taking care of a sick mess-company.
>   But as for
> stewing trotters, snouts, feet . . .

Anaxilas in *Circe* (fr. 13):

> It's terrible, my friend,
> to have a pig's snout and need to scratch!

Also in *Calypso* (fr. 11):

> Then I realized I had a pig's snout.

Anaxandrides mentions ears in *Satyrias* (fr. 44). And Axionicus says in *The Chalcidian* (fr. 8):

---

[97] See 3.107a. [98] Quoted in a more complete form at 10.417b. [99] About three pounds.

συντιθεὶς οἴνῳ τε ῥαίνων, ἔντερ᾽ ἁλὶ καὶ σιλφίῳ
σφενδονῶν, ἀλλᾶντα τέμνων, παραφέρων χορδῆς
    τόμον,
ῥύγχος εἰς ὄξος πιέζων, ὥστε πάντας ὁμολογεῖν
τῶν γάμων κρείττω γεγονέναι τὴν ἔωλον
    ἡμέραν. |

d

Ἀριστοφάνης Προαγῶνι·

ἐγευσάμην χορδῆς ὁ δύστηνος τέκνων·
πῶς ἐσίδω ῥύγχος περικεκαυμένον;

Φερεκράτης Λήροις·

ὡς οὐχὶ τουτὶ ῥύγχος ἀτεχνῶς ἐσθ᾽ ὑός.

καὶ τόπος δέ τις οὕτω καλεῖται Ῥύγχος περὶ Στράτον
τῆς Αἰτωλίας, ὥς φησι Πολύβιος ἐν ἕκτῃ Ἱστοριῶν.
Στησίχορός τέ φησιν ἐν Συοθήραις·

    κρύψαι δὲ ῥύγχος
e   ἄκρον γᾶς ὑπένερθεν. |

ὅτι δὲ κυρίως λέγεται ῥύγχος ἐπὶ τῶν συῶν προ-
είρηται. ὅτι δὲ καὶ ἐπ᾽ ἄλλων ζῴων Ἄρχιππος Ἀμφι-
τρύωνι δευτέρῳ κατὰ παιδιὰν εἴρηκε καὶ ἐπὶ τοῦ προσώπου οὕτως·

καὶ ταῦτ᾽ ἔχων τὸ ῥύγχος οὑτωσὶ μακρόν.

---

[100] The point has not in fact been made explicitly.

                          I'm making broth
by warming up some fish, adding half-eaten
left-overs, sprinkling it all with wine, tossing in some
     entrails
seasoned with salt and silphium juice, cutting up a
     sausage, adding a slice of tripe,
and soaking a snout in vinegar, my goal being to make
     them all admit
that the day after is better than the wedding feast
     itself.

Aristophanes in *The Proagon* (fr. 478):

Wretched me! I tasted my children's guts;
how shall I look upon a scorched snout?

Pherecrates in *Jewelry* (fr. 107):

that this is not, simply put, a pig's snout.

There is also a place called "Snout" near Stratus in Aetolia, according to Polybius in Book VI (59 Buettner-Wobst) of the *Histories*. Stesichorus says in *Boar-Hunters* (*PMG* 221):

          to conceal the tip
of its snout beneath the earth.

That the word *rhunchos* ("snout") is properly used of pigs was noted above.[100] But that it can also be used in reference to other animals, and even of the human face, is said humorously by Archippus in his second *Amphitryon* (fr. 1), as follows:

and with a snout as big as this at that!

καὶ Ἀραρὼς Ἀδώνιδι·

ὁ γὰρ θεὸς τὸ ῥύγχος εἰς ἡμᾶς στρέφει.

Ἀκροκωλίων δὲ μέμνηται Ἀριστοφάνης Αἰολοσί-
κωνι·

καὶ μήν, τὸ δεῖν᾽, ἀκροκώλιά γε σοι τέτταρα
f   ἥψησα | τακερά.

καὶ ἐν Γηρυτάδῃ·

ἀκροκώλι᾽, ἄρτοι, κάραβοι.

Ἀντιφάνης Κορινθίᾳ·

           (Α.) ἔπειτα κἀκροκώλιον
ὕειον Ἀφροδίτῃ; γελοῖον. (Β.) ἀγνοεῖς·
ἐν τῇ Κύπρῳ δ᾽ οὕτω φιληδεῖ ταῖς ὑσίν,
<ὦ> δέσποθ᾽, ὥστε σκατοφαγεῖν ἀπεῖρξε < . . . >
τὸ ζῷον < . . . >, τοὺς δὲ βοῦς ἠνάγκασεν.

ὅτι δ᾽ ὄντως Ἀφροδίτῃ ὗς θύεται μαρτυρεῖ Καλλίμαχος ἢ Ζηνόδοτος ἐν Ἱστορικοῖς Ὑπομνήμασι γράφων
96 ὧδε· ‖ Ἀργεῖοι Ἀφροδίτῃ ὗν θύουσι, καὶ ἡ ἑορτὴ
καλεῖται Ὑστήρια. Φερεκράτης δ᾽ ἐν Μεταλλεῦσι·

σχελίδες δ᾽ ὁλόκνημοι πλησίον τακερώταται
ἐπὶ πινακίσκοις, καὶ δίεφθ᾽ ἀκροκώλια.

Ἄλεξις Κυβευταῖς·

                                    ἠριστηκότων

520

Also Araros in *Adonis* (fr. 1):

> Because the god is turning his snout toward us.

Aristophanes mentions trotters in *Aeolosicon* (fr. 4):

> In fact, I boiled four whatchamacallits—trotters—
> for you until they were soft.

And in *Gerytades* (fr. 164):

> trotters, loaves of bread, crayfish.

Antiphanes in *The Girl from Corinth* (fr. 124):

>   (A.) Then a pig's
> trotter for Aphrodite? Ridiculous. (B.) You're
>   misinformed.
> On Cyprus she's so fond of pigs,
> master, that she keeps the animal
> from eating shit, and makes the cows do it instead.

That pigs are actually sacrificed to Aphrodite is attested by Callimachus (cf. fr. 200a) or Zenodotus in the *Historical Commentary*, writing as follows: The Argives sacrifice a pig *(hus)* to Aphrodite, and the festival is referred to as the *Hustēria*. Pherecrates in *Miners* (fr. 113.13–14):[101]

> Very tender whole-leg hams were nearby
> on platters, and also boiled trotters.

---

[101] Quoted in more complete form at 6.268d.

σχεδόν τι δ' ἡμῶν ἐξ ἀκροκωλίου τινός.

κἂν Παννυχίδι ⟨ἢ⟩ Ἐρίθοισιν·

ἡμίοπτα μὲν
b   τὰ κρεᾴδι' ἐστί, τὸ περίκομμ' ἀπόλλυται, |
ὁ γόγγρος ἐφθός, τὰ δ' ἀκρωκώλι' οὐδέπω.

τῶν δ' ἐφθῶν ποδῶν μνημονεύει Φερεκράτης ἐν Δου-
λοδιδασκάλῳ·

(Α.) † ὡς παρασκευάζεται δεῖπνον πῶς ἂν εἴπαθ'
ἡμῖν. †
(Β.) καὶ δῆθ' ὑπάρχει τέμαχος ἐγχέλειον ὑμῖν, τευθίς, ἄρ-
νειον κρέας, φύσκης τόμος,
ποὺς ἐφθός, ἧπαρ, πλευρόν, ὀρνίθεια πλήθει πολλά, τυ-
ρὸς ἐν μέλιτι, μερὶς κρεῶν.

Ἀντιφάνης Παρασίτῳ·

(Α.) χοιρίων
c   σκέλη καπύρ'. (Β.) ἀστεῖόν γε, νὴ τὴν Ἑστίαν, |
ἄριστον. (Α.) ἐφθὸς τυρὸς ἐπεδόνει πολύς.

Ἐκφαντίδης δ' ἐν Σατύροις·

πόδας ἐπεὶ δέοι πριάμενον καταφαγεῖν ἐφθοὺς
ὑός.

Γλώσσης δὲ μέμνηται Ἀριστοφάνης ἐν Ταγηνι-
σταῖς διὰ τούτων·

Alexis in *Dice-players* (fr. 123):

> after we had just
> lunched on a pig's trotter.

Also in *The All-Night Festival or Hired Workers* (fr. 180):

> The chunks of meat
> are half-roasted; the mincemeat's ruined;
> the conger eel's stewed, but the trotters aren't done
>   yet.

Pherecrates mentions boiled feet in *The Slave-Teacher* (fr. 50):

> (A.) † How tell us how the preparations for dinner
>   are coming. †
> (B.) Well, there's an eel-steak
> for you, a squid, some
> lamb, a slice of sausage,
> a boiled foot, a liver, a rib, a
> large number of birds, some
> cheese in honey, and a serving of chunks of meat.

Antiphanes in *The Parasite* (fr. 183):

> (A.) Dry-roasted
> pork hams. (B.) A sophisticated lunch,
> by Hestia! (A.) A lot of cheese is sizzling on top.

Ecphantides in *Satyrs* (fr. 1):

> when he had to buy boiled pigs' feet and gobble them
>   down.

ἄλις ἀφύης μοι·
  παρατέταμαι γὰρ
  τὰ λιπαρὰ κάπτων.
ἀλλὰ † φέρετατ᾽ ἀπόβασιν † ἡπάτιον ἢ
  καπριδίου νέου
  κόλλοπά τιν᾽· εἰ δὲ μή, πλευρὸν ἢ γλῶτταν ἢ
  σπληνά γ᾽ ἢ νῆστιν ἢ δέλφακος ὀπωρινῆς

d ἠτριαίαν φέρετε δεῦρο μετὰ | κολλάβων
  χλιαρῶν.[53]

Τοσούτων λεχθέντων καὶ περὶ τούτων οὐδὲ τῶν
ἰατρῶν οἱ παρόντες ἀσύμβολοι μετειλήφασιν. ἔφη
γὰρ ὁ Διονυσοκλῆς· Μνησίθεος ὁ Ἀθηναῖος ἐν τῷ
Περὶ Ἐδεστῶν ἔφη· κεφαλὴ καὶ πόδες ὑὸς οὐ πολὺ τὸ
τρόφιμον καὶ λιπαρὸν ἐν ἑαυτοῖς ἔχουσι. καὶ ὁ Λεω-
νίδης· Δήμων ἐν τετάρτῃ Ἀτθίδος, Ἀφείδαντα, φησί,
βασιλεύοντα Ἀθηνῶν Θυμοίτης ὁ νεώτερος ἀδελφὸς
νόθος ὢν ἀποκτείνας αὐτὸς ἐβασίλευσεν. ἐφ᾽ οὗ Μέ-
e λανθος Μεσσήνιος ἐκπεσὼν τῆς πατρίδος | ἐπήρετο
τὴν Πυθίαν ὅπου κατοικήσει. ἡ δὲ ἔφη, ἔνθα ἂν
ξενίοις πρῶτον τιμηθῇ τοὺς πόδας αὐτῷ καὶ τὴν κεφαλὴν ἐπὶ τῷ δείπνῳ παραθέντων. καὶ τοῦτ᾽ ἐγένετο
αὐτῷ ἐν Ἐλευσῖνι· τῶν ἱερειῶν γὰρ τότε πάτριόν τινα
ἑορτὴν ἐπιτελουσῶν καὶ πάντα τὰ κρέα καταναηλω-
κυιῶν, τῶν δὲ ποδῶν καὶ τῆς κεφαλῆς ὑπολοίπων

[53] At this point A includes a marginal note: τῶν εἰς λ΄ τέλος
τοῦ ε΄ ἀρχὴ τοῦ ζ΄ ("Of the division into 30, the end of number 5
and the beginning of number 6"). See Introduction.

Aristophanes mentions tongue in *Frying-Pan Men* (fr. 520), in the following verses:

I've had enough small-fry;
>   because I'm worn out with
>   gulping down greasy food.
But [corrupt] a little liver or some flesh from a young
>   boar's
>   neck. Otherwise, bring me here a rib or a tongue
>   or
>   a spleen or a jejunum or a paunch of a pig
>   butchered in the fall, along with some hot
>   rolls.

Although a large number of remarks had already been made on these topics, the physicians present did not fail to contribute. For Dionysocles said: Mnesitheus of Athens said in his *On Edible Substances* (fr. 40 Bertier): Pigs' heads and feet do not contain much nutrition or fat. And Leonidas said: Demon reports in Book IV of his *History of Attica* (*FGrH* 327 F 1) that Apheidas, the king of Athens, was killed by his illegitimate younger brother Thymoetes, who then became king himself. In his time Melanthus of Messene was banished from his fatherland and asked the Pythia where he should settle. She told him to do so in the first place where they showed him hospitality by serving him the feet and head for dinner (Delphic oracle L79

ὄντων ταῦτα τῷ Μελάνθῳ ἀπέστειλαν.

Μήτρα ἑξῆς ἐπεισηνέχθη, μητρόπολίς τις ὡς ἀλη-
θῶς οὖσα καὶ μήτηρ τῶν Ἱπποκράτους υἱῶν, οὓς εἰς
f ὑῳδίαν | κωμῳδουμένους οἶδα. εἰς ἣν ἀποβλέψας ὁ
Οὐλπιανός, ἄγε δή, ἔφη, ἄνδρες φίλοι, παρὰ τίνι
κεῖται ἡ μήτρα; ἱκανῶς γὰρ γεγαστρίσμεθα καὶ και-
ρὸς ἤδη 'στὶ καὶ λέγειν ἡμᾶς. τοῖς δὲ κυνικοῖς τοῦτο
παρακελεύομαι σιωπᾶν κεχορτασμένοις ἀφειδῶς,
πλὴν εἰ μὴ καὶ τῶν σιαγόνων καὶ τῶν κεφαλῶν κατα-
τρῶξαι βούλονται καὶ τὰ ὀστᾶ, ὧν οὐδεὶς φθόνος
αὐτοῖς ἀπολαύειν ὡς κυσί· τοῦτο γάρ εἰσι καὶ εὔ-
97 χονται καλεῖσθαι. ‖

νόμος δὲ ⟨δείπνου⟩ λείψαν' ἐκβάλλειν κυσίν,

ἐν Κρήσσαις ὁ Εὐριπίδης ἔφη. πάντα γὰρ ἐσθίειν καὶ
πίνειν θέλουσιν, ἐπὶ νοῦν οὐ λαμβάνοντες ὅπερ ὁ
θεῖος Πλάτων ἔφη ἐν Πρωταγόρᾳ· τὸ περὶ ποιήσεως
διαλέγεσθαι ὁμοιότατον εἶναι τοῖς συμποσίοις τοῖς
τῶν φαύλων καὶ ἀγοραίων ἀνθρώπων. καὶ γὰρ οὗτοι
διὰ τὸ μὴ δύνασθαι ἀλλήλοις δι' αὑτῶν συνεῖναι ἐν τῷ
πότῳ μηδὲ διὰ τῆς ἑαυτῶν φωνῆς καὶ λόγων τῶν
ἑαυτῶν ὑπὸ ἀπαιδευσίας τιμίας ποιοῦσι τὰς αὐλητρί-
b δας, πολλοῦ μισθούμενοι ἀλλοτρίαν φωνὴν | τὴν τῶν
αὐλῶν, καὶ διὰ τῆς ἐκείνων φωνῆς ἀλλήλοις ξύνεισιν.

---

[102] Melanthus then drove Thymoetes (the last Athenian king
descended from Theseus) from the throne and became king in his
place (Paus. 2.18.9).

Fontenrose). This happened to him in Eleusis. For at that time the priests were celebrating a traditional festival and had eaten all the meat; but since the feet and head were left over, they sent them to Melanthus.[102]

A sow's womb (*mētra*) was brought in next, a veritable metropolis and a mother (*mētēr*) of the sons of Hippocrates, who I know are ridiculed in comedy for their swinishness.[103] Ulpian looked at it and said: Come now, my friends; in what author is the word *mētra* attested?[104] For we've stuffed our bellies enough, and now it is time for us to have some conversation. But I encourage the Cynics, since they have been lavishly foddered, to keep quiet, unless they want to gnaw on the jawbones and skulls, which they are welcome to enjoy in their guise of dogs. Because that is what they are, and they take pride in the name.

> It's customary to throw the dinner left-overs to the
> dogs,

said Euripides in *Cretan Women* (fr. 469). For they are willing to eat and drink anything, and do not keep in mind what the divine Plato said in the *Protagoras* (347c–d): Arguing about poetry is like the symposia of low, working-class people. For their lack of education makes them unable to enjoy one another's company over their wine by relying on their own voices and conversation; they there-

---

[103] *Huōdia* ("swinishness") puns on *huioi* ("sons") above. The Hippocrates in question is not the famous physician, but Hippocrates son of Ariphron of the deme Cholargeus (*PAA* 538615), a nephew of the Athenian politician Pericles; his three sons are ridiculed as fools at Ar. *Nu.* 1001 (where see Dover's n.; and cf. Ar. fr. 116 with K–A ad loc.).   [104] Cf. 1.1e.

ὅπου δὲ καλοὶ καὶ ἀγαθοὶ ξυμπόται καὶ πεπαιδευμένοι
εἰσίν, οὐκ ἂν ἴδοις οὔτε αὐλητρίδας οὔτε ὀρχηστρίδας
οὔτε ψαλτρίας, ἀλλ' αὐτοὺς ἑαυτοῖς ἱκανοὺς ὄντας
συνεῖναι ἄνευ τῶν λήρων τε καὶ παιδιῶν τούτων διὰ
τῆς ἑαυτῶν φωνῆς, λέγοντάς τε καὶ ἀκούοντας ἐν μέρει
ἑαυτῶν κοσμίως, κἂν πάνυ πολὺν οἶνον πίωσι. τοῦτο
δ' ὑμεῖς ποιεῖτε, ὦ Κύνουλκε· πίνοντες, μᾶλλον δ'
ἐκπίνοντες αὐλητρίδων καὶ ὀρχηστρίδων δίκην ἐμπο-
c δίζετε | τὴν διὰ τῶν λόγων ἡδονήν, ζῶντες κατὰ τὸν
αὐτὸν Πλάτωνα, ὃς ἐν τῷ Φιλήβῳ φησίν, οὐκ ἀνθρώπου βίον, ἀλλά τινος πλεύμονος ἢ τῶν ὅσα θαλάττια
μετ' ὀστρείνων ἔμψυχά ἐστι σωμάτων. καὶ ὁ Κύνουλ-
κος ὀργισθείς, γάστρων, ἔφη, καὶ κοιλιόδαιμον ἄν-
θρωπε, οὐδὲν ἄλλο σὺ οἶσθα, οὐ λόγους διεξοδικοὺς
εἰπεῖν, οὐχ ἱστορίας μνησθῆναι, οὐ τῆς ἐν λόγοις
χάριτος ἀπάρξασθαί ποτε, ἀλλὰ τὸν χρόνον ἅπαντα
περὶ ταῦτα κατετρίβης ζητῶν "κεῖται, οὐ κεῖται; εἴρηται, οὐκ εἴρηται;" ἐξονυχίζεις τε πάντα τὰ προσπί-
d πτοντα | τοῖς συνδιαλεγομένοις τὰς ἀκάνθας συν-
άγων,

ὡς ἀπ' ἐχινόποδας καὶ ἀνὰ τρηχεῖαν ὄνωνιν

ἀεὶ διατρίβων, ἀνθέων τῶν ἡδίστων μηδὲν συναθροίζων. ἢ οὐ σὺ εἶ ὁ καὶ τὴν ὑπὸ Ῥωμαίων καλουμένην
στρήναν κατά τινα πατρίαν παράδοσιν λεγομένην καὶ

---

105 Cf. 1.1d–e.

fore put a premium on pipe-girls, and hire someone else's voice, that of the pipes, at great expense, and use that voice when they are in one another's company. But wherever educated men from good backgrounds drink together, pipe-girls, dancing-girls, and harp-girls are nowhere to be seen; they have sufficient resources of their own to spend time with one another without such nonsense and foolishness, relying on their own voices, and speaking and listening to one another in turn in an orderly way, even if they drink a great deal of wine. This is what you Cynics do, Cynulcus. When you drink—or, rather, when you drink too much— you prevent pleasant conversation in the same way pipe-girls and dancing-girls do, and you live in the style this same Plato refers to, when he says in his *Philebus* (21c): not the life of a human being, but that of a jellyfish or one of the shellfish that live in the sea. Cynulcus got angry and said: Glutton! Worshipper of your own belly! That's all you know how to do—not how to have a careful discussion, or recall historical events, or offer graceful words on occasion. Instead, you spend all your time asking "Is it attested or is it not? Is the word used or is it not?"[105] And you scratch away at whatever occurs to the rest of the group to discuss, collecting all the thorns,

just as amid urchin's-foot and rough rest-harrow,[106]

always wasting time and collecting none of the sweetest

[106] The first half of an anonymous elegiac couplet quoted in full at Plu. *Mor.* 44e–f; 485a; 621e.

[107] Latin *strena*, a New Year's gift; Ulpian's name for it is perhaps intended to mark it as something given over and above any normal obligation.

διδομένην τοῖς φίλοις ἐπινομίδα καλῶν; καὶ εἰ μὲν τὴν
Πλάτωνος ζηλώσας, μαθεῖν βουλόμεθα < . . . > εἰ δὲ
παρά τινι οὕτως εὑρὼν λεγομένην, ἐμφάνισον τὸν
εἰπόντα. ἐγὼ γὰρ οἶδα ἐπινομίδα καλουμένην καὶ
μέρος τι τῆς τριήρους[54], ὡς Ἀπολλώνιος ἐν Τριηρικῷ

e παρατέθειται. | οὐ σὺ εἶ ὁ καὶ τὸν καινὸν καὶ οὐδέπω
ἐν χρείᾳ γενόμενον φαινόλην—εἴρηται γάρ, ὦ βέλτιστε, καὶ ὁ φαινόλης—εἰπὼν "παῖ Λεῦκε, δός μοι τὸν
ἄχρηστον φαινόλην"; εἰς βαλανεῖον δέ ποτε πορευό-
μενος οὐκ ἔφης πρὸς τὸν πυνθανόμενον "ποῖ δή;",
"ἀπολούμενος, ἦν δ᾽ ἐγώ, ἐπείγομαι"· κἀκείνης σοι τῆς
ἡμέρας ὁ καλὸς καννυσῖνος ὑπὸ λωποδυτῶν ἀνηρπά-
σθη, ὡς γέλωτα πάμπολυν ἐν τῷ βαλανείῳ γενέσθαι
ἀχρήστου ζητουμένου φαινόλου. ἄλλοτε δέ, ὦ ἑταῖροι
φίλτατοι—πρὸς γὰρ ὑμᾶς εἰρήσεται τἀληθῆ—προσ-

f έπταισε | λίθῳ καὶ τὴν κνήμην ἔλυσε· θεραπευθεὶς οὖν
προῄει καὶ πρὸς τοὺς πυνθανομένους "τί τοῦτο, Οὐλπιανέ;", "ὑπώπιον" ἔλεγε. κἀγὼ—ξυνῆν γὰρ αὐτῷ—
τότε τὸν γέλωτα φέρειν οὐ δυνάμενος παρά τινι τῶν
φίλων ἰατρῷ ὑπαλειψάμενος τὰ ὑπὸ τοὺς ὀφθαλμοὺς
παχεῖ φαρμάκῳ πρὸς τοὺς πυνθανομένους "τί δὲ σύ;",
"πρόσκομμα" ἔφασκον. τῆς δ᾽ αὐτῆς ταύτης σοφίας

---

[54] τῆς τριήρους ACE

108 A lost work attributed to Plato was entitled *Epinomis*; and
the lost portion of the text of Athenaeus probably said something
like "what connection there is between the two."

flowers. Is it not you who uses the term *epinomis* for what
the Romans refer to as a *strēna*[107], the name of which is a
matter of ancestral tradition, and which we present to our
friends? And if you are imitating the work of Plato,[108] we
would like to learn . . . But if you found it referred to in this
way in an author, tell us who uses the word! Because I am
aware that *epinomis* is also used of a part of a trireme and
is cited in that sense by Apollonius in *On Triremes*. Are
you not also the man who, referring to his new cloak—for
the word is used in the masculine, my friend, as well as
the feminine[109]—that had not been used yet, said "Slave!
Leucus! Give me my useless[110] cloak!" And once when you
were on your way to the baths and someone asked you
"Where are you off to?", did you not say "I'm hurrying,
quoth I, unto destruction"?[111] That same day your beautiful robe of Canusian wool was taken by clothes-thieves; the
result was tremendous laughter in the bathhouse, as the
search went on for your "useless cloak." On another occasion, my dear friends—because what you are going to hear
is the truth—he bumped into a stone and hurt his shin. After getting it cared for, he went on his way; and when people asked "What's this, Ulpian?", he said "I've got a black
eye." I was with him and could not keep from laughing at
the time; and when I was visiting one of my friends, who is

---

[109] *Paenula* is feminine in Latin, but Greek *phainolē* can be
either masculine or feminine.   [110] *achrēstos*, which Ulpian—
an allegedly unsuccessful devotee of a "pure Attic style"—intended in the sense "unused"; cf. 3.98b (confusion of a different
sort); Luc. *Lex*. 9.   [111] Ulpian meant "to wash myself off"
(< *apolouō*; cf. 3.98a; Luc. *Lex*. 2), and was perhaps quoting the
beginning of an iambic trimeter line.

καὶ ἕτερός ἐστι ζηλωτής, Πομπηιανὸς ὁ Φιλαδελφεύς,
98 ἄνθρωπος οὐκ ἀπάνουργος, ὀνοματοθήρας δὲ ‖ καὶ
αὐτός. ὅστις πρὸς τὸν οἰκέτην διαλεγόμενος μεγάλῃ
τῇ φωνῇ καλέσας τοὔνομα, "Στρομβιχίδη", ἔφη, "κό-
μιζέ μοι ἐπὶ τὸ γυμνάσιον τὰς βλαύτας τὰς ἀφορή-
τους καὶ τὴν ἐφεστρίδα τὴν ἄχρηστον. ἐγὼ γὰρ ὑπο-
δησάμενος τὸν πώγωνα προσαγορεύσω τοὺς ἑταίρους·
ὀπτὸς γάρ ἐστί μοι Λάριχος. κόμιζε δὲ τοῦ ἐλαίου τὴν
λήκυθον· πρότερον γὰρ συντριβησόμεθα, ἔπειθ᾽ οὕτως ἀπολούμεθα." ὁ δ᾽ αὐτὸς οὗτος σοφιστὴς Φε-
b βρουαρίῳ μηνί, ὡς Ῥωμαῖοι λέγουσι—τὸν δὲ μῆνα ǀ
τοῦτον κληθῆναί φησιν ὁ Μαυρούσιος Ἰόβας ἀπὸ τῶν
κατουδαίων φόβων κατ᾽ ἀναίρεσιν τῶν δειμάτων—ἐν
ᾧ τοῦ χειμῶνός ἐστι τὸ ἀκμαιότατον, καὶ ἔθος τότε
τοῖς κατοιχομένοις τὰς χοὰς ἐπιφέρειν πολλαῖς ἡμέραις, πρός τινα τῶν φίλων "οὐκ εἶδές με", ἔφη, "πολλῶν
ἡμερῶν διὰ τὰ καύματα." τῆς δὲ τῶν Παναθηναίων
ἑορτῆς ἐπιτελουμένης, δι᾽ ἧς καὶ τὰ δικαστήρια οὐ
συνάγεται, ἔφη "γενέθλιός ἐστι τῆς ἀλέκτορος⁵⁵ καὶ

---

⁵⁵ ἀλέκτορος Ἀθηνᾶς ACE

112 Perhaps the model for Lucian's Lexiphanes, who speaks in the same way and makes many of the same errors.
113 Pompeianus meant "unworn"; cf. Luc. Lex. 9.
114 Pompeianus apparently intended to tie his beard up out of the way somehow, but used a verb properly applied only to shoes and sandals; cf. Luc. Lex. 5.

a physician, I had some heavy salve applied beneath my eye, and when people asked "What happened to you?", I said "I bruised my leg." Another man devoted to learning of this sort is Pompeianus of Philadelphia,[112] an individual full of guile and himself a hunter of words. When he was speaking to his slave, he called his name in a loud voice and said "Strombichides! Take my unbearable[113] slippers and my useless mantle to the wrestling school for me! I'm going to tie my beard under my feet[114] and speak to my friends. For I have to cook up[115] Larichus. And bring my oilflask; because first the two of us are going to get beaten up,[116] and then in this way we'll be destroyed."[117] In the month of February, as the Romans call it—Juba of Mauretania (*FGrH* 275 F 96) says that the month gets it name from the terrors lurking beneath the earth, as a way of removing fear of them[118]—which is the coldest part of the winter and a time when it was customary to make libations to the dead for a number of days, this same learned gentleman said to one of his friends: "You haven't seen me for many days because of the heat."[119] When the Panathenaic festival, during which the lawcourts do not meet, was being celebrated, he said "It's the birthday of the Rooster,[120] and on

---

[115] Pompeianus meant "look up," as if *optos* ("roasted") were from *horaō, opsomai* ("see"); cf. Luc. *Lex*. 9.   [116] Pompeianus meant "get a massage"; cf. Luc. *Lex*. 5.   [117] Cf. 3.97e n.

[118] As if the Latin *Februarius* were derived from the Greek *phobous audaious airein*, a preposterous etymology.

[119] Pompeianus meant "the burnt offerings I had to make"; cf. Luc. *Lex*. 2.   [120] Pompeianus meant "the Unwedded One" *(alektros)*, i.e. Athena, whose name was added above the line by a scribe as an explanatory note that eventually made its way into the text.

ATHENAEUS

c ἄδικος ἡ τῆτες ἡμέρα." ἐκάλεσε δέ ποτε καὶ τὸν | ἐκ
Δελφῶν ἐπανελθόντα ἡμῶν ἑταῖρον οὐδὲν αὐτῷ χρή-
σαντος τοῦ θεοῦ ἄχρηστον. δεῖξιν δέ ποτε λόγων
δημοσίᾳ ποιούμενος καὶ ἐγκώμιον διεξερχόμενος τῆς
βασιλευούσης πόλεως ἔφη "θαυμαστὴ δ᾽ ἡ Ῥωμαίων
ἀρχὴ ἡ ἀνυπόστατος." τοιοῦτοί τινές εἰσιν, ὦ ἑταῖροι,
οἱ Οὐλπιάνειοι σοφισταί, οἱ καὶ τὸ μιλιάριον καλούμενον ὑπὸ Ῥωμαίων, τὸ εἰς θερμοῦ ὕδατος κατεργασίαν κατασκευαζόμενον, ἱπνολέβητα ὀνομάζοντες,
d πολλῶν⁵⁶ ὀνομάτων | ποιηταὶ καὶ πολλοῖς παρασάγ-
γαις ὑπερδραμόντες τὸν Σικελιώτην Διονύσιον, ὃς τὴν
μὲν παρθένον ἐκάλει μένανδρον, ὅτι μένει τὸν ἄνδρα,
καὶ τὸν στῦλον μενεκράτην, ὅτι μένει καὶ κρατεῖ,
βαλλάντιον δὲ τὸ ἀκόντιον, ὅτι ἐναντίον βάλλεται, καὶ
τὰς τῶν μυῶν διεκδύσεις μυστήρια ἐκάλει, ὅτι τοὺς
μῦς τηρεῖ. Ἄθανις δ᾽ ἐν πρώτῃ Σικελικῶν τὸν αὐτόν
φησι Διονύσιον καὶ τὸν βοῦν γαρόταν καλεῖν καὶ τὸν
χοῖρον ἴακχον. τοιοῦτος ἦν καὶ Ἀλέξαρχος ὁ Κασ-
σάνδρου τοῦ Μακεδονίας βασιλεύσαντος ἀδελφός, ὁ
e τὴν Οὐρανόπολιν | καλουμένην κτίσας. ἱστορεῖ δὲ

⁵⁶ πολλῶν A: καλῶν C: πολλῶν γρ(άφεται) καινῶν E: "perhaps πολλῶν καινῶν" Kaibel

---

121 Cf. Luc. *Lex*. 9.
122 Pompeianus used *achrēstos* as if it were derived from
chraō ("pronounce an oracle"). 123 Pompeianus intended
the word in the sense "unshakeable."
124 Latin *miliarium*; used in bathhouses.

534

this day of the year there's no justice."[121] He once referred to a friend of ours who came back from Delphi without getting a response from the god as "useless."[122] On another occasion, when he was making a display-speech in public and was offering extended praise of the imperial city, he said "One has to marvel at the insecure[123] dominion of the Romans." This, my friends, is what Ulpianic intellectuals are like—men who call what the Romans refer to as a *miliarion*,[124] which serves to produce hot water, an "oven-cauldron,"[125] and who in their creation of new vocabulary go many miles[126] beyond Dionysius of Sicily. He referred (*TrGF* 76 F 12f–g, a, h) to an unmarried girl as *menandros*, because she is waiting *(menei)* for her husband *(andra)*; to a column as *menekratēs*, because it remains in one place *(menei)* and supports *(kratei)* something; to a javelin as a *ballantion*,[127] because it is thrown against *(balletai enantion)* someone; and to mouse-holes as *mustēria*,[128] because they protect mice *(mus tērei)*. Athanis in Book I of the *History of Sicily* (*FGrH* 562 F 1) says that this same Dionysius (*TrGF* 76 F 12i–k) referred to an ox as a *garotas*,[129] and to a pig as an *iakchos*.[130] Alexarchus the brother of Cassander king of Macedon[131] and the founder of the city of Oura-

---

[125] Lucian's *Lexiphanes* (8) also uses the word, which is otherwise attested only in the diminutive in Pollux.

[126] Literally "parasangs," a Persian measure of distance (cf. 3.121f–2a with n.) = 30 stades or about 3.5 miles.

[127] The word normally means "purse."

[128] The word normally means "mystic rites."

[129] < *ga* ("earth") and *aroō* ("plow").

[130] < *iakcheō* ("cry aloud," and thus "squeel").

[131] See 1.19c n.

περὶ αὑτοῦ Ἡρακλείδης ὁ Λέμβος ἐν τῇ τριακοστῇ
ἑβδόμῃ τῶν Ἱστοριῶν λέγων οὕτως· Ἀλέξαρχος ὁ τὴν
Οὐρανόπολιν κτίσας διαλέκτους ἰδίας εἰσήνεγκεν, ὀρ-
θροβόαν μὲν τὸν ἀλεκτρυόνα καλῶν καὶ βροτοκέρτην
τὸν κουρέα καὶ τὴν δραχμὴν ἀργυρίδα, τὴν δὲ χοίνικα
ἡμεροτροφίδα καὶ τὸν κήρυκα ἀπύτην. καὶ τοῖς Κασ-
σανδρέων δὲ ἄρχουσι τοιαυτά ποτ᾽ ἐπέστειλε· Ἀλέξαρχος † ὁ μάρμων⁵⁷ † πρόμοις γαθεῖν. τοὺς ἡλιο-
f κρεῖς οἰῶν οἶδα † λιπουσαθεωτων | † ἔργων †
κρατιτορας † μορσίμῳ τύχᾳ κεκυρωμένας † θεουπο-
γαις † χυτλώσαντες αὑτοὺς καὶ φύλακας ὀριγενεῖς. τί
δὲ ἡ ἐπιστολὴ αὕτη δηλοῖ νομίζω ᾽γὼ⁵⁸ μηδὲ τὸν
Πύθιον διαγνῶναι. κατὰ γὰρ τὸν Ἀντιφάνους Κλεο-
φάνη·

> τὸ δὲ τυραννεῖν ἐστιν ‹ . . . ›
> ἢ τί ποτε; τὸν σπουδαῖον ἀκολουθεῖν ἐρεῖς
> ἐν τῷ Λυκείῳ μετὰ σοφιστῶν νὴ Δία
99 λεπτῶν, ἀσίτων, συκίνων, λέγονθ᾽ ὅτι ‖
> τὸ πρᾶγμα τοῦτ᾽ οὐκ ἔστιν, εἴπερ γίγνεται,
> οὐδ᾽ ἔστι γάρ πω γινόμενον ὃ γίγνεται,
> οὔτ᾽ εἰ πρότερον ἦν, ἔστιν ὅ γε νῦν γίγνεται,
> ἔστιν γὰρ οὐκ ὂν οὐδέν· ὃ δὲ μὴ γέγονέ πω,

---

⁵⁷ Ὁμαιμέων Wilamowitz   ⁵⁸ νομίζω ᾽γὼ A: δοκῶ CE

---

[132] A dry measure equivalent to slightly more than a liter, and
conventionally the amount of barley a man needed for a day.
[133] Cf. Homeric ēputa ("loud-voiced"; of a herald at Il. 7.384).

nopolis was also like this. Heracleides of Lembos in Book XXXVII of his *Histories* (fr. 5, *FHG* iii.169) offers the following information about him: Alexarchus the founder of Ouranopolis introduced peculiar vocabulary, referring to a rooster as a "dawn-crier," a barber as a "mortal-shearer," a drachma as "worked silver," a *choinix*[132] as a "daily-feeder," and a herald as an *aputēs*.[133] He once wrote something of the following sort to the public authorities in Casandreia:[134] Alexarchus [obscure] to the foremost men: Joy to you! I am aware that our sun-fleshed sheep [obscure], masters of the worked lands, have met their fated doom [obscure], washing them and their mountain-bred guardians." As for what this letter says, in my opinion not even the Pythian god[135] could make sense of it. To quote Antiphanes' *Cleophanes* (fr. 120):

> to be a tyrant is . . .
> Or else what is it? You'll say that the serious man
>   trails along
> at the Lyceum with a crowd of sophists, by Zeus—
> thin, hungry good-for-nothings—and says that
> this thing doesn't exist, if it's coming into existence,
> since what's coming into existence hasn't already
>   done so;
> nor, if it existed previously, can it be what is now
>   coming into existence,
> since nothing exists that isn't in existence. And
>   whatever hasn't come into existence

---

[134] The letter is as incomprehensible to us as it apparently was to Heracleides.   [135] Apollo in his guise as god of oracles (and thus master of riddles).

οὐκ ἔστ᾿ ἔωσπερ γέγονε † ὃ δὲ μὴ γέγονέ πω †.
ἐκ τοῦ γὰρ εἶναι γέγονεν· εἰ δ᾿ οὐκ ἦν ὅθεν,
πῶς ἐγένετ᾿ ἐξ οὐκ ὄντος; οὐχ οἷόν τε γάρ.
† εἰ δ᾿ αὐτόθεν ποι γέγονεν, οὐκ ἔσται
κηποι δεποτις εἴη, πόθεν γενήσεται
τοὐκ ὂν εἰς οὐκ ὄν· εἰς οὐκ ὂν γὰρ οὐ

b   δυνήσεται †. |

ταυτὶ δ᾿ ὅ τι ἐστὶν οὐδ᾿ ἂν Ἀπόλλων μάθοι.

οἶδα δ᾿ ὅτι καὶ Σιμωνίδης που ὁ ποιητὴς ἀρίσταρχον
εἶπε τὸν Δία καὶ Αἰσχύλος τὸν Ἅιδην ἀγησίλαον,
Νίκανδρος δὲ ὁ Κολοφώνιος ἰοχέαιραν τὴν ἀσπίδα τὸ
ζῷον. διὰ ταῦτα καὶ τὰ τοιαῦτα ὁ θαυμασιώτατος
Πλάτων ἐν τῷ Πολιτικῷ εἰπὼν ξηροβατικά τινα ζῷα
καὶ ἀεροβατικὰ < . . . > ἄλλα, ξηροτροφικόν τε καὶ
ὑγροτροφικὸν καὶ ἀερονομικὸν⁵⁹ ἐπὶ ζῴων χερσαίων
καὶ ἐνύγρων καὶ ἐναερίων ἐπιλέγει, ὥσπερ παρακελευ-
c   όμενος τούτοις τοῖς ὀνοματοποιοῖς | φυλάττεσθαι τὴν
καινότητα γράφων καὶ κατὰ λέξιν τάδε· κἂν διαφυ-
λάξῃς τὸ μὴ σπουδάζειν ἐπὶ τοῖς ὀνόμασι, πλουσιώ-
τερος καὶ εἰς γῆρας ἀναφανήσῃ φρονήσεως. οἶδα δὲ
καὶ Ἡρῴδην τὸν Ἀττικὸν ῥήτορα ὀνομάζοντα τροχο-
πέδην τὸ διαβαλλόμενον ξύλον διὰ τῶν τροχῶν, ὅτε

---

⁵⁹ ἀερονομικὸν Schweighäuser: ξηρονομικὸν ACE

136 More often a divine epithet, "arrow-shooter."

doesn't exist until it has done so. † And whatever
　　hasn't come into existence. †
Because it has come into existence from existence;
　　but if there was no source for it,
how did it come into existence from what doesn't
　　exist? This is impossible.
† But if it came into existence from the same source
　　somewhere, it will not be
[corrupt], whence will what doesn't exist
turn into what isn't? Because it won't be able to into
　　what isn't †.
And what all this means not even Apollo could
　　understand.

I am aware that the poet Simonides (*PMG* 614) refers
somewhere to Zeus as *aristarchos* ("best-ruler"); that Aeschylus (fr. 406) calls Hades *agēsilaos* ("leader of the people"); and that Nicander of Colophon (fr. 33 Schneider)
calls an asp *iocheaira* ("venom-shooter").[136] Because of
these and similar coinages, the marvellous Plato in his
Politicus (264d), referring to certain creatures that "traverse the dry land" and "traverse the air" . . . others, and
uses the terms "dry-raised," "moist-raised," and "air-
dwelling" for land-animals, marine animals, and birds,
respectively, as if he were encouraging those who enjoy
coining words to beware of novelty, writing specifically as
follows (261e): And if you maintain your indifference to
names, you will appear richer in wisdom in your old age. I
am also aware that the orator Herodes Atticus[137] used the
word *trochopedēs* ("wheel-shackle") for the piece of wood

---

[137] *PAA* 573240 (fl. mid-2nd century CE).

κατάντεις τόπους ὀχούμενος πορεύοιτο[60], καίτοι Σιμα-
ρίστου ἐν τοῖς Συνωνύμοις ἐποχέα τὸ ξύλον τοῦτο
ἐπονομάσαντος. καὶ Σοφοκλῆς δέ που ὁ ποιητὴς τὸν
d φύλακα μοχλὸν φόβου[61] ὠνόμασεν | ἐν τούτοις·

θάρσει· μέγας σοι τοῦδ᾽ ἐγὼ φόβου μοχλός.

κἂν ἄλλοις δὲ τὴν ἄγκυραν ἰσχάδα κέκληκεν διὰ τὸ
κατέχειν τὴν ναῦν·

ναῦται δ᾽ ἐμηρύσαντο νηὸς ἰσχάδα.

καὶ Δημάδης δὲ ὁ ῥήτωρ ἔλεγε τὴν μὲν Αἴγιναν εἶναι
λήμην τοῦ Πειραιῶς, τὴν δὲ Σάμον ἀπορρῶγα τῆς
πόλεως, ἔαρ δὲ τοῦ δήμου τοὺς ἐφήβους, τὸ δὲ τεῖχος
ἐσθῆτα τῆς πόλεως, τὸν δὲ σαλπικτὴν κοινὸν Ἀθη-
e ναίων ἀλέκτορα. ὁ | δ᾽ ὀνοματοθήρας οὗτος σοφιστὴς
καὶ ἀκάθαρτον ἔφη γυναῖκα ἧς ἐπεσχημένα ἦν τὰ
γυναικεῖα. πόθεν δέ σοι, ὦ Οὐλπιανέ, καὶ "κεχορ-
τασμένοι" εἰπεῖν ἐπῆλθε, δέον τῷ κορεσθῆναι χρήσασθαι;

Πρὸς ταῦτα ὁ Οὐλπιανός πως ἡδέως γελάσας,
ἀλλὰ μὴ βάυζε, εἶπεν, ὦ ἑταῖρε, μηδὲ ἀγριαίνου τὴν

---

[60] πορεύοιτο CE: ἐπορεύετο A
[61] φόβου Kaibel: που ACE

---

[138] The word normally means "dried fig," but is here derived
from ischō ("hold, stay"), as also at Luc. Lex. 15.
[139] The remark is elsewhere attributed to Pericles (e.g. Arist.
Rh. 1411a14–15; Plu. Per. 8.5).

put through his wheels when he was travelling through steep territory in his carriage, although Simaristes in his *Synonyms* calls this piece of wood an *epocheus* ("brake"). Likewise the poet Sophocles (fr. 760) somewhere called a guard a bar against fear, in the following words:

Take courage; I am your great bar against this fear.

And elsewhere (fr. 761) he refers to an anchor as an *ischas* ("stay"),[138] because it holds the ship in place:

The sailors drew up the ship's anchor (*ischas*).

So too the orator Demades said that (fr. LXVII de Falco) Aegina was pus in the eye of the Peiraeus;[139] that (fr. XXVIII de Falco) Samos was a piece broken off of Athens;[140] that (fr. LXVIII de Falco) the young men just coming of age were the spring of the people;[141] that (fr. XXX de Falco) the wall was the city's clothing; and that (fr. XXXI de Falco) the public trumpeter was the common rooster of the Athenians. This word-hunting sophist also described a woman whose menstrual periods had ceased as uncleansed.[142] But where did you get the idea, Ulpian, of saying "foddered,"[143] when you should have used the word "sated"?

In response, Ulpian smiled rather sweetly and said: Don't bark, my friend, or go wild and unleash your canine

---

[140] An allusion to the settlement of Athenian cleruchs on the island in 365 BCE.   [141] This remark as well is elsewhere attributed to Pericles (Arist. *Rh.* 1365a31–3, 1411a1–4).

[142] Cf. Luc. *Lex.* 19. The "word-hunting sophist" in question is presumably Pompeianus (cf. 3.98a), last referred to in 3.98c.

[143] 3.96f.

κυνικὴν προβαλλόμενος λύσσαν τῶν ὑπὸ κύνα οὐσῶν
ἡμερῶν, δέον αἰκάλλειν μᾶλλον καὶ προσσαίνειν τοὺς
συνδείπνους, μὴ καί τινα Κυνοφόντιν ἑορτὴν ποιησώ-
f μεθα ἀντὶ τῆς παρ᾽ Ἀργείοις | ἐπιτελουμένης. χορτα-
σθῆναι εἴρηται, ὦ δαιμόνιε ἀνδρῶν, παρὰ μὲν Κρατίνῳ ἐν Ὀδυσσεῦσιν οὕτως·

ἦσθε πανημέριοι χορταζόμενοι γάλα λευκόν.

καὶ Μένανδρος δὲ ἐν Τροφωνίῳ ἔφη χορτασθείς. Ἀριστοφάνης δ᾽ ἐν Γηρυτάδῃ·

θεράπευε καὶ χόρταζε τῶν μονῳδιῶν.

Σοφοκλῆς τε ἐν Τυροῖ·

100   σίτοισι παγχόρτοισιν ἐξενίζομεν. ‖

Εὔβουλος δ᾽ ἐν Δόλωνι·

ἐγὼ κεχόρτασμαι μέν, ἄνδρες, οὐ κακῶς,
ἀλλ᾽ εἰμὶ πλήρης, ὥστε καὶ μόλις πάνυ
ὑπεδησάμην ἅπαντα δρῶν τὰς ἐμβάδας.

Σώφιλος δ᾽ ἐν Φυλάρχῳ·

γαστρισμὸς ἔσται δαψιλής· τὰ προοίμια
ὁρῶ ⟨ . . . ⟩ χορτασθήσομαι.
νὴ τὸν Διόνυσον, ἄνδρες, ἤδη στρηνιῶ.

καὶ Ἄμφις ἐν Οὐρανῷ·

εἰς τὴν ἑσπέραν

distemper during the Dog-days![144] You should instead be fawning on your fellow-guests and wagging your tail at them to keep us from having a Dog-slaughter festival like the one celebrated in Argos. The word "foddered" is used, my good sir, by Cratinus in *Odysseuses* (fr. 149.1), as follows:

> You sat there all day long, foddered on white milk.

Menander also said "foddered" in *Trophonius* (fr. 353). Aristophanes in *Gerytades* (fr. 162):

> Take care of him and fodder him on some of the monodies.

Also Sophocles in *Tyro* (fr. 666):

> We entertained them with grain, which fodders all.

Eubulus in *Dolon* (fr. 29):

> I've not been foddered badly, gentlemen.
> I'm full; and as a result, despite my efforts,
> I was barely able to tie my shoes.

Sophilus in *Phylarchus* (fr. 7):

> There's going to be a lot of gorging. I see
> what comes first . . . I'm going to be foddered,
> by Dionysus, gentlemen; I'm already running wild.

Also Amphis in *Heaven* (fr. 28):

> Foddered

[144] Referring to the fact that Cynulcus is a Cynic; cf. 1.1d; 1.22e n.

χορταζόμενα πᾶσιν ἀγαθοῖς.

b τοῦτα μὲν οὖν, ὦ Κύνουλκε, | εἰπεῖν προχείρως ἔχω
σοι τὰ νῦν, αὔριον δὲ ἢ ἔνηφι—τὴν γὰρ εἰς τρίτην
Ἡσίοδος εἴρηκεν οὕτως—πληγαῖς σε χορτάσω, ἐάν-
περ μὴ εἴπῃς ὁ κοιλιοδαίμων παρὰ τίνι κεῖται. σιω-
πήσαντος δ᾽ ἐκείνου, ἀλλὰ μὴν καὶ τοῦτο αὐτός σοι, ὦ
κύον, ἐρῶ ὅτι Εὔπολις τοὺς κόλακας ἐν τῷ ὁμωνύμῳ
δράματι οὕτω κέκληκε· τὸ δὲ μαρτύριον ἀναβαλοῦμαι,
ἔστ᾽ ἂν ἀποδῶ σοι τὰς πληγάς.

Ἡσθέντων οὖν ἐπὶ τοῖς πεπαιγμένοις ἁπάντων,
c ἀλλὰ μήν, ἔφη ὁ Οὐλπιανός, καὶ τὸν περὶ τῆς | μήτρας
λόγον ἀποδώσω. Ἄλεξις γὰρ ἐν τῷ Ποντικῷ ἐπιγραφομένῳ δράματι Καλλιμέδοντα τὸν ῥήτορα, Κάραβον
δὲ ἐπικαλούμενον κωμῳδῶν—ἦν δ᾽ οὗτος εἷς τῶν κατὰ
Δημοσθένη τὸν ῥήτορα πολιτευομένων—φησίν·

ὑπὲρ πάτρας μὲν πᾶς τις ἀποθνῄσκειν θέλει,
ὑπὲρ δὲ μήτρας Καλλιμέδων ὁ Κάραβος
ἐφθῆς ἴσως προσεῖτ᾽ ἂν ἀποθανεῖν.

d ἦν δὲ ὁ Καλλιμέδων καὶ ἐπὶ ὀψοφαγίᾳ διαβόητος. |
μνημονεύει τῆς μήτρας καὶ Ἀντιφάνης ἐν Φιλομήτορι
οὕτως·

---

[145] Used by Cynulcus at 3.97c.
[146] Ulpian never returns to the point; but cf. Eup. fr. *190.
[147] Answering the question he himself posed at 3.96f.

until evening on good food of every sort.

These, then, are the citations I have ready at hand for you at the moment, Cynulcus. But tomorrow or *enēphi*—because Hesiod (*Op.* 410) refers this way to the day after tomorrow—I will fodder you with blows, unless you tell me in what author the word "Worshipper of your own belly"[145] is attested. Cynulcus was silent, and Ulpian said: Well, my dog, I myself will tell you this too; Eupolis (fr. 187) refers this way to flatterers, in the play by the same name. But I will put off providing proof of this until I give you the beating you are owed.[146]

Everyone was pleased with these jokes, and Ulpian said: Well, I will also offer an account of the sow's womb.[147] Alexis in the play entitled *The Man from Pontus* (fr. 198) ridicules the orator Callimedon, nicknamed Crayfish—he was one of those active in politics in Demosthenes' time[148]—and says:

Everyone is willing to die for his fatherland.
But Callimedon the Crayfish would perhaps
submit to death for the sake of a stewed sow's womb
  (*mētra*).[149]

Callimedon was notorious for his gluttony. Antiphanes too mentions sow's womb in *The Man Who Loved His Mother* (fr. 219), as follows:

[148] Callimedon son of Callicrates (*PAA* 558185) was a pro-Macedonian opponent of Demosthenes. Athenaeus preserves a number of comic fragments that refer to him at 3.104c–d; 8.339e–40e.

[149] With a pun on *mētēr* ("mother").

ἔμμητρον ἂν ᾖ τὸ ξύλον, βλάστην ἔχει·
μητρόπολίς ἐστιν, οὐχὶ πατρόπολις ⟨πόλις⟩·
μήτραν τινὲς πωλοῦσιν ἥδιστον κρέας·
Μητρᾶς ὁ Χῖός ἐστι τῷ δήμῳ φίλος.

Εὔφρων δ᾽ ἐν Παραδιδομένῃ·

οὑμὸς διδάσκαλος δὲ μήτραν σκευάσας
παρέθηκε Καλλιμέδοντι, κἀσθίονθ᾽ ἅμα
e ἐπόησε πηδᾶν, ὅθεν ἐκλήθη Κάραβος. |

Διώξιππος δ᾽ ἐν Ἀντιπορνοβοσκῷ·

οἵων δ᾽ ἐπιθυμεῖ βρωμάτων, ὡς μουσικῶν·
ἤνυστρα, μήτρας, χόλικας.

ἐν δὲ Ἱστοριογράφῳ·

τὴν στοὰν διεξέπαιον. Ἀμφικλῆς μήτρας δύο
κρεμαμένας δείξας "ἐκεῖνον πέμπε," φησίν, "ἂν
ἴδῃς".

Εὔβουλος δ᾽ ἐν Δευκαλίωνι·

ἡπάτια, νῆστις, πλεύμονες, μήτρα.

Λυγκεὺς δ᾽ ὁ Σάμιος, ὁ Θεοφράστου γνώριμος, καὶ
f τὴν σὺν ὀπῷ χρῆσιν αὐτῆς | οἶδεν. ἀναγράφων γοῦν
τὸ Πτολεμαίου συμπόσιόν φησιν οὕτως· μήτρας τινὸς

---

150 Otherwise unknown.   151 Callimedon, who is identified with the food he loves.   152 According to 4.128a, he
was one of the students of Theophrastus (c.371–c.287 BCE).

If wood contains the heart of the tree (*emmētron*), it's
    capable of growth;
a city is a metropolis, not a patropolis;
the sweetest meat they sell is sow's womb (*mētra*);
and Metras of Chios[150] is a friend to the Athenian
    people.

Euphron in *The Girl Who Was Handed Over* (fr. 8):

My teacher prepared a sow's womb
and served it to Callimedon. It made him
leap about as he ate it, and he's therefore called
    Crayfish.

Dioxippus in *The Anti-Pimp* (fr. 1):

The sort of food he's eager for! How refined!
Fourth stomachs, sows' wombs, sausages.

And in *The Historian* (fr. 3):

They were bursting through the colonnade.
    Amphicles pointed to two
sows' wombs hanging there, and said "Send him,[151] if
    you see him!"

Eubulus in *Deucalion* (fr. 23):

livers, jejunum, lungs, sow's womb.

Lynceus of Samos, who knew Theophrastus,[152] is aware
that sow's womb is eaten with silphium juice. In his description of Ptolemy's[153] symposium, at any rate, he says

[153] Presumably Ptolemy II Philadelphus (reigned 285–246
BCE).

περιφερομένης ἐν ὄξει καὶ ὀπῷ. τοῦ δὲ ὀποῦ μέμνηται
Ἀντιφάνης ἐν Δυσέρωσι περὶ Κυρήνης τὸν λόγον
ποιούμενος·

ἐκεῖσε διαπλέω
ὅθεν διεσπάσθημεν, ἐρρῶσθαι λέγων
ἅπασιν, ἵπποις, σιλφίῳ, συνωρίσιν,
101   καυλῷ, κέλησι, μασπέτοις, πυρετοῖς, ὀπῷ. ||

τῆς δὲ διαφορᾶς τῆς περὶ τὴν ἐκτομίδα μνημονεύει
Ἵππαρχος ὁ τὴν Αἰγυπτιακὴν Ἰλιάδα συνθεὶς ἐν
τούτοις·

ἀλλὰ λοπάς μ᾽ εὔφραιν᾽ ἢ μήτρης καλὰ
    πρόσωπα
ἐκβολάδος, δέλφαξ <δ᾽> ἐν κλιβάνῳ ἡδέα ὄζων.

Σώπατρος δ᾽ ἐν μὲν Ἱππολύτῳ φησίν·

ἀλλ᾽ οἷα μήτρα καλλίκαρπος ἐκβολὰς
δίεφθα λευκανθεῖσα τυροῦται δέμας.

ἐν δὲ Φυσιολόγῳ·

b   μήτρας ὑείας εὖ καθεψηθεὶς τόμος, |
τὴν δηξίθυμον ἐντὸς ὀξάλμην ἔχων.

ἐν δὲ Σίλφαις·

μήτρας ὑείας ἐφθὸν ὡς φάγῃς τόμον,
δριμεῖαν ὠθῶν πηγανῖτιν εἰς χολήν.

the following (fr. 5 Dalby): A sow's womb in vinegar and silphium juice made its way around. Antiphanes mentions silphium juice in *Men Who Were Unlucky in Love* (fr. 88), in a speech about Cyrene:

> I'm sailing to the place
> we were torn away from; I'm saying goodbye
> to everything—horses, silphium, teams of horses,
> silphium stalk, race horses, silphium leaf, fevers,
> silphium juice.

Hipparchus, the author of the *Egyptian Iliad* (*SH* 496), mentions the excellence of the womb of a sow that has miscarried[154] in the following verses:

> But let a casserole-dish or the lovely face of a
> miscarried sow's womb
> cheer me up, and a pig smelling delicious in a baking-
> shell!

Sopater says in *Hippolytus* (fr. 8):

> But how the fruitful miscarried sow's womb,
> stewed until it turned white, is curdling!

And in *The Scientist* (fr. 20):

> a slice of sow's womb, well stewed,
> with heart-biting vinegar sauce inside it.

And in *Cockroaches* (fr. 17):

> that you may eat a stewed slice of sow's womb,
> pushing it into pungent rue gall.

[154] Cf. Plin. *Nat.* 11.210–11; Plu. *Mor.* 997a.

549

Οἱ μέντοι ἀρχαῖοι πάντες πρὸ τοῦ δειπνεῖν οὐ
παρέφερον οὔτε μήτρας οὔτε θρίδακας οὔτ᾽ ἄλλο τι
τῶν τοιούτων, ὥσπερ νῦν γίνεται. Ἀρχέστρατος γοῦν
ὁ ὀψοδαίδαλος μετὰ τὸ δεῖπνον καὶ τὰς προπόσεις καὶ
τὸ μύροις χρήσασθαί φησιν·

c   ἀεὶ δὲ στεφάνοισι κάρα παρὰ δαῖτα πυκάζου |
παντοδαποῖς, οἷς ἂν γαίας πέδον ὄλβιον ἀνθῇ,
καὶ στακτοῖσι μύροις ἀγαθοῖς χαίτην θεράπευε,
καὶ σμύρναν λιβανόν τε πυρὸς μαλακὴν ἐπὶ
   τέφραν
βάλλε πανημέριος, Συρίης εὐώδεα καρπόν,
ἐμπίνοντι δέ σοι φερέτω τοιόνδε τράγημα,
γαστέρα καὶ μήτραν ἐφθὴν ὑὸς ἔν τε κυμίνῳ
ἔν τ᾽ ὄξει δριμεῖ καὶ σιλφίῳ ἐμβεβαῶσαν

d   ὀρνίθων τ᾽ ὀπτῶν ἁπαλὸν γένος, ὧν ἂν | ὑπάρχῃ
ὥρη. τῶν δὲ Συρακοσίων τούτων ἀμέλησον,
οἳ πίνουσι μόνον βατράχων τρόπον, οὐδὲν
   ἔδοντες.
ἀλλὰ σὺ μὴ πείθου κείνοις, ἃ δ᾽ ἐγὼ λέγω ἔσθε
βρωτά· τὰ δ᾽ ἄλλα γ᾽ ἐκεῖνα τραγήματα πάντα
   πέφυκε
πτωχείης παράδειγμα κακῆς, ἐφθοί τ᾽ ἐρέβινθοι
καὶ κύαμοι καὶ μῆλα καὶ ἰσχάδες. ἀλλὰ

e   πλακοῦντα |
αἰνῶ Ἀθήνησιν γεγενημένον· εἰ δὲ μὴ αὐτοῦ
αὐτὸν ἔχῃς, ἑτέρωθι μέλι ζήτησον ἀπελθὼν
Ἀττικόν, ὡς τοῦτ᾽ ἐστὶν ὃ ποιεῖ κεῖνον ὑβριστήν.

None of the ancients, however, served sows' wombs,
lettuce, or anything else of this sort before they had dinner,
as happens now. The culinary genius Archestratus (fr. 60
Olson–Sens = *SH* 192), for example, mentions it after the
dinner, the toasts, and the use of perfume:

Always cover your head at a feast with garlands
of every variety, with which the earth's rich plain
　　blooms;
treat your hair with fine perfumes dispensed in drops;
and all day long cast myrrh and frankincense,
the fragrant fruit of Syria, upon the fire's soft ash.
And to you, as you are drinking your fill, let someone
　　bring a dainty such as
a stomach-sausage, or a stewed sow's womb that has
　　embarked
in cumin and in pungent vinegar and silphium,
or the tender race of whatever roasted birds are in
season. Pay no attention to these Syracusans,
who act like frogs and merely drink without eating
　　anything.
Pay them no heed, but eat the foods
I mention. All those other dainties are
evidence of wretched beggary—boiled chickpeas,
fava beans, apples, and dried figs. But I praise
the flat-cake born in Athens; if you do not have it
　　there,
go off elsewhere and look for Attic honey,
since that is what makes it saucy.

οὕτω τοι δεῖ ζῆν τὸν ἐλεύθερον ἢ κατὰ τῆς γῆς
καὶ κατὰ τοῦ βαράθρου καὶ Ταρτάρου ἐς τὸν
   ὄλεθρον
ἥκειν καὶ κατορωρύχθαι σταδίους ἀναρίθμους.

Λυγκεὺς δὲ διαγράφων τὸ Λαμίας τῆς αὐλητρίδος
δεῖπνον, ὅτε ὑπεδέχετο Δημήτριον τὸν Πολιορκητήν,
εὐθέως τοὺς εἰσελθόντας ἐπὶ τὸ δεῖπνον ἐσθίοντας
ποιεῖ ἰχθῦς παντοίους καὶ κρέα. ὁμοίως καὶ τὸ Ἀντι-
f γόνου | τοῦ βασιλέως δεῖπνον διατιθεὶς ἐπιτελοῦντος
Ἀφροδίσια καὶ τὸ Πτολεμαίου τοῦ βασιλέως ἰχθῦς
πρῶτον παρατίθησι καὶ κρέα. θαυμάζειν δ᾽ ἐστὶν
ἄξιον τοῦ τὰς καλὰς ὑποθήκας παραδιδόντος ἡμῖν
Ἀρχεστράτου, ὡς Ἐπικούρῳ τῷ σοφῷ τῆς ἡδονῆς
καθηγεμὼν γενόμενος κατὰ τὸν Ἀσκραῖον ποιητὴν
γνωμικῶς καὶ ἡμῖν συμβουλεύει τισὶ μὲν μὴ πείθε-
σθαι, αὐτῷ δὲ προσέχειν τὸν νοῦν, καὶ ἐσθίειν παρακελεύεται τὰ καὶ τά, οὐδὲν ἀποδέων τοῦ παρὰ Δαμο-
ξένῳ τῷ κωμῳδιοποιῷ μαγείρου, ὃς ἐν Συντρόφοις
102 φησίν· ||

            (Α.) Ἐπικούρου δέ με
ὁρᾷς μαθητὴν ὄντα τοῦ σοφοῦ, παρ᾽ ᾧ
ἐν δύ᾽ ἔτεσιν καὶ μησὶν οὐχ ὅλοις δέκα
τάλαντ᾽ ἐγώ σοι κατεπύκνωσα τέτταρα.
(Β.) τοῦτο δὲ τί ἐστιν; εἰπέ μοι. (Α.) καθήγισα.
μάγειρος ἦν κἀκεῖνος † οὐκ ᾔδει θεοί †.
(Β.) ποῖος μάγειρος; (Α.) ἡ φύσις πάσης τέχνης

That is how a free man ought to live, or else go down
unto destruction beneath the earth and beneath the
Pit and Tartarus,
and be buried countless stades deep.

Lynceus (fr. 4 Dalby), in his description of the dinner given
by the pipe-girl Lamia[155] when she entertained Demetrius
Poliorcetes, represents them as eating all kinds of fish and
meat as soon as they came in to dinner. Likewise in his account of the dinners given by King Antigonus when he was
celebrating the Aphrodisia and by King Ptolemy, he serves
them fish and meat at the very start.[156] There is good reason to admire Archestratus (cf. fr. 60.10–13 Olson–Sens =
SH 192.10–13, above), who passes on to us his excellent in-
structions and, as a forerunner of the wise Epicurus on the
subject of pleasure, advises us in a didactic fashion remi-
niscent of Hesiod not to put any confidence in certain people, but to pay attention to him, and urges us to eat this and
that, exactly like the cook in the comic poet Damoxenus,
who says in Foster-brothers (fr. 2):

> (A.) You see that I'm
> a student of the wise Epicurus, in whose house
> in less than two years and ten months,
> I'd have you know, I "condensed" four talents.
> (B.) What does this mean? Tell me! (A.) I "sanctified"
> them.
> He was a cook, too [corrupt].
> (B.) What do you mean, "a cook"? (A.) Nature is the
> fundamental source

155 PAA 601325; cf. 4.128b.   156 For the letters containing these descriptions, see 4.128a–b; and cf. 3.100e–f.

ἀρχέγονόν ἐστ'. (Β.) ἀρχέγονον, ὦλιτήριε;
(Α.) οὐκ ἔστιν οὐθὲν τοῦ πονεῖν σοφώτερον,
ἦν τ' εὐχερὲς τὸ πρᾶγμα τοῦ λόγου τριβὴν |
ἔχοντι τούτου· πολλὰ γὰρ συμβάλλεται.
διόπερ μάγειρον ὅταν ἴδῃς ἀγράμματον
μὴ Δημόκριτόν τε πάντα διανεγνωκότα,
καὶ τὸν Ἐπικούρου Κανόνα, μινθώσας ἄφες
ὡς ἐκ διατριβῆς. τοῦτο δεῖ γὰρ εἰδέναι,
τίν' ἔχει διαφορὰν πρῶτον, ὦ βέλτιστε σύ,
γλαυκίσκος ἐν χειμῶνι καὶ θέρει, πάλιν |
ποῖος περὶ δύσιν Πλειάδος συνειδέναι
ἰχθὺς ὑπὸ τροπάς τ' ἐστὶ χρησιμώτατος.
αἱ μεταβολαὶ γὰρ αἵ τε κινήσεις κακὸν
ἠλίβατον ἀνθρώποισιν ἀλλοιώματα
ἐν ταῖς τροφαῖς ποιοῦσι, μανθάνεις; τὸ δὲ
ληφθὲν καθ' ὥραν ἀποδίδωσι τὴν χάριν.
τίς παρακολουθεῖ ταῦτα; τοιγαροῦν στρόφοι
καὶ πνευμάτια γινόμενα τὸν κεκλημένον |
ἀσχημονεῖν ποιοῦσι. παρὰ δ' ἐμοὶ τρέφει
τὸ προσφερόμενον βρῶμα καὶ λεπτύνεται,
ὀρθῶς τε διαπνεῖ. τοιγαροῦν εἰς τοὺς πόρους
ὁ χυμὸς ὁμαλῶς πανταχοῦ συνίσταται—
(Β.) χυμός; (Α.) λέγει Δημόκριτος—οὐδ'
    ἐμφράγματα
γινόμενα ποιεῖ τὸν φαγόντ' ἀρθριτικόν.

---

[157] See 2.62d n.

of every technical skill. (B.) The "fundamental
    source," you sinner?
(A.) There's nothing wiser than hard work,
and anyone who devotes himself to this saying finds
his business easy; for he gets help from many
    quarters.
So if you ever see a cook who's uneducated
and hasn't read Democritus from beginning to end,
along with Epicurus' *Canon*—smear his nose with
    shit and kick him out,
like they kick people out of philosophical schools!
    Because this is what he needs to know:
first of all, my good sir, how the *glaukiskos*[157]
is different in the winter and the summer; he also
has to understand what kind of fish is best
when the Pleiades set and at the solstice.
For changes and movements produce alterations
in the food people eat, which is an
abysmal evil for them, don't you know? But
    whatever's
eaten at the proper time brings a benefit.
Who understands this? The result is upset stomachs
and gas, which make the guest
disgrace himself. But when I'm there, the food
they eat is nourishing and digestible,
and everyone can breath normally. And the result is
    that its humour
is distributed evenly into the pores everywhere—
(B.) Its "humour"? (A.) Thus Democritus—and there
    are
no obstructions that give the man who eats it gout.

(Β.) καὶ τῆς ἰατρικῆς τι μετέχειν μοι δοκεῖς.

e (Α.) καὶ πᾶς ὁ φύσεως ἐντός. ἡ δ᾽ ἀπειρία |
τῶν νῦν μαγείρων κατανόει, πρὸς τῶν θεῶν,
οἷα 'στίν. ἅλμην ὅταν ἴδῃς ἐξ ἰχθύων
ὑπεναντίων αὐτοῖσι ποιοῦντας μίαν
καὶ σήσαμ᾽ ὑποτρίβοντας εἰς ταύτην, λαβὼν
ἕκαστον αὐτῶν κατὰ μέρος προσπαρδέτ᾽. (Β.)
    ἐγώ;

ὥς μοι κέχρησαι. (Α.) τί γὰρ ἂν εὖ γένοιτ᾽ ἔτι,
τῆς ἰδιότητος πρὸς ἑτέραν μεμιγμένης

f καὶ συμπλεκομένης οὐχὶ συμφώνους ἀφάς; |
τὸ ταῦτα διορᾶν ἐστιν ἐμψύχου τέχνης,
οὐ τὸ διανίζειν λοπάδας οὐδ᾽ ὄζειν καπνοῦ.
ἐγὼ γὰρ εἰς τοὐπτάνιον οὐκ εἰσέρχομαι.
(Β.) ἀλλὰ τί; (Α.) θεωρῶ πλησίον καθήμενος,
πονοῦσι δ᾽ ἕτεροι. (Β.) σὺ δέ; (Α.) λέγω τὰς
    αἰτίας
καὶ τἀποβαῖνον. "ὀξὺ τὸ περίκομμ᾽, ἄνες."
(Β.) ἁρμονικός, οὐ μάγειρος. (Α.) "ἐπίτεινον. τὸ
    πῦρ

103 ὁμαλιζέτω τοῖς τάχεσιν. ἡ πρώτη λοπὰς ‖
ζεῖ ταῖς ἐφεξῆς οὐχὶ συμφώνως." νοεῖς
τὸν τύπον; (Β.) Ἄπολλον. (Α.) καί τι φαίνεται
    τέχνη;
εἶτ᾽ οὐθὲν εἰκῆ παρατίθημι (μανθάνεις;)
βρῶμ᾽, ἀλλὰ μείξας πάντα κατὰ συμφωνίαν.

(B.) Apparently you also know something about
    medicine.
(A.) As does anyone with insight into Nature. But
    consider
the ignorance of today's cooks, by the gods!
If you ever see them making a single broth
out of fish with opposed characters
and grinding sesame seed into it—grab them
and fart on each of them, one after another! (B.) Me?
I can't believe how you're treating me. (A.) What
    good could result,
when one characteristic is mingled with another
and entangled in an unharmonious mix?
Distinguishing these things is a mark of inspired
    craftsmanship,
not washing casserole-dishes or smelling like smoke.
Because I don't go into the kitchen.
(B.) What *do* you do? (A.) I sit nearby and watch;
the other people do the work. (B.) What about you?
    (A.) I identify causes
and results. "The mincemeat's too tart; lower it a
    note!"
(B.) You're a composer, not a cook! (A.) "Raise the
    pitch! Get the fire
in time with the beat! The first casserole-dish
is boiling out of time with the ones next to it!" Do
    you see
what I'm driving at? (B.) Apollo! (A.) Does this look
    anything like a technical skill?
And I don't serve the food at random, do you
    understand?
Instead, I arrange everything harmoniously.

(B.) πῶς; (A.) ἔστιν αὐτοῖς ἃ διὰ τεττάρων ἔχει
κοινωνίαν, διὰ πέντε, διὰ πασῶν πάλιν.
ταῦτα προσάγω πρὸς αὐτὰ τὰ διαστήματα
καὶ ταῖς ἐπιφοραῖς εὐθὺς οἰκείως πλέκω.
ἐνίοτε δ' ἐφεστὼς παρακελεύομαι· "πόθεν
b ἅπτει; τί τούτῳ μειγνύειν μέλλεις; ὅρα, |
διάφωνον ἕλκεις· οὐχ ὑπερβήσῃ;" † σοφὸν †
Ἐπίκουρος οὕτω κατεπύκνου τὴν ἡδονήν·
ἐμασᾶτ' ἐπιμελῶς. εἶδε τἀγαθὸν μόνος
ἐκεῖνος οἷόν ἐστιν· οἱ δ' ἐν τῇ στοᾷ
ζητοῦσι συνεχῶς, οἷόν ἐστ' οὐκ εἰδότες.
οὐκοῦν ὅ γ' οὐκ ἔχουσιν, ἀγνοοῦσι δέ,
οὐδ' ἂν ἑτέρῳ δοίησαν. (B.) οὕτω συνδοκεῖ·
ἀφῶμεν οὖν τὰ λοιπά· δῆλα δὴ πάλαι.

καὶ Βάτων[62] δ' ἐν Συνεξαπατῶντι δυσχεραίνοντα ποι-
c ήσας μειρακίου πατέρα ὡς διαφθαρέντος | κατὰ τὴν
δίαιταν ὑπὸ τοῦ παιδαγωγοῦ φησίν·

(A.) ἀπολώλεκας τὸ μειράκιόν μου παραλαβών,
ἀκάθαρτε, καὶ πέπεικας ἐλθεῖν εἰς βίον
ἀλλότριον αὐτοῦ· καὶ πότους ἑωθινοὺς

---

[62] Βάτων Casaubon: Πλάτων ACE

---

[158] Quoted again at 7.279a–c.

(B.) How? (A.) Some items have a four-part
structure, others a five-part, others a structure that
    combines everything.
I bring them together in ways that suit these precise
    dimensions,
and weave them in appropriately with what comes
    next.
Sometimes when I'm supervising I give orders like:
    "What does this
connect to? What are you going to mix with this?
    Watch out!—
you're hitting a false note! Leave that out!" [corrupt]
This is how Epicurus "condensed" pleasure:
he chewed carefully. He's the only person
who knew what the Good is. The Stoics
are always looking for it, although they don't know
    what it's like.
And since they don't have it and aren't able to
    recognize it,
they can't give it to anyone else. (B.) We agree about
    that.
But let's let the rest go; it's been clear for a long time.

Bato too says in *The Partner in Deception* (fr. 5)[158], in
which he presents a father upset about his son, who has descended into a life of debauchery under the influence of
his slave guardian:

(A.) You've taken my boy and ruined him,
you bastard; and you've convinced him to adopt a
    lifestyle
that's foreign to him. He's drinking in the morning

πίνει διὰ σὲ νῦν, πρότερον οὐκ εἰθισμένος.
(B.) εἶτ' εἰ μεμάθηκε, δέσποτα, ζῆν, ἐγκαλεῖς;
(A.) ζῆν δ' ἐστὶ τὸ τοιοῦθ'; (B.) ὡς λέγουσιν οἱ
   σοφοί.

ὁ γοῦν Ἐπίκουρός φησιν εἶναι τἀγαθὸν
d   τὴν ἡδονὴν δήπουθεν· οὐκ ἔστιν δ' ἔχειν |
ταύτην ἑτέρωθεν, ἐκ δὲ τοῦ ζῆν παγκάλως
† ευσωσιαπαντη † τυχὸν δώσεις ἐμοί.
(A.) ἑόρακας οὖν φιλόσοφον, εἰπέ μοι, τινὰ
μεθύοντ' ἐπὶ τούτοις θ' οἷς λέγεις κηλούμενον;
(B.) ἅπαντας· οἱ γὰρ τὰς ὀφρῦς ἐπηρκότες
καὶ τὸν φρόνιμον ζητοῦντες ἐν τοῖς περιπάτοις
καὶ ταῖς διατριβαῖς ὥσπερ ἀποδεδρακότα,
οὕτως, ἐπὰν γλαυκίσκος αὐτοῖς παρατεθῇ,
e   ἴσασιν οὗ δεῖ πρῶτον ἅψασθαι τόπου |
καὶ τὴν κεφαλὴν ζητοῦσιν ὥσπερ πράγματος,
ὥστ' ἐκπεπλῆχθαι πάντας.

καὶ παρ' Ἀντιφάνει δ' ἐν Στρατιώτῃ ⟨ἢ⟩ Τύχωνι
παραινέσεις εἰσφέρων ἄνθρωπος τοιοῦτός ἐστιν, ὅς
φησιν·

          ὅστις ἄνθρωπος δὲ φὺς
ἀσφαλές τι κτῆμ' ὑπάρχειν τῷ βίῳ λογίζεται,
πλεῖστον ἡμάρτηκεν· ἢ γὰρ εἰσφορά τις ἥρπακεν

---

159 Literally "who have raised eyebrows"; cf. 2.35d n.

now, because of you, which isn't something he used
     to do.
(B.) Are you complaining, master, because he's
     learned how to live?
(A.) Is this kind of behavior "living"? (B.) That's what
     the wise say.
Epicurus, for example, identified the Good
with pleasure, I believe. And you can't get
pleasure from anywhere else; but by living very well
[corrupt] you'll grant me is to the point.
(A.) Tell me, then—have you ever seen a philosopher
drunk or enchanted by the sort of actions you're
     describing?
(B.) All of them! Because the ones with a haughty
     expression,[159]
who are on the look-out for the "prudent man" in
     their discussions
and their debates, as if he were a runaway slave—
if they're served a *glaukiskos*,
they're so knowledgeable about where to take hold of
     it first,
and they get to the "head of the matter," as it were, so
     fast,
that everyone's stunned.

Also in Antiphanes' *The Soldier or Tychon* (fr. 202) there is
a person of this type, who offers advice and says:

              Any human being
who thinks that anything he owns is his for life
is very much in error. For either a special levy
     snatches away

f τἄνδοθεν πάντ', ἢ δίκῃ τις περιπεσὼν ἀπώλετο, |
   ἢ στρατηγήσας προσῶφλεν, ⟨ἢ⟩ χορηγὸς
   αἱρεθεὶς
   ἱμάτια χρυσᾶ παρασχὼν τῷ χορῷ ῥάκος φορεῖ,
   ἢ τριηραρχῶν ἀπήγξατ', ἢ πλέων ἥλωκέ ποι,
   ἢ βαδίζων ἢ καθεύδων κατακέκοφθ' ὑπ' οἰκετῶν.
   οὐ βέβαιον οὐθέν ἐστι, πλὴν ὅσ' ἂν καθ'
104   ἡμέραν ||
   εἰς ἑαυτὸν ἡδέως τις εἰσαναλίσκων τύχῃ.
   οὐδὲ ταῦτα σφόδρα τι· καὶ γὰρ τὴν τράπεζαν
   ἁρπάσαι
   κειμένην ἄν τις προσελθών· ἀλλ' ὅταν τὴν
   ἔνθεσιν
   ἐντὸς ἤδη τῶν ὀδόντων τυγχάνῃς κατεσπακώς,
   τοῦτ' ἐν ἀσφαλεῖ νόμιζε τῶν ὑπαρχόντων μόνον.

   τὰ αὐτὰ εἴρηκε καὶ ἐν Ὑδρίᾳ. εἰς ταῦτ' οὖν τις ἀπο-
b βλέπων, ἄνδρες φίλοι, εἰκότως ἂν ἐπαινέσειεν | τὸν
   καλὸν Χρύσιππον κατιδόντα ἀκριβῶς τὴν Ἐπικούρου
   φύσιν καὶ εἰπόντα μητρόπολιν εἶναι τῆς φιλοσοφίας
   αὐτοῦ τὴν Ἀρχεστράτου Γαστρολογίαν, ἣν πάντες οἱ
   τῶν φιλοσόφων γαστρίμαργοι Θέογνίν[63] τινα αὐτῶν

---

63 Θέογνίν Welcker: θεογονίαν A

---

160 *Chorēgoi* (literally "chorus-leaders") were wealthy individuals required to provide financial support for a set of tragedies, a comedy, or a dithyramb at one of Athens' state festivals.
161 Trierarchs ("trireme commanders") were required to outfit

everything he's accumulated; or he gets involved in a
    lawsuit and is ruined;
or he serves as a general and is fined; or he's selected
    as a *chorēgos*,[160]
and provides golden clothing for his chorus but is
    reduced to rags himself;
or he hangs himself while serving as a trierarch;[161] or
    he's captured as he's sailing somewhere;
or his slaves cut him to pieces when he's walking
    along the street or fast asleep.
Nothing is certain, except what a man spends
on enjoying himself on a day-by-day basis.
And even that's not completely secure, because
    someone could come up
and steal the table while it's sitting in front of him. So
    when you've got
a mouthful past your teeth and swallowed down,
you can consider that the one possession you've got
    firm control of.

He says the same in *The Pitcher* (Antiph. fr. 211). Someone
who pays attention to these matters, my friends, would
with good reason praise the noble Chrysippus (fr. 709,
SVF iii.178), who understands Epicurus' "Nature" precisely and says that the original source of his philosophy
is the *Gastrology* of Archestratus (test. 6 Olson–Sens), a
lovely bit of epic poetry which all gluttonous philosophers
claim as their particular Theognis.[162] Theognetus too is re-

---

and man one of the city's fighting ships for a year, potentially at ru-
inous expense.   [162] I.e. as a fundamental source of moral
and social instruction.

εἶναι λέγουσι τὴν καλὴν ταύτην ἐποποιίαν. πρὸς οὓς
καὶ Θέογνητος ἐν Φάσματι ἢ Φιλαργύρῳ φησίν·

ἐκ τούτων < . . . >,
ἄνθρωπ᾽, ἀπολεῖς με· τῶν γὰρ ἐκ τῆς ποικίλης
στοᾶς λογαρίων ἀναπεπλησμένος νοσεῖς.
"ἀλλότριόν ἐσθ᾽ ὁ πλοῦτος ἀνθρώπῳ, | πάχνη·
σοφία δ᾽ ἴδιον, κρύσταλλος. οὐθεὶς πώποτε
ταύτην λαβὼν ἀπώλεσ᾽." ὦ τάλας ἐγώ,
οἵῳ μ᾽ ὁ δαίμων φιλοσόφῳ συνῴκισεν.
ἐπαρίστερ᾽ ἔμαθες, ὦ πόνηρε, γράμματα·
ἀντέστροφέν σου τὸν βίον τὰ βιβλία·
πεφιλοσόφηκας γῇ τε κοὐρανῷ λαλῶν,
οἷς οὐθέν ἐστιν ἐπιμελὲς τῶν σῶν λόγων.

Ἔτι τοῦ Οὐλπιανοῦ διαλεγομένου παῖδες ἐπεισῆλ-
θον φέροντες ἐπὶ δίσκων καράβους μείζονας | Καλλι-
μέδοντος τοῦ ῥήτορος, ὃς διὰ τὸ φιληδεῖν τῷ βρώματι
Κάραβος ἐπεκλήθη. Ἄλεξις μὲν οὖν αὐτὸν ἐν Δορκίδι
ἢ Ποππυζούσῃ φίλιχθυν εἶναι κοινῶς παραδίδωσι,
καθάπερ καὶ ἄλλοι τῶν κωμῳδιοποιῶν, λέγων οὕτως·

τοῖς ἰχθυοπώλαις ἐστὶν ἐψηφισμένον,
ὥς φασι, χαλκῆν Καλλιμέδοντος εἰκόνα

---

163 Frequented by the philosopher Zeno, whose sect accordingly came to be called the "Stoics."

164 For Callimedon and his fondness for seafood, cf. 3.100c n.

165 Athenaeus refers to this play in the same way at 10.431a,
but at 9.395b gives the first of the two alternative titles as either

ferring to these people when he says in *The Phantom or The Man Who Loved Money* (fr. 1):

> You'll be the death of me,
> sir, with these arguments! You're stuffed full of little speeches
> from the Stoa Poicile,[163] and they've made you sick.
> "Wealth doesn't really belong to a person, whereas wisdom
> is our own; it's frost versus ice. No one ever
> lost his wisdom after he got it." Miserable me—
> what a philosopher the gods forced me to share a house with!
> You learned your letters backwards, fool!
> Your books turned your life upside-down!
> You've offered your philosophical babbling to earth and heaven,
> and they're completely uninterested in what you have to say.

As Ulpian was still speaking, slaves came in carrying platters full of crayfish larger than the orator Callimedon, who got the nickname Crayfish because of his fondness for this food.[164] Alexis in fact reports in *Dorcis or The Girl Who Popped Her Lips* (fr. 57)[165] that he was fond of fish in general, as other comic poets also record. He says the following:

> The fish-sellers have voted,
> so people say, to erect a bronze statue

Rhodion ("Little Rose"; presumably a courtesan's name) or *The Man from Rhodes*.

στῆσαι Παναθηναίοισιν ἐν τοῖς ἰχθύσιν,
ἔχουσαν ὀπτὸν κάραβον ἐν τῇ δεξιᾷ,
e   ὡς αὐτὸν ὄντ᾽ αὐτοῖσι τῆς τέχνης μόνον |
σωτῆρα, τοὺς ἄλλους δὲ πάντας ζημίαν.

περισπούδαστος δὲ ἦν πολλοῖς ἡ τοῦ καράβου βρῶ-
σις, ὡς ἔστι δεῖξαι διὰ πολλῶν τῆς κωμῳδίας μερῶν·
ἀρκέσει δὲ τὰ νῦν Ἀριστοφάνης ἐν ταῖς Θεσμοφο-
ριαζούσαις οὕτως λέγων·

(Α.) ἰχθὺς ἐώνηταί τις ἢ σηπίδιον
ἢ τῶν πλατειῶν καρίδων ἢ πουλύπους;
ἢ νῆστις ὀπτᾶτ᾽ ἢ γαλεὸς ἢ τευθίδες;
(Β.) μὰ τὸν Δί᾽, οὐ δῆτ᾽. (Α.) οὐδὲ βατίς; (Β.) οὔ
f   φημ᾽ ἐγώ. |
(Α.) οὐδὲ χόρι᾽ οὐδὲ πυὸς οὐδ᾽ ἧπαρ κάπρου
οὐδὲ σχαδόνες οὐδ᾽ ἠτριαῖον δέλφακος
οὐδ᾽ ἐγχέλειον οὐδὲ κάραβος; μέγα
γυναιξὶ κοπιώσαισιν ἐπεκουρήσατε.

πλατείας δὲ καρίδας ἂν εἴη λέγων τοὺς ἀστακοὺς
καλουμένους, ὧν μνημονεύει Φιλύλλιος ἐν Πόλεσι.
καὶ Ἀρχέστρατος γὰρ ἐν τῷ διαβοήτῳ ποιήματι οὐδ᾽
ὅλως που κάραβον ὀνομάζων ἀστακὸν προσαγορεύει,
105 ὥσπερ κἂν τούτοις· ||

ἀλλὰ παρεὶς λῆρον πολὺν ἀστακὸν ὠνοῦ

---

166 I.e. the lost *Women Celebrating the Thesmophoria II*,
rather than the preserved play.

of Callimedon in the fish-market during the
    Panathenaic festival,
holding a roasted crayfish in its right hand,
since he is the sole savior
of their trade, and everyone else is a loss.

Many people were very eager to eat crayfish, as can be
demonstrated from numerous passages from comedy; but
for the moment Aristophanes will suffice to make the
point. He says the following in *Women Celebrating the
Thesmophoria*[166] (fr. 333):

> (A.) Has any fish been bought? Or a little cuttlefish
> or some broad shrimp or an octopus?
> Or has a dogfish been roasted? Or a mullet or some
>   squid?
> (B.) Certainly not, by Zeus. (A.) No skate? (B.)
>   Absolutely not.
> (A.) No haggis, beestings, boar's liver,
> honeycomb, pork belly,
> eel, or crayfish? This is great aid
> you've lent to wearied women!

By "broad shrimp" he must be referring to what are called
astakoi ("lobsters"), which Philyllius mentions in *Cities* (fr.
12.1).[167] Because Archestratus (fr. 25 Olson–Sens = *SH*
155) as well refers to the crayfish by name nowhere in his
much-celebrated poem, but calls it an *astakos*, as in the
following lines:

> But pass over much rubbish and buy yourself an

[167] Quoted at 3.86e.

τὸν τὰς χεῖρας ἔχοντα μακρὰς ἄλλως τε
βαρείας,
τοὺς δὲ πόδας μικρούς, βραδέως δ᾽ ἐπὶ γαῖαν
ὀρούει.
εἰσὶ δὲ πλεῖστοι μὲν πάντων ἀρετῇ τε κράτιστοι
ἐν Λιπάραις· πολλοὺς δὲ καὶ Ἑλλήσποντος
ἀθροίζει.

καὶ Ἐπίχαρμος δ᾽ ἐν Ἥβας Γάμῳ τὸν προειρημένον
ἀστακὸν ὑπὸ τοῦ Ἀρχεστράτου δηλοῖ ὅτι κάραβός
ἐστι λέγων οὕτως·

b   ἐντὶ δ᾽ ἀστακοὶ κολύβδαιναί τε | χὢς τὰ πόδι᾽
ἔχει
μικρά, τὰς χεῖρας δὲ μακράς, κάραβος δὲ
τὤνυμα.

ἴδιον δ᾽ ἐστὶ γένος καράβων καὶ ἀστακῶν ἄλλο, ἔτι δὲ
καρίδων. τὸν δ᾽ ἀστακὸν οἱ Ἀττικοὶ διὰ τοῦ ō ὀστακὸν
λέγουσι, καθάπερ καὶ ὀσταφίδας. Ἐπίχαρμος δὲ ἐν
Γᾷ καὶ Θαλάσσᾳ φησίν·

    < . . . > κἀστακοὶ γαμψώνυχοι.

Σπεύσιππος δὲ ἐν δευτέρῳ Ὁμοίων παραπλήσιά φησιν εἶναι τῶν μαλακοστράκων κάραβον, ἀστακόν,
νύμφην, ἄρκτον, καρκίνον, πάγουρον. Διοκλῆς δ᾽ ὁ
Καρύστιός φησι· καρίδες, καρκίνοι, κάραβοι, ἀστακοὶ
c εὐστόμαχα καὶ διουρητικά. | κολύβδαιναν δ᾽ εἴρηκεν
Ἐπίχαρμος ἐν τοῖς προεκκειμένοις, ὡς μὲν Νίκανδρός

> *astakos*,
> the one that has large and, in addition, heavy hands,
> although its feet small and it rushes along slowly
>   on land.
> They are most numerous and of the highest quality
> in the Lipari Islands; but the Hellespont as well
>   assembles many of them.

Epicharmus in *The Wedding of Hebe* (fr. 50) makes it clear that the *astakos* referred to by Archestratus above is a crayfish, when he says the following:

> There are *astakoi* and *kolubdainai*[168] and the one that
>   has little
> feet but large hands, whose name is crayfish.

Crayfish are a distinct family, lobsters *(astakoi)* another, and shrimp a third. Attic authors refer to the *astakos* as an *ostakos*, with an *omicron*, like *ostaphides*.[169] Epicharmus says in *Earth and Sea* (fr. 27):

> and crook-clawed lobsters *(astakoi)*.

Speusippus in Book II of *Similar Things* (fr. 9 Tarán) says that the crustaceans that resemble one another are the crayfish, lobster, *numphē*, bear-crab, crab *(karkinos)*, and common crab *(pagouros)*. Diocles of Carystus (fr. 224 van der Eijk) says: Shrimp, crabs, crayfish, and lobsters are easy on the stomach and diuretic. Epicharmus in the passage quoted above (fr. 50.1, quoted at 3.105b–c) uses the word *kolubdaina* to refer to the sea-phallus, according to

---

[168] For this word, see 3.105c.
[169] "Raisins," normally *astaphides*.

φησι, τὸ θαλάσσιον αἰδοῖον, ὡς δ' ὁ Ἡρακλείδης ἐν
Ὀψαρτυτικῷ, τὴν καρίδα. Ἀριστοτέλης δ' ἐν <πέμ-
π>τῳ Ζῴων Μορίων, τῶν μαλακοστράκων ὀχεύονται,
φησί, κάραβοι, ἀστακοί, καρίδες καὶ τὰ τοιαῦτα,
ὥσπερ καὶ τὰ ὀπισθουρητικὰ τῶν τετραπόδων. ὀχεύονται δὲ τοῦ ἔαρος ἀρχομένου πρὸς τῇ γῇ (ἤδη γὰρ
ὦπται ἡ ὀχεία πάντων τῶν τοιούτων), ἐνιαχοῦ δὲ ὅταν
τὰ σῦκα ἄρχηται πεπαίνεσθαι. γίνονται δ' οἱ μὲν
d κάραβοι ἐν τοῖς τραχέσι | καὶ πετρώδεσιν, οἱ δ'
ἀστακοὶ ἐν τοῖς λείοις, ἐν δὲ τοῖς πηλώδεσιν οὐδέ-
τεροι. διὸ καὶ ἐν Ἑλλησπόντῳ μὲν καὶ περὶ Θάσον
ἀστακοὶ γίνονται, περὶ δὲ τὸ Σίγειον καὶ τὸν Ἄθω
κάραβοι. εἰσὶ δ' οἱ κάραβοι μακρόβιοι πάντες. Θεόφραστος δ' ἐν τῷ Περὶ τῶν Φωλευόντων τοὺς ἀστακοὺς καὶ καράβους καὶ καρίδας ἐκδύεσθαί φησι τὸ
γῆρας.

Περὶ δὲ τῶν καρίδων, ὅτι καὶ πόλις ἦν Καρίδες
περὶ Χίον τὴν νῆσον Ἔφορος ἐν τῇ τρίτῃ[64] ἱστορεῖ,
κτίσαι φάσκων αὐτὴν τοὺς διασωθέντας ἐκ τοῦ ἐπὶ
e Δευκαλίωνος | γενομένου κατακλυσμοῦ μετὰ Μάκα-
ρος, καὶ μέχρι νῦν τὸν τόπον καλεῖσθαι Καρίδας. ὁ δὲ
ὀψοδαίδαλος Ἀρχέστρατος παραινεῖ τάδε·

ἦν δέ ποτ' εἰς Ἴασον Καρῶν πόλιν εἰσαφίκηαι,
καρίδ' εὐμεγέθη λήψει· σπανίην δὲ πριᾶσθαι.

[64] τρίτῃ Marx: πρώτῃ A

Nicander (fr. 139 Schneider); but Heracleides in the *Art of Cooking* says that he means the shrimp. Aristotle in Book V of *Parts of Animals* (*HA* 541^{b}19–24) says: Of the crustaceans, crayfish, lobsters, shrimp, and the like copulate in the same way that those quadrapeds that urinate backwards do. They copulate in early spring near the land (because the copulation of all such creatures has been observed); but in some places this takes place when the figs begin to ripen. (*HA* 549^{b}13–17) Crayfish are found in rough, rocky areas, whereas lobsters are found in areas free of rocks; neither is found in muddy areas. As a result, lobsters are found in the Hellespont and around Thasos, whereas crayfish are found around Sigeum and Athos. (*HA* 549^{b}28) All crayfish are long-lived. Theophrastus in his *On Animals That Live in Holes* (fr. 367) says that lobsters, crabs, and shrimp shed their outgrown shells.

As for shrimp, Ephorus in Book III (*FGrH* 70 F 11) reports the existence of a city by that name near the island of Chios; he claims that survivors of the flood that occurred in Deucalion's time, joined by Macar,[170] founded it, and that it was still called Shrimp in his time. The culinary genius Archestratus (fr. 26 Olson–Sens = *SH* 156) offers the following advice:

> But if you ever come to the Carian city of Iasus,
> you will buy a nice big shrimp, although it is rarely
>   for sale there.

---

[170] Also called Macareus, and better known for settling Lesbos (and from there Chios, Samos, and Cos) after the great flood (D.S. 5.81.3–8).

ἐν δὲ Μακηδονίη τε καὶ Ἀμβρακίῃ μάλα πολλαί.

ἐκτεταμένως δ᾽ εἴρηκε καρίδα Ἀραρὼς μὲν ἐν Καμπυ-
λίωνι·

αἵ τε καμπύλαι
f   καρῖδες ἐξήλλοντο δελφίνων δίκην |
εἰς σχοινόπλεκτον ἄγγος.

καὶ Εὔβουλος ἐν Ὀρθάννῃ·

καρῖδα καθῆκα κάτω κἀνέσπασ᾽ αὖθις.

Ἀναξανδρίδης Λυκούργῳ·

καὶ συμπαίζει καριδαρίοις
μετὰ περκιδίων καὶ θρᾳττιδίων,
† καὶ ψιτταδίοις μετὰ κωβιδαρίων
καὶ σκινδαρίοις μετὰ κωβιδίων †.

106 ὁ δ᾽ αὐτὸς κἀν Πανδάρῳ φησίν· ‖

οὐκ ἐπικεκυφὼς ὀρθός, ὦ βέλτιστ᾽, ἔσῃ·
αὕτη δὲ καριδοῖ τὸ σῶμα καμπύλη,
ἄγκυρά τ᾽ ἐστὶν ἄντικρυς τοῦ σώματος.

ἐν δὲ Κερκίῳ·

ἐρυθρότερον καρῖδος ὀπτῆς σ᾽ ἀποφανῶ.

Εὔβουλος Τιτθαῖς·

καρῖδάς τε τῶν
κυφῶν.

But in Macedon and Ambracia they are quite
numerous.

Araros used the word *karis* ("shrimp") with a long *iota* in
Campulion (fr. 8.2–4):[171]

> and the bent
> shrimp leapt out like dolphins
> into a container woven out of rushes.

Also Eubulus in *Orthannes* (fr. 78):

> I lowered a shrimp down and pulled it up again.

Anaxandrides in *Lycurgus* (fr. 28):

> And he plays with little shrimp
> accompanied by tiny perch and *thrattai*,
> † and with little flatfish accompanied by tiny gobies,
> and with little maigres accompanied by little gobies. †

The same author says in *Pandarus* (fr. 38):

> You'll be straight, not bent over, my good sir.
> But she curls her body so she's bent like a shrimp
> and is an outright anchor for your body.

In *Cercion* (fr. 23):

> I'll make you look redder than a roasted shrimp!

Eubulus in *Wet-Nurses* (fr. 110):

> some of the curved
> shrimp.

---

[171] Additional portions of the fragment are preserved at 3.86d.

καὶ Ὠφελίων Καλλαίσχρῳ·

κυρταὶ δ' ὁμοῦ καρῖδες ἐν ξηρῷ πέδῳ.

καὶ ἐν Ἰαλέμῳ·

b   ὠρχοῦντο † ὥσπερ † καρῖδες ἀνθράκων ἔπι |
πηδῶσι κυρταί.

συνεσταλμένως δ' εἴρηκεν Εὔπολις ἐν Αἰξὶν οὕτως·

                                        πλὴν
ἅπαξ ποτ' ἐν Φαίακος ἔφαγον καρίδας.

καὶ ἐν Δήμοις·

ἔχων τὸ πρόσωπον καρίδος μασθλητίνης.

ὠνομάσθησαν δὲ καρῖδες ἀπὸ τοῦ κάρα· τὸ πλεῖστον
γὰρ μέρος τοῦ σώματος ἡ κεφαλὴ ἀπηνέγκατο. καρί-
c δες δὲ βραχέως οἱ Ἀττικοὶ | ἀναλόγως· παρὰ γὰρ τὸ
κάρη γέγονε διὰ τὸ μείζονι κεχρῆσθαι κεφαλῇ. ὡς οὖν
παρὰ τὸ γραφὴ γραφὶς καὶ βολὴ βολίς, οὕτως καὶ
παρὰ τὸ κάρη καρίς. ταθείσης δὲ τῆς παρατελευταίας
ἐτάθη καὶ τὸ τέλος, καὶ ὁμοίως λέγεται τῷ ψηφὶς καὶ
κρηπίς[65].

Περὶ δὲ τῶν ὀστρακοδέρμων τούτων Δίφιλος μὲν ὁ
Σίφνιος οὕτω γράφει· τῶν δ' ὀστρακοδέρμων καρίς,

[65] κρηπίς καὶ τευθίς A

Also Ophelio in *Callaeschrus* (fr. 2):[172]

> curved shrimp along with them on the dry ground.

And in *The Dolt* (fr. 1):

> They were dancing † just like † curved shrimp
> jumping around on the coals.

But Eupolis uses the word with a short *iota* in *Nanny-Goats* (fr. 2), as follows:

> except that
> I once ate shrimp in Phaeax' house.

And in *Demes* (fr. 120):

> with the face of a shrimp that's red as leather.

Shrimp *(karîdes)* got their name from the word *kara* ("head"), because their head occupies the largest portion of their body[173]. Attic authors use the form *karides* with a short *iota* for a similar reason: the word is derived from *karē* ("head"), because the shrimp has a very large head. So just as *graphis* ("stylus") is derived from *graphē* ("writing"), and *bolis* ("missile") from *bolē* ("throw"), so too *karis* is derived from *karē*. For when the penultimate syllable was lengthened, the end of the word was as well, and it is pronounced like *psēphîs* ("pebble") and *krēpîs* ("high boot").

Regarding these crustaceans, Diphilus of Siphnos writes as follows: Of the crustaceans, the shrimp, lobster, cray-

---

[172] Probably a personal name, but perhaps *Handsome Yet Ugly*.   [173] Far more likely the word was originally a diminutive of *karabos* ("crayfish").

ἀστακός, κάραβος, καρκίνος, λέων τοῦ αὐτοῦ γένους
d ὄντα διαφέρουσι. μείζων δ᾽ ἐστὶν | ὁ λέων τοῦ ἀστα-
κοῦ. οἱ δὲ κάραβοι καὶ γραψαῖοι λέγονται· τῶν καρκί-
νων δ᾽ εἰσὶν σαρκωδέστεροι. ὁ δὲ καρκίνος βαρὺς καὶ
δύσπεπτος. Μνησίθεος δ᾽ ὁ Ἀθηναῖος ἐν τῷ Περὶ
Ἐδεστῶν, κάραβοι, φησί, καὶ καρκίνοι καὶ καρῖδες
καὶ τὰ ὅμοια δύσπεπτα μὲν πάντα, τῶν δ᾽ ἄλλων
ἰχθύων εὐπεπτότερα πολλῷ. πρέπει δ᾽ αὐτοῖς ὀπτᾶ-
σθαι μᾶλλον ἢ ἕψεσθαι.

Κουρίδας δὲ τὰς καρίδας εἴρηκε Σώφρων ἐν Γυναι-
e κείοις οὕτως· ἴδε καλᾶν κουρίδων, ἴδε καμμάρων, ἴδε |
φίλα· θᾶσαι μὰν ὡς ἐρυθραί τ᾽ ἐντὶ καὶ λειοτριχιῶσαι.
Ἐπίχαρμος δ᾽ ἐν Γᾷ καὶ Θαλάσσᾳ·

⟨ . . . ⟩ κουρίδες τε φοινίκιαι.

ἐν δὲ Λόγῳ καὶ Λογίννᾳ διὰ τοῦ ω εἴρηκεν·

⟨ . . . ⟩ ἀφύας τε κωρίδας τε καμπύλας.

Σιμωνίδης δέ·

θύννοισι τευθίς, κωβιοῖσι κωρίδες.

fish, crab, and "lion" are different from one another, although they belong to the same family. The "lion" is larger than the lobster. Crayfish are also called *grapsaioi*; they are meatier than crabs. Crabs are heavy and difficult to digest. Mnesitheus of Athens says in his *On Edible Substances* (fr. 37 Bertier): Crayfish, crabs, shrimp, and the like are all difficult to digest, but are much easier to digest than other types of fish. They are more suited to roasting than to stewing.

Sophron refers to shrimp as *kourides* in the *Women's Mimes* (fr. 25),[174] as follows: Look at the lovely shrimp (*kourides*)! Look at the lobsters! Look, my dear! See how red and smooth they are! Epicharmus in *Earth and Sea* (fr. 28):

and red shrimp *(kourides)*.

But in *Male and Female Logos* (fr. 78) he has the word with an *omega*:

both small-fry and curved shrimp *(kōrides)*.

Simonides (Semon. fr. 15 West[2]):

a cuttlefish for tuna, shrimp *(kōrides)* for gobies.

[174] Cited again at 7.306c.

Index

INDEX

585

INDEX

589

INDEX

591

INDEX

Scylla, 1.13b

Scymnus of Tarentum, 1.20a

Seasons, 2.36d, 38c, 60a

Seleucus, *grammarian* (ed. Müller), fr. 26: 1.24b; fr. 42: 2.50a; fr. 45: 3.76f; fr. 61: 2.52c; fr. 63: 3.77c–d; fr. 81: 1.20d

Seleucus I, 1.18d–e

Seleucus of Tarsus, 1.13c

Semele, 2.39b n.

Semonides (West[2] ed.), fr. 11: 2.57d; fr. 15: 3.106e

Semus of Delos (*FGrH* 396), F6a: 1.30c–d; F16: 2.38a–b; F17: 2.71c

Septimius Severus, vii; x

Seuthes of Thrace, 1.15e; 2.49b n.

Sicinnus, 1.20e

Silenus, 2.45c

Simaristes, 3.99c

Simonides (*PMG*), 515: 1.3e; 614: 3.99b; 647: 2.40a–b; (West[2] ed.) fr. 24: 1.32b–c

Sirens, 1.14d

Sitalces of Thrace, 1.27e

Socrates of Athens, xii; 1.20f–1a

Sopater, test. 1: 2.71a–b; fr. 7: 3.86a; fr. 8: 3.101a; fr. 17: 3.101b; fr. 20: 3.101a; fr. 21: 2.71a–b

Sophilus, fr. 7: 3.100a; fr. 9: 2.54f

Sophocles, 1.17f; (Radt ed.) test. 28: 1.20e–f; test. 52b: 1.22a–b; *Tr.* 781–2: 2.66a–b; fr. 112: 3.94e; fr. 181: 3.76c–d; fr. 314.281–2: 2.62f–3a; fr.

324: 3.86c–d; fr. 348: 2.70a; fr. 395.1–2: 2.51d; fr. 565: 1.17d; fr. 606: 2.67c; fr. 666: 3.99f; fr. *675: 2.67f; fr. 718: 2.70a, c; fr. 757: 1.33c; fr. 758: 2.39f–40a; fr. 759: 2.52b; fr. 760: 3.99c–d; fr. 761: 3.99d; fr. 765: 1.23d; fr. dub. 1122: 2.67f–8a

Sophron of Syracuse, fr. 23: 3.86d–e; fr. 24: 3.87a; fr. 25: 3.106d–e; fr. 43: 3.86a–b; fr. 62: 3.89a; fr. 94: 2.44b; fr. 95: 2.48c; fr. 96: 3.86a; fr. 97: 3.91b

Soroadeios, 1.27d and n.

Sosibius of Sparta (*FGrH* 595), F10: 3.78c; F11: 3.81f

Sosicrates, fr. 4: 1.31e

Sostratus, 1.19c–d

Soterides, 1.7d

Speusippus (Tarán ed.), 2.59d; test. 47: 1.3f; fr. 6: 2.61c; fr. 7: 2.68e; fr. 8: 3.86c–d; fr. 9: 3.105b

Staphylus of Naucratis (*FHG* iv), fr. 9: 2.45c–d

Stesichorus of Himera (*PMG*), 187: 3.81d; 221: 3.95d

Straton of Tarentum, 1.19f

Strattis, fr. 23.1: 1.32b; fr. 43: 3.76e; fr. 64: 1.30f; fr. 71: 2.68f–9a

Susarion, 2.40a–b n.

Sycē and Syceas, 3.78a–b

Tantalus, 1.25a

Teiresias, 2.41e

Telamon, 1.23e

595